Summarized below (and continuing on the inside back cover) are important statistical equations and tools described in this text and used widely in behavioral and social research:

CHAPTER 6

Spearman-Brown internal-consistency reliability: $\quad R^{SB} = \dfrac{nr_{ii}}{1 + [(n - 1)r_{ii}]}$

CHAPTER 9

Approximate 95% confidence interval for a proportion: $\quad prop \pm 2\sqrt{\dfrac{prop(1 - prop)}{n}}$

CHAPTER 10
Stem-and-leaf chart:

Stems	Leaves
.9	5 6
.8	2
.7	0 1 1 1 1 2 7
.6	0 0 2 7 7 8 8 8 9
.5	4 4 5 7
.4	3 4 7
.3	
.2	5
.1	
.0	0

Variability		Found at
Maximum	.96	Highest score
Q_3 (75th percentile)	.71	.75(N + 1)
Mdn (Median)	.675	.50(N + 1)
Q_1 (25th percentile)	.54	.25(N + 1)
Minimum	.00	Lowest score

CHAPTER 10
Mean: $\qquad M = \dfrac{\Sigma X}{N}$

CHAPTER 10
95% confidence interval for a mean: $\quad M \pm \dfrac{\left(t_{(.05)}\right)(S)}{\sqrt{n}}$

CHAPTER 10
Variance and standard deviation of a population:

$$\sigma^2 = \frac{\Sigma(X - M)^2}{N} \quad \text{and} \quad \sigma = \sqrt{\sigma^2} = \sqrt{\frac{\Sigma(X - M)^2}{N}}$$

CHAPTER 10
Unbiased estimator of the population variance: $\quad S^2 = \dfrac{\Sigma(X - M)^2}{N - 1}$

CHAPTER 10
Standard score:

$$z = \frac{X - M}{\sigma}$$

CHAPTER 11
Pearson r correlation coefficient:

$$r_{xy} = \frac{\Sigma z_x z_y}{N}$$

CHAPTER 11
Spearman rho:

$$r_s = 1 - \frac{6(\Sigma D^2)}{N^3 - N}$$

CHAPTER 11
Phi coefficient:

$$\phi = \frac{BC - AD}{\sqrt{(A + B)(C + D)(A + C)(B + D)}}$$

CHAPTER 12
95% confidence interval for effect size r:

$$\text{Fisher } z_r \pm (1.96)\left(\frac{1}{\sqrt{N - 3}}\right)$$

CHAPTER 13
Binomial effect-size display (BESD) for $r_{\text{effect size}} = .20$:

	Above	Below	Sum
Treatment	60	40	100
Control	40	60	100
Sum	100	100	

CHAPTER 13
Independent t test and pooled variance:

$$t = \frac{M_1 - M_2}{\sqrt{\left(\frac{1}{n_1} + \frac{1}{n_2}\right)S^2}} \quad \text{and} \quad S^2 = \frac{\Sigma(X_1 - M_1)^2 + \Sigma(X_2 - M_2)^2}{n_1 + n_2 - 2}$$

CHAPTER 13
Cohen's d and Hedges's g:

$$d = \frac{M_1 - M_2}{\sigma_{\text{pooled}}} \quad \text{and} \quad g = \frac{M_1 - M_2}{S_{\text{pooled}}}$$

CHAPTER 13
Paired (correlated) t test and population variance estimate:

$$t = \frac{M_D}{\sqrt{\left(\frac{1}{N}\right)S_D^2}} \quad \text{and} \quad S_D^2 = \frac{\Sigma(D - M_D)^2}{N - 1}$$

CHAPTERS 13 AND 14
$r_{\text{effect size}}$ of t or F comparing 2 groups: $r_{\text{effect size}} = \sqrt{\frac{t^2}{t^2 + df}} = \sqrt{\frac{F}{F + df_{\text{within}}}}$

FIFTH
EDITION

Beginning Behavioral Research

A Conceptual Primer

RALPH L. ROSNOW
Emeritus, Temple University

ROBERT ROSENTHAL
University of California, Riverside

PEARSON
Prentice
Hall

Upper Saddle River, New Jersey 07458

Library of Congress Cataloging-in-Publication Data

Rosnow, Ralph L.
   Beginning behavioral research : a conceptual primer / Ralph L. Rosnow.—5th ed.
      p. cm
   Includes bibliographical references and indexes.
   ISBN 0-13-114730-7
  1. Psychology—Research—Methodology—Textbooks.   2. Social
sciences—Research—Methodology—Textbooks.   I. Rosenthal, Robert, 1933– II. Title.

BF76.5.R64 2004
300′.72—dc22

2004002944

> To our students and colleagues
> in research methods
> past, present, and future

Sr. Acquisitions Editor: Jayme Heffler
Editor-in-Chief: Leah Jewell
Editorial Assistant: Jennifer M. Conklin
Marketing Director: Beth Mejia
Asst. Managing Editor: Maureen Richardson
Production Liaison: Fran Russello
Permissions Coordinator: Michael Farmer

Manufacturing Buyer: Tricia Kenny
Cover Design: Bruce Kenselaar
Composition/Full-Service Project
  Management: Jessica Balch/Pine Tree Composition
Printer/Binder: RR Donnelley and Sons, Inc.
Cover Printer: Phoenix Color Corp.

Pearson Prentice Hall is a trademark of Pearson Education, Inc.
Pearson® is a registered-trademark of Pearson plc
Prentice Hall® is a registered trademark of Pearson Education, Inc.

Pearson Education Ltd., London
Pearson Education Singapore, Pte. Ltd
Pearson Education, Canada, Ltd
Pearson Education—Japan
Pearson Education Australia PTY, Limited

Pearson Education North Asia Ltd
Pearson Educación de Mexico, S.A. de C.V.
Pearson Education Malaysia, Pte. Ltd
Pearson Education, Upper Saddle River,
  New Jersey

10 9 8 7 6 5 4 3 2 1
0-13-114730-7

Contents

3 Ethical Considerations and Guidelines   59

PART II OBSERVATION AND MEASUREMENT

4 Strategies of Systematic Observational Research   84

5 Methods for Looking Within Ourselves   109

6   Reliability and Validity in Measurement and Research   139

PART III DESIGN AND IMPLEMENTATION

9 Survey Research and Subject Recruitment   220

PART IV DESCRIBING DATA AND MAKING INFERENCES

10 Summarizing the Data   247

11 Quantifying and Interpreting Relationships Among Variables   272

PART V STATISTICAL TESTS

Appendix A   Communicating Your Research Findings   384

Appendix B   Statistical Tables   408

Preface

Robert Rosenthal   Ralph L. Rosnow

Welcome to the fifth edition of *Beginning Behavioral Research*. This book was originally conceived as an undergraduate text for students who, as part of an introductory course in research methods, are required to plan an empirical study, to analyze and interpret the data, and to present their findings and conclusions in a written report. It is also intended to encourage students to be analytical and critical not only in interpreting their own research findings, but in seeing and understanding what is behind the research reported in newspaper, TV, and Internet stories of scientific (and pseudoscientific) results and claims. Boyce Rensberger (2000), a prominent science journalist and author of several popular science books, commented on the general public's relative lack of discrimination about science and pseudoscience:

> Without a grasp of scientific ways of thinking, the average person cannot tell the difference between science based on real data and something that resembles science—at least in their eyes—but is based on uncontrolled experiments, anecdotal evidence, and passionate assertions. They like it all. (p. 61)

Our hope is that this book will teach students to understand the difference between real science and pseudoscience and the exacting standards of good scientific research.

Thus, although the primary emphasis of this text is on behavioral research, we have tried to connect this approach with the empirical reasoning used in other fields in order to underscore the broad base of scientific thinking. The examples we have chosen give a sense not only of traditional ways of doing, analyzing, and thinking about research, but also of some recent developments that may not be as well known. For example, we introduce students to statistical methods that, while enormously useful, do not yet generally appear in many methods texts: contrast analysis and interpretable indices of effect size, the distinction between intrinsic and nonintrinsic repeated measures, interval estimates of effect sizes, meta-analysis, and so on. The emphasis of these discussions is intended to resonate with the spirit and substance of the guidelines recommended by the American Psychological Association's Task Force on Statistical Inference (Wilkinson et al., 1999), which is reflected in the most recent edition of the *Publication Manual of the American Psychological Association* (APA, 2001).

Although *Beginning Behavioral Research* was conceived as a text for students assigned an empirical research project, we have been pleasantly surprised to learn that it has been successfully used in ways that go far beyond its original purpose. For example, it has been used in courses in which the production of a research project was not a major goal, as well as by master's degree students in several fields as a primary methods text and by doctoral students to slip into our advanced text, *Essentials of Behavioral Research* (Rosenthal & Rosnow, 1991). *Beginning Behavioral Research* has also been used to teach research methods and data analysis to several thousand students in distance learning programs.

Organization

As in earlier editions, the chapters in this edition are presented in a linear sequence corresponding to the steps involved in conducting an empirical research study and in analyzing and reporting the results. The beginning researcher is led step by step through the following process:

1. *Crafting a research idea that can be empirically tested.* Understanding empirical reasoning, the scientific method, levels of empirical investigation, and the scientific outlook (Chapter 1); creating, shaping, and polishing a research idea, and conducting a search of the relevant literature for the research proposal and the project itself (Chapter 2); weighing and balancing ethical considerations, and preparing for an ethics review (Chapter 3)

2. *Choosing methods of data collection and measurement.* Knowing what methods are available for watching and recording behavior in laboratory and field research, using archival data and outside observers, and preparing a research proposal (Chapter 4); collecting data in which the participants describe their own behavior or state of mind (Chapter 5); assessing the reliability and validity of measuring instruments and research designs (Chapter 6)

3. *Designing and implementing the research study.* Designing a randomized experiment while controlling for artifacts and other threats to validity (Chapter 7); using time-series, single-case, longitudinal, and correlational designs (Chapter 8); surveying opinions and behavior, controlling for self-selection bias, and testing the methods and instruments (Chapter 9)

4. *Approaching the research data.* Using graphics and statistical summary procedures to develop an overall picture of the results (Chapter 10); identifying relationships (Chapter 11); testing hypotheses, estimating effect sizes, creating confidence intervals around obtained effects, using the BESD as an aid in interpreting importance, and doing a power analysis (Chapter 12)

5. *Testing hypotheses and exploring the results.* Using t to compare two independent or two correlated conditions (Chapter 13); computing F and t in designs with

more than two conditions, examining the simple effects, interpreting an obtained interaction, computing contrasts and effect sizes, and analyzing designs with repeated measures (Chapter 14); analyzing tables of frequencies by chi-square and related procedures (Chapter 15); comparing and combining effect sizes, obtaining an overall significance level, and doing a file-drawer analysis to estimate the tolerance for future null results (Appendix C)

6. *Reporting the research project in a paper or in a poster.* Writing up the findings and conclusions in the spirit and style of the APA publication manual and developing a poster (Appendix A)

Our Approach

In our long experience of teaching research methods and data analysis, we have noted the questions and uncertainties of students' first attempts at empirical research. The vast majority of undergraduate students have not planned to pursue a career in research, but most of them have recognized the vitality and ubiquitousness of scientific research in their daily lives. So we have tried to anticipate and confront questions and uncertainties from their perspective not as potential professional producers of empirical research, but as intelligent consumers of scientific findings. For example, we describe procedures that can be used to analyze the results reported in published articles (including, in some cases, the meager ingredients in news stories), and thus possibly to reach beyond the original researcher's (or the journalist's) published conclusion or interpretation. It is also essential for educated consumers to understand the limitations of particular research methods, and therefore, at the same time that we explain the utility of various methods, we also mention some of their limitations. We are not wedded to any single scientific method, theory, or unit of analysis, and indeed the mantra of our approach in this book is *methodological pluralism and theoretical ecumenism.*

Instructors who know our earlier work will recognize that this book—as well as our more advanced text (*Essentials of Behavioral Research*)—grew out of a 117-page paperback book that we wrote many years ago: *Primer of Methods for the Behavioral Sciences* (Rosenthal & Rosnow, 1975a). Over the intervening period, we have developed and refined that material. Most of our undergraduate students have been psychology majors who were required to take a methods course as part of their concentration, but others majored in fields as diverse as communication, social work, urban studies, criminal justice, computer science, physical education, mathematics, statistics, accounting, nursing, biology, education, sociology, marketing, management, and even English, art, and theology. Whether they took this course as part of their major or as an elective, many of them dreaded the thought of having to wrestle with statistics. On the assumption that few readers have total recall of statistics or have come away from a statistics course with an intuitive understanding of what was taught, we review basic aspects of data analysis procedures, purposely avoiding the use of any mathematics beyond the high school level. We focus primarily on the most popular procedures (t, F, and chi-square), but in a way that can also be used outside a research methods course to examine the implications of a set of results.

Guided by their instructor's lectures, even students with little or no training in statistics should find that they can master basic data-analytic skills by reading the chapters and repeating the exercises in the order in which they are presented. In this age of the computer, the speediest method of doing complex calculations is with the aid of SPSS, SAS, SYSTAT, Minitab, or some other program. As statistician John W. Tukey (1977) noted, we can also learn much by simply changing our point of view and exploring the data in different ways. Our own philosophy of data analysis is to treat statistics (in Chapters 10–15 and Appendix C) by showing, through intuitive reasoning and clear examples, what the results tell us. Instructors who plan to teach students to perform their main calculations on a computer will find that our emphasis on the concrete and arithmetical aspects of data analysis will complement any statistics program they choose. We also describe useful data-analytic procedures that might not yet be available in basic computer packages but can be easily performed with a good calculator.

Instructors familiar with *Essentials of Behavioral Research* will recognize that *Beginning Behavioral Research* can be used for students up to, but just below, the level of *Essentials,* and that the conceptual and philosophical treatment of methods and data analysis is similar in the two texts. We emphasize the utility of the correlational family of effect size indices, which includes (a) the point-biserial r when one variable is continuous and one variable is dichotomous; (b) the phi (ϕ) coefficient when both variables are dichotomous; and (c) other variants that are described in Chapter 14, including $r_{\text{effect size}}$, r_{contrast}, and r_{alerting}. For a comprehensive discussion of these indices, see Rosenthal, Rosnow, and Rubin (2000); for an introduction to alternative effect size estimators in experimental psychology, see Rosnow and Rosenthal (2003). We also introduce students to statistical power analysis in a way that many should be able to apply in their research. Chapter 3, on ethics, draws on recently discussed guidelines (Sales & Folkman, 2000) and also raises a number of questions to prompt students' thinking about ethical issues that project well beyond this text. Students interested in pursuing any of these topics will find more detailed discussions in the books and articles that are mentioned. Throughout this book, we have also sought to communicate the richness, diversity, and excitement of research that we ourselves find so challenging and stimulating.

Other Features and New Additions

In an effort to make this book more useful and user-friendly to a wide variety of students, we have incorporated several pedagogical devices. Each chapter begins with a set of *preview questions,* which students can refer to as they progress. The introduction to each chapter states the purpose of the chapter and gives an overview of its content. *Box discussions* highlight and enliven concepts with practical examples and illustrations. Each chapter ends with a *summary* of the main ideas, followed by a list of *key terms* pegged to particular pages (shown in boldface in the text), and finally a number of *review questions* to stimulate thought and discussion, with the answers located at the end of the chapter. A *glossary* at the end of the book lists and defines all the key terms and notes the primary location where each term is discussed. Selected Web activities are listed at the end of each chapter. There is an Instructor's Manual, which was prepared by David B. Strohmetz of Monmouth University, and a set of diskettes available to instructors from their Prentice Hall representative. As with the previous edition, a Web site, connected to Prentice Hall's Web site (http://www.prenhall.com/rosnow), provides students with study aids for each chapter and convenient links to other useful Internet resources.

There are a number of changes and new additions in this edition of *Beginning Behavioral Research*. We have tightened the writing by eliminating some boxes and superfluous material in all chapters. The sample report in Appendix A has been tightened and rewritten to reflect recent APA guidelines for the analysis and reporting of research, and the proposal and final report also emphasize the importance of consulting the instructor in all phases of the project. There are new boxes and several new examples, which we believe are particularly illustrative and poignant. In response to instructors' requests, we have added material on repeated measures analyses (Chapter 14), focused data analyses (contrast *t* and *F* tests), and associated effect sizes, and on computing and interpreting confidence intervals for proportions, means, and effect sizes. The discussion of reliability and validity in Chapter 6 has been reorganized and rewritten to improve the flow of this material and to accentuate connections in the following chapters. There are new chapter titles, headings, and subheadings to reflect the spirit of these changes, and we refer back and forth to ideas so that connections are emphasized and built upon.

Acknowledgments

We have benefited once again from working with David Strohmetz, who prepared the Instructor's Manual and contributed to the Web site. As with the previous edition, Margaret Ritchie did the copy editing, and Mary Lu Rosenthal prepared the indexes; we are grateful for their creative, elegant, and helpful assistance. We thank Bruce Rind for again allowing us to include an edited version of his empirical work in Appendix A and this time to represent it as that of a fictitious student named "Mary Jones." We thank Robert E. Lana for permission to borrow or adapt ideas from *Introduction to Contemporary Psychology* (Lana & Rosnow, 1972). We thank a long line of excellent teaching assistants and students at Temple University, the University of California, Riverside, and Harvard University for their valuable comments on and criticisms of the lectures, handouts, drafts, and earlier editions on which this fifth edition was based. We thank the reviewers of this edition for their feedback: Laura Carlson, University of Notre Dame; George M. Kapalka, Monmouth University; Thomas E. Malloy, Rhode Island College; and Kevin Thomsen, Concordia University. We also thank the following reviewers of one or more previous editions of this book for their constructive feedback: Bernard C. Beins, Ithaca College; B. LaConyea Butler, Spelman College; Patricia R. DeLucia, Texas Tech University; Paul W. Foos, University of North Carolina at Charlotte; Allan J. Kimmel, Groupe École Supérieure de Commerce de Paris; Wilson McDermut, William Patterson University; Anthony

Uzwiak, Rutgers University; John W. Webster, Towson State University; Paul J. Wellman, Texas A. & M. University; and Jon L. Williams, Kenyon College. We thank Jayme Heffler and Jennifer Conklin at Prentice Hall and Jessica Balch at Pine Tree Composition for their editorial and production support. And finally, we thank Mimi Rosnow and Mary Lu Rosenthal for counseling us in ways too numerous to mention.

Certain tables, figures, and passages (specifically noted in the text) have by permission been reproduced in part or in their entirety, for which we thank the following authors, representatives, and publishers: Jacob Cohen; Mihaly Csikszentmihalyi; J. A. Hagenaars; R. Vance Hall; Howard Kahane; Paul Slovic; Alan Sockloff; Robert Weisberg; Academic Press; American Association for the Advancement of Science; American Psychological Association; American Sociological Association; American Statistical Association; Biometrika Trustees of the Imperial College of Science, Technology & Medicine; Brooks/Cole Publishing Company; Cambridge University Press; Elsevier Science Publishers; HarperCollins Publishers; Helen Dwight Reid Educational Foundation and Heldref Publications; Holt, Rinehart & Winston; Houghton Mifflin Company; Iowa State University Press; *Journal of Applied Behavior Analysis;* Lawrence Erlbaum Associates, Inc.; McGraw-Hill, Inc.; W. W. Norton & Company, Inc.; Oxford University Press; Pergamon Press; The Rand Corporation; Sussex Publishers, Inc., and Psychology Today Magazine; The University of Chicago Press; Wadsworth Publishing Company; and John Wiley & Sons, Inc. We are also grateful to the Longman Group UK Ltd., on behalf of the Literary Executor of the late Sir Ronald Fisher, F.R.S., and Dr. Frank Yates, F.R.S., for permission to reprint Table V from *Statistical Tables for Biological, Agricultural, and Medical Research* (6th ed., 1974).

This is our 15th book together in a collaboration that began many years ago, and the beat goes on!

Ralph L. Rosnow
Robert Rosenthal

CHAPTER 1

Behavioral Research and the Scientific Method

Preview Questions

- What is the purpose of knowing about the fourth R—researching?

- What is distinctive about the method of tenacity, the method of authority, and the a priori method, and how do they differ from the scientific method?

- Why is the expression "the scientific method" considered a misnomer?

- What is empirical reasoning?

- What is the role of analogical thinking in the rhetoric of science?

- What is the term *behavioral science* meant to connote?

- How do the descriptive, relational, and experimental orientations differ from one another?

- What are some of the traits of good researchers?

Why Study Research Methods?

Reading, 'riting, and 'rithmetic—the three Rs—are viewed as the fundamentals of education. Beginning in grade school, we are taught these basic skills, and it is not hard to figure out why they are considered important. A fourth R, "researching" (i.e., exploring a problem systematically), is now regarded as another crucial skill for any educated person (Hult, 1996). In high school, you were introduced to the processes involved in "researching" a term paper. In college science courses, the term *researching* implies the use of a strategy traditionally called the **scientific method** to explore a problem. Though this strategy transcends all branches of science, its applications vary from one field to another. Researchers in fields as varied as psychology, biomedicine, business, education, communication research, economics, sociology, anthropology, physics, biology, and chemistry all use some variation of this method. However, you may be wondering why you need to know about the scientific method or to study techniques of research if you do not plan to become a scientific researcher. There are at least five good reasons.

One is that our modern way of life is largely the creation of science and technology, and we enhance our understanding of the full range of this influence by learning about the logic and evidence used by scientists to open up the world to scrutiny and explanation. By analogy, viewing paintings, drawings, and sculpture in a museum becomes more meaningful when we know something about the processes and creative ideas that were involved in producing the works of art. Similarly, reading that a voter survey found Candidate X ahead of Candidate Y by 4 percentage points with a 5% margin of error, or that educational researchers say they have ways of fostering reading skills in young children, or that a medical study found a significant relationship between health problems and exposure to some environmental substance has more meaning when we understand how the conclusions were reached.

Besides providing a richer appreciation of the information that science brings to our lives, a second reason for studying research methods is that *not* having a clear understanding of how researchers cast and address questions can sometimes cost us dearly. Doctors, teachers, lawyers, the clergy, politicians, the police—these people also have an influence on our daily lives, and everyone seems to be familiar with how people in these fields go about their work. But few seem to have even a vague idea of how scientific researchers in vastly different fields create and test hypotheses and theories that enlarge our understanding of the world. As a consequence, people often succumb to misleading recommendations based on bogus data that purport to be scientific. Having the opportunity to do an empirical research study under the watchful eye of an experienced guide will begin to sensitize you to the difference between good scientific research and **pseudoscience** (i.e., dubious claims masquerading as scientific fact).

A third reason is to acquire information and skills you can use later. For example, once you understand the logic of controlled, randomized, double-blind experiments, you sharpen your powers of causal reasoning. Similarly, learning how researchers come up with ideas "through hunch, analogy, insight, and creativity" (Baltimore, 1997, p. 8) may stimulate your own creative thinking. And improving your data-analytic skills will enable you to think of probing questions to ask about the basis of research claims, whether they are consultants' reports in work situations or news reports intended to inform the general public. For example, there are often enough basic details in newspaper stories of medical experiments to enable us to perform simple calculations (described later in this book) to estimate the effect size of a reported outcome (i.e., quite apart from whether it had "statistical significance"). By also using the other essential information that is usually reported as well (for example, what kind of study and what kind of participants), you should be better able to make sense of the findings and decide whether they may apply to you (Brody, 2002).

A fourth reason for studying and doing research is to learn about the limits of particular studies. All study designs are limited in some ways, but an important question is the degree to which those limitations affect the meaning and the generalizability of the results. For example, correlations in epidemiological studies may be due to variables other than those measured, and findings in experimental studies of new drugs administered to young, healthy, mobile volunteer participants may not apply to aged, infirm, hospitalized people with advanced diseases (Brody, 2002). In Chapter 3, we will discuss the limitations imposed by institutional review boards that are responsible for overseeing the ethical responsibilities of researchers. In research with human participants, another limitation occurs when the people whose behavior is being studied know they are being observed for some scientific purpose; they may behave quite differently than if they don't know. In a later chapter, we will describe specific techniques used by psychological researchers to address this problem, but these techniques are also limited in some ways. However, despite these limits, behavioral and social researchers have formulated reliable principles about how and why humans feel, think, and behave as they do (see also Box 1.1).

A final reason for studying and doing research is that some students will find this activity so much fun and so absorbing that they may want to make a career of it!

 ## Peirce's "Methods of Fixing Beliefs"

The scientific method is not the only approach used to make sense of things and give us information. For example, philosophers, novelists, and theologians also seek to give us a coherent picture of our world, but they do not use the scientific method to organize their ideas and explain things. What is distinctive about the different strategies used by scientists and nonscientists to formulate a sense of

---

BOX 1.1 The Provisional Nature of Scientific Knowledge

Because even the most carefully designed study is limited in some ways, it is generally accepted that scientific knowledge is in a constant state of development. For many years, philosophers and historians of science have wrestled with the pattern of this development. Thomas S. Kuhn (1962, 1977), a physicist turned scientific historian, theorized that major advances in science appear as "paradigm shifts" resulting from revolutionary insights. Philosopher Karl Popper (1963, 1972), on the other hand, compared progress in science with Charles Darwin's idea of "survival of the fittest." Popper's idea is that the fittest theories withstand falsification in what resembles an evolutionary process of competition and survival. No matter whether we view the development of science as revolutionary or evolutionary, on one point all seem to agree: Scientific knowledge is relative and provisional. As one leading biomedical researcher put it, "Scientists know that questions are not settled; rather, they are given provisional answers for which it is contingent upon the imagination of followers to find more illuminating solutions" (Baltimore, 1997, p. 8).

understanding and belief? This question has long perplexed philosophers, some of whom even argue that there are no real differences between scientific and nonscientific thinking. By contrast, another answer was proposed many years ago by a famous American philosopher, Charles Sanders Peirce (1839–1914), who said that the scientific method is one of four distinctive strategies that provide a foundation for strongly held beliefs—he called this "the fixation of beliefs." Peirce (pronounced "purse") called the other three the *method of tenacity*, the *method of authority*, and the *a priori method*. Each, he contended, is characterized by a particular formulaic way of thinking and behaving (Peirce, 1966).

Peirce thought the **method of tenacity** the most primitive strategy of all, because it involves clinging stubbornly (tenaciously) and mindlessly to claims or beliefs just because they have been around for a while. This kind of knee-jerk thinking is like that of an ostrich that buries its head in the sand, he said, because these kinds of people go through life excluding anything that might challenge or alter their beliefs. Sometimes it seems that a whole society has fallen victim to some peculiar notion, and it is not easy to shake fixed beliefs or to open up closed minds (Mitchell, 1985). For example, beginning with the Ptolemaic treatise in the 2nd century A.D., people were convinced that the earth was fixed, immobile, and at the center of the universe. It was one of the ancient astronomer Ptolemy's few misconceptions, but it was a whopper that endured for over a thousand years. It was not until Copernicus's insight that the sun, not the earth, is the center of the universe that the geocentric (i.e., earth-centered) design was challenged, although the Copernican system also left much room for improvement (it neglected to show that the sun was a center of force). Indeed, it was not until the advent of modern astronomy, or what one historian called the "witness of the naked eye" (Boorstein, 1985, p. 305), that the geocentric design was finally swept away by the scientific method.

In our own time, we recognize that the method of tenacity still has a pernicious hold on many people's convictions and superstitions (see Box 1.2). Peirce thought that superstitions and other dogmatic beliefs are like the cadence that concludes a musical phrase in a symphony and provides closure. Sometimes this closure seems to be based on what social psychologists call a "false consensus" or "pluralistic ignorance"; it means that people have a tendency to misperceive, and frequently overestimate, the extent to which others believe the same thing (Kelley & Thibaut, 1969; Ross, Greene, & House, 1977). Telling themselves that only their beliefs are correct, they dismiss counterarguments as deviant and seek out information that is consistent with their own biases about how the world should be understood (Marks & Miller, 1987; Ross et al., 1977; Sherman, Presson, & Chassin, 1984).

The **method of authority** was Peirce's term for the presumption that something is true because someone in a position of authority says it is. Peirce saw that blind obedience to authority was similar in some ways to the method of tenacity (because both imply inflexible compliance), but he thought the method of authority superior in some ways, although flawed. To illustrate blind obedience, he described the horrible atrocities that resulted when ordinary people obeyed the word of authority to cruelly punish those accused of witchcraft. Present-day examples include unscrupulous people who pose as authorities, preying on human weakness by using fakery. Think of medical quacks, food faddists, faith healers, TV psychics, cult leaders, and eccentric sexual theorists (M. Gardner, 1957; Shermer, 1997). The authority of these fakers and hucksters is in the eyes of their victims, however, so that it behooves the buyer to beware.

Peirce thought the method of authority was at least a small improvement on the method of tenacity because civilized society would cease to exist without people's willingness to obey laws and to carry out reasonable orders. In the behavioral and social sciences, researchers are subject to the benevolent authority of an ever-evolving "social contract" between science and society concerning the rights of research participants and the privileges granted to researchers (Rosnow, 1997). Other examples on the positive side are the physician who prescribes a drug or regimen to cure an illness, the electrician who advises the replacement of wiring that is about to burn out, and the mechanic who warns that the brakes on a car are worn and need replacing; we depend on their honesty and the authority of

BOX 1.2 Flying Saucers, Bigfoot, and Other Odd Beliefs

Myth, folklore, and superstition illustrate the method of tenacity's powerful hold on beliefs that can endure for centuries. The noted Swiss psychiatrist and psychologist Carl G. Jung (1910, 1959)—one of Sigmund Freud's students—theorized about the persistence of stories of "flying saucers," unidentified flying objects (UFOs) piloted by extraterrestrials. This stubborn rumor, he argued, is merely an expression of people's fears and uncertainties about the world situation and their wish for a redeeming supernatural force. Interestingly, the UFO story usually takes one of two forms: It is said either that benevolent superior beings from another planet have come to save humanity (as represented in the 1951 movie *The Day the Earth Stood Still*), or that menacing creatures threaten humanity and this threat will unify people of diverse ideologies to make a stand against a common foe (represented in the 1996 movie *Independence Day*). Like UFO believers, some people also still insist that the earth is flat, that sunrise and sunset are optical illusions, and that the moon landing was an elaborate hoax staged in a hangar in Arizona (D. Martin, 2001). In another fascinating case, it was revealed recently that a prankster named Ray L. Wallace had created the modern myth of Bigfoot (or Sasquatch), the name for the giant, hairy, upright biped rumored to be living in the woods of the Pacific Northwest. After Wallace's death in November 2002, his family displayed the carved wooden feet that he had used to stamp a track of oversized footprints. What is so remarkable about this case is that, despite all the evidence to the contrary, Bigfoot defenders continue to insist that the creature exists (Egan, 2003).

their expertise. Even if we know very little about medicine, wiring, or brakes, we can nevertheless use the third method (i.e., the a priori method) to ask questions to help us better understand the particular authoritative recommendations.

In the **a priori method**, people rely on their individual powers of reason and logic to make sense of the world and to explain it to others. This method, Peirce (1966) argued, is "far more intellectual and respectable" than the previous two (p. 106); it has proved itself quite robust in the hands of mathematicians and philosophers. In fact, we use the a priori method all the time. When we balance our checkbooks, ruminate on what career path to take, or figure out the amount of a tip in a restaurant, we presumably bring reason and logic into play. Thinking rationally and logically can also be an effective defense against hoaxes and hucksters who depend on human gullibility (see, for example, Box 1.3). We can approach dubious claims with a questioning mind that, as one psychologist put it, "resists being overly impressed" (Gilovich, 1991, p. 187). For example, when we hear a sensational rumor, we can ask how the story got started. The person who tells it to us may be quite reliable, but we may question the credibility of the person who originated it. Despite the old chestnut about there being a "kernel of truth" in every rumor, rumors often turn out to be nothing more than urban legends and pranks (Brunvand, 2000; Fine & Turner, 2001; Kimmel, 2004).

It is hard to find fault with the a priori method, but Peirce cautioned that it is constrained by the limits of pure reason. Suppose you conclude that A causes B,

---

BOX 1.3 Debunking False Rumors and Hoaxes

False rumors and hoaxes can now be spread instantaneously on the Internet. An insidious case (which one of us learned about firsthand) involves something called the "teddy bear virus." The hoax arrives in an e-mail warning from a friend urging you to delete a contaminated file (Jdbgmgr.exe) identified by a teddy bear logo, and to forward this message to everyone in your address book. Your friend received the warning from another friend, and so on. According to the message, the virus defies detection by antivirus software (which should make the story seem a little fishy to you), is sent automatically by your server and address book, and stays dormant for 14 days before damaging your system. In fact, the story is a hoax that your friend was snookered into believing. "Jdbgmgr.exe" is a valid Windows file for Java, not a harmful virus, but deleting it essentially gets *you* to do what a virus would do in a way. If the "virus" were real, it would be virtually impossible to eradicate, because someone is still bound to have and innocently transmit it, and the cycle will begin again. Incidentally, using reason and logic, you will probably want to seek out information on the Symantec or McAfee virus information Web sites (http://securityresponse.symantec.com or http://vil.nai.com).

and I disagree. Do we just have to let it go at that? What we need, Peirce said, is a way of drawing on nature to help us resolve our dispute. This is presumed to be the role of the scientific method, to provide a framework for drawing on independent realities to evaluate claims rather than to depend on armchair reasoning or a source that one of us rejects. In behavioral science, as a noted social psychologist once said, we use the scientific method to help us sort out what we know about human nature from what we only think we know (Milgram, 1977).

Empirical Reasoning and the Scientific Method

The term *scientific method* is actually a misnomer. It is not synonymous with any single, fixed procedure for settling disputes; instead, it is a strategy that embraces many different empirical techniques (**empirical** means based on observation or experience). In particular, however, it can be distinguished by what we call **empirical reasoning**, that is, a combination of logic, carefully organized observation, and measurement. One scientist used the following analogy to describe the role of the scientific method: Suppose we are trying to unlock a door with a set of previously untried keys. A person reasons, "If this key fits the lock, then the lock will spring when I turn the key" (Conant, 1957, p. xii). Similarly, the scientist has a choice of "keys" in the form of hunches and empirical techniques, logically decides on one, and then says, "Let's try it." The implication is that the scientific method relies on techniques that are available to any researcher who is skilled enough to use them to open up the world for scrutiny and measurement. It is this dependence on logic, observation, and measurement (i.e., empirical reasoning) that is the essential connection among scientists working on many different problems, even though they use quite different procedures and measurements in their work. Furthermore, there is often more than just one "right" key even in the same field, because each key can open up only some limited domain.

The use of empirical reasoning goes back several centuries in natural science, but a little over 100 years in behavioral science. If you took a physics course in high school, you will recall the legendary story of how, back in the 16th century, Galileo dropped two objects of different weights from the Leaning Tower of Pisa to prove that Aristotle was wrong when he insisted that heavier objects fall faster than lighter ones. (When American astronauts landed on the moon, they successfully repeated this experiment for all to see.) Another famous procedure, which you may have experimented with in high school, was Newton's use of a prism to show that white light is a combination of different colors (not a pure form of light as Aristotle had claimed), and that each color remained pure when refracted through a second prism. If you have visited a science museum, you may recall seeing a perpetually swinging iron ball suspended from a wire, with a stylus on the ball tracing a slightly different clockwise pattern in the sand beneath it with each revolution. This construction goes back to the mid-19th century and the idea of a French scientist named Jean-Bernard-Léon Foucault, who wanted to show in a dramatic way that the earth revolves on its axis. (Incidentally, in the Southern Hemisphere the rotation of "Foucault's pendulum" is counterclockwise, and on the equator, it would not move at all.) (See also Box 1.4.)

Empirical reasoning entered into behavioral science at the end of the 19th century, when the creative advances inspired by the applications of the scientific method in physics and biology led to the development of psychology as a distinct science. In Leipzig, Germany, Wilhelm Wundt (1832–1920), trained in medicine and experimental physiology, developed the first formal experimental laboratory to study psychological behavior. Around the same time, William James (1843–1910), who had a background in philosophy and physiology, announced a graduate course in psychology at Harvard University in which students participated in experiments that he arranged. To be sure, empirical reasoning was not practiced only in the laboratory or only experimentally. In Britain, Francis Galton (1822–1911) was demonstrating its application to questions that had been thought to lie completely outside science.

In one of his many fascinating investigations, Galton decided to explore possible empirical grounds for believing that prayers are answered. He reasoned that one way to get at this problem was to look at something prayed for with tremendous frequency. In England, the health and longevity of the royal family were prayed for weekly or even daily nationwide. Galton asked: Do members of the British royal family therefore live longer than individuals of humbler birth? In 1872, he published the results of his empirical inquiry (Forrest, 1974). What he found, after a painstaking gathering and analysis of actuarial data, was that, of 97 members of royal families, the mean age attained by males had been 64.04 years. Compared to 945 members of the clergy, who had lived to a mean age of 69.49,

---

BOX 1.4 The Beauty of Science

The poet John Keats wrote that "Beauty is truth, truth beauty," which for many researchers is also a metaphor of worth in science (Chandrasekhar, 1987; Garfield, 1989a, 1989b; Gombrich, 1963; Nisbet, 1976; Wechler, 1978). Einstein's theory of general relativity was said by one eminent mathematician (Paul Dirac) to be so beautiful that it *had* to be true (Kragh, 2002). In a 2002 article in *Physics World*, Robert P. Crease invited readers to submit candidates for the "most beautiful experiment in physics" (www.physicsweb.org). Among the 10 winners were Galileo's Tower of Pisa experiment, Newton's prism experiment, and Foucault's pendulum. Respondents offered a range of definitions of beauty, such as emphasizing the "economy" of a procedure and what they called "deep play" (i.e., the demonstration was incredibly absorbing and engaging). The 10 winning experiments, in particular, were said to epitomize beauty in the classical sense, in that the logical simplicity of the apparatus and analysis seemed "as inevitable and pure as the lines of a Greek monument" (G. Johnson, 2002, p. F3).

294 lawyers who had lived to 68.14, 244 physicians who had lived to 68.14, and so forth, the members of the royal family had actually fared worse than Galton expected based on the many prayers on their behalf. Of course, Galton could not control for differences in the sincerity of prayers, nor did he reject the idea that religious faith can have a powerful effect in other ways. It can, for example, strengthen people's resolution to face hardships, though for some it can also be a source of stress or confusion (Exline, 2002; Myers, 2000; Pargament, 2002).

Applications in Behavioral Research

Since the time of Wundt, James, and Galton, there has been phenomenal growth in the application of empirical reasoning to questions about human nature, cognition, perception, and behavior. Throughout this book, we will mention examples of both classic and contemporary applications. To get us started, here are two well-known studies: a recent one by Cornell University researcher Stephen J. Ceci and his coworkers in developmental psychology, and an older study by Solomon Asch in social psychology. Although the study designs and research participants were quite different, each study in its own way illustrates the experimental application of controlled observation and measurement to the study of human suggestibility.

The focus of Ceci's research was the accuracy of children's eyewitness testimony. To study this problem in a real-life setting, he and his coworkers designed an elegant experiment in which a character named "Sam Stone" was described to 3- to 6-year-olds as someone who was very clumsy and broke things (Ceci & Bruck, 1993, 1995; White, Leichtman, & Ceci, 1997). Then, a person identified as Sam Stone visited the children's nursery school, where he chatted briefly with them during a storytelling session—but did not behave clumsily or break anything. The next day, the children were shown a ripped book and a soiled teddy bear and were asked if they knew how the objects had been damaged. Over the course of the next 10 weeks, the children were reinterviewed. Each time, they were asked two leading questions, such as "I wonder whether Sam Stone was wearing long pants or short pants when he ripped the book?" or "I wonder if Sam Stone got the teddy bear dirty on purpose or by accident?"

What the researchers observed (and videotaped so others could see for themselves) was that the planted stereotype of Sam Stone carried over into the children's eyewitness reports. When asked, 72% of the 3- to 4-year-olds said that Sam Stone had ruined either the book or the teddy bear, and 45% of these children claimed they had actually seen him do it (and they embellished their accounts with other details). The researchers used a comparison condition, called a **control group**, against which to evaluate the effect of their experimental manipulation. The control group received the suggestive interviews but no planted stereotypical information about Sam Stone. As we would predict, children in the control group made fewer false claims than the children in whom the stereotype had been planted.

Asch (1952) was primarily interested in conformity and the reasons why people go along with certain consensual opinions. In this famous experiment, a

BOX 1.5 Conformity Outside the Lab

Asch's research showed that, at least in the psychological laboratory, subjects can be pressured into making ridiculous perceptual judgments. But an important question is whether the finding is applicable outside Asch's experimental lab. Allen Funt, who for years produced the popular television show *Candid Camera*, showed that the answer to our question is yes. His 1970 film, *What Do You Say to a Naked Lady?* contained a sequence that resembles the Asch findings. A man serving as the subject of the demonstration is sent to a waiting room in which three accomplices are seated. After a few minutes the accomplices stand and remove their shirts, then their shoes and socks. Soon they have all stripped down to their shorts—and, just as Asch's study would imply, so has the subject of the demonstration.

subject arrived at the psychology laboratory along with several other participants, who were actually accomplices of the experimenter. Once seated together at the same table, all of the participants were told by the experimenter that they would be asked to make judgments about the length of several lines. Each person was to judge which of three lines was closest in length to a standard line. The accomplices always stated their opinions first, after which the subject expressed an opinion. The accomplices, acting in collusion with the experimenter, sometimes gave obviously incorrect opinions, but they were always unanimous in their responses. A third of the subjects, Asch found, gave the same opinion as the accomplices in the study. When interviewed later, these people gave three distinct reasons for yielding to the apparent pressure exerted by the incorrect majority: (a) unawareness of being incorrect; (b) doubts about their own perceptions and lack of confidence in them; and (c) a wish to appear the same as the majority. Thus, using a controlled experimental manipulation, Asch produced conformity in the laboratory and observed that going along with a consensus may come about for a variety of reasons (see also Box 1.5).

Rhetoric and Analogical Thinking

Although the scientific method is primarily identified by its reliance on empirical procedures, it has some additional features in common with other methods used by nonscientists. One of these is that opinions and arguments are articulated in the accepted **rhetoric** (i.e., the informative and persuasive language) of the particular field that they represent (A. G. Gross, 1990; Pera & Shea, 1991). In other words, lawyers argue like lawyers, philosophers like philosophers, doctors like doctors, and scientists like scientists. Although each branch of science has its own distinctive set of terms, many technical terms are commonly used in more than one field. Thus, to have an understanding of the rhetoric of science, we must understand how various technical terms are used. For example, what do psychological researchers mean when they refer to *effect sizes* and *confidence intervals,* or when they say that a study used a *repeated measures design* or a *Latin-square design,* or that they observed a *statistical interaction* or used *contrasts?* In subsequent chapters, we will define these and many other terms that are commonly used in behavioral science.

Another aspect of this rhetoric is that researchers are expected to publish their findings in *peer-refereed journals* (i.e., before the articles are actually accepted for publication, they undergo reviews by experts in the field). In Appendix A (beginning on page 384), you will find a sample research report that follows the logical progression used in many research journals in psychology and other fields. Notice how the section headings organize the student's report. This basic structure, which has evolved over many years, consists of an abstract, an introduction, a methods section, a results section, a discussion section, and a list of the references that are cited in the report. The purpose of this organization is to allow busy researchers to read research articles more easily (because they conform to a similar structure) and to enable authors to organize their thoughts as they summarize their research for others.

Although all scientists place enormous emphasis on precision in specification, another aspect of the rhetoric of science is that researchers (like all of us) have a penchant for poignant analogies and metaphors for visualizing one thing in terms of another. "Her life was an uphill climb" and "He is between a rock and a hard place" are everyday examples of **analogical rhetoric** (i.e., they invite us to visualize one thing in terms of another). In fact, much has been written about the use of analogical rhetoric (and analogical thinking) in science, psychotherapy, and everyday life (Barker, 1996; Billow, 1977; Gentner, Holyoak, & Kokinov, 2001; Gentner & Markman, 1997; Gigerenzer, 1991; Holyoak & Thagard, 1997; Kolodner, 1997; Lakoff & Johnson, 1980; Leary, 1990; A. I. Miller, 1986, 1996; Oppenheimer, 1956; Randhawa & Coffman, 1978; Weiner, 1991). A famous example in physics occurred when the quantum theorists first tried to convince the physical determinists that, given a great many atoms, all capable of certain definite changes, it was possible to estimate the proportion of atoms undergoing each change but not the particular changes that any given atoms would undergo. Albert Einstein's pungent metaphor to express his visceral dislike of the idea that, at the level of atomic processes, activity is ruled by pure chance was that God "does not play dice with the world" (Clark, 1971; Jammer, 1966). What makes this imagery so affecting is that we can perceive in our "mind's eye" what he meant (Bauer & Johnson-Laird, 1993; Johnson-Laird, 1983; Johnson-Laird & Byrne, 1991; Robin, 1993).

The Context of Behavioral Science

The examples we have mentioned so far cover a wide range of disciplines, including psychology, physics, and astronomy. However, this book is not just a trip into the realm of science in general; it is a journey into the domain of behavioral science in particular. **Behavior** is what you do and how you act; **behavioral science** is an umbrella term that also includes cognitive and emotional functioning as well as social behavior (social science) and behavioral economics. As the term is defined in this broad way, the range of interests of behavioral scientists includes the study of early primitive humans, and of humans as political animals, financial animals, social animals, talking animals, and logicians. These aspects of human nature are the concern of psychologists (e.g., clinical, cognitive, counseling, developmental, educational, experimental, industrial-organizational, and social), mass communication researchers, sociologists, physical and cultural anthropologists, economists, psycholinguists, behavioral biologists, neuroscientists, and even some statisticians. The objective in all these branches of behavioral and social science is the same: to describe and explain how and why humans think, feel, and behave as they do (Kimble, 1989).

For many purposes, it may not matter much whether we can distinguish among the various branches, but there are differences nonetheless. In experimental psychology, researchers often study human experiences in controlled laboratory settings. Social and industrial-organizational psychologists, particularly those trained in a psychology graduate program, frequently conduct experiments, but these are likely to be performed in a field setting as well as in a laboratory setting. By contrast, sociologists are more likely to perform survey studies in the field or to do qualitative research. Nonetheless, many behavioral researchers borrow from one another's storehouse of methods: Sociologists also conduct experiments, and psychologists perform survey and qualitative research. Though these researchers teach in different departments in colleges and universities, the boundary lines in behavioral and social science are by no means rigid. As one recent illustration, there is a new project called TESS (Time-sharing Experiments for the Social Sciences), funded by the National Science Foundation, which allows experimenters in the social sciences to compete for the opportunity to **replicate** (repeat) their laboratory findings in large populations using telephone and Internet-based survey interviews (for on-line information, visit www.ExperimentalCentral.org).

Some research questions seem especially suitable to experimental investigation in the lab and also have real-life applications. For example, in the area known as **psychophysics** (the study of the relationship between physical stimuli and our human experience of them), experimenting psychologists working in the laboratory discovered many years ago that the amount by which stimulus intensity must be increased to produce a just-noticeable change in the perception of the stimulus is a constant proportion of the intensity of the original stimulus. Following this line of discovery and reasoning, they showed that it is possible to write a mathematical statement of the theoretical relationship between the intensity of a stimulus and the intensity of a sensation, a statement that can then be applied to a range of real-life situations. If, say, your dormitory room is lighted by a 100-watt bulb, and if 15 watts of light must be added before you can just detect a difference in the amount of the light, then in a room with a 50-watt bulb, 7.5 watts must be added before the difference is detectable.

The philosopher Hans Reichenbach observed how scientists, inspired by different ideas and often using different techniques, amass "concatenations of evidence" to explain things. This observation also applies to behavioral and social scientists. In many areas, research has evolved since the early 1970s to embrace what we describe as methodological pluralism and theoretical ecumenism (Jaeger & Rosnow, 1988; Rosnow, 1981, 1986; cf. Houts, Cook, & Shadish, 1986). By **methodological pluralism**, we mean that behavioral scientists frequently use more than one method to zero in on phenomena of interest, on the assumption that any single method is limited in some ways. Using multiple methods is a way of attempting to have one method's strengths compensate for another's limitations (e.g., the TESS project noted above, which allows researchers to use large populations, thereby compensating for the small, highly select samples they originally used in their lab experiments). By **theoretical ecumenism**, we mean there is often more than one "right way" to view the causes of behavior, since human nature can be quite complex and behavior may be motivated by more than one cause or the pursuit of more than one objective. As scientists in different disciplines strive to develop a more complete and integrated picture of human behavior, we have begun to see more interdisciplinary research. Sometimes a whole new field is created. Examples include behavioral medicine, psychobiology, ethnopsychology, psycholinguistics, psychological anthropology, and, perhaps most broadly, cognitive neuroscience.

Another prime example recently has been the application of psychological principles to the understanding of economic behavior. Psychologists Daniel Kahneman (who was awarded a Nobel Prize in economics in 2002) and his coworker for many years, the late Amos Tversky, did seminal research on how people commonly use information-processing rules of thumb (called *cognitive heuristics*) to quickly make judgments that not only defy logic but are often wrong (Kahneman & Tversky, 1973; Tversky & Kahneman, 1974). Later on in this book (Chapter 11), we refer to risk judgments, which show that people frequently think things are more risky or less risky than they are in actuality (Kahneman, Slovic, & Tversky, 1982). When people frame an event in their minds, they frequently make predictions and then behave in ways that are generally consistent with their expectations, such as overestimating the likelihood of a particular economic outcome merely because instances of it are salient at that moment. Previously, we mentioned the false consensus effect (Ross et al., 1977), which is another example of a cognitive heuristic (in this case, overestimating the extent to which others share your beliefs). Once people behave in accordance with their predictions, their predictions become what sociologist Robert Merton (1948, 1968) called a *self-fulfilling prophecy* (we will refer to this term again). Thus, we see how hybrid branches of behavioral science grow creatively from new interdisciplinary ventures.

Three Lines of Empirical Research

We have touched on a number of research techniques, such as the use of actuarial data to study the efficacy of prayer, the "Sam Stone" manipulation in the study of children's eyewitness testimony, the experimental simulation of conformity, and the laboratory investigation of physical stimuli and our perception of them. But even a cursory glance at any of the hundreds of different journals in psychology will reveal that there are countless techniques of empirical inquiry. To give an overview, we will lump together the orientations of behavioral and social research into three general types: descriptive, relational, and experimental. Table 1.1 provides illustrations of each type in three research areas (psycholinguistics, the psychology of rumor, and research on a methodological issue). As you study these illustrations, you will see that descriptive conclusions tell us *how things are*, relational (also often called *correlational*) conclusions tell us *how things are in rela-*

Table 1.1   Descriptive, Relational, and Experimental Conclusions in Three Research Areas

Psycholinguistics

Descriptive: When a 2-year-old child listens to a message spoken by his or her mother and is asked to repeat it, the child typically repeats only part of the message (Brown, 1965).
Relational: On the average, frequently used words tend to be shorter than infrequently used words; this statement is called *Zipf's law* (G. A. Miller & Newman, 1958; Zipf, 1935, 1949).
Experimental: When interfering background noise is present, a speaker tends to use more words and fewer abbreviations than when there is no interfering background noise (Heise & Miller, 1951).

Psychology of Rumor

Descriptive: In rumor chat groups on the Internet, individuals tend to adopt transient roles, described as the skeptical disbeliever, the positivist, the apprehensive believer, the curious, the anxious, the prudent initiator, and the investigator (Bordia & Rosnow, 1998).
Relational: In some circumstances, rumors that forecast unpleasant consequences are passed to others with greater frequency than rumors that predict pleasant consequences (Rosnow, Esposito, & Gibney, 1987; C. J. Walker & Blaine, 1991).
Experimental: College students who were made to feel anxious required less verbal prodding to repeat a rumor than students who had been told the rumor but were not made to feel anxious (C. J. Walker & Beckerle, 1987).

Methodological Research

Descriptive: It has been estimated that perhaps 80% of psychological research on normal adults has used college and university students as research participants (Higbee & Wells, 1972; J. Jung, 1969; McNemar, 1946; Schultz, 1969; Sears, 1986; Sieber & Saks, 1989; Smart, 1966).
Relational: People who volunteer to participate in behavioral and social research are usually higher than nonvolunteers in education, social class, intelligence, and the need for social approval (Rosenthal & Rosnow, 1975b; Rosnow & Rosenthal, 1997).
Experimental: Research participants made to experience a conflict between "looking good" and cooperating with the experimenter are likely to try to look good, whereas participants not made to experience such a conflict are likely to help the experimenter (Rosnow, Goodstadt, Suls, & Gitter, 1973; Sigall, Aronson, & Van Hoose, 1970).

tion to other things, and experimental conclusions tell us *how things are and how they got to be that way.*

As you become better acquainted with the literature in your area of interest, you will see that the research usually involves more than one line of attack, although a given study can often be described as primarily one of these three in terms of its general orientation. As any program of research progresses, the investigators may need to alternate among these three general types, or they may follow a systematic progression from descriptive to relational to experimental. The hypothetical case presented in the following paragraphs on instructional research in educational psychology will show more clearly what we mean by a systematic progression in a program of empirical studies.

The Descriptive Orientation

In **descriptive research**, the goal of the investigation is the careful mapping out of a situation or a set of events, that is, a description of what is happening behaviorally. Causal explanations are not of direct concern except perhaps speculatively. For example, if we are interested in the study of children's failure in school, we may spend a good deal of time measuring and evaluating the classroom behavior of children who are doing poorly. We would then describe as carefully as possible what we have observed. Our careful observation of failing pupils may lead to some revision of our traditional concepts of classroom failure, to suggestions about factors that may contribute to the development of failure, and perhaps to speculative ideas for the redemption of failure.

This descriptive orientation is often considered a necessary first step in the development of a program of research because it establishes the foundation of any future undertaking. But it is rarely regarded as sufficient, because sooner or later someone will want to know *why* something happens or *how* what happens is related to other events. If our interest is in children's classroom failure, we are not likely to be satisfied for very long with even the most careful description of that failure. We will want to know the antecedents of the failure and the outcomes of procedures designed to reduce it. Even if we were not motivated directly by the practical implications of knowing the causes and cures of failure, we would believe our understanding to be considerably improved if we knew the conditions that increase and decrease its likelihood. To learn about the increase or decrease of failure, or any other behavior, we must focus on at least two variables at the same time; that is, we must make two sets of observations that can be related to one another.

The Relational Orientation

At this point, the second broad type of approach, **relational research**, begins. Research is called relational (or **correlational**) when two or more variables or conditions are measured and related to one another. As we continue with the classroom example, let us suppose we have noted that the teachers of many of the failing students rarely looked at or addressed the students and seldom exposed them to new academic information. At this stage, we may have only an impression about the relation between learning failure and teaching behavior. Such impressions are a frequent, and often valuable, by-product of descriptive research. If they are to be taken seriously, however, they cannot be left at the impressionistic level for very long.

Because we want to find out whether the researcher's impressions are accurate, we now arrange a series of coordinated observations on a sample of pupils who effectively represent the target population of pupils (i.e., the pupils to whom we would like to generalize our findings). We note whether or not each pupil in the sample is learning anything or to what degree the pupil has been learning; we also note to what degree the teacher has been exposing the pupil to the material to be learned. From these coordinated observations, we should be able to make a quantitative statement concerning the relationship, or degree of correlation, between the amount of the pupils' exposure to the material to be learned and the amount of this material they have in fact learned. We will then indicate not just (a) whether "X and Y are significantly related" (i.e., whether this nonzero relationship is unlikely to have occurred by chance alone), but also (b) the pattern of the relationship (e.g., linear or nonlinear) and (c) the strength of the relationship in terms of the size of the correlation between X and Y. (Later in this book, we will define and illustrate in a more precise way what these statistical terms mean.)

The Experimental Orientation

To carry the example into the third general approach, **experimental research**, suppose that the pupils exposed to less information are also those who tend to learn less. The discovery of this relationship may tempt us to conclude that children learn less because they are taught less. Such an **ad hoc hypothesis** (i.e., a conjecture or supposition developed on the spot "for this" special result), although plausible, is not warranted by the relationship reported. It may be that teachers teach less to those they know to be less able to learn; that is, differences in teaching behavior may be a result of the pupils' learning as much as a determinant of that learning. To pursue this idea, we will need to make further observations that will allow us to infer whether differences in the information presented to the pupils, apart from any individual differences among them, affect their learning. We can best answer such questions by manipulating the conditions that we think are responsible for the effect. In other words, we will introduce some change into the situation, or we will interrupt or terminate the situation in order to identify some causes.

This process is what is generally meant by the term *experimental research,* the objective of which is the identification of causes (i.e., what leads to what). Relational research only rarely provides such information, and then only under very special conditions. The difference between the degree of focus on a causal explanation in relational and experimental research can be expressed in the difference between the statements "*X* is *related* to *Y*" (relational research) and "*X* is *responsible* for *Y*" (experimental research). In our example, teaching is *X* and learning is *Y*. Our experiment will be designed to reveal the effects of teaching on pupil learning. We will select a sample of youngsters and, by tossing a coin, or by some other unbiased method of selection, divide them into two equivalent groups (see also Box 1.6). The teachers will give more information to one of these groups (the experimental group) and will give the other group (the control group) less information. We can then assess whether the experimental group surpassed the control group in learning achievement. If we find this to be true, we can say that giving the experimental group more information was *responsible* for the outcome.

There might still be a question of what it was about the better procedure that led to the improvement. Indeed, it is characteristic of research that, when a new procedure is shown to be effective, many questions arise about what specific aspects of the procedure are producing the benefits. In the case of increased teaching, we may wonder whether the improvement was due to (a) the nature of the additional material; (b) the teacher's increased attention to the pupil while presenting the additional material; (c) any accompanying increases in eye contact, smiles, or warmth; or (d) other possible correlates of increased teaching behavior. In fact, these alternative hypotheses have already been investigated. The findings indicate that the amount of new material that teachers present to their pupils is sometimes predictable not so much by the children's learning ability as by the teachers' beliefs or expectations about their pupils' learning ability. In other words, teachers' expectations about their pupils' performance may become a self-fulfilling prophecy, in which teachers' expectations become responsible for the outcome in their students'

BOX 1.6 Random Selection and Random Assignment

Two important concepts that students new to research methods sometimes find confusing are *random selection* and *random assignment*. In the relational example, we described arranging for a series of observations "on a sample of pupils who effectively represent the target population of pupils." To ensure the likelihood that the sample will be representative of the population from which it was drawn, we use a **random selection** procedure (i.e., the kind of procedure used by pollsters or survey researchers). In the experimental example just discussed, we said that we could divide a sample of students into two equivalent groups by tossing a coin to decide which condition each student would be in. Using a randomizing procedure (e.g., a coin toss) to allocate participants to different conditions is called **random assignment**. We will have more to say about both of these strategies later in this book.

performance (Babad, 1993; Raudenbush, 1984; Rosenthal, 1966, 1976, 1985, 1991; Rosenthal & Jacobson, 1968; Rosenthal & Rubin, 1978).

Some Traits of Good Researchers

Whether they are students, teachers, spouses, parents, workers, and so on, some people are better at what they do than others. This is no less true of researchers, many of whom excel in what they do. Judith A. Hall (1984), a Northeastern University psychology professor, noted that many textbooks are filled with guidelines for good research but rarely mention what makes a good researcher. We will end this chapter by borrowing her list and adding a little to it, because these characteristics should also serve us well in everyday life:

1. *Enthusiasm*. Being enthusiastic about what you do is contagious and self-motivating, whereas being apathetic can also sap the passion and zeal of everyone around you. This is also true in science. As a wise researcher, experimental psychologist Edward C. Tolman (1959), astutely commented, "In the end, the only sure criterion is to have fun" (p. 152). He did not mean that the good researcher views science as just fun and games without any ethical or societal responsibilities, implications, or consequences. What he meant was that for researchers who excel in what they do, choosing a topic, doing research, and analyzing and reporting the results are as absorbing and as much fun as any game that requires skill and concentration and that fills a person with enthusiasm.

2. *Open-mindedness*. It is also more satisfying to be with someone who is open-minded, listens to what you have to say, and, when responding, is reasonable rather than dogmatic or a know-it-all. The good researcher is also open-minded, because it is by experiencing the world with a keen, attentive, inquisitive, and open mind that scientists come to perceive things in novel ways. Another characteristic of an open mind is the ability to learn from one's mistakes and from the sensible advice and keen insights of others.

3. *Common sense*. Common sense is a prized characteristic in every aspect of life. There is an old axiom called the **principle of the drunkard's search**: A drunkard lost his house key and began searching for it under a street lamp although he had dropped the key some distance away. Asked why he didn't look where he dropped it, he answered, "There is more light here." Much effort is lost when researchers fail to use common sense and instead look in a convenient place, rather than in the most likely place (i.e., the place where common sense would lead them), for the answers to their questions. Similarly, Hall (1984) mentioned that many students ask only if their research plan is technically correct, not whether it makes sense.

4. *Role-taking ability*. The ability to see things from others' viewpoints is crucial to success in a wide variety of situations. In behavioral and social research, it means being able to see your study from the viewpoint of the participants. It also means seeing it from the viewpoint of the person who will evaluate it (in this case, the instructor who will grade it). For students who plan to present

their results in a poster, role-taking ability also means seeing it from the vantage point of those who will view the poster.

5. *Creativity and inventiveness.* The good researcher is also creative and inventive, that is, adept at finding solutions to problems of financial resources, equipment, recruitment, research space, and scheduling of participants. The good researcher also responds appropriately in emergencies and, of course, raises interesting questions.

6. *Confidence in one's own judgment.* Since there is seldom only one right way to do things, as Hall (1984) also noted, "There is no inherent reason why you must do as others in a research tradition have done" (p. v). As another writer put it, "You have to believe that by the simple application of your own mind to the facts of experience, you can discover the truth—a little part of it anyway" (Regis, 1987, p. 209).

7. *Ability to communicate.* Given the provisional nature of scientific truths, the end of one study may very well be the starting point for another study. Therefore, it is essential to be able to communicate clearly so that one's findings will be plain to others (Barrass, 1978). As Hall perceptively commented, "Research is not just the doing, it's the telling. If no one knows about your study, or if they can't figure out or remember your results, then you might as well never have done it" (p. vi).

8. *Care about details.* Being careful about details is another characteristic that serves us well, because others know they can have confidence in our conscientiousness, thoroughness, and the accuracy of our work. The good researcher is always careful about details, whether preparing a poster for a meeting, a paper in a course, or an article for a scientific journal. It also means keeping complete records, carefully organizing the data, copying and adding numbers correctly, stating facts accurately, and proofreading patiently.

9. *Integrity and honest scholarship.* Finally, every good researcher knows that integrity and honesty are paramount (American Association for the Advancement of Science, 1988; American Psychological Association, 1973, 1982; Bridgstock, 1982; Koshland, 1988; R. Rosenthal, 1994b). Because "rigged" experiments or the presentation of faked results undermines the basic respect for the literature on which the advancement of science depends, either one is devastating to science. It is the duty of all scientists to safeguard against dishonesty, and this responsibility is taken very seriously. (As you think about ethical problems in research, you are also forced to confront your own moral presuppositions.)

Summary of Ideas

1. Five reasons for studying research methods are (a) to provide a richer appreciation of the information that science and technology bring to modern life; (b) to avoid falling prey to hucksters and imposters whose showy claims are counterfeit; (c) to learn information and skills that are transferable beyond the research setting; (d) to learn that scientific knowledge is relative and provisional; and (f) to consider research as a career.

2. Peirce's four methods for the "fixation of belief" (the formation of strong beliefs or convictions) are (a) the method of tenacity (i.e., stubbornly and mindlessly clinging to myth, folklore, and superstition, like believing in UFOs or the geocentric design of the universe); (b) the method of authority (i.e., complying with the word of authority, as in Peirce's witchcraft example, or, on the positive side, obeying reasonable laws that are the basis of civilized society); (c) the a priori method (i.e., the use of reason and logic to make sense of things and debunk hoaxes, as in discrediting the "teddy bear virus" hoax); and (d) the scientific method.

3. The *scientific method* is a misnomer, in that it is not any single, fixed procedure but is instead a strategy primarily distinguished by *empirical reasoning* (a combination of logic and the use of careful observation and measurement, e.g., Galton's study of prayer, Ceci's experimental study of children's eyewitness testimony, and Asch's use of accomplices in his laboratory demonstration of conformity).

4. The informative and persuasive language (or *rhetoric*) of science often takes the form of written reports of research findings, which conform to an accepted basic structure that is illustrated in Appendix A.

5. Scientists often use analogical rhetoric to explain things (e.g., Einstein's statement) and are also attuned to the beauty of science (Box 1.4).

6. *Behavioral science* comprises a variety of different fields, which enlist the use of multiple methods and theories (called *methodological pluralism* and *theoretical ecumenism*) to explain things by zeroing in (converging) on phenomena of interest. What all these fields have in common is that they are concerned with how and why people behave, feel, and think as they do.

7. *Descriptive research* tells us "how things are" (e.g., describes children's failure in school; other examples are given in Table 1.1).

8. *Relational research* tells us "how things are in relation to other things" (e.g., describes the relation between student failure and teaching behavior; see other examples in Table 1.1).

9. *Experimental research* tells us "how things are and how they got to be that way" (e.g., by studying the effects of teaching on pupil learning by manipulating the hypothesized causes of student failure; see other examples in Table 1.1).

10. *Random selection* refers to choosing an unbiased sample that is representative of a population, whereas *random assignment* refers to how subjects are allocated by an unbiased procedure to different groups or conditions in an experiment (Box 1.6).

11. Hall listed nine traits of good researchers: enthusiasm, open-mindedness, common sense, role-taking ability, a combination of creativity and inventiveness, confidence in one's own judgment, the ability to communicate, care about details, and integrity and honest scholarship.

 Key Terms

ad hoc hypothesis   p. 16
analogical rhetoric   p. 11
a priori method   p. 6
behavior   p. 11
behavioral science   p. 11
control group   p. 9
correlational research   p. 15
descriptive research   p. 15
empirical   p. 7

empirical reasoning   p. 7
experimental research   p. 16
method of authority   p. 4
method of tenacity   p. 4
methodological pluralism
   p. 13
principle of the drunkard's
   search   p. 18
pseudoscience   p. 2

psychophysics   p. 12
random assignment   p. 17
random selection   p. 17
relational research   p. 15
replicate   p. 12
rhetoric   p. 10
scientific method   p. 1
theoretical ecumenism   p. 13

WEB ACTIVITY

Want to improve your critical thinking? Check out University of Melbourne philosopher Tim van Gelder's Web site at http://www.philosophy.unimelb.edu.au/reason/critical/index.htm. To learn about "strange beliefs, amusing deceptions, and dangerous illusions," visit Sacramento City College philosopher Robert T. Carroll's http://www.skepdic.com.

Multiple-Choice Questions for Review (answers appear at the end of this chapter)

1. John believes that women are more emotionally expressive than men. When asked why he believes this, John says it is because he has "always" believed it, and because "everybody knows it is true." John is using the (a) method of tenacity; (b) scientific method; (c) a priori method; (d) method of authority.

2. Some philosophers have suggested that we can understand the universe by using only pure reason and logic. These philosophers would advocate using the (a) method of tenacity; (b) scientific method; (c) a priori method; (d) method of authority.

3. Julie believes that everyone dreams every night because her psychology professor told her this is true. Julie is using the (a) method of tenacity; (b) scientific method; (c) a priori method; (d) method of authority.

4. Dr. Smith believes that psychotherapy is generally very effective in treating mental disorders. She claims that her belief is based on empirical research in which therapy was given to some patients but not others, and in which the degree of mental disorder was carefully measured. Dr. Smith's belief is based on the (a) method of tenacity; (b) scientific method; (c) a priori method; (d)method of authority.

5. Which of the following is the *most* distinctive characteristic of science? (a) empirical inquiry; (b) analogical imagery; (c) the rhetoric of science; (d) statistical explanation

6. Behavioral science (a) encompasses many scientific disciplines that study behavior; (b) emphasizes multiple methods of observation and explanation; (c) has seen a growth in the number of interdisciplinary fields; (d) all of the above.

7. Which approach to empirical research is generally considered a necessary first step in conducting research but is rarely considered sufficient by itself? (a) relational research; (b) experimental research; (c) descriptive research; (d) none of the above

8. A researcher at the College of the Southwest conducts a research project on the study habits of students. She reports that, on average, college students study 20 hours per week. This is an example of (a) relational research; (b) experimental research; (c) descriptive research; (d) none of the above.

9. Experimental research (a) can support cause-effect conclusions; (b) involves the manipulation of variables; (c) involves randomly assigning subjects to conditions; (d) all of the above.

10. Flipping a coin to decide whether each person in a sample of participants will be assigned to the experimental or the control group is an illustration of (a) random sampling; (b) random assignment; (c) both random assignment and randomization because they are synonyms; (d) none of the above.

Discussion Questions for Review (answers appear at the end of this chapter)

1. Philosopher Charles Sanders Peirce described four approaches (he called them *methods*) on which strong beliefs are ostensibly based. What are these "methods"? Give an example of a belief based on each method.

2. What are the characteristics of the scientific method? Can any one of them be considered "more fundamental" than the others?

3. A Wayne State researcher is interested in the effects of children's viewing TV violence on the children's level of aggression on the playground. The amount and type of viewing will be assessed through a standard procedure: TV diaries sent to parents. Aggression will be rated by two judges. The researcher hypothesizes that children who spend more time watching violent TV at home are more aggressive on the playground than their peers who watch relatively little violent TV at home. Of the three general research types (i.e., descriptive, relational, and experimental), which type is this?

4. A Wichita State researcher plans to assign fifth-grade children to one of two conditions. Half the children (Group A) will be shown a relatively violent movie at 10:30, and half (Group B) will be shown a nonviolent movie at the same time. Each film will be equally engaging. Two observers will code the children's behavior when both groups are brought back together on the playground for their 11:00 recess. This procedure will continue daily for six weeks. The researcher predicts that Group A will be more aggressive than Group B. What type of research is this?

5. A researcher at the University of New Hampshire wants to measure the prevalence of shyness in the undergraduate community. She administers the well-standardized Shyness Scale to volunteers in a main dining hall, collecting data on a respectable 35% of all undergraduates. What type of research is this?

6. A North Dakota State student wants to study other students' creativity, and he wants to use all three types of research approaches (descriptive, relational, and experimental) in this project. Think of a concrete example of each type that he could use.

7. A student at Foothill College claims that it is not possible to study such nonscientific concepts as prayer because prayer falls in the domain of theology rather than of science. Is the student correct?

8. The chapter ended by describing Hall's nine "traits of good researchers." List as many as you can recall.

Answers to Review Questions

Multiple-Choice Questions

1. a	3. d	5. a	7. c	9. d
2. c	4. b	6. d	8. c	10. b

Discussion Questions

1. First, the method of tenacity: believing something because it is an idea that has been around for a long time (e.g., Elvis is alive). Second, the method of authority: believing something told to you by an expert in the field (e.g., cutting back on fatty foods because the doctor told you to do so and you believe that doctors know about this). Third, the a priori method: using pure reason as a basis of belief (e.g., reasoning that $12 \times 100 = 120 \times 10 = 1 \times 1200$). Fourth, the scientific method:

using empirical reasoning as a basis of belief (e.g., believing the earth is round because you have circled the globe by foot, boat, and vehicle and not fallen off).

2. Empirical reasoning is considered the "most fundamental" characteristic of the scientific method. Other characteristics include the technical terms and special language that scientists use (i.e., the rhetoric of science, which often includes the use of perceptible metaphors and analogies) and the beauty of science.

3. This is relational research because the relation of two sets of observations (TV diary entries and playground aggression) is examined. It is not experimental because neither of the variables is manipulated by the investigator.

4. This is experimental research because the investigator has manipulated the type of movie shown.

5. This is descriptive research because the data are collected on student shyness, but these scores are not examined for their relation to any other variable.

6. For his descriptive research, he might collect data on the creativity scores of other students. For his relational research, he might examine the relationship between creativity scores and SAT scores. For his experimental research, he might experimentally manipulate the type of music being played in the background while the students' creativity is being measured to see whether Mozart makes students more creative than does hard rock.

7. No, it certainly *is* possible to study the concept of prayer, and Galton conducted a relational study of prayer and longevity. An experimental study might employ prayer for a randomly chosen half of 20 people who are ill and no prayer for the remaining people to see whether prayer brings about faster recovery.

8. The nine traits are (a) being enthusiastic about the topic and process of research; (b) being open-minded so as not to miss a promising lead, and so as to learn from your mistakes and others' criticisms; (c) using good sense rather than doing something only because it is convenient; (d) taking the role of the research participant, the person who grades your paper, and, if you are presenting a poster, the poster's viewers; (e) being inventive and creative during the planning and implementation of your research and in asking interesting questions; (f) having confidence in your own judgment after applying your mind to the facts; (g) learning to communicate clearly; (h) being careful about details in all phases of your research; and (i) being honest in every aspect of the research.

CHAPTER 2

Creative Ideas and Working Hypotheses

Preview Questions

- How do ideas for hypotheses and empirical research get started?
- What belongs in my research proposal?
- How do I find and use reference materials to do a literature search?
- How should I go about defining concepts and variables?
- What is the difference between a theory and a hypothesis?
- What are the criteria of scientific hypotheses?
- What is the purpose of a construct?
- What is meant by *independent variable* and *dependent variable?*

Discovery and Justification

The purpose of this chapter is to give you a sense of what philosopher Hans Reichenbach (1938) called the "discovery phase" of the scientific method and, if you will be doing empirical research, to get you thinking about a suitable hypothesis and give you a preview of the research proposal and the final report. Thus, if you have not yet studied Appendix A, now is the best time to read it, as it contains a sample research report (beginning on p. 384) and also provides tips that will help you organize your time. The student whose name is indicated ("Mary Jones") is fictitious, but the results shown are real data (from an unpublished study conducted by Dr. Bruce Rind, who gave us permission to use the data). Notice that the report begins by describing how "Mary" got the idea for her study from watching lawyers on TV who were at loggerheads on a controversial issue. She tells how she developed a testable hypothesis based on a particular social psychological theory. The remainder of Mary's report describes her study design, her empirical findings and the results of her statistical calculations, and then her interpretation of the overall study. Notice that there is also a special section at the end of the report (called an *appendix*) that contains her raw data and an overview of her statistical analyses. Not all instructors require their students to include an appendix, but many now do. However, even if you are not required to report the raw scores and your calculations, it is very important that you keep all your notes and raw data, at least until the instructor has returned your report and you have received a grade in the course—just in case there are any questions about your work.

As Mary's introduction illustrates, suitable leads for research ideas are all around us. One source of creative ideas is the research literature, and later in this chapter, we will describe how to do a literature search. Another way to uncover problems that need probing or questions that have gone unanswered is to attend colloquium talks in the psychology department and paper and poster presentations at psychology meetings. You may suddenly think of an interesting new way of looking at something, or of a way of turning some phenomenon or relationship on its head. For example, social psychologists have long believed that attitudes shape behavior (e.g., Kraus, 1991), but Daryl Bem, a Cornell University social psychologist, proposed reversing this relationship when he raised the possibility that reflecting on one's behavior can also shape one's attitude. Suppose a politician takes a stand on an issue for the sake of expediency and, after defending it repeatedly, thinks to himself, "I guess I really believe this." Or suppose you wolf down a sandwich and *then* it occurs to you, "Gee, I must have been starving" (Brehm & Kassin, 1996). Bem (1965, 1972) designed and conducted experiments to test and confirm what he called "self-perception theory."

We will be describing a number of other examples of what Yale University social psychologist William J. McGuire (1973, 1997) called "hypothesis-generating heuristics," that is, the circumstances or the strategies that were the basis of hypotheses for empirical research. Sometimes ideas almost seem to be thrust on us by a set of circumstances (see also Box 2.1), and at other times we are moved to replicate a published study by designing a study with a new twist. We will have more to say about replication later in this book, but it can be especially useful early in the history of a research question (Rosenthal, 1990c). Suppose all replications were weighted equally, in which case the first replication would essentially double the amount of information on the topic found in the original research. Once the number of replications grows to be substantial, we can use a statistical approach called *meta-analysis* (introduced in Appendix C) to develop an overall picture of the findings. For example, the effectiveness of psychotherapy was, at one time, questioned by some psychologists (e.g., Eysenck, 1952, 1961). However, by the 1970s, there were enough empirical studies available, including many replications, for University of Colorado researchers Mary Lee Smith and Gene Glass (1977) to use meta-analysis to synthesize the results of nearly 400 controlled evaluation studies of psychotherapy and counseling. Among their findings was that the average patient who received psychotherapy showed improvement that far exceeded that shown by the untreated controls. Meta-analysis is also used as an exploratory tool to develop hypotheses regarding the conditions that strengthen or weaken a relationship, called **moderator variables**.

BOX 2.1   When Circumstances Evoke Ideas

In a famous case, clinical psychologist Leo Kanner (1943) was working with some disturbed children when he noticed a similarity in their behavior. Not only did they tend to be socially isolated, but they had also failed to develop appropriate language skills. Calling this *syndrome* (i.e., a set of symptoms) "infantile autism," Kanner and others began to do research on it. It is now listed in the diagnostic manual that clinical psychologists and psychiatrists use. Similar creative insights that were evoked by circumstances have been documented in the business world. For example, Edwin H. Land was with his 3-year-old daughter when she asked him why a camera could not produce pictures instantly. Thinking about her question while out for a walk, he suddenly hit on the idea for the Polaroid Land Camera. In another famous case, George deMestral was picking cockleburs from his jacket after a stroll in the Swiss countryside when he noticed that they were covered with tiny hooks that had become embedded in the loops of the fabric of his jacket. Suddenly he saw a way to create something useful out of a nuisance—the Velcro fastener (R. M. Roberts, 1989).

Reichenbach chose the term **discovery phase** to capture the idea of the scientist as a kind of "Christopher Columbus" who is venturing into the unknown. In later chapters, we will focus on what Reichenbach (1938) called the **justification phase**, in which researchers test their **working hypotheses** (i.e., testable suppositions or conjectures) and logically defend their conclusions (often with the aid of statistics and graphs). Another philosopher (Kordig, 1978) suggested dividing the discovery phase into three stages: initial thinking, plausibility, and acceptability. Although we use these terms in this chapter, it is important to keep in mind that the discovery/justification division, as well as the three stages of discovery, are merely a convenient way of thinking about this process and are not without controversy in the philosophy of science. At the end of this chapter, we will illustrate that not all research proceeds in this linear way. We will explain concepts such as *hypotheses, theories,* and *independent* and *dependent variables* in more detail, but we begin by illustrating six hypothesis-generating heuristics: (a) the use of an intensive case study approach; (b) the effort to make sense of a paradoxical incident; (c) the use of analogical thinking; (d) the resolution of conflicting results; (e) the effort to improve on older ideas; and (f) the exploitation of unexpected observations (serendipity).

Using an Intensive Case Study

By **intensive case study**, we simply mean an in-depth examination of an individual or a group of people with a common identity (Davison, 2000; Ragin, 1992; Ragin & Becker, 1992). For example, anthropologists describe their studies of particular cultures as "case studies," on the assumption that each culture can be presumed to have an internal consistency, broadly speaking (Platt, 1992). Beginning with the work of Sigmund Freud (1856–1939), psychoanalytic ideas about human motivation have come from case studies using the free association method (i.e., the patient tells whatever passes through his or her mind) to tease out the concealed psychological bases of neurotic symptoms that apparently have no organic cause. Case studies are also widely used in educational research, policy making, organizational and management analysis, and city and regional planning (Merriam, 1991; Yin, 1989). In Chapter 8, we will describe a quantitative variant of the case study called *single-case experimental research* (see also Box 2.2). Case studies have also spawned hypotheses and research in such diverse areas of behavioral science as memory, animal behavior, and cognitive development (Kazdin, 1980, 1992).

An intensive case study of a quite different kind was done by Perry London, a clinical psychologist. A book about the trial of a notorious World War II Nazi criminal (Arendt, 1963) had generated considerable interest in developing an understanding of the character traits and motivations of Christians in Germany who saved Jews from the horrors perpetrated by the Nazis during World War II. London and his colleagues carried out intensive case studies of 27 rescuers and 42 rescued people by tape-recording and analyzing interviews with each of them. Because the respondents were not a random sample, the researchers could not generalize from this group of rescuers to the majority of those who aided Jews during World War II. At best, then, the case study could be used only to generate some tentative hypotheses, or as London (1970) described it, "The lacunae in our data are so great that we cannot even conjecture about the generality of our hypotheses" (p. 249).

Nonetheless, a number of valuable hypotheses came out of this work. Among London's many insights was that the behavior of the rescuers could not be boiled

 BOX 2.2   XOT, BOK, LUM, ZAT

An early example of single-case experimental research is a classic investigation conducted by Hermann Ebbinghaus (1850–1909). Using himself as the case studied, Ebbinghaus developed theoretical curves to describe the rates at which certain information is learned and forgotten. To do this, he measured his own ability to learn and relearn thousands of nonsense syllables, each consisting of a random combination of two consonants and a middle vowel, pronounceable as words but uniformly lacking in meaning (e.g., *xot, bok, lum, zat*). With himself as the sole subject, he first recorded how long it took him to master a list of nonsense syllables. He waited until he had forgotten the syllables and then relearned the list. He then repeated the procedure, each time making a careful record of his learning and forgetting.

down to any simplistic description. Some of them had been well compensated for their efforts, others had spent fortunes and had been left destitute, and still others had started out with little and had shared their meager resources with the rescued. Motives were even harder to pin down. Some of the rescuers were fanatically religious, and others were atheists; some of the rescuers had deep affiliations with the Jewish community, and others were anti-Semites. Three promising clues emerged as the basis of a plausible hypothesis to be evaluated more critically at a later time. First, almost all the rescuers interviewed possessed a spirit of adventure. Second, they also had an intense identification with a parental model of moral conduct. Third, they appeared to be socially marginal in terms of German culture. London (1970) hypothesized a scenario in which a zest for adventure and chance had been important in the initiation of the rescue behavior, but what gave the rescuers the impetus and endurance to do what they did was their strong identification with a very moralistic model and their experience of social marginality.

Making Sense of a Paradoxical Incident

A **paradoxical incident** is an event that seems contradictory. Social psychologists Bibb Latané and John Darley were puzzled by contradictory aspects of the circumstances surrounding a lurid murder in Queens, New York, in the spring of 1964. A 28-year-old nurse, Catherine (Kitty) Genovese, was coming home from work at 3 A.M. when she was attacked by a man who stabbed her repeatedly. When they heard her cries of terror, more than three dozen of her neighbors came to their windows to see what was happening, but no one went to her aid, even though it took the stalker over half an hour to murder her. Latané and Darley were struck by the paradox that, even though there were so many witnesses, none had bothered to call the police. The social psychologists wondered whether *so many* people failed to intervene because each believed someone else was likely to. On the basis of this idea, they developed their hypothesis—which they called the "diffusion of responsibility"—predicting that the more the witnesses to an emergency, the less likely it is that any one of them will offer help.

Latané and Darley (1970) then went on to test their diffusion-of-responsibility hypothesis in a series of experiments. For example, in a study at Columbia University, they demonstrated that the larger the number of students present, the less likely any of them was to volunteer to help in an emergency. The students in this experiment had agreed to take part in a discussion of problems related to life at an urban university. As the discussion progressed, a stream of smoke began to puff into the room through a wall vent. The researchers found that, when one student was in the room, she or he was about twice as likely to report the emergency as when the student was in the room with as few as three others. Instead of reporting the emergency, students in a group tended to be passive and to dismiss their fears through rationalization (Latané & Darley, 1968). In a similar study with introductory psychology students at New York University, who had also agreed to take part in a discussion group, each was much more likely to report a (simulated) epileptic seizure that he or she happened to hear if alone than if he or she believed that others were also aware of the emergency (Darley & Latané, 1968).

Analogical Thinking Revisited

In Chapter 1, we mentioned that metaphors and analogical thinking are often reflected in the rhetoric of science (see also Box 2.3); they can also serve as hypothesis-generating heuristics. McGuire (1964) used an inoculation metaphor as a basis of hypotheses he developed concerning ways of inducing resistance to propaganda messages. He began by assuming that some beliefs (he called them "cultural truisms") are so widely accepted in American society that they are perceived as indisputably true. Examples are "Mental illness is not contagious," "It's a good idea to brush your teeth after every meal," and "Cigarette smoking is bad for your health." Using the inoculation metaphor as a point of departure, McGuire theorized that beliefs like these are especially vulnerable to counterpropaganda for two reasons. First, recipients of propaganda attacking cultural truisms, seldom having been called on to defend their beliefs, are unpracticed in mustering a defense. Second, they are not motivated to develop a defense because they view such beliefs as established and unassailable.

McGuire drew an analogy between believing some cultural truisms and not having been vaccinated for smallpox. Like the unvaccinated person, who is highly vulnerable to an attack of the smallpox virus, a person who has not given very much thought to *why* he or she believes that something is true may also be highly

BOX 2.3 The Spiral in Nature and Analogy

A favorite analogy is the spiral because it seems to have such a prominent place in nature. For example, economists speak of "inflationary spirals," and in football, we have "spiral passes." A noted developmental psychologist, Heinz Werner (Werner & Kaplan, 1963), proposed a "psychogenetic principle of spirality," which he derived from an earlier philosophical analogy about the unfolding of historical events. In nature, of course, there are many examples of spirality: Storms that arise in the Northern Hemisphere typically display a counterclockwise spiral rotation, whereas those that arise in the Southern Hemisphere typically display a clockwise rotation. Human hair forms a spiral pattern on the scalp that is generally clockwise in men and counterclockwise in women. Spiral forms are also found in pinecones and other varieties of plants. One author (Robin, 1993) told of a researcher who blindfolded a right-handed friend and told him to walk a straight line across a country field; the man walked in a clockwise spiral, that is, until he stumbled on a tree stump.

vulnerable to a massive attack of counterpropaganda. Just as vaccinating a person with a weakened dose of smallpox virus stimulates the person's defenses so that he or she can later overcome an attack, perhaps a similar kind of technique would work to "immunize" people's attitudes. McGuire theorized that, to immunize people against "viral-like" counterpropaganda, we can simply expose them to some small form of the counterpropaganda in advance, thus stimulating them to build up their own "logical defenses" by rehearsing arguments against the counterpropaganda. Exposing them to too much preliminary counterpropaganda may, however, produce the opposite effect, causing them to reverse their attitude (i.e., it would be like accidentally giving them the disease). The problem, which McGuire worked out in a systematic program of research studies, was to establish the amount of "live virus" in an "inoculation" that, without giving people the "disease," would help build a defense against a future massive attack of the same "virus."

Resolving Conflicting Results

In a fourth hypothesis-generating heuristic, the scientist develops insights by trying to **account for conflicting results**. You will recall that we mentioned in Chapter 1 that there is frequently more than one "right way" to explain the causes of behavior, and thus it is possible that both sides of a theoretical dispute may be right when they are arguing about what processes are involved in some behavior. As an illustration, during the 1940s, there was a protracted dispute between two leading experimentalists, Clark L. Hull and Edward C. Tolman, concerning the nature of animal learning. Hull, inspired by Pavlov's research on conditioned reflexes, had developed a systematic behavior theory that asserted that the stimulus (S) affects the organism (O), but that the resulting response (R) depends on O as well as on S. According to this "S-O-R model," learning is a process in which S-R connections are automatically strengthened only because they occur in association with reinforcement. On the other hand, Tolman's "S-S model" stressed the cognitive nature of learning: Behavior is goal-directed and makes use of environmental supports, but this process is a discontinuous one that depends on exploratory behaviors from which the animal learns what leads to what. The appearance of docility, Tolman argued, is thus a mark of purpose, because the animal gradually learns by acquiring expectations and forming "cognitive maps."

Not only were there distinct theoretical and methodological differences between the two camps, but they also used different strains of selectively bred rats. The Tolmanians, centered at the University of California, used a strain of rats that had been selectively bred by the mating of wild males and laboratory albino females. The Hullians, at Yale University under Hull's direction and in a second camp at the University of Iowa under Kenneth W. Spence, used another strain of rats that had originally been bred for nonemotionality. To resolve these differences, another team of experimental researchers, Marshall B. Jones and Robert S. Fennell (1965), hypothesized that genetic differences might explain the different results obtained by the Tolmanians and the Hullians, as the two strains of rats used in this research had been separated for over 30 years (during which time they had been differently and selectively bred). To test this idea, Jones and Fennell used rats from both strains to duplicate the animal learning experiments done by the Tolmanians and the Hullians. The Hullian rats, Jones and Fennell observed, quickly exited the start box, ambled down the runway and around the turn, and ended up in the goal box, whereas the Tolman rats were more docile and seemed oblivious of their environment. In other words, Jones and Fennell concluded, Hull and Tolman were both right (see also Box 2.4).

Another prominent example of how behavioral scientists sometimes come up with an innovative hypothesis by trying to account for conflicting results is the work of Robert Zajonc (pronounced "zy-ence," rhymes with *science*), a social psychologist at Stanford University. He proposed a hypothesis that he termed "social facilitation" (Zajonc, 1965) to account for some conflicting published data: Some reports indicated that performance in humans and animals improved when passive observers were present, whereas other reports showed performance becoming poorer in the presence of others. For instance, in one old experiment, the participants were required to learn a list of nonsense syllables, either alone or in the

---

BOX 2.4 The Dayyan's Decree and Empirical Jeopardy

Jones and Fennell's resolution of the Tolman-Hull conflict reminds us of an old Yiddish anecdote, which might be called *the dayyan's decree* (Rosnow & Rosenthal, 1996b). A dayyan, or rabbinical judge, was asked by a couple to mediate a conflict in which they were embroiled. The woman told her side, and the dayyan commented, "You are right." Then the man told his side, and the dayyan said, "You are right." A young student, who happened to overhear the conversations, meekly pointed out to the dayyan, "Surely, sir, they both can't be 100% right." To which the dayyan replied, "You are right, too." The lesson of the dayyan's decree is not to foreclose on the possibility of more than one right answer. The physicist Neils Bohr stated that "the opposite of a great truth is also true," while psychologists Donald T. Campbell and Julian C. Stanley (1963) put it this way:

> When one finds, for example, that competent observers advocate strongly divergent points of view, it seems likely on a priori grounds that both have observed something valid about the natural situation, and that both represent a part of the truth. (p. 3)

Of course, even the agreement of all is no certain proof of accuracy or precision. In science, tests for accuracy and precision always include subjecting ideas to the jeopardy of empirical evaluation.

presence of others. The number of trials needed to learn the list was the criterion variable. Those participants who learned the list alone averaged more than 9 trials, and those who learned the syllables before an audience averaged more than 11 trials (Pessin, 1933). In later experiments, participants who performed a familiar task in groups did better than when they performed the task alone (Bergum & Lehr, 1963). It seemed that the presence of others enhanced performance on some tasks but not on others.

How could these seemingly inconsistent results be explained? One important finding in experimental psychology is that a high drive level causes people to give the dominant response to a stimulus. When the task is familiar and well learned, the dominant response is usually the right one. However, when the task is novel and the correct responses are unknown or not well learned, the dominant response will probably be wrong. Zajonc started with the idea that the presence of others serves to increase the individual's drive level and this increase leads to dominant responses. Therefore, Zajonc hypothesized, the presence of others must inhibit the learning of new responses but facilitate the performance of well-learned responses. If this hypothesis is valid, it follows that students should study alone, preferably in an isolated cubicle, and then (having learned all the correct responses) take examinations with many other students on a stage before a large audience.

Improving Earlier Theories and Methods

A fifth hypothesis-generating heuristic involves **improving on older ideas**. For example, one of many contributions by the noted experimentalist B. F. Skinner was to show that it was possible to look at two classical theories in a new light, the ideas of the Russian physiologist Ivan Pavlov and those of the American psychologist E. L. Thorndike. In the 1930s, Skinner's clear distinction between Pavlov's and Thorndike's ideas of conditioning opened the way to a long series of studies by Skinner and others (e.g., Ferster & Skinner, 1957; Skinner, 1938).

Pavlov had done pioneering work on classical conditioning. In the experimental procedure that produces this type of conditioning, a neutral stimulus is paired with one that always brings about some desired behavior or response. Suppose we, like Pavlov, wish to condition a hungry dog to salivate at the sound of a bell. After the animal becomes accustomed to the apparatus, we sound the bell to make sure that the dog does not automatically salivate to it. The dog pricks up its ears or barks, but it does not salivate. We now know that the bell will not cause the animal to respond as it does to food. The next step is to ring the bell and present meat to the dog. If we do this a number of times, we find that the dog begins to salivate at the sound of the bell, before we present the meat.

In contrast, E. L. Thorndike, who experimented at about the same time as Pavlov, in the early 1900s, worked with what he called "trial-and-error learning." For example, he studied how cats learned to escape from a puzzle box to gain food. He was convinced that the cats did not reason out a solution. Instead, he thought that their getting out and eating the food he provided somehow strengthened the connection between successful escape movements and the actual escape.

Skinner recognized a clear distinction between Pavlov's and Thorndike's types of conditioning. Skinner perceived that, in Pavlovian conditioning, the major factor is the stimulus that precedes the response. The response is elicited reflexively. In Thorndike's trial-and-error conditioning, the major factor is the stimulus consequence (i.e., the reinforcement of escaping the puzzle box), which follows the response. Skinner focused his own work on the latter type of conditioning, called *operant* or *instrumental*. In this type of conditioning, first, the organism responds to a stimulus, and then something is done that will either increase or decrease the probability of the organism's making the same response again. Say that we wish to train a dog to sit on command, and we prepare the animal by withholding food for a time. An operant conditioning procedure requires that we reward the dog *after* it sits (or approximates sitting) following the command. The work on operant conditioning, in turn, paved the way for applications in the military, in educational institutions, and in the treatment of behavior disorders. In his novel, *Walden II,* Skinner (1948b) described a whole society organized according to known principles of conditioning.

Another classic illustration of this fifth hypothesis-generating heuristic was Stanley Milgram's (1974) series of experiments on how far people will go in subjecting another person to pain at the order of an authority figure. We will have more to say about this research in the next chapter, but it will suffice here to note that Milgram came up with the idea for his studies as a way of improving on Asch's earlier conformity experiments (which we mentioned in the previous chapter). Milgram (1977) explained that he had wanted to make the work done by Asch "more humanly significant" (p. 12). Asch had designed his investigation to determine under what conditions people will remain independent of their groups and when they will conform. It will be recalled that Asch used accomplices to influence an individual subject's expressed judgment concerning which of three lines was closest in length to a standard line.

Milgram (1977) recalled the moment when he suddenly hit on the idea for his own experiments:

> I was dissatisfied that the test of conformity was judgments about *lines*. I wondered whether groups could pressure a person into performing an act whose human import was more readily apparent, perhaps behaving aggressively toward another person, say by administering increasingly severe shocks to him. But to study the group effect you would also need an experimental control; you'd have to know how the subject performed without any group pressure. At that instant, my thought shifted, zeroing in on this experimental control. Just how far *would* a person go under the experimenter's orders? It was an incandescent moment, the fusion of a general idea on obedience with a specific technical procedure. Within a few minutes, dozens of ideas on relevant variables emerged, and the only problem was to get them all down on paper. (p. 12)

Serendipity

The name for a felicitous insight or lucky discovery is **serendipity**; the term originally derived from a fairy tale about three princes of Serendip (an ancient name for Sri Lanka) who were constantly making lucky findings (R. M. Roberts, 1989). Previously, we mentioned deMestral's sudden insight that led to the invention of Velcro fasteners. Serendipity is also something that everyone seems to benefit from at one time or another (see Box 2.5), and like others, we have benefited from it in our research. In the previous chapter, we referred to the finding that teachers' expectations about their pupils' performance can sometimes become a self-fulfilling prophecy, that is, that the expectations become responsible for the outcome in behavior (Babad, 1993; Raudenbush, 1984; Rosenthal, 1966, 1976, 1985, 1991; Rosen-

BOX 2.5 Serendipity in the Art World

One day in May 1984, a young artist named J. S. G. Boggs was sitting in a Chicago diner having a doughnut and coffee and doodling on a napkin. As the waitress kept refilling his cup, the doodle evolved into an abstracted one-dollar bill. Fascinated, the waitress asked if she could buy it, causing Boggs to wonder why anyone would want a greasy napkin covered with coffee stains and perspiration. "Tell you what," he said, "I'll pay you for my doughnut and coffee with this drawing." To his astonishment she took the "dollar" and gave him a dime's change! Inspired by this serendipitous incident, Boggs began using colored ink and pencils to launch a career of drawing fairly exact representations of existing denominations of actual currency, and then photocopying them and successfully "spending" them in a kind of artistic performance for goods and services (Weschler, 1988). That is, he always insists on receiving a receipt and change in real money; he then sells the change and receipts to collectors, who in turn track down the people who accepted the art currency. The performance ends when all the elements are encased in a frame on the collector's wall.

The story does not end here, however. According to a news report in *The New York Times* (December 6, 1992), Boggs suddenly found himself under scrutiny of the law in several countries. In 1987, he was tried in England on charges of producing counterfeit British currency. When he was found not guilty, he paid his lawyers in drawings. He was also prosecuted in Australia and, this time, was found not guilty and awarded $20,000 in damages. In the United States, the Secret Service seized some of his work, calling it "counterfeit money." They also searched his office and stopped him as he was leaving his apartment one day to attend a ceremony where he planned to announce a new project to print $1 million in his own bills. Boggs was quoted in the *Times:* "They said I was a counterfeiter; they don't understand the difference between art and crime."

thal & Jacobson, 1968; Rosenthal & Rubin, 1978). In a later chapter, we will discuss other implications of self-fulfilling prophecies in research, given that some prophecy of how an investigation will turn out is virtually a constant in science (e.g., the scientist's hypothesis). What is generally known as **experimenter expectancy bias** began to be studied systematically in the 1950s, and its study had a lot to do with serendipity. The idea for a series of studies of this phenomenon was inspired by an unexpected result in Rosenthal's dissertation research (which at the time did not seem so lucky or felicitous).

Rosenthal was studying the defense mechanism of projection in college men and women and in a group of hospitalized patients with paranoid symptomatology. Each of these three groups was subdivided into three subgroups receiving a success, failure, or neutral experience on a task structured as, and simulating, a standardized test of intelligence. Before the participants' treatment conditions were imposed, they were asked to rate the degree to which they perceived success or failure in the faces of individuals pictured in photographs, and immediately after the experiment, the participants rated another set of faces on their degree of success or failure. Rosenthal's hypothesis was that being in the success condition would lead the participants to perceive other people as prone to success, and that being in the failure condition would lead those participants to perceive others as being more prone to failure (as measured by the difference between the preratings and postratings). Digging into the results, he did a number of statistical analyses, and in one of these, to his great surprise and dismay, he discovered that the preratings were biased in favor of his hypothesis even *before* the experimental treatments were implemented. After discussing the problem with his research adviser, Rosenthal began a frantic search of journals and books for references to this problem, which he called "unconscious experimenter bias." He learned that, as far back as Ebbinghaus (1885), psychologists had alluded to something like this problem, though no one had explicitly designed and conducted experiments to test the hypothesis of unconscious experimenter bias. In a long series of studies of how experimenters' hypotheses might unwittingly influence their results (which began at the University of North Dakota, in work with Kermit L. Fode, and continued at Ohio State University and then at Harvard University), the concept of unconscious experimenter bias evolved into the concept of experimenter expectancy bias (Rosenthal, 1966, 1976, 1993).

Rosnow's brush with serendipity occurred in 1969, when the Beatles were at the height of their popularity and a rumor concerning them began to circulate. The rumor alleged that, leaving the recording studio tired and dejected, Paul McCartney had been decapitated in an automobile accident; to maintain the group, the accident had been covered up, and he had been replaced by a double. The Paul-is-dead rumor, although a preposterous fiction, swept across U.S. colleges with numerous variants and deviations (Rosnow & Fine, 1974, 1976). What made the rumor so intriguing was that it was not at all like rumors that had been previously analyzed by psychologists and sociologists. The standard textbook on the social psychology of rumor insisted that, in view of the porosity of human memory, rumors must *always* become shorter (Allport & Postman, 1947). However, the Paul-is-dead rumor was not shrinking but growing by leaps and bounds as people improvised details and the "clues" multiplied. This progression raised the interesting possibility that the traditional understanding of the psychology of rumor might be incomplete, perhaps even wrong in some respects, and this possibility in turn opened the way to further research and new hypotheses that challenged and built upon aspects of the traditional theory. According to one recent theory, rumors are an attempt to deal with anxieties and uncertainties by generating and passing stories and suppositions that explain things, address anxieties, and provide a rationale for behavior (Rosnow, 1980, 1991, 2001). People have a tendency to spread rumors they themselves perceive as credible (even the most ridiculous stories), though when their anxiety is intense, they seem less apt to monitor what they are transmitting, which has important implications for how malicious rumors can be effectively combatted (Fine & Turner, 2001; Kimmel, 2004).

The Research Proposal

Let us assume you have an initial idea for a research study, and the next step is to decide whether the idea is plausible and worth investigating. As you search and retrieve relevant literature and discuss your idea with your instructor, you will get a better sense of how to develop a rationale for your hypotheses (in the way that Mary Jones explains the basis of her hypothesis in Appendix A). Once you have retrieved relevant work, developed your hypothesis, and have a research design and a plan to implement it, you must tell your instructor what you would like to study and how you propose to go about it, including how you propose to deal with ethical issues (discussed in Chapter 3). In other words, you are required to submit a proposal, possibly along the lines of the sample proposal in Exhibit 2.1. However, you should think of the research proposal not as a one-way communication, but as a mutual understanding between you and the instructor. Your instructor may require additional information or some variation on the sample proposal, but this exhibit will give you an idea of the way to organize it. Once the proposal has been approved, it is customary that you first consult with your instructor should you decide to make changes, as the proposal constitutes a formal agreement you have made with the instructor.

Note that Mary's proposal begins with an obviously tentative title, which provides a focus for her ideas but can be changed when she writes her final report. Next, she tells how she came up with her initial idea, so that its originality is not in question. She then cites the basis of her hypothesis. The next section describes her proposed design (including details and technical terms that we will explain later in this book). She describes the experimental manipulation, making clear that it is closely tied to her hypothesis. She tells how she proposes to measure the responses and why she chose this range of responses. In describing her proposed data analysis, she mentions her intention to meet with the instructor "to discuss any difficulties" she encounters. She then implies that she has given more than just cursory attention to ethical issues. The proposal concludes with a brief list of references,

(text continues on p. 40)

Research Proposal for (Course No.)

Submitted by Mary Jones

(Date Submitted)

Working Title

Is There a Biasing Effect of Drug-Testing Results on Bail Judgments?

Objective

    While watching television one evening, I happened to see two lawyers disagreeing about whether judges impose higher bail on defendants who test positive for drug use. One lawyer insisted that, even when positive information from mandatory drug testing is not directly related to the crime in question, it will nevertheless bias the judge's bail decision. This lawyer further argued that mandatory drug testing is therefore a serious threat to the criminal justice system's ideal of being just and unbiased in all its aspects. Moved by this dispute, I began perusing texts and searching PsycINFO for some relevant literature.

    To develop a directional hypothesis, I have been thinking about Jones and Davis's (1965) correspondent inference theory, which states that observers focus on certain types of behavior to infer traits because they believe that only certain behaviors are indicative of traits. Among the questions that observers presumably ask themselves is whether the behavior is low in social desirability. Baron and Byrne (1987) also mentioned that observers have a tendency to focus on socially undesirable behavior in judging the actor's traits and, once having inferred these traits, use this information to predict the actor's future behavior. On the assumption that drug usage is generally considered low in social desirability in our society, my hypothesis is that positive results from a drug test will result in harsher bail judgments than when no such information is made available.

Exhibit 2.1   Sample Research Proposal Based on Mary Jones's Project (Appendix A)

(continued)

Proposed Method

I propose to use a simple randomized design in which the research participants are assigned to one of two conditions. The sample will consist of approximately 30 students in an undergraduate class. I have been given permission by the course instructor to invite the students to participate. I have also developed a "crime scenario" that the participants will read; it describes a man seen running from a burglarized house.

In the experimental condition, the scenario will state that the suspect tested positive for drugs while in custody:

A man was arrested as a suspected burglar. He fit the description of a man seen running from the burglarized house. While in custody the man submitted to a blood test, and it was determined that he had very recently used drugs.

In the control condition, neutral information (i.e., the suspect ate and phoned someone) will be presented in lieu of the information about having tested positive for drugs:

A man was arrested as a suspected burglar. He fit the description of a man seen running from the burglarized house. The man spent enough time in custody so that he received two meals and made three phone calls.

Following these conditions, I will measure the dependent variable by asking the participants to respond to the following question:

If you were the bail judge, what would you set the bail to be? Choose a dollar amount from $0 to $50,000.

My reason for specifying a range is to give the participants a common metric, and I chose this range because it seemed realistic and sufficiently wide to produce differences between the experimental and control groups. At the beginning of the questionnaire, the participants will be asked their age, sex, year in college, and estimated GPA. No name will be asked for, because I believe that the partici-

Exhibit 2.1 *(continued)*

Mary Jones 3

pants will be more forthcoming if they know they are responding anonymously.

Proposed Data Analysis

I plan to analyze the results using an independent t test and to report not only the associated p value but also the effect size and its 95% confidence interval. However, as I get into this study, I will meet with Professor Rind to discuss any difficulties I happen to encounter. As these calculations are pretty simple, I expect to do them by using Foster's (2003) software. As a precaution, I will go over the planned analysis with Professor Rind once I have the raw data and have calculated the means and standard deviations.

Ethical Considerations

Though I have obtained permission to run my study in another instructor's class, I will emphasize at the outset (as part of the informed-consent procedure) that students who do not wish to participate may decline to respond. I will point out that all responses will be anonymous. The study does not involve deception; nevertheless, I will debrief the students and answer any questions at the end of the study.

Preliminary List of References

Baron, R. A., & Byrne, D. (1987). *Social psychology: Understanding human interaction.* Boston: Allyn & Bacon.

Foster, E. K. (2003). METASTATS: Behavioral science statistics for Microsoft Windows and the HP49G programmable calculator. *Behavior Research Methods, Instruments, & Computers, 35,* 325-328.

Jones, E. E., & Davis, K. E. (1965). From acts to dispositions: The attribution process in person perception. In L. Berkowitz (Ed.), *Advances in experimental social psychology* (Vol. 2, pp. 219-266). New York: Academic Press.

Exhibit 2.1   *(continued)*

which she will presumably expand as she gets further into the study, resumes her literature search, and begins to sketch out her final report.

Retrieving and Using Reference Materials

Since you will be using the resources available in your college library when you do your literature search, now is the time to familiarize yourself with what is on hand. Most college libraries have fact sheets that indicate where books, journals, and other work are stored in the stacks (i.e., the shelves in the library). You also need information on the material that has restricted access and the books and periodicals that are available only for browsing, which you can ask about at the information desk or by going on-line to the library's Web page. If you need a book or journal that is unavailable in your library or on-line, you need to find out how to use the interlibrary loan to request it. All of the library's material is referenced in its auto-mated card catalog, which not only gives you basic information but also tells you where things can be found. It is easy to use the automated catalog, but if you have a question, click on the Help key or ask for assistance at the information desk. In-formation librarians like to be helpful, and they will know the right answer or know where to send you for the answer. Since it is a lot easier to photocopy pages or paragraphs from journals and books than to copy lengthy passages by hand, you will also want to know where copying machines are located and whether you need to bring coins or purchase a card in order to use them. Another good reason to photocopy material is that it is a way to ensure that you have information ex-actly as it appears in the original text.

For psychology students, the easiest way of searching the literature is to use **PsycINFO**, an extensive reference database maintained by the American Psycholog-ical Association, to which your library subscribes. The PsycINFO database now goes back to 1872 and contains abstracts as well as full-text materials. You can access PsycINFO in your college library using one of their desktop computers, but you may also be able to do so in your room using your own computer. To find out how to do this, ask at the information desk. Once you are into PsycINFO, you need search terms (sets of words or phrases, also called *descriptors*) to pull up relevant abstracts; PsycINFO can even help you with this if you click on its Thesaurus icon. The trick in using PsycINFO is not to get too much or too little information; you will have to use patience in combining terms until you feel you have the records you need. There is a tiny box at the beginning of each record that you can check for later printing or saving, or you can save the whole file without checking any of the boxes. If you bring a blank disk with you, you can save everything, read it again at your leisure, and then print out what you need (this plan can be a great time saver if your college library's printers are busy).

Once you feel comfortable using PsycINFO, other computerized databases will be a snap. By going to your library's Web page, you will be able to find out what other reference and full-text databases are available to you on-line. You will find reference databases for just about anything you can think of, for example, census information (Census Lookup), government publications (GPO Access), medical information (Harrison's Online and Internet Grateful Med, for instance), news reports by topic areas (LEXIS-NEXIS), and even dictionaries and encyclopedias. Another useful database is the Web of Science, which allows access to the Social Sciences Citation Index (SSCI) and the Science Citation Index (SCI). SSCI and SCI can be used to do a very thorough *ancestry search,* which means tracking "ancestral" citations of an article or a book back to a specified year. Even the most hard-to-find material (called the *fugitive literature*)—like technical reports, dissertations, and master's theses—can often be identified and later retrieved once you know what reference databases are available to you. It is a good idea to keep a record as you search, so you do not backtrack without realizing it; list the abstract or index you used, the years you searched, and the various search terms you used (see also Box 2.6).

BOX 2.6 Starting Your Literature Search

Here are some tips that we borrowed from Rosnow and Rosnow's (2003) writing manual to help you get started on your literature search:

- Be realistic in deciding how much material you really need; too much material will overwhelm you and too little will result in a weak foundation for your report. How can you find out what is a happy medium? Tell your instructor what you plan to do, and ask whether your plan sounds realistic.

- Ask the instructor if she or he can suggest key works that you should read or consult. Missing a key work will stick out like a sore thumb when you submit your final report.

- Do not expect to complete your literature search in one sitting; you will only feel overly anxious and rush a task that should be done patiently for the best result.

- If you cannot find something you are looking for in the stacks, ask a librarian whether the material is lost or checked out (and due back shortly). If you really think you need it, ask whether the librarian can borrow the material from another college library. The problem is that it can take a long time to get something, so it is important not to put off the next step in your project while you are waiting for the elusive material. You may miss the deadline set by your instructor, and it is not an acceptable excuse to say that you had to wait for the library to turn up something.

- Keep a running checklist of all the sources you searched and the search terms you used so that you do not waste effort accidentally retracing your steps.

Another important point is that you should not stop with the abstract (i.e., the summary) but go to the work itself and read it. This advice applies even to a summary of a classic work that you find consistently cited and described by many authors. Mark Twain once defined a classic as a book that people praise and don't read. Read what you are citing, if only to make sure that you are not passing on a misreported account in a secondary source (Treadway & McCloskey, 1989). Another reason to go to the original work, particularly in the case of a research article, is to make sure you agree with the researcher's conclusion: There is no rule that says you *must* agree with something just because it is in print.

It is particularly important not to depend on media accounts of research as the final word; scientific findings reported in the media are often oversimplified. Go to the original and examine the findings yourself. Similarly, in public lectures, the speaker usually does not have the opportunity to provide the details that are required by scientific journals. By the time an article has been published in a quality journal, the report has gone through a process of review by several independent consultants. Nevertheless, published research reports are not guaranteed to be error-free; even though the aim of the review process is to detect errors and to raise questions that the author is required to address. There is also a "pecking order" of journals, and when a manuscript is rejected by a high-prestige journal, the author may try a somewhat lesser journal that may be willing to overlook some flaws (Sternberg, 2000). As the philosopher Francis Bacon advised more than 350 years ago, "Read not to contradict and confute; nor to believe and take for granted . . . but to weigh and consider" (Vickers, 1996, p. 438). As you study the material you have gathered, think carefully about the plausibility of your initial idea in the context of the published work.

Defining Terms and Variables

At this juncture, you also need to think about naming and defining the things you want to study, because how you describe something tells others how you conceptualize it, and whether you perceive it the same way they do. Researchers usually distinguish between two types of definitions, called *operational* and *theoretical*. First, **operational definitions** "link concepts to observable events" (Stanovich, 1986, p. 42). That is, this type of definition identifies terms on the basis of the empirical conditions (i.e., operations) used to measure or to manipulate them. For example, an experimental psychologist may define hunger operationally (empirically) by using laboratory equipment to measure stomach contractions. A social psychologist may define racial or gender bias by a person's score on a specially designed attitude test or questionnaire (see, e.g., www.UnderstandingPrejudice.org), or by the person's behavior in a particular group setting. A developmental psychologist may define frustration operationally by stopping a child from playing with a set of attractive new toys.

In another example, a team of clinical psychologists (Kendall, Howard, & Hays, 1989), interested in studying clinical depression (also known as unipolar depression), looked for a way to define this disorder operationally. To do this, they had college students and inpatients at a psychiatric institution respond to an inventory of "thoughts" by indicating how frequently, if at all, each thought had occurred to them over the past week. Some thoughts listed were positive ("I feel very happy" and "This is super!"); others were negative ("My life is a mess" and "There must be something wrong with me"). Comparing their results with previous data, these researchers developed a way of empirically defining the general concept of *clinical depression* in terms of reportable events (i.e., positive and negative thoughts).

Next, **theoretical definitions** (also called **conceptual definitions**) assign the meaning of terms more abstractly or more generally, for example, defining *hunger* by a connection between the reported feeling of being hungry and the experience of certain internal and external cues. The social psychologist interested in race bias might conceptualize it in theoretical terms that link it to "an indirect neural or behavioral preference for one racial group over another" (Phelps et al., 2000). The developmental psychologist may conceptualize *frustration* as "the condition that exists when people feel their goals are blocked by internal or external barriers." In their research, the team of clinical investigators mentioned above (Kendall et al., 1989) theoretically defined *clinical depression* as "a preponderance of negative thinking." In their research they found that people who had been clinically identified as depressed reported a high proportion of negative thoughts and a low proportion of positive thoughts. On the other hand, there are also different types of depressive disorders that vary in their severity and recurrence, that are treated in different ways in clinical practice, and that require further theoretical explanation to distinguish them from one another (Hollon, Thase, & Markowitz, 2002).

How can you get started in your quest for good operational and theoretical definitions of the things you want to study? Before you find yourself reinventing the wheel, you might look in standard references to see how others have conceptualized the same thing. You will find most relevant concepts in psychology defined in recently published encyclopedias such as Kazdin's *Encyclopedia of Psychology* (2000), Smelser and Baltes's *International Encyclopedia of the Social and Behavioral Sciences* (2002), Lewis-Beck, Bryman, and Liao's *Encyclopedia of Research Methods for the Social Sciences* (2003), and Friedman's *Encyclopedia of Mental Health* (1998). Your library may also have earlier encyclopedic works, such as Ramachandran's *Encyclopedia of Human Behavior* (1994), Harré and Lamb's *Encyclopedic Dictionary of Psychology* (1983), Wolman's *International Encyclopedia of Psychiatry, Psychology, Psychoanalysis, and Neurology* (1977), and Corsini's *Encyclopedia of Psychology* (1984). Another excellent source of information is the *Annual Review of Psychology,* which contains integrative literature reviews in various specialized areas. Other valuable literature reviews can be found in the *Psychological Bulletin,* the *Review of General Psychology, Behavioral and Brain Sciences, Personality and Social Psychology Review,* and *Psychological Science in the Public Interest*. All these reference sources will also provide further leads for you to track down in the library. Be sure to make a careful record of whatever you plan to quote or paraphrase, including the source and page number where the original material appeared.

A Summary Illustration

Before we move on, let us illustrate what we have discussed so far (i.e., coming up with an idea, doing a literature search, and defining the idea in operational and theoretical terms). Suppose we are interested in studying what we view as a particular aspect of intelligence that is different from academic intelligence. We know that people from different countries and cultures have different ideas about intelligence, but they all seem to view "dealing with other people" as an aspect of intelligence. In North American society, for example, we speak of some people as being "street smart" (i.e., astute in the ways of the world) and others as having "business savvy" or "political sense." All of these qualities seem to use social skills, such as being able to figure out others' motives or intentions. Given this crude conception, where do we go next?

Because every scientific idea has a lineage, the next step is to do a literature search to find out how specialists in this area may have viewed intelligence as encompassing multiple abilities. This search, let us say, turns up the early work of J. P. Guilford (1967), who envisioned 120 different ways of being intelligent. We have made a promising beginning, but even these 120 ways do not relate specifically to the "intelligence" we have in mind. It appears that we will have to be more dogged in our literature search. We continue by browsing texts and handbooks; by speaking with faculty who work in developmental, educational, and social psychology; and by using search terms to retrieve abstracts from PsycINFO and other on-line databases (e.g., another relevant database is ERIC, an acronym for Educational Resources Information Center, which contains bibliographic records of research reports, conference papers, teaching guides, books, and journal articles in education). If we continue in this way, we will turn up a relatively recent paper written by an American Psychological Association task force, which provides a list of scientific "knowns" and "unknowns" about intelligence (Neisser et al., 1996). We will also hit pay dirt by turning up a substantial body of work on "multiple intelligences" by cognitive, developmental, educational, and social psychologists, and by identifying leading researchers and theorists whose books and journal articles we can track down by using these and other databases (e.g., Cantor & Kihlstrom, 1989; Ceci, 1990, 1996; H. Gardner, 1985, 1993; Gardner, Kornhaber, & Wake, 1996; Sternberg, 1985, 1990, 1997; Sternberg & Detterman, 1986; Wyer & Srull, 1989).

All these specialists stress the existence of intellectual capacities beyond mathematical and language skills (i.e., beyond academic intelligence). We are interested only in one particular set of skills, however, which some include in the category of "social intelligence" (e.g., Cantor & Kihlstrom, 1989; Wyer & Srull, 1989) or "interpersonal intelligence" (H. Gardner, 1985). One theorist, Howard Gardner (1985), describes the core capacity of interpersonal intelligence as "the ability to notice and make distinctions among other individuals and, in particular, their moods, temperaments, motivations, and intentions" (p. 239). This sounds like a good description of what we are interested in, and we also find other conceptual definitions that we might be able to quote later. Gardner (1985) also states that interpersonal intelligence is a system that "turns outward, to other individuals" (p. 239); another specialist, Robert Sternberg, writes that it involves "understanding and acting upon one's understanding of others" (Sternberg, 1990, p. 265). All of these descriptions are quite consistent with our idea of socially skilled intelligence.

All we need now are a researchable idea and an operational definition, and we will find promising leads throughout this work—as well as by watching (and thinking about) how people interact. What interests us most is the idea of levels of interpersonal intelligence. Gardner (1985) theorized that, in its most elementary form, interpersonal intelligence entails the ability "to discriminate among individuals . . . and to detect their various moods" (p. 239); in its advanced form, it "permits a skilled adult to read the intentions and desires—even when these have been hidden—of many individuals and, potentially, to act upon their knowledge" (p. 239). We cannot study everything, and so we need to narrow our ideas and conceptualization. To differentiate what we want to study from the broader conceptualizations of interpersonal and social intelligence, we decide to study *interpersonal acumen,* so named because it refers to an individual's ability to discern (*acumen* means "discernment") another's intentions and behavior. Researchers have identified "levels" of this ability and implied operationally accessible variables (Aditya & House, 2002; Rosnow, Skleder, Jaeger, & Rind, 1994). Reading this work stimulates us to think of other operationally accessible situations that might tap interpersonal acumen, such as the ability of teachers to discern their students' motivations to act in certain ways, or the ability of children to discern the mood of a parent, or the ability of salespeople to spot impulse buyers. We need to connect our ideas with specific measurable events, but we have made a beginning.

Theories and Hypotheses

We are ready to tackle the acceptability stage, in which the researcher, having decided the initial idea is plausible and having a context for it, molds it into a testable supposition, or **working hypothesis** (also called an **experimental hypothesis** in experimental research). Before we go on, we should clarify the distinction usually made between **hypotheses** and **theories** (e.g., Lana, 1991; N. Miller & Pollock, 1994; Overton, 1991a, 1991b). To help us understand this difference, we look at another example, a classic formulation called *social comparison theory.* This important psychological theory was created by Leon Festinger (1954), and like all scientific theories, it comprises a number of explicit and implicit assumptions and predictions.

Most basically, social comparison theory assumes that all people need to evaluate their own opinions and abilities. People want to know whether they are like or unlike others, or better or worse than others. There are objective standards for many opinions and abilities to help people decide where they stand in relation to others. But for many others, such as opinions about ethnic or racial groups, religion, sex, or environmental pollution, not many objective criteria are immediately available. It follows, Festinger reasoned, that when no immediate objective standard exists, people attempt to evaluate their opinions and abilities by comparing themselves to others. He also theorized that the tendency to compare oneself with another person decreases as the expected difference between oneself and another increases. Thus, if you wanted to evaluate your opinions about the existence of God, you would be more likely to compare yourself with another college student, for example, than with a member of the clergy. The theory also states that you will be less attracted to groups in which the members' way of thinking is very different from your own than to groups in which the members think more as you do. One reason, according to Festinger, is that people are motivated to elicit feedback (reinforcement) about the legitimacy of their own opinions.

We see what a "theory" can look like (at least in social psychology), and now let us see what working hypotheses look like. Previously, we said that they take the form of conjectures or suppositions; their goal is to "select" what the researcher should observe (see also Box 2.7). In the case of Festinger's social comparison theory, he and many other researchers have developed their own working hypotheses. Here are a couple of examples that Festinger (1957) developed: "Given a range of possible persons for comparison, someone close to one's own ability or opinion will be chosen for comparison" (p. 151) and "The existence of a discrepancy in a group with respect to opinions or abilities will lead to action on the part of the members of that group to reduce the discrepancy" (p. 124).

What does this illustration teach us about scientific theories and hypotheses? First, it illustrates that a hypothesis is a conjectural statement or supposition, while a theory is a larger set of such statements in the context of certain assumptions, or presuppositions. Second, we see that hypotheses can be derived from a theory and that they give direction to researchers' systematic observations. Third, we see that a theory postulates a kind of conceptual pattern, which can then serve as a logical framework for the interpretation of the larger meaning of our observations (Hoover & Donovan, 1995). Finally, it is true of *seminal theories* (i.e., those that shape or stimulate other work) that they are constantly evolving as new findings, hypotheses, and interpretations emerge. Good scientific theories are also described as

BOX 2.7 "Selecting" What to Observe

To illustrate this function, the philosopher Karl Popper (1934, 1963) told his students, "Take pencil and paper; carefully observe, and write down what you have observed." They immediately asked *what* it was he wanted them to observe, because a directed observation needs a chosen object, a definite task, an interest, a point of view, and a problem. Popper explained to them that this was why the scientist develops hypotheses: to give direction to his or her observations, a direction researchers cannot do without.

generative, which means they allow others to generate further hypotheses and encourage additional observations; social comparison theory measures up well to this standard (e.g., Buunk & Gibbons, 1997; Suls, Martin, & Wheeler, 2000; Suls & Miller, 1977; Wheeler, Martin, & Suls, 1997; Wood, 1989).

Molding Ideas into Acceptable Hypotheses

In the final phase of the discovery process, the objective is to mold the plausible idea into a working hypothesis that can direct the researcher's observations. To pass muster as an acceptable scientific proposition, the working hypothesis must satisfy three basic standards: correspondence with reality, the joint criterion of coherence and parsimony, and falsifiability.

First, **correspondence with reality** refers to the extent to which the hypothesis agrees with accepted truths (e.g., other respected scientific theories and reliable empirical data). The working hypotheses that correspond most closely to accepted scientific truths are understood to have a higher "payoff potential" when subjected to empirical jeopardy. That is, such hypotheses are expected to be more easily corroborated than conjectures that come out of the blue. It is impossible to be absolutely certain that our working hypothesis will pay off when it is tested, but the idea is to maximize the odds in our favor by ensuring that our conjectures are consistent with accepted scientific truths. This first criterion is illustrated by another well-known proposition in social psychology, called the "similarity-leads-to-liking principle"—which in recent years has been most closely associated with the work of Donn Byrne (1971) and his students.

In 1961, Byrne began a series of studies proceeding from a theoretical idea he called the "similarity-attraction principle." This idea could be easily viewed as quite compatible with accepted wisdom in scientific psychology. For instance, in a classic study, Francis Galton (1869) observed that the marital customs of eminent Englishmen implied a pattern of "like-to-like" in the women they chose as mates. Similarly, an early test of social comparison theory by Festinger and others (Festinger, Gerard, Hymovitch, Kelley, & Raven, 1952) was also consistent with the similarity-attraction principle. The participants wrote their opinions on a specific social issue and were then given a slip of paper that supposedly contained a summary of the opinions of other group members. Some of the participants were led to believe that the others in the group held opinions similar to their own, whereas the remaining subjects were told that the opinions of the others were considerably different. All participants were then asked to state how much they liked the others in the group. The results showed that those who thought the others held divergent opinions were less attracted to the group. Byrne (1961) himself cited a number of other studies with similar results, and he pointed out again that we generally seem to be attracted to people who reward us and to dislike people who punish us. Byrne theorized that knowing that someone has attitudes similar to one's own should be personally rewarding, whereas dissimilarity is "punishing." Thus, the reason we are attracted to people with attitudes similar to our own is the desire for rewards. By ensuring that his theoretical ideas were consistent with accepted scientific findings, Byrne had attempted to maximize the payoff potential of finding the hypothesized relationship between similarity and attraction.

We will return to Byrne's ideas in a moment, but the second standard—also used by him in formulating working hypotheses—is a combination of coherence and parsimony. **Coherence** simply means that the statement of the hypothesis "sticks together" in a logical way; **parsimony** means the statement is not overly wordy or unduly complicated. Most scientists believe that, to be acceptable, hypotheses must be logically coherent and only as wordy or complicated as is absolutely necessary. Therefore, they "cut away" what is superfluous by means of a ruminative and winnowing process called **Occam's razor**, after a 14th-century Franciscan philosopher named William of Occam (also Ockham, known to his fellow friars as "doctoral invincibilis"), who insisted that we cut away what is unwieldy. What can be stated or explained in fewer words or on the basis of fewer principles is stated or explained needlessly by more, he argued. A word of caution, however: Occam's razor is not a description of nature (because nature is often very complicated); it is only a prescription for the wording of acceptable scientific hypotheses. It is important not to cut off too much—"beards" but not "chins." How can you find out whether your statement of the working hypothesis cuts off too much or does not cut off enough? The best way is to ask your instructor for feedback and suggestions.

The third criterion used by scientists to assess the acceptability of their working hypotheses comes from another of philosopher Karl Popper's insights, which he called **falsifiability** (synonymous with *refutability*). Realizing that it was possible for those with a fertile imagination to find support for even the most preposterous allegations, Popper argued that falsifiability is the most essential standard of all. Conjectures that cannot, in principle, be refuted by *any* means are not within the realm of empirical science, he argued (e.g., Popper, 1934, 1961). An example of such a conjecture would be "Behavior is a product of the good and evil lying within us," since it is not refutable in an empirical way. As you peruse the relevant literature in your area, you will find many examples of falsifiable working hypotheses that guided the research. You will see that scientific conjectures are "risky" because they go out on a limb by hypothesizing what *should* happen (Stanovich, 1986); examples are Byrne's similarity-attraction principle and Festinger's working hypotheses based on social-comparison theory (see also Box 2.8).

Constructs and Variables

Two other specialized terms, which refer to key elements of scientists' theories and hypotheses, are *constructs* and *variables*. **Constructs** are theoretical concepts formulated (i.e., constructed) to serve as causal or descriptive explanations. We discuss constructs and their validation more fully in a subsequent chapter, but Latané and Darley's "diffusion of responsibility" (mentioned in the previous chapter) represents a construct. You will recall that they used this concept to explain why each

BOX 2.8 The Evolution of Conjectures

Going out on a limb allows other scientists to use your work as a point of departure for further insights, and Byrne's work illustrates this evolutionary pattern of scientific conjectures. Milton Rosenbaum (1986a, 1986b), another noted social psychologist, challenged the similarity-attraction principle on theoretical and empirical grounds. Rosenbaum argued that, although dissimilarity can lead to repulsion, similarity *never* leads to attraction. In an answer reminiscent of the principle of the dayyan's decree (Box 2.4), Byrne and his coworkers responded by proposing that similarity-attraction and dissimilarity-repulsion are *both* right, depending on the particular stage of a relationship (Byrne, Clore, & Smeaton, 1986). The dispute between Byrne and Rosenbaum is still unresolved, but later results (e.g., Klohnen & Mendelsohn, 1998; Tan & Singh, 1995) implied that attraction and repulsion may be far more complex than was once thought.

bystander in a group felt that he or she was not responsible for summoning help, and that others should and would help. Constructs serve as a theoretical scaffolding between variables, particularly independent and dependent variables.

A **variable** is an event or condition that the researcher observes or measures or plans to investigate that is likely to vary (or change). The rhetoric of behavioral and social science also recognizes a classic distinction between dependent variables and independent variables (R.A. Fisher, 1973, p. 129). The **dependent variable** (usually symbolized as Y) is the "effect" (or outcome) in which the researcher is interested; the **independent variable** (usually symbolized as X) is the presumed "cause," changes in which lead to changes in the dependent variable. For example, in the statement "Jogging makes you feel better," the independent variable (X) is *jogging or not jogging,* and the dependent variable (Y) is *feeling better or not feeling better.* This does not mean that particular variables are always either dependent or independent but is simply another conceptual convenience in the rhetoric of science. In fact, *any* event or condition may be an independent variable *or* a dependent variable.

For example, it is easy to imagine how some independent variable might be transformed into a dependent variable, and vice versa, because a variable derives its label from its context. By way of illustration, in the 1960s, a commission was established by President Lyndon B. Johnson to study the roots of racial rioting in the United States. It was called the Kerner Commission (after its chairman, Governor Otto Kerner of Illinois), and one of its chief conclusions was that rumors had significantly aggravated tensions and disorder in a substantial proportion of civil disorders (Kerner et al., 1968, p. 136). Earlier in this chapter, we mentioned that rumors appear to be triggered by a combination of anxiety and uncertainty (i.e., in that case, anxiety and uncertainty were both independent variables, and rumor was the dependent variable). In the Kerner Commission's conclusion, rumors are the independent variable (i.e., the aggravating condition) and anxiety and uncertainty are the dependent variables (i.e., the aggravated tension). In the blink of an eye, our independent and dependent variables have switched places. Thus, the causal pattern is no longer linear (i.e., cause leads to effect); it now becomes a vicious circle in which some rumors can be viewed as "causes" (independent variables) one moment and "effects" (dependent variables) the next (Rosnow, 2001).

Examples of Independent Variables

You may be wondering whether in behavioral science there is an agreed-upon way of classifying independent variables, in the way, for instance, that chemists can turn to the periodic table to find out how an element is classified. The answer is no. There are, in fact, scores of independent and dependent variables in the literature of behavioral and social research. As simply an illustration, two general categories of independent variables that encompass a great many specific forms are biological and social variables. We will use eating behavior to illustrate these two categories.

One classic example of a biological independent variable is seen when blood from a well-fed animal, as compared to the blood of a hungry animal, is injected into another animal that is hungry. The hungry animal stops feeding (Davis, Gallagher, & Ladove, 1967). This finding suggested that a biological independent variable for satiation is somehow carried by the blood: Information about a cell need must be transmitted to a part of the central nervous system that is well supplied with blood and that can control and organize the food-getting activities of the whole animal.

Another classic independent variable affecting eating behavior was first identified by physicians who observed that tumors in the region of the brain near the hypothalamus and the pituitary gland caused the symptoms (described as *Froehlich's syndrome*) of tremendous obesity and atrophy of the genital organs. It was unclear, before experiments on animals, whether the syndrome was due to damage of the pituitary or to damage of the hypothalamus by the tumor. When the pituitary gland of normal animals was surgically removed, no obesity resulted, but subsequent damage to the hypothalamus was followed by obesity (Bailey & Bremer, 1921). The status of the hypothalamus, not the pituitary gland, was the independent biological variable involved in the physiological regulation of food intake.

There are also many examples of social variables affecting eating behavior. The reason, of course, is that feeding by both humans and other species is affected not only by internal factors but also by many external conditions, including attitudes toward food in different cultures. For example, when people in Flemish Belgium, France, the United States, and Japan were surveyed about their beliefs about the diet–health link, whether they worried about food, and other issues related to the consumption of foods perceived as "healthier," the results revealed clear country differences in all domains except the importance of diet to health. Interestingly, Americans associated food most with health and least with pleasure among these cultural groups (Rozin, Fischler, Imada, Sarubin, & Wrzesniewski, 1999).

Having learned to eat at particular times of the day is another social variable that affects one's experiences of hunger (e.g., Schachter, 1968), as anyone who has ever crossed several time zones during an airplane trip can testify. Taste, appearance, and consistency are other obvious independent variables that strongly influence what foods humans prefer and how much food they will eat.

Independent variables can also occur in combinations, or **interactions** of independent variables. For example, approximately half of the 40%–50% of North American women who crave chocolate or sweets do so primarily during the part of the menstrual cycle surrounding the onset of menstruation, but it is not yet clear whether this craving is due to biological or social factors, or maybe to a combination of both (Michener, Rozin, Freeman, & Gale, 1999). Another illustration implying an interaction is that, if ice cream is adulterated with quinine in increasing quantities, obese people tend to refuse it before normal-weight people refuse it. Obese people also tend to eat more of an expensive, good-tasting ice cream than do normal-weight people, but obese people do not work as hard as normal-weight or underweight people to obtain food (Schachter, 1968).

Examples of Dependent Variables

Dependent variables also have no single classification system. Suppose an animal behaviorist wanted to study pain avoidance as a source of "drive" somewhat different from the appetitive drives of hunger, thirst, and sex. (A *drive* is another example of a construct; it is a theoretical idea referring to the state of readiness of an organism to engage in physiologically connected behavior.) As no distinct element is characteristic of pain avoidance and compares with the drive for food, water, or a mate, what should the researcher choose as the dependent measure?

Imagining yourself quickly withdrawing your hand from a shock-producing stimulus suggests that measuring the time it takes to withdraw from the stimulus (i.e., the *latency,* or delay, of withdrawal) is a good dependent measure. However, suppose the researcher were interested instead in the pain connected with extreme sexual deprivation. This topic seems more complex than food or water deprivation, though similarities certainly exist. If the subjects were hungry, sexually starved male rats, the researcher might record their actions as they were faced with choosing between food and a female rat in heat.

In animal learning and conditioning experiments, four broad categories of dependent variables have frequently served as outcome measures: (a) the *direction* of any observed change in behavior, (b) the *amount* of the change, (c) the *ease* with which this change is effected, and (d) the *persistence* of the change over time. For example, in a learning experiment that consists of teaching a thirsty rat to run through a complex maze toward a thimbleful of water, the measures might focus on (a) the direction the rat chooses on each trial (i.e., whether it turns toward or away from the water); (b) the amount of change, as reflected in how long the rat persists in the correct response when the water is no longer available at the end of its run; (c) the ease with which the rat reacquires the correct response when the reward is again made available; and (d) how long the correct response persists after it is reacquired and the reward is permanently removed.

We can imagine parallels of these dependent variables in a social psychology experiment. A researcher interested in attitude change might, for example, measure participants' reactions to a message treatment or to a no-treatment comparison condition. The independent variable in this case is exposure (experimental group) or nonexposure (control group) to the message. Among the researcher's outcome (dependent) measures would be (a) the direction of each participant's attitudinal response (which determines whether the results in the experimental group point to different directions from those in the control condition); (b) the intensity of the new attitude, or how deeply felt it is; (c) the ease with which the participants are able to express or defend their newly acquired attitude; and (d) how long the new attitude lasts and whether the level of belief diminishes with time.

When you peruse the journal literature in your field, you will see that these examples barely scratch the surface of the many kinds of dependent variables examined by behavioral scientists. Here is a more exotic example from the field of developmental psychology: Infants have always fascinated their parents by balancing precariously on the edge of a chair or table in apparent imitation of a tightrope walker. The fascination is usually liberally mixed with fear for the safety of the infant. Obviously, an infant is not yet a fully competent and accurate judge of size and distance in its exploration of the space around it. The child's ability to perceive depth was a subject of intense interest to Eleanor J. Gibson and Richard D. Walk. These investigators worked with a "visual cliff," a board laid across a large sheet of glass that was raised a foot or more above the floor. A checkerboard pattern covered half the glass. On the other half, the same checkerboard pattern appeared on the floor directly under the glass. The visual cliff was created by the perceptual experience of the difference between the two sides. In one classic study, Gibson and Walk (1960) tested infants ranging in age from 6 to 14 months on the visual cliff. Each child was placed on the central board and was called by its mother from the "cliff" side and the "shallow" side successively. Most of the infants moved off the central board onto the glass, and all of these crawled out to the "shallow" side at least once. Only a few moved to the glass suspended above the pattern on the floor; most infants would not cross the apparent chasm to their mothers. The dependent variable was *crossing versus not crossing the apparent chasm*. As a consequence of having developed this not-so-ordinary dependent variable, Gibson and Walk discovered that most human infants discriminate depth as soon as they are able to crawl. This research also illustrates how developmental researchers often define their dependent variable in terms of incremental stages or levels of cognitive and behavioral development (e.g., Fischer, Pipp, & Bullock, 1984).

Discovery as Exploration

So far in this chapter, we have characterized discovery as a linear process of inspiration, library research, and critical rumination. But no rule says the scientist cannot explore by simply keeping his or her eyes and ears open and then developing a very tentative hypothesis to serve as an ad hoc explanation of an observed effect or phenomenon. A prototypical example of this approach was the creative style of Stanley Milgram. In his words, "You try to determine whether particular incidents lead up to the myriad surface phenomena . . . . You generalize from your own experience and formulate a hypothesis" (Milgram, 1977, p. 2).

In fact, Milgram was a master of exploratory discovery. In an interview with Carol Tavris for *Psychology Today* magazine,* he described how the routine incidents that he encountered while commuting to work in Manhattan by train led him to hit on what he called the "familiar stranger" phenomenon and to research questions with societal implications:

Milgram: I noticed that there were people at my station whom I had seen for many years but never spoken to, people I came to think of as *familiar strangers*. I found a peculiar tension in this situation, when people treat each other as properties of the environment rather than as individuals to deal with. It happens frequently. Yet there remains a poignancy and discomfort, particularly when there are only two of you at the station: you and someone you have seen daily but never met. A barrier has developed that is not readily broken.

Tavris: How can you study the phenomenon of the familiar stranger?

Milgram: Students in my research seminar took pictures of the waiting passengers at one station. They made duplicates of the photographs, numbered each of the faces, then distributed the group photographs the following week to all the passengers at the station. We asked the commuters to indicate those people whom they knew and spoke to, those whom they did not recognize, and those whom they recognized but never spoke to. The commuters filled out the questionnaires on the train and turned them in at Grand Central Station.

Well, we found that the commuters knew an average of 4.5 strangers, and the commuters often had many fantasies about these people. Moreover, there are sociometric stars among familiar strangers. Eighty percent of the commuters recognized one person, although very few had ever spoken to her. She was the visual high point of the station crowd, perhaps because she wore a miniskirt constantly, even in the coldest months.

Tavris: How do your dealings with familiar strangers differ from those with total strangers?

---

*Reprinted with permission from *Psychology Today Magazine,* Copyright 1974 (Sussex Publishers, Inc.).

Milgram: The familiar-stranger phenomenon is not the absence of a relationship but a special kind of frozen relationship. For example, if you wanted to make a trivial request or get the time of day, you are more likely to ask a total stranger, rather than a person you had seen for many years but had never spoken to. Each of you is aware that a history of noncommunication exists between you, and you both have accepted this as the normal state.

But the relationship between familiar strangers has a latent quality to it that becomes overt on specific occasions. I heard of a case in which a woman fainted in front of her apartment building. Her neighbor, who had seen her for 17 years and never spoken to her, immediately went into action. She felt a special responsibility; she called the ambulance, even went to the hospital with her. The likelihood of speaking to a familiar stranger also increases as you are removed from the scene of routine meeting. If I were strolling in Paris and ran into one of my commuter strangers from Riverdale, we would undoubtedly greet each other for the first time.

And the fact that familiar strangers often talk to each other in times of crisis or emergency raises an interesting question: Is there any way to promote solidarity without having to rely on emergencies and crises? (Milgram, 1977, pp. 3–4)

By simply observing people—keeping his eyes and ears open and coming up with a tentative causal explanation to describe the events—Milgram created ad hoc hypotheses. Such hypotheses must then stand up to the challenges of empirical testing in order to be absorbed into the scientific literature as valid generalizations (i.e., accepted scientific wisdom).

Summary of Ideas

1. Reading the sample research report in Appendix A, as well as the research proposal in this chapter, will give you a useful overview of these assignments.

2. In philosophy, a traditional (but nevertheless controversial) way to organize our thinking about the scientific method is in terms of (a) a *discovery* phase (in which testable ideas are fashioned) and (b) a *justification* phase (in which the ideas are tested and any conclusions defended).

3. In this chapter, drawing again on philosophy, we described three stages in the discovery phase as (a) initial thinking, (b) plausibility, and (c) acceptability.

4. In Stage 1 (*initial thinking*), some general scenarios that produce good research ideas are (a) an intensive case study (e.g., Freud's psychoanalytic studies of neurotic symptoms, London's interview study of rescuers, and Ebbinghaus's single-case studies with nonsense syllables); (b) a paradoxical incident (e.g., Latané and Darley's work on bystander intervention); (c) a metaphorical theme (e.g., McGuire's inoculation model of propaganda resistance); (d) a conflicting result (e.g., Jones and Fennell's adjudication of the Tolman-Hull debate and Zajonc's social facilitation hypothesis); (e) an old idea that needs improving (e.g., Skinner's work on traditional learning theories and Milgram's refinement of Asch's classic research); and (f) serendipity, or an unexpected insight

or observation (e.g., Rosenthal's work on the self-fulfilling nature of interpersonal expectations and Rosnow's on rumor).

5. There is often more than one right answer; sometimes two researchers can disagree and yet both be right (e.g., the adjudication of the Tolman-Hull debate; also Box 2.4).

6. The research proposal is an agreement made between the student and the instructor regarding the student's plans to do a research study; it describes (a) the rationale and hypotheses of the proposed investigation, (b) the proposed method and data analysis, and (c) the ethics of the proposed plan of investigation.

7. In Stage 2 of discovery (*plausibility*), the literature search begins to play an important role as you evaluate your initial ideas and plan your research proposal (using PsycINFO and other reference sources).

8. Operational and theoretical (or conceptual) definitions are the two primary kinds of definitions used by behavioral and social researchers.

9. Coming up with the plausible concept of *interpersonal acumen* provided a summary case illustrating the first two stages of discovery.

10. Theories are sets of statements, generally including some hypotheses, connected by a logical argument (e.g., Festinger's social comparison theory). Hypotheses are testable suppositions that are usually derived from a theory and that give direction to the researcher's observations. Theories provide conceptual patterns and a framework for the interpretation of the larger meaning of the observations.

11. Basic standards to be met by scientific hypotheses in Stage 3 of discovery (*acceptability*) are (a) that they correspond with accepted scientific wisdom, (b) that they be coherent and parsimonious, and (c) that they be potentially refutable, or falsifiable (e.g., Byrne's similarity-leads-to-attraction hypothesis or Rosenbaum's dissimilarity-leads-to-repulsion hypothesis in Box 2.8).

12. Constructs are explanatory concepts (e.g., *diffusion of responsibility*) that provide a scaffold or theoretical connection between variables, whereas the variables are what the researcher observes or measures (and, as the term implies, are apt to vary).

13. The independent variable (X) is the status of the determining event or condition (e.g., biological and social determinants of eating behavior); such events or conditions may also occur in combinations (*interactions*).

14. The dependent variable (Y) is the status of the effect or consequence (e.g., direction, amount, ease, and persistence of changes in behavior). However, there is an infinite variety of dependent variables (e.g., crossing a "visual cliff" in studies of young children).

15. In exploratory discovery, the idea is to keep one's eyes and ears open and to develop plausible ad hoc hypotheses as your observations progress (e.g., Milgram's insights about "familiar strangers").

Key Terms

accounting for conflicting results   p. 30
coherence   p. 48
conceptual definitions   p. 43
constructs   p. 48
correspondence with reality   p. 47

dependent variable   p. 49
discovery phase   p. 26
experimental hypothesis   p. 45
experimenter expectancy bias   p. 35
falsifiability (refutability)   p. 48
generative   p. 47

hypotheses   p. 45
improving on older ideas   p. 32
independent variable   p. 49
intensive case study   p. 26
interactions   p. 41
justification phase   p. 26

WEB ACTIVITY

For a portal to search engines, directories, reference sites, databases, graphics, periodicals, governmental information, book dealers, and other useful research tools on the Web, visit http:virtualsalt.com/search.htm. For a portal to Web sites of national and international scholarly societies in psychology, visit Waterloo University's Scholarly Societies Project at http://www.lib.uwaterloo.ca/society/psychol_soc.html. For links to a variety of resources in psychology, visit http://www.psywww.com or http://www.psychology.org. For APA-style writing tips and links to other relevant information on the APA on-line site, visit http://www.apastyle.org/previoustips.html.

Multiple-Choice Questions for Review

1. Paul has suffered brain damage in a car accident. Dr. Thaler studies Paul intensively, giving him many clinical interviews and tests to measure his cognitive functioning. Based on his work with Paul, Dr. Thaler comes up with a brilliant new theory of brain functioning, which he and others can test further in empirical research. Based on what we know so far, we would say that the doctor's theory came about primarily through the process of (a) serendipity; (b) analogical thinking; (c) an intensive case study; (d) the examination of a paradoxical incident.

2. A professor at the University of Colorado is interested in studying dynamics in small groups (typically consisting of two to five people). She begins by thinking that people in small groups relate to each other much as the governments of large countries relate to each other. She develops hypotheses about small-group dynamics by thinking about how people in small groups are similar to diplomats at the United Nations. Her hypothesis came about through the process of (a) attempting to resolve conflicting results; (b) improving on older ideas; (c) using analogical thinking; (d) serendipity.

3. A researcher at Monmouth University conducts a study of high school students and finds there is no relationship between the amount of time spent watching TV and grade point average. A researcher at Emporia University conducts a study of elementary school students and finds that those who watch a lot of TV tend to have very low grades. A third researcher, from Providence College, now develops a new theory stating that the relationship between watching TV and grade point average depends on other variables, including the age of the subject. This third researcher's theory has come about through the process of (a) serendipity; (b) using analogical thinking; (c) attempting to resolve conflicting results; (d) examining intensive case studies.

4. A medical researcher at Johns Hopkins University sets out to find a new treatment for cancerous brain tumors. She accidentally discovers a treatment for Parkinson's disease, a disease that is totally unrelated to cancer. Her new discovery has come about through the process of (a) improving on older ideas; (b) using analogical thinking; (c) examining intensive case studies; (d) serendipity.

5. Finding and using references (a) begins to play a role during the plausibility stage; (b) is a way of focusing your ideas; (c) is an opportunity to use PsycINFO; (d) all of the above.

6. "Intelligence can be defined as a person's general ability to adapt to his or her environment." This statement illustrates (a) an operational definition; (b) a theoretical definition; (c) a dimensional definition; (d) none of the above.

7. "Intelligence can be defined as a person's score on the WAIS (Wechsler Adult Intelligence Scale)." This statement is an example of (a) an operational definition; (b) a theoretical definition; (c) a dimensional definition; (d) none of the above.

8. _____ is to operational definition as _____ is to theoretical definition. (a) Construct, variable; (b) Coherence, parsimony; (c) Parsimony, coherence; (d) Variable, construct

9. Dr. Gomez conducts an experiment with two groups of subjects. Half the subjects are given 1 ounce of alcohol; the other half are given 4 ounces of alcohol. He then gives all subjects a test of physical and motor coordination. In this experiment, the test of physical and motor coordination is the _____ variable. (a) control; (b) dependent; (c) independent; (d) none of the above

10. In Dr. Gomez's experiment, the amount of alcohol is the _____ variable. (a) control; (b) dependent; (c) independent; (d) none of the above

Discussion Questions for Review

1. A Northern Illinois University student wants to see whether self-esteem affects academic performance. He asks 30 randomly selected students from his dormitory to fill out a self-esteem measure, and he divides the students into groups having high and low self-esteem on the basis of their test scores. He then compares the self-reported grade point average (GPA) of the two groups and concludes that high self-esteem does lead to a higher GPA. How has he operationalized his independent and dependent variables? If he finds these variables to be highly related, how well justified will he be in claiming that self-esteem affects academic performance?

2. A Virginia Tech student is interested in the personality trait of extraversion. Give an example of both an operational and a theoretical definition of this construct that she can use.

3. A friend tells a George Washington University student that astrology is a science and reminds her that President Ronald Reagan consulted an astrologer. How should the student respond to her friend? Can you think of a way for her to do an empirical study to test her friend's assertion?

4. A San Diego State student is interested in studying revenge. Can you devise a causal hypothesis for her to test? How can you assess your hypothesis on scientific grounds of acceptability before passing it to her?

5. A "wolf boy" was discovered in Alaska and brought to a learned doctor for study. The doctor conducted many exploratory tests to determine the boy's reactions. The doctor slammed the door, and though everyone else flinched, the boy remained calm and unmoving. The doctor called out to his secretary, who was taking notes, "Write: Does not respond to noise." A nurse who was looking after the boy protested, "But, sir, I have seen the boy startle at the sound of a cracking nut in the woods 30 feet away!" The doctor paused and then instructed his secretary, "Write: Does not respond to *significant* noise." How was the doctor's explanatory observation flawed? How would you instead propose to study the wolf boy?

Answers to Review Questions

Multiple-Choice Questions

1. c	**3.** c	**5.** d	**7.** a	**9.** b
2. c	**4.** d	**6.** b	**8.** d	**10.** c

Discussion Questions

1. His independent variable was operationalized by scores on the self-esteem scale; his dependent variable was operationalized by self-reported GPA. Because this is a relational study rather than an experimental study, he would not be justified in drawing the causal inference that either variable led to or affected the other.

2. An operational definition might be "score earned on Hans Eysenck's test." A theoretical definition might be "the degree of social ease and smoothness shown in a group setting."

3. Science is defined by its procedures rather than by the status of a person who labels a particular belief system a science. One study of the accuracy of astrological forecasts might ask a panel of "expert" astrologers to prepare a brief description of the personality of persons born under each of the 12 signs of the zodiac. A large number of students would then be asked to rate each of these 12 descriptions on the extent to which each of the descriptions applied to them. As long as the students know nothing about astrology, evidence of the accuracy of astrology would be obtained if the students rated the personality descriptions of their sign as more characteristic of them than the average of the other 11 descriptions. These students' roommates or friends could also rate the students, assuming the roommates or friends also knew nothing about astrology.

4. A causal hypothesis might be that revenge is more likely to occur when people feel they have been harmed intentionally by another. To evaluate the acceptability of this hypothesis, we would examine the correspondence with reality of this hypothesis, its coherence and parsimony, and its falsifiability. On these grounds, it seems we are ready to proceed to the stage of operationalizing our independent and dependent variables.

5. The doctor did not take the boy's cultural background or context into account. We might study the boy by administering standard medical, neurological, and psychological evaluations; by giving him a wide choice of cultural artifacts (toys, tools, foods, pictures, videos, etc.) to observe, use, and explore; and by accompanying him to settings (e.g., parks, lakes, and forests) more like those in which he grew up in order to observe his behavior in a habitat to which he was more accustomed.

CHAPTER 3

Ethical Considerations and Guidelines

Preview Questions

- What is the role of ethical guidelines in scientific research?
- What is an informed-consent agreement, and when am I expected to use it?
- How can I prepare for an ethics review?
- What are ethical dilemmas in research?
- What are active and passive deception, and how are they evaluated?
- What is the purpose of debriefing, and how do I go about it?
- How is animal research governed by ethical rules?
- What are plagiarism and lazy writing, and how can they be avoided?

Ethical Issues in Research

In Chapter 1, we discussed three general research approaches (descriptive, relational, and experimental), and you learned that any single study may be focused on one objective of these three types (i.e., to describe, to identify relationships, or to infer causality) or that the study might encompass more than one approach. We noted that, within these three approaches, there are many different strategies and options (some of which are further illustrated in the next two chapters). In Chapter 2, we examined the "discovery" process, in which tightly reasoned, falsifiable hypotheses are created. In the sample proposal (pp. 37–39), under the heading "Ethical Considerations," Mary Jones stated her intention to use an informed-consent procedure, to tell the participants that their responses would be anonymous, and, at the end of study, to debrief them and answer any of their questions. Once your instructor is satisfied that your research question is worth studying and that it can be formulated in a scientifically meaningful way, you are ready to consider the ethics of the empirical strategy that you will pursue. The purpose of this chapter is get you thinking about this challenge, and also to acquaint you with other ethical issues in empirical research with human or animal subjects.

The term **ethics** (from the Greek *ethos,* meaning "character" or "disposition") generally refers to the values by which people morally (from the Latin *moralis,* meaning "custom" or "manner") evaluate character or behavior. As the term is used in modern science, *ethics* refers to the values by which the conduct of researchers, as well as the morality of the empirical strategies they use, are evaluated. To help us in this process, we can consult legal, institutional, and professional **ethical guidelines** that contain rules and specifications pertaining to the question "Should I conduct this study?" when conducting the study involves a moral issue (Kimmel, 1996, p. 5). The guidelines that have figured most prominently in psychological research in the United States are those adopted by the American Psychological Association (APA; American Psychological Association, 1973, 1982, 1992). An APA task force recently addressed newly emerging ethical issues; the results of those deliberations were published in an informative book edited by Bruce D. Sales and Susan Folkman (2000); it also contains (a) the APA's 1992 ethical principles and code of conduct, (b) the U.S. government's regulations for the protection of human subjects, and (c) a government document that is well known to researchers, the "Belmont Report" (see Box 3.1). The Sales and Folkman book is not an official statement of the APA, but we will use its five principles as a springboard for our discussion of ethics: (a) respect for persons and their autonomy, (b) beneficence and nonmaleficence, (c) justice, (d) trust, and (e) fidelity and scientific integrity (M. B. Smith, 2000).

No set of guidelines can anticipate every possible case, but the idea of an ethics code is to have an agreed-upon focal point from which to examine "matters of right or wrong, ought or ought not, a good action or a bad one" (Kimmel, 1996, p. 5). Collectively, the five principles constitute a kind of "social contract" of do's and don'ts which are designed to remind us of our responsibility *not to do* harm to the research participants and to try *to do* beneficial research in a way that will produce valid results (Rosnow, 1997). We will give a flavor of the rigorous review process that research proposals are subjected to, which (at least in theory) is presumed to involve a risk-benefit assessment. We will also discuss the ethics of animal experimentation, though the main focus of this chapter is research with human participants. The chapter concludes with a discussion of ethical issues that are relevant to the reporting of research, with particular emphasis on plagiarism and how to avoid it. Throughout this chapter we will also pose various questions to stimulate your thinking (see Box 3.2).

Principle I. Respect for Persons and Their Autonomy

The term **autonomy** connotes "independence" and, in the context of research ethics, refers to a prospective participant's right as well as ability "to choose" whether to take part in the study or to continue in the study. The researcher's ethi-

BOX 3.1 The Belmont Report and the Tuskegee Study

The **Belmont Report** was developed in 1974 by a national commission that was given the task of formulating guidelines that would protect the rights and welfare of participants in biomedical and behavioral research. The document takes its name from discussions that were held in Washington, D.C., at the Smithsonian Institution's Belmont Conference Center (National Commission for the Protection of Human Subjects of Biomedical and Behavioral Research, 1979). Prior to this report, there had been some safeguards to protect subjects in medical research, but serious violations had occurred nonetheless. In a notorious study done by the U.S. Public Health Service from 1932 to 1973, the course of syphilis in more than 400 low-income African-American men in Tuskegee, Alabama, had been monitored without the researchers' informing the men they had syphilis (they were told only that they had "bad blood") and without giving them penicillin when, in 1947, it was found to be an effective treatment for syphilis. Although given free health care and a free annual medical exam, they were warned that they would be dropped from the study if they sought treatment elsewhere; the researchers even got local doctors to promise not to provide antibiotics for subjects in the study (Stryker, 1997). The Tuskegee study was terminated after details were made public by a lawyer who had once been an epidemiologist for the Public Health Service. By this time, however, the disease had progressed in its predictable form without treatment: The men had experienced skeletal, cardiovascular, and central nervous system damage, and, in some cases, death (J. H. Jones, 1993). As a consequence of this horrendous episode, there remains a "legacy of mistrust" of government and medicine in many minority communities (Stryker, 1997, p. E4).

cal and legal responsibility is to ensure that potential participants know what they will be getting into, and that they are free to decide whether or not to participate. In practice, the way this works is to tell them about the study and to obtain their written agreement to participate (called **informed consent**). There are, however, situations in which obtaining the informed consent of the prospective participants is unnecessary or impossible, such as in research that uses certain public records (illustrated in the next chapter). Another exempt case would be risk-free experiments in which informed consent would be counterproductive. For example, a team of social psychologists who were interested in tipping behavior had servers in a restaurant-diner draw or not draw a happy face on the back of customer checks before presenting them (Rind & Bordia, 1996). Before initiating the study, the researchers explained everything to the servers and the owner of the restaurant and obtained their permission to proceed, but no effort was made to inform the

BOX 3.2 Confronting Your Own
         Presuppositions

Thinking about ethical issues in science also forces us to confront our own moral presuppositions. For example, how would you answer the following three questions?

1. Is it right to withhold information from participants if I think that a full disclosure will bias their responses?
2. Am I justified in misleading participants by using a deception if misleading them is necessary to study an important issue?
3. Is it permissible for me to invade the privacy of participants if there is no other way to gather essential facts?

In fact, ethicists and researchers in behavioral science wrestle with difficult questions like these all the time (e.g., Blanck et al., 1992; Kimmel, 1981, 1988, 1991, 1996; Parloff, 1995; Rosenthal, 1994b; Rosnow, Rotheram-Borus, Ceci, Blanck, & Koocher, 1993; Schuler, 1982; Sieber, 1982a, 1982b, 1983, 1992, 1994; Stanley, Sieber, & Melton, 1987). As philosopher John Atwell (1981) noted, one thing that is sure is that research with human participants always treads "on thin moral ice" inasmuch as researchers "are constantly in danger of violating someone's basic rights, if only the right of privacy" (p. 89).

customers or to get them to sign a consent form, as telling them about the research would have destroyed the credibility of the manipulation and rendered the experiment meaningless. (Incidentally, the results were that drawing the happy face was associated with increased tips for the female server but did not increase tips for the male server.)

In most cases, however, informed consent is a requirement of the research procedure. In biomedical experiments in which the participants are randomly assigned to a treatment group or a control group, they are told that they will be blindly given an active drug or a placebo but are not told which one they will receive. In the recruitment of people for psychological experiments, the prospective participants are given a form that describes (a) the nature of the study; (b) any potential risk or inconvenience to them; (c) the procedure for ensuring the confidentiality of the data; and (d) the voluntary nature of their cooperation and their freedom to withdraw at any time without prejudice or consequence. The person is asked to sign a form in order to indicate that he or she understands the study and is willing to participate. Figure 3.1 shows in Section A an example of the consent portion of an informed-consent agreement and, in Section B, a form on which the participant may be asked about being "debriefed" after the study has been com-

Instructions to participant: Before you participate in this study, please print and then sign your name in the space provided in Section A. Once the study is over and you have been debriefed, you will be asked to initial the three statements in Section B to indicate your agreement.

Section A

I, _____, voluntarily give my consent to participate in this project. I have been informed about, and feel that I understand, the basic nature of the project. I understand that I may leave at any time and that my anonymity will be protected.

_____   _____

Signature of Research Participant   Date

Section B

Please initial each of the following statements once the study has been completed and you have been debriefed:

_____I have been debriefed.

_____I was not forced to stay to complete the study.

_____All my questions have been answered satisfactorily.

Figure 3.1   Example of the written-consent portion of the informed-consent agreement.

pleted. (We will return to debriefing later in this chapter.) However, because of increased scrutiny by regulatory groups, the disclosure form and procedure in some studies have become so detailed and cumbersome that they could defeat the purpose for which they were intended (Imber et al., 1986). If the participants are confused about the nature of their participation, it cannot be said that the researcher complied with the spirit of the law.

Suppose the prospective participants have a limited or diminished capacity to understand the consent form. For example, young children may have difficulty understanding the consent agreement (e.g., Dorn, Susman, & Fletcher, 1995; Susman, Dorn, & Fletcher, 1992). Whenever research calls for children or adolescents to participate, the researcher is required to obtain parental consent before proceeding and is not permitted to make appeals to children to participate before this consent is obtained (Scott-Jones & Rosnow, 1998). If the children do not live with their parents (e.g., if they are wards of some agency), the researcher can speak with an advocate who is appointed to act in the best interests of the child. Once the informed consent of the parent or advocate has been obtained, the researcher asks the child on the day of the study whether he or she wishes to participate—assuming the child is mature enough to be asked about participation. Incidentally, some

BOX 3.3 Freedom of Choice for Intro Psych Students

Freedom of choice must also be factored in when students in college or university classes are required to participate in a certain number of hours of research. Students taking introductory psychology are used frequently in studies by psychologists because such students are so readily available. They must be given a choice whether to participate in the study or to select some alternative requirement, and there must be an educational benefit to the students who participate in the research (e.g., a deeper understanding of the research process and, presumably, the results they are learning about in the course). To prevent coercion or the appearance of coercion, the alternative requirement must be educational and no more arduous than the research participation (e.g., reading one or more journal papers or attending a special lecture).

participants may mistakenly assume that, by signing an informed-consent agreement, they have relinquished their legal right to sue the researcher for negligence (T. Mann, 1994). In fact, the right to sue is protected by federal regulations on the use of human subjects (Department of Health and Human Services, 1983). (See also Box 3.3.)

Principle II. Beneficence and Nonmaleficence

Beneficence means the "doing of good"; **nonmaleficence** means "not doing harm." This second principle implies that, just as in the Hippocratic oath that physicians take, behavioral and social researchers must agree to "do no harm." In addition, the researchers are expected to maximize the benefits of their studies. The researcher submits a proposal of the planned research to a panel of evaluators, called an **institutional review board (IRB),** which provides an oversight mechanism by performing a **risk-benefit analysis** of the proposed study. Studies classified by the IRB as of **minimal risk** (i.e., the likelihood and extent of harm to participants is no greater than that typically experienced in everyday life) are eligible for an **expedited review** (i.e., they can be evaluated without undue delay). Studies involving more than minimal risk automatically raise a red flag that signals the need for a more detailed assessment by the IRB. Student projects in research courses typically fall in the no-risk category and are typically evaluated by either the instructor or a surrogate committee.

Figure 3.2 shows a **decision-plane model** that helps us conceptualize how this process is presumed to work, ideally. After their review of a detailed description of the proposed study, and after the researchers have responded to specific questions, the IRB members consider aspects of the study that may have risk-

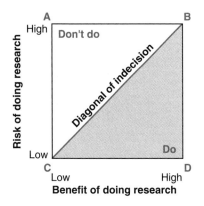

Figure 3.2   **Representation of an idealized risk-benefit ethical evaluation.** Studies falling at A are not carried out; studies falling at D are carried out; and studies falling along the B–C diagonal require further elaboration.

benefit implications. The questions that researchers must answer vary from one institution to another (see Table 3.1). Basically, the risks and benefits of doing a particular study are evaluated on scales of perceived methodological and societal values or interests. The "risks of doing the research" might include annoyances or inconveniences to the subjects and the loss of privacy, whereas the "benefits of doing the research" might include educational or psychological advantages to the participants, to other people at other times and places, and to the advance of scientific knowledge. Studies that are well thought out and are of minimal risk, and that address important issues, will be judged to be more beneficial than studies that are not well thought out, that involve physical or psychological risks, or that address trivial issues. In Figure 3.2, studies falling in the upper left area (labeled A) are *not* approved because the risks are high and the benefits low; studies falling in the lower right area (labeled D) *are* approved because the benefits are high and the risks low. Studies falling along the B–C diagonal (the "diagonal of indecision") are too hard to decide about and are returned for changes or further information.

A limitation of this idealized assessment is that it focuses only on the risks and benefits of "doing" research and ignores the societal and scientific costs of "not doing" important research. In view of this limitation, some critics have argued that IRBs are typically held to a less rigorous standard of accountability than are researchers (Haywood, 1976; Rosnow, 1997). Bureaucrats and pressure groups may also obstruct important scientific research (Brooks-Gunn & Rotheram-Borus, 1994). For example, a study involving a sexual survey of adolescents was terminated prematurely on the grounds that it "violated community norms," though stopping this research deprived the community of fundamental data that were needed to address vital health problems (Wilcox & Gardner, 1993). Another issue is that IRBs may ignore potential benefits altogether and use only a "risk analysis" as the basis of their decision making. Given the subjectivity of an ethical review, there is considerable

Table 3.1	Sample Questions for Ethics Review

Investigator

1. Who is the primary investigator, and who is supervising the study?
2. Will anyone be assisting you in this investigation?
3. Have you or the others whose names are listed above had any experience with this kind of research?

Nature of the study

4. What is the purpose of this research? What is it about?
5. What will the research participants be asked to do, or what will be done to them?
6. Will deception be used? If the answer is yes, why is it necessary?
7. What is the nature of the deception, and when will the debriefing (dehoaxing) take place?
8. Will the participants risk any harm (physical, psychological, legal, or social) by taking part in this research?
9. If there are any risks, how do you justify them? How will you minimize the risks?

Research participants

10. How will you recruit the research participants?
11. How do you plan to explain the research to your potential participants and obtain their informed consent?
12. What should be the general characteristics of your research participants (e.g., age range, sex, and institutional affiliation) and the projected number of participants?
13. What, if any, are the special characteristics you need in your research participants (e.g., children, pregnant women, racial or ethnic minorities, mentally retarded persons, prisoners, or alcoholics)?
14. Are other institutions or individuals cooperating in or cosponsoring the study?
15. Do the participants have to be in a particular mental or physical state to participate usefully?

Material

16. If electrical or mechanical equipment will be used, how has it been checked for safety?
17. What standardized tests, if any, will be used? What information will be provided to the participants about their scores on these tests?

Confidentiality

18. What procedure will you use to ensure the confidentiality of the data?

Debriefing

19. How do you plan to debrief the participants?

variability in the decision making of different IRBs. Getting a sensitive proposal approved is often a matter of the luck of drawing a particular group of IRB members whose values happen to be congruent with the values of the researchers (Ceci, Peters, & Plotkin, 1985; Kimmel, 1991).

Principle III. Justice

The spirit of the principle of justice is that the burdens as well as the benefits of any proposed study are expected to be distributed fairly. In the case of the Tuskegee study (Box 3.1), none of the men who participated could have benefited in any significant way; they alone bore the awful burdens. Based on the model in Figure 3.2, this study would clearly fall at A. But suppose it had been a medical experiment that tested the effectiveness of a new drug to cure syphilis, and suppose the strategy was to give half the men at random the new drug and the other half a **placebo** (a fake "pill" masquerading as the real thing). Do you think it is acceptable to deprive some people (e.g., those in the control group) of the benefits of a potentially lifesaving drug? This is a divisive question in our society, but one alternative that has been used is to give the control group the best currently available medicine, so that the comparison is between the new drug and the best available option.

Justice also implies **fair-mindedness,** or impartiality, but this is usually a matter of one's perception or subjective judgment. Even if the objective is desirable, some people might see the study as unfair. For example, in the 1970s, there was a field experiment, known as the **Rushton study,** that was designed to improve the quality of work life in a mining operation owned by the Rushton Mining Company in Pennsylvania (Blumberg & Pringle, 1983). After months of careful preparation by the researchers and the managers of the mine, an appeal was made for volunteers for a work group that would have direct responsibility for the production in one section of the mine. The experiment called for the workers in this group to abandon their traditional roles and to coordinate their own activities after extensive training in safety laws, good mining practices, and job safety analysis. They were also given the top-rate wages, those paid for the highest skilled job classification in that section. Not surprisingly, they were enthusiastic proponents of "our way of working."

Unfortunately, trouble soon reared its head. Workers in the rest of the mine (who were the control group) were resentful of the "injustice" of the situation: "Why should inexperienced volunteers receive special treatment and higher pay than other miners with many more years on the job?" Rumors circulated through the mine that the volunteers were "riding the gravy train" and being "spoon-fed," and that the project was a "communist plot" because all the volunteers received the same rate and the company was "making out" at their expense. As a consequence, the study had to be terminated prematurely. Yet, is it reasonable to expect that *full justice* can be achieved in any research situation? As life constantly reminds us (see Box 3.4), the principle of justice is an ideal that is unlikely to be fully achieved in a world that is never fully just (Sales & Folkman, 2000).

Principle IV. Trust

The fourth principle refers to the establishment of a relationship of trust with the research participants. It is based on the assumption that people will be told what they are getting into (i.e., informed consent) and that nothing will be done to

BOX 3.4   Unfairness in Daily Life

It is not always easy to distribute benefits and burdens equally. For example, a drug company announces a new medicine that slows the course of multiple sclerosis, but the company is unable to produce enough of the new medicine to treat everyone who wants it (Lewin, 1994). The ethical question is how to select people for treatment. The company's answer is to have people register for a lottery and then to draw names at random as the medicine becomes available. Each person in the lottery has the same likelihood of being chosen—in the same way, for example, that a lottery may be used in wartime to select conscripts for the military. Is this a "just" procedure because everyone who is eligible has an equal chance of being selected for life or death? Suppose people are selected to receive the new medicine not randomly, but on the grounds of who is most likely to benefit from it. Similarly, suppose that conscripts for the military were selected on the basis of who is the biggest and strongest (Broome, 1984). Which approach, in your view, is *more ethical*—a random lottery or selection on the basis of who is more likely to benefit or survive?

jeopardize this trust. And yet we asked in Box 3.2, "Is it right to withhold information from participants if I think that a full disclosure will bias their responses?" To deal with this situation, researchers *debrief* people after their participation in the study (described later in this chapter). One procedure for establishing trust is to protect the confidentiality of participants' disclosures. **Confidentiality** means that participants' disclosures are protected against unwarranted access; it is a way of ensuring their privacy and may be a way of improving the data they provide, since it seems to lead to more open and honest responding (e.g., Esposito, Agard, & Rosnow, 1984).

To maintain confidentiality in your research, you need to seek advice from your instructor to set procedures in place that will protect your data. For example, you can devise a coding system in which the names of your participants are represented by a sequence of numbers that no one else can identify. When participants are not asked to give any personal information that would identify them, their privacy is automatically protected. In government-funded biomedical and behavioral research, it may be possible for the researcher to obtain a **certificate of confidentiality,** which is a formal agreement that requires the researcher to keep the data confidential (and exempts the data from subpoena). The extent to which such a certificate can actually provide legal protection has not been established in the courts, however, and is complicated by the existence of laws that require the reporting of certain sensitive information. For example, the Child Abuse Prevention and Treatment Act of 1974 and its revisions and amendments mandate that each state pass laws to require the reporting of child abuse and neglect. The nature and wording of such statutes is left to the discretion of the states, but the lists of people who are now obligated to report suspected cases in each state has expanded over the years (Liss, 1994). Suppose you were a member of a team of developmental researchers that was studying child abuse, and you wanted to protect the privacy and confidentiality of your participants. Your legal responsibility is to report suspected cases of child abuse, but reporting a suspected culprit means violating the trust you established with the participants when you promised to hold their disclosures confidential. Furthermore, it is possible that charges of abuse will not be proven, although this possibility does not excuse you from your legal responsibility (Liss, 1994).

Principle V. Fidelity and Scientific Integrity

The goal of the fifth principle is to foster scientific advances that lead to valid knowledge (Rosenthal, 1994b). Poor-quality research is an ethical problem because it is wasteful of resources and may be misleading and even potentially damaging to society. But what about something as seemingly innocent as implying a causal relationship where the data do not support it? Is this also an "ethical issue" and not just a design issue? Suppose an IRB receives a proposal for a study that, according to the researchers' own statement, "will test whether private schools improve children's intellectual functioning more than public schools do." Children from randomly selected private and public schools will be tested extensively, and the hypothesis will be tested by a comparison of the scores earned by students from private and public schools. The research design and proposal raise ethical problems because it is clear that the design does not permit reasonable causal inference (e.g., "intellectual functioning" might be due to intrinsic differences in the different populations). Resources will be wasted (e.g., money will be wasted, and people's time will be taken from potentially more beneficial educational experiences), and conclusions that are unwarranted and inaccurate will result. Were it not an ethical and practical absurdity, an alternative would be to propose an experiment in which children would be randomly assigned to either private or public schools. However, another choice is to accurately state in the proposal exactly what the study design can tell us. If the research proposal had stated that the purpose of the investigation was to learn about *performance differences* between students in private and public schools, then the original design would have been quite suitable (Rosenthal, 1994b).

Deception

Another example of the interrelationship between ethics and scientific integrity involves the use of deception. Although deception is commonly used in everyday life, it is considered an ethical problem in science. Recall that Mary Jones (sample proposal in Chapter 2) made a point of noting that her proposed study design did not involve deception. As an illustration of its use by investigative journalists, CBS's news program *60 Minutes* used an elaborate deception to study claims made by polygraph examiners (Saxe, 1991). On the pretense that they represented a photography magazine owned by CBS, the *60 Minutes* people recruited four polygraph examiners randomly chosen from the telephone directory and asked each of them to identify which of the magazine's employees had stolen more than $500 worth of camera equipment. No one, in fact, had stolen anything, and a different person was "fingered" by the *60 Minutes* staff for each of the polygraphers. The "culprits" were confederates who were paid $50 by the program staff if they could convince the polygrapher of their innocence. A hidden camera filmed the testing situation without the polygraphers' knowing they were being recorded. The film record showed each polygraph examiner *trying* to get the "guilty" person to confess. Dramatically, the *60 Minutes* report showed that the polygraphers did not necessarily "read" the psychophysiological polygraph information to make their diagnoses of deception. (See also Box 3.5.)

If this had been a scientific study, it would have been a source of contention because of the moral conflict between the respect for persons and their autonomy and a duty to scientific integrity (Principles I and V). As one researcher put it,

> The demonstration was very clever, but dishonest: CBS lied to the polygraphers. The four polygraphers unwittingly starred in a television drama viewed by millions . . . yet it is hard to think of a way to do this study without deception. (Saxe, 1991, p. 409)

Informing the polygraphers that they were subjects for a *60 Minutes* exposé would have made the study—and no doubt the results—quite different. Were this study to be submitted for approval to an IRB, it is unlikely that it would be approved in this form. Would you say that the deception used was justified by the study's purpose (i.e., to expose fraud), or would you instead argue that the ends did not justify the means? Do you think using any form of deception is ever justified in scientific re-

---

 BOX 3.5 Go Directly to Jail

Deception is also used by defense lawyers who manipulate the truth in court on behalf of their clients, and by police who use sting operations to capture fugitives. For example, the New York City police used an elaborate deception to capture 261 fugitives (M. Cooper, 1997). One of the captured fugitives, who had been arrested for selling marijuana, had skipped his court date and fled to New Mexico. He was sent an official-looking letter informing him there was a check for $6,000 waiting for him to pick up in the Bronx office of the "State of New York Division of Abandoned and Unclaimed Funds." When he showed up, after traveling 2,025 miles by bus, he was handed a check marked "Go Directly to Jail. Do not pass go, do not collect $200." He was then searched, handcuffed, and booked.

search? In fact, its use by leading social psychologists in a number of classic studies has been a source of controversy for years (cf. A.E. Gross & Fleming, 1982; Kelman, 1968; Menges, 1973; Z. Rubin, 1974; I. Silverman, 1977).

Some argue that deception in *any* form is morally wrong, whereas others argue that there are special circumstances in which it is needed to ensure the integrity of important scientific data. In general, two broad types of deception have been used in behavioral and social research: active and passive. In **active deception** (sometimes characterized as **deception by commission**), the subjects are actively misled, as when they are given false information about the purpose of the research, or when they unwittingly interact with confederates (recall, in Chapter 1, Asch's use of confederates to make ridiculous perceptual judgments), or when they are secretly given a placebo. In **passive deception** (sometimes characterized as **deception by omission**), certain information is withheld from the participants, as when they are not informed of the meaning of their responses when they are given a projective test or when they are not told the full details of the study (Arellano-Galdames, 1972). In order to be allowed to use a deception, researchers must have no acceptable alternative, and its proposed use must be approved by an IRB. A famous controversy in psychology regarding the use of deception involved Stanley Milgram's (1974) work on obedience.

Milgram's Use of Deception

In contrast to Asch's studies (though stimulated in part by them), Milgram's work sparked ethical debate both inside and outside behavioral and social science from the moment it was first published. He did not make the decision to perform the experiments lightly; he had important societal and scientific questions in mind. His interest in this research stemmed from his profound dismay about the horrifying results of blind obedience to Nazi commands in World War II. During that nightmarish period, the unthinkable became a reality when millions of innocent men, women, and children were systematically slaughtered. Milgram's purpose in performing his experiments was to study the psychological mechanism that links blind obedience to destructive behavior. In particular, he wanted to determine how far *ordinary adults* would go in carrying out the orders of a legitimate authority to act against a third person.

Milgram tricked volunteer participants, placed in the role of the "teacher," into believing that they would be giving varying degrees of painful electric shock to a third person (the "learner") each time the learner made a mistake in a certain task. Milgram also varied the distance between the teacher and the learner, to see whether the teachers would be less ruthless in administering the electric shocks as they got closer and the learner pressed the teacher to quit. The results were, to Milgram as well as to others, almost beyond belief. A great many participants (the "teachers") unhesitatingly obeyed the experimenter's "Please continue" or "You have no choice, you must go on" and continued to increase the level of the shocks no matter how much the learner pleaded with the "teacher" to stop. What particularly surprised Milgram was that no one ever walked out of the room in disgust or protest. This remarkable obedience was seen time and time again in a number of different settings where the experiment was repeated. "It is the extreme willingness of adults to go to almost any lengths on the command of an authority that constitutes the chief finding of the study and the fact most urgently demanding explanation," Milgram wrote (1974, p. 5).

Although the "learner" in these studies was a confederate of Milgram's and no electrical shocks were actually transmitted by the "teacher," concerns about ethics and values have dogged these studies ever since they were first reported. Psychologist Diane Baumrind (1964) quoted Milgram's descriptions of the reactions of some of his participants—such as "a twitching, stuttering wreck, who was rapidly approaching a point of nervous collapse" (Milgram, 1963, p. 377). Baumrind argued that once Milgram had seen how stressful his deception was, he should have immediately terminated the research. She insisted that there was "no rational basis" for ever using this kind of manipulation, unless the participants were fully aware of the psychological dangers to themselves and effective steps were taken to ensure the restoration of their well-being afterward.

Milgram responded that the chief horror was not that a stressful deception was carried out, but instead that participants obeyed. The signs of extreme tension in some participants were quite unexpected, but his intention had not been to create anxiety, he explained. Indeed, before carrying out the research, he had asked professional colleagues about their expectations, and none of the experts had anticipated the blind obedience that resulted. Like the experts, he had thought the participants would refuse to follow orders. Moreover, he was skeptical about Baumrind's contention that there had been psychologically injurious effects on the participants, in spite of the dramatic appearance of anxiety in some of them. To ensure that the participants would not feel worse after the experiment than before, he had taken elaborate precautions to debrief them. They were given an opportunity for a friendly reconciliation with the "learner" after the experiment was concluded and were shown that the "learner" had not received dangerous electric shocks but had only pretended to receive them.

To find out whether there were any delayed negative effects, Milgram sent questionnaires to the participants to elicit their reactions after they had read a full report of his investigation. Less than 1% of those who received this questionnaire said they regretted having participated; 15% were neutral or ambivalent, and over 80% said they were glad to have participated. Milgram interpreted these results as providing another good reason for his research:

> The central moral justification for allowing my experiment is that it was judged acceptable by those who took part in it. Criticism of the experiment that does not take account of the tolerant reaction of the participants has always seemed to me hollow. This applies particularly to criticism centering on the use of false illusion (or "deception," as the critics prefer to say) that fails to relate this detail to the central fact that subjects find the device acceptable. The participants, rather than the external critics, must be the ultimate source of judgment in these matters. (Milgram, 1977, p. 93)

Is Deception Ever Justified?

In arguing that research participants, not the experimenter, are the ultimate arbiters of whether a particular deception is morally acceptable, Milgram was speaking before the advent of IRBs. In fact, *when* Milgram did his work, it was well within the norms of deception then in use. But suppose the study had never been done, and it was you who wanted to do it. The IRB rejects your proposal and responds that the use of deception in any form is unacceptable. "Be open and honest with your participants, and have them sign an informed-consent agreement that indicates they fully understand what the research is about," the IRB admonishes you. Is getting rid of the deception, and being open and honest, a reasonable requirement in this case, or could it present a further ethical dilemma? Before you answer, imagine an experiment like Milgram's in which the experimenter instead greeted the participants by saying something like the following:

> Hello. Today we are going to do a study on blind obedience to a malevolent authority, particularly emphasizing the effects of physical distance from the victim on willingness to inflict pain on her or him. You will be in the "close" condition, which means that you are expected to be somewhat less ruthless in your behavior. In addition, you will be asked to fill out a test of your fascist tendencies because we believe there is a positive relation between scores on our fascism test and blind obedience to an authority who requests that we hurt others. Any questions?

A completely open and honest statement to a research participant of the intention of the experiment might involve a briefing of this kind, but would it result in fewer problems? Clearly, such a briefing would be absurd if you were serious in your wish to learn about blind obedience to authority. If the participants had full information about your experimental purpose, plans, procedures, and hypotheses, it seems unlikely they would behave as Milgram's participants did. They might instead base their behavior on what they *thought* the world was like or what they believed *you* thought the world was like. This is not to say that any scientists would advocate the use of deception merely for its own sake. At the same time, however, there may be few who feel that they can do entirely without certain minimal-risk deceptions (e.g., disguising the name of the "California Fascism Scale" by calling it the "Personal Reaction Inventory"). Certainly no behavioral or social scientist would seriously advocate giving up the study of prejudice or discrimination. However, would it be worth the effort and expenditure if all measures of prejudice and discrimination had to be openly labeled? If you answered yes, what about the ethical dilemma of reporting results that would be misleading because the subjects were not open and honest regarding their beliefs and behavior? Adopting an uncompromising moral orientation that decries deception as wrong would mean banishing *all forms* of deception or producing misleading results in some cases.

Surely, most people—scientists included—would be willing to weigh and measure the "sins" of commission and omission resulting from the use of deception, and to judge some to be larger than others. For example, refraining from telling diners that you are doing a study of tipping behavior, or not telling a participant that an "experiment in the learning of verbal materials is designed to show whether earlier, later, or intermediate material is better remembered," does not seem to be an especially heinous deception. The reason most of us would probably not view these deceptions with alarm seems, on first glance, that they involve an omission (a passive deception) rather than a commission (an active deception). A truth is left unspoken; a lie is not told. But what if the verbal learning experiment were instead represented as a "study of the effects of the meaningfulness of verbal material on retention or recall"? That is a direct lie, designed to misdirect the participant's attention from a crucial aspect of the experimental treatment to another factor that really does not interest the scientist. Even this change, however, does not seem to make the deception appalling, though the "sin" is now one of commission and the scientist has not withheld information from, but actively lied to, the participant. It is not simply the active or passive style of a deception that is significant, but its effect on the participant. Few people would care whether participants focused on a noncrucial aspect of verbal material rather than on a crucial aspect, because this deception seems to have no perilous consequence. Similarly, not telling diners they are participating in an experiment on tipping behavior does not seem shocking in any way. It is not deception so much as it is potentially *harmful* deception that we would like to minimize. But how shall we decide what is potentially harmful? Does it come down to someone's opinion, and if so, whose opinions should prevail? Individual investigators, their colleagues, IRBs, and, to some extent, ultimately, the general society that supports the research must decide whether a particular deception is worth a possible increase in knowledge.

Debriefing Participants

We mentioned that Milgram's participants were given the opportunity to have a friendly reconciliation with the "learner." They were also given an opportunity to engage in an extended discussion with the experimenter about the purpose of the study (i.e., a **debriefing**), and about why it was necessary to use the particular deception (see also Box 3.6). The debriefing session gives us an opportunity to remove any misconceptions and anxieties the participants may have, so that their sense of dignity remains intact and they feel that their time has not been wasted (Blanck et al., 1992; Harris, 1988). If deception has been used, it is also important to remove any "detrimental impact on the participant's feeling of trust in interpersonal relationships" (APA, 1973, p. 77). However, just as there were situations in which informed consent seemed impossible or counterproductive, there are also situations in which the use of debriefing seems impossible or inadvisable (e.g., the tipping study). For example, a full debriefing is inadvisable if it would produce stress or be ineffective, such as when the participants are children, are mentally ill, or are retarded (Blanck et al., 1992).

In many instances, however, debriefings not only are ethically essential but can also provide an opportunity to explore what participants thought about the

---

BOX 3.6 Debriefing

The word *debrief* was first used by the British military in World War II to describe the procedure used by Royal Air Force (RAF) interrogators of pilots who had returned from bombing missions. Before the mission, the pilot was "briefed" and, after the mission, "debriefed." You can see that the term *debriefing*, when it refers to informing research participants of the nature and purpose of the deception used in a study is a misnomer; such a session should be called a *briefing session*. However, when researchers use this opportunity to interrogate the participants about their perceptions, the term *debriefing session* is more appropriate (Harris, 1988).

---

study, providing the researcher with an experiential context in which to interpret the data and with good ideas for further investigation (Blanck et al., 1992; Jones & Gerard, 1967. Milgram's debriefings were unusually extensive—far more so, in fact, than is characteristic of most experiments. Because he duped the participants into believing that they were administering painful electric shocks to another person, he felt it necessary to go to elaborate lengths to remove any lingering stresses or anxieties. He told the participants that their behavior was normal and that any conflict or tension that they may have experienced had been felt by other participants. At the conclusion of the research, all received a comprehensive written report detailing the experimental procedures and findings and, of course, treating the participants' own part in the research with dignity. They were also administered a questionnaire that asked them again to express their thoughts and feelings about their behavior in the research. A year later, a psychiatrist interviewed 40 of the participants, to identify any possible injurious effects resulting from the experiment.

Most studies do not require debriefing covering so wide an area or so great a span of time as Milgram's study, but the debriefing procedure used should be sufficiently focused to satisfy the participants about having cooperated in the investigation. The following guidelines (Aronson & Carlsmith, 1968; Sieber, 1982a, 1983) may be incorporated into more typical debriefings:

First, if your study involved some form of deception, you should give whatever explanation is needed to reveal the truth about the research and your carefully considered use of the deception. You might explain that science is the search for truth and that it is sometimes necessary to resort to deception to uncover truth.

Second, despite your sincere wish to treat your participants responsibly, some of them may have left the study feeling gullible, as if they have been "had" by a fraudulent procedure. Whatever kind of deception you used, you should clearly explain it and assure participants that being taken in does not reflect in any way on their intelligence or character but simply shows the effectiveness or validity of the study's design. You presumably went to some pains to achieve an effective design in order not to waste the participants' time and effort in your search for truth.

Third, you should proceed gradually and patiently, with the chief aim of gently unfolding the details of any deception that you used. A patient discussion will go far to reduce the subjects' negative feelings. Instead of thinking of themselves as "victims," they may more correctly realize that they have been "coinvestigators" in the search for truth.

Fourth, never use **double deception,** that is, a second deception in what the participant thinks is the official debriefing. Double deception can be terribly damaging: Instead of restoring your participants to the frame of mind in which they entered the study, you are leaving them with a lie. It is also unethical.

The Use of Animals in Research

Although the primary focus of this book is on research with human subjects, we did mention in Chapter 2 the Pavlovian conditioning of a dog, Thorndike's studies of cats in puzzle boxes, and the use of rat subjects by the Tolmanians and Hullians. Given the biological continuities between animals and human beings, animals are used as research subjects in about 8% of psychological research (Kimmel, 1996). The use of animals in experiments has been vigorously debated in recent years (Slife & Rubinstein, 1992) because the very assumption of biological continuity raises ethical dilemmas. That is, it should follow that animals, like humans, must experience some measure of pain and suffering. As a consequence of concerns about the treatment of animals, federal laws and licensing requirements now spell out the responsibilities of researchers and animal facilities to protect the well-being of experimental animals, consistent with advancements made possible by research.

For example, the Animal Welfare Act sets specific standards for the use of animals in research, such as their handling, housing, feeding, and use in the study of drugs. Research institutions are also subject to unannounced inspections by the U.S. Department of Agriculture at any time, and if violations are uncovered, the institution's license to run animal facilities may be revoked. Beyond these federal regulations, animal researchers are subject to institutional and professional requirements. Institutions with animal care facilities make a point of underscoring the experimenter's responsibilities, and any proposed animal research also routinely undergoes ethical review. In addition, the APA and other professional and scientific organizations around the world have expanded on the ethical obligations of investigators of animal behavior. For example, the APA insists that researchers make every effort to minimize discomfort, illness, and pain in their experimental animals. Any procedure that subjects animals to pain, stress, or privation may be used only when no alternative procedure is available and the goal of the research is justified by its prospective scientific, educational, or applied value.

Nevertheless, the confrontation between those who argue for and those who argue against experiments using animals is often quite heated. One point of disagreement concerns whether the interests of human beings supersede the interests of animals. At one extreme, many animal rights activists argue that animals and humans have equal rights and that benefits to humans are not a justification for animal experimentation. On the other side, it has been argued that animals have often benefited from the research, such as from discoveries in veterinary medicine (e.g., vaccines for deadly diseases) and experimental insights that have helped to preserve some species from extinction (e.g., the wild condor). Scientists point out that the use of animals in a variety of behavioral and biomedical studies has directly benefited humans in a great many ways. In medical research, for example, the development of vaccines for rabies and yellow fever was made possible by the use of animal proxies (Paul, Miller, & Paul, 2000).

In behavioral science, research with animals has led to advances in the rehabilitation of persons suffering from spinal cord injuries, in the treatment of disease and eating disorders, and in improvements in communication with the severely retarded. For example, Roger Sperry, who won a Nobel Prize for his work, did experiments with cats and monkeys that demonstrated that severing the fibers connecting the right and left hemispheres of the brain (resulting in a so-called split brain) did not impair a variety of functions, including learning and memory. This important discovery led to a treatment for severe epilepsy and made it possible for people who would have been confined to hospitals to lead a normal life instead (Gazzaniga & LeDoux, 1978; Sperry, 1968).

Animal rights activists argue that enterprising researchers would be forced to think of alternative methods if they were banned from using animals (see also Box 3.7). In fact, such advances have been made without any ban on animal experimentation. It has been possible, for example, to use anthropomorphic "dummies" (e.g., in car crash tests), to simulate tissue and bodily fluids in research situations, to use computer models of human beings, to use lower order species (e.g., fruit flies in experiments on genetics), and to study animals in their natural habitats (such as Dian Fossey's studies of gorillas; Fossey, 1981, 1983) or else in zoos, rather than to breed animals for laboratory research. In a fascinating set of studies,

BOX 3.7 Another Three Rs

Some years ago, the British zoologist William M. S. Russell and microbiologist Rex L. Burch made the argument that, given scientists' own interest in the humane treatment of the animals used in research, it would be prudent to search for ways to (a) *reduce* the number of animals used in research, (b) *refine* the experiments so that there was less suffering, and (c) *replace* animals with other procedures whenever possible. Called the "**three Rs principle**" by Russell and Burch (1959), this argument defines modern research on animal subjects.

comparative psychologists were able to generate new theoretical insights into the functions of yawning behavior simply by comparing Siamese fighting fish in the lab, lions and baboons in the zoo, and students who kept daily logs of yawning behavior (Baenninger, 1987; Baenninger, Binkley, & Baenninger, 1996; Greco, Baenninger, & Govern, 1993).

In sum, just as the scientific community recognizes both an ethical and a scientific responsibility for the general welfare of human subjects, it also assumes responsibility for the humane care and treatment of animals used in research. There are laws and ethical guidelines to protect animals in research, and it is also evident that humans and animals have benefited by discoveries made in experiments with animals. Thus, even though there is a heated debate about the use of animals in scientific research, it is clear that society has benefited in terms of biomedical and behavioral advances and that the ethical consciousness of science and society has been raised with regard to the conduct of this research.

Ethics of Writing and Reporting

In this chapter, we have concentrated on the data collection phase of the research process, but ethical guidelines have implications for all aspects of the research process. As mentioned in Chapter 1, a fundamental ethical principle of good researchers is integrity and honesty, an essential aspect of the research process, from the implementation of the study to the final report of the procedures used, the results, and their implications. As we have also tried to show, many of the ethical guidelines discussed in this chapter, although directed specifically at professional researchers, have implications for students who are conducting research to satisfy a requirement in a methods course.

Some ethical rules have implications for the final phase of the process, in which you will be writing up your results (Rosnow & Rosnow, 2003). For example, professional researchers are responsible for making available the data on which their conclusions are based. The implication for students writing research reports is that they are expected to produce all of their raw data as required by the instructor. It is also considered unethical to misrepresent original research by publishing it in more than one journal and implying that each report represents a different study. The implication for students is that it is unethical to submit the same work for additional credit in different courses. Also, authors of published articles are expected to give credit where it is due, and the implication for the student is that if someone gave you an idea, you should credit that person in a footnote. Should your research become part of an article authored by your instructor, the decision about whether you will be listed as a coauthor or in a footnote acknowledgment will depend on the nature of your contribution to the research. Analyzing data that the instructor provided may be a minor contribution deserving a footnote acknowledgment, but if the article is substantially based on your individual efforts, you will usually be listed as a coauthor, possibly as the principal author of a multiple-authored piece (if the circumstances warrant).

Avoiding Plagiarism

The most nagging ethical concern of most instructors, however, is conveying to students the meaning and consequences of plagiarism and how to avoid it. The term **plagiarism** comes from a Latin word meaning "kidnapper," and to plagiarize means to kidnap another person's idea or work and to pass it off as one's own. **Accidental plagiarism** occurs when one copies someone else's work but "forgets" to credit it or to put it in quotes. It is crucial that you know what constitutes plagiarism, because it is not an acceptable defense to claim that you do not understand what plagiarism is, nor is it ethically defensible to lift a passage (without putting it in quotes) because it was not easy to think of a way to express a thought or concept in your own words. Even if the plagiarism was "accidental," it is important to understand that stealing someone else's work is wrong and that, even if it is unintentional, the penalty may be severe.

Of course, you can use other's people's ideas or work in your research and writing, but you must always give the author of that material full credit for originality and not misrepresent (intentionally or accidentally) that material as your own original work. For example, suppose a student did a study on cognitive dissonance and then turned in a report that, without a citation, contained the following passage in the introduction:

> Dissonance—that is, the existence of nonfitting relations among cognitions—is a motivating factor in its own right. By *cognition* is generally meant any knowledge, opinion, or belief about the environment, about oneself, or about one's behavior. Cognitive dissonance can be seen as an antecedent condition that leads to activity oriented toward dissonance reduction, just as hunger leads to activity oriented toward hunger reduction.

The student has cheated by committing plagiarism and will pay the consequences: an F in the course. The reason is that, except for a changed word here and there, the student has lifted this passage directly from Leon Festinger's *Theory of Cognitive Dissonance* (1962). On page 5, Festinger wrote:

> In short, I am proposing that dissonance, that is, the existence of nonfitting relations among cognitions, is a motivating factor in its own right. By the term *cognition,* here and in the remainder of the book, I mean any knowledge, opinion, or belief about the environment, about oneself, or about one's behavior. Cognitive dissonance can be seen as an antecedent condition which leads to activity oriented toward dissonance reduction just as hunger leads to activity oriented toward hunger reduction.

How might the student have used Festinger's work without falling into plagiarism? The student would simply indicate what is his or hers and what is Festinger's. For example, this student could have written:

> In his book *A Theory of Cognitive Dissonance,* Festinger (1962) described cognition as "any knowledge, opinion, or belief about the environment, about oneself, or about one's behavior" and defined cognitive dissonance as "the

BOX 3.8 Avoiding Lazy Writing

Some students, on hearing that cited material is not construed by definition as plagiarism, submit papers that are saturated with quoted material. However, such papers are viewed by instructors as **lazy writing.** Although the penalty for lazy writing is not as severe as that for plagiarism, often it means a reduced grade. You may need to quote or paraphrase some material (with a citation, of course), but your written work is expected to result from your own individual effort. Quoting a simple sentence that can easily be paraphrased signals lazy writing (Rosnow & Rosnow, 2003).

existence of nonfitting relations among cognitions" (p. 5). He added, "Cognitive dissonance can be seen as an antecedent condition which leads to activity oriented toward dissonance reduction" (p. 5).

If you find something on the Internet you want to use, the same considerations of honesty apply. Electronic plagiarizing is no more acceptable than plagiarizing from printed matter. (See also Box 3.8.)

Summary of Ideas

1. Legal, institutional, and professional ethical guidelines help us evaluate the moral "rights" and "wrongs" of particular strategies of doing and reporting research.
2. In general, researchers are obliged *not to do* physical or psychological harm to research participants and *to do* research in a way that is most likely to produce valid results of benefit to society.
3. Principle I of the APA's task force on ethics in research with human participants ("Respect for Persons and Their Autonomy") tells us to respect the freedom of individuals to participate in the study and to be told what they are getting into (i.e., the informed-consent agreement).
4. Principle II ("Beneficence and Nonmaleficence") instructs us to maximize the benefits and minimize the risks of the research we do.
5. The review process serves as a control mechanism, and in a proposal submitted for review, the questions to be answered concern many aspects of the research (including the way in which the participants will be recruited, the procedures to be used, confidentiality, and the risks to the participants).
6. The insufficiency of the idealized decision-plane model used to weigh the risks and benefits of doing research (in Figure 3.2) is that it ignores the societal and scientific costs of not conducting (or of being prevented from conducting) some potentially valuable studies.
7. Principle III ("Justice") urges that the benefits and burdens of research be distributed as fairly as possible, although (as is true of life itself) full justice can seldom be achieved.
8. Principle IV ("Trust") tells researchers not to do anything that will jeopardize the trusting relationship with participants and to protect their disclosures against unwarranted access (i.e., to maintain confidentiality).

9. Principle V ("Fidelity and Scientific Integrity") defines the promulgation of valid knowledge as an ethical pursuit.

10. Assuming that Milgram's research was worth doing, then he had no alternative but to use deception, because being open and honest with the participants would have jeopardized the validity of the results.

11. The measure of the acceptability of deception seems to be whether it may harm participants rather than whether the deception is active or passive.

12. Debriefing participants after the data have been collected is the final step in the data collection process and is considered essential when there has been a deception or when there is likely to be any residual anxiety.

13. Just as the scientific community has an ethical and scientific responsibility for the general welfare of human subjects, it also assumes responsibility for the humane care and treatment of animals used in research.

14. Ethical guidelines also require that researchers (a) make available the data on which their conclusions are based (while protecting the confidentiality of their participants); (b) not imply that a study published in more than one journal represents different studies; and (c) give credit where it is due.

15. *Plagiarism* means lifting another person's idea or work, and it is severely punished. To avoid "accidental plagiarism," it is essential to make careful notes and to cite the sources of any ideas, work, or quotations used in your report.

16. Avoid the "lazy writing" of repeatedly quoting sentences that can be paraphrased in your own words (and referenced, of course).

 ## Key Terms

accidental plagiarism   p. 79
active deception (deception by commission)   p. 71
autonomy   p. 60
Belmont Report   p. 61
beneficence   p. 64
certificate of confidentiality   p. 68
confidentiality   p. 68
debriefing   p. 74
deception by commission   p. 71

deception by omission   p. 71
decision-plane model   p. 64
double deception   p. 76
ethical guidelines   p. 60
ethics   p. 60
expedited review   p. 64
fair-mindedness   p. 67
informed consent   p. 61
institutional review board (IRB)   p. 64
lazy writing   p. 80

minimal risk   p. 64
nonmaleficence   p. 64
passive deception   p. 71
placebo   p. 67
plagiarism   p. 79
risk-benefit analysis   p. 64
Rushton study   p. 67
three Rs of humane animal experimentation   p. 77

WEB ACTIVITY

For the American Psychological Association's ethics home page, containing links to the APA code as well as other information concerning human and animal research, visit http://www.apa.org/ethics/code.html. To learn more about animal rights, visit Michigan State University's College of Law site for relevant cases, laws, and other information at http://www.animallaw.info.

Multiple-Choice Questions for Review

1. Which of the following methodological procedures can cause moral conflicts to arise? (a) invasion of privacy; (b) deception; (c) withholding information from research participants; (d) all of the above

2. Deliberately withholding information from research participants is called _____; deliberately misinforming participants is called _____. (a) active deception, passive deception; (b) active deception, double deception; (c) double deception, passive deception; (d) passive deception, active deception

3. In the Milgram experiments, which of the following actually received electrical shocks? (a) the "teacher"; (b) the "learner"; (c) both a and b; (d) neither a nor b

4. Ethical questions were raised about the Milgram experiments because (a) participants were deceived and apparently stressed; (b) some participants received severe shocks; (c) some participants were physically injured; (d) all of the above.

5. The Rushton study, conducted in a mining company, raised the ethical issue of (a) deception; (b) fair-mindedness; (c) invasion of privacy; (d) all of the above.

6. The participants who objected to the Rushton study were (a) in the control group; (b) in the experimental group; (c) in both the experimental and control groups; (d) subjected to severe shocks.

7. According to the decision-plane diagram in the text, if the risks of doing a research project are equal to the benefits of doing the research, then the study is said to fall on (a) the diagonal of ambivalence; (b) the diagonal of equality; (c) the diagonal of indecision; (d) none of the above.

8. Research at virtually all colleges and universities has to be approved by (a) the president of the institution; (b) the U.S. government; (c) professors in the psychology department; (d) an IRB.

9. The procedure of disclosing the full purpose of a study after individuals have participated is called (a) debriefing; (b) peer review; (c) the Milgram procedure; (d) double deception.

10. Which of the following help ensure that animals used as subjects in research are treated ethically? (a) federal laws; (b) professional codes of ethics; (c) institutional (e.g., university) policies; (d) all of the above

Discussion Questions for Review

1. A study proposal is submitted to the Tufts University IRB for review. The researchers plan to administer a two-hour-long questionnaire to people hanging out on the street in the red light district in Boston. The questionnaire contains items asking about these people's lifestyles and attitudes toward criminal behavior. What are some potential risks to the subjects for their participation in the study?

2. A University of Richmond student is interested in studying helping behavior. She designs an experiment to take place in a corner drugstore. Enlisting the aid of the owner, the student has confederates, varying in age and manner of dress, commit a robbery at the store. Another confederate, posing as a customer, observes the real customers, noting which of them help, what they do, how long it takes, and so on. What are some ethical problems in this research? What risks and benefits would you consider in deciding whether this project should be done?

3. A UCLA student wants to run a study in which he will deceive subjects into believing that they have done poorly on a test of their sensitivity to others. At the end of the experimental session, he plans to pay the subjects, thank them for participating, and tell them they can call him later if they

have questions about the study. How does the student fail in his ethical responsibilities to the participants? What should he do?

4. Your instructor tells you that, in her view, your proposed study falls on the "diagonal of indecision." What does she mean, and what are the implications for you?

5. An Arlington University student proposes to use Texas students to replicate Asch's experiment. His IRB requires an informed-consent agreement from his participants. What does this mean, and what are the implications for the student?

6. A Whittier College student is interested in conducting a study of the effects of various financial incentive programs in a large organization. Because his research involves no deception or invasion of privacy, he tells his adviser that no ethical issues are raised by his research. The adviser's reply is "Remember the Rushton study!" What does she mean?

7. An instructor at Temple University tells her students that they have ethical responsibilities when writing up their research. What are those responsibilities?

Answers to Review Questions

Multiple-Choice Questions

1. d	3. d	5. b	7. c	9. a
2. d	4. a	6. a	8. d	10. d

Discussion Questions

1. Two possible risks include (a) embarrassment at "being studied" in an unsavory location or occupation and (b) the danger of discovery of subjects' criminal behavior because someone in law enforcement obtains the questionnaire and can link it to the respondents.

2. Observing the thefts might be quite upsetting to the real customers, who may be put at risk of, say, anxiety reactions or heart attacks. The confederate "robbers" may also be put at risk of being shot by an armed shopkeeper or attacked by a customer trying to foil the robbery. We need to ask whether what we might be able to learn from this research is really worth the risk to the real customers, the shopkeeper, and the confederate "robbers."

3. The student has failed to debrief the participants, so that they may feel that they are really insensitive to others. He should, of course, debrief them.

4. She means that the risks and benefits are in such balance that it is very difficult for her to decide whether to let you go ahead with the research. For removal of the study from the diagonal of indecision, you need to decrease the risks of the study, increase the benefits, or both. If there are significant risks, however, start by eliminating them.

5. The participant must understand what the research will require from her or him, that she or he may leave at any time, and that he or she will remain anonymous.

6. The Rushton study also raised no questions of deception or invasion of privacy. However, the issue of fair-mindedness was raised. Were some of the organization's workers going to be "treated specially," or would they get to ride "the gravy train" in the eyes of other workers?

7. Their responsibilities include (a) producing all of their raw data if she asks for it, (b) not submitting the paper for credit in another course, (c) giving credit to anyone who helped, and (d) not committing plagiarism, even accidentally.

CHAPTER 4

Strategies of Systematic Observational Research

Preview Questions

- How does systematic observation differ from everyday noticing or watching?
- How do ethnographic researchers simultaneously participate and observe?
- How is content analysis used to impose structure on archival data?
- What is the role of laboratory experimentation, and what is meant by *rival hypotheses?*
- How do researchers do experiments in field settings?
- What is the distinction between reactive and nonreactive observation?
- What is meant by *unobtrusive observation,* and how do researchers go about it?
- How are judges or raters used to code behavior, and how are they chosen?

The Researcher as Observer

In preceding chapters, we gave you a flavor of different types of research strategies. The purpose of this chapter is to examine perhaps the most common qualitative and quantitative observational strategies in more detail. Within the descriptive, relational, and experimental framework that we outlined in Chapter 1, there are several different ways of carving up the many creative approaches used in systematic observational research. For example, we can think of naturalistic and artificial observation, or primary and secondary observation, or qualitative and quantitative observational research. However, whenever we examine a particular set of observational studies, we are likely to find that it encompasses more than one type of approach. For example, studies in which raters or judges are used (called *judgment studies*) can involve primary or secondary observations, and judges may be used in descriptive, relational, or experimental research. Furthermore, the same systematic observational study might generate both qualitative and quantitative data. Thus, for the sake of convenience, we will focus on four common strategies of systematic observational research: participation observation, secondary observation, experimental observation in the lab, and field experiments in naturalistic settings.

The term **systematic observation** simply means that what the researcher observes, and how it is recorded, uses a methodology that can be evaluated on the basis of certain technical standards (e.g., those discussed in Chapter 6) and that these observations are, at least in part, guided by certain preexisting questions or hypotheses (as contrasted with the more casual and haphazard nature of most of our everyday observations). Within this broad definition, the overall strategy presumably calls for resourcefulness as the researcher makes plans to use more than one method in the spirit of a "let's-try-it-and-see" orientation (see also Box 4.1). As noted earlier, the reason for multiple methods is that all procedures and techniques are limited, and therefore the use of a single method will only confine our observations. By using multiple methods (called *methodological pluralism* in Chapter 1), the researcher attempts to develop a comprehensive picture of the phenomenon of interest by zeroing in on it from different perspectives, a process known as **methodological triangulation** in psychological science (Campbell & Fiske, 1959). In this chapter, we will also discuss some of the limitations of specific observational procedures and the role of unobtrusive observations (i.e., the people observed are unaware of being studied for research).

BOX 4.1 Does Anything Go?

Paul Feyerabend (1988), a philosopher of science, described how the scientific method seems to depend on researchers' bending or breaking rules and doing whatever works. As Feyerabend put it, "Not every discovery can be accounted for in the same manner, and procedures that paid off in the past may create havoc when imposed on the future. Successful research . . . relies now on one trick, now on another" (p. 1). Feyerabend's description has been called the **anything-goes view of science,** but it does not simply mean that there are no dependable criteria for evaluating good science and weeding out bad science or pseudoscience. All it means is that doing research *does* seem to involve a "let's-try-it-and-see" strategy. The scientist experiments with one procedure and then another before deciding that a theoretical prediction is correct or should be junked. The challenge is to find (or create) and properly implement methods and techniques that address the theoretical question or hypothesis of interest, while recognizing that no method or technique is perfect.

Another common distinction, as alluded to above, is that made between qualitative and quantitative research. The term **qualitative research** is another umbrella concept in behavioral and social research; the term is meant to encompass procedures and techniques for collecting data that exist in other than a numerical form (e.g., recorded conversation, videotaped or filmed behavior, and written communication). There is a burgeoning literature on qualitative research, including its use in feminist studies, social work, organizational management, social psychology, anthropology, aging, and family studies (e.g., H. R. Bernard, 1994; Crabtree & Miller, 1992; Denzin & Lincoln, 1994, 2000; Gilgun, Daly, & Handel, 1992; Gubrium & Sankar, 1993; Morse, 1993; Riessman, 1993; D. Silverman, 1993; Taylor & Bogdan, 1998). By contrast, the term **quantitative research** encompasses procedures and techniques in which the observed data are recorded in a numerical form. Because it is usually possible for creative researchers to think of ways of quantifying qualitative data, these two strategies are not sharply distinct. For example, we will describe how a counting method can be used to quantify qualitative data in the form of written communications and pictorial stimuli (called *content analysis*), and in a later chapter, we will describe a popular statistical procedure (chi-square) for analyzing tables of counts. In this chapter, we will also describe procedures for choosing judges and raters to observe and code qualitative information or observed behavior.

Observing While Participating

When the observer takes a role in the situation under study, the procedure is generally referred to as **participant observation** (where the prefix *participant* refers to the investigator as opposed to the research participants, or *informants* as they are frequently called in sociology). In one famous participant observation study in social psychology, the researchers observed a cult from within (as members) for approximately 2 months preceding and 1 month after the date that the cult leader had predicted that the world would end (Festinger, Schachter, & Riecken, 1956). The leader told her followers, who fervently believed every word, that she had received written messages from extraterrestrials that told about gods and spiritual vibrations on other planets and that, on a specified day, just before dawn, a flood would engulf most of the continent. In the days prior to this predicted cataclysm, many members quit their jobs, discarded their possessions, and were careless about their money, believing they would have no need for these things. What gave them emotional consolation was the leader's word that they would be evacuated by a flying saucer that would land in her backyard at 4:00 P.M. on a particular day to transport the "chosen ones" to another planet. Although they waited in anticipation with coats in hand, no flying saucer arrived and the world did not end. Nonetheless, they did not lose faith, reinterpreting the experience as a drill and a rehearsal for the real pickup. Leon Festinger (1957) discussed this study in his seminal book on cognitive dissonance, using it as evidence of how people often cling to beliefs even in the face of disconfirmation by, for example, seeking out new reasons to justify their beliefs.

As this study illustrates, one advantage of participant observation research is that it lets us record events as they occur rather than relying on public records of past events (usually made by nonscientists); it is also a way of watching natural events in their "wholeness," particularly those that would be impossible to simulate in a lab, or that might be too sensitive or too risky to try to manipulate experimentally (Weick, 1968). It has been said that participant observers attempt to approach the field of observation without any preconceived ideas, and that the hypothesizing occurs only later (Taylor & Bogdan, 1998). However, it is hard to see how social researchers would realistically know where, when, how, or what to study without having at least some theoretical preconception, even if the purpose of the research were descriptive and exploratory. If for no other reason, having some ideas in advance encourages serendipity, or as Fine and Deegan (1996) put it, "The prepared participant observer hoping to maximize the chances of obtaining data selects just the right time and just the right place" (p. 439).

As another illustration of this qualitative research strategy, Temple University social psychologist Louise H. Kidder (1972) was fascinated by what she called the "aura of power that surrounds hypnosis and hypnotists" (p. 317), and especially by the intriguing question, "How do I know if I was hypnotized?" (which people often ask after coming out of hypnotic induction for the first time). In most situations in which participant observation is used, gaining access to a group and establishing rapport require diligence and patience; as Taylor and Bogdan (1998) cautioned, "It is not uncommon for researchers to 'spin their wheels' for weeks, even months, trying to break into a setting" (p. 27). Kidder, however, found a quite accessible participant-observation setting in which to explore the questions that interested her. She simply signed up for a 3-day hypnosis workshop and observed the steps that 20 practicing psychologists went through as they learned how to hypnotize someone, during which they also gradually learned to become hypnotized. Using a tape recorder and written notes to make a permanent record of her observations, Kidder kept verbatim accounts of the interactions between the experienced hypnotists and the psychologists.

Although this research was descriptive and exploratory, what Kidder selectively recorded was guided by two questions of interest to her: (a) How do people (including skeptics) become convinced that they have been hypnotized? And (b) does becoming convinced reflect a change in the person's definition of hypnosis, a change in definition of the experience, or both? As the workshop progressed, Kidder's (1972) interest in these questions was reinforced by the vagueness and ambiguity she perceived in the reactions of most people coming out of hypnosis for the first time: "How do I know if I was hypnotized?" or "I still don't consider it an experience any different from others" (p. 317). At one point, for example, Kidder observed and recorded the interaction between a "guest subject" (who had been brought into the workshop to be hypnotized by one of the experts) and several other workshop participants, who were given an opportunity to interview the guest subject:

Question: How did it feel?

Answer: Just very good. Very, very relaxed.

Question: Have you felt anything like this before?

Answer: Yeah, well it's sort of like smoking grass. The first few times I used it I just fell asleep.

Question: I want to ask what other experiences it was like.

Answer: It's like being very tired. Or like sitting in an airport and feeling tired and hearing other people around you talking—sort of hazy. (p. 321)

Kidder noted that the experts gave a great deal of feedback to the workshop participants, seemingly manipulating the participants' attitudes, just as they might be shaped in a conditioning study. Her interpretation was that, by the last session, most of the participants had learned how to *behave* like good hypnotic subjects and had come to accept the experts' definitions of hypnosis and new definitions of their own feelings. She hypothesized that becoming hypnotized is similar to a social interaction and that those who are most hypnotizable will proceed through the learning cycle more rapidly than others. In effect, Kidder's ad hoc hypothesis was that they learn to notice new sensations and to *feel* that maybe they have been hypnotized, whereas some people never go beyond the "I-don't-think-I-was-hypnotized state" (p. 322). Although not a substitute for a series of tightly controlled experiments (see Orne, 1970), Kidder's conversational records flesh out her explanation of how people learn to become hypnotized. Not all groups are studied as easily by participant observation, and in many cases it is hard to distinguish this strategy of observation and questioning from what journalists do. However, Kidder's study is an instructive example of the use of this qualitative methodology.

Ethnographic Field Research

Participant observation has played a particularly prominent role in qualitative research known as **ethnography,** so called because the researchers are interested in "cultures" (a term that is very broadly defined). In feminist ethnographic research, for example, a popular area of investigation is cultures that are defined as "living in oppression." Some ethnographers have even studied their own culture, calling it "autoethnography" (Tedlock, 2000). Most of this research has traditionally been done by anthropologists and sociologists, but it has attracted the interest of psychologists as well (see, for example, Box 4.2). As an illustration of its use in anthropology and communication research, Table 4.1 shows a small portion of the meticulous field notes made by John Haviland (1977), who lived for 10 years in Zinacantan, a small village in Mexico. The table shows excerpts of some of the conversations he recorded and translated, along with his interpretation of each fragment. He was interested in the social control and "sense making" functions of ordinary gossip in this culture. Among his many observations was that gossiping in Zinacantan encouraged spying between households at the same time that it isolated households from one another.

In the early development of ethnographic research, there was not yet a tradition of how to ensure the most credible qualitative data. Back in those days, it was

BOX 4.2 Being Sane in Insane Places

Psychologist David Rosenhan (1973) was interested in how people who are labeled "mentally ill" get to be stigmatized and what determines the way they are treated. Rosenhan and a number of volunteer coworkers feigned psychiatric symptoms in order to be admitted as patients to mental hospitals. Once they were admitted, however, they behaved quite normally. They kept detailed records of their observations and interactions with the psychiatrists, psychologists, and resident physicians. One fascinating observation of these researchers was that the staff members actually seemed to avoid interacting with their patients. The researchers agreed that they all felt "depersonalized" by this experience, a feeling, Rosenhan surmised, probably similar to the powerlessness felt by mental patients.

common for researchers not even to describe how they had collected their data, leaving it to readers to try to figure out what had been done (Hallett & Fine, 2000). Nowadays, researchers are required to give a detailed description of the procedures they used. Another early criticism was that researchers might be biased and their observations slanted. Ethnographic researchers now often work in teams and employ checks and balances to try to control for biases in observations and interpretations; careful field notes are also made by each member of the team. For example, one rule of thumb is to indicate for each written note referring to a conversation whether it is based on a verbatim quote or is the researcher's paraphrase. The risk in paraphrases is that observers may have unwittingly distorted what the informants meant. Whenever possible, ethnographers usually make audio or video recordings (with the permission of the informants). When the informants are to be interviewed or given questionnaires to answer, it is vitally important that the questions be phrased accurately in their own language. When the language of the informants is not the native language of the researchers, **translation and back-translation** are used. That is, one bilingual person first translates the questions from the source to the target language, and then another bilingual person translates the questions back into the source language. In this way, we can compare the original with the twice-translated version (i.e., the back-translation) to see whether anything has been lost in the translation.

One of the principal objectives of ethnographic research is to make sense of what is going on in a "cultural" situation (generally referred to as *sensemaking* by sociologists). Ethnographers seem particularly adept in the use of dramatic metaphors and analogical thinking (Fine & Deegan, 1996). However, there are also formulaic questions they can use to impose structure and order on observations. For example, listed below are some broadly stated questions (Goodenough, 1980), and after each, we have indicated how it might be addressed in Haviland's study of gossiping in Zinacantan:

	Table 4.1	Fragments of Zinacanteco Gossip and Their Analysis

Examples	Interpretations
"Didn't I hear that old José was up to some mischief?"	
"Perhaps, but that never became public knowledge. It was a secret affair."	
"The magistrate settled the whole business in private."	Shows how some villagers even gossip about gossip.
"Yes, when a dispute is settled at the townhall, then a newspaper report goes out to every part of town. . . . Ha ha ha."	
"Yes, then we all hear about it on the radio. . . . Ha ha ha."	
"But when the thing is hushed up, then there's on the radio. There are no newspapers. Then we don't hear about it. Ha ha ha."	
"Is it true that old Maria divorced Manuel?"	
"Yes. She complained that she awoke every morning with a wet skirt. Old Manuel used to piss himself every night, just like a child."	Shows how some gossip trades on a separation, but also on a connection, between the public and the private domains.
"When he was drunk, you mean?"	
"No, even when he was sober. 'How it stinks!' she said."	
"Ha ha ha. She spoke right out at the townhall."	
"This is what I told him: All right, I'll see how deeply I must go into debt to take this office. But I don't want you to start complaining about it later. If I hear that you have been ridiculing me, saying things like: 'Boy, he is just pretending to be a man; he is just pretending to have money to do ritual service. He stole my office, he took it from me.' . . . If you say such things, please excuse me, but I'll drag you to jail. I'll come looking for you myself. I don't want you to tell stories about me, because you have freely given me your ritual office. If there is no dispute, then I too will behave the same way. I won't gossip about you. I won't ridicule you. I won't say, for example, 'Hah, I am replacing him; he has no shame, acting like a man, asking for religious office when he has no money.' I won't talk like that. 'He wanted to serve Our Lord, but he ran away. I had to take over for him.' I won't say things like that, if we agree to keep silent about it . . ."	Shows a common theme in gossip about shady dealings and how the villagers take pains to ensure that the matter is kept quiet.

Source: Reproduced from "Gossip as Competition in Zinacantan" by J. B. Haviland, 1977, *Journal of Communication, 27,* pp. 186–191. Copyright © 1977; *Journal of Communication,* Oxford University Press. Used with permission of the publisher.

1. *What is the purpose of the activity?* (For example, what are the goals and their justifications?) In his study, Haviland classified several objectives of gossiping in Zinacantan, which led him to conclude that, despite the actual fences erected between households, the neighbors were constantly scrutinizing one another's dealings.

2. *What procedures are used to perform the activity?* (For example, what are the operations performed, the media or raw materials used, the skills and instruments involved, if any?) In Haviland's study, the medium of gossip was word of mouth; he carefully categorized the linguistic and psychological skills required in gossipmongering in this community.

3. *What are the time and space requirements of the activity?* (For example, how much time is needed for each operation, what areas or facilities are required, and are there any obstacles in the way of the activity?) Haviland noted when and where gossiping occurred, as well as what natural obstacles there were to the transmission of information.

4. *What are the personnel requirements of the activity?* (For example, how many actors participate, and what is each person's specialization, if any?) Haviland classified and evaluated the elaborate conversational devices by which people in positions of authority protected themselves. In other words, the person's "specialization" was that he or she was someone of authority.

5. *What is the nature of the social organization?* (For example, what are the categories of the actors; their rights, duties, privileges, and powers; and the types of sanctions or restrictions used by them?) Haviland classified and evaluated the ways in which gossip was used by the villagers to manage their social faces (i.e., how they wanted to appear to others) and at the same time to protect their privacy.

6. *What are the occasions for performance of the activity?* (For example, when is the activity mandatory, permitted, and prohibited, and what is the relationship of the initiator's role to the roles of others?) Haviland noted the occasions that were most and least conducive to gossiping, and he categorized and analyzed the particular role interactions of the gossips within those circumstances.

Secondary Observation and Content Analysis

Observational methods can sometimes involve the use of **archival material** rather than firsthand observations of behavior. The most convenient source of such data is a college library, which has encyclopedias, biographical dictionaries, histories, anthologies, print collections, and manuscripts (Simonton, 2000). Other archival material that may be available in your college library, or that is accessible by means of a computer, includes (a) actuarial records (e.g., birth, marriage, and death records); (b) political and judicial records (e.g., voting records of legislators and speeches printed in the *Congressional Record*); (c) various other government records (weather reports, invention records, and crime reports); and (d) information from the mass media (stories, news reports, advertising, and editorials). Still other valuable archival material might include (e) sales records (e.g., sales at airport bars, sales of trip insurance policies, and decreased sales of airline tickets, all constituting plausible indicators of increased anxiety); (f) industrial and institutional records (e.g., sicknesses and absences, complaints, unsolicited commendations from the public, and accident reports); and (g) various other written documents (e.g., diaries and letters of captured soldiers in wartime or letters of protest to large companies).

The use of archival material in social science falls into the category known as **secondary observation,** which means that the observation of the researcher is usually twice removed from the source. That is, the person who originally recorded the information is once removed from the source, and the researcher is removed from the recorder by another degree. A popular method of studying written messages and pictorial documents involves the classification and evaluation of their content, called **content analysis.** It requires precise, objective classification of material (see Box 4.3 for an example). The customary procedure consists of using judges (also called *raters* or *coders*) to tabulate symbols, words, sentences, ideas, or any other type of data (Berelson, 1952, 1954; Boyatzis, 1988; Holsti, 1969; Krippendorff, 1980; C. W. Roberts, 1997; Rosengren, 1981; C. P. Smith, 1992; Stone, Dunphy, Smith, & Ogilvie, 1966; Weber, 1985). Computer programs that have been

BOX 4.3   Gender Roles in Children's Picture Books

In an illustration of the use of content analysis with pictorial material, Peter B. Crabb and Dawn Bielawski (1994) explored how visual presentations in influential books for children portrayed female and male roles. They chose for their study all picture books that had gotten a prestigious award (the Caldecott Medal) over a 53-year period, on the assumption that these books have had a high profile in libraries and bookstores. The books contained 1,613 illustrations, including 416 of female characters and 1,197 of male characters. For their sampling procedure, the researchers drew a proportionate sample of 300 representative illustrations of gender and decade. The judges, who were first rehearsed in the coding system, coded the sex of the characters shown in the pictures, the nature of any household tools (such as those used in food preparation, cleaning, repair, and family care), nonhousehold tools (e.g., the kind that are used in construction, agriculture, and transportation), any tools not falling into the above two categories, and features of the characters using the tools and the situation (e.g., age of character: child, teenager, adult). The judges' ratings were in strong agreement, indicating good intercoder reliability. One finding was that household tools tended to be associated more with female characters, whereas nonhousehold tools tended to be associated more with male characters. Also, the proportion of male characters shown using household tools had increased over time, though the proportion of female characters using nonhousehold tools had not changed very much over time.

specially designed for use in content analysis research can sort through written material based on particular research specifications.

If you think you might like to do a content analysis, there are three general guidelines to keep in mind:

1. It is important that the analysis of content be consistent among the judges; that is, the different coders should produce close to the same results. Assuming that each category and unit has been precisely defined, and that the judges were properly trained, the **intercoder reliability** (i.e., the consistency among the judges who do the coding or rating) should be satisfactorily high. We will have more to say about how to choose judges later in this chapter (and more on reliability in Chapter 6).

2. It is essential that the specific categories and units be relevant to the questions or hypotheses of the study. In choosing categories for written records, for example, it is a good idea to ask, "What is the communication about?" and "How is it said?" Questions like these will help to focus the analysis on the substance (the *what*) and the form (the *how*) of the subject matter. It is also prudent to consider several different units of analysis before settling on any one unit. For example, you might consider coding words and word compounds (or phrases) or perhaps themes (or assertions), as illustrated by the pictorial themes alluded to in Box 4.3.

3. And finally, it is important to decide on a good sampling procedure. Because content analysis is so time-consuming, you must be sure that the materials to be analyzed are representative enough to justify the effort. We will have more to say about different sampling plans later in this book, including approaches that call for (a) random sampling from listings of all relevant units; (b) stratified samples, which break up units into subgroups and sample from them; and (c) systematic samples, which involve selecting every *n*th unit of a list.

As we said before, all strategies and procedures are limited in some ways, and the method of content analysis is no exception. Most basically, it is limited by the quality, dependability, and relevance of the material to be analyzed. However, it also has four definite advantages when used properly (Woodrum, 1984). First, developing a coding system and then implementing it requires little more than commonsense logic. Second, content analysis is a "shoestring" methodology in that, although labor-intensive when done by hand, it does not require much capital investment. Third, it is a "safe" methodology, because you can add necessary information if it is missed or incorrectly coded (if there are changes in what is being measured over time, it is not usually possible to do this in the typical experimental or survey study). Fourth, it forces researchers to scrutinize the material that they are evaluating and classifying.

Experimental Simulations

In Chapter 2, we mentioned examples of laboratory experimental observation, particularly the use of animals in learning and conditioning studies. In human experimental research, it is frequently possible to *simulate* (or mimic) a causal relationship in a controlled experimental setting in which we can manipulate the causal condition (the independent variable). Suppose we were interested in why people's ears buzz and tickle as they listen to a hard rock band up close. We could position a loudspeaker next to one or more subjects in a laboratory setting, manipulate the carefully calibrated sounds, and ask the subjects to report the sensations they feel. If they report that their ears buzz and tickle, the sound pressure may well be above 120 decibels, which can produce feelings of discomfort, prickling, and pain. After each exposure to such sounds, the sensitivity of the ear may be temporarily reduced. (If we wanted to find out whether people who have a steady diet of hard rock have hearing difficulties, we could design a relational study in which we sampled a population of people and recorded the minimal audible noise detected by those who said they routinely listened to a lot of hard rock or no hard rock.)

Another interesting example of experimental simulation were classic studies conducted by social psychologists Irving Janis and Leon Mann (1965; Mann, 1967; Mann & Janis, 1968), who were interested in whether the "saying is believing" principle might be used to get people to modify their smoking behavior. In particular, they experimented with a simulation procedure to increase the participants' emotional involvement. The volunteer participants were young women, all between the ages of 18 and 23, none of whom knew that the objective of the research involved modifying their smoking habits and attitudes toward smoking. Before the study began, the people who participated had averaged approximately a pack of cigarettes a day. Randomly assigned to an experimental or a control group, the participants were told at the beginning of the study that the research was intended to examine two important problems about the human side of medical practice: (a) how patients react to bad news and (b) how they feel when a physician tells them to quit an enjoyable habit like smoking.

Each participant in the experimental condition was told to imagine that the experimenter was a physician who had been treating her for a persistent cough, and on this "third visit" he was going to give her the results of x-rays and other diagnostic tests that had been previously carried out. The experimenter then outlined five different scenes, and he instructed the participant to "act out" each scene as realistically as possible. The first scene took place in the doctor's office while the patient awaited the diagnosis. She was asked to imagine and express aloud her thoughts, her concern, her feelings about whether to give up cigarettes. The second scene was the imagined interaction with the physician. The participant was told that according to the results of diagnostic tests, there was a small malignant mass in her right lung. She was also told that there was only a moderate chance of surgical success in treating this condition. She was then encouraged to ask questions. In the next scene she was instructed to express her feelings about her misfortune. The physician could be overheard in the background phoning for a hospital bed. In the fourth scene the physician described the details of imminent hospitalization. He told the participant that chest surgery typically required a long convalescent period, at least 6 weeks. He then raised questions about the woman's smoking history and asked whether she was aware of the relationship between smoking and cancer. He stressed the urgent need for her to stop smoking and encouraged her to talk freely about the problems she felt she might encounter in trying to break the smoking habit.

Participants assigned to the control group were exposed to similar information about lung cancer from a tape recording of one of the experimental sessions. However, they were not given an opportunity to engage in emotional role playing. As Janis and Mann hypothesized, the impact of the experimental manipulation in the role play condition exceeded that in the control condition. There was greater fear of personal harm from smoking, a stronger belief that smoking causes lung cancer, and a much greater willingness and intent to quit smoking in the experimental group. To find out about long-term effects, the researchers conducted follow-up interviews at different points over 18 months. The results were essentially as before. On the average, the women in the emotional role play sessions reported that they had reduced their daily cigarette consumption by more than twice the amount of those randomly assigned to the control group; this difference persisted even after a year and a half.

In many cases, doing research in a laboratory setting is a convenient and effective way of studying a phenomenon of interest in behavioral science (Mook, 1983). However, it is important to proceed with some caution when generalizing from laboratory simulations to situations outside the lab. For example, suppose we were interested in the effect of frustration on aggression in a controlled laboratory setting. Because frustration can make a person display hostile behavior, we might design a simulation experiment in which two subjects engage in a competitive task and are given an opportunity to administer a mild electric shock to one another. We frustrate one subject by withdrawing some particular desired object and then see whether the person administers shock to the other participant. Recent meta-analytic findings suggest that simulating aggression in the laboratory yields a faithful representation of certain effects in the real world, but these laboratory simulations of aggression may overestimate the effects of situational variables (e.g., media violence) and underestimate the effects of individual difference variables (C. A. Anderson & Bushman, 1997). Efforts to improve the generalizability of experimental simulations are currently under way in a number of areas of psychology (see Box 4.4.)

Rival Interpretations and Hypotheses

Later in this book, we will discuss how to anticipate and control for certain experimental design problems. However, it is not too soon to begin to sharpen your intuitive skills or to get an idea of what your instructor may expect as you begin to put together a background review of the literature on your research topic or write the discussion section of your research report. The instructor will expect you to think carefully about flaws and alternative explanations (also called **rival interpretations** or **rival hypotheses**) for the reported results and about possible ways of improving the studies you review. To get you thinking about rival interpretations, let us look at two more examples of laboratory research (although the process of

BOX 4.4 Microworlds for Experimental Research

So-called **microworld simulations,** which use computer-generated environments, are becoming increasingly popular in psychology because they seem to hold the promise of reducing concerns about realism and generalizability (e.g., Brehmer & Dörner, 1993; DiFonzo, Hantula, & Bordia, 1998; Funke, 1991; Omodei & Wearing, 1995). Simulations of perceptual and social phenomena might be improved by the use of virtual reality technology similar to that found in some arcades (e.g., Biocca & Levy, 1995; Carr & England, 1995; Loomis, Blascovich, & Beall, 1999; Steuer, 1992). The person wears a helmet with a 3-D video card that displays and receives tactile, motion, and audio stimulation designed to immerse the person in a "world" that feels the same as the real world. This approach has been used for years by the U.S. military and aerospace programs to train pilots and astronauts. However, there are time constraints on this methodology, as many subjects in psychology studies find the simulation uncomfortable after a period of time; also, the cost of routinely using it in psychological research may be prohibitive for many years. Still, the potential advantages are that (a) subjects may be made to "feel" the same way they do in a real-world setting; (b) naturally occurring variables can be manipulated in a controlled setting; (c) the situation is dynamic (rather than static) in the way that real-world settings are; and (d) we can study questions that may otherwise be too sensitive to study except in passive observational studies or in experiments using written vignettes or videotapes (Pierce & Aguinis, 1997).

critical evaluation is typical of the scrutiny given all research studies). The first example focuses on how human beings' life experience influences what they select from their perceptual environment as objects and events that are significant to them.

Several classic studies in psychology have shown that individuals' personal values affect how they perceive aspects of their environment. In one classic study, the researchers began by giving a questionnaire to a group of participants to measure each person's values, for example, whether the person's value orientation was predominantly aesthetic, theoretical, economic, social, political, or religious (Postman, Bruner, & McGinnies, 1948). Participants who valued the search for truth above most other things would have received a high "theoretical" score, and participants whose values were dominated by the usefulness of things would have a high "economic" score. The "political" participants were concerned about power, "social" participants about the needs of others, "aesthetic" participants about criteria of beauty, and "religious" participants about the meaning of life as it related to their conception of God. All participants were then presented with a series of words through a tachistoscope projector, a device that briefly presents various stimuli by flashing them on a screen for a fraction of a second. The words chosen reflected the six value orientations of the participants.

On the whole, participants identified words associated with their own value orientation more rapidly than words not so associated. This outcome was taken as evidence of subliminal perception, but can you think of a rival interpretation to the idea that people visually perceive certain words more quickly subliminally merely because of their value orientation? In fact, this interpretation was challenged by other researchers (Solomon & Howes, 1951), who argued that people with a specific value orientation may have been exposed to these words in print more often than other people (presumably, individuals read more literature relevant to their particular values). Therefore, a person oriented to "political" words would recognize them more rapidly than other words because of their familiarity and not because they were subliminally perceived more quickly. This notion paved the way for follow-up studies that were specifically designed to reconcile such differences in interpretation.

Here is another research example on which to practice identifying flaws and considering plausible rival interpretations. Although a great deal is now known about how marijuana acts (e.g., L. L. Iversen, 2000), in the 1960s, when this experiment was conducted, there were volumes of statistics on the relationship between alcohol use and accident rates, but comparable data for marijuana use were unavailable. A laboratory experiment to investigate the effects of drugs on simulated driving performance was deemed ethically acceptable and could be controlled. What was lost, however, was the actual stress of driving in traffic. In this study (Crancer, Dille, Delay, Wallace, & Haybin, 1969), the effects of marijuana, alcohol, and no drug were compared in three simulated driving tests.

In Test 1, experienced marijuana smokers were tested for 30 minutes after smoking two marijuana cigarettes, and the same people were tested when their blood alcohol concentration reached 0.10% (the legally defined intoxication level in 1969), the equivalent of about 6 ounces of 86-proof liquor in a 120-pound person. In the no-drug control condition, neither marijuana nor alcohol was given. In the driving test, the participant sat in a specially constructed console mock-up of a recent-model car and observed a large screen on which a driver's-eye motion picture was projected. Normal and emergency situations on urban and suburban streets appeared on the screen, and the participant was instructed to respond to them by operating the accelerator, brake, turn signals, and steering, and by checking the speedometer. It was possible to make up to 405 errors during the 23-minute film. Test 2 was taken by the participant 2½ hours after taking the first test, and Test 3 was taken 1½ hours after Test 2. All tests were the same.

Here are the results: Under the effects of alcohol, the participants did worse than in either the marijuana or no-drug condition. In the alcohol condition over all three tests, they made a mean of 97 errors; they made a mean of 85 errors in the control condition. In the marijuana condition, compared to the control condition, the only bad effect was an increase in speedometer errors. Under the effects of alcohol, there was an increase in all types of errors except steering errors. The

BOX 4.5 How Was the Experiment Flawed?

The research subjects were experienced marijuana users, were probably moti-vated to do well in the marijuana condition, and may even have been motivated to do poorly in the alcohol condition. A second flaw is that the drug doses may not have been comparable. Two marijuana cigarettes may not have made the participants nearly as "high" as 6 ounces of 86-proof alcohol. Moreover, if the al-cohol and marijuana treatments had made the participants equally "high," the er-rors might have been more nearly equal, and both might have been greater than those accumulated in the no-drug condition.

results were revealing, but ambiguous. What problems do you see in this research? (Compare your answer with Box 4.5.)

Mundane and Experimental Realism in Field Experimentation

As we cautioned before, do not get the idea that only laboratory research is subject to critical scrutiny for rival interpretations or hypotheses. The purpose of this exer-cise was to illustrate the kind of critical evaluation done routinely on all studies. Experimentation is also not limited to the laboratory; it can also be done in a natu-ralistic setting. In such **field experiments,** the researcher evokes behavior by modifying some aspect of the situation or by introducing an experimental variable (i.e., a manipulated independent variable) in a real-world setting. The advantage of this strategy is that it may have more mundane and experimental realism than an analogous laboratory experiment. **Mundane realism** means that the various di-mensions of the experiment are very similar to those in the real world, and **experi-mental realism** refers to the extent to which the participant is drawn into or is affected by the treatment (Aronson & Carlsmith, 1968). The more the manipulation of the independent variable resembles the real-world phenomenon, the greater the mundane realism is. The more involving the manipulation of the independent vari-able, or the greater the degree to which the participant's attention is "turned on" by the treatment, the more experimental realism there is.

Illustrative of the field experiment is a study done by Rosenthal and Jacobson (1968) to investigate whether elementary school teachers' expectations of their stu-dents' intellectual performance might come to serve as self-fulfilling prophecies (Merton, 1948). In the spring of 1964, all the children in a public elementary school in South San Francisco were given a standard nonverbal intelligence test. The test was represented to the teachers as a measure of intellectual "blooming," and ap-proximately 20% of the children (the experimental group) were said to be capable of marked intellectual growth. The difference between the supposed potential bloomers and the other students (the control group) existed solely in the minds of their teachers, because the bloomers had been picked entirely at random. The dependent variable in this study was the children's performance on the same intelligence test after one semester, again after a full academic year, and again after 2 full academic years.

The overall results revealed that, although the greatest differential gain in total measured intelligence appeared after 1 school year, the bloomers clearly held an advantage over the other children, the control participants, even after 2 years. To account for this finding, Rosenthal and Jacobson speculated that the teachers had been more encouraging and friendly to the children in whom they expected greater gains, and in this way, the teachers had unwittingly motivated the children to greater achievement (see also Box 4.6). In the same way that the expectations of the teachers became self-fulfilling prophecies, so can a researcher's hypothesis serve as a self-fulfilling prophecy. In that case, we need to control for this problem in some way, and we will return to this predicament in a later chapter.

BOX 4.6 Pygmalion in the Classroom

Rosenthal and Jacobson (1968) called the educational self-fulfilling prophecy they observed the "Pygmalion effect" because it reminded them of George Bernard Shaw's play *Pygmalion*—which was made into the Broadway musical *My Fair Lady*. In the story, Eliza Doolittle, a poor street girl who sells flowers, becomes the object of a self-fulfilling prophecy when she captures the attention of Henry Higgins, a language professor, because she has the most atrocious accent he has ever heard. He bets that, by changing her accent, he can transform her into a "lady" in English high society. He wins his bet and imagines himself as the mythic sculptor, Pygmalion, who created a statue of a woman so lovely he could not resist her. In Shaw's play, Higgins argues that, "apart from the things anyone can pick up (the dressing and the proper way of speaking, and so on), the difference between a lady and a flower girl is not how she behaves, but how she's treated." It was the way that the students in Rosenthal and Jacobson's study were treated by their teachers, because of their expectations for their students, that was the reason those expectations became a self-fulfilling prophecy. More recently, using the methodology of meta-analysis (see Appendix C), Stephen W. Raudenbush (1984) made further investigations of the Pygmalion effect and found that it is less likely to occur if the teacher has had prior contact with the student, a finding suggesting that the teachers' impressions (and prior prophecies) may have hardened by the time they received the expectancy suggestion.

Reactive and Nonreactive Observation

A further distinction is made between **reactive observation** and **nonreactive observation;** the terms are used to differentiate between observations that do (reactive) from those that do not (nonreactive) affect the behavior being observed. For example, in a clinical experiment on therapy for weight control, the initial weigh-in might be a reactive stimulus to weight reduction, even without the therapeutic intervention (Campbell & Stanley, 1963). Any use of **concealed measurement** illustrates nonreactive observation, such as using a hidden recording device to eavesdrop on conversations. A variant of concealed measurement is also sometimes called **partial concealment;** the researcher does not conceal the fact that he or she is making observations but does conceal who or what is being observed. For example, in studies of mother-child interaction, the researcher implies that it is the child who is being observed when both the mother *and* the child are being studied (Weick, 1968).

A classic example of a field experiment that used nonreactive observation was conducted by psychologist George W. Hartmann (1936). He examined the role of emotional and rational persuasive communications in an actual voting campaign and election. Hartmann was struck by the fact that much of the persuasive communication to which we are subjected in advertisements and political speeches is designed to appeal more to our emotions than to our reason. The purpose of such communication seems to be to arouse certain needs and to offer simple solutions that, if we adopt them, will supposedly satisfy those needs. Every day we are bombarded by a host of advertisements on TV, radio, and so forth, each commercial in its own way claiming that it will make us feel better because we will be more sexually appealing or more companionable or more sweet-smelling. Around election time, political commercials become a complex fusion of excitement, resentment, vague enthusiasm, aroused fears, and hopes. While he was working at Columbia University in the 1930s as a postdoctoral fellow, Hartmann decided to test whether emotional or rational advertisements are more persuasive in politics.

During the 1935 statewide election campaign in Pennsylvania, Hartmann's name had been placed on the ballot as a Socialist Party candidate in Allentown. To study the effects of emotional and rational messages, he created two political leaflets, one designed to appeal to Allentown voters' reason and the other to appeal to their emotions. The leaflets were distributed in different wards matched on the basis of their size, population density, assessed property valuation, previous voting habits, and socioeconomic status. The nonreactive observation in this study was the objective record of the polls. The results of Hartmann's analysis of these data were that the wards that had received the emotional leaflet increased their Socialist votes more than the wards receiving the rational leaflet. In a more in-depth comparison, Hartmann also found that even the "rational" wards showed a greater increase in Socialist votes than a number of control wards that had received neither leaflet.

Another classic example of a nonreactive measurement, called the "lost letter" technique, involves dropping addressed, stamped, but unposted letters in public places. The person who comes across such a letter must decide whether to read it, mail it, disregard it, or destroy it. In the first field experiment that used this technique (Merritt & Fowler, 1948), two kinds of stamped, fully addressed envelopes, one containing a trivial message and the other a lead slug about the size of a half-dollar, were "lost." By recording the return rates, the experimenters attempted to gauge the honesty of various samples of respondents in large cities around the country without the respondents' suspecting that they were participating in an experiment. The result was that fewer letters with slugs than without them were mailed. Variations on this strategy have been used by other researchers, including using lost letters (Milgram, Mann, & Harter, 1965) and lost e-mail on the Internet to study attitudinal responses (Stern & Faber, 1997) and using lost post cards to study the spread of rumors (Walker & Blaine, 1991).

Unobtrusive Observation

Hartmann's use of voting behavior and the lost-letter technique are also examples of what is termed **unobtrusive observation,** so called because those being studied are unaware that they are being observed for the purpose of research. Unobtrusive observation, because it involves the use of concealment, causes ethical conflicts, which need to be carefully considered. For example, the threat to privacy is made worse by the lack of permission in this situation and by the fact that debriefing is not typically used. The defense of unobtrusive observation usually assumes that the individuals observed are anonymous, so that their privacy is protected. That is, the behavioral or social scientist's goal (unlike, for example, the investigative reporter's) is not to obtain individually identified information. The code of ethics that governs psychological researchers (Chapter 3) reminds us that individual researchers are responsible for protecting the dignity of those they study. Thus, the ethical obligation of researchers who use unobtrusive observation is to ensure that any information to be published will not damage a person by subjecting him or her to ridicule or scorn.

A major work on unobtrusive observation was written by a team of interdisciplinary authors headed by Eugene J. Webb (Webb, Campbell, Schwartz, & Sechrest, 1966; updated by Webb, Campbell, Schwartz, Sechrest, & Grove, 1981). It is a fascinating gem of a book that contains hundreds of unobtrusive measures collected by Webb and his group. In general, they classified all their measures into four broad categories: (a) archival records, (b) physical traces, (c) simple observations, and (d) contrived observations. Previously, we discussed archival records, and we will conclude this section by giving examples of the other classes described by Webb and his coauthors.

Physical traces include the kind of material evidence that a detective might use as a clue in solving a crime. For example, in one detective case, a car's radio buttons were clues to the driver's geographic location. By studying the commercial station frequencies to which the buttons were turned, the detectives could identify the general area where the car had been garaged. In one commercial application of this strategy, a car dealer used radio dial settings in an audience measurement study. The dealer had his mechanics record the position of the dial in all the cars brought in for service. He then used this information to choose the radio stations that would carry his advertising to old and potentially new customers.

Other examples of the use of physical traces include measuring the wear and tear (particularly on the corners of pages) of library books as an unobtrusive measure of what books are actually read (not just books checked out and possibly never opened, never read, or never finished). In another case, the relative popularity of children's museum exhibits was measured unobtrusively. The exhibits had glass fronts, and each evening they were dusted for children's noseprints. Those exhibits with more noseprints on the glass were more frequently or more closely observed, the researchers speculated. The distance of the noseprints from the floor even provided a crude index of the ages of the children. Another example in this category might be studying language behavior by analyzing the content of messages that people have composed trying out floor models of personal computers on display in stores.

Simple observation occurs when one observes events unobtrusively without trying to affect them in any way. For example, Webb's group described a correlation between the methodological and theoretical disposition of psychologists and the length of their hair. The researchers in that study unobtrusively evaluated and classified the hairstyles of psychologists at professional meetings and also categorized the research. They reported that the "tough-minded" psychologists had shorter hair than the "tender-minded" psychologists.

In **contrived observation,** the researcher introduces some variable of interest into a situation and then unobtrusively observes its effect on behavior. It is what Hartmann did in his field experiment, described earlier. For example, you might estimate the degree of fear induced by a ghost story by observing the shrinking diameter of a circle of seated children. In the past, before the days of the IRBs and informed consent, some investigators "bugged" cocktail parties and recorded the conversations after introducing some variable of interest (e.g., introducing a stranger or an oddly dressed guest). Before the days of audiotapes, Francis Galton, the pioneering English empiricist mentioned in Chapter 1, carried with him paper in the shape of a cross and a small needle for punching holes in the paper. He used this device to count whatever he was observing at the time; a hole at the head of the cross meant "greater," on an arm "equal," and at the foot "less."

Using Judges as Observers

Except for secondary observations using archival records, we have considered only the researcher himself or herself as the primary observer. Among other observational "instruments" that are used in field and laboratory studies are independent **judges** (coders, raters, decoders, etc.) who assist in describing and categorizing ongoing events or existing records of events (film records, narratives, etc.). Judges use **checklists** and **tally sheets** to impose a sense of structure on their observations; as the names imply, these are simply systematic ways of counting (checking off or tallying) the frequency of occurrence of particular acts or events. In Box 4.3, we mentioned how a team of researchers used judges to content-analyze a sample of pictures from children's books. In a classic series of observational studies on how people interact in small groups, Robert F. Bales and his coworkers (1950a, 1950b; Bales & Cohen, 1979) developed a system for having judges observe and code people's relations with one another. Among the many findings was that small groups tend to have more than one leader, usually a task leader and one who is a socioemotional leader (someone who is witty and cheerful and serves to reduce tension and keep interpersonal relations harmonious for others in the group). Another interesting finding was that when there seemed to be too much task or problem-solving behavior in the group, socioemotional relations between members became strained, and there was then a tendency to alternate to socioemotional behavior until a kind of psychological equilibrium was reached.

In general, researchers choose judges in one of three ways: (a) on the basis of intuition, (b) by consulting the research literature for relevant criteria to help them choose, or (c) by doing pilot testing.

The first approach is to decide intuitively on the type of judges needed (e.g., graduate students, community members, college students, clinical psychologists, linguists, mothers) and then to regard each judge within that sample as equivalent to (or interchangeable with) any other judge within the sample. For example, if you wanted a sample of raters educated at a certain level, you might be content to select college students. If you wanted ratings of nonverbal expressions of neuroses, you would choose as your judges experienced professionals, such as clinical psychologists, psychiatrists, or psychiatric social workers. If you wanted ratings of nonverbal expressions of discomfort in infants, you might select pediatricians, developmental psychologists, or mothers. If you wanted ratings of nonverbal cues of persuasion, you might invite trial lawyers, Fundamentalist ministers, or salespersons. You would also want to make sure that the judges are not relying on stereotypes that might not be accurate (e.g., salespersons recruited to watch people give persuasive messages might rely on stereotypes to tell you which of the nonverbal cues were most persuasive).

A second approach is to consult the relevant research literature, in which case you might do even better by making a special selection of judges. For example, if you wanted to obtain the highest possible general accuracy in judgments of nonverbal cues, your selection of judges might be based on prior research that had identified the characteristics of people who are more sensitive to nonverbal cues. This research suggests that, to optimize overall sensitivity to nonverbal cues, you should probably select judges who are (a) female, (b) college-aged, and (as measured by psychological tests) both (c) cognitively complex and (d) psychiatrically unimpaired (Rosenthal, Hall, DiMatteo, Rogers, & Archer, 1979). A more recent study has added another characteristic to this list: *field independence,* which means that the person chosen to do the rating is able to impose organization on information and is not dependent only on the external or ostensible organization. Field-independent persons, identified by an instrument designed to measure this characteristic (the Group Embedded Figures Test), appear to be more accurate raters than field-dependent persons (Härtel, 1993).

A third way to select judges is to do a **pilot test,** in which you compare all recruits in your pool of potential judges for their accuracy of judgments on some relevant criterion. Suppose you were interested in selecting raters for a study in which they would have to categorize the emotions expressed by participants in group therapy sessions. You might begin by showing your pool of potential raters pictures of people exhibiting different emotions, such as anger, disgust, fear, happiness, sadness, and surprise. You would ask them to identify the emotion expressed in each picture, score the answers given by them, and then use the most accurate judges in your study.

A Final Note

You have seen from the wide variety of examples in this chapter (and in previous chapters) that systematic observational methods provide much of the empirical content of behavioral and social science, yet our discussion has barely scratched the surface of what is possible. Before we turn to strategies in which the observations are directed "inward" rather than "outward," we want to add a word of caution about the use of observational strategies. Scientists, like all human beings, are susceptible to the biases imposed by limitations of perception and cognition. Human imagination and expectations powerfully affect perceptions, or as one scientist put it, "Our assumptions define and limit what we see, i.e., we tend to see in such a way that they will fit in with our assumptions even if this involves distortions or omission" (M. L. Johnson, 1953, p. 79). This is another reason why scientists emphasize the importance of independent observations as a way of checking on the accuracy of any single observation or set of observations. We will have more to say about this topic in Chapter 6, when we discuss the role of replication in research. We began this chapter by urging that you not harbor illusions about the power of any single research method or tool but instead be mindful of the fact that all are limited in some ways. It is a constant challenge to try to figure out ways of effectively opening up our world for scientific scrutiny, to evaluate the validity and reliability of these strategies, and, ultimately, to make prudent generalizations that do not mislead by exaggerating what we think we know.

Summary of Ideas

1. Systematic observation is characterized by a plan of action and by preexisting questions or hypotheses in naturalistic and artificial situations, primary and secondary observational research, and qualitative and quantitative research.
2. Feyerabend's "anything-goes view of science" (Box 4.1) means that doing research *does* involve a "let's-try-it-and-see" attitude.

3. Because each observational method is limited in some ways, we use multiple methods to try to fill in the gaps through triangulation, that is, by converging on the phenomenon or research question from more than one perspective.

4. Participant observers study a social situation from within by watching and recording how people behave and what they talk about (e.g., Festinger et al.'s observational study of a cult that predicted the end of the world on a specified date and Kidder's study of participants in a hypnosis workshop).

5. Ethnographic research uses participant observation to study people in a "cultural setting" (a term that is broadly defined, e.g., Rosenhan's study of patients in mental hospitals, noted in Box 4.2).

6. In making sense of the qualitative data, ethnographers may be guided by questions about (a) the purpose of the activity being observed; (b) the procedures used to perform the activity; (c) the time and space requirements of the activity; (d) the personnel requirements; (e) the nature of its social organization; and (f) the occasions for performance (e.g., Haviland's study of gossiping in a small village in Mexico).

7. Content analysis is used in archival research to code and sort secondary observations (or, in the case of Crabb and Bielawski's study of gender roles in children's picture books, pictorial representations of behavior, as noted in Box 4.3).

8. In designing a content analysis, it is important (a) to ensure intercoder reliability; (b) to develop specific, relevant content categories for the judges to code; and (c) to choose a good sampling plan.

9. Observational research in a laboratory experiment means testing or trying out something in a tightly controlled setting in order to study causality, and in many cases using a simulation (e.g., the experiment to simulate the effects of marijuana and alcohol use on automobile driving).

10. All research studies, including tightly controlled laboratory experiments, are subject to critical reexamination for potential flaws and rival interpretations (e.g., the study in Number 9 above and the tachistoscopic study of word recognition).

11. Field experiments are a variant of naturalistic observational research (e.g., Rosenthal and Jacobson's experimental study of teachers' expectations as unwitting determinants of their students' intellectual performance and Hartmann's field study of the effects of emotional and rational political communications on voting behavior).

12. Nonreactive observation includes concealed measurement and partial concealment (e.g., Hartmann's study and the lost-letter technique).

13. Unobtrusive observation is nonreactive; examples include (a) archival records, (b) physical traces, (c) simple observation, and (d) contrived observation.

14. When choosing judges to classify events or to rate behavior, we can use (a) intuition; (b) previous results that help us select the most accurate individuals (e.g., college-aged women who are cognitively complex, psychiatrically unimpaired, and field-independent); or (c) pilot testing.

Key Terms

anything-goes view of science (Feyerabend) p. 85	content analysis p. 92	intercoder reliability p. 93
archival material p. 91	contrived observation p. 102	judges p. 102
checklists p. 103	ethnography p. 88	methodological triangulation p. 85
concealed measurement p. 100	experimental realism p. 98	microworld simulations p. 96
	field experiments p. 98	

WEB ACTIVITY

Visit a fascinating site about perceptual illusions at http://www-bc.mit.edu (note there is a hyphen, not a period, after www). To participate in a study of the small world problem, visit Columbia University's http://www.smallworld.sociology.columbia.edu.

Multiple-Choice Questions for Review

1. In a classic study, several social psychologists "joined" a religious cult that believed that the world would soon end. After they were accepted as members of the group, they made careful observations of the behavior of the group. This type of research is known as (a) a field experiment; (b) participant observation; (c) ethnocentric research; (d) back-translation.

2. A student at the University of Hawaii wants to study gossip and rumor among Asian cultures. In this research, interview questions must be translated from English into other languages. To ensure that the translations are accurate, the researcher must use the procedure of (a) ethnographic research; (b) linguistic relativism; (c) back-translation; (d) dual translation.

3. In 1935, social psychologist George Hartmann ran for political office in Pennsylvania. In some areas, he distributed leaflets with an emotional appeal to voters. In other areas, he distributed leaflets with a rational appeal. He then observed the voting records in these different areas. In this study, the type of leaflet was the _____ variable, and the voting records were the _____ variable. (a) independent, experimental; (b) experimental, independent; (c) dependent, independent; (d) independent, dependent

4. Suppose you are conducting an observational study, and you want judges (or raters) who are very sensitive to nonverbal cues. You should choose judges who are (a) psychiatrically unimpaired; (b) college-aged; (c) female; (d) all of the above.

5. A researcher at Montclair State University carefully observes whether or not people lock their car doors when parked in the university's parking lot. The people do not realize that they are being observed for a research study. This is an example of (a) reactive observation; (b) partial concealment; (c) unobtrusive observation; (d) none of the above.

6. A researcher at Florida International University conducts an observational study of job satisfaction in a large corporation. She tells the research participants that she is studying their behavior but does not tell them what aspect of their behavior she will be observing. This is an example of (a) quasi disclosure; (b) partial concealment; (c) unobtrusive observation; (d) residual disclosure.

7. To determine which classrooms are used most heavily at Akron University, a researcher measures the amount of wear on floor tiles. This is an example of the use of (a) physical traces; (b) simple observations; (c) contrived observations; (d) archival records.

8. A researcher at Colby College observes how far apart people stand from each other at a party. This is an example of the use of (a) physical traces; (b) simple observations; (c) contrived observations; (d) archival records.

9. A researcher at the University of Colorado at Denver reports that marriage rates are associated with the size of the city. She obtained both the marriage rates and the population estimates from government statistics available in the library. This is an example of the use of (a) physical traces; (b) simple observations; (c) contrived observations; (d) archival research.

10. Webb and his colleagues described four types of unobtrusive measures. Which of the following is *not* one of these types? (a) physical traces; (b) simple observations; (c) contrived observations; (d) interview schedules

Discussion Questions for Review

1. An Iowa State student is given the task of describing two possible uses of archival measures not mentioned in this chapter. Can you suggest some possibilities?

2. An Arizona State student wants to test the hypothesis that people's level of aggression predicts their preference of sports; that is, more aggressive people like more aggressive sports. How might the student test this hypothesis using nonreactive measures?

3. A Towson State student wants to use content analysis to study the comic pages in *The Baltimore Sun*. Can you think of a particular hypothesis to guide the data collection? What steps would you advise the student to take in carrying out her study?

4. A Fitchburg State College student wants to do a participant observer study of tourists and local residents in Provincetown. What advice would you give him about systematizing his observations?

5. A student at the University of Massachusetts at Boston wants to illustrate the application of methodological triangulation to the question of whether inhaling cigarette smoke is unhealthy. Can you help by giving an example of a descriptive, a relational, and an experimental study, all addressing the same question?

6. An Ohio State University student has found that teachers' ratings of their students' intellectual ability are highly correlated with the students' IQ test scores and concludes that this correlation reflects the effects of teachers' expectations on students' intellectual performance. What might be a plausible rival hypothesis to that interpretation?

Answers to Review Questions

Multiple-Choice Questions

1. b	3. d	5. c	7. a	9. d
2. c	4. d	6. b	8. b	10. d

Discussion Questions

1. To learn the "effects" of legislation on some outcome behavior (e.g., drunk driving) by comparing the changes in behavior in states (or counties) changing their laws with the change in behavior in states not changing their laws. To predict legislators' votes from an analysis of their past votes or the style of communication revealed in their earlier speeches. To predict future intelligence, personality, and psychopathology from archived early childhood drawings.

2. The student could correlate the frequency of reported fights, stampedes, and riots with the aggressiveness of various sports as defined by the average number of injuries per player sustained in each sport.

3. To examine the hypothesis that comic strips featuring children are designed for a younger readership, the mean word length in comic strips featuring children is compared to the mean word length in comic strips not featuring children. The student should check the reliability of two judges' (a) classifying the strips as featuring or not featuring children and (b) counting the word lengths and computing their average. The student might also want to sample the comic strips over a period of several weeks or months.

4. The most important advice is that he should be clear about what he wants to learn from this research. In addition, he should consider the general questions suggested by Goodenough and described on pages 89–91.

5. A descriptive study may reveal a high rate of wheezing, coughing, illness, and death among those exposed to cigarette smoke. A relational study may show that those who are exposed to greater amounts of cigarette smoke suffer from higher rates of illness and death. An experimental study may show that animals experimentally exposed to higher dosages of cigarette smoke have higher rates of illness and death than do animals exposed to lower dosages.

6. The teachers' ratings of their students' intellectual ability were nothing more than the teachers' accurate diagnosing of IQ. It would take an experimental manipulation of teachers' expectations to demonstrate that these expectations played a causal role.

CHAPTER 5

Methods for Looking Within Ourselves

Preview Questions

- What are the uses and limitations of self-report measures?

- What are open-ended and fixed-choice measures?

- How are projective tests and personality inventories used?

- What are different kinds of rating scales, and how are rating errors controlled?

- What is the purpose of semantic differentials, Likert scales, and Thurstone scales?

- When is a questionnaire used in research, and how should it be constructed?

- How are face-to-face and telephone interviews done?

- How are *behavioral diaries* used in research?

 ## Self-Report Measures

Researchers who study human behavior not only watch and record, frequently calling on judges (raters or coders) to make systematic observations, but they often ask participants to look within themselves and disclose their own attitudes, feelings, perceptions, and beliefs, a kind of information that no one else can claim to know as well (Baldwin, 2000). These observations are described as **self-report measures,** and their use in behavioral and social research goes back over a century. In the formative years of psychological science, experimental researchers had subjects reflect and verbally report on their sensations and perceptions (a process known as *introspection*). Later on, with the development of behavioral methodology, verbal reports fell out of favor for some years in experimental psychology and were largely replaced by behavioral responses and observational methods.

Nonetheless, self-report is used quite regularly in many areas. When you go to the eye doctor to be fitted for glasses, after you are shown the letter chart you will

BOX 5.1 Personality Testing

Psychologists have shown that it is possible to estimate future performance in some occupations from well-constructed measures of normal personality, given to potential employees before employment (Hogan, Hogan, & Roberts, 1996). Some National Football League teams even give personality tests to prospective draft choices to help in judging the draftees. The New York Giants organization gives its own test to prospective players, including asking them to answer true or false to statements like "When a person 'pads' an income tax report so as to get out of some taxes, it is just as bad as stealing money from the Government," and "I am often said to be hotheaded" (T. W. Smith, 1997, p. 11). The prospective player's responses to these and other items are used to create a personality profile. These profiles are believed to be as informative as the physicals the draftees take.

be shown a series of paired images and asked which ones you find easier to see. When you go to your family doctor, you are asked how you feel. In a similar way, psychological researchers who use **standardized measures** (i.e., they were developed and are administered and scored according to certain rules, or standards) to study subjective well-being also ask people how they feel (e.g., Diener, 2000). Many behavioral and social researchers use a variety of self-report measures in their work (A. A. Stone et al., 2000), including personality inventories that estimate future performance (see Box 5.1), attitude and opinion questionnaires, and procedures in which people are asked to reflect on their inner feelings or to "think aloud" (Ericsson & Simon, 1993).

The purpose of this chapter is to familiarize you with a range of self-report measures and to discuss the advantages and limitations of each. Most of the instruments described are readily available to students, but some require supervised training and someone certified as qualified to use them, such as the Rorschach, Thematic Apperception Test, and the Minnesota Multiphasic Personality Inventory (all described in this chapter). Among the other methods to be discussed are simple rating scales, questionnaires that measure attitudes, and interviews and behavioral diaries. We will also describe types of rating errors and how they are controlled, but we begin by mentioning three issues to keep in mind when using self-report measures.

Three Important Issues

One issue is the dependability of self-report data. A basic assumption in the use of a self-report measure is that what the research participants say about themselves is true and not merely a strategy to "look good." However, when people feel apprehensive about being evaluated, they are often evasive or not completely forth-coming. Called **evaluation apprehension** (Rosenberg, 1969), this anxious state may be reduced a little if they are allowed to answer privately (Schaeffer, 2000). In experimental studies that contain an element of surprise or have an aura of mystery, the level of evaluation apprehension may be intensified (Rosenberg, 1969). Some researchers believe that one way to encourage more open and hon-est responses is to assure people that what they say will be held in strict confi-dence (Esposito et al., 1984; Singer, Von Thurn, & Miller, 1995). However, there is also evidence that the more elaborate the assurance of confidentiality in survey re-search, the more expectations may increase that the questions will touch on highly sensitive topics that the person is reluctant to talk about (Frey, 1986; Singer, Hip-pler, & Schwarz, 1992).

A second issue is that it is vital not to use self-report methods (or undertake any research) without thinking carefully about ethical implications. For example, if sensitive information will be revealed, we must try to anticipate potentially risky consequences. People have the right to withhold information, and they also have the right not to have the information they disclose made public or used against them (Bersoff & Bersoff, 2000). However, suppose that we are studying young chil-dren or adolescents, and we learn that the child has a suicidal tendency or that the parents are abusing the child (LaGreca, 1990). Because such situations are possible, a concern of ethicists is whether it is appropriate for an untrained researcher (such as a college student) to ask participants about such things as depression, anxiety, sexuality, and traumatic life experiences (Bersoff & Bersoff, 2000). As we discussed in Chapter 3, virtually all proposed research is now subject to an ethical evaluation. Your instructor will be sensitive to ethical issues and conflicts that your inexperi-ence may cause you to overlook.

A third issue is whether research participants, even the most well intentioned, *can* provide information that can be considered as valid and reliable as other be-havioral data. Some psychologists have argued that people simply cannot look within themselves or have a clear sense of themselves apart from the immediate situation (e.g., Nisbett & Wilson, 1977). Another side of this issue is the accuracy of people's memories and the unintentional fabrication of information (Greenwald, 1980; Karney & Coombs, 2000; Loftus & Palmer, 1974; Neisser & Fivush, 1994). In one study, parents were interviewed as they were leaving an HMO immediately after their children had received one or more vaccinations; the parents' reports of what had occurred a few minutes earlier were riddled with errors of recall (Willis, Brittingham, Lee, Tourangeau, & Ching, 1999). In another study, men were asked about particular experiences they had reported 30 years earlier when they were adolescents (Offer, Kaiz, Howard, & Bennett, 2000). While 61% of them, as adoles-cents, had reported that sports and other physical activities were their favorite pas-times, only 23% of them as adults gave the same answer when asked to recollect their favorite pastimes. When they were young, 28% of them had reported that they disliked schoolwork, but 58% as adults "remembered" they hated it. As ado-lescents, 70% had said they found religion personally helpful, but as adults, only 26% of them remembered it the same way (see also Box 5.2).

BOX 5.2 The Seven Sins of Memory

Daniel L. Schacter (1999), a Harvard cognitive psychologist, described what he called the "seven sins of memory." Three of them refer to types of forgetting: (a) absent-mindedness, (b) blocking out certain information, and (c) the gradual deterioration of details over time. Another three refer to different kinds of distortions or inaccuracies: (d) attributing something to the wrong source, (e) unconscious biases due to stereotypes and prejudices, and (f) human suggestibility to implanted ideas. The final memory "sin" does not refer to forgetting or memory gaps, but instead to (g) the nagging persistence of images that are instantaneously, and seemingly forever, imprinted in our memory (like the shocking images of September 11, 2001). Schacter theorized that these sins of memory are like "spandrels," an architectural term referring to the leftover spaces in structural components of buildings, except that these memory spandrels are leftover effects gone astray in an evolutionary process that is imperfect.

Open Versus Closed Questions

All of the methods that are described in this chapter, whatever their limitations, have been used in both basic and applied behavioral research. In fact, few people escape the opportunity to participate in one of these two types of research, although not everyone agrees to participate. For example, suppose you receive the following telephone call:

> Hello, is this ____? My name is ____, and I'm calling from the Survey Institute at Central University. We are conducting a short random survey to determine how people feel about gun control issues so that we can get a true picture of people's attitudes. It will take only about 5 minutes, and we would greatly appreciate your help. May I ask you some questions?

If you answer yes, you will be a participant in a study using self-report data to measure people's behavior or state of mind.

You will be read a series of questions and asked to say how you personally behave, feel, or think (Lavrakas, 1987). Some of the questions you are asked may be **open-ended,** so called because they offer you an opportunity to express your feelings and impressions spontaneously. Other questions, called **fixed-choice measures** (also called *structured, precoded,* or *closed*), will use a more controlled approach, giving you specified options such as yes-no or multiple-choice alternatives. Later, we will describe how open-ended and fixed-choice measures are used in personality inventories, attitude and survey questionnaires, interviews, and behavioral diaries. The rule of thumb is that the measures chosen should match the dimensions of interest and the kind of information that is desired.

The doctor's asking, "How do you feel?" is an example of an open-ended question. Your answer not only gives the doctor a clue about *what* to observe or diagnose but also gives her or him a sense of how *you* (as an individual) experience things. In the telephone survey example, the researcher is looking for individual responses, although the goal is to generalize (cautiously) about similar individuals in some specified population. An example of an open-ended question that the researcher might ask is "How do you feel about the National Rifle Association?" When analyzing the data, the researcher will categorize responses to this question and then correlate the coded data with the responses to other questions (another example of relational research).

Like any observational or self-report method, an open-ended format has advantages and disadvantages (Scott, 1968). The advantages of open-ended measures are that (a) they do not lead the respondent by suggesting specific answers; (b) their approach is exploratory, allowing the researcher to find out whether the person has anything at all to say; and (c) they invite the person to answer in his or her own language, a procedure that sometimes helps to increase rapport. Disadvantages of open-ended measures are that (a) they are time-consuming for both the researcher (who must code and analyze the responses) and the participants; (b) they often elicit rambling and off-the-mark responses that may never actually touch on the topic the researcher is interested in (but see Box 5.3); and (c) they may be hard to assess for reliability (discussed in the next chapter).

BOX 5.3 The Critical Incident Technique

A procedure for eliciting more focused responses to open-ended questions is called the **critical incident technique,** which was developed by organizational psychologist John Flanagan (1954). It involves asking the participant to give an open-ended description of an observable action, the purpose of which must be fairly clear to the observer, and the consequences sufficiently definite to leave little doubt about the action's effects. For example, a team of researchers used the critical incident technique in their study of company managers in the United States and India who were interviewed as part of an investigation of how managers cope with destructive rumors (DiFonzo, Bordia, & Rosnow, 1994). Managers were asked to describe as concretely and fully as possible an actual situation that had been important to their company in which they had been required to confront a harmful or a potentially harmful rumor. The data revealed some circumstances in which rumor control strategies are likely to succeed and that were also found to be consistent with empirically based theorizing. For a detailed description of the critical incident technique, see Flanagan's seminal article (published in the *Psychological Bulletin* in 1954).

An example of a fixed-choice item would be "How do you feel about a 10-day waiting period for permission to buy a gun? Would you say you are strongly in favor, moderately in favor, moderately against, or strongly against this idea?" A response that would not be read to you is "Don't know," but if that is your spontaneous answer, the interviewer will note it down. Advantages and disadvantages of fixed-choice measures are usually understood to be the reverse of those of open-ended measures. For most researchers, the major advantage of the fixed-choice format is that it forces the participants' answers into the dimensions of interest to the researcher rather than producing irrelevant or uncodable answers (Scott, 1968). We will continue our discussion of self-report measures by describing some specialized instruments used by researchers, clinical and counseling psychologists, school psychologists, and others to get people to reveal aspects of their personality.

The Rorschach, TAT, and MMPI

As ideas of personality have developed, from the time of Sigmund Freud to the present, methods of assessing various personality characteristics, particularly as part of the therapeutic process, have also evolved. Much of the early testing of personality consisted of diagnosing the mental state of the individual by examining that part of the personality relevant to therapy, a process that led to the development of a variety of personality inventories. The particular configuration of an individual's personality is believed to have profound consequences for her or his behavior. Although there is disagreement about the factors that are most influential in a given situation, there is theoretical speculation that a small number of factors may transcend cultural differences (McCrae & Costa, 1997). That is, there is presumed to be a human universal in the structure of personality, similar to the universality of the human skeletal structure—even though individuals differ from one another in, for example, their girth and height (see Box 5.4).

Measures of the structure of personality take many different forms, including the use of open-ended and fixed-choice formats. One of the oldest psychological measures of personality is the **projective test.** This class of instruments, of which the **Rorschach test** is perhaps the most familiar, uses an open-ended format. The Rorschach comprises inkblots produced on pieces of cardboard; the inkblots are presented to the respondent one by one in a standard order, each for as long as the respondent likes. The Rorschach test is *open-ended* because the researcher instructs the respondent to describe *whatever* he or she sees in the blot. The researcher keeps a verbatim record of everything the person says, also noting any peculiarity of facial expression or bodily movement. Once the person has responded to all the inkblots, the task of scoring begins. Psychiatrist Hermann Rorschach, who created this instrument, also provided a scoring procedure for the responses, and the scoring method has been modified and expanded by other researchers over the years (e.g., Beck, Beck, Levitt, & Molish, 1961; Exner, 1993; Harrower & Bowers, 1987; Kleinmuntz, 1982; Klopfer & Kelley, 1942). Scoring and interpreting the Rorschach calls for professionally supervised experience, so the

BOX 5.4 OCEAN: The Big Five

Current thinking in personality assessment generally supports the idea of five broad domains of individual personality, called the **Big Five factors** (Goldberg, 1993; McCrae & Costa, 1997; Wiggins, 1996). The acronym *OCEAN* is an easy way to remember these five factors, although each factor may be made up of hundreds of specific traits:

1. *Openness to experience* (O), or the degree of imagination, curiosity, and creativity.
2. *Conscientiousness* (C), or the degree of organization, thoroughness, and reliability.
3. *Extraversion* (E), or the degree of talkativeness, assertiveness, and activity.
4. *Agreeableness* (A), or the degree of kindness, trust, and warmth.
5. *Neuroticism* (N), or the degree of nervousness, moodiness, and temperamentality.

Rorschach test is out of the reach of undergraduate students doing research. Illustrative of its use in other research was a study by George A. De Vos, an anthropologist, and L. Bryce Boyer, a psychiatrist. They used a scoring system that they developed to analyze the verbal responses of Japanese, Algerian Arabs, and Apache Native Americans in order to identify certain universal concepts and symbols (De Vos & Boyer, 1989).

Another open-ended projective test, but one not as well known to the general public, is the **Thematic Apperception Test (TAT).** Created by Henry Murray, it consists of a number of pictures of people in various life contexts, and the respondent is asked to make up a story explaining each picture. Because the situations depicted are adaptable to a large number of interpretations, different stories are appropriate. The stories the respondent tells are presumed to reveal certain concerns and personality characteristics. In a classic study in personality research, David McClelland and his coworkers (McClelland, Atkinson, Clark, & Lowell, 1953) used the TAT to profile people who were high and low in the "need to achieve." The researchers asked college students to construct a story from TAT pictures. As each picture was presented, the student was asked: (a) What is happening? Who are the persons? (b) What has led up to this situation? That is, what has happened in the past? (c) What is being thought? What is wanted? By whom? and (d) What will happen? What will be done? Once the students had made up their stories, they were scored on the need for achievement. The researchers used other tools of personality measurement to elicit the respondents' high and low levels of need for achievement. McClelland and his colleagues described the structure and intensity of the need for achievement in each respondent and developed a model of the situational factors that may increase or decrease a need for achievement.

Another well-known personality measure with a fixed-choice format is the **Minnesota Multiphasic Personality Inventory (MMPI).** It contains hundreds of statements such as "I often cross the street to avoid meeting people," "I am afraid of losing my mind," "I believe I am no more nervous than most others," and "I have a great deal of stomach trouble." The test taker responds true or false to each statement. The statements were originally selected by researchers after studies had determined which items best differentiated normal individuals from various types of psychiatric patients. Some statements were also selected to reflect general health, sexual attitudes, emotional states, and so on. From these statements, clinical scales were created, which are related to diagnostic categories such as depression, paranoia, and schizophrenia. Those taking the MMPI are usually scored on all scales, and the scores are then compared with those of normal control respondents.

All of the tools described in the remainder of this chapter can be used quite routinely by most students (with the ethical stipulation noted previously), but the Rorschach, the TAT, and the MMPI call for professional training and supervised experience that will prevent the occurrence of negative consequences. Access to the Rorschach, TAT, and MMPI requires certification to the publisher that the user has had such training. Students who are interested in learning more about professional testing principles will find a detailed discussion in the most recent edition of the American Psychological Association's *Standards for Educational and Psychological Testing* (see also Box 5.5). The point of describing these tools is that you may find them referred to in your literature search, and knowing something about them will give you a better sense of the research in which they have been used.

BOX 5.5 Ethical Testing Practices

A joint committee on testing practices, representing several professional organizations, recently proposed a code that spells out the ethical requirements of test developers and test users. Among the requirements of test developers are that they (a) define what each test measures and the people for whom it is appropriate, (b) accurately represent its uses and limitations, (c) tell how the test was developed and evaluated, and (d) provide scientific evidence that the test measures what it is purported to measure. Among the requirements of test users are that they (a) know all these basic details about the tests they use, (b) use the tests only in the way that they are designed to be used, and (c) not use the tests if they lack the skills to use them. For further information about the *Code of Fair Testing Practices in Education,* address your request to the National Council on Measurement in Education, 1230 Seventeenth Street, NW, Washington, DC 20036.

Rating Scales and How to Interpret Them

Researchers who want to have people rate themselves (or to have judges rate others, as discussed in the previous chapter) often use simple **rating scales.** The most commonly used rating scales in observational research are the numerical and graphic kinds, but we will also describe a third kind, the forced-choice rating scale. Whether you are testing people and scoring the results yourself or are using a computer to administer and score rating scales, you will find these three types easy to use, easy to score, and widely applicable. Many standardized questionnaires also use one of these three formats. Where there are response options that are labeled with **cue words** (guiding labels), it is prudent to give the respondent an example (illustrated later in this chapter). However, before we describe these three types of rating scales, there are two related issues of importance.

The first issue is the interpretation of individual scores. Suppose we were using a standardized test for which there were **norm-referenced** values of respondents in some specified population (such as the Scholastic Assessment Test you took when you were applying to college). By comparing a person's score with that of the normative group, we can estimate the percentile in which the person's score falls (more about *percentiles* in a later chapter). But what if we constructed our own rating instrument? It might be misleading to compare rating scores of one person with those of another person (Bartoshuk, 2002). Suppose that Persons A and B independently rated the extent to which they were "feeling stress" as 3 on a scale from 0 (no stress) to 7 (extreme stress). Although both gave the same response, how do we know that A's score means the same thing as B's? Suppose they have different thresholds of stress. On the other hand, if all we want to know is whether each person's feeling of stress changed over time, we have the original scores as base rates in a repeated-measures design (more about repeated-measures designs later in this book). Similarly, there is no problem if all we want to do is compare the average rating scores for stress in two randomly assigned groups, because we presume that randomly occurring differences (called *random errors* in the next chapter) will cancel out (Norwick, Choi, & Ben-Shachar, 2002).

Second, there are certain minimal considerations when researchers set out to construct a questionnaire (Robinson, Shaver, & Wrightsman, 1991). For example, the various items that the researchers create must sample the *universe of content* that the questionnaire claims to represent. One way to assess the adequacy of the sampling is to ask knowledgeable people to examine the questionnaire for possible omissions. The items must also be easily understood; that is, they must be expressed in plain language without any double-talk (ambiguities) or out-of-date expressions. As a check, the researchers do **pilot testing** of the questionnaire with a sample of individuals from the target population. And finally, the researchers need to make sure that the respondents are giving appropriate answers, which can also be assessed during the pilot-testing phase.

Numerical, Forced-Choice, and Graphic Scales

Numerical scales, which are the most popular form of rating scales, are distinguished by the fact that respondents work with a sequence of defined numbers. The numbers may be stated for the person to see and use, or they may be implicit (e.g., 1 vs. 0 for yes vs. no). To illustrate, here is a 5-point item from a questionnaire that was designed to measure attitudes toward mathematics (Aiken, 1963):

My mind goes blank, and I am unable to think clearly when working with math.

_____ strongly disagree

_____ disagree

_____ undecided

_____ agree

_____ strongly agree

In this example, the numbers are implicit rather than explicit. For instance, we can score *strongly disagree* as -2, *disagree* as -1, *undecided* as 0, *agree* as +1, and *strongly agree* as +2. Or we can score *strongly disagree* as 1, *disagree* as 2, *undecided* as 3, *agree* as 4, and *strongly agree* as 5. Either way, we will get equivalent results when we analyze the data.

Notice in the item above that the respondent was given the option to answer "undecided" (neutral). However, some researchers prefer pushing respondents to one or the other side rather than giving them the neutral option, for example,

My mind goes blank, and I am unable to think clearly when working with math.

_____ strongly disagree

_____ disagree

_____ agree

_____ strongly agree

Most survey researchers regard neutral responses as a form of missing data that reduces their ability to detect statistical differences (Schuman & Presser, 1996). In the illustrative item above, the positive and negative scoring will remain the same, but there is no zero. Alternatively, we can score *strongly disagree* as 1, *disagree* as 2, *agree* as 3, and *strongly agree* as 4.

To illustrate the second form of rating scales, called **forced-choice scales,** suppose you were asked to respond to the following question:

Which characteristic *best* describes you—honest or intelligent?

This question forces you to choose between two positive attributes (thereby implying that the one you did not choose is less characteristic of you). Since many people dislike having to make such a choice, you might ask why use forced-choice scales at all? The answer is that they were created to overcome a type of response bias called the **halo effect,** which occurs when the person doing the rating of someone (the target person) forms a very favorable impression of the target person based on one central trait and extends that impression to the target person's other characteristics. For example, suppose a target person who is athletic and good-looking is judged to be far more popular than she or he really is. A numerical scale would allow the rater to pile up favorable scores, but on a forced-choice scale the rater is required to make a difficult choice (see also Box 5.6). The forced-choice format that seems to arouse the least antagonism (and produces the most valid results) presents four positively-valenced options and asks respondents to select the two *most descriptive* ones in this group (Guilford, 1954).

For example, suppose we were interested in evaluating a new incentive program designed to improve the reward system and morale in a company. To test the effectiveness of the projected program, we expose a sample of workers (i.e., the experimental group) to a 1-month treatment condition and compare their reactions with those of other workers (i.e., the control group) who did not receive the experimental treatment. In the spirit of methodological pluralism, our dependent measures consist of self-ratings, ratings by managers, and nonreactive measures of performance, which we will use to triangulate on the effectiveness of the new program. Among the self-ratings are some forced-choice items, such as:

Circle the *two* characteristics that *best describe* how you feel in your work:
rewarded   relaxed   appreciated   trusting

Our hypothesis is that, if the incentive program has the effect of improving the reward system and morale, the experimental group will be more likely than the control group to circle characteristics such as "rewarded" and "appreciated."

 ## BOX 5.6 The Halo Effect

In recent years, some researchers have questioned the seriousness of the halo effect and whether it is as ubiquitous as earlier researchers claimed (Murphy, Jako, & Anhalt, 1993). Should it occur, it may be likely to do so when there is a substantial delay between observation and judgment, so that the rater relies on global impressions rather than on recently observed behavior. Halo errors may also occur when the rater is only casually acquainted with the person being rated, or when earlier judgments involve dimensions that are logically related to the rater's global evaluation of the person. Early research suggested some other situations in which halo errors may occur, such as when the trait or characteristic to be rated cannot be easily observed, or is not clearly defined, or involves relations with other people, or is of some moral importance (Symonds, 1925).

Graphic scales are a third basic type of rating scale. Usually a graphic scale is a straight line resembling a thermometer, presented either horizontally or vertically. It can be used as either an observational or a self-report method (just as numerical and forced-choice scales can also be used in both situations). For example, school-teachers might use the following items to rate each student in their homeroom (an observational method), or each student might be asked to rate himself or herself (a self-report method):

Unpopular   _____   Popular

Shy   _____   Outgoing

Solitary   _____   Gregarious

The respondent makes a check mark, and the researcher then transforms that mark into a number by placing a ruler under the line and reading the number from the ruler. Notice that another characteristic of these items is that they are **bipolar;** that is, the cue words at the ends of these scales are extreme opposites.

It is much easier, however, to divide the straight line into segments, thereby transforming the "thermometer-scale" into a numerical rating scale (or a **segmented graphic scale**), as in the following 6-point example:

Unpopular   ____:____:____:____:____:____   Popular

Shy   ____:____:____:____:____:____   Outgoing

Solitary   ____:____:____:____:____:____   Gregarious

Here, we ask the teacher or student to make a decision that reflects only positively or negatively on the person being rated, because a scale with an even number of segments does not allow for an undecided response. This example is, in a way, reminiscent of a forced-choice measure, except that it gives the person a range of positive and negative options.

Rating Errors and How to Control Them

The use of rating scales assumes that respondents are capable of an acceptable de-gree of rating precision and objectivity. In constructing questionnaires that use such measures, it is important to think about how to overcome certain **rating er-rors** (also called **response biases** or **rater biases**), such as the halo effect men-tioned above. Statistical adjustments may be possible (Hoyt, 2000), but there are also simpler ways of attempting to overcome the biases by choosing or modifying a particular numerical or graphic rating scale.

For example, another type of rating error is called **leniency bias** because it occurs when judges rate someone who is very familiar, or someone with whom they are ego-involved, in an unrealistically positive manner. If we were using a graphic scale, a way to overcome this bias would be to give only one unfavorable cue word (e.g., *poor*); the rest of the range is then made up of favorable responses in different degrees (e.g., *fairly good, good, very good, excellent*), as in the following extended scale:

Poor	Fairly good	Good	Very good	Excellent

However, we treat or analyze the cue words numerically so that *Good* is only a 3 on a 5-point scale from *Poor* (scored 1) to *Excellent* (scored 5).

Another type of rating error, **central tendency bias,** occurs when the respondent hesitates to give extreme ratings and instead clusters her or his responses around the center choice. This potential bias can be addressed in the same way that the positive range was expanded in the case above. Suppose we wanted to have a range of at least 5 points in a segmented-graphic scale, in which case we might use a 7-point scale, on the assumption that some respondents may be reluctant to use the end points in any circumstances. Similarly, if we wanted to have a range of at least 7 points, we might instead use a 9-point scale. Another circumstance is a rating scale used as a before-and-after measure in an experimental situation; we gauge where the respondents generally score on the before measure, and we include enough points on the scale to ensure them room to move their scores on the after measure. We do not want them to be restricted by a ceiling or floor effect (see discussion in Box 5.7).

In another type of response bias, the **logical error in rating,** the respondents give similar ratings for variables or traits that they connect as logically related in their own minds but that may not occur together in the person being rated. This bias is similar in a way to the halo effect in that both erroneously intercorrelate variables or traits that are being rated. The difference between the two is that, in the halo effect, the respondent extends one favorable trait to the person as a whole, whereas in the logical error, the respondent interrelates certain variables or

BOX 5.7 Ceiling and Floor Effects

Suppose we wanted to use 5-point numerical or segmented-graphic scales as before-and-after measures (or "tests") in an experiment using a manipulation designed to move the participants' responses in a given direction. If the participants make extremely high or extremely low scores on the *pretest* (i.e., the measure taken before the manipulation), there will be a problem if we then want to produce further change in that direction. That is, we have a **ceiling effect** or a **floor effect,** which restricts the amount of change that can be produced. We could try extending the ends of the scale after pilot-testing it, so that a 5-point scale becomes a 9-point or an 11-point scale. If we find no changes from pretest to posttest, we must make sure the data were not artificially restricted by a ceiling or floor effect.

traits irrespective of the individuals being rated. The standard way to overcome a logical error in rating is to construct very precise definitions and to make the instructions as explicit as possible.

In still another type of response bias, the **acquiescent response set,** some respondents (called **yea-sayers**) go along with almost any statement. If they are asked whether they agree or disagree with even the most unlikely item, they will almost invariably agree with it. We address this bias simply by using both anti and pro items. Yea-sayers can easily be identified (and, in most cases, eliminated from the study) by their agreement with both types of items.

The examples above give a flavor of response biases and their control, but there are other possibilities as well. In the next chapter, we will describe classic research on "socially desirable responding," in which the person answering has a tendency to give responses that will make him or her look good. The MMPI, mentioned earlier in this chapter, has a set of items (called the **L Scale,** or **Lie Scale**) that was designed to identify respondents who are *trying* to appear socially desirable. Socially desirable responding was originally seen by researchers as simply a nuisance variable to be controlled or eliminated in some way (e.g., R. J. Fisher, 1993), but it is also viewed as a personality variable of interest in a wide variety of settings (Crowne, 1979; Nouri, Blau, & Shahid, 1995; Ones, Viswesvaran, & Reiss, 1996). We now turn to three traditional approaches to developing specialized attitude questionnaires: the semantic differential method, the Likert method of item analysis, and the Thurstone equal-appearing interval method.

The Semantic Differential

The **semantic differential method** was conceived by Osgood, Suci, and Tannenbaum (1957) for the study of attitudes about the subjective (or representational) meaning of things in everyday life. For example, your open-ended, subjective associations about a "puppy" might be "a warm, furry animal that shows unconditional acceptance of its master." The semantic differential, however, uses not an open-ended format, but a fixed-choice format using segmented-graphic scales. The inventors of this method found that most things in life (dogs, chairs, continents, ethnic groups, flowers, undergraduate majors, and so forth) are universally perceived in terms of three primary dimensions of subjective meaning, which they named **evaluation, potency, and activity,** and which they defined in terms of bipolar cue words. There are some other dimensions, but they seem to account for only a tiny portion of our subjective associations.

Suppose we wanted to compare people's attitudinal associations about two music groups in terms of their respective evaluative, potency, and activity meanings to samples of different age groups. To tap the evaluative dimension, we could choose from among the following bipolar anchors: *bad-good, unpleasant-pleasant, negative-positive, ugly-beautiful, cruel-kind, unfair-fair,* and *worthless-valuable.* To measure the potency dimension, we could choose from among *weak-strong, light-*

heavy, small-large, soft-hard, and *thin-heavy.* For the activity dimension, any of the following could be used: *slow-fast, passive-active,* and *dull-sharp.*

The 7-point bipolar scales might look as follows, though we would want to use more than just these three items (because, as explained in the next chapter, increasing the number of items will increase the *reliability* of the instrument as a whole):

Ugly ____:____:____:____:____:____:____ Beautiful

Soft ____:____:____:____:____:____:____ Hard

Dull ____:____:____:____:____:____:____ Sharp

We would instruct participants to rate each music group by checking the appropriate space. To score people's responses, we would assign numbers to their ratings as follows,

Ugly ____:____:____:____:____:____:____ Beautiful
$$-3 \quad -2 \quad -1 \quad \; 0 \quad +1 \quad +2 \quad +3$$

We can then compute a composite index such as a median (the midmost score) or mean, both of which are discussed later in this book.

Previously, we noted the importance of ensuring that the participants understand what each response category signifies, particularly when the segments in graphic scales are unlabeled. In this example, the numbers above stand for something like "extremely beautiful music" (+3), "quite beautiful music" (+2), "slightly beautiful music" (+1), "neutral" (0), "slightly ugly music" (−1), "quite ugly music" (−2), and "extremely ugly music" (−3). If these labels make sense to you in terms of the purpose of your study, then the rating scale will do. Figure 5.1 shows a typical set of instructions based on those provided by the inventors of the semantic differential, which would appear on the front page of our questionnaire booklet. Notice that these instructions incorporate a number of examples so that respondents will know what each checkmark is intended to represent.

The Likert Scale

The semantic differential gives us a multidimensional picture (evaluation, potency, and activity), whereas another traditional scaling procedure, called the **summated ratings method,** gives us a one-dimensional picture of people's attitudes on controversial issues. The method of summated ratings was developed by Rensis Likert (1932), and attitude questionnaires that are created using this method are known as **Likert scales.** Many researchers have gotten into the habit of referring to 5-point numerical items with responses ranging from *strongly agree* to *strongly disagree* as "Likert items" because this is the form of the items typically used in Likert scales, but this usage is misleading if the summated ratings method is not also used.

The purpose of this questionnaire is to measure the *meanings* of some music groups to various people by having them judge these groups against a set of descriptive scales. We would like you to judge each group on the basis of what the group listed means *to you*. On each page of this booklet, you will find a different group to be judged and beneath it a set of scales. You are to rate the group on each of these scales in order.

If you feel that the group at the top of the page is *very accurately described* by the word at one end of the scale, place your check mark as follows:

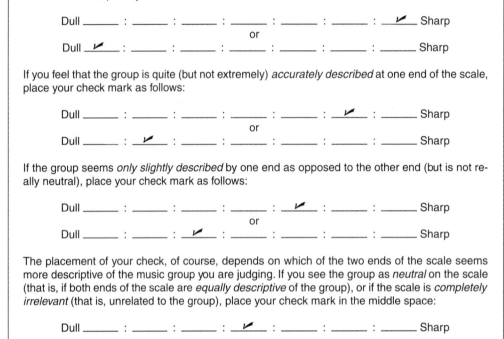

Figure 5.1 Semantic differential instructions.

Though most students will not have occasion to construct their own Likert scales, it is useful to know how they are constructed in case you refer to a published one in your work.

Briefly, the first step in using the summated ratings method is to write a large number of statements on the controversial issue. These statements are given to a sample of people from the target population, who indicate their evaluations of each statement, usually by means of a 5-point numerical scale (*strongly agree, agree, undecided, disagree, strongly disagree*). The researcher sorts through the data in order to select the best 20 or so statements for the final questionnaire. This task consists of finding out the extent to which all of the responses to individual statements are correlated with the total score (the sum of the scores for all the items). The statements that correlate well with (i.e., show a strong relationship to) the total score are prospects for the final questionnaire. The theory behind the summated ratings method is that statements that have low correlations with the total score will not discriminate those people with positive attitudes from those with negative attitudes.

The result of using this method is illustrated in Figure 5.2. It shows a questionnaire that was pared down to 20 items (Mahler, 1953). Items 2, 4, 6, 9, 10, 11, 14, and 15 (called "pro-socialized medicine" statements by the author of this scale) are in favor of a compulsory health program and against the system of private practice. Items 1, 3, 5, 7, 8, 12, 13, 16, 17, 18, 19, and 20 (called "anti-socialized medicine" statements) are against a compulsory health program and in favor of the system of private practice. In using this attitude scale, we weight the responses to the pro-socialized-medicine statements from 5 (*strongly agree*) to 1 (*strongly disagree*). For the anti-socialized-medicine statements, we simply reverse this scoring procedure. A person's score is the sum of the weighted responses, a high score indicating an accepting attitude toward a compulsory health program and a low score indicating an unaccepting attitude toward a compulsory health program. In this example, the highest and lowest possible scores, respectively, will be 100 (most strongly in favor of a compulsory health program) and 20 (most strongly against a compulsory health program).

The Thurstone Scale

Another traditional procedure for developing an attitude questionnaire was called the **method of equal-appearing intervals** by its inventor, L. L. Thurstone (1929, 1929–1934). It takes its name from the idea that judges, who are asked to sort statements into different piles, are able to keep the piles psychologically equidistant. Attitude questionnaires developed by this method are also known as **Thurstone scales.** Thurstone also invented other scaling methods and conceptualized theoretical rationales for all these methods, and his seminal ideas have been absorbed into modern scaling methodology and theory (a field known as *psychometrics*). However, when you see some reference to a "Thurstone attitude scale," you can usually assume that the writer means that a questionnaire was constructed by the method of equal-appearing intervals. Once again, we will describe this method not because you are likely to use it to construct a questionnaire, but because you are likely to come across attitude or personality measures developed in this way that may be relevant to your interests (see Box 5.8).

Briefly, this method also begins with a large number of statements, each one printed on a separate slip of paper or an index card. Judges (not the people to be given the questionnaire) then sort the statements into 11 piles, numbered from 1 (labeled "most unfavorable statements") to 11 ("most favorable statements"). The judges are allowed to place as many statements as they wish in any pile. A scale value is obtained for each statement and is usually calculated as the median of the responses of all the judges to that item. In selecting statements for the final questionnaire, the idea is to try to choose those (a) that are most consistently rated by the judges and (b) that are spread relatively evenly along the entire attitude range.

Instructions to Subjects

Please indicate your reaction to the following statements, using these alternatives (circle your choice):

Strongly agree = SA

Agree = A

Undecided = U

Disagree = D

Strongly disagree = SD

1. The quality of medical care under the system of private practice is superior to that under a system of compulsory health insurance.

    SA   A   U   D   SD

2. A compulsory health program will produce a healthier and more productive population.

    SA   A   U   D   SD

3. Under a compulsory health program there would be less incentive for young men and women to become doctors.

    SA   A   U   D   SD

4. A compulsory health program is necessary because it brings the greatest good to the greatest number of people.

    SA   A   U   D   SD

5. Treatment under a compulsory health program would be mechanical and superficial.

    SA   A   U   D   SD

6. A compulsory health program would be a realization of one of the true aims of a democracy.

    SA   A   U   D   SD

7. Compulsory medical care would upset the traditional relationship between the family doctor and the patient.

    SA   A   U   D   SD

8. I feel that I would get better care from a doctor whom I am paying than from a doctor who is being paid by the government.

    SA   A   U   D   SD

9. Despite many practical objections, I feel that compulsory health insurance is a real need of the American people.

    SA   A   U   D   SD

10. A compulsory health program could be administered quite efficiently if the doctors would cooperate.

    SA   A   U   D   SD

11. There is no reason why the traditional relationship between doctor and patient cannot be continued under a compulsory health program.

    SA   A   U   D   SD

12. If a compulsory health program were enacted, politicians would have control over doctors.

    SA   A   U   D   SD

13. The present system of private medical practice is the one best adapted to the liberal philosophy of democracy.

    SA   A   U   D   SD

14. There is no reason why doctors should not be able to work just as well under a compulsory health program as they do now.

    SA   A   U   D   SD

15. More and better care will be obtained under a compulsory program.

    SA   A   U   D   SD

16. The atmosphere of a compulsory health program would destroy the initiative and the ambition of young doctors.

    SA   A   U   D   SD

17. Politicians are trying to force a compulsory health program upon the people without giving them the true facts.

    SA   A   U   D   SD

18. Administrative costs under a compulsory health program would be exorbitant.

    SA   A   U   D   SD

19. Red tape and bureaucratic problems would make a compulsory health program grossly inefficient.

    SA   A   U   D   SD

20. Any system of compulsory insurance would invade the privacy of the individual.

    SA   A   U   D   SD

Figure 5.2   The Socialized Medicine Attitude Scale.

Source: Reproduced from "Attitudes Toward Socialized Medicine" by I. Mahler, 1953, *Journal of Social Psychology, 38,* 273–282. Copyright © 1953. Used by permission of the Helen Dwight Reid Educational Foundation. Published by Heldref Publications, 1319 Eighteenth Street NW, Washington, DC 20036-1802.

BOX 5.8 Useful Reference Books

A particularly valuable resource is the *Directory of Unpublished Experimental Mental Measures,* a series of volumes edited by Bert A. Goldman, David Mitchell, and their colleagues, and published by the American Psychological Association from 1995–2003. It contains brief descriptions of several thousand noncommercial psychological instruments that are available for use in a variety of research situations, such as measures of educational, psychological, social, and vocational adjustment, and measures of aptitude, attitude, concept meaning, creativity, personality, problem solving, status, and so on. If you are looking for an attitude or personality measure developed by the Likert or Thurstone procedure, you will find many such measures in the public domain. One source of information is Shaw and Wright's *Scales for the Measurement of Attitudes* (1967), which also reproduces specific instruments and describes their characteristics (e.g., reliability and validity) and scoring. Another compendium is Robinson et al.'s *Measures of Personality and Social Psychological Attitudes* (1991); it contains original tests and information about their scoring, validation, reliability, and use, including tests of subjective well-being, self-esteem, social anxiety, shyness, depression and loneliness, alienation, interpersonal trust, authoritarianism, sex roles, and personal values.

Shown in Figure 5.3 is an attitude questionnaire that, although developed during World War II, is still topical (Day & Quackenbush, 1942). Notice that we are asked to reply to each statement three times, that is, once for each type of war. Using the method of equal-appearing intervals, Shaw and Wright (1967) obtained scale values for these 13 items by having 15 women and 35 men respond to each statement; these values are shown in Table 5.1. The lowest scale value (0.8 for Statement 3) corresponds to the most "promilitaristic" item, and the highest scale value (8.4 for Statement 6) to the most "antimilitaristic" item in this set. If we decided to use this scale in research, the attitude score for each referent (defensive war, cooperative war, and aggressive war) would be the median scale value of the statements endorsed (i.e., checked) by the respondent for the referent. The higher the median, the more unfavorable the respondent's attitude toward that particular war referent. For example, if the person checks Statements 2, 4, 6, and 11 under Roman numeral I, you know that the person is very strongly opposed to defensive war (median = 8.05, or midway between the scale values of 7.9 for Statement 4 and 8.2 for Statement 11).

Pilot-Testing Your Questionnaire

In developing a questionnaire—as much as in developing an interview (discussed next)—pilot testing is absolutely essential. This testing will enable the researcher to determine whether the items are worded properly, for example, whether terms like

Instructions to Subjects

This is a study of attitudes toward war. Below you will find a number of statements expressing various degrees of attitudes toward war or tendencies to act in case of war.

In expressing your agreement or disagreement with the statements, please put yourself in three possible situations. First, imagine that the United States had declared a *Defensive War* (war for the purpose of defending the United States in case of an attack). Please indicate in the first set of parentheses, designated by roman numeral I, your agreement, disagreement, or doubt. Put a check mark (✓) if you agree with the statement, put a minus sign (−) if you disagree with the statement, and a question mark (?) if you are in doubt about the statement.

Second, imagine that the United States has declared a *Cooperative War* (war in cooperation with the democratic countries of Europe for the defense of democracy). Go over the statements again and indicate in the second set of parentheses, designated by roman II, your agreement, disagreement, or doubt in a similar way.

Third, imagine that the United States has declared an *Aggressive War* (war for the purpose of gaining more territory). Read the statements again and indicate in the third set of parentheses, designated by roman III, your agreement, disagreement, or doubt by a similar method.

I	II	III	
( )	( )	( )	1. I would support my country even against my convictions.
( )	( )	( )	2. I would immediately attempt to find some technicality on which to evade going to war.
( )	( )	( )	3. I would immediately go to war and would do everything in my power to influence others to do the same.
( )	( )	( )	4. I would rather be called a coward than go to war.
( )	( )	( )	5. I would offer my services in whatever capacity I can.
( )	( )	( )	6. I would not only refuse to participate in any way in war but also attempt to influence public opinion against war.
( )	( )	( )	7. I would take part in war only to avoid social ostracism.
( )	( )	( )	8. I would not go to war unless I were drafted.
( )	( )	( )	9. If possible, I would wait a month or two before I would enlist.
( )	( )	( )	10. I would go to war only if my friends went to war.
( )	( )	( )	11. I would refuse to participate in any way in war.
( )	( )	( )	12. I would disregard any possible exemptions and enlist immediately.
( )	( )	( )	13. I would not enlist but would give whatever financial aid I could.

Figure 5.3   The Attitudes Toward War Scale.

Source: Reproduced from "Attitudes Toward Defensive, Cooperative, and Aggressive War" by D. D. Day and O. F. Quackenbush, 1942, *Journal of Social Psychology, 16,* 11–20. Copyright © 1942. Used by permission of the Helen Dwight Reid Educational Foundation, Heldref Publications, 1319 Eighteenth Street NW, Washington, DC 20036-1802.

Table 5.1	Scale Values for the Questionnaire in Figure 5.3		
Statement	Scale value	Statement	Scale value
1	2.5	8	5.9
2	7.5	9	4.6
3	0.8	10	5.1
4	7.9	11	8.2
5	2.5	12	1.4
6	8.4	13	3.5
7	6.3		

Note. The scale values are median scores (or midmost values), based on the responses of 15 women and 35 men to each particular item (Shaw & Wright, 1967).

approve and *like* (or *disapprove* and *dislike*) are being used as synonyms or whether there are differences in implication. Suppose that a company president wants to examine a team of workers' opinions of the quality of a manager's job performance, and the president directs that a fixed-choice item be phrased as follows: "How do you feel about the manager? ____I like him. ____I dislike him." The item is useless because it does not distinguish between liking and approving. It is possible to like someone without approving of his or her job performance, and vice versa (Bradburn, 1982).

If you were assigned the job of writing questions, you would also have to be sure that the way in which your items are worded and presented does not lead the respondent into giving an unrealistically narrow answer. A poor question will produce a very narrow range of responses or will be misunderstood by the respondents. Take the following item: "Do you approve of the way the manager is handling her duties? ____Yes. ____No." Respondents might approve of the way she handled one crisis but not another, or they might disapprove of the way she handled the dress code but not the rumor about possible layoffs. Thus, a number of different items are needed to cover the various issues on which you want an opinion about the manager's effectiveness, and the issues must be spelled out if you are to avoid misunderstanding by the respondents. Suppose the dress code crisis was resolved amicably, but the layoff crisis involved union confrontations. You need a separate question, or set of questions, regarding each situation and whether the respondent approved or disapproved of its handling.

You must also avoid asking **leading questions** (i.e., questions that "lead" the respondent to answer in a particular way), because they can constrain responses and produce biased answers. An example of a leading question is "Do you agree that the manager has an annoying, confrontational style? ____Yes. ____No." The phrasing of the question practically directs the respondent to be overly negative or critical. How should the question be properly phrased? The answer depends on what you are trying to find out. However, in coming up with an alternative, you want to be sure that the new question is not worded so as to produce another meaningless answer: "Do you agree with the manager's work philosophy? ____Yes. ____No." What would a yes or no really tell you? You need to be more precise and specific, and also to do some probing to get meaningful information.

Problems such as these can be identified during the pilot testing and can often be resolved with rewording or with a set of probing items instead of a single item. The question of whether to use open-ended or more structured items (or a combination of both) can also be answered in pilot testing. Like personality measures, the questionnaires used by many survey researchers come in a variety of open and fixed-choice formats. The latter may, for example, be multiple-choice, yes-no, either-or, or acceptable-unacceptable items. A fill-in-the-blank form is useful when more specific, unprompted responses are sought. Of course, these structured forms are effective only if the material to be covered allows this amount of simplification.

In your pilot testing, you might think about asking exploratory questions such as "What did the whole item mean to you?" "What was it you had in mind when you said '____'?" "Consider the same item this way, and tell what you think of

it:_____"; "You said '_____,' but would you feel differently if the question read
'_____'?" (Converse & Presser, 1986, p. 52). It is also important that the information
elicited reflect what the respondent *really* feels or believes. As a rule, people have
not thought very much about most issues that do not affect them directly; their answers may reflect a superficial understanding, or they may try to "put on a good
face." Thus, survey researchers may also ask the respondent how he or she feels
about a topic (e.g., "How *deeply* do you feel about it?"). In this way, they attempt
to determine whether the respondent believes what he or she has reported
(Labaw, 1980). Still another technique is to ask respondents to rate their confidence
in their answer so that they reveal how much they are guessing.

The Research Interview

We turn now to the **face-to-face interview,** but first we should say a few words
about the relative advantages of interviews over questionnaires. Questionnaires are
useful because (a) they can be efficiently administered to large numbers of people
(e.g., in mail surveys, assuming that they'll be mailed back to you); (b) they are relatively economical (since a mail survey eliminates travel time and cost); and (c)
they provide a type of "anonymity" (i.e., instead of meeting the researcher face to
face, the respondent returns the completed survey, for example, to an impersonal
research center). The face-to-face interview is useful because (a) it provides an opportunity to establish rapport with people and to stimulate the trust and cooperation needed to probe sensitive areas; (b) it provides an opportunity to clarify
questions (if participants are confused); and (c) it allows flexibility in determining
the wording and sequence of questions by giving the researcher greater control
(e.g., by letting the interviewer determine on the spot the amount of probing required).

Just as researchers who use questionnaires need to do pilot testing, researchers
who use an **interview schedule** (i.e., a script containing the questions to be asked
in the interview) must also try it out before actually implementing the study. This
pilot testing and all the planning that precedes it typically involve four steps: (a)
stating the objectives of the research (the questions and hypotheses to be addressed); (b) formulating a plan to recruit the interviewees; (c) structuring the interview schedule; and (d) testing it and making appropriate revisions. The first step
is self-explanatory. The second step is simply a matter of defining the population
to which we want to generalize, and then devising a plan for recruiting a representative sample from that population (discussed in more detail in Chapter 9). In the
final step (pilot testing), we interview a few people from the target population and
listen *analytically* to their responses to each item (Downs, Smeyak, & Martin,
1980). Good interviewers have good listening skills; that is, they are patient, hear
the facts, and do not jump in or interrupt before the person being interviewed has
developed an idea (Weaver, 1972).

The third step (structuring the interview schedule) needs a little more explanation because it involves writing the items and checking each one for relevancy, de-

termining ranges of responses for some fixed-choice items, and establishing the best sequence and wording of questions. Each question must be carefully considered for its bearing on the specific hypotheses or exploratory aims of the research. Because fatigue or boredom is apt to set in after an hour or more of being interviewed, the interview schedule may require the pruning of undesirable or unnecessary items. If we need to know income levels, then we need to decide on ranges of responses rather than bluntly ask for an exact amount. If we are planning to ask questions that rely on people's memories, we want to make sure that we are not making unrealistic demands. One researcher who has studied and written extensively about memory errors in survey research mentioned that the best cues to jog a person's memory about a particular event are those that help the person to differentiate the event from others that might be brought to mind (Tourangeau, 2000). However, this same researcher cautioned that even the best cues to help people recall experiences cannot trigger the retrieval of a memory that was not fully or accurately stored in the person's memory in the first place.

The sequence in which sets of questions should be presented also needs to be established. Specific questions appear to be less affected by what preceded them than are general or broadly stated questions (Bradburn, 1982; Schuman & Presser, 1996). When sensitive issues are touched on, it is usually better to ask these questions at the end of the interview. Some people may view questions about their age, education, and income as an invasion of their privacy. When asked at the beginning of an interview, questions like these may interfere with the establishment of trust. Even when they are asked at the end of the interview, it is usually helpful to preface such questions with a reassuring statement. In one study, the interviewer was unusually candid: "Some of the questions may seem like an invasion of your privacy, so if you'd rather not answer any of the questions, just tell me it's none of my business" (C. Smith, 1980). The researcher also needs to work out the best wording of the items. It is essential that all the interviewees readily understand the wording in equivalent ways. The final step (the pilot testing) should reveal what jargon and expressions are inhibitors and facilitators of communication. Especially important is the phrasing of the opening question, which should show the person immediately that the interviewer is pursuing the stated purpose. Finally, as noted in Chapter 3, we want to be as open and honest as possible in our communications with our participants, just as we want them to be open and forthcoming in their responses.

Interviews by Telephone

Beginning in the 1960s, various changes in American society led many researchers in the United States to turn to the **telephone interview** and the mail survey as substitutes for the face-to-face interview method. Among the changes contributing to this shift were (a) the increased costs of conducting face-to-face interviews (because interviewing is a labor-intensive activity); (b) the invention of random digit-dialing methods for the random sampling of telephone households; and (c) the development of computer-assisted methods of recording responses, in which questions are flashed on a computer screen and the interviewer directly keys in responses for computer scoring (Rossi, Wright, & Anderson, 1983).

Like all research methods, telephone interviewing has both advantages and disadvantages (Downs et al., 1980; Lavrakas, 1987; P. V. Miller & Cannell, 1982). Among the advantages are that it allows a quick turnaround (i.e., information can be obtained more promptly than by a face-to-face interview or a mail survey). It has also been reported that refusal rates are usually lower in telephone interviewing because it is not necessary to allow a stranger into one's home. Among the disadvantages are that interviewing is restricted, first, to households that own a telephone and, then, to those that answer the telephone (instead of having an answering machine or caller ID constantly on duty to screen calls). A further disadvantage is that fewer questions (and less probing questions) can be asked because it is harder to establish rapport than in a face-to-face interview and people are more impatient to conclude a telephone interview.

Generally speaking, whether telephone or face-to-face interviewing is used, the same procedures are followed in developing an interview schedule and training the interviewers. One difference, however, is that telephone interviewers have less time to establish rapport; the person called can always immediately hang up without listening to the introduction. If the person does not immediately hang up, then a strategy used to foster "commitment" on the part of the person is to point out the important goals of the research and to use positive feedback to reinforce what the researcher perceives as good responding: "Thanks . . . this is the sort of information we are looking for in this research . . . it's important to us to get this information . . . these details are helpful" (P. V. Miller & Cannell, 1982, p. 256).

Memory and the Use of Behavioral Diaries

As we said before, a nagging problem when using self-report measures is that autobiographical questions may yield inaccurate answers when the participants are asked to rely on memory (e.g., how often they have done something or how much of something they have bought or consumed). Some examples are "How many weeks have you been looking for work?" and "How much have you paid for car repairs over the previous year?" As noted in Box 5.2, problems surface because the storing of events in memory is fallible, memory is porous, recall is limited, and people fill in the gaps of what they cannot retrieve (H. B. Bernard & Killworth, 1970, 1980; Reed, 1988; Schacter, 1999; A. A. Stone et al., 2000; Tourangeau, 2000; Webber, 1970; Zechmeister & Nyberg, 1982). Suppose we wanted to study lying in everyday life. If we asked people to estimate, for example, the number of "little white lies" they tell each day, the results could hardly be considered valid because of all the factors mentioned above and also their possible wish to give a socially desirable response.

An innovative tool that is thought by its users to overcome the various memory problems is the **behavioral diary** (e.g., Conrath, 1973; Wickesberg, 1968), a method based on the use of field diaries and field notes in ethnographic research (discussed in the previous chapter). The basic procedure is to ask people to keep diaries of certain events at the time they occur. As an illustration, social psychologists Bella M. DePaulo and Deborah A. Kashy, and their coworkers, used this method in studies of the lies that college students tell (DePaulo & Kashy, 1998; DePaulo, Kashy, Kirkendol, Wyer, & Epstein, 1996; Kashy & DePaulo, 1996). The participants in this research were asked to keep meticulous records of their lying. Assuming that the records they turned in were themselves truthful, the findings were quite revealing. For example, people who indicated they had told more lies were also found to be more manipulative and more concerned with self-presentation and, not surprisingly, to have told more self-serving lies.

Another recent study that used this method was conducted by Mihaly Csikszentmihalyi and Reed Larson (1984), who were interested in teenagers' day-to-day lives. The participants in this study were 75 teenagers, who were given beepers and were then signaled at random by the researchers. When the beeper went off, the teenager was supposed to record his or her thoughts and feelings at that moment. Figure 5.4 shows a week in the life of one participant. This person had hoped to spend her first year after high school studying abroad but learned that she would not be allowed to go. The scale at the top shows a continuum from self-reported bad to good moods, and the zig-zagged line reveals that this person's mood fluctuated tremendously as she tried to cope with everyday events. Clearly, she was happiest when with friends and unhappiest when alone.

Researchers who use this method assume that such a diary gives more reliable data than questionnaires or interviews that elicit answers to autobiographical questions. To evaluate this assumption, a team of researchers (Conrath, Higgins, & McClean, 1983) collected data from managers and staff personnel in three diverse organizations (a manufacturer of plastic products, an insurance brokerage company, and a large public utility). Each participant was instructed to keep a diary of 100 consecutive interactions, beginning on a specific date and at a specific time. The instructions were to list the other party to the interaction, the initiator of the activity, the mode of interaction, the elapsed time, and the process involved. The diary was constructed in such a way that the participant could quickly record all this information with no more than four to eight check marks next to particular items. At a later time, each participant was asked to answer a questionnaire covering the same interactions.

The data from all the behavioral diaries and questionnaires were compared afterward. If one person reported talking to others, the researchers checked the diaries and questionnaires of those others to see whether they had also reported that activity. In this way, a separate measure of reliability was obtained for the behavioral diary and for the questionnaire data (i.e., concerning the reporting of specific events at the time of the events as opposed to a later time). The results were that the questionnaire data (the recalls from autobiographical memory) were less reliable than the behavioral diary data. In spite of these encouraging results, other researchers have challenged the accuracy of diary information and have argued that the participants may be overly attentive to events that "stick out" in their minds and

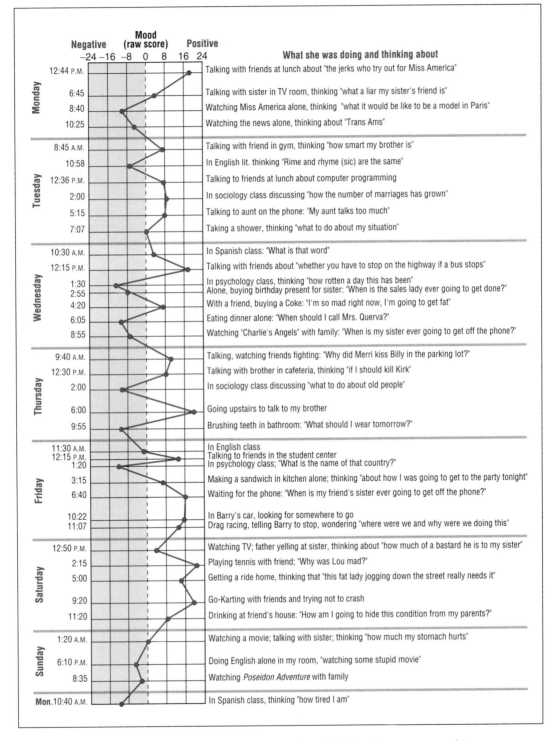

Figure 5.4 The self-recorded diary record of a week in the life of one teenage subject.

Source: Figure 8.4 in "The Week of Lorraine Murawski" from *Being Adolescent: Conflict and Growth in the Teenage Years,* by Mihaly Csikszentmihalyi and Reed Larson. Copyright © 1984 by Basic Books, Inc. Reprinted by permission of Basic Books, a division of HarperCollins Publishers, Inc.

may underreport other behavior (Maurer, Palmer, & Ashe, 1993). Nonetheless, it is another interesting method that, in conjunction with observational methods, might be used to triangulate on the behavior in question.

Summary of Ideas

1. Three fundamental issues when using self-report measures concern (a) the truthfulness of what people report, especially when the information is personal and sensitive; (b) the ethical and potentially risky implications of such information, particularly when the researchers have not been professionally trained; and (c) the validity of information that depends on remembering some past event (Schacter's "seven sins of memory" in Box 5.2).

2. Two forms of self-report measures are those that allow respondents to express their feelings and impressions quite spontaneously (i.e., *open-ended*) and those that use a structured format with precoded response options (i.e., *fixed-choice*); the general advantages and limitations of open-ended measures are essentially the reverse of the advantages and limitations of fixed-choice measures. The *critical incident technique* (Box 5.3) is a way of holding open-ended responses in check by concentrating on an actual incident and asking the respondent a series of focused (though open-ended) questions.

3. The Big Five factors of personality (OCEAN) are openness to experience, conscientiousness, extraversion, agreeableness, and neuroticism (Box 5.4).

4. The Rorschach inkblot test and the TAT (which are both open-ended measures) operate on the principle that, in the spontaneous responses that come to his or her mind, the respondent will project some unconscious aspect of his or her life experience and emotions onto ambiguous stimuli. The MMPI (which has a fixed-choice format) contains hundreds of statements to which the respondent answers true or false.

5. Three kinds of popular rating scales are the numerical (in which the numbers may be implicit or explicit), the forced-choice (which was developed to overcome the halo effect, discussed in Box 5.6), and the graphic (resembling a thermometer that may or may not be segmented).

6. Other rating biases (besides the halo effect) include the error of leniency, the error of central tendency, the logical error in rating, and the acquiescent response set—each of which can be controlled in a particular way by choosing or modifying a numerical or graphic rating scale.

7. The semantic differential, which is a multidimensional segmented-graphic scale, is designed to measure attitudes about the subjective meaning of things, usually in terms of the dimensions of evaluation, potency, and activity.

8. Likert's method of summated ratings is used to construct a one-dimensional numerical attitude scale (e.g., the Socialized Medicine Attitude Scale in Figure 5.2).

9. Thurstone's method of equal-appearing intervals is another traditional procedure that is used to construct attitude scales (e.g., attitudes about three kinds of war in Figure 5.3).

10. The purpose of pilot-testing a questionnaire or interview schedule is to enable the researcher to fine-tune the data collection instrument and procedures. The four steps in developing an interview schedule are (a) working out the objective; (b) formulating a general strategy of data collection; (c) writing the questions and establishing the best sequence; and (d) pilot-testing the material.

11. Telephone interviews have become popular because they are more cost-efficient than face-to-face interviews and can also be implemented easily with random digit-dialing and computer-assisted interviewing and data-recording methods.

12. The behavioral diary is a procedure for recording events as they happen, and there is no need to rely on longer term recall (e.g., the study about lying and the study of teenagers' day-to-day lives).

Key Terms

acquiescent response set   p. 122
behavioral diaries   p. 132
Big Five factors (OCEAN)
  p. 115
bipolar rating scales   p. 120
ceiling effect   p. 121
central tendency bias   p. 121
critical incident technique
  p. 113
cue words   p. 117
evaluation apprehension   p. 111
evaluation, potency, and activity
  p. 122
face-to-face interview   p. 130
fixed-choice (structured)
  measures   p. 112
floor effect   p. 121
forced-choice scales   p. 118

graphic scales   p. 120
halo effect   p. 119
interview schedule   p. 130
leading questions   p. 129
leniency bias   p. 120
Lie (L) Scale   p. 122
Likert scales   p. 123
logical error in rating   p. 121
method of equal-appearing
  intervals   p. 125
Minnesota Multiphasic
  Personality Inventory
  (MMPI)   p. 116
norm-referenced   p. 117
numerical scales   p. 118
open-ended measures   p. 112
pilot testing   p. 117

projective test   p. 114
rater biases   p. 120
rating errors   p. 120
rating scales   p. 117
response biases   p. 120
Rorschach test   p. 114
segmented graphic scale   p. 120
self-report measures   p. 109
semantic differential method
  p. 122
standardized measure   p. 110
summated ratings method   p. 123
telephone interview   p. 131
Thematic Apperception Test
  (TAT)   p. 115
Thurstone scales   p. 125
yea-sayers   p. 122

WEB ACTIVITY

To learn more about interviewing methods and questionnaire design, visit the Creative Research Systems Web site at http://www.surveysystem.com/sdesign.htm.

Multiple-Choice Questions for Review

1. A researcher at Southwestern University decides to use self-report methods in his study of caffeine use. His survey contains the following question: "In the past week, did you drink any coffee? Yes or no." This question is an example of (a) a fixed-choice question; (b) an open-ended question; (c) a neutrally worded question; (d) a negatively worded question.

2. A researcher at Baylor is conducting a study about the self-concept of college students. His survey contains the following question: "In your own words, please describe your self-concept. In other words, what kind of person are you?" This question is an example of (a) a negatively worded question; (b) an open-ended question; (c) a neutrally worded question; (d) a fixed-choice question.

3. A researcher at Case Western Reserve gives a participant an ambiguous picture of people in a social situation and asks the participant what the people in the picture are doing, what they are thinking, and what they will be doing in the future. This is an example of a (a) fixed-choice format question; (b) reverse-scored question; (c) projective test; (d) none of the above.

4. Some research participants are likely to agree with almost any question that is asked of them. This tendency is generally referred to as (a) an acquiescent response set; (b) an affirmation bias; (c) a nonnegation bias; (d) an affirmation tendency.

5. To avoid problems with the "halo effect," a researcher might want to use (a) forced-choice scales; (b) graphic rating scales; (c) equal-appearing interval scales; (d) segmented graphic scales.

6. Observers often assume that, if a person is physically attractive, he or she also has many other positive qualities, including being intelligent and outgoing. This is an example of (a) the error of central tendency; (b) the halo effect; (c) the error of misperception; (d) none of the above.

7. According to research on the semantic differential method, which of the following is a major dimension of subjective meaning? (a) potency; (b) activity; (c) evaluation; (d) all of the above

8. Which of the following is also known as the method of summated ratings? (a) the semantic differential method; (b) the Thurstone method; (c) the Likert method; (d) the equal-appearing interval method

9. Which of the following is also known as the method of equal-appearing intervals? (a) the semantic differential method; (b) the Thurstone method; (c) the Likert method; (d) the graphic rating method

10. Imagine that you are asked to do the following during an interview: "Describe as fully and concretely as possible a real situation that was important to you in which you acted in some way that was a cover for your true feelings." This is an example of (a) a self-recorded diary; (b) the critical incident technique; (c) the semantic differential method; (d) an interview schedule.

 ## Discussion Questions for Review

1. An Austin Peay student wants to develop numerical and graphic items to measure attitudes about abortion. What advice would you give the student on how to get started?

2. A Central Michigan student is asked by the instructor to tell which rating error each of the following descriptions represents: (a) rating someone you know too positively (b) tending to respond in an affirmative direction (c) not using the extremes of a scale (d) rating a central trait and other traits in the same way. Do you know the answers? Do you also know how to control for each of these errors?

3. A Northwestern University student who has a job selling used cars is thinking about developing a questionnaire to discover the motivations of people who buy and don't buy used cars. What methodological pointers would you give the student?

4. A Wheaton College student wants to develop a Thurstone scale to measure attitudes about eliminating final exams for graduating seniors. Describe the steps she will need to take in developing this scale.

5. The student in Question 4 has a boyfriend who is a psychology major at Rhode Island College. He tells her that he is planning to develop a Likert scale to measure the same attitudes. Do you know the difference between these two approaches?

6. A student at the City University of New York wants to use the semantic differential to study people's reactions to certain *New York Times* advertisements. If you were this student, how would you design this instrument?

7. A student with a dual major in psychology and political science at Ohio Wesleyan, who is running for student body president, reads *The Selling of the President,* in which Joe McGinniss wrote about the use of the semantic differential by advertising researchers who worked for Richard M. Nixon when he began assembling a team for his 1968 presidential campaign. The researchers traveled all through the United States asking people to evaluate the presidential candidates (Nixon, Hubert Humphrey, and George Wallace). They then plotted an "ideal presidential curve" (i.e., a line connecting the points that represented what the researchers thought would be the ideal candidate) and compared the candidates' profiles with this ideal. The Ohio Wesleyan student is also running against two rivals and wonders whether it might be possible to do a similar study. What methodological pointers would you give her?

8. A student at the University of South Africa, a correspondence university, works in a company that wants to study the morale of its employees. The student thinks it might be instructive to ask a sample of the employees one or two critical incident questions. How should they be worded?

9. A Haverford College student is asked by his instructor to state, in one succinct sentence, the major advantage of the behavioral diary method over using a questionnaire. How should he answer?

Answers to Review Questions

Multiple-Choice Questions

1. a	3. c	5. a	7. d	9. b
2. b	4. a	6. b	8. c	10. b

Discussion Questions

1. Define the aspects of attitudes about abortion you want to have covered by your measure, and be sure the items are easily understood. Decide how many response categories you want to use in your numerical and segmented graphic scales.

2. Leniency bias, acquiescent response set, central tendency bias, and halo effect (or logical error in rating), respectively. The section on rating errors gives suggestions on how to control for each of these rating concerns.

3. Most of the chapter contributes to an answer to this question, but you might begin with the answer to discussion Question 1 above.

4. Have a large number of judges sort a large number of items into 11 piles numbered 1 to 11 in order of item favorableness. The median rating of favorableness of each item is computed, and items are selected for the final scale on the basis of (a) the judges' agreement on each item's degree of favorableness and (b) the items' being spread fairly evenly throughout the range of attitudes from 1 to 11.

5. The major difference is that the Likert 5-point (or 7-point or 9-point) rating scale is used only if it correlates highly enough with the total score.

6. Select a sample of bipolar cue words from the lists in this chapter that seem to best represent the evaluative, potency, and activity dimensions.

7. Instead of supposing what the ideal candidate might be like, it might be better to ask respondents which characteristics of candidates would elicit their votes.

8. One wording might be: Describe in detail a situation in which you felt pleased and proud to be an employee of the company. What led up to the situation, and what was its outcome? The same question might well be asked again, this time with "unhappy and ashamed" substituted for "pleased and proud."

9. It has been shown to lead to more accurate data.

CHAPTER 6

Reliability and Validity in Measurement and Research

Preview Questions

- What is the difference between validity and reliability?

- What are random and systematic errors?

- What is the purpose of test-retest and alternate-form reliability?

- What is internal-consistency reliability, and how is it estimated and increased?

- How is reliability related to replication and external validity?

- What is the difference between content validity and criterion validity?

- What is the role of construct validity in test development and experimental research?

- What role do statistical-conclusion validity and internal validity play in causal inference?

Multiple Uses of Validity and Reliability

The purpose of this chapter is to explain several different applications of two important criteria of how well measurements and certain research designs fulfill their functions. One of these criteria, **validity,** in the most general terms, is how well the measure or research design does what it purports to do. The measure might be a psychological test or a personality inventory of some kind, a group of judges who rate things, an encephalogram for monitoring brain waves, or any other instrument or measuring tool. Consider an aptitude test that is designed to predict whether applicants to law school will succeed if admitted. We would be interested in the test's *criterion validity,* as it would tell us how well scores on the test are correlated with the particular standard of success used to assess it. We would also be interested in the test's *construct validity,* as it would tell us how well the test can be understood as measuring the theoretical aptitude in question. There are other kinds of validity that may interest us as well, such as the test's *content validity,* that is, how well it has sampled the "universe of content" it purports to measure.

By the same token, the concept of validity also has several different uses in research design, and in the following chapters we will examine specific experimental and nonexperimental designs and how well each fulfills its function. For example, suppose that a new report found a statistically significant correlation between the living habits and the health outcomes in a particular society and implied that the relationship was causal. We are skeptical about the *internal validity* of this study, however, as we can imagine a plausible rival hypothesis for the implied causal relationship. Quite apart from the causal relationship, we would also be interested in the generalizability (or *external validity*) of the observed association between living habits and health outcomes. That is, we would still want to know how dependable the data were, for example, whether the correlational findings could be replicated and generalized across different societies. We will have much more to say about these and other kinds of validity, all of which are previewed in Table 6.1.

The second important criterion, **reliability,** generally implies consistency or stability, but it may also imply dependability. Thus, the concept of external validity (noted above) can be said to be a bridge between reliability and validity because it often implies not only generalizability, but also dependability (e.g., whether an observed causal relationship can be replicated with different participants and in a different setting). By stability, we mean, for example, that if we measure a person's IQ as 110 in January, we would expect to obtain a similar score when we test the person again in December. That is, we expect the IQ test to give us temporally stable results—though we anticipate seeing some random fluctuations in the IQ scores (discussed next). We would also be interested in the reliability of the test as a whole (i.e., its *internal-consistency reliability*), or how well all of the items in the test "hang together." Were we using judges to make ratings, we would want to know how coherent all their ratings were as a group (*their* internal-consistency reliability) as well as the average reliability of any *single* judge. These and other applications of the concept of reliability, which are discussed in this chapter, are also previewed in Table 6.1.

If the measure we want to use is unreliable, it is often less likely to be valid. However, it is quite possible for a measure to be reliable and *not* be valid with regard to a particular criterion. For example, it is possible to imagine that people blink their eyes roughly the same number of times a minute under a variety of circumstances (the measure has high reliability), but we cannot predict someone's IQ or success in law school from the person's eye-blink rate (i.e., it is neither a valid measure of IQ nor a forecaster of grades in law school). Generally speaking, when assessing the measuring tools of behavioral research (whether they are based on physical measures, test items, or judges' ratings, etc.), researchers usually like both validity and reliability to be as high as possible. The bottom line criterion is always validity, however, as it rarely serves the researcher's objectives to have a highly reliable measure that correlates with nothing of any consequence.

Table 6.1	Types of Reliability and Validity

Reliability

Alternate-form reliability: The degree of relatedness of different forms of the same test.

Internal-consistency reliability: The overall degree of relatedness of all items in a test or all raters in a judgment study (also called *reliability of components*).

Item-to-item reliability: The reliability of any single item on average (analogous to *judge-to-judge reliability*, which is the reliability of any single judge on average).

Test-retest reliability: The degree of temporal stability (relatedness) of a measuring instrument or test, or the characteristic it is designed to evaluate, from one administration to another.

Validity

Construct validity: The degree to which the conceptualization of that which is being measured or experimentally manipulated is what is claimed, such as the constructs that are measured by psychological tests or that serve as a scaffolding between independent and dependent variables.

Convergent and discriminant validity: The grounds established for a construct based on the convergence of related tests or behavior (convergent validity) and the distinctiveness of unrelated tests or behavior (discriminant validity).

Content validity: The adequate sampling of the relevant material or content that a test purports to measure.

Criterion validity: The degree to which a test or questionnaire is correlated with outcome criteria in the present (its *concurrent validity*) or the future (its *predictive validity*).

External validity: The generalizability of an inferred causal relationship over different people, settings, manipulations (or treatments), and research outcomes.

Face validity: The degree to which a test or other instrument "looks as if" it is measuring something relevant.

Internal validity: The soundness of statements about whether one variable is the cause of a particular outcome, especially the ability to rule out *plausible rival hypotheses*.

Statistical-conclusion validity: The accuracy of drawing certain statistical conclusions, such as statistical significance or an estimation of the magnitude of the research results (i.e., the *effect size*).

Random and Systematic Error

Before we turn to the specialized uses of reliability and validity listed in Table 6.1, there are two other important concepts that are not only related to reliability and validity but are also relevant to the statistical procedures discussed in later chapters. These are the concepts of random error and systematic error. **Random error** (also called *noise*) is the name for chance fluctuations, or haphazard errors. **Systematic error,** on the other hand, is the name for fluctuations that are not random but are slanted in a particular direction (thus, another name for systematic error is **bias**). In classical test theory, the idea is that the scores obtained (also called the

BOX 6.1 The Logic of Classical Test Theory

In the language of classical test theory, if we use the symbol Y_o to represent an observed (or raw) score on some dependent measure, Y_t for the true score, and e for random error, the relationship among these variables can be expressed as $Y_o = Y_t + e$. This model presumes that the variability of true scores and their random errors of measurement are independent of each other (i.e., they are uncorrelated). If you have had a course in statistics, you know that one popular measure of variability is the variance (σ^2) of a set of scores (discussed in Chapter 10). The classical model is based on the idea that the variance of observed scores (σ_o^2) is equal to the variance of true scores (σ_t^2) plus their random error variance of measurement (σ_e^2), that is, $\sigma_o^2 = \sigma_t^2 + \sigma_e^2$. Thus, the proportion of variance due to true scores (σ_t^2/σ_o^2) plus the proportion of variance due to their random errors of measurement (σ_e^2/σ_o^2) must equal 1. The smaller the random error variance (i.e., the less the noise), the more reliable the raw scores will be, and therefore, the more precise our estimate of any particular true score should be.

raw scores or *observed scores*) comprise the theoretically "true scores" (i.e., the actual or "real" values) and random errors (called *errors of measurement*). Errors of measurement are understood as randomly pushing the raw scores up and down around the true scores. The greater these random fluctuations (i.e., the more noise there is), the less consistent or dependable (i.e., the less reliable) the raw scores are (see also Box 6.1).

Random errors are not confined to psychological measures; they are characteristic of all measurements, no matter how well controlled and precisely calibrated the instruments. As an illustration, the National Bureau of Standards in Washington, D.C., checks the weights and measures that people use by comparing them with prototypes that are owned by the bureau. One such prototype is called *NB10* because it is the standard weight of 10 grams (the weight of two nickels). This prototype, which was acquired around 1940, has been weighed approximately once a week ever since. At each weighing, an attempt has been made to control all the factors known to affect the results (like air pressure and temperature), but still there have been detectable fluctuations. In one series of five weighings, for example, the results were:

9.999591 grams

9.999600 grams

9.999594 grams

9.999601 grams

9.999598 grams

As you can see, although the first four digits are identical, the numbers are shaky in the last three digits. As careful and precise as these measurements were, we can see errors of measurement in the form of chance fluctuations (random error) (Freedman, Pisani, Purves, & Adhikari, 1991).

As an illustration of systematic error (or bias), suppose the measuring instrument is off by a known percentage. Since all the results will be biased by the same percentage, we can easily correct for it. However, it is also possible to imagine a situation in which we know the direction but not the amount of the bias. For example, suppose we bought a bunch of grapes from a grocer who had an annoying habit of putting his thumb on the scale every time he weighed something, thus inflating the cost of our grapes (but we don't know by exactly how much). It is also possible to imagine a situation where the systematic error occurred quite innocently. Suppose your sample of participants consisted only of men, but you wanted to generalize your results to women *and* men. Systematic error due to a biased sample could jeopardize your conclusions.

Another way of thinking about the difference between systematic and random errors is that (a) random errors are likely to cancel one another, on the average, over many repeated measurements (i.e., they are likely to have an average of about zero), whereas (b) systematic errors do not cancel one another and do affect all measurements in roughly the same way (i.e., they do *not* have an average of about zero). Thus, if we wanted a single, unbiased estimate of the true weight of NB10, all we need do is calculate the arithmetic mean of all the different values, on the assumption that (a) the random errors will cancel out, and (b) the measurement apparatus is unbiased (i.e., there is no systematic error). In the case of the dishonest grocer with the heavy thumb, perhaps we could figure out whether his thumb on the scale inflates what he has weighed. Simply by using another scale to weigh several bunches of grapes that he has weighed, we can use the average difference in values to estimate the bias imposed by his heavy thumb. But imagine we have two scales, and we know that one is consistently too high and the other is inconsistent all the time. Which scale is better? We would prefer using the first scale, because a little bias is better than a lot of random error when we know the amount of bias and can adjust for it (J.C. Stanley, 1971).

Test-Retest and Alternate-Form Reliability

As noted in Table 6.1, one type of reliability is **test-retest reliability** (also sometimes referred to simply as *retest reliability*). Suppose you wanted to use a psychological test or other assessment procedure to empirically examine some prediction of interest. Test-retest reliability is an estimate of the degree of fluctuation of the instrument, or of the characteristic it is designed to measure, from one administration to another. If it is a standardized test (such as an IQ test, or a personality test like the MMPI), you should be able to find out about its test-retest reliability in your literature search. You can also estimate the test-retest reliability simply by administering the instrument to a sample of people and then administering it again to the

BOX 6.2 Retesting the Same People Is Sometimes Impossible

Test-retest reliability requires that the same measure be administered on separate occasions to the same individuals. However, circumstances beyond our control sometimes prevent us from doing so, such as when people are no longer available. A biblical case (which also illustrates the ancient roots of behavioral assessment) involved the Gileadites, who used a one-item ability test to ferret out the Ephraimites who were hiding in their midst (Wainer, 1990). The test was to pronounce the word *shibboleth;* the Ephraimites could not pronounce *sh* (which came out as *s*), and those who failed this test were put to death. The grotesque practice may have cut down on the number of Ephraimites, but it obviously left no opportunity to check on the test's retest reliability.

same people later on (but see Box 6.2). The test-retest reliability can be represented by a **correlation coefficient** between the scores on the test administered at those two different times.

We will have more to say about correlation in Chapter 11, but if you have had a course in statistics, you know that the basic measure of association is the Pearson *r* correlation coefficient. If you are unfamiliar with the Pearson *r*, or need your memory about correlation jogged a little, all you need to know at this point is that the Pearson *r* measures the strength of association (i.e., the degree of relatedness) of two variables, such as height and weight. One characteristic of the Pearson *r* is that it ranges from −1.0 through 0 to +1.0. A value of 0 means that the two variables being correlated have no linear relation, for example, that taller people are not heavier (or lighter) on average than shorter people. A value of +1.0 means that the two variables have a perfect positive relation: As the scores on one variable increase, there are perfectly predictable increases in the scores on the other variable. A value of −1.0 means the opposite: As the scores on one variable increase, there are perfectly predictable decreases in the scores on the other variable.

Knowing these characteristics of the Pearson *r*, what would you want the correlation *(r)* between the scores at the initial testing and at the retesting to be if you were thinking about using a particular instrument in your research? The answer is that you would probably want the *r* to be a positive value as high as possible, as the higher the test-retest coefficient, the more dependable or temporally stable is the instrument. By temporal stability or dependability, we mean that those who scored high initially scored high on retest, and that those who scored low initially scored low on retest. Thus, the retest reliability depends on maintaining one's *relative* position from initial test to retest; it is not affected by changes in *everyone's* scores from pretest to retest. If everyone earns, for example, 10 points more on retest because of practice effects (or 10 points less on retest because of fatigue effects), retest reliability is not affected even though scores have changed quite a bit from pretest to retest. If you are measuring something that you believe is very stable over time, the closer the r is to +1.0, the more impressive is the temporal stability of the measuring instrument. On the other hand, if you are measuring a volatile or very changeable variable (such as mood), you would expect much lower test-retest reliability if there have been changes in relevant circumstances affecting that variable. That is, you would want a measuring instrument that is sensitive to the volatility or change. Thus, reports of test-retest reliability ordinarily indicate not only the interval over which the retesting was done, but also the nature of the sample on which the test-retest reliability is based.

However, a common concern when people take the same test twice is that the test-retest r may be artificially inflated because of their familiarity with the test items. One way to avoid this problem is to create two statistically and theoretically comparable forms of the test with different items that are measuring the same content. Not all tests, of course, have more than one form, but many of the most popular ones do. If the forms are reliable, higher scores on one form should be associated with higher scores on the other forms as well. The correlation coefficient is again used to assess the reliability of the sets of scores, that is, their **alternate-form reliability.** To illustrate, say we wanted to test vocabulary skills. We could randomly draw several samples of words from the dictionary and let each random sample constitute one form of our test. The correlation between each form with another form at a particular time would be one indication of their comparability (Guilford, 1954). Other indications would be that the forms also have similar variances as well as similar intercorrelations with theoretically relevant criteria (Gulliksen, 1950; Nunnally & Bernstein, 1994).

Before we turn to another very important application of reliability, we want to reiterate the conceptual difference between the simple correlations we have just discussed. In the case of test-retest reliability, the correlation is between scores on the same form administered to the same people at different times. Thus, it can be understood as a measure (or coefficient) of *stability*. In the case of alternate-form reliability, the correlation is between scores on different forms that were administered to the same people at approximately the same time. Thus, it is conceptualized as a measure (or coefficient) of *equivalence*. The situation becomes more complicated, however, if the correlation is between one form of the test at Time 1 and another form at Time 2, which is called a *cross-lag correlation*. We will have more to say about it later in this book (Chapter 8), but you may already perceive how a cross-lagged correlation can be affected by instability, nonequivalence, or both.

Internal-Consistency and Item-to-Item Reliability

The **internal-consistency reliability** of a test is a general expression that refers to the degree of relatedness of the individual items. As it tells us how well the separate items (or *components*) of the test "hang together," it is also called the

reliability of components. There are several ways of estimating this reliability. One traditional approach (illustrated below) is to use the Spearman-Brown formula, which in turn is based on the average intercorrelation of all the items symbolized as r_{ii} to denote the mean item-to-item Pearson (r) correlation. Two other traditional approaches, which you may come across in your reading, are K-R 20 and Cronbach's alpha coefficient, which are described briefly in Box 6.3. It has been demonstrated that when all the item variances are equal, the estimates of internal-consistency reliability obtained from the two methods in Box 6.3 and the Spearman-Brown formula should be identical (Li & Wainer, 1998). In this discussion, we use the capital letter R to denote an estimate of internal-consistency reliability (to emphasize that it refers to the composite, or overall, measure of reliability), and we use the superscript SB to indicate that the estimation procedure is based on the Spearman-Brown formula (R^{SB}).

To illustrate, suppose you have made up a three-item questionnaire in which people are to indicate their agreement or disagreement with three attitudinal statements on a 5-point numerical scale from *strongly agree* to *strongly disagree*. You want to have a single summary score for each respondent based on your assumption that the items tap into conceptually related aspects of the attitudinal issue. You administer the questionnaire to a sample of people, score the results, and then correlate responses to Item 1 with responses to Item 2, Item 1 with Item 3, and Item 2 with Item 3. We can represent these Pearson correlations by the letter r with nu-

---

BOX 6.3 K-R 20 and Cronbach's Alpha as Estimates of Internal-Consistency Reliability

K-R 20 gets its name from its originators, G. F. Kuder and M. W. Richardson, and the *20* comes from the fact that it was their 20th-numbered equation. K-R 20 is useful when the test items are scored dichotomously, for example, scored 1 if marked correctly and 0 if not marked correctly. **Cronbach's alpha,** named after Lee J. Cronbach (1951), is not restricted to only dichotomously scored items. Cronbach's alpha is frequently referred to simply as the **alpha coefficient.** If you have had a course in statistics, you may recall that another name for the p value is *alpha*. That alpha, which refers to the probability of a Type I error (reviewed in Chapter 12), is not the same thing as Cronbach's alpha, which refers only to internal-consistency reliability. It is beyond the scope of this text to give examples of how K-R 20 or Cronbach's alpha are calculated. However, the same rule applies whether we use K-R 20, Cronbach's alpha, or the Spearman-Brown formula: The more comparable items there are in a test and the longer the test, the greater will be its internal-consistency reliability.

merical subscripts indicating the specific items that were correlated with one another. Let us say you find r_{12} = .45 between Items 1 and 2; r_{13} = .50 between Items 1 and 3; and r_{23} = .55 between Items 2 and 3. Summing the values gives us .45 + .50 + .55 = 1.50. Dividing this sum by the number of pairs (three pairs) tells us the *mean* item-to-item correlation (i.e., r_{ii} = 1.50/3 = .50), that is, the **item-to-item reliability.** Think of this value as the estimate of the *reliability of any single item on average.*

To estimate the internal-consistency reliability of the three-item test from the information at hand, we will use the **Spearman-Brown formula** (created by Charles Spearman and William Brown, who came up with it independently and simultaneously published their work in the same issue of the *British Journal of Psychology* in 1910), as expressed by

$$R^{SB} = \frac{nr_{ii}}{1 + [(n-1)r_{ii}]},$$

where n = the number of items in the test, and r_{ii} = the average intercorrelation of the items. To use the results noted above, we set n equal to 3 (because you have a three-item test) and r_{ii} equal to .50. Substituting in the expression above, we find

$$R^{SB} = \frac{3(.50)}{1 + [(3-1).50]} = \frac{1.5}{1 + 1.0} = .75.$$

The beauty of this formula is that we can try out different values of n and predict what the effect will be on the internal-consistency reliability when the length of the test is changed. Thus, the formula is also known as the Spearman-Brown *prophecy formula.* For example, suppose we were to use six items instead of three. Assuming the average intercorrelation is still r_{ii} =.50, we predict as follows:

$$R^{SB} = \frac{6(.50)}{1 + [(6-1).50]} = .86.$$

What if we wanted to further increase the length of our test, going to nine items? With n = 9 and the same average intercorrelation, our prediction is:

$$R^{SB} = \frac{9(.50)}{1 + [(9-1).50]} = .90.$$

There is not much difference between .90 and .86. However, what is striking is that we can keep on improving the internal-consistency reliability by steadily adding new items, as long as the average item-to-item correlation (r_{ii}) remains unchanged. If the new items are not as relevant or as reliable as items already in the test, then r_{ii} will be reduced, and if this reduction is great enough, the internal-consistency reliability will be reduced (Li, Rosenthal, & Rubin, 1996). If some items have very low test-retest reliability, this will further increase the error of measurement and also reduce the internal-consistency reliability (Wainer & Thissen, 1993). Of course, we cannot add items ad infinitum, since there is a psychological limit to how long a test should be. If we make the test too long, the respondents will become fatigued and lose their concentration.

What Is Acceptable Test-Retest and Internal-Consistency Reliability?

Just how many items are optimal to achieve the reliability we want, without making the test or questionnaire so cumbersome as to burden the respondents or give them headaches? Unfortunately, there is no simple answer. The acceptable range depends on the context in which the instrument is to be used and the objective of the research. For example, if we needed an instrument with a high degree of test-retest reliability, we might not settle for a test-retest correlation less than .80. And yet, there are many acceptable instruments with test-retest correlations below .80, including many medical tools for detecting or diagnosing illness (e.g., the instrument used for measuring blood pressure). Scores on many medical tests vary as a function of feelings of anxiety, changes in one's diet, and so on. Besides asking your instructor for guidance, you can develop a sense of the answer in any particular case by looking up relevant test reviews in sourcebooks (such as the *Mental Measurements Yearbook*) or by perusing the *Directory of Unpublished Experimental Mental Measures* for relevant measures (described in the previous chapter in Box 5.8).

To give you a context, the test-retest *r* on the Scholastic Assessment Test (SAT) for essay scores in the humanities is usually between .3 and .6, and for chemistry, it is usually between .6 and .8 (Braun & Wainer, 1989). In the previous chapter, we described the Minnesota Multiphasic Personality Inventory (MMPI) and the Rorschach inkblot test. A team of psychologists (Parker, Hanson, & Hunsley, 1988) compared the internal consistency and test-retest reliability of these instruments and another well-known psychological test, the **Wechsler Adult Intelligence Scale (WAIS),** based on the information they found in articles between 1970 and 1981. Developed by David Wechsler (a clinical psychologist who was connected with New York City's Bellevue Hospital for many years), the WAIS is the most widely used individually administered intelligence test. It is divided into verbal and performance subtests, the verbal part depending more on school-related abilities than the performance part. Parker et al. estimated that the average internal-consistency reliability was .87 for the overall WAIS, .84 for the MMPI, and .86 for the Rorschach test. They also estimated the average test-retest correlation as .82 for the overall WAIS, .74 for the MMPI, and .85 for the Rorschach. Internal-consistency reliability is usually expected to be higher than test-retest reliability, unless the test-retest intervals are very short. These findings, then, are consistent with that expectation, although in the case of the Rorschach the difference is hardly noticeable.

More is known about the reliability (and the validity) of the WAIS, the MMPI, and the Rorschach than about that of most other psychological tests in current use, including the two attitude questionnaires displayed in the previous chapter. Regarding the Thurstone questionnaire that was designed to measure attitudes toward defensive, cooperative, and aggressive war (Figure 5.3 on p. 128), the developers of this scale (D. D. Day & Quackenbush, 1942) reported only its internal-consistency reliability, which was in the .80 to .87 range for all three referents measured. For the Likert questionnaire measuring socialized-medicine attitudes (displayed in Figure 5.2, p. 126), the internal-consistency reliability was reported by its developer (Mahler, 1953) to be .96. This 20-item questionnaire is interesting for another reason having to do with alternate-form reliability because the test in Figure 5.2 actually comprises two comparable 10-item forms, with the alternate-form reliability in the .81 to .84 range.

Application to Reliability of Judges

As mentioned in Chapter 4, reliability is also a basic consideration in observational studies that use raters, as well as in all judgment studies. To cite an instance, in one popular observational procedure used by developmental psychologists to study attachment behavior in infants and the maternal responses, the judges code positive and negative actions in a number of situations. They may do this coding, for example, when the mother and the infant are together, when the mother leaves the infant in the presence of a stranger, when the mother returns, and when the infant is left alone (Ainsworth, Blehar, Waters, & Wall, 1978; de Wolff & Van Ijzendoorn, 1997; Main & Solomon, 1990). Suppose a developmental researcher has three judges (A, B, and C) code the maternal behavior of five mothers (Smith, Jones, Brown, Kelly, and Blake) in one situation on a 7-point scale from "very secure" (1) to "very anxious" (7). The hypothetical results are shown in Part A of Table 6.2. After calculating the correlations between all pairs of judges (A with B; A with C; and B with C), the researcher obtains the mean of these correlations. The results are given in Part B of Table 6.2, in which the mean correlation is shown as r_{jj} = .676 (the subscript j stands for *judge*). This mean correlation is the **judge-to-judge reliability,** or the *reliability of any single judge on average.*

We would also like to know the reliability of the group of three judges as a whole, that is, the internal-consistency reliability. We obtain the answer by using the Spearman-Brown formula, now expressed as

$$R^{SB} = \frac{nr_{jj}}{1 + [(n-1)r_{jj}]},$$

where n = the number of judges and r_{jj} = the average judge-to-judge reliability. Substituting in the formula gives us

$$R^{SB} = \frac{3(.676)}{1 + [(3-1).676]} = \frac{2.028}{1 + 1.352} = .862.$$

We now know that the reliability of the three judges' ratings as a whole (their internal-consistency reliability) is .862 and that the reliability of any single judge is .676 (the average judge-to-judge reliability). We would report both reliabilities and, of course, label each to prevent reader misunderstandings. Suppose we want to predict the amount by which internal-consistency reliability will increase if we use

Table 6.2	Ratings and Intercorrelations for Three Judges

A. Judges' ratings

Mothers	Judges		
	A	B	C
Smith	5	6	7
Jones	3	6	4
Brown	3	4	6
Kelly	2	2	3
Blake	1	4	4

B. Judge-to-judge correlations

r_{AB} = .645
r_{AC} = .800
r_{BC} = .582
r_{jj} = .676

Note. We typically report correlations to two decimal places, but when we are going to use correlations in further calculations, it is often helpful to employ three decimal places.

one more judge whose ratings are also correlated approximately .68 with the other judges. We find the answer to our question by substituting in the Spearman-Brown formula, with the number (n) of judges now 4 instead of 3 and the average reliability (r_{jj}) rounded to .68:

$$R^{SB} = \frac{4(.68)}{1 + [(4 - 1).68]} = .895.$$

Using four instead of three judges is predicted to boost the internal-consistency reliability from .86 to roughly .90, assuming the judge-to-judge reliability is not reduced by the addition of this fourth judge.

Using a Table of Estimated Values

Table 6.3 shows the Spearman-Brown internal-consistency estimates for values of n ranging from 1 to 20 judges, or 1 to 20 items in a test. When $n = 1$, we see that internal-consistency reliability (R^{SB}) is equivalent to the reliability of a single judge (r_{jj}), or a single test item (r_{ii}). To show how to use this table, we will start with three questions about judges and then ask a fourth one dealing with test items.

1. Given an obtained or estimated mean reliability, r_{jj}, and a sample of n judges, what is the approximate Spearman-Brown internal-consistency estimate, R^{SB}, of the mean of the judges' ratings? The value of R^{SB} is read from the table at the intersection of the appropriate row (n) and column (r_{jj}). Suppose we want to work with a variable believed to show a mean reliability of $r_{jj} = .50$ and can

| Table 6.3 | Estimation of Spearman-Brown Reliability (R^{SB}) Based on Number (n) of Judges or Test Items and Mean Judge-to-Judge (r_{jj}) or Item-to-Item (r_{ii}) Reliability |

Mean judge-to-judge (r_{jj}) or item-to-item (r_{ii}) reliability

N	.05	.10	.15	.20	.25	.30	.35	.40	.45	.50	.55	.60	.65	.70	.75	.80	.85	.90	.95
1	.05	.10	.15	.20	.25	.30	.35	.40	.45	.50	.55	.60	.65	.70	.75	.80	.85	.90	.95
2	.10	.18	.26	.33	.40	.46	.52	.57	.62	.67	.71	.75	.79	.82	.86	.89	.92	.95	.97
3	.14	.25	.35	.43	.50	.56	.62	.67	.71	.75	.79	.82	.85	.88	.90	.92	.94	.96	.98
4	.17	.31	.41	.50	.57	.63	.68	.73	.77	.80	.83	.86	.88	.90	.92	.94	.96	.97	.99
5	.21	.36	.47	.56	.62	.68	.73	.77	.80	.83	.86	.88	.90	.92	.94	.95	.97	.98	.99
6	.24	.40	.51	.60	.67	.72	.76	.80	.83	.86	.88	.90	.92	.93	.95	.96	.97	.98	.99
7	.27	.44	.55	.64	.70	.75	.79	.82	.85	.88	.90	.91	.93	.94	.95	.97	.98	.98	.99
8	.30	.47	.59	.67	.73	.77	.81	.84	.87	.89	.91	.92	.94	.95	.96	.97	.98	.99	.99
9	.32	.50	.61	.69	.75	.79	.83	.86	.88	.90	.92	.93	.94	.95	.96	.97	.98	.99	.99
10	.34	.53	.64	.71	.77	.81	.84	.87	.89	.91	.92	.94	.95	.96	.97	.98	.98	.99	.99
12	.39	.57	.68	.75	.80	.84	.87	.89	.91	.92	.94	.95	.96	.97	.97	.98	.99	.99	1.0
14	.42	.61	.71	.78	.82	.86	.88	.90	.92	.93	.94	.95	.96	.97	.98	.98	.99	.99	1.0
16	.46	.64	.74	.80	.84	.87	.90	.91	.93	.94	.95	.96	.97	.97	.98	.98	.99	.99	1.0
18	.49	.67	.76	.82	.86	.89	.91	.92	.94	.95	.96	.96	.97	.98	.98	.99	.99	.99	1.0
20	.51	.69	.78	.83	.87	.90	.92	.93	.94	.95	.96	.97	.97	.98	.98	.99	.99	.99	1.0

afford only four judges. We believe we should go ahead with our study only if the internal-consistency reliability (R^{SB}) will reach or exceed .75. Shall we go ahead? The answer is yes, because the table shows R^{SB} = .80 for an n of 4 and an r_{jj} of .50.

2. Given the value of the obtained or desired internal-consistency reliability, R^{SB}, and the number of judges actually available, n, what will be the predicted value of the mean reliability, r_{jj}? The table is entered in the row corresponding to the n of judges available and is read across until the value of R^{SB} closest to the one desired is reached; the value of r_{jj} is then read as the corresponding column heading. Suppose we will settle for internal-consistency reliability no less than R^{SB} = .90 and we have a sample of n = 20 judges available. For each of the variables to be rated by these judges, what should be the judges' minimally acceptable average individual reliability? From this table we see the answer is r_{jj} = .30.

3. Given an obtained or estimated mean reliability, r_{jj}, and the obtained or desired internal-consistency reliability, R^{SB}, what is the approximate number of judges (n) required? The table is entered in the column corresponding to the mean reliability, r_{jj}, and is read down until the value of R^{SB} closest to the one desired is reached; the value of n is then read as the corresponding row title. For example, we know our choice of variables to have a mean reliability of .40, and we want to achieve internal-consistency reliability of .85 or higher.

How many judges must we allow for in our preparation of a research budget? The answer is $n = 9$ judges.

4. Table 6.3 can be used equally well in estimating the increase in internal-consistency reliability of tests when new, relevant items are added. In that case, we redefine the n of judges as the n of items, r_{ii} as the average intercorrelation of items (i.e., the item-to-item reliability), and R^{SB} as the Spearman-Brown internal-consistency estimate with n items. In the previous section, we gave the example of a three-item test (i.e., $n = 3$) with an average item-to-item correlation of $r_{ii} = .50$; the researcher wanted to estimate the overall effect of using three, six, or nine items. The table is entered in the column corresponding to this mean reliability, and we then read down the column until we reach the Spearman-Brown value closest to the one desired. Let us say we want to achieve internal-consistency reliability of $R^{SB} = .90$ or higher. How many new, relevant items will we need? When we read across the row, the answer is $n = 9$.

Reliability, Replication, and External Validity

We turn now to the concept of validity, beginning with an application that is sometimes a source of confusion, as it encompasses aspects of both reliability *and* validity. Called **external validity** by Donald T. Campbell and Julian C. Stanley (1963), in its most recent iteration it was defined specifically to refer to "inferences about the extent to which a *causal relationship* [our emphasis] holds across variations in persons, settings, treatments, and outcomes" (Shadish, Cook, & Campbell, 2002, p. 82). It is one of four types of validity that are presumed to play an essential role in causal inference (statistical-conclusion validity, construct validity, and internal validity are the other three), though for now we will concentrate only on external validity and its relevance to the importance of **replication.** Just as we are interested in the dependability of measurements, we are also interested in the dependability of causal generalizations in experimental research (or external validity) based on replicable findings.

More is said in the next chapter about the logic of causal inference in experimental research, but suppose we obtain a particular result in a psychology or educational or child development experiment. We want to know not only whether it will stand up over time, but also whether it is generalizable across different kinds of participants and different investigators (see also Box 6.4). Or suppose we have successfully conducted not one, but a series of experiments on learning or cognition, and although the causal results are reliable, the subjects in these experiments were psychology students. Can we assume that the same results will apply to a general population that is not as literate or as well educated? Suppose the participants in a biomedical experiment are male volunteers. Can we generalize to women, or even to men who may not have been inclined to volunteer to participate in the research? Or suppose we use one standard experimental treatment in all experiments. Can we assume that the causal result will hold up across other

BOX 6.4 Independent and Nonindependent Replications

In the evaluation of a set of replication studies, it is often assumed that replications are independent of one another. But what does "independence" really mean? The usual minimum requirement is that the study participants be different persons. But what about the independence of the people who conducted the research? Are 10 replications conducted by one investigator as independent of one another as 10 replications each of which is conducted by a different investigator? One way to address this concern is to separate the replications into subsets (a procedure called *blocking*) and to compare and contrast the different subsets. For example, we might block on the particular interests of the investigators (Do they hold similar views, or are they at odds with one another?) or their background and training (Are they all affiliated in some way?). Once such characteristics have been identified, it is possible to assign a set of weights to the results that reflect some theoretically defined degree of independence, and to use these weights in the analysis (Rosenthal, 1990c).

treatment variations in other settings? These are the kinds of questions that external validity addresses.

The problem is that the *same* experiment can never be "exactly" duplicated, because at the very least the participants will be older. Thus, researchers think of all replications, even the ones most closely modeled on the original study, as *relative replications* (Cook & Campbell, 1979; Rosenthal, 1990c; Shadish, Cook, & Campbell, 2002; Sidman, 1960). In the case of external validity, the issue is whether the size of the effect of an independent variable (X) on a dependent variable (Y) is similar in both the original and the replication study. One convenient way to operationalize the concept of **effect size** is to compute the correlation between X and Y. Effect size correlations that scattered around zero would tell us that not much was going on between X and Y in either study. However, suppose we wanted to replicate an experiment in which the effect size was $r_{XY} = .50$ (the subscripts indicate that the correlation is between variable X and variable Y), and say the effect size in our replication attempt is $r_{XY} = .40$. The two correlations are positive, far from zero, and not that far apart, a result leading us to conclude that the replication attempt was successful. We can also compare the two effect sizes statistically (using a procedure described in Appendix C) in order to rule out chance variation.

Although we said that replications are possible only in a relative sense, we can think of a distribution of possible replications in which their overall variability is a function of the degree of similarity to the original study that characterizes each possible replication. If researchers choose the study designs of their replications to be as similar as possible to the study being replicated, they may be more true to the original ideal of replication but they may also pay a price. That price is limited generalizability across other variations in settings and treatments. Broadly speaking, the kinds of threats to the external validity of causal inferences that experimenters worry about fall into two categories (Shadish et al., 2002): (a) variables that *were not* in the experiment (i.e., variations in persons, settings, and treatments) and (b) those that *were* in the experiment (e.g., operationalizing the variable of interest too narrowly, or using a specialized group of participants, or conducting the research in a setting that is quite unlike the circumstances to which the experimenters want to generalize). Though it would be impossible to rule out every possible threat, researchers must be sensitive to the logical limitations of their study designs and not make false or imprudent causal generalizations.

Validity in Test and Instrument Construction

Before turning to the three other applications of the concept of validity in experimental research, we will first examine its application in test and instrument construction. Previously, we said that *validity* refers to whether a test or measuring instrument actually does what it purports to do. This assessment is considered the most important criterion in instrument construction and, in test and questionnaire construction, involves accumulating evidence in three categories, called *content validity, criterion validity,* and *construct validity.* Test developers are expected to provide this kind of information so that test users know the capabilities and limitations of the instruments before using them, and so that test takers are not misled or their time and effort wasted when they are administered these instruments.

Content Validity

Content validity means that the test or questionnaire items represent the kinds of material (or content areas) they are supposed to represent, usually a basic consideration in the construction phase of any test or questionnaire. Thus, saying that a test or questionnaire has "good content validity" means that it adequately covers all major aspects of the content areas that are relevant. For example, when the MMPI was developed, the researchers tried to select a range of statements that would be endorsed in a certain direction by each of several different clinical groups. For this purpose, they began by developing a set of specifications, with the idea that the items could then be judged against these specifications. In this way, they hoped to differentiate among a number of different clinical conditions by including a wide range of items that tapped different content areas. To assess whether test items were consistent with the original specifications, they called on expert judges to make subjective evaluations of the relevance or appropriateness of each item for assessing different content areas (see also Box 6.5).

Less formal methods can be used in other situations. For instance, suppose an instructor is making up a final exam and wants it to have content validity. The instructor may start simply by asking, "What material should my students have mas-

BOX 6.5 What Does the Test Look Like?

Another type of validity you may come across in your reading is **face validity.** It simply means whether the test seems on the surface (or "face") to be measuring something relevant. It should not be confused with content validity; face validity refers not to what the test measures but only to how it looks. In other words, does it "look like" a valid measure of what we are interested in? If a test does not *appear* to be relevant, some people may not take it seriously in a practical situation (Anastasi & Urbina, 1997). Of course, there are many tests (e.g., the Rorschach and the TAT) that purposely do not contain a clue to what they are supposed to be measuring.

tered by studying the readings and taking my course?" The instructor would make a list of the material the exam should cover and then make up questions to represent this material. As students we have all experienced exams with poor content validity. They are the ones about which we say, "The instructor never even mentioned this material; and it appeared in a two-line footnote in the appendix!" Thus, content validity has little to do with statistical aspects of the test or questionnaire (Cronbach & Quirk, 1971). The instructor is not interested in items that are highly intercorrelated, because such intercorrelation would impose restrictions on the range of material the instructor wants to cover. Also, a test that is content-valid one semester is not necessarily going to be content-valid when the course is taught again, because there may be a new textbook or the instructor may have updated the lectures. The instructor must also make sure that all items can be easily understood, so that if a student gives the wrong answer, it is not because of some "irrelevant difficulty" but because the student did not know the right answer (Cronbach & Quirk, 1971, p. 168).

Criterion Validity

Criterion validity has more to do with statistical aspects of the test, as it refers to the degree to which the test or questionnaire is correlated with one or more outcome criteria (a variable with which the instrument should be reasonably correlated). For example, suppose researchers were interested in developing a test of college aptitude. They might use as their criterion the successful completion of the first year of college or maybe the grade point average (GPA) after each year of college. If they were developing a test to measure anxiety, they might use as their criterion the pooled judgments of a group of highly trained clinicians who rated (e.g., on a numerical rating scale) each person to whom the researchers administered the test. In assessing criterion validity, researchers select the most sensitive and meaningful criterion in the

BOX 6.6 Criteria Evaluated Against Criteria

Frequently, researchers must consider the validity of the criterion itself. Suppose a personality researcher wants to develop a short test of anxiety that will predict the scores on a longer test of anxiety. The longer test serves as the researcher's criterion, and the new short test may be relatively valid with respect to the longer test. But the longer test may be of dubious validity with respect to some other criterion (e.g., clinicians' judgments). In other words, criteria must often be evaluated with respect to other criteria, but there are no firm rules (beyond the use of logic and the consensus of other researchers in that area) about what constitutes an "ultimate" criterion.

present (called **concurrent validity**) or future (called **predictive validity**) and then correlate performance on the test or questionnaire with that criterion.

For example, clinical diagnostic tests are ordinarily assessed for concurrent validity, as the criterion of the patient's "real" diagnostic status is in the present with respect to the test being validated. The concurrent validity of shorter forms of longer tests is also typically evaluated, the longer test being used as the criterion (see also Box 6.6). The practical advantage to researchers of using a criterion in the present is that it is less expensive and less time-consuming than using a criterion that is in the future. It also controls for any possible complicating effect of temporal instability (Anastasi & Urbina, 1997).

Nevertheless, predictive validity also plays an important role in measurement. Tests of college aptitude are normally assessed for predictive validity because the criteria of graduation and GPA are of the future. The aptitude test scores would be saved until the future-criterion data become available, and the test scores are then correlated with the future-criterion data. The resulting correlation coefficient serves as an index of criterion validity. GPA tends to be a fairly reliable criterion, but clinicians' judgments (e.g., about complex behavior) may be a less reliable criterion. Previously, we showed how the internal-consistency reliability of pooled judgments can be increased if more judges are used, assuming they are similar to the other judges. In the same way, we can increase the internal-consistency reliability of pooled clinical judgments by adding similar clinicians to the group whose pooled judgments is going to serve as their criterion (Rosenthal, 1973, 1982, 1987).

Construct Validity in Test Development

More sophisticated views of the validation of tests require that researchers be sensitive not only to the correlation between their measures and some appropriate criterion, but also to the correlation between their measures and some "inappropriate" criterion. Suppose that a researcher in clinical psychology developed a new test of psychological adjustment, which she wanted to use in a field experiment. She would do some pilot studies to ensure the validity of the new test. In one aspect of the pilot work, she could have expert clinicians rate the psychological adjustment of a group of clients who have just been given the test. Say she finds that the test scores correlated positively and substantially with the pooled judgment of the expert clinicians. She could correctly interpret this correlation as an attractive outcome of a concurrent validation effort.

However, suppose she had also given the clients a standard test of verbal aptitude and found that their scores on this test and on her new test of psychological adjustment correlated positively and substantially with one another. Should she conclude that the new test would be a reasonably valid measure of psychological adjustment, of verbal aptitude, of both, or of neither? This question is difficult to answer, but she could not claim on the basis of such results to understand the new test very well. It was not intended, after all, to be a measure of verbal aptitude. In short, the new test has good concurrent validity but fails to discriminate: It does not correlate differentially with criteria for different types of observation. This "ability to discriminate" is a vital characteristic of **construct validity** in test development, which in turn is generally considered the most "fundamental and all-inclusive validity concept, insofar as it specifies what the test measures" (Anastasi & Urbina, 1997, p. 114). To put it another way, construct validity has to do with what a test *really* does assess. In current usage, content and criterion validity provide valuable information in their own right but are generally regarded as improving our understanding of the construct assessed by the test. (We will turn to another use of *construct validity* at the end of this chapter.)

How one should establish the construct validity of a test has been debated for many years in psychology. One traditional way is to use logical analysis, while another procedure involves manipulating the respondents' experience before the test or during the test to see whether it will produce differences in responding as the construct would imply (Cronbach & Quirk, 1971). In a seminal article, Donald T. Campbell and Donald W. Fiske (1959) proposed a way of formalizing the construct validation procedure. To achieve this statistically, they suggested that researchers use two essential kinds of validation evidence: (a) the testing for *convergence* across different measures or manipulations of the same behavior (called **convergent validity**) and (b) the testing for *distinctiveness* between measures or manipulations of related but conceptually different traits or behaviors (**discriminant validity**). For example, the finding that the new test of psychological adjustment correlated positively and substantially with expert clinicians' ratings would be seen as convergent validation evidence. Finding that the new test correlated positively and substantially with a test of verbal aptitude (which is distinct from the construct of psychological adjustment) would be seen as contrary to the necessary discriminant validation evidence. Recently, measures besides simple correlation have been applied to the quantification of construct validity (Westen & Rosenthal, 2003).

Detailed Example: Crowne and Marlowe's Research

To give a clearer sense of the process of construct validation, we turn to a classic program of research by personality psychologists Douglas Crowne and David Marlowe, in which a number of different strategies were used, including logical analysis, correlation, and laboratory studies. The original purpose of this research was to develop a psychological scale that would measure *socially desirable responding*. As noted in the previous chapter, in this type of behavior people respond in ways that make them look good (rather than give their most candid and honest responses). As their work progressed, Crowne and Marlowe realized that the scale they were building might be assessing a more general personality variable, which they termed the **need for social approval** (to reflect the idea that people differ in their need to be thought well of by others). In developing this scale—called the **Marlowe-Crowne Social Desirability Scale (MCSD)**—the researchers wanted not only to measure the degree to which people vary on the need-for-approval dimension independent of their level of psychopathology, but also to validate the need-for-approval construct.

Crowne and Marlowe began by considering hundreds of personality test items (including a few from the MMPI) that could be answered true or false. To be included, an item had to reflect socially approved behavior but also almost certainly be untrue (behavior too good to be true). In addition, answers to the items could not have any implications of psychological abnormality or psychopathology. By having a group of psychology graduate students and faculty judge the social desirability of each item, Crowne and Marlowe developed a set of items that would reflect behavior that was too virtuous to be probable, but that would not be primarily influenced by personal maladjustment.

The final form of the MCSD scale, which consisted of 33 items chosen by item analysis and ratings by experienced judges (Crowne, 1979; Crowne & Marlowe, 1964), showed a high degree of relationship to those variables with which the scale scores were expected to converge (i.e., convergent validation evidence). For example, high scorers on the final MCSD preferred low-risk behaviors and avoided the evaluations of others. The final form also showed only a low degree of relationship to those variables with which the scale was expected not to converge. For example, correlations with measures of psychopathology were smaller in magnitude than was the case for an earlier developed scale of social desirability, a result implying that the MCSD was a better measure of social desirability because it was not confounded by psychopathology. Also encouraging was an impressive correlation ($r = .88$) between the responses of a group of participants who were tested 1 month apart (i.e., evidence of test-retest reliability).

These were promising beginnings for the MCSD, but it remained to be shown that the concept of need for social approval (and the scale developed to measure it) was meaningful beyond predicting responses on other paper-and-pencil measures. As part of their program of further validating their new scale and the construct that was its basis, the researchers undertook an ingenious series of varied replications relating scores on the MCSD to participants' behavior in a number of non-paper-and-pencil test situations. They reasoned that "dependence on the approval of others should make it difficult to assert one's independence, and so the approval-motivated person should be susceptible to social influence, compliant, and conforming" (Crowne, 1991, p. 10). A series of relational studies produced results that were generally consistent with this logical expectation.

In the first of these studies, the participants began by completing various tests, including the MCSD, and then were asked to get down to the serious business of the experiment. This "serious business" required them to (a) pack a dozen spools of thread into a small box, (b) unpack the box, (c) repack the box, (d) unrepack the box, and so on for 25 minutes while the experimenter appeared to be timing the performance and making notes about them. After these dull 25 minutes had elapsed, the participants were asked to rate how "interesting" the task had been, how "instructive," and how "important to science" and how much they wanted to participate in similar studies in the future. Those persons who scored above the mean on social desirability said they found the task more interesting, more instructive, and more important to science and were more eager to participate again in similar studies than those persons who had scored below the mean. In other words, just as Crowne and Marlowe had predicted, the people higher in the need for social approval were more compliant and said nicer things to the experimenter about the task that he had set for them.

In still other research, Crowne and Marlowe used a variant of Asch's (1952) conformity procedure (described in Chapter 1). That is, a group of people are required to make judgments on specific issues, and all the confederates make the same uniform judgment, one that is quite clearly in error. Conformity was defined as the real subject's "going along with" the majority in his or her own judgment rather than giving the objectively correct response. In one study, Crowne and Marlowe had the real subject listen to a tape recording of knocks on a table and then report his or her judgment of the number of knocks. Each subject was led to believe that he or she was the fourth participant. To create this illusion, the experimenter played for the subject the tape-recorded responses of three prior participants to each series of knocks that was to be judged. The earlier three participants were the confederates, and they all gave an incorrect response in 12 of 18 trials. It was therefore possible to count the number of times out of 12 that the real subject yielded to the wrong but unanimous majority. The results were consistent with Crowne and Marlowe's hypothesis that the approval-motivated person is conforming: The subjects who had scored higher in the need for social approval went along with the majority judgment more than did the subjects who scored lower in the need for social approval.

Many additional studies were performed by these and other investigators (e.g., Allaman, Joyce, & Crandall, 1972; Crowne, 1979; Crowne & Marlowe, 1964; Paulhus, 1991; Weinberger, 1990), and some of the follow-up studies produced different results. In current usage, the word *need* in Crowne and Marlowe's *approval need* construct is no longer fashionable (Paulhus, 1991), and researchers have also suggested relabeling the construct *evaluative dependence* (Millham & Jacobson, 1978) or simply calling it *approval motivation* (Strickland, 1977). These

---

BOX 6.7   The Marlowe-Crowne Scale

If you would like to see the final form of the MCSD, you will find it in Robinson et al.'s *Measures of Personality and Social Psychological Attitudes* (1991) (along with commentary by D. L. Paulhus on related measures). The respondent reads each statement and decides whether it is true or false as it pertains to the person himself or herself. In about half the items, a "true" answer reflects the socially desirable response (i.e., the higher need for approval), and in the remainder, a "false" answer reflects this type of response. An example of the former type of item is "I have never intensely disliked anyone," whereas an example of the latter type is "I sometimes feel resentful when I don't get my way."

---

developments are consistent with the course of any successful research program, in which researchers build on, and attempt to improve our understanding of, the earlier seminal work. However, the main point of this example is to pull together some of the ideas that we have discussed in this chapter and to illustrate a systematic approach to construct validity. (See also Box 6.7.)

Validity and Causal Inference in Experimental Design

External validity and construct validity are of major interest to experimenters; two other types of validity that are of great interest to experimenters are statistical-conclusion and internal validity (Shadish et al., 2002). Construct validity is concerned with the conceptualization of variables. In research in which causal generalizations are the primary objective, **construct validity** refers to the validity of the hypothetical idea linking the independent (X) and dependent (Y) variables, but it also refers to the conceptualization of X and Y. An illustration was Latané and Darley's (1968, 1970) experiments (in Chapter 2) using the concept of "diffusion of responsibility" to explain why the more witnesses there are to an emergency (X), the less likely it is that any one of them will offer help (Y). Among the more common threats to construct validity are vagueness in defining or operationalizing the concepts or variables of interest. For example, what precisely is meant by "diffusion of responsibility," "witnesses," and an "emergency"? In the case of the idea of diffusion of responsibility, another question would be how well conceptualized this "theoretical scaffolding" between X and Y is (Cronbach & Meehl, 1955).

While in the past some leading psychologists have claimed that it is quite possible to do research without using constructs, Shadish et al. (2002) argued that it is a logical impossibility for three reasons. First, researchers need constructs to connect the operations they use in their studies to pertinent theory and to the way that causal generalization will be used in practice. Not using constructs to connect operations is like speaking in gobbledygook, that is, without any substance or meaning that makes sense to anyone. Second, constructs shape our perceptions and, because they also invariably have rich connotations, invite discourse and debate that stimulate further ideas for operationalizing and measuring these constructs. Third, the "creation and defense of basic constructs" is the very essence of what science is about (Shadish et al., 2002, p. 65). In chemistry, the periodic table is a basic construct; in physics, the atom is another basic construct; and in psychology, there are countless constructs that are considered essential (the *self,* the *body, groups, society, culture, environment, evolution,* and on and on). Indeed, the very idea of a *construct* is itself a basic construct in our thinking, and that we can talk about it in a meaningful way is further evidence of the validity of Shadish et al.'s argument.

Another major application of validity in research is called **statistical-conclusion validity** because it refers to whether certain statistical conclusions are well grounded, such as conclusions about the size of the effect (i.e., the correlation between treatment and outcome, or between the independent variable and the dependent variable) or conclusions about its statistical significance (Shadish et al., 2002). For example, when a statement is made about a correlation, the question pertaining to statistical-conclusion validity is whether there is a likely relationship between two variables or whether some observed statistical association is merely due to chance fluctuations. When experimenters are interested in making a causal inference (i.e., that X causes Y), they first need to show that the presumed cause and the presumed effect actually occur together (an effect called *covariation*). A "real" causal relationship may be occurring, but the statistical circumstances may not be conducive to observing (or "detecting") it at the given level of significance (more about this topic in later chapters).

The final type of validity in experimental research, **internal validity,** is concerned with ruling out **plausible rival hypotheses.** As defined by Shadish et al. (2002), internal validity refers specifically to whether observed covariation between X and Y actually reflects a causal relationship from X to Y. There are a number of threats to internal validity, some of which we will discuss in the following chapter. To anticipate, suppose a team of students (one male student and one female student) decide to conduct an experiment on verbal learning. Their particular interest is in the causal effect of stress, in the form of loud noise, on the learning of certain prose material. In order to divide the work fairly, the students flip a coin to determine which of them will run the participants in the stress condition and which of them will run those in the no-stress condition. The problem is that, even if they find the hypothesized relationship, they cannot ascribe it to the experimental stress, because there are plausible rival hypotheses. One rival hypothesis would be that the results are merely due to experimenter differences (e.g., personality and gender differences). This rival hypothesis could have been ruled out if each of the students had run half the participants in the stress condition and half the participants in the no-stress condition. Such a design would prevent the *confounding* (or intermixing) of the effects of stress and the effects of plausible experimenter differences and, in turn, strengthen the internal validity of the argument.

If you are confused about the difference between internal validity and construct validity, one way to separate them in your mind is to remember that *ruling*

BOX 6.8 Being Wrong Versus Being in a Weak Position

Judith A. Hall (1984), whose intuitive ideas about what makes a good researcher were discussed in Chapter 1, has also proposed a good intuitive distinction between four kinds of validity in experimental research. When either construct or internal validity is poor, researchers may be actively misled because they are at risk of making causal inferences that are plain "wrong." When statistical-conclusion or external validity are poor, researchers are at risk of being in a "weak position" to make *any* causal inferences or sweeping conclusions because limits are imposed on what can be learned or what can be generalized to other situations.

out plausible rival hypotheses is the essential characteristic of internal validity. That is, internal validity concerns whether we can logically rule out competing explanations for the observed covariation between the presumed independent variable (X) and the presumed effect of X on the dependent variable (Y). Construct validity, on the other hand, concerns the validity of the theoretical concepts we use in our measurements and causal explanations. Whenever you ask what is *really* being measured (e.g, "What does this test really measure?") or what is *really* being investigated (e.g., "What is this experiment really investigating?"), you are asking about construct validity rather than about internal validity. Stated still another way, construct validity concerns whether the concepts being measured or manipulated are properly identified (i.e., do we have a clear conception of what we are measuring or manipulating?), and internal validity concerns whether a variable other than X (the causal variable we *think* we are studying) may have caused Y to occur (see also Box 6.8.)

Summary of Ideas

1. Generally speaking, *validity* refers to the degree to which something does (or is) what it claims to do (or to be), whereas *reliability* refers to consistency, stability, or dependability.
2. All measurements are subject to random errors (also called *noise*), which are presumed to cancel out, on the average, over many repeated measurements. By contrast, systematic error (called *bias*) pushes measurements in one direction.
3. According to the logic of classical test theory, observed (raw) scores comprise the true scores and their random errors of measurement (Box 6.1).
4. Test-retest reliability (a measure of *stability*) is the correlation between scores on a test given to the same people on two different occasions; alternate-form reliability (a measure of *equivalence*) is the correlation between scores on different forms of the same test given to the same people at approximately the same time.

5. Internal-consistency reliability is the overall degree of relatedness of the components of a test (also called *reliability of components*) or a group of judges. One way to measure it is to use the Spearman-Brown formula, which is based on the average item-to-item or judge-to-judge correlation and the number of items or judges. Other common measures of internal consistency are K-R 20 and Cronbach's alpha (Box 6.3), which (along with the Spearman-Brown procedure) give similar results when the item variances are equal.

6. The degree of reliability of widely used tests (e.g., the MMPI, the Rorschach, and the WAIS) provides standards by which to assess what convention specifies as acceptable reliability.

7. External validity, one of four major types of validity in causal inference based on empirical research, is the dependability of causal generalizations across persons, settings, and treatment and outcome variations.

8. To say that a replication attempt was successful generally implies that the research procedure was modeled on the original study, the overall pattern of results was similar, and the effect sizes (i.e., the correlation between the independent variable, X, and the dependent variable, Y) of the studies were fairly similar.

9. Validity in test development usually means accumulating evidence in three categories: (a) content-related validity, (b) criterion-related validity (e.g., predictive, concurrent), and (3) construct validity (based, for example, on convergent and discriminant validity, as illustrated by Crowne and Marlowe's validation of the construct of "approval need" and the test they created to measure it).

10. Besides external validity and construct validity, two other major types of validity of interest to experimenters are statistical-conclusion validity (whether certain statistical conclusions are well grounded, such as the effect size and the p value) and internal validity (whether plausible rival hypotheses can be logically ruled out).

Key Terms

alpha coefficient   p. 146
alternate-form reliability   p. 145
bias   p. 141
concurrent validity   p. 156
construct validity   pp. 157, 160
content validity   p. 154
convergent validity   p. 157
correlation coefficient   p. 144
criterion validity   p. 155
Cronbach's alpha   p. 146
discriminant validity   p. 157
effect size   p. 153
external validity   p. 152
face validity   p. 155

internal-consistency
   reliability   p. 145
internal validity   p. 161
item-to-item reliability (r_{ii})
   p. 147
judge-to-judge reliability (r_{jj})
   p. 149
K-R 20   p. 146
Marlowe-Crowne Social Desirability Scale (MCSD)   p. 158
need for social approval   p. 158
plausible rival hypotheses
   p. 161
predictive validity   p. 156

random error   p. 141
reliability   p. 140
reliability of components   p. 146
replication   p. 152
Spearman-Brown prophecy
   formula   p. 147
statistical-conclusion
   validity   p. 161
systematic error   p. 141
test-retest reliability   p. 143
validity   p. 139
Wechsler Adult Intelligence
   Scale (WAIS)   p. 148

WEB ACTIVITY

Learn more about measurement and validity by clicking on the relevant links at Professor William M. K. Trochim's http://www.trochim.human.cornell.edu/tutorial/TUTORIAL.HTM.

Multiple-Choice Questions for Review

1. Random error is error that (a) isn't worth worrying about; (b) is always in the same direction; (c) has an average of about zero; (d) is also known as *bias*.

2. Broadly speaking, _____ refers to the consistency or stability of measurement: (a) validity; (b) modulation; (c) reliability; (d) invalidity

3. A researcher at Wheelock College administers a test of chronic anxiety. One month later, she administers the same questionnaire and finds that scores on the two administrations of the test correlate highly ($r = .85$). This outcome demonstrates the _____ of the test. (a) internal validity; (b) internal-consistency reliability; (c) external validity; (d) test-retest reliability

4. A researcher at Roosevelt University constructs a five-item measure of attitudes toward national health insurance. The average intercorrelation among the items is $r_{ii} = .40$. Using the Spearman-Brown equation, he calculates that $R^{SB} = .77$. This researcher has calculated the _____ of the attitude scale. (a) internal validity; (b) internal-consistency reliability; (c) test-retest reliability; (d) convergent validity

5. In the question above, in which the researcher determined that $R^{SB} = .77$, what is the reliability of the scale as a whole? (a) .77; (b) .50; (c) .40; (d) cannot be determined from the information given

6. One intelligence test has two separate forms. Both measure intelligence, but they contain different questions. Scores of Eastern University students on Form A correlate highly with their scores on Form B ($r_{AB} = .92$). This correlation demonstrates the _____ reliability of the test. (a) internal consistency; (b) external consistency; (c) test-retest; (d) alternate-form

7. In determining whether or not one study replicates the results of another, scientists often examine _____, which are statistics that reflect the magnitude of the relationship between X and Y. (a) significance levels; (b) alpha coefficients; (c) effect sizes; (d) data on the manipulation checks

8. "A test should correlate with theoretically related external variables; for example, the SAT should correlate with grade point average." This statement defines _____ validity. (a) statistical-conclusion; (b) content; (c) consistency; (d) criterion

9. A test should not correlate with variables from which it is theoretically distinct." This statement defines _____ validity. (a) convergent; (b) content; (c) discriminant; (d) criterion

10. The generalizability of the causal results of a study is referred to as the _____ of the study. (a) internal validity; (b) external validity; (c) construct validity; (d) discriminant validity

Discussion Questions for Review

1. An Emory University student is trying to make her mark in the field of psychology by developing a new scale measuring fear of public speaking. How might she assess her scale's predictive and construct validity?

2. On a quiz, a University of Lethbridge student is asked how we know that the Marlowe-Crowne scale (MCSD) measures need for social approval. What is the answer?

3. A University of Houston student has piloted his observational study using two judges and has found a moderate judge-to-judge reliability ($r_{jj} = .50$). Because he wants to achieve a higher reliability coefficient, he is distressed by the prospect of having to modify his coding criteria and training procedures. Another student suggests, "Don't bother with all that. Simply add two more judges to improve the reliability." Would you consider the second student's advice sound?

4. A Pennsylvania State University researcher wants to study the effects of the texture of toys on the frequency with which toddlers touch them. She uses the following toys: a brown teddy bear, a

smooth blue plastic ball, a green wooden cube, and an orange corduroy-covered rattle. She finds that male toddlers are more likely to touch the ball and the cube than the teddy bear and the rattle, whereas female toddlers are more likely to touch the teddy bear and the rattle than the other two toys. When she reports the results, a member of the audience raises the possibility that male toddlers must therefore prefer hard, less variegated textures to soft, more variegated textures, whereas female toddlers show the reverse preference. What is one rival hypothesis that would also be consistent with the researcher's results? How might the rival hypothesis be ruled out?

5. A Northeastern University researcher wants to build a 20-item test to measure need for power. She assigns several students to use the Spearman-Brown formula to measure the internal-consistency reliability of her new test from data recently collected from a large sample. They tell her that R^{SB} = .50 and that the mean interitem reliability (r_{ii}) equals .40. She asks them to check their work. Why?

6. A student at the State University of New York at Binghamton is interested in assessing a new 20-item scale of optimism-pessimism. How should she assess the reliability of this scale? The student is also advised by her instructor to measure several different traits using several different methods to demonstrate empirically the convergent and discriminant validity of the new scale. Why did the instructor give this advice?

7. A student at Bridgewater State College weighs a 10-pound object 5 times and obtains readings on the scale of 14, 8, 7, 10, and 11 pounds. Describe the systematic error and the random errors characterizing the scale's performance.

Answers to Review Questions

Multiple-Choice Questions

1. c	**3.** d	**5.** a	**7.** c	**9.** c
2. c	**4.** b	**6.** d	**8.** d	**10.** b

Discussion Questions

1. By showing that her scale correlates substantially with future symptoms of fear when people are asked to speak in public (predictive and convergent validity). In addition, the new scale should not correlate substantially with such less relevant variables as height, spatial relations abilities, and political party preference (discriminant validity). Convergent and discriminant validity are aspects of construct validity.

2. Because it correlates highly with behaviors defined as reflecting high need for social approval, but not as highly with behaviors not reflecting high need for approval.

3. Yes, because a total of four judges will yield an internal-consistency reliability of .80 when the typical judge-to-judge reliability is .50 (see Table 6.3).

4. Perhaps female toddlers prefer more complex shapes than do male toddlers. A new study might add four new stimuli: a smooth, hard teddy bear and rattle, and a soft, fuzzy ball and cube. If the plausible rival hypothesis is correct, female toddlers will prefer the new smooth, hard teddy bear and rattle to the new fuzzy ball and cube. Considering all eight stimuli, then, female toddlers will prefer the four complexly shaped stimuli, whereas male toddlers will prefer the four simply shaped stimuli if the rival hypothesis is accurate. Still another rival hypothesis is that color differences in the toys determine the frequencies with which toddlers touch them. To address this alternative, similar toys would have to be created in different colors, such as wooden cubes that are brown, blue, green, and orange but are identical in all other respects.

5. Because Table 6.3 shows that, for 20 items, a mean item-to-item reliability of .40 is associated with internal-consistency reliability of .93, not .50.

6. The test-retest reliability can be computed by administering the test twice to the same people (for example, 4 weeks apart) and computing the correlation between the two administrations. The internal-consistency reliability can be computed by correlating all the items with each other and then applying the Spearman-Brown formula to the average intercorrelation of the items (or using Table 6.3) to get the overall internal-consistency reliability. The reason for administering several different measures is that the student could show convergent validity with the measures with which his new scale should correlate substantially and discriminant validity with the measures with which his new scale should not correlate substantially.

7. There is no systematic error because the average reading is accurate (10 pounds). The random errors are +4, −2, −3, 0, and +1 on the five readings, or errors of +40%, −20%, −30%, 0%, and +10%, respectively, a not very precise performance.

CHAPTER 7

Randomized Experiments and Causal Inference

Preview Questions

- What is the purpose of randomly assigning the sampling units, and how is it done?

- What are between-subjects and within-subjects randomized designs?

- Why is causation said to be "shrouded in mystery, controversy, and caution"?

- What three criteria do scientists use to justify causal inferences?

- What can the Solomon design teach us about control group design?

- What is characteristic of "preexperimental designs"?

- How are history, maturation, instrumentation, and selection threats to internal validity?

- What do demand characteristics have to do with the "good subject" and quasi-control subjects?

- How are experimenter expectancy effects addressed by "blind" designs and expectancy control designs?

The Framework of This Chapter

Now that you have an understanding of some general methods of data collection, we turn to the design of your research. One design option, which is the focus of this chapter, may be to conduct a randomized experiment. This chapter will give you a sense of the wide variety of randomized experimental designs and the logic of drawing causal inferences when employing such designs. For students who have had a course in psychological statistics, we will also briefly mention what statistical procedures are typically used to analyze these designs. However, if you have not taken a statistics course or can hardly remember the difference between t and F, you can think of these brief previews as an introduction to procedures explained in more detail later in this book. In the preceding chapter, we discussed the difference between random and systematic errors, and this chapter concludes with a discussion of sources of systematic error that can produce *artifacts* in the research (and are not limited to randomized experiments).

As you learned in the preceding chapters, the term *experiment* is used in different ways in science. In Chapter 1, we mentioned the classic demonstration experiments of Galileo, Newton, and Foucault in physics. Psychologists may also do nonrandomized demonstration experiments, for example, classic demonstrations in social psychology of how information is distorted when a message is passed from one person to another without the opportunity for feedback and correction (Allport & Postman, 1947) or, in Gestalt psychology, of how people presented with incomplete perceptual images have a mental tendency to fill in the cognitive gaps (Koffka, 1935; Köhler, 1929). In medical research, common variants are laboratory experiments that use animals to test the effects of suspected carcinogens, such as administering saccharin to mice to see whether it causes cancer. If you have taken a course in chemistry, you know that studies in the laboratory often consist of mixing reagents in test tubes to produce predicted reactions. In behavioral and social research, still other variants are *single-case experiments* (discussed in the next chapter), such as those performed in an area of research called the *experimental analysis of behavior*. A single-case experiment might involve shaping (controlling) the responses of a rat that receives reinforcement in the form of a food pellet, or shaping the responses of a person or a small group by manipulating an important situational contingency.

Randomized experiments, on the other hand, are those kinds of experiments in which the participants have been randomly assigned to one or another group or condition. In the sample report in this book, Jane Doe's experiment takes this form, or what she described in her proposal (in Chapter 2) as a "simple randomized design in which the research participants are assigned to one of two conditions." In medical science, randomized experiments in the field are described as the "gold standard" of research, such as investigating the effects of a new drug in a "clinical trial" (which is another name for this sort of randomized experiment). Typically, the participants in a clinical trial are randomly assigned to receive either the new drug or a **placebo** (i.e., a substance without any pharmacological benefit that is given as a pseudomedicine to a control group). This is not to say that randomized clinical trials are without flaws or limitations, however. Just as the value of gold can fluctuate, randomized experiments also fluctuate with respect to their potential value (see Box 7.1). Furthermore, although randomized experiments are often referred to as "true experiments" in psychological research (a term originally suggested by Campbell & Stanley, 1963), the other examples above remind us that "scientific truths" have also been established in experiments without random assignment (D. B. Rubin, 1974). Suppose we wanted to study the effects of high dietary cholesterol on human longevity. It would be an ethical absurdity to think that we can randomly assign people to a high-cholesterol diet in order to see how many more will die than those assigned to a low-cholesterol diet. One research option, discussed in the next chapter, is to do a longitudinal study, such as those done by epidemiologists, who observe groups of people (called *cohorts*) for many years to identify conditions that are associated with illness.

BOX 7.1 Imperfect Experiments

Judea Pearl (2000), a professor of computer science and statistics at the University of California, Los Angeles, noted three ways in which randomized clinical trials may be marred. First, perfect control is often hard to achieve because subjects who experience adverse reactions to an experimental drug may decide to reduce their assigned dosage, or if they suspect they are in a placebo control group, they may try to obtain the experimental drug on their own from other sources. Second, assigning people with a terminal illness to a placebo group has moral and legal ramifications, as they are being denied access to a potentially lifesaving drug or experimental treatment. As we mentioned in Chapter 3, one option in many cases is to give the control group the best available treatment, so the comparison is between the experimental drug or treatment and the best available alternative. Third, merely knowing that randomization is being used may make some people wary of volunteering and could thus jeopardize the generalizability of the results if volunteers and nonvolunteers would respond differently to the treatment (discussed in Chapter 9).

Though you will read about how various randomized designs are typically analyzed, it is also important to keep in mind that it is not just the research design that determines the statistical procedure you should use to analyze your results. Your statistical procedures should always be guided by your hypotheses or questions of interest. The design is the blueprint for your data collection and is a way of ensuring that the data you collect will be logically connected to a particular conceptualization in your mind. After you have gone to the considerable effort of developing specific hypotheses and questions, it would be foolish to ignore them. For example, suppose your hypothesis called for three levels of some variable of interest (e.g., three levels of arousal), and say you predicted better performance on the dependent variable in the middle level than in the two extreme levels. What you want to know is not whether there were "some differences" among these three groups (i.e., the question that would be addressed by an overall F test on all three groups), but whether the middle group actually performed better on the dependent variable than the other two groups. Later in this book, we will show how such an analysis can be done with a t or F test that is specifically focused on the "curvilinear" relation between group membership and performance.

After outlining some basic randomized experimental designs and defining a number of pertinent terms, we will turn once more to the idea of causal inference and causal generalization in science. In the previous chapter, we explained the concept of *internal validity*, which has to do with bias within experiments, and ruling out plausible alternative hypotheses for the presumed causal relation. We also explained the concept of *external validity*, which has to do with causal generalizability. Although there are circumstances in which a researcher may be interested only in evaluating a particular experimental result in the here and now, and not in making any causal generalizations beyond that limited situation, for the most part researchers are usually interested in generalizing to a population of some kind or to other settings and other treatment variations. Later in this chapter, we will discuss some further limitations on internal validity. However, we first examine the challenging idea of *causality* and how controlled experiments are used to tease out a particular kind of causal relation. Although the idea of causality continues to be a source of discussion and debate in philosophy of science, most researchers (if they think about it at all) think of the justification of causality in terms of certain general criteria (described in this chapter).

Random Assignment and Matching of Sampling Units

There are traditionally three reasons for using **random assignment** (also called **randomization**). One is that, as conceived by the statisticians who invented it, random assignment provides a safeguard against the possibility of experimenters' subconsciously letting their opinions and preferences influence which of the sampling units will receive any given treatment (Gigerenzer et al., 1989). The term **sampling units** is a general way of referring to the participants, subjects, groups, or objects being studied (i.e., the units sampled from the population), though these units might also be animals, schools, countries, or agricultural crops. The term **treatment** is simply another name for the manipulated variable. For example, in a clinical trial, the treatment might be a new drug, which the subjects (the sampling units) in the experimental group (the treatment group) receive and the subjects in the control group do not receive.

A second reason, which is the one that most experimenters would give, is that random assignment distributes the characteristics of the sampling units over the treatment and control conditions in a way that will not bias the outcome of the experiment (Kirk, 2000). There is no absolute guarantee, however, for it is always possible (especially when sample sizes are small) that some characteristic related to the dependent variable will occur more frequently in one group than in another. For example, suppose there are two conditions (a treatment and a control group) with only five people in each, and that two subjects who are unusually tense also happen to end up in the treatment group (rather than one ending up in the treatment group and the other in the control group). If tenseness were a plausible confounding variable in the experiment, it might also be a suspected threat to the internal validity of the study. Random assignment does not guarantee equality in the characteristics of the sampling units assigned to different conditions, but the idea is to give each unit an equal chance of being assigned to any condition.

The third reason, which is also the one that psychological statisticians and textbooks in statistics underscore, is that random assignment permits the computation of statistics that require certain characteristics of the data (Kirk, 1995, 2000; Maxwell & Delaney, 2000). In particular, it provides a mechanism to derive probabilistic properties (*p* values) of estimates based on the data by controlling for extraneous variables (D. B. Rubin, 1974). To be sure, randomized experiments are not the only method that can be used to control for extraneous variables. Another procedure is **matching,** in which the sampling units are matched either before initiation of the treatment or, if there is a large enough number of sampling units, after the experiment has been completed. To do this effectively, the experimenter must think carefully about threats to internal validity, that is, about plausible variables or conditions besides the experimental treatment that might conceivably causally affect scores on the dependent variable (see also Box 7.2).

Experimenters use a variety of procedures to achieve random assignment. Imagine an experimental design with two conditions (a treatment and a control condition), and each condition is presented in the form of a booklet or questionnaire. One convenient procedure presorts the booklets into pairs so that each pair contains a treatment booklet (or questionnaire) and a control booklet (or questionnaire). The first person receives Booklet A or B (by a flip of a coin), and the next person receives the other booklet. For the next two participants this random procedure is repeated, so that the experimenter ends up with an equal number of subjects in each of the treatment conditions. Or the experimenter can arrange the stimulus materials so that, of every four or six or eight booklets, half will be As and

BOX 7.2 Matching on Propensity Scores

Matching the sampling units requires that we have accurate data on the characteristics on which we want to match them. One procedure that has captured the imagination of researchers in the social and biomedical sciences, as well as the statistical community, is the use of a particular method of subclassification based on what are called *propensity scores* (P. R. Rosenbaum & Rubin, 1983; D. B. Rubin, 1973; Rubin & Thomas, 1996). Suppose, in a nonexperimental investigation, we were interested in comparing the mortality rates for nonsmokers, cigarette smokers, and cigar and pipe smokers in several different populations, but we think that age may be a confounding variable in the interpretation of a causal relationship. That is, age may be a plausible rival hypothesis to the hypothesis that smoking increases morbidity. In the propensity score procedure, the populations would be subdivided into age categories of approximately equal size, and the death rates would then be compared within these age categories. Although this is an example of relational research, a similar kind of reasoning is used for matching sampling units in experimental investigations. The basic idea of the propensity score procedure is to reduce all the characteristics on which the treated and the untreated participants differ into a single composite variable, and then to estimate the treatment effect by comparing the results in subclassifications of this composite variable.

half will be Bs (determined by coin flips). If the same experiment were being run on a computer, randomizing would be easier because the machine could be programmed to randomly assign the treatment conditions and could also tabulate the results.

Suppose that, instead of a booklet or a questionnaire, the subjects in one condition receive a new drug and the subjects in the second condition receive a placebo. An easy way to assign people in equal numbers to these two conditions is, first, to write each person's name on a slip of paper and then to "blindly" draw pairs of names. The experimenter flips a coin or consults a table of random numbers to decide which member of a pair will receive the new drug.

To illustrate, let us assume the experimenter wants to use a table of random numbers to assign 40 subjects at random to either an experimental or a control condition. You will find such a table on p. 227, from which the following 120 random digits were taken:

10097	32533	76520	13586	34673
37542	04805	64894	74296	24805
08422	68953	19645	09303	23209
99019	02529	09376	70715	38311
12807	99970	80157	36147	

The researcher decides to read across and down the first five-digit column (10097, 37542, 08422, 99019, 12807) and have the numbers 1, 3, 5, 7, 9 designate the participants to be randomly assigned to the experimental group (and 0, 2, 4, 6, 8 designate those in the control group). The researcher would assign Subject 1 to the experimental group (1), Subjects 2 and 3 to the control group (0, 0), Subjects 4 through 8 to the experimental group (9, 7, 3, 7, 5), Subjects 9 through 15 to the control group (4, 2, 0, 8, 4, 2, 2), Subjects 16 and 17 to the experimental group (9, 9), Subject 18 to the control group (0), Subjects 19 and 20 to the experimental group (1, 9), and so forth.

Some Basic Designs and Pertinent Terms

When the subjects are exposed to one condition each, this arrangement is known as a **between-subjects design.** For example, Jane Doe's experimental design may be described as a "two-group between-subjects design." The basic design is illustrated in Part A of Table 7.1, where we see that 5 subjects receive Condition A and 5 other subjects receive Condition B. Another statistical name for the between-subjects design is **nested design,** because the subjects are "nested" within their own groups or conditions. A popular way of analyzing the data from such two-condition between-subjects designs is to calculate a t test for independent samples (illustrated in Chapter 13).

However, suppose all the subjects receive both Condition A and Condition B. This basic design is illustrated in Part B of Table 7.1, where we see that all 10 sub-

Table 7.1	Examples of Between- and Within-Subjects Designs

A. Between-subjects design

Condition A	Condition B
Subject 1	Subject 2
Subject 3	Subject 4
Subject 5	Subject 6
Subject 7	Subject 8
Subject 9	Subject 10

B. Within-subjects design

Condition A	Condition B
Subject 1	Subject 1
Subject 2	Subject 2
Subject 3	Subject 3
Subject 4	Subject 4
Subject 5	Subject 5
Subject 6	Subject 6
Subject 7	Subject 7
Subject 8	Subject 8
Subject 9	Subject 9
Subject 10	Subject 10

jects receive A and then B. This arrangement is called a **within-subjects design;** the *t* test can again be used, but this time the research design calls for a *t* test for nonindependent samples (illustrated in Chapter 13). Because the subjects' reactions are measured after each condition, this is also called a **repeated measures design.** Another name for a basic within-subjects design is **crossed design,** because the subjects are thought of as "crossed" by conditions (i.e., observed under two or more conditions) rather than nested within them.

Between- and within-subjects designs are not simply limited to two groups or conditions, however. For example, suppose an experimenter who is interested in the effects of nutrition on academic performance decides to randomly assign children to one of four different conditions in a between-subjects design. One condition will receive a hot lunch daily, another condition will get free milk, a third condition will get a vitamin supplement, and the fourth will get nothing (it will serve as an untreated control, or "zero control" condition). In a later chapter, we will discuss the statistical analysis of this very study with hypothetical data. Although there are several ways of analyzing it, if we had a specific hypothesis, we would want to compute a contrast *t* or contrast *F* (as illustrated in Chapter 14). Still another name for this type of design is a "one-factor" or "one-way" between-subjects design, where the term *factor* is simply a general name for the variable of interest.

In within-subjects designs with repeated treatments and measurements, a problem is that the *order* in which the treatments are administered to the same subjects may be **confounded** with the treatment effect. Suppose the treatment conditions are administered to young children who are immediately measured after each treatment (i.e., in a repeated-measures design). The children may be nervous when first measured, and they may perform poorly. Later on, they may be less nervous, and they may perform better. To address the problem of systematic differences between successive treatments (or measurements), the experimenter would use **counterbalancing,** which means rotating the sequences. In other words, some children would randomly receive Condition A before Condition B, and the others would randomly receive B before A (see also Box 7.3).

It is also possible to have designs with more than one factor. For example, suppose that women and men were randomly assigned to either a drug or a placebo group. We now have a two-factor design with two *levels* of the factor of gender (women vs. men) and two levels of the manipulated factor (drug vs. placebo). This arrangement, called a **factorial design,** is represented in Table 7.2. When there are two levels of each of two factors, we describe the arrangement as a

---

BOX 7.3 Latin Square Designs

A specific statistical design that has counterbalancing built in is called the **Latin square design.** It is characterized by a square array of letters (representing the treatment conditions) in which each letter appears once and only once in each row and in each column. Illustrated below is a Latin square representing a case in which four treatments (A, B, C, and D) will be administered to all the subjects in a counterbalanced pattern:

	Order of administration			
	1	2	3	4
Sequence 1	A	B	C	D
Sequence 2	B	C	D	A
Sequence 3	C	D	A	B
Sequence 4	D	A	B	C

The subjects randomly assigned to Sequence 1 receive the treatments in the sequence A, then B, then C, and finally D. In Sequences 2 through 4, the treatments are administered in different sequences, BCDA, CDAB, and DABC, respectively. In Chapter 14, we use hypothetical data to illustrate the analysis of this type of design by the *F* statistic. You will also find more detailed discussions of Latin square designs in Keppel (1991), Kirk (1995), Maxwell and Delaney (2000), and Rosenthal and Rosnow (1991).

Table 7.2	Two-by-Two Factorial Design	
	Manipulated conditions	
Gender	Drug	Placebo
Women	A	B
Men	C	D

"2 × 2 factorial design" (where "2 × 2" is read as "two by two") or "2^2 factorial design." When analyzing this sort of design, we also have several options (discussed in Chapter 14), depending on the hypotheses or questions of interest to us. We can, for example, compute a 2 × 2 analysis of variance (ANOVA), in which we analyze (a) the between-group variation of women versus men (the two levels of the *row factor* in Table 7.2), (b) the between-group variation of the drug versus the placebo (the two levels of the *column factor* in Table 7.2), and (c) the interaction of these two factors (i.e., the interaction of the two levels of the row factor with the two levels of the column factor).

There are also combinations of these design formats, as well as more complex designs. For example, we could have a two-factor design in which one factor was between subjects and the other was within subjects (called a *mixed factorial design*). We could also have a randomized design with more than two factors and more than two levels within each factor, although it might be stretching the number of subjects rather thinly. For example, if all we had to work with were 24 sampling units, in a two-group between-subjects design with equal sample sizes, there would be 12 subjects in each group. But if we had a 3 × 4 factorial design and only the same number of units, there would be 12 conditions and 2 units in each condition. Suppose we had a randomized factorial design with three between-subjects factors (A, B, and C) and two levels of each factor. We now have eight pertinent sources of variation to look into: (a) between levels of Factor A; (b) between levels of Factor B; (c) between levels of Factor C; (d) interaction of levels of Factor A with levels of Factor B; (e) interaction of levels of Factor A with levels of Factor C; (f) interaction of levels of Factor B with levels of Factor C; and (g) interaction of all three factors. One final point is that, though we have mentioned only *t* and *F* tests, a data analysis would be incomplete without reporting the sizes of the effects, when appropriate, and interval estimates for these effect sizes (more about this later in this book).

Four Kinds of Causation

You know that the purpose of scientific experiments is to show "what causes what," and before going any further in this chapter, it is important that you understand what scientists usually mean by *causation*. This is not an easy concept to define precisely, even though it is basic to behavior and human thought. As one author put it, "Causality is a notion shrouded in mystery, controversy, and caution, because scientists and philosophers have had difficulties defining when one event *truly causes* another" (Pearl, 2000, p. 331). To illustrate, imagine the flight of a curve ball thrown by a pitcher at a baseball game. The batter swings and misses, and we ask ourselves, "What *caused* the ball to break that way?" This is a question also pondered by Isaac Newton—not about baseballs, but about tennis balls. When we think carefully about questions of causation (such as this one), we begin to see that they have more than a single answer. Indeed, more than 2,300 years ago, Aristotle thought carefully about questions of causation (but it was not baseballs or tennis balls that stimulated his interest) and came to realize that they can be answered in four distinct ways.

One answer concerns what Aristotle called the **material cause,** by which he meant the substance or substances that are necessary for the movement or coming into being of the effect. According to the physics of baseball (R. K. Adair, 1990), the roughness on the surface of the ball and the nature of fluid flow constitute the material cause of the ball's unusual movement—and make it hard to hit. A ball with a smooth surface would tend to have a smooth flight, especially if it passes through air at a speed of less than 50 miles per hour. A ball with rough seams that travels at a speed over 50 miles per hour begins to encounter turbulence, particularly when it is thrown in a special way to take advantage of the nature of airflow.

The second answer concerns what Aristotle called the **formal cause,** which is the plan or development that gives meaning to the event. In this instance the idea of throwing a curve ball is formally initiated in the mind of the catcher, who then communicates the plan to the pitcher, who in turn thinks "curve ball" up to the moment the ball is released.

The third answer, Aristotle termed the **final cause** (also called *teleological,* which means the action is "goal-directed") because it refers to the objective or end purpose of the event. In this case, it is the objective of having a ball "break" as it nears the plate, so that the batter will not be able to hit the pitch squarely. Aristotle was particularly fond of the teleological way of thinking about causality, because it explained causality in terms of a *purpose* for an observed action or event.

And finally, the fourth answer is the **efficient cause,** or the activating force or event that was responsible for the effect. In the baseball example, the efficient cause is the actual throwing of the ball, which causes it to travel at an optimal velocity and causes its trajectory to deviate from the original horizontal direction of motion.

How may we translate these four "causes" in the case of human behaviors? For human development, for instance, we may say that (a) cellular structure is the material cause (i.e., the "stuff" of development); (b) DNA or genetics is the formal cause (i.e., the biological blueprint); (c) physiological maturation is the final cause (i.e., the end "purpose" or goal); and (d) parenting as an environmental variable is the efficient (i.e., activating or instigating) cause. All four kinds of Aristotelian causation are of interest to different behavioral and social scientists. However, it is the fourth cause, in particular, that experimenting scientists frequently have in mind when they theorize that manipulated treatment "produces an effect" (i.e., *causes* something else to occur).

Three Criteria of Efficient Causation

How do scientists actually arrive at the conclusion that something produces an effect or that one thing causes something else to occur, for example, that "taking a pill will lower your cholesterol" or that "hearing the same message over and over will make it seem more believable" or the idea that "frustration often causes aggression to occur"? The answer to this question goes back to the great 18th-century Scottish philosopher David Hume, who wrestled with the idea of causality and ultimately concluded that, although it is a learned habit of thinking about things, there are certain "rules" we can use to judge causes and effects (Hume, 1739–1740). In current thinking, the rules he conceived have been boiled down to three essential criteria: covariation, temporal precedence, and internal validity (see also Box 7.4).

First, we look for evidence that the independent variable (X) and the dependent variable (Y) are mutually related (or "covary"). That is, we ask whether the presence (and absence) of X (the presumed cause) is actually associated with the presence (and absence) of Y (the presumed effect). If we do indeed find that X and Y show a satisfactory correlation, we have evidence of **covariation.** What constitutes a "satisfactory correlation"? There is no simple answer to this question, because it depends on the nature of X and Y. If I push you, and you fall down, it seems clear that there is a high degree of association between my pushing you (X) and your falling (Y). If we are talking about taking a particular pill to lower cholesterol, the degree of correlation may be relatively small and yet still be considered a

BOX 7.4 Hume's "Rules"

In his classic work entitled *A Treatise of Human Nature,* David Hume (1739–1740, pp. 173–175) listed eight "rules by which to judge causes and effects." They include the assumption that "the cause and effect must be contiguous in space and time," and also that "there must be a constant union betwixt the cause and effect" (i.e., what we now call *covariation*). What we call *temporal precedence*, he stated as "the cause must be prior to the effect." Hume went on to explain how the perception of causation can be understood as the mere product of observations of contiguous events that occur in a certain temporal sequence. Causation is in the mind's eye, he thought, or as Pearl (2000, p. 336) put it, for Hume the idea of a causal connection was "a learnable habit of the mind, almost as fictional as optical illusions and as transitory as Pavlov's conditioning" (p. 336). Many cognitive neuroscientists today would probably argue that we are "prewired" by the evolution of human nature to perceive causal connections, for it is hard to imagine how we could hope to survive without causal inferences and causal generalizations, no matter whether they are mental and sociocultural constructions.

"satisfactory correlation" in a clinical trial if it is indeed meaningful. Later in this book, we will illustrate this idea with very small correlations between X and Y that are considered quite meaningful in medical research. Of course, although causation implies covariation (i.e., correlation), observing a correlation does not automatically imply causation.

Second, we also look for evidence that Y did not occur until after X occurred or was set in motion, a sequence referred to as **temporal precedence** among variables. Because a later event cannot be the cause of an earlier one, we are interested in whether there is clear-cut evidence that X actually came before Y. In relational research it is often hard to find incontrovertible evidence of temporal precedence, because we are looking at X and Y in retrospect (i.e., looking back at them). We will have more to say about this issue in the next chapter, but sometimes it can be argued on logical grounds, even retrospectively, that X must surely have come before Y. Say we have found satisfactory evidence of covariation between sex and height and now want to say which is the independent variable and which is the dependent variable. Common sense leads us to conclude that sex is more likely to determine height than height is to determine sex, as a person's sex is biologically established at conception.

Of course, temporal precedence and covariation alone cannot tell us whether an event is the cause of another event. For example, "the barometer falls before it rains yet does not cause the rain" (Pearl, 2000, p. 42). Thus, a third thing we look for is logical and evidential ways to rule out competing explanations of the causal relation between X and Y. In other words, we will try to rule out plausible rival hypotheses that may undermine our causal interpretation (i.e., we look for evidence of **internal validity**). None of us are clairvoyant, however, and therefore there is a human limit on how successful this effort can be. That is, we cannot realistically expect to anticipate all plausible rival hypotheses, because we cannot look into the future. Nevertheless, beginning with Donald T. Campbell and Julian C. Stanley's (1963) seminal work, followed by that of Thomas D. Cook and Campbell (1979), and more recently that of William R. Shadish, Cook, and Campbell (2002), psychological methodologists have compiled lists of the conditions that undermine the four types of validity in behavioral and social research described (in Chapter 6) as statistical-conclusion validity, internal validity, construct validity, and external validity.

The bottom line, however, is that working even within the limited framework of these three criteria (covariation, temporal precedence, and internal validity), scientists find they must settle for the most pertinent and compelling evidence *available* to define efficient causation, even if that evidence is inconclusive. Thus, causal inference (i.e., the act or process of inferring that X causes Y) is always subject to some degree of uncertainty. This uncertainty is not surprising, as we know that all ideas and methods are limited in some ways. In fact, some degree of uncertainty is a constant in science, just as it is in everyday life, and it makes clear causal inferences difficult in many situations. Nonetheless, the idea of controlled randomized experiments is that it should be possible to tease out patterns of causal relationships based on the logic of something known as *Mill's methods*.

Mill's Methods and the Logic of Experimental Control

Mill's methods is the name given to certain "logical methods" (or propositions) popularized by the 19th-century English philosopher John Stuart Mill. Two of these methods—agreement and difference—together provide the logical basis of causal inferences made in all two-group between-subjects randomized experiments.

First, the **method of agreement** states, "If X, then Y," X symbolizing the presumed cause and Y the presumed effect. The statement means that, if we find two or more instances in which Y occurs, and if only X is present on each occasion, it follows that X is a **sufficient condition** of Y. Calling X a sufficient condition means that it is *adequate* (i.e., capable or competent enough) to bring about the effect. Stated another way, an effect will be present when this sufficient cause is present. In baseball, we would say there are several sufficient conditions for getting the batter to first base, such as getting a hit (X_1), being walked by the pitcher (X_2), or being struck by a pitch (X_3).

Second, the **method of difference** states, "If not-X, then not-Y." The statement implies that if the presumed effect (Y) does not occur when the presumed cause (X) is absent, then X is a **necessary condition** of Y. Calling X a necessary condition means that it is *indispensable*; that is, X is absolutely essential to bring about the effect. Stated another way, the effect will be absent when the necessary cause is absent. To win in baseball (Y), since a tie is not possible, it is *necessary* to score more runs than the other team (X); not scoring any runs (not-X) will therefore result in not winning (not-Y).

To take these ideas one step further, suppose that X represents a new and highly touted tranquilizer, and Y represents a change in measured tension. We give people who complain of tension a certain dosage of X, and they show a reduction in measured tension. Can we conclude from this before-and-after observation that the tranquilizer caused the reduction in tension? Not yet, because even if we repeatedly find that giving X is followed by tension reduction, we imply only that X is a sufficient condition of Y. What we seem to need is a control group with which to compare the reaction in the first group. For our control group, we need a group of comparable individuals to whom we do not give drug X. If these people show no tension reduction, we have implied that X may be a necessary condition of Y.

We can diagram this simple randomized design as follows, and we see that it corresponds precisely to Mill's methods of agreement and difference:

Experimental group	**Control group**
If X, then Y	If not-X, then not-Y

Can we now conclude that taking the drug led to tension reduction? Yes, but with the stipulation that "taking the drug" implies something more than getting a chemical into the bloodstream. "Taking the drug" means among other things (a) having someone give the person a pill; (b) having someone give the person the attention that goes with pill giving; (c) having the person believe that relevant medication has been administered; and (d) having the ingredients of the drug find their way into the person's blood system.

Usually, when testing a drug in a randomized clinical trial, the researcher is interested only in the subjects' physical reactions to the active ingredients of the medication. The researcher does not care whether the subjects will feel better if they merely *believe* they are being helped, because this fact (i.e., the power of suggestion) has already been established. But if researchers know about the power of suggestion, how are they to separate the effects of the drug's ingredients from the effects of pill giving, of the subjects' expectations of being helped, and of other factors that may be sufficient conditions of *Y*? The answer is by the choice of a different (or additional) control group. So this time, we use not a group given nothing, but a group given something that differs only in lacking the ingredients whose effects we would like to know (i.e., a **placebo control group**). The general finding, incidentally, is that placebos are often effective and are sometimes even as effective as the far more expensive drug for which they serve as the control (see also Box 7.5).

In this research, we use a no-pill control group (i.e., a zero control group) and a group that received a placebo. Assuming there is often a choice of groups, how can we decide what design to use? If there are two groups, the groups should be as similar as possible except for the effect of interest. If the groups to be compared differ on some pertinent characteristic other than that effect, the influence of this characteristic (or factor) is said to be **confounded** (i.e., mixed up or confused) with the effect of interest. In settling on a randomized experimental design, the researcher tries to control for potentially confounding effects while isolating the effect of interest. Let us see how this done.

BOX 7.5 "I Shall Please"

The word *placebo* means in Latin "I shall please," and it is now widely recognized that **placebo effects** (i.e., the "healing" effects of inert substances or nonspecific treatments) are ubiquitous in clinical practice and research, including the healing effects of a placebo on angina, blood pressure, the common cold, cough, fever, panic disorder, headache, psoriasis, insomnia, pain, rheumatoid arthritis, the effects of vaccines, and warts (Turkkan & Brady, 2000). If people are told they are receiving a placebo, there is less of a placebo effect. Also, if they receive a real treatment but *believe* it to be a placebo, the treatment is usually less effective (White, Tursky, & Schwartz, 1985). Although expectations and the context of the situation play an important role in the placebo effect, the biobehavioral mechanism mediating the healing remains unexplained (but there is speculation that it might involve classical conditioning or interactions of the central nervous system with organ systems, e.g., Turkkan & Brady, 2000).

Teasing Out Effects

Suppose we were interested in studying whether giving children a lesson on the rules of correct spelling will improve their spelling ability. We can design an experiment in which we assign a group of children to either an experimental or a control group at random. We then teach those in the experimental group the rules of correct spelling and do not teach these rules to the children in the control group. Using the logic of Mill's methods, we then compare the mean scores of these two groups using an independent *t* test. As the groups are presumed to be similar in all pertinent characteristics except for the experimental treatment, any difference between them on the posttest must be due to the experimental treatment. This between-groups design can also be described as an "after-only" (or "posttest-only") design because no measurements were made before the experimental manipulation (i.e., there was no *pretesting* of the children).

However, suppose we are also interested in knowing how the children responded before they were randomly placed in those two groups, because we feel we need a "baseline" to tell us exactly how much improvement occurred on the average, or how much improvement occurred in each child. Instead of an after-only design, we would use a "before-after design" (or "pre-post design"). We would begin by pretesting the children on a list of words of equal difficulty by having them spell the words. We then teach half the children at random (the experimental group) the rules of spelling (the experimental treatment) and do not teach these rules to the other children (the control group), and afterward we test all of them on the same list of words. Because we used random assignment, we assume the two groups scored about the same (i.e., on the average) on the pretest, but we now have a way of checking this assumption. We also have another data analysis option. Instead of simply comparing the means of the two groups on the posttest, we can compute for each child a "difference score" based on the child's posttest-minus-pretest score and then use our independent *t* test on these scores. A positive difference score tells us that there was an achievement gain in spelling ability, and a negative difference tells us the opposite. We are mildly curious to find out whether there was a gain in the control group, which received nothing of substance but did take the same kind of spelling test twice (a practice effect?).

A possible problem with the before-after design is that pretesting the experimental group may "sensitize" them to the experimental treatment (known as **pretest sensitization**) and distort the outcome in this group. That is, children in this group may perform better or worse on the posttest relative to the control group than if they have not been pretested. To find out whether this is true, we would need to redesign our study, using all four groups above (assuming we have enough children to do so). That is, we need to use the two after-only groups as well as the two before-after groups, assigning each child at random to one of these four groups. With the new design, which we can conceptualize as a 2×2 factorial design, we can see whether there was a **pretest-treatment interaction**, which is the combination of the levels of certain factors (as explained next).

Table 7.3	The Solomon Four-Group Design	
	Pretested?	
Experimentally treated?	**Yes**	**No**
Yes	Group I	Group II
No	Group III	Group IV

Thus, two questions interest us. The primary question is whether being given a lesson on spelling rules will improve children's spelling ability. We want to know the answer without worrying about a possible contaminating effect of pretesting. However, we are also curious about what these children's original spelling ability was like, so we need to pretest some of them at least. The second question is a methodological one, which is of interest to us because it may have implications for whether we use a before-after or an after-only design in future research. This question is whether there was a pretest-treatment interaction effect. Once we know the answer, we may be able to control for this confounding effect, or to estimate the resulting bias, in any future investigation (Bonate, 2000; Lana, 1969). The design we will use is shown in Table 7.3. Known as the **Solomon design** (after its developer, Richard L. Solomon, 1949), it is a 2 × 2 between-subjects factorial design that was created for the specific purpose of addressing questions like these.

The Solomon Design

In this design, the subjects are randomly assigned to one of the four conditions in Table 7.3. Notice that Group I is pretested, receives the experimental treatment, and is then retested. Group II is not pretested but undergoes the same experimental treatment as Group I. Group III is pretested and retested but does not receive the experimental treatment. Group IV gets only the posttest. If we wanted to do so, we could compute a two-factor analysis of variance on the posttest scores to obtain the three F tests for (a) the main effect of the two levels of the row factor; (b) the main effect of the two levels of the column factor; and (c) the interaction effect of the levels of the row and column factors. (If you are unfamiliar with these terms, they are discussed in detail in Chapter 14, where we turn to the F test.). The first F test above answers the question of primary interest in *both* pretested and un-pretested subjects, whereas comparing only Groups II and IV (using a t test or an F test) addresses the primary question without the concern of pretest sensitization (because neither group was pretested).

The success of this design is predicated on the assumption that randomization has created groups that are similar to begin with. If this assumption has not been met, then the interpretation of the results will be questionable. However, assuming that all of the groups are similar in terms of pretreatment characteristics and performance, we can estimate the pretreatment performance in Groups II and IV (the unpretested groups) using the average value of the pretest in Groups I and

III. In other words, without actually pretesting Groups II and IV, we can make a reasonable guess of the *average* pretest scores in both groups. This guess will require a leap of faith, because we cannot be *absolutely* sure what the mean pretest performance in the unpretested groups would have been. Even if the average value of the pretest in Group I is identical to that in Group III, we can only *assume* that these values are close to those that would have been obtained by Groups II and IV. Furthermore, even if the average pretest values in Groups I and III differ greatly (which can happen easily when sample sizes are small or when randomization was not carried out properly), there is still a possibility that the unknown pretest scores in Groups II and IV would have been similar to the mean of Groups I and III.

From our estimation of the average pretest performance levels in Groups II and IV, we can enrich our understanding of the average posttest performance in these groups. That is to say, we can now interpret the average pre-to-post benefit of the experimental treatment without having contaminated these experimental and control groups by pretesting. Of course, the test we computed, as noted above, was simply a comparison of the mean performance scores in Groups II and IV (on the assumption of comparability on the pretests because of the use of randomization). Our hypothesis was that the spelling ability performance of Group II would surpass that of Group IV on the posttest.

Finally, this design can tell us whether there was a pretest-treatment interaction (i.e., any combined effects of treatment and pretesting). The interaction F test in the analysis of variance gives us one partial answer, but we still need to interpret the data to see whether the obtained interaction resulted in a positive or negative effect. In a later chapter, we will describe how this interpretation is done generally in any kind of factorial design, but the most concise answer in the case of the 2×2 factorial design is to use a subtraction-difference procedure in which we compare the four posttest means to identify whether the interaction was positive or negative. A positive interaction may imply that pretest sensitization caused subjects to respond more favorably to the experimental treatment than if they had not been pretested, whereas a negative interaction may imply just the opposite. If we were interested in comparing different experimental situations where pretest sensitization was a concern, we would also be interested in the magnitude of the positive or negative effect of the pretest-treatment interaction. For example, we may be interested in whether pretest sensitization is a potential problem in attitude change experiments and, if so, whether it is equally a problem when the subjects are all nonvolunteers or all volunteers (Rosnow & Suls, 1970).

To illustrate how this is done, we refer to Table 7.4. The rows show the four plausible antecedent events affecting the outcome measure in each group. Note that the outcome in Group I can be affected by the pretest, the experimental treatment, pretest sensitization (i.e., in part, the pretest-treatment interaction), and any unaccounted-for extraneous effects. The outcome in Group II can be affected by the treatment and any extraneous effects, but by no other conditions because there was no pretest to produce a pretest effect or a pretest sensitization. The outcome in Group III can be affected by the pretest and any extraneous effects, but by no

Table 7.4	Plausible Causal Events in the Solomon Design in Table 7.3			
	Plausible effects			
Causal events	Group I	Group II	Group III	Group IV
Pretest	Yes	No	Yes	No
Treatment	Yes	Yes	No	No
Sensitization	Yes	No	No	No
Extraneous effects	Yes	Yes	Yes	Yes

other conditions because there was no treatment to produce a treatment effect or a pretest sensitization. The outcome in Group IV can be affected by extraneous effects, but by no other conditions.

To identify the magnitude and direction of the pretest-treatment interaction, we simply isolate the effect of sensitization in Table 7.4. To do this, we subtract the posttest means of the four groups as follows: (Group I − Group III) − (Group II − Group IV). First we do subtractions within the parentheses, and then we subtract what remains in the right parentheses from what remains in the left parentheses. That is, we first subtract the posttest mean of Group III from the posttest mean of Group I, thereby canceling out the pretest and the extraneous effects and leaving the treatment and sensitization effects. Next, we subtract the posttest mean of Group IV from the posttest mean of Group II, canceling out the extraneous effects and leaving the treatment effect. When we subtract what remains on the right from what remains on the left, the remainder is the effect of the pretest-treatment interaction effect, which is strongly related to the effect of pretest sensitization. Another name for leftover effects is *residual effects*, a term that you will see again in Chapter 14.

Preexperimental Designs

Previously, we mentioned that leading psychological methodologists have developed master lists of variables to help experienced researchers check for plausible threats to validity when choosing a randomized or nonrandomized research design (Campbell & Stanley, 1963; Cook & Campbell, 1976, 1979; Shadish, Cook, & Campbell, 2002). In their initial work on this problem, Campbell and his associates used symbols to represent the design templates (or models) and speculated on threats to statistical-conclusion validity, internal validity, construct validity, and external validity that are (or are not) controlled in each general case. In the case of the Solomon design's ability to control for pretest sensitization, Campbell et al. conceptualized the interaction of the pretest and the treatment as one of a number of plausible threats to external validity controlled by this design.

Campbell et al. also described two templates, or models, that are so deficient in control as to be labeled **preexperimental designs.** One of these preexperimental designs, called the **one-shot case study,** is symbolized as **X-O,** where

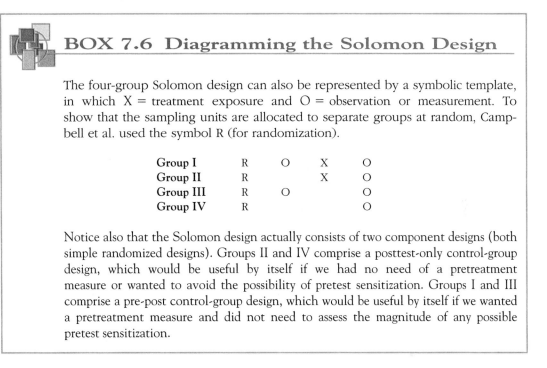

BOX 7.6 Diagramming the Solomon Design

The four-group Solomon design can also be represented by a symbolic template, in which X = treatment exposure and O = observation or measurement. To show that the sampling units are allocated to separate groups at random, Campbell et al. used the symbol R (for randomization).

Group I	R	O	X	O
Group II	R		X	O
Group III	R	O		O
Group IV	R			O

Notice also that the Solomon design actually consists of two component designs (both simple randomized designs). Groups II and IV comprise a posttest-only control-group design, which would be useful by itself if we had no need of a pretreatment measure or wanted to avoid the possibility of pretest sensitization. Groups I and III comprise a pre-post control-group design, which would be useful by itself if we wanted a pretreatment measure and did not need to assess the magnitude of any possible pretest sensitization.

X = the exposure of a treatment group to an event or experimental variable, and O = an observation or measurement (see also Box 7.6). An illustration is the introduction of a new educational treatment (X) designed to improve concentration and then the use of an achievement test (O) to measure students' performance after receiving this treatment. No allowance is made by this design for a comparison with the reactions of students who have not received the educational treatment, nor do we know the students' pretreatment levels of achievement. On the other hand, although called *preexperimental,* this X-O design also resembles an acceptable type of demonstration experiment in chemistry, in which X may refer to mixing chemical reagents in a test tube, and O is the observation of the chemical reaction.

Campbell et al. argued that a slight improvement on the one-shot case study in behavioral or social research would be a preexperimental design that at least measured the subjects before and after exposure to the treatment. Called a **one-group pre-post design,** it is symbolized as **O-X-O.** It was still viewed as preexperimental by Campbell et al. because of the lack of comparison conditions (i.e., beyond the pretreatment measure). We still cannot rule out uncontrolled events between X and O, as well as some other threats to internal validity. In fact, there are a number of specific conditions that, Campbell et al. noted, can jeopardize the internal validity of a study. For a flavor of some of these conditions, let us look at four: history, maturation, instrumentation, and selection.

History, Maturation, Instrumentation, and Selection

First, the term **history** implies a plausible source of error attributable to an uncontrolled event that occurs between the premeasurement (the pretest) and the postmeasurement (the posttest) and that can bias the postmeasurement. History is a threat to internal validity when the inferred causal relationship is confounded by the irrelevant, uncontrolled event. Suppose a sudden snowstorm results in an unexpected cancellation of classes. Neither preexperimental design would allow us to isolate the effects on motivation of a school closing, or to assess that factor apart from the effects of the new educational treatment designed to improve concentration. The Solomon design, as well as its two component designs (noted in Box 7.6), does allow us to assess this factor in the treated groups apart from the untreated groups.

Second, **maturation** refers to certain intrinsic changes in the research participants, such as their growing older, wiser, stronger, or more experienced between the premeasurement and the postmeasurement. Maturation becomes a threat to internal validity when it is not the variable of interest but the inferred causal relationship is nevertheless confounded by the presence of these changes. Imagine a study in which the posttest is given 1 year after the pretest. If the students' concentration has improved as a result of their getting older, so that they have become better at the task, neither of the preexperimental designs will tell us whether the gains are due to the students' maturing or to their being subjected to a particular educational treatment. The Solomon design (or either of the component designs in Box 7.6) controls for maturation bias by virtue of the randomization shown in Box 7.6.

Third, **instrumentation** refers to the intrinsic changes in the measuring instruments, such as deterioration. Instrumentation is a threat to internal validity when an effect may be due to unsuspected changes in the instruments over time. In the case of our educational treatment, we might ask whether the effect is due to instability (i.e., deterioration) of the achievement test or to changes in the students that are caused by the treatment. Or suppose the "instruments" are actually judges who are asked to rate the subjects. Over time, judges may become better raters of student concentration, in which case the confounding is due not to instrument deterioration but to instrument improvement. Instrumentation bias is not a relevant issue in the case of the X-O design because the test is administered only once, but it is both relevant and uncontrolled in the O-X-O design, and both relevant and specifically identifiable (i.e., controlled) in the Solomon design and its component designs.

Fourth, **selection** also refers to the subjects or participants, but in this case, the threat to internal validity comes from the selection of the participants for their assignment to particular treatments. Selection is a threat to internal validity when there are important, unsuspected differences between the participants in each condition. In the X-O design there is no way of knowing beforehand anything about the state of the participants because they are observed or measured only after the treatment has been administered. The addition of an observation before the treatment in the O-X-O design results in an improvement over the X-O design; it enables us to ascertain the prior state of the participants. The Solomon design and its two component designs specifically control for selection bias by randomly allocating the participants.

The Social Psychology of the Experiment

In Chapter 4, the terms *reactive* and *nonreactive* were used to distinguish measurements or observations that do (reactive) from those that do not (nonreactive) affect the behavior being measured or observed. When an engineer carefully takes the dimensions of a large piece of metal, we do not suppose that the act of measurement will have an effect on the metal. Similarly, when a biologist observes the movements of a paramecium, we do not expect the paramecium to change its behavior when the scientist is looking at it through a microscope. However, one may be less sure of the risks of reactive observation when humans or primates are the object of study (see also Box 7.7).

The term used to refer to this problem is **artifact,** which in this context means a finding that results from conditions other than those intended by the experimenter (e.g., Blanck, 1993; Fiske, 2000; Orne, 1959; Rosenthal, 1966; Rosenthal & Rosnow, 1969; Rosnow, 2002; Rosnow & Rosenthal, 1997; Rosnow, Strohmetz, & Aditya, 2000). Artifacts are not simply serendipitous findings, however, but findings resulting from uncontrolled conditions that may jeopardize the validity (internal, construct, and external) of the researcher's conclusions about what went on in the study or about the implications of the results. In the remainder of this chapter we will touch on some of the work in this area (called the *social psychology of the experiment*) and note some ways that so-called subject- and experimenter-related artifacts are handled.

BOX 7.7   Reactive Observations in Animal Research

The risks of reactive observation are not limited only to research with humans and primates. For example, one researcher reported that experienced observers in an animal laboratory could judge which of several experimenters had been handling a rat by the animal's behavior while running a maze or when being picked up (Christie, 1951). Another researcher observed that a dog's heart rate would drop dramatically simply because a certain experimenter was present (Gantt, 1964).

Subject-Related Artifacts

The notion of subject-related artifacts proceeds from the idea that much of the complexity of human activity described by behavioral scientists lies in the nature of the human organisms that serve as the model: the research participants. We know, for example, that no two people behave identically, and therefore, the "same" careful experiment conducted in one place at one time may yield results very different from those of an experiment conducted in another place at another time. Although it is generally accepted that much of this complexity is due to the complexities of human nature, it is recognized that most people know perfectly well that they are research participants and that they are to play out this role in interaction with the experimenter. The role of "research subject" appears to be well understood by most normal adults who find their way into behavioral scientists' subject pools. Thus, what one researcher interprets as a causal relation between X and Y another researcher may theorize to be the plausible relation between some role variable and Y (J. G. Adair, 1973; Danziger, 1988; Gniech, 1976; Rosenthal & Rosnow, 1969, 1975b; I. Silverman, 1977; Strohmetz & Rosnow, 1994; Suls & Rosnow, 1988).

Pioneering work in the social psychology of the experiment was done by Martin T. Orne, whose interests in subject-related artifacts grew out of his research on hypnosis. Observations in that research led him to theorize that the trance manifestations that people exhibit on entering hypnosis are partly determined by their motivation to "act out" the role of a hypnotized person. Both their preconceptions of how a hypnotized person ought to act and the cues communicated by the hypnotist of how the subjects should behave, called **demand characteristics,** were viewed by Orne (1962, 1969, 1970) as plausible determinants of the subjects' expectations concerning how this role was to be enacted. In particular, Orne postulated that typical volunteers for hypnosis have a tendency to act out the role of the **good subject,** that is, the kind of research participant who is sensitive to demand characteristics and tries to give experimenters what they seemingly want to find.

In Chapter 5, we spoke of Milton Rosenberg's (1969) view of the human participants in psychological research as typically being apprehensive about being evaluated, a condition that he called **evaluation apprehension.** Although Rosenberg argued that typical subjects are motivated to "look good" rather than to help the cause of science (Orne's view), he and Orne agreed that typical subjects frequently find meaning in even the most meaningless cues (see Box 7.8). Orne theorized that most research subjects (especially volunteers for research participation) reason that, no matter how trivial and inane the task outwardly seems, the experimenter must surely have an important scientific purpose that justifies their experimental participation. Feeling that they have a stake in the outcome of the study, the "good subjects" believe that they are making a useful contribution to science by complying with the demand characteristics of the experiment, Orne argued. The puzzle for the researcher is to figure out what demand characteristics may have been inadvertently operating in the experiment.

To help us in this quest, Orne (1962, 1969) proposed that **quasi-control subjects** be used. These are research subjects who are asked to step out of their tradi-

BOX 7.8 The Good Subject

The extent to which some research participants will comply with demand characteristics sometimes surprises even the experimenter. At one point in his hypnosis
research, Orne (1962) tried to devise a set of dull, meaningless tasks that non-
hypnotized persons either would refuse to do or would try for only a short time.
One task was to add thousands of rows of two-digit numbers. Five and a half
hours after the subjects began, the experimenter gave up. When the subjects
were told to tear each worksheet into a minimum of 32 pieces before going on
to the next, they *still* persisted.

tional roles and to serve as "coinvestigators" (that is, rather than as "objects of
study" for the experimenter to investigate). Such subjects are usually drawn from
the same population as the experimental and control subjects, but the quasi-control
subjects are asked to reflect on the context in which the experiment is being conducted. They then free-associate about how the situation might have influenced
their behavior if they were in the experimental group. For example, the participation of a few subjects in the experimental group may be terminated at different
points during the course of the study. They then become quasi-control subjects,
who are carefully interviewed about what they thought were the demand characteristics of the experiment.

Experimenter Expectancy and Its Control

On the other side of the artifact coin are experimenter-related artifacts, that is, sources
of bias (or systematic error) resulting from the uncontrolled intentions or actions of
the experimenters. A number of such sources have been identified (Rosenthal, 1966),
though the one we describe here is particularly intriguing because it occurs when
people's expectations unwittingly serve as *self-fulfilling prophecies* (discussed in
Chapter 4). That is, someone expects an event to occur, and this expectation then
shapes the expecter's behavior in such a way as to make the predicted event more
likely to occur. In the Pygmalion experiment (Box 4.6 on p. 99), teachers who believed that certain pupils were especially bright may have acted more warmly toward
them, taught them more material, and spent more time with them. Over time, this behavior resulted in greater gains in IQ test performance for those students than occurred in the absence of the teachers' positive expectations.

When the "prophet" is the experimenter and the study participants' behavior is
at issue, the self-fulfilling prophecy is called an **experimenter expectancy effect.**
In one early study of experimenter expectancy, a dozen student experimenters
were each given five rats that were to be taught to run a maze with the aid of visual cues (Rosenthal & Fode, 1963). Half the students were told their rats had been

specially bred for maze-brightness, and the remaining students were told their rats had been bred for maze-dullness. Actually, there were no differences in the rats; they had been randomly given the labels of maze-bright and maze-dull. At the end of the experiment, however, there were clear differences. The rats run by experimenters who expected bright behavior did, in fact, perform better than the rats run by experimenters who expected dull behavior.

The study was repeated, this time using a series of learning experiments, each conducted in a Skinner box (Rosenthal & Lawson, 1964). Half the student experimenters were led to believe their rats were "Skinner-box bright," and half were led to believe their animals were "Skinner-box-dull." Once again, there were not really any differences in the two groups of rats, at least not until the end of the study. Then, the allegedly brighter animals really were brighter, and the alleged dullards were really duller. We should emphasize that the experimenters' expectations acted on the actual performance of the animals, not simply on the perception of the animals' performance. In addition, neither of these studies showed any evidence that the experimenters were trying to generate false data (i.e., there was no evidence of cheating).

One strategy for dealing with the experimenter expectancy problem is to use **blind experimenters,** that is, experimenters who are unaware of ("blind" to) which subjects are to receive the experimental treatment and which the control treatment. The idea is that, if the experimenters do not know what treatment the subject has received, they are unlikely to communicate expectancies about the nature of that treatment. The necessity of keeping the experimenters blind (i.e., unaware) is well recognized in randomized drug trials. In fact, no drug trial is taken completely seriously unless it has followed elaborate **double-blind procedures** (in which neither the subjects nor the experimenters know who is in the experimental and control groups). (See also Box 7.9.)

Another approach to the experimenter expectancy problem is to use a factorial design that not only assesses whether an expectancy effect is present but also allows a direct comparison of that effect with the phenomenon of theoretical interest. Called an **expectancy control design,** this approach usually takes the form of the 2 × 2 factorial arrangement shown in Table 7.5. Group A represents the condition in which the experimental treatment is administered to subjects by data collectors who expect the occurrence of the experimental effect in this group. Group D represents the condition in which the absence of the experimental treatment is associated with data collectors who expect the nonoccurrence of the experimental effect in this group. But ordinarily, researchers are interested in the experimental effect unconfounded with experimenter expectancy; the addition of the appropriate expectancy control groups permits the researchers to evaluate the experimental effect separately from the expectancy effect. Subjects in Group B receive the experimental treatment but are contacted by data collectors who do not expect an experimental effect in this group. Subjects in Group C do not receive the experimental treatment but are contacted by data collectors who expect an experimental effect.

You can see that it is an expensive design, because it calls for many data collectors who are randomly assigned to the four cells. However, it has been used in a

BOX 7.9 Blindfolding to Ensure "Blindness"

The principle of ensuring "blindness" may also be applicable to the role of other participants in the research. For example, cognitive psychologists Kathy Hirsh-Pasek and Robert Michnick Golinkoff (1993, 1996) used a novel method to study language comprehension in infants and toddlers, a model that the researchers called the "preferential looking paradigm." Suppose we want to study noun comprehension in order to find out how early in their lives infants and toddlers are able to distinguish a shoe from a hat. An infant is seated on a blindfolded parent's lap approximately $2\frac{1}{2}$ feet away from a pair of television monitors. By means of a concealed speaker, the word *shoe* is sounded at the same time that one of the monitors shows a shoe and the other monitor shows a hat. A camera records the child's preferential looking behavior over a series of paired-comparison trials using many different stimuli. Blindfolding eliminates the possibility of the parent's unintentionally signaling the correct responses.

number of experimental situations. Illustrative of its use in animal research is a study reported by J. Randolph Burnham (1966), with the results shown in Table 7.6. Each of about two dozen student-experimenters ran one rat in a discrimination task in a T maze (i.e., a runway with the starting box at the base and the goal at one end of the crossbar). Portions of the brains of approximately half the rats had been surgically removed (by *lesioning*). The remaining rats had received only sham surgery, which involved a cut through the skull but no damage to brain tissue (so that it was impossible for the student-experimenters to tell which rats had actually undergone brain lesioning). The purpose of the study was explained to the student-experimenters as an attempt to learn the effects of lesions on discrimination learning. Expectancies were manipulated by the labeling of each rat as "lesioned" or "unlesioned." Some of the really lesioned rats were labeled accurately as lesioned, but some were falsely labeled as unlesioned. Similarly, some of the really unlesioned rats were labeled accurately as unlesioned, but others were falsely labeled as lesioned.

By comparing the means in the row and column margins, we get an idea of the relative effectiveness of the surgical and the expectancy treatments. The higher

Table 7.5	Basic Expectancy Control Design	
	Expectancy conditions	
Treatment conditions	**Experimental treatment**	**Control treatment**
Experimental	Group A	Group B
Control	Group C	Group D

| Table 7.6 | Expectancy Control Design Used by Burnham (1966) to Study Discrimination Learning in Rats | | |

Treatment conditions	Expectancy conditions Lesioning of brain	No lesioning of brain	Row means
Lesioning of brain	46.5	49.0	47.75
No lesioning of brain	48.2	58.3	53.25
Column means	47.35	53.65	

these scores, the better was the rats' performance in that row or column. We see that rats that had been surgically lesioned did not perform as well as those that had not been lesioned. We also see that the rats that were *believed* to be lesioned did not perform as well as those that were believed to be unlesioned. The logic of this design is that it enables the researcher to compare the magnitude of the effect of experimenter expectancy with the magnitude of the effect of actual removal of brain tissue. We see that, in this case, the two effects were similar. Of course, we are not limited to comparing the differences in row means and column means, and later in this book, we will see how it is possible statistically to compare individual cell means in a factorial design.

Summary of Ideas

1. Randomized experimental designs are characterized by the assigning of subjects to treatments so as to guard against potential sources of allocation bias by giving each sampling unit an equal chance of being assigned to any group or condition.
2. Randomization (i.e., random assignment) procedures include coin flipping and using a table of random digits to allocate the sampling units or treatment conditions in an unbiased way.
3. Random assignment does not guarantee equality of the different groups or conditions (Box 7.1); another procedure is matching the subjects on propensity scores (Box 7.2).
4. Between-subjects designs (nested designs) and within-subjects designs (crossed designs) are distinguished, respectively, by whether each sampling unit is observed once or more than once.
5. Between- and within-subjects designs are not limited to two groups or conditions; they also include combinations (mixed factorial designs) as well as counterbalanced repeated measures designs (Latin square designs, Box 7.3).
6. Aristotle described four kinds of causality: material, formal, efficient, and final; subsequently, inspired by Hume's "rules by which to judge causes and effects," specific criteria evolved out of these earlier ideas (the criteria of covariation, temporal precedence, and internal validity).
7. The logic of using a control condition in two-group between-subjects designs embodies Mill's methods of agreement and difference.
8. Using the Solomon design, we can define and display the pretest-treatment interaction effect by using a subtraction-difference procedure.
9. The Solomon design is used to identify the magnitude and direction of the pretest sensitization effect by a subtraction-difference procedure, which is also the most parsimonious description of the

pretest-treatment interaction; this design can also be understood as a combination of a pre-post control group design and a posttest-only control group design.

10. Preexperimental designs, as illustrated by the one-shot case study (X-O) and the one-group pre-post study (O-X-O), make no effort to control for threats to internal validity.

11. Campbell et al. developed checklists of threats to validity, including threats to internal validity such as history, maturation, instrumentation, and selection.

12. The name for subjects who are sensitive and accommodating to the demand characteristics of an experiment is the *good subject* (a term coined by Martin Orne).

13. The use of quasi controls, in addition to regular control groups, helps us to ferret out demand characteristics.

14. Experimenter expectancy may cause the experimenter's working hypothesis to become a self-fulfilling prophecy.

15. Blind procedures are used to control for expectancy effects, and an expectancy control design is used to isolate and compare the expectancy effect with the effect of the main independent variable (e.g., Burnham's study of discrimination learning in rats).

 ## Key Terms

artifact   p. 187
between-subjects design   p. 172
blind experimenters   p. 190
confounded   pp. 174, 180
control group   p. 179
counterbalancing   p. 174
covariation   p. 177
crossed design   p. 173
demand characteristics   p. 188
double-blind procedures   p. 190
efficient cause   p. 176
evaluation apprehension   p. 188
expectancy control design   p. 190
experimental group   p. 179
experimenter expectancy
  effect   p. 189
factorial design   p. 174
final cause   p. 176
formal cause   p. 176

good subject   p. 188
history   p. 186
instrumentation   p. 186
internal validity   p. 178
Latin square design   p. 174
matching   p. 171
material cause   p. 176
maturation   p. 186
method of agreement   p. 179
method of difference   p. 179
Mill's methods   p. 179
necessary condition   p. 179
nested design   p. 172
one-group pre-post design
  (O-X-O)   p. 185
one-shot case study (X-O)   p. 184
placebo   p. 168
placebo control group   p. 180

placebo effect   p. 180
preexperimental designs   p. 184
pretest sensitization   p. 181
pretest-treatment interaction
  p. 181
quasi-control subjects   p. 188
random assignment   p. 170
randomization   p. 170
randomized experiments   p. 168
repeated measures design
  p. 173
sampling units   p. 170
selection   p. 186
Solomon design   p. 182
sufficient condition   p. 179
temporal precedence   p. 178
treatments   p. 170
within-subjects design   p. 173

WEB ACTIVITY

Learn more about randomized designs and validity by clicking on the relevant links at Professor William M. K. Trochim's http://www.trochim.human.cornell.edu/tutorial/TUTORIAL .HTM. To read Martin Orne's classic article and learn more about demand characteristics in clinical practice and human subjects research, visit the American Psychological Association e-journal, *Prevention and Treatment,* at http://www.journals.apa.org/prevention/volume5/ toc-oct18-02.html.

Multiple-Choice Questions for Review

1. Which of the following is considered a defining characteristic of randomized clinical trials in medical research? (a) random sampling of subjects; (b) random assignment of subjects to the experimental conditions; (c) the use of a placebo control group; (d) the use of a quasi control group

2. Randomization is (a) selecting a sample at random from a larger population; (b) manipulating a random sample of variables within an experiment; (c) ensuring that each subject has an equal chance of being assigned to any condition; (d) randomly determining which experimenter will conduct which experimental condition.

3. Which of the following was a type of cause identified by Aristotle? (a) final; (b) efficient; (c) formal; (d) all of the above

4. To conclude that X causes Y, scientists must be able to rule out plausible rival hypotheses. This is called the criterion of (a) covariation; (b) temporal precedence; (c) internal validity; (d) material causation.

5. Philosopher J. S. Mill stated, "If X, then Y." This is known as Mill's method of (a) agreement; (b) disagreement; (c) difference; (d) covariation.

6. Which of the following is a common threat to internal validity? (a) maturation; (b) covariation; (c) time series data; (d) none of the above

7. Campbell et al.'s name for a research design in which there is only one group, and that group is measured only after the treatment, is the (a) Solomon design; (b) one-shot case study; (c) one-group pre-post study; (d) factorial design.

8. A study is conducted in which there is only one group, and that group is measured both before and after the treatment. This design is vulnerable to which of the following threats to internal validity? (a) history; (b) maturation; (c) selection; (d) all of the above

9. Which of the following research designs allows the scientist to examine the possibility of pretest sensitization? (a) Solomon four-group design; (b) one-shot case study; (c) one-group pre-post design; (d) factorial design

10. Cues given off by an experimental procedure and context that communicate to participants how they should behave are called (a) artifacts; (b) demand characteristics; (c) experimenter expectancy effects; (d) none of the above.

Discussion Questions for Review

1. A Colby College student wants to evaluate the effectiveness of a popular method of boosting self-esteem called I'm-better-than-OK therapy. In this therapy, clients read pop psychology books, compliment themselves while looking in a mirror, and have group touch-a-lot sessions. What kind of control group(s) would you recommend?

2. A Villanova University student believes that positive reinforcement increases self-esteem. To test this hypothesis, she administers a self-esteem scale to 40 other students and correlates the scores with their grade point averages. Can you think of any limitations in this research design?

3. An Auburn University student tells his participants that he is interested in identifying the characteristics associated with good leadership skills. He then administers two measures titled the Social Intelligence Survey and Interpersonal Problem-Solving Ability. Do you see any potential problem in this method?

4. A student at the University of New Mexico wants to prove that eating chocolate chip cookies will cure depression. What basic requirements of inference would he have to meet, according to J. S. Mill?

5. An American University student wants to use an expectancy control design to assess a program offering individual tutoring to enhance students' performance on achievement tests. How might she set up this design?

6. A manufacturer of pain relievers wants to market what seems to be a revolutionary new product: a near-cure for the common cold. Researchers in the R & D division select 1,000 persons to participate in a test study. Each participant is observed for 6 months. For the first 3 months, baseline data are collected. For the last 3 months, the participants take a weekly dose of the common-cold cure. Sure enough, 15% of the participants contract a cold during the first 3 months, whereas only 5% do in the second 3 months. The investigators rush their findings to the company president, who must decide whether the data are convincing enough for the product to be put on the market. Can you think of any weakness in the research design?

7. On a quiz, University of Arkansas students are asked how the Solomon design allows researchers to rule out the possibility of confounding the pretest and the results of the treatment. What is the answer? The same students are also asked to define the following threats to internal validity: history, maturation, selection, and instrumentation. Do you know the answers?

8. A Howard University medical student designs an experiment to test the effects of a new drug. In consultation with her faculty mentor, she decides to include both a placebo control and a zero control group. Do you know the difference?

Answers to Review Questions

Multiple-Choice Questions

1. b	3. d	5. a	7. b	9. a
2. c	4. c	6. a	8. d	10. b

Discussion Questions

1. A placebo control group might be used to which clients would be randomly assigned. This placebo control group would receive a pseudomethod of boosting self-esteem for example, reading material believed to be irrelevant to self-esteem and watching irrelevant movies. The clients assigned to this placebo control group should believe that their "treatment" will have beneficial effects to the same degree as do the clients assigned to the "real" treatment.

2. Because the positive reinforcement (grades) was not experimentally manipulated, there is no basis for her concluding that it "caused" the self-esteem scores even if there is a positive correlation between self-esteem and GPA. Self-esteem may as well "cause" grades, or some other variable may "cause" both grades and self-esteem.

3. Telling participants the hypothesis and the names of the measuring instruments is likely to result in strong demand characteristics.

4. According to Mill's methods, the student would have to show that eating chocolate chip cookies is followed by a reduction in depression (method of agreement) and that not eating chocolate chip cookies is not followed by a reduction in depression (method of difference).

5. The basic plan could be implemented by use of the following four conditions, analogous to those shown in Tables 7.5 and 7.6:

	Expectancy	
Actual treatment	Experimental	Control
Tutoring	A	B
Control	C	D

6. As in all one-group pre-post studies, history, maturation, and instrumentation all threaten the internal validity of the research.

7. The Solomon design allows researchers to use the subtraction-difference procedure to compare the difference between the experimental and control groups obtained when pretests have and have not been used. The four threats to internal validity were described as part of Campbell et al.'s analysis in this chapter.

8. A placebo control group offers a treatment-like condition that serves to control for subjects' beliefs or expectations about the efficacy of any treatments that might be administered. A zero control group is characterized by the absence of any intervention, "real" or "pseudo" (placebo).

CHAPTER 8

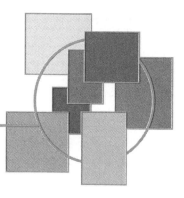

Categories of Nonrandomized Research

Preview Questions

- How do studies with nonequivalent groups address questions of causality?

- What is the role of time-series designs and "found experiments" in social research?

- What design strategies are used in single-case experiments?

- What are the limitations of cross-lagged panel designs?

- What is the purpose of longitudinal research?

- What is the risk in generalizing from cross-sectional research to long-term changes?

The Role of Nonrandomized Research

In the previous chapter, we saw how researchers use randomized experimental designs to attempt to create the equivalence they need to make causal inferences. The idea was to use an unbiased procedure (e.g., a table of random digits or the flipping of a coin) to allocate the sampling units (e.g., human or animal subjects) to the different conditions so that the groups presumably differ only with respect to the condition being studied. Though these kinds of experiments are regarded as the "gold standard" in medical research, for practical or ethical reasons it is not always possible to conduct randomized experiments in order to tease out causal relationships. Say we wanted to study whether smoking causes heart disease and cancer in humans. A randomized experiment might mean assigning nonsmokers to either an experimental condition that requires them to smoke for many years or to a nonsmoking control group. That procedure would be an ethical absurdity. Instead, we might use a combination of different methods and procedures, each giving us a different perspective on the question of causality.

As a further illustration, imagine that we have discovered an outbreak of strange medical symptoms and want to explain them in causal terms. Time is of the essence, but we do not want to mislead (and possibly cause further harm) by making an incorrect causal inference. We might begin by drawing a representative sample of those afflicted (using a procedure described in the next chapter) and then interview them, with the aim of finding some event they have in common (i.e., a clue to the covariation of an event and the strange symptoms). Suppose we find that all have been taking a new prescription medicine whose side effects have not yet been fully established. We now suspect that the new drug may be the cause of the symptoms, in some persons at least. We could, of course, easily confirm our suspicion if we simply arranged to take a sample of asymptomatic people (i.e., people without this particular symptom) and randomly give half of them the suspected drug. This procedure would allow us to compare these two groups of people to see whether those given the new drug are more likely to develop the strange symptoms. Once again, however, the ethical cost of such a randomized experiment would be too high, as we would not be willing to expose people to a drug we had good reason to believe was harmful.

As a practical alternative, we can track down patients who were originally diagnosed as having the illness or disease for which the new drug was prescribed for some patients. We can then compare the patients who were given the new drug by their physicians with those patients whose physicians did not prescribe the new drug. If only those given the new drug develop the strange medical symptoms, the new drug is more seriously implicated. However, its causal role is still not fully established, because those patients given the new drug may still differ in some other ways from those not given the drug. That is, using the same logic we used when thinking about rival hypotheses in randomized experiments (threats to internal validity), we think it is plausible that not the new drug but an unknown correlate of being given the new drug might be the causal variable.

Suppose in our exploratory research we discover that not all patients who took the new drug were given the same dosage levels. Another strategy would correlate the dosage levels with the outcome variable. If it turns out that patients on larger dosages suffer more severely from the strange medical symptoms, would this evidence implicate the drug more strongly as the cause of those symptoms? Unfortunately, the answer is the same as the one above, which is that we still cannot be sure about the causal role of the new drug, as those given larger dosages may have initially been more severely ill. In this case, the illness for which the new drug was prescribed, rather than the drug itself, might be the cause of the strange medical symptoms.

How have we done so far? "Not very well," you might answer. To establish temporal precedence, we need to show that taking the new drug preceded the strange medical symptoms. Unless our medical records go back far enough, we might not be able to prove that the symptoms did not occur until after the drug was taken. The covariation assumption requires us to show that the new drug is related to the strange medical symptoms. However, even if we can show that taking the new drug is correlated with the mysterious symptoms, it might be argued that, in order to be susceptible to the drug, a patient already had to be in a given state of distress. According to this argument, it is not the new drug, or *not only* the drug, that is related to the strange symptoms. If the patients who were in a state of distress are the only ones given the new drug, it might be possible to explain the observed relationship on the basis of **self-selection;** that is, it could be argued that the patients' state of distress determined the particular group in which they found themselves.

Despite the difficulty of clear inference in this example, we might still be convinced by strong circumstantial, though inconclusive, evidence. If people taking the new drug are more likely to show the strange medical symptoms, if those taking more of the new drug show more of the symptoms, and if those taking it over a longer period of time show more of the symptoms, we would be reluctant to say that the new drug was *not* the cause of the symptoms. Even if we were unwilling to say that the new drug was *surely* at the root of the strange medical symptoms, at least on the basis of the type of evidence outlined above, it might well be prudent to act "as though" it were. On this basis, perhaps we can design a randomized experiment using primates in order to try to simulate the strange medical symptoms, as we now have a causal model with which to work. Of course, failure to produce those symptoms in primates would not rule out a causal relationship in human patients.

The purpose of this chapter is to illustrate four categories of nonrandomized designs in behavioral and social research: (a) studies with nonequivalent groups, (b) time-series designs, (c) single-case designs, and (d) correlational designs. A traditional way of referring to these general categories is **quasi-experimental research,** following the suggestion of Campbell and Stanley (1963). The term *quasi-experimental* should not be viewed as a snubbing (or put-down) of this research, as *quasi* merely means "resembling." Campbell and Stanley's notion was that quasi-experimental research resembles randomized experimental research because quasi-experimental designs generally have outcome measures, sampling units, and something comparable to the "treatment" condition (called an *intervention*); what identifies them as quasi-experimental is that they do not use randomization to assign the units to different conditions. We will describe the causal reasoning in simple quasi-experimental designs, which sometimes resembles the reasoning used by a family doctor (see Box 8.1), or that of an epidemiologist trying to uncover the cause of an outbreak of some malaise by using only circumstantial evidence.

Nonequivalent-Groups Designs

Nonequivalent-groups designs are traditionally between-subjects designs in which the participants are assigned to experimental and control groups by means other than randomization and are tested before and after the experimental treatment. For example, suppose we want to study the effect of some new therapy for

---

BOX 8.1   Causal Reasoning in the Doctor's Office

Suppose your hand has been bitten by a dog. You go to a doctor, who prescribes a tetanus shot and an oral antibiotic. You ask the doctor to give the tetanus shot in your bad arm so that you have your good arm to use. But the doctor points out that if she did so and you had a reaction to the tetanus, she would not be able to separate it from the possible continued reaction to the dog bite—which could, in the worst-case scenario, also cause the arm, not the hand, to swell. For this reason, she gives the shot in your good arm, so any swelling due to an allergy to the tetanus will not be confounded with a possible reaction to the dog bite. Her causal reasoning is based on a comparison of her before-and-after observations.

---

hyperactive children. If this is a randomized experiment, we will use an unbiased procedure to assign hyperactive children to a treated experimental group or an untreated control group. But suppose the circumstances dictate that we *must* use two intact groups: one group of children at School A and one at School B. We can flip a coin to decide which school will be assigned to the experimental group, but we cannot use randomization to assign the children *within* each school to the two groups.

The children in the two schools are measured at the beginning and the end of the study according to this diagram:

School 1	NR	O	X	O
School 2	NR	O		O

where X = the treatment or intervention, O = the observation or measurement, and NR = the nonrandomized allocation of subjects to the treatment conditions. Our study resembles a randomized experiment in most respects, but because the groups are not equivalent, the design does not control for certain threats to internal validity (e.g., the history of the groups may be different).

How might we increase the likelihood that the two groups will be similar to one another? In Chapter 7, we mentioned matching groups by the propensity score method (see again Box 7.2 on page 171). This important approach is predicated on the assumption that there will be a sufficient number of subjects in the subcategories, not always a feasible proposition in all research situations. A further problem is that matching sometimes requires us to drop some of the subjects, so that a certain number of people will not be included in the data analysis. As discussed in a later chapter, tests of statistical significance (like t, F, and chi-square) are very much affected by the size of the samples to be compared. If the sample size is too small, the statistical test may not have enough "power" to detect a real difference at the preferred level of significance.

Sometimes when researchers must work with intact groups, the problem is depriving some participants of the benefits of the experimental treatment by assigning them to a control condition. Rather than settle for a nonequivalent-groups design, we might propose a randomized design with a **wait-list control group.** Those assigned to the experimental condition (Group 1) are given the experimental treatment during the regular period of the experiment, and (assuming the treatment is found to be beneficial) those assigned to the control condition (Group 2) are given the experimental treatment sometime after the period of the experiment. Depending on the extent of the delay before the second group receives the treatment, if we measure the first group after the treatment and again after the second group receives the treatment we may gain valuable information about the long-term effect of the treatment in the first group. This design can be diagrammed as follows:

Group 1	R	O	X	O		O
Group 2	R	O		O	X	O

where R = the randomized allocation of participants to treatment conditions, and O and X are defined as before.

Inferring Causation in an Epidemiological Investigation

At the beginning of this chapter, we illustrated the problem of trying to infer causation when the only information we have is circumstantial evidence of covariation and temporal precedence. This problem is quite common in epidemiological research, but investigators frequently attempt to emulate the causal reasoning of the randomized experimental approach in order to reach causal inferences that are as sound as possible (i.e., working within the intrinsic limitations of the research; see Cook & Campbell, 1979; Shadish et al., 2002). The hypothetical data in Table 8.1 help us to illustrate this approach (adapted from Kahane, 1989). They represent a situation in which 12 people ate at the same fast-food restaurant, and the problem is to determine the cause (X) of food poisoning (Y) that was subsequently diagnosed in 5 of them (Mimi, Nancy, Michele, John, and Sheila). The table shows that Michele had a milkshake, but we cannot think of a way that the milkshake might have caused food poisoning. Furthermore, Gail and Greg also had milkshakes, and they did not get sick or even get an upset stomach. Of the 5 people who got sick, 3 (Nancy, Michele, and John) ate a salad, and it is remotely possible that it contained spoiled dressing that did not taint any other salads. Of the 5 people who got sick, the table also shows that 4 ate greasy french fries, which could have produced stomach upsets, but Connie and Richard also ate french fries and were not affected. The most striking finding in this table is that all those who got sick ate a rare hamburger (which no one else ordered). It is easy to imagine that a rare hamburger might have contained bacteria that were not destroyed in the cooking process.

Table 8.1	Illustration of Agreement and Difference Methods					
Name	Ate burger	Ate tuna sandwich	Ate fries	Ate salad	Drank shake	Got food poisoning
Mimi	Yes	No	Yes	No	No	Yes
Gail	No	No	No	Yes	Yes	No
Connie	No	No	Yes	No	No	No
Jerry	No	Yes	No	Yes	No	No
Greg	No	Yes	No	No	Yes	No
Dwight	No	No	No	Yes	No	No
Nancy	Yes	No	Yes	Yes	No	Yes
Richard	No	Yes	Yes	Yes	No	No
Kerry	No	No	No	Yes	No	No
Michele	Yes	No	Yes	Yes	Yes	Yes
John	Yes	No	Yes	Yes	No	Yes
Sheila	Yes	No	No	No	No	Yes

Source: Based on a similar example in *Logic and Philosophy: A Modern Introduction* (6th ed.) by H. Kahane, 1989, Wadsworth. Used by permission of Howard Kahane and Wadsworth Publishing Co.

What should we conclude? If we can safely assume that all 12 people in Table 8.1 would have been found healthy in a pretest diagnosis, maybe we have a "kind" of nonequivalent-groups design (i.e., poisoned group vs. nonpoisoned group). On the surface, the one common factor is the rare hamburger. But the owner tells us that one of the food handlers was feeling ill the day these people were served. The food handler worked for a while, but then he asked to be excused after complaining of feeling dizzy and nauseous. Is it possible that this food handler was the culprit? Suppose he touched some but not all of the foods eaten that day; maybe he passed on his germs in this way. His possible handling of Mimi's and Sheila's burger, Nancy's salad dressing, and Michele's and John's fries would be another factor common to all the cases. By the logic of Mill's methods of agreement and difference (discussed in Chapter 7), it is possible, in other words, that these particular foods were the *sufficient* conditions to bring about poisoning (*Y*), but that this food handler's handling of them (*X?*) was the *necessary* condition.

Once we think about this problem some more, we believe we can safely rule out the food handler because he must have touched many more items than those implicated above. If he were the cause (*X*), then others who ate at the restaurant should have become ill (*Y*). However, Table 8.1 shows that 7 people did not get food poisoning (not-*Y*) even though they ate some of the same things the others ate (*X*)—except for the rare hamburger (the true *X?*). Only the burger was absent in every case in which there was no food poisoning. On the basis of this circumstantial evidence, we now believe more strongly that the burger was probably the necessary and sufficient condition (*X*) that brought about food poisoning (*Y*). However, perhaps there are also *moderating variables* affecting the likelihood that others, had they also eaten the rare hamburger, would have contracted food poisoning (see Box 8.2). (We will return to these data in Chapter 11, where we will

BOX 8.2 Identifying Moderator Variables

Moderator variables are factors associated with variations (i.e., increases or decreases) in the magnitude of a relationship between two variables (H. M. Cooper, 1984, 1989). For example, social psychologist Alice H. Eagly (1978) used the methodology of meta-analysis (see Appendix C) to discover a fascinating moderator variable. Textbooks in her field had long asserted that women were more conforming and more easily influenced than men, presumably because socialization processes had taught men to be independent thinkers, a cultural value seldom suggested as suitable for women. Reasoning that the historical period in which the results had been collected might be a moderator of the association between sex and influenceability, Eagly meta-analyzed all the relevant studies she could find. She discovered a pronounced difference in the correlation between sex and influenceability in studies published before 1970 from those published during the era of the women's movement in the 1970s. In contrast to the older studies, which found greater influenceability among females than among males, the newer studies found few sex differences in influenceability.

show how the association between eating the burger and becoming sick can be quantified by a special case of the Pearson r correlation).

Time-Series Designs and "Found Experiments"

A second broad category of quasi-experimental research includes various **time-series designs.** The defining characteristic of all these designs is that the effects of some "treatment" are inferred from a comparison of the outcome measures obtained at different time intervals before and after the treatment (or intervention) occurred. This data structure is called a *time series* because there is a single data point for each point in time, and it is frequently called an "interrupted time series" when there is a clear dividing line at the beginning of the intervention (i.e., a line analogous to the start of the treatment). Although some users of these designs make and analyze simple tables and charts, others use quite sophisticated statistical procedures that go beyond the scope of this text (see, e.g., Cryer, 1986; Judd & Kenny, 1981).

A number of fascinating applications of this approach were reported by sociologist David P. Phillips, who called his investigations "found experiments" because they were essentially *found* quasi experiments in naturally occurring situations (Phillips & Glynn, 2000). In one set of studies, Phillips and others investigated the clustering of imitative suicides after televised news stories and televised movies about suicide (see, e.g., Phillips, Lesyna, & Paight, 1992, for a review). The results showed interesting variations, which were not easy to explain. For example, a New

York City study found that suicides by teenagers increased after three televised fictional films about suicide (Gould & Shaffer, 1986), but then an attempted replication by Phillips and Paight (1987) in California and Pennsylvania found no evidence of an increase in teenage suicides after the same three films were televised. In an Austrian study, however, Phillips and Carstensen (1986) found evidence of what seemed to be copycat imitations of suicides in news stories.

In Vienna, Austria, there was a sharp increase in the number of subway suicides in 1984. Persuaded by the evidence generated by Phillips and others, the Austrian Association for Suicide Prevention, Crisis Intervention, and Conflict Resolution argued that there might be a connection between this increase and a sudden heavy emphasis in newspaper stories on subway suicides. The organization drew up media guidelines and persuaded two large-circulation Viennese newspapers to curtail the publicity given to subway suicides. This change in policy occurred in June 1987, and Figure 8.1 contains time-series data that show the dramatic reduction in subway suicides and suicide attempts after this policy was enacted (Sonneck, Etzersdorfer, & Nagel-Kuess, 1994). Using the same symbols used earlier, we can diagram this interrupted time-series design as:

O O O O O O O O O X O O O O O

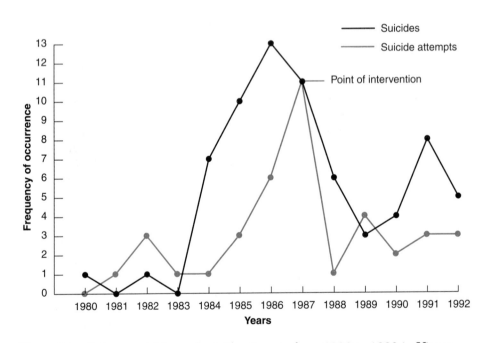

Figure 8.1   **Subway suicides and suicide attempts from 1980 to 1992 in Vienna, Austria.**

Source: Based on data in G. Sonneck, E. Etzersdorfer, and S. Nagel-Kuess, "Imitative Suicide on the Viennese Subway," *Social Science and Medicine,* 1994, *38,* p. 454. Copyright © 1994. Reprinted with permission of Elsevier Science.

BOX 8.3 When Death Takes a Holiday

Phillips also studied how mortality rises and dips during certain symbolically meaningful periods in people's lives. In one study, Phillips and King (1988) found that Jewish mortality fell sharply below the expected level just before Passover and rose by an equal amount above the expected level immediately afterward. To replicate this study, Phillips and Smith (1990) next gathered data about Chinese mortality during the Harvest Moon Festival and found that mortality among Chinese dipped by 35% in the week before the festival and peaked by the same amount in the week after. As a result of these time-series studies, Phillips and Smith hypothesized that some people may actually be able to prolong their lives until the arrival of some important, personally meaningful event.

where Os denote observations of the number (or frequency of occurrence) of subway suicides and suicide attempts per calendar year, and the X is the intervention of the media curtailment agreed to by leading newspapers (see also Box 8.3).

Single-Case Experimental Designs

A very popular class of within-subjects designs is called **single-case experimental research** (also called **small-N experimental research** and **N-of-1 experimental research**), although Campbell and Stanley (1963) conceptualized it as a subcategory of interrupted time-series designs. Single-case designs have long been a mainstay of behavior modification research. What is distinctive about this research is that it does not involve found experiments; instead, it incorporates treatments that are manipulated (and controlled for within the repeated measures designs). Generally speaking, all single-case experiments have the following characteristics: (a) only one sampling unit is studied or only a few units are studied; (b) repeated measures are taken of the unit (a within-subjects design); and (c) random assignment is rarely used. It would, of course, be impossible to assign a single subject at random to the various treatment procedures; instead, the occasions (e.g., at intervals of days, weeks, or months) may be assigned at random to the various treatment procedures, and the results are then compared (Hineline & Lattal, 2000).

Although the sampling unit in single-case designs is frequently a single subject (human or animal), it may also be a group, such as an assembly line, a class of students, one shift in a plant, or even a set of hungry pigeons (see Box 8.4). In one case, for example, the unit was the offensive backfield on a football team of 9- to 10-year-olds, the purpose of the study being to test a schedule of feedback to improve their execution of plays (Komaki & Barnett, 1977). In another case, the unit

BOX 8.4   Superstition in the Pigeon and the Financial Market

In a fascinating single-case study by B. F. Skinner (1948a), the unit was eight hungry pigeons. The birds were housed in cages in which there was a food hopper (containing grain) that swung into and away from the cage at regular intervals. A timing mechanism automatically moved the hopper into the cage so that all the pigeon had to do was reach into the hopper and eat. But six of the birds developed "superstitious" movements, in that whatever they had been doing in the moment when they were first rewarded with food became imprinted. One pigeon made counterclockwise motions about the cage before taking the grain; another performed a tossing motion of the head; and others persisted in making pendulum-type motions of the head and body or brushing movements toward the floor. Some behavioral economists theorize that this behavior is similar to what goes on in financial markets, where people make causal connections between two occurrences when, in fact, there is no causal link (Fuerbringer, 1997).

was a community, and the objective was to encourage drivers to obtain and use child safety seats by presenting them with coupons they could exchange for a seat and training in its use (Lavelle, Hovell, West, & Wahlgren, 1992). In another situation, a single-case design was used to evaluate the Great American Smokeout campaign's effect on smoking behavior in a large urban hospital (Hantula, Stillman, & Waranch, 1992).

Single-case experimental designs are particularly popular in educational, clinical, and counseling settings for evaluating the effects of operant conditioning interventions (Barlow, 1984; Bellack, Hersen, & Kazdin, 1982; Hersen & Barlow, 1976; Iversen & Lattal, 1991; Johnston & Pennypacker, 1993a, 1993b; Kazdin, 1992; Kazdin & Tuma, 1982). In operant conditioning (described in Chapter 2), one way to strengthen behavior is to use positive reinforcement (i.e., to reward the behavior), and one way to weaken behavior is to use extinction (i.e., no longer reinforcing the response). Such designs use as a **behavioral baseline** observations of a consistent pattern in the subject's behavior before the experimental treatment (or intervention) has been applied. That is, the observation of a relatively stable pattern of behavior before the treatment or intervention serves as a kind of "pretest" with which information about the pattern of behavior after the treatment can be compared. In this way, the unit (e.g., the subject or group) serves as its own control in a simple within-subjects design.

To illustrate, R. Vance Hall, Diane Lund, and Dolores Jackson (1968) used a single-case design to track the effects of interventions used in the classroom to shape the behavior of a child named Robbie. The results of this study are shown in Figure 8.2. During the baseline period (a class spelling period), the psychologists

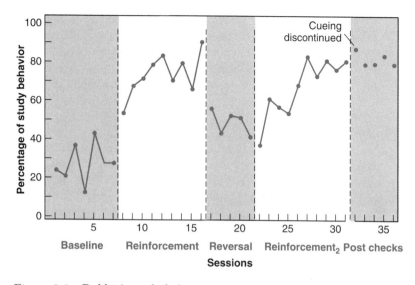

Figure 8.2   Robbie's study behavior record.

Source: Reproduced from R. V. Hall, D. Lund, and D. Jackson, "Effects of Teacher Attention on Study Behavior," *Journal of Applied Behavior Analysis,* 1968, *1,* 1–12. Used by courtesy of R. Vance Hall and the *Journal of Applied Behavior Analysis.*

recorded that Robbie's study behavior was consistently low, ranging from a low point of about 15% of the time to a high point of slightly over 40%, with an average of about 25%. The rest of the time, they observed, Robbie's behavior was disruptive: He snapped rubber bands, played with toys in his pocket, slowly drank his milk and played with the milk carton, and laughed with those around him. Almost 55% of his teacher's attention was absorbed by this disruptive behavior.

The psychologists believed that the teacher's attention was actually maintaining Robbie's disruptive behavior. To modify his poor behavior, they decided to use a twofold intervention: (a) ignoring the nonstudy and disruptive behavior (extinction) and (b) attending to the study behavior (positive reinforcement). Whenever Robbie engaged in 1 minute of continuous study, the observer would quietly signal the teacher and she would come over and compliment Robbie, saying such things as "Good work, Robbie." The second part of Figure 8.2 shows Robbie's increased study behavior during the nine sessions of this stage of the experiment. Then, to verify the effect of the teacher's attention, the consequences were reversed. The teacher ignored Robbie, remaining with the group. His study behavior decreased to about 50% over these sessions. When reinforcement was restored, Robbie's study behavior increased to and leveled off at about 75%. A checkup over the following weeks, when the teacher continued to praise his study behavior, showed that Robbie continued to study. Robbie's spelling performance also improved, with a jump from fewer than 5 words correct out of 10 to 9 correct out of 10 (although this improvement might also be attributed to certain uncontrolled sources of internal invalidity).

Instead of Xs and Os, single-case researchers use a different notation system to represent their specific designs. The basic model is called an **A-B-A design,** which evolved out of an even simpler prototype, the **A-B design** (which is the simplest of all single-case designs). In the A phase, no treatment (or intervention) is in effect, and in the B phase, a treatment (or intervention) is operating. The first A in the A-B-A and A-B designs is, therefore, the baseline period. Once the researcher observes steady, continuous behavior in the baseline phase, the treatment (B) is introduced. In other words, the researcher is observing and recording the behavior repeatedly within all phases of the design: the A phase *and* the B phase. In an A-B design, the dependent variable is measured repeatedly throughout the baseline and intervention phases of the study. In the A-B-A design, the treatment is withdrawn at the end of the B phase and the behavior is measured; that is, there are repeated measures before the treatment, during the treatment, and then when the treatment has been withdrawn.

A number of other single-case designs are used in clinical intervention assessment. In the **A-B-BC-B design,** for example, B and C are two different therapeutic interventions. The symbols tell us that the individual's behavior is measured or observed (a) before the introduction of either intervention, (b) during Intervention B, (c) during the combination of Intervention B and Intervention C, and (d) during B alone. The purpose of this design is to evaluate the effect of B both in combination with C and apart from C. Notice in this case that the sequence ends with a treatment phase, the reason being that, if the intervention is beneficial, the researcher does not want to end the study on a negative note.

Still another basic variant is the **A-B-A-B design.** The strategy again ends in a treatment phase of B, but this model provides two occasions (B to A and then A to B) for demonstrating the positive effects of the intervention (Hersen & Barlow, 1976). Returning to the illustrative study in Figure 8.2, we can see that it is a simple variant on this design, that is, an **A-B-A-B-A design.** Robbie's behavior was observed (a) before the reinforcement intervention, (b) during the intervention, (c) after removal of the invention, (d) during its restoration, and (e) after the desired behavior had been shaped by the prior intervention. The advantage of this design is that it allows us to compare Robbie's behavior during different phases, although, as noted, it does not control for threats to internal validity (such as the instrumentation problem). Although the interpretation of single-case results typically depends on visual inspection, there are also statistical techniques for testing focused predictions when evaluating these within-subjects designs (see, e.g., Kazdin, 1976; Kratochwill & Levin, 1992; Rosenthal & Rosnow, 1985; Rosenthal, Rosnow, & Rubin, 2000). (See also Box 8.5.)

Catchall Category of Correlational Research

The largest general class of quasi-experimental designs is called **correlational research,** which is actually a catchall category for odds and ends of quasi-experimental studies. Some of these studies have characteristics of the other two

BOX 8.5 Randomization in Single-Case Research

We mentioned that, on occasion, single-case researchers have used designs that are hard to distinguish from randomized experimental designs. An example is a study done by researchers at the University of Notre Dame (Anderson, Crowell, Hantula, & Siroky, 1988), in which the unit consisted of workers in a student-managed bar. The bar was a haunt of many students and faculty members, but the state board of health threatened to close it after citing health problems (e.g., pervasive accumulations of grease, and garbage disposal areas strewn with debris). The researchers agreed to try to modify the behavior of the students who worked at the bar, and they used a variant on the A-B-C design, in which the B phase consisted of exposing workers to a task clarification treatment, and the C phase was a feedback period. What is particularly striking about this single-case research is that the researchers allocated the workers to three groups at random in an effort to control for the delay of feedback. The A phase was the baseline period, in which the workers' usual behavior was recorded. During the B phase, all the workers were instructed in how to work more neatly, and a set of criteria was posted for all to see (e.g., put refrigerated items in the refrigerator, pick up garbage in the men's bathroom, clean bar utensils, and wipe off all games). A week later, each worker in Group 1 was given feedback, which continued for 2 more weeks. The feedback treatment in Group 2 did not begin until 1 week after it had been initiated in Group 1, and the feedback in Group 3 was initiated a week later. Thus, it was possible to compare the effects of immediate and delayed feedback in this combination of a between-groups (i.e., delay of feedback) and within-groups (i.e., A-B-C) design. The result of the behavior modification effort was that sanitary conditions in the bar improved markedly, so much that it was not closed—to the gratification of the students and the researchers.

categories but do not fall neatly into either one of them. In fact, the term *correlational* is not really a helpful description, because we know that correlations are also looked for in randomized experiments (i.e., the covariation of X and Y). We will give some examples that would be generally lumped together in this category, beginning with a correlational study that was done by Robert W. Weisberg (1994), a cognitive psychologist who was interested in an old theory that asserted that madness fosters creativity.

One way we might test this theory in a quasi-experimental correlational fashion would be to compile lists of all the musical compositions by a number of great and ordinary composers; we would then have expert critics rate the quality of each composition. We should find a relationship between the fame of the composer and the number of quality works by that composer. We would next do a search of biographical and autobiographical archives (e.g., books and letters) in order to find further data about any episodes of "madness" (which we would conceptualize as a moderator variable) affecting the creativity of these composers. Specifically, we hypothesize that the great composers were most creative when they were quite mad. We can also hypothesize that, when they were not mad, the quality and quantity of their work were no different from those of ordinary composers.

Weisberg did not conduct this particular study. Instead he did a correlational case study of one noted composer rather than of a great many composers. He chose for his case the musical compositions of the German composer Robert Schumann (1810–1856), who suffered from manic-depression (called *bipolar disorder*) and eventually committed suicide. Weisberg compiled an exhaustive list of Schumann's musical compositions, noted those that experts consider works of genius, and also documented the specific years in which Schumann suffered from depression or hypomania (i.e., a mild form of mania, characterized by elation and quickness of thought). Weisberg found no support for the causal model that madness fostered brilliance in Schumann's work; that is, the quality of his work seemed unaffected. However, as Table 8.2 shows, the specific state of Schumann's mental health seemed to be linked with the *quantity* of music he produced. That is, he had a tendency to produce more compositions when he was in a hypomanic than when he was in a depressive state. (You will see these results again in Chapter 10 when we discuss the use of graphics in data analysis.)

Weisberg's study is clearly correlational, but it also has features of an interrupted time-series design, where Schumann's career is interrupted periodically by bouts of depression and hypomania. In the designs we turn to next, each can be more clearly identified as a particular subtype of correlational design: the cross-lagged panel design and the longitudinal design using cohorts.

Table 8.2	Robert Schumann's Bouts of Depression and Hypomania and His Compositional Productivity		
Periods of depression		Periods of hypomania	
Year	Number of compositions	Year	Number of compositions
1830	1	1829	1
1831	1	1832	4
1839	4	1840	25
1842	3	1843	2
1844	0	1849	28
1847	5	1851	16
1848	5		

Source: Reproduced from R. W. Weisberg, "Genius and Madness? A Quasi-Experimental Test of the Hypothesis That Manic-Depression Increases Creativity," *Psychological Science,* 1994, *5,* 361–367.

Cross-Lagged Panel Designs

A **cross-lagged panel design** is called *cross-lagged* because, while it is basically another variant of a correlational design, some data points are treated as temporally "lagged" (or delayed) values of the outcome variable. It is called a *panel design* because, in social survey terminology, a *panel study* is another name for a **longitudinal study** (i.e., a study that examines the change in a person or a group of people over an extended period of time), and the roots of this design are in longitudinal investigations in sociological survey research (Lazarsfeld, 1978). (See also Box 8.6.)

You will recall that the correlation coefficient is a measure of the degree of association of two variables or measurements; we gave as an example the Pearson *r*. It will be recalled that *r*s can range from -1.0 (a perfect negative relationship) through 0 (no relationship) to $+1.0$ (a perfect positive relationship). As illustrated in Figure 8.3, A and B represent two variables, each of which has been measured individually at two successive time periods. Three sets of paired correlations are also represented, generally described as test-retest, synchronous, and cross-lagged correlations.

The two **test-retest correlations** (r_{A1A2} and r_{B1B2}) indicate the reliability of A and B over time; that is, they refer to the relationship, respectively, between A1 and A2 and between B1 and B2. The two **synchronous correlations** (r_{A1B1} and r_{A2B2}), when compared, indicate the reliability of the association between A and B over time; that is, they refer to the relationship, respectively, between A1 and B1 and between A2 and B2. The two **cross-lagged correlations** (r_{A1B2} and r_{B1A2})

BOX 8.6 The Framingham Heart Study

Longitudinal research has come to play a significant role in medicine as well as in behavioral and social science. In medical research, for example, an important longitudinal study was started by the U.S. Public Health Service in 1948—known as the *Framingham heart study*. Responding to concerns about the soaring coronary disease rate in the United States, this study has followed several thousand residents of Framingham, Massachusetts. The findings have helped to improve our understanding of risk factors that predict cardiovascular disease. In 1960, cigarette smoking was first revealed to be a risk factor, and in 1961, high blood pressure was found to be another risk factor. The correlational findings in this study have led to randomized clinical trials that have confirmed the preventive approach to combating heart disease by exercising, not smoking, lowering harmful cholesterol, and reducing stress, blood pressure, and obesity (National Heart Institute, 1966).

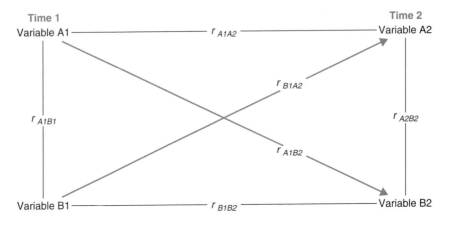

Figure 8.3   **Design for cross-lagged and other correlations between Variables A and B.**

Source: From p. 99 in *Essentials of Behavioral Research: Methods and Data Analysis,* 2e, by Robert Rosenthal and Ralph L. Rosnow. © 1991. Reprinted by permission of The McGraw-Hill Book Companies.

show the relationships between two sets of data points, where one is treated as a lagged value of the outcome variable, in this case the association, respectively, between A1 and B2 and between B1 and A2.

The causal question concerns whether A is a more likely cause of B than B is of A, or whether A causes B to a greater extent than B causes A. The basic logic used to arrive at the answer is that, given equally reliable test-retest correlations and synchronous correlations equal in magnitude, comparing the cross-lagged correlations should enable us to conclude which is the more likely causal direction, or which variable shows the preponderance of causal influence. Presumably, we would conclude that A is a more likely (or more important) cause of B than B is of A if r_{A1B2} is appreciably higher than r_{B1A2}. On the other hand, we would conclude that B is a more likely (or more important) cause of A than A is of B if r_{B1A2} is appreciably higher than r_{A1B2}. Let us use a real-life example to show how this design is used, and also to reveal the hidden problem of *confounded hypotheses* (i.e., competing confounded pairs of hypotheses).

Figure 8.4 is taken from a study by Louise H. Kidder, Robert L. Kidder, and Paul Snyderman (1976). These investigators used archival data in the *FBI Uniform Crime Reports* for 1968–1969; the variables noted are the number of police (A) and the number of burglaries (B) in 724 U.S. cities during each year. Looking first at the test-retest correlations (.86 and .89), we see that both the number of police and the number of burglaries were reliable during this 2-year period. That is, cities with a lot of police in 1968 had a lot of police in 1969, and also cities with a lot of burglaries in 1968 continued to have a lot of burglaries in 1969. The synchronous correlations of .47 and .39 between the number of police and the number of burglaries for 1968 and 1969, respectively, were substantial in magnitude.

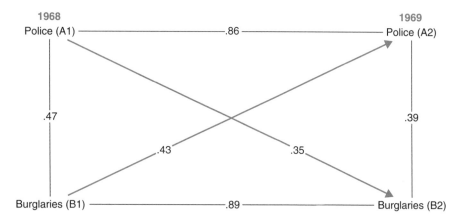

Figure 8.4   **Correlation of number of police and number of burglaries per capita measured in 1968 and 1969 in 724 cities.**

Source: Adapted from Kidder, Kidder, and Snyderman, 1976, by permission of L. H. Kidder.

At first glance, our intuition says that burglaries may cause an increase in the number of police. The problem of confounded hypotheses is that it might just as well be hypothesized that police increase burglaries, because the more police there are available, the more opportunities there are to keep thorough records of all the burglaries reported. That is, when there are not many police, some reported burglaries may go unrecorded. The cross-lagged correlations do not allow us to definitively rule out either competing hypothesis and, in fact, provide some support for both (.43 and .35). If you think carefully, you are sure to come up with other rival hypotheses. There are statistical ways of trying to rule out rival causal hypotheses in cross-lagged designs, but they also are not without problems (Campbell & Stanley, 1963; Kenny, 1979; Pelz & Andrew, 1964; Rozelle & Campbell, 1969). While the cross-lagged panel strategy is no longer as popular as it once was, some leading methodologists continue to emphasize its usefulness as an exploratory procedure in the analysis of longitudinal data (Campbell & Kenny, 1999; cf. Kenny & Campbell, 1984, 1989).

Longitudinal Designs Using Cohorts

Suppose we wanted to study the *life course* of some variable of interest. One possibility would be to estimate maturational effects by using a **cross-sectional design,** that is, a design that takes a slice of time and, in this case, examines several age groups during one period. An example would be a cross-sectional survey performed in 1999 to study the maturational effects of the variable of interest in cohorts (see also Box 8.7) born in 1959, 1969, 1979, and 1989. The purpose of the survey is to develop a growth curve of the effects of interest in people who are 10, 20, 30, and 40 years old. This approach would be a lot easier than, for example,

BOX 8.7 Cohorts and Generation Gaps

In ancient times, a **cohort** was a company of soldiers in the Roman legions. In behavioral and social science, the term means any group sharing a given trait, usually age. Thus, a group of people born around the same time and having had similar life experiences constitutes a cohort or generation. As shown in Table 8.3, a generation is usually defined as 20 years, so a "generation gap" implies a 20-year differential between cohorts.

examining people's responses or behavior over an extended period of time (i.e., a longitudinal study).

The problem with our cross-sectional design is that those who were 40 in 1999 may have had different life experiences at age 10 (in 1969), from those who were 10 years old in 1999. That is, it is likely that children who are born and grow up in one period have life events quite different from those of children who are born and grow up in another period. Some of these experiences (such as schooling, repeated exposure to TV, and growing up with the Internet) may, in turn, systematically alter what is considered "normal" in the two groups. The problem in research is that a possible confounding of cohort and maturation would be hidden in a design that failed to look at several cohorts longitudinally. Insofar as such experiences are associated with the variable of interest, we may be led to spurious conclusions about maturational effects if we rely solely on a cross-sectional design to find them.

Table 8.3 illustrates how the relationship between maturation (age) and another variable may be misinterpreted because of a reliance on the results of cross-sectional studies instead of on the results of longitudinal studies of cohorts. This table shows the results of a study done in the Netherlands by Jacques A. Hagenaars and Niki P. Cobben (1978), in which data were compiled on the percentages of women with no religious affiliation, by age and time period. The results are shown for seven different cohorts (or generations) of women in the Netherlands. The values in the vertical rectangle beneath Period 4 provide the basic data for a cross-sectional analysis, and the values in the parallelogram for Cohort 4 provide the basic data for a longitudinal analysis. Notice that the trends are opposite in these two sets of values and therefore lead to completely opposite conclusions.

A graph showing this difference appears in Figure 8.5; it allows us to compare the cross-sectional data for Period 4 (1969) with the longitudinal data for Cohort 4 in Table 8.3. The cross-sectional curve would mislead us to the conclusion that, with the passing of years and the approach of the end of life, religious observance increased (i.e., the percentage of nonaffiliation decreased) in these women. By contrast, the cohort curve tells us that the opposite is true: Religious observance actually decreased (i.e., the percentage of nonaffiliation increased) in these women as they became older.

Table 8.3	Percentages of Women in the Netherlands with No Religious Affiliation According to Age and Time Period			
	Period 1 (1909)	Period 2 (1929)	Period 3 (1949)	Period 4 (1969)
Age 20–30	Cohort 4 4.8%	Cohort 5 13.9%	Cohort 6 17.4%	Cohort 7 23.9%
Age 40–50	Cohort 3 3.1%	Cohort 4 11.9%	Cohort 5 17.2%	Cohort 6 22.0%
Age 60–70	Cohort 2 1.9%	Cohort 3 6.7%	Cohort 4 11.9%	Cohort 5 19.4%
Age 80-	Cohort 1 1.2%	Cohort 2 3.8%	Cohort 3 6.6%	Cohort 4 12.2%

Note: An example of a cross-sectional design is shown by the vertical analysis (Period 4), and an example of a longitudinal design is shown by the diagonal analysis (Cohort 4).

Source: Reproduced from "Age, Cohort and Period: A General Model for the Analysis of Social Change" by J. A. Hagenaars and N. P. Cobben, 1978, *Netherlands Journal of Sociology, 14*, pp. 58–91. Used by permission of J. A. Hagenaars and Elsevier Science Publishers.

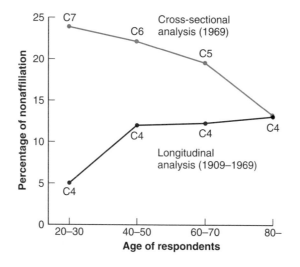

Figure 8.5   **Percentages of nonaffiliation with church of women in the Netherlands, as shown by a cross-sectional design in 1969 and a longitudinal design from 1909 to 1969.** Cohorts are symbolized as C7 (Cohort 7), C6 (Cohort 6), and so forth.

Source: Reproduced from J. A. Hagenaars and N. P. Cobben, "Age, Cohort and Period: A General Model for the Analysis of Social Change," *Netherlands Journal of Sociology*, 1978, *14*, pp. 58–91. Used by permission of J. A. Hagenaars and Elsevier Science Publishers.

Researchers who like to use longitudinal designs—including animal researchers (e.g., Fairbanks, 1993)—also attempt, whenever possible, to examine several cohorts cross-sectionally and longitudinally. In this way they learn about cohort changes as well as age group changes as a function of period. Other informative uses of longitudinal designs are possible, although each is limited in some predictable ways (for discussion, see Rosenthal & Rosnow, 1991, pp. 105–109). Thus, as stated earlier, it is a good idea to use several different strategies that allow convergence on the phenomenon of interest. Each strategy will be limited in some way, but the objective is to use procedures whose strengths and weaknesses will compensate for one another.

Summary of Ideas

1. Quasi-experimental research is said to resemble randomized experimental research in some respects, except that quasi-experimental research does not use a randomization procedure.

2. Four broad categories of nonrandomized research are (a) studies with nonequivalent groups, (b) time-series designs, (c) single-case designs, and (d) correlational designs.

3. In nonequivalent-groups designs, matching may be used to create comparability of the subjects found in the treatment and control conditions.

4. The use of wait-list controls can sometimes overcome objections to randomized experiments that use placebo controls.

5. Inferring causation in epidemiological research emulates the logic of Mill's methods of agreement and difference (e.g., the study of a case of food poisoning).

6. Moderator variables are factors that alter the magnitude of a relationship (e.g., Eagly's meta-analytic study of how a period of history moderated the relationship between gender and influenceability).

7. Interrupted time-series designs compare the effects of an intervention in the situation before and after it occurred (e.g., Phillips's work on the delay of death and on imitative suicide, and the latter's implications for the Vienna subway system).

8. Single-case experimental designs come in many different forms (e.g., A-B-BC-B and A-B-A-B); the unit of study may be an N of 1 (e.g., the study of Robbie) or a few subjects (e.g., Skinner's study of superstition in pigeons) or several groups of individuals with one of the treatments randomized (Box 8.5).

9. Correlational research includes many designs that do not easily fit into the other two categories (e.g., Weisberg's study of Robert Schumann's hypomania and musical productivity).

10. In the cross-lagged panel approach, some data points are treated as temporally delayed values, and the cross-lagged correlations are analyzed along with the test-retest and the synchronous correlations for the direction of causation (e.g., Kidder et al.'s study of the number of police and the number of burglaries).

11. Longitudinal research means that the variable of interest is observed in such as a way as to uncover changes that occur over time.

12. In studies in which age is the independent variable, a cross-sectional analysis may lead to spurious conclusions (e.g., the study of women's religiosity in the Netherlands).

Key Terms

WEB ACTIVITY

Learn more about nonexperimental and nonrandomized research by visiting Professor William M. K. Trochim's http://www.trochim.human.cornell.edu/tutorial/TUTORIAL.HTM and clicking on the relevant links.

Multiple-Choice Questions for Review

1. Which of the following is definitely not characteristic of quasi-experimental designs? (a) an experimental group; (b) randomization; (c) a control group; (d) repeated measurement

2. A researcher at North Carolina State University develops a new treatment program for alcoholism. He allows participants to choose whether they want to be in the experimental group or the control group. This is an example of a (a) correlational design; (b) nonequivalent-groups design; (c) time-series design; (d) cohort design.

3. In the case directly above, which threat to internal validity is the study least able to rule out? (a) selection; (b) history; (c) maturation; (d) instrumentation

4. One type of research design involves measuring a single variable on many separate occasions and assessing the impact of interventions on this variable. This type of design is called a (a) correlational design; (b) cohort design; (c) cross-sectional design; (d) time-series design.

5. A behavioral therapist at Northeastern University is working with autistic children. He decides first to observe their baseline levels of disruptive behavior and then to observe their behavior several times after administering his intervention. He then removes his intervention to determine whether disruptive behavior will return to baseline levels. This type of design can be described as an (a) A-B design; (b) A-B-C design; (c) A-B-A design; (d) A-B-A-C design.

6. A study examining changes in individuals over an extended period of time is called a (a) longitudinal study; (b) quasi-longitudinal study; (c) nonequivalent-groups design; (d) time-series study.

7. A researcher at the University of Montana conducts a study on the relationship between watching TV (Variable A) and violent behavior (Variable B). She measures both variables at two points in

time. She calculates the correlation between watching TV at Time 1 and watching TV at Time 2. This is an example of a(n) _____ correlation. (a) internal validity; (b) test-retest; (c) synchronous; (d) cross-lagged

8. The same researcher calculates the correlation between watching TV at Time 2 and violent behavior at Time 2. This is an example of a(n) _____ correlation. (a) internal consistency; (b) test-retest; (c) synchronous; (d) cross-lagged

9. In the study above, this researcher also calculates the correlation between watching TV at Time 2 and violent behavior at Time 1. This is an example of a(n) _____ correlation. (a) internal validity; (b) test-retest; (c) synchronous; (d) cross-lagged

10. The researcher finds that r_{A1B2} = .30 and r_{B1A2} = .02. These results suggest that (a) it is more likely that watching TV causes violent behavior; (b) it is more likely that violent behavior causes TV watching; (c) there is no causal relationship between watching TV and violent behavior; (d) watching TV and violent behavior have reciprocal causal effects.

Discussion Questions for Review

1. A University of Toledo student wants to assess the possible causal relationship between therapist approval, expressed in tone of voice, and degree of patient progress. Using a sample of 45 therapist-patient dyads, he measures these variables at the beginning and end of treatment. Based on results shown below, what do you think he will conclude?

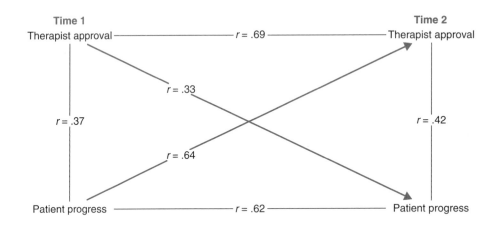

2. Using a cross-sectional design, an Oklahoma University student found a lower degree of androgyny in women aged 40–45 than in women aged 20–25. What confounding variable prevents him from concluding that androgyny decreases with age? Can you think of a better way to do the study?

3. A University of Nevada student wants to evaluate the effects of an educational intervention that is purported to motivate elementary-school children to do their homework. She had hoped to perform an experiment in which she would randomly assign large numbers of children in Reno either to the intervention treatment or to a large control group. However, she ran into complications and found that she would not be able to use randomization. Can you think of some other way that she might evaluate the effects of the intervention without the use of randomization? What are the limitations of this way?

4. A Catholic University student wants to do a time-series analysis of the effects of assassination attempts against U.S. presidents but cannot decide on the dependent variable. What dependent variable would you advise her to track, and how would you suggest she locate the kind of data she needs for such a study?

Answers to Review Questions

Multiple-Choice Questions

1. b	**3.** a	**5.** c	**7.** b	**9.** d
2. b	**4.** d	**6.** a	**8.** c	**10.** a

Discussion Questions

1. Since (a) the test-retest correlations are similar to each other, (b) the synchronous correlations are similar to each other, and (c) the cross-lagged correlations differ appreciably from each other (.64 versus .33), it might be reasonable for him to conclude a preponderance of causal influence of the patient progress variable over the therapist approval variable.

2. The cohort of women is confounded with their age, so the student cannot tell whether age or cohort differences or both are reflected in the obtained differences. For example, it may be that the women aged 40–45 have been showing an *increasing* degree of androgyny as they developed from age 20–25 to age 40–45. A longitudinal design of the type represented, for example, by the diagonal analysis shown in Table 8.3 would be a better way to do this study.

3. She might try to match the children finding their way into each of the two conditions on as many relevant variables as possible and then perform her data analysis only on the subset of children in whom there are very close matches. Because of the large proportion of children for whom there may be no good matches, and who would therefore be omitted from the design, the generalizability of the study may be decreased substantially. In addition, the lack of randomization could seriously limit the internal validity of the study.

4. Some dependent variables that may reflect presidential assassination attempts are stock market figures, mental-health-facility-usage data, gun-control legislation activity, the number of people announcing for elective positions, views of the United States reflected in the foreign press, and changes in party affiliation. Reference librarians can help her find the government and other documents that carry the needed information. These documents would also be a rich source of ideas for other dependent variables for which data are available.

CHAPTER 9

Survey Research and Subject Recruitment

Preview Questions

- What is meant by the avoidance of bias and instability in survey designs?
- What is the difference between simple random sampling and stratified random sampling?
- What is characteristic of an unbiased sampling plan?
- How are point estimates and 95% confidence intervals calculated and interpreted in survey research?
- What is nonresponse bias, and how is it minimized?
- How is nonresponse bias related to volunteer subject bias?
- How is volunteer bias addressed outside survey research?

Selecting the Research Participants

In the two preceding chapters, we examined the logic and limitations of various randomized and nonrandomized designs for empirical studies. As a leading statistician remarked, "In a sense all studies lie on a continuum from irrelevant to relevant with respect to answering a question" (D. B. Rubin, 1974, p. 699). For example, a randomized experiment in a college setting may have a restricted sample of subjects but more control over the variables of interest. On the other hand, a nonrandomized experiment in a natural setting may have less control over the particular treatment (or intervention) but may be less constrained as to the participants. In this chapter, we turn our attention to the selection of research subjects. Most experimenters in psychology would probably say they are interested in learning about human nature in general, a statement explaining why they often use **opportunity samples** (groups made up of the first units that are available) rather than special sampling procedures to select participants. By contrast, survey researchers would say that, as they are interested in generalizing their findings to a specified larger pool (or **population**) of people, using an opportunity sample can produce spurious results and misleading conclusions. Instead, survey researchers recruit participants from *sampling lists* (or *frames*) that identify the relevant units or subgroups in the population (e.g., census information).

For example, pollsters often use survey designs to map out some specified population's opinions on important societal issues, such as people's fears of crime or their choice of political candidates. Similar methods are sometimes used in epidemiological research, forensic research, economic research, and many other areas. When health officials wanted to find out about trends in cases of tuberculosis contracted on the job, they did surveys of hospitals to make a count of reported employees with TB (Kilborn, 1994). As the federal courts became inundated with mass torts involving asbestos cases (averaging 1,140 per month in 1990, or one third of the federal criminal caseload), one solution was to sample asbestos cases from the larger pool within a court's jurisdiction. The assessed damages in randomly chosen cases from each of five disease categories were then applied to each larger pool (Saks & Blanck, 1992).

Instead of questioning every member of the population (which is usually impossible), this type of research focuses on a segment (or **sample**) that is believed to be typical of the population. How can researchers be certain that the segment is **representative** (or typical) of the population? How can they be certain, for example, that fears of crime in the sample are typical of percentages in a specified population or know that reported TB cases in sampled hospitals are representative of trends in all similar hospitals? The answer is that they can never be 100% sure. They can make a reasonable guess, however, by first developing an accurate sampling frame defining the population and then relying on a carefully designed blueprint (called the **sampling plan**) for selecting the sample by means of probability sampling. The term **probability sampling** implies that randomness enters into the selection process (i.e., **random selection**) at some stage so that the laws of mathematical probability apply; **probability** refers to the mathematical chance of an event's occurring. Examples would be the likelihood of getting "heads" when you flip a coin once (1 chance in 2), or getting a 2 when you throw a die once (1 chance in 6), or knowing what a 20-to-1 shot is at the racetrack (see Box 9.1).

Although survey studies can take many different forms, all use sampling plans in which some method of probability sampling determines the random selection of subjects. Such plans enable the researcher to assume reasonably—but with no guarantee of being correct—that the sample is representative of its population. However, practical problems may impose limits on the representativeness of the sample. For example, even in the most carefully conducted survey study, not everyone who is asked to participate will agree to do so. Later in this chapter, we will discuss how survey researchers confront this problem, and how experimenters cope with a similar problem. We will begin by describing some basic concepts in survey sampling and then illustrate the logic of probability sampling plans. (Incidentally, remember not to confuse random selection with random assignment. As explained previously, random assignment is the unbiased allocation of units to

BOX 9.1 What Are Racetrack Odds?

A "20-to-1 shot" means that, in the eyes of the odds setters, this particular long shot will win about once in every 21 races, given the conditions under which the horse is currently running. Why should a horse ever beat other horses that are faster? The lead horse might stumble, the jockey on the second horse might fall off, and so forth. Unlikely? Yes—but that is why the track management is willing to pay 20-to-1 odds. This example gives us two ideas about probability: (a) It implies relative uncertainty, and (b) it deals with chance. We will have more to say about this concept in later chapters.

groups or conditions; its purpose is to control differences in the groups or conditions to be compared.)

Basic Concepts in Survey Samples

Survey research is done not only by private organizations (the Gallup Organization and Louis Harris & Associates, among others), but by individual researchers working alone or with ties to private organizations (e.g., the Research Triangle Institute in North Carolina), and in the United States at university-based institutes that are equipped to implement face-to-face and telephone interviewing in national probability surveys (such as the University of Chicago's National Opinion Research Center, the University of Michigan's Institute for Social Research, and Temple University's Institute for Survey Research). Although this research can take many different forms, all valid survey research is characterized by sampling plans in which every element, or sampling unit, in the population has a known nonzero probability of being selected. Two important statistical requirements of a probability sampling plan are (a) that the sample values be unbiased and (b) that there be stability in the samples.

To be **unbiased,** the values produced by the sample must, on average, coincide with the "true" values of the population—although we can never actually be sure that this requirement has been met in a given study unless we already know those values. **Stability,** on the other hand, means that there is not much variability (or spread) in the sample values. Stability can be estimated by statistical procedures such as the variance and the standard deviation (which are described in the next chapter). Figure 9.1 will help you to understand these two technical requirements more clearly. In the design, the O is a particular sampling unit, the X represents the true population mean, and the horizontal line represents the underlying continuum on which the relevant values are determined.

Suppose we were trying to estimate the number of widgets that teams of assembly-line workers make in a given period. In the diagram, O = a work team's

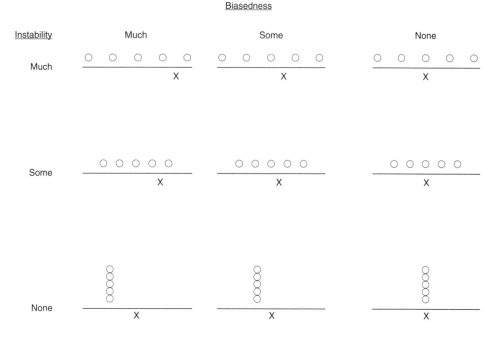

Figure 9.1   Illustrations of bias and instability in sampling.
The circles represent sampling units located on some dimension, and X represents the population mean.

Source: From p. 208 in *Essentials of Behavioral Research: Methods and Data Analysis*, 2nd. ed. by Robert Rosenthal and Ralph L. Rosnow. Copyright © 1991. Reprinted by permission of The McGraw-Hill Book Companies.

output, X = the value we are trying to estimate, and the continuum ranges from a low to a high number. The distance between the true population value and the midpoint of the sampling units indicates the amount of **bias** (i.e., systematic error). The spread (variability) among the sampling units indicates their degree of instability. We see that the amount of instability is constant within each row, going from a high amount of instability (or spread) in row 1 to no instability in row 3. The amount of bias is constant in each column, going from a high bias in column 1 to zero bias in column 3. Thus, in the three cases in column 3, the sample values are balanced around the population mean, but with much instability in row 1, some in row 2, and none in row 3. In the three cases in row 3, there is no instability, but there is much bias in column 1, some in column 2, and none in column 3. The hypothetical case at the intersection of row 3 and column 3 represents the best of all situations, although it is unlikely that we will ever find such complete agreement.

Generally speaking, the more homogeneous (alike) the members of the population are, the fewer of them need to be sampled (see also Box 9.2). If all widget makers were exactly alike (the case in row 3, column 3), *any* sampling unit would provide complete information about the population as a whole. The more hetero-

BOX 9.2 The Wine Taster

In the manufacture of red wine, grapes are crushed and the residue is put into huge vats in which fermentation occurs. The wine is then drawn off into barrels, where fermentation continues, and the product is periodically sampled by the wine taster. The wine taster needs to draw only a small sample in order to evaluate the quality of the wine in the barrel. It is the same in survey research: The more homogeneous the population, the smaller the sample that needs to be drawn.

geneous (dissimilar) the different teams are, the more sampling units are needed to ensure that we will sample the full range of dissimilarity.

In connection with our never knowing "for sure" whether there is bias in the results, it is sometimes said that election forecasting allows us to know for sure because we can compare the predicted results with the actual results. For example, Gallup Survey records in U.S. presidential elections show discrepancies that are remarkably small. In the 1996 election, the final election poll conducted by the Gallup Organization for *USA Today* and CNN, using 1,448 "likely voters" who were sampled on November 3–4, 1996, predicted that Bill Clinton would win 48%, Robert Dole 40%, and Ross Perot 6% of the vote. The prediction that Clinton would top Dole by 8% was right on the mark, and the specific vote predictions were close to the actual election result of 49% for Clinton, 41% for Dole, and 8% for Perot (Kagay, 1996). Polls that are conducted very close to the election are bound to be better predictors than early polls, but there is no guarantee that voters will not change their minds between the poll and the election. In fact, in the 1996 election, many early polls reported a landslide 15% point lead by Clinton, which may have made some Clinton supporters complacent and therefore less likely to show up. In the 2000 election, the final difference between George W. Bush and Al Gore was razor thin in some states, and not surprisingly, even the final polls were in some disagreement about which candidate would ultimately be the victor.

Simple Random Sampling

There is one sure way to know whether a sample is biased, and that is to examine every member of the population and the sample *at the same time* the sampling is conducted. If the pattern of replies in the sample exactly matches the pattern of replies in the population, we know for certain that there is no sampling bias in the survey sample. Such a procedure, of course, makes no sense, practically speaking. That is, we would have no need of a sample if we knew the responses of everyone in the population. Thus, we use a selection process involving probability sampling.

The basic prototype of probability sampling is called **simple random sampling.** The *simple* tells us that the sample is selected from an undivided population, and *random* means that the sample is to be chosen by a process that will give every sampling unit in the population the same chance of being selected (see also Box 9.3). In order for this to occur, the selection of one unit must have no influence on the selection of other units. In simple random sampling, a further requirement is that we have knowledge of the existence of all the units in the population. The idea is to draw units (e.g., names) one at a time until we have as large a sample as we require. The actual method of selecting people might consist of throwing dice, using a table of random digits, or even spinning a roulette wheel or drawing capsules from an urn. In connection with telephone interviewing (described in Chapter 5), **random digit dialing** is used to include people with unlisted numbers; the researcher selects the first three digits according to the geographic area of interest and then uses a computer program to select the last four digits.

Procedures such as drawing capsules from an urn provide the least complex approach, but they are not without potential problems. A famous case illustrating the hazards of inadequate randomization occurred in 1970. The previous year, while the war in Vietnam was in progress, the U.S. Congress had passed a bill allowing the use of a random lottery to select conscripts for the armed forces. To give each individual an equal chance of being selected or not selected, the planners decided to pick birthdays out of an urn. The 365 days of the year were written on slips of paper and placed inside tiny cylindrical capsules. Once all the capsules were inside the urn, it was shaken for several hours, and then the capsules were

BOX 9.3 Randomness and Aimlessness

Don't confuse randomness with *aimlessness*, or "hit-or-miss" sampling, which, in fact, can seldom be called random. You can prove the difference to yourself by asking a friend to write down "at random" several hundred one-digit numbers from 0 to 9. Afterward, tabulate the 0s, 1s, 2s, and so on. If the numbers were truly random, there would be few obvious sequences, and each digit would occur approximately 10% of the time. You will find, however, that the results are inconsistent with the hypothesis of randomness. You will see obvious sequences, and some digits will occur with high frequency, whereas others will appear hardly at all (Wallis & Roberts, 1956). Interestingly, however, psychologist Allen Neuringer, using a single-case experimental strategy, was able to reinforce pigeons in making left-right choices that looked pretty random (Neuringer, 1992). He then used feedback to reinforce individual Reed College students to generate sequences of numbers that also closely resembled random sequences (Neuringer, 1996; Neuringer & Voss, 1993).

removed, one by one. However, the results were biased in spite of the precautions taken to ensure a random sample: The birth dates in December tended to be drawn first, those in November next, then those in October, and so on. The reason was that the January capsules were put in the urn first, the February capsules next, and so forth, and layers were formed with the December capsules on top. Even shaking the urn for several hours did not ensure a thorough mixing of the capsules (Broome, 1984; Kolata, 1986).

The use of a table of random digits, such as Table 9.1, helps us to avoid such pitfalls. The 2,250 digits in this list came from a million random digits that were generated by an electronic roulette wheel programmed to produce a random frequency pulse every tiny fraction of a second (Rand Corporation, 1955). As a check on the hypothesis of randomness, the computer also counted the frequency of 0s, 1s, 2s, and so on in the final results. A probability method that is impartial would produce an approximately equal number of 0s, 1s, 2s, and so on in the overall table of a million random digits. This equality is exactly what was observed.

In Chapter 7, we showed how to use the random numbers in this table to allocate subjects to experimental and control conditions (i.e., random assignment). To see how you might use this table if you were doing a survey (i.e., a random selection), imagine you want to conduct a public opinion poll, and you decide to interview 10 men and 10 women individually after choosing them at random from a list of 96 men and a list of 99 women. You begin by numbering the population of men consecutively from 01 to 96 and the population of women from 01 to 99. You are now ready to use the random digits in Table 9.1. To do so, you put your finger blindly on a starting position. You can start anywhere in the table and then move your finger in any direction, as long as you do not pick a set of numbers because they "look right" or avoid a set of numbers because they "do not look right." Suppose you put your finger on the first five-digit number in row 5, column 1. Beginning with this number, 12807, you will read across the line two digits at a time, selecting the men numbered 12, 80, 79, 99, and so on, until you have randomly chosen the 10 male interviewees. You do the same thing, beginning at another blindly chosen point, to select the 10 female interviewees. If you have fewer than 10 persons on each list, you will need to read only one digit at a time; if you have between 100 and 999 persons on your list, you will need to read three digits at a time, and so forth.

Random Sampling Options

Suppose you choose the same two-digit number more than once, or suppose you choose a two-digit number not represented by any member of the population. In either case, you go on to the next two-digit number in the row (that is, unless you are sampling with replacement, as discussed next). What if your population is so small that you are forced to skip many numbers in the table because they are larger than the largest number of people in your population? For example, what if there are 450 people in the population and you want to select 50 people at

Table 9.1 — 2,250 Random Digits

Rows	1–5	6–10	11–15	16–20	21–25	26–30	31–35	36–40	41–45	46–50
1	10097	32533	76520	13586	34673	54876	80959	09117	39292	74945
2	37542	04805	64894	74296	24805	24037	20636	10402	00822	91665
3	08422	68953	19645	09303	23209	02560	15953	34764	35080	33605
4	99019	02529	09376	70715	38311	31165	88676	74397	04436	27659
5	12807	99970	80157	36147	64032	36653	98951	16877	12171	76833
6	66065	74717	34072	76850	36697	36170	65813	39885	11199	29170
7	31060	10805	45571	82406	35303	42614	86799	07439	23403	09732
8	85269	77602	02051	65692	68665	74818	73053	85247	18623	88579
9	63573	32135	05325	47048	90553	57548	28468	28709	83491	25624
10	73796	45753	03529	64778	35808	34282	60935	20344	35273	88435
11	98520	17767	14905	68607	22109	40558	60970	93433	50500	73998
12	11805	05431	39808	27732	50725	68248	29405	24201	52775	67851
13	83452	99634	06288	98083	13746	70078	18475	40610	68711	77817
14	88685	40200	86507	58401	36766	67951	90364	76493	29609	11062
15	99594	67348	87517	64969	91826	08928	93785	61368	23478	34113
16	65481	17674	17468	50950	58047	76974	73039	57186	40218	16544
17	80124	35635	17727	08015	45318	22374	21115	78253	14385	53763
18	74350	99817	77402	77214	43236	00210	45521	64237	96286	02655
19	69916	26803	66252	29148	36936	87203	76621	13990	94400	56418
20	09893	20505	14225	68514	46427	56788	96297	78822	54382	14598
21	91499	14523	68479	27686	46162	83554	94750	89923	37089	20048
22	80336	94598	26940	36858	70297	34135	53140	33340	42050	82341
23	44104	81949	85157	47954	32979	26575	57600	40881	22222	06413
24	12550	73742	11100	02040	12860	74697	96644	89439	28707	25815
25	63606	49329	16505	34484	40219	52563	43651	77082	07207	31790
26	61196	90446	26457	47774	51924	33729	65394	59593	42582	60527
27	15474	45266	95270	79953	59367	83848	82396	10118	33211	59466
28	94557	28573	67897	54387	54622	44431	91190	42592	92927	45973
29	42481	16213	97344	08721	16868	48767	03071	12059	25701	46670
30	23523	78317	73208	89837	68935	91416	26252	29663	05522	82562
31	04493	52494	75246	33824	45862	51025	61962	79335	65337	12472
32	00549	97654	64051	88159	96119	63896	54692	82391	23287	29529
33	35963	15307	26898	09354	33351	35462	77974	50024	90103	39333
34	59808	08391	45427	26842	83609	49700	13021	24892	78565	20106
35	46058	85236	01390	92286	77281	44077	93910	83647	70617	42941
36	32179	00597	87379	25241	05567	07007	86743	17157	85394	11838
37	69234	61406	20117	45204	15956	60000	18743	92423	97118	96338
38	19565	41430	01758	75379	40419	21585	66674	36806	84962	85207
39	45155	14938	19476	07246	43667	94543	59047	90033	20826	69541
40	94864	31994	36168	10851	34888	81553	01540	35456	05014	51176
41	98086	24826	45240	28404	44999	08896	39094	73407	35441	31880
42	33185	16232	41941	50949	89435	48581	88695	41994	37548	73043
43	80951	00406	96382	70774	20151	23387	25016	25298	94624	61171
44	79752	49140	71961	28296	69861	02591	74852	20539	00387	59579
45	18633	32537	98145	06571	31010	24674	05455	61427	77938	91936

Source: From *A Million Random Digits with 100,000 Normal Deviates,* 1955, New York: Free Press. Reprinted by permission of the Rand Corporation.

BOX 9.4 Sampling With or Without Replacement

To do random sampling with replacement, we would have to be selecting items one at a time. For example, suppose the sampling units are days of the year sealed in tiny capsules in an urn stirred so completely that there are no layers or nonrandom clusters. We simply select a capsule, read it, and put it back, so that the same capsule may be selected more than once. For random sampling without replacement, we do not need to select items one at a time. For example, if we scooped a handful of capsules, recorded each, and then discarded them all and called it quits, this would be sampling without replacement. The wine taster (Box 9.2) who draws and then spits out a small sample of wine is also doing simple random sampling without replacement. We wouldn't have it any other way!

random? Because the population is numbered from 001 to 450, you will have to skip approximately one half the three-digit numbers in the section of the table you have chosen (i.e., those from 451 to 999). As a simple solution (also acceptable in terms of randomness), you may mentally subtract 500 from any number in the range from 501 to 999. This additional option will result in fewer unusable selections.

Another option in some situations is sampling with or without replacement (see also Box 9.4). **Sampling with replacement** means that the selected names are placed in the selection pool again and may be reselected on subsequent draws. Thus, every unit in the population continues to have the same probability of being chosen every time a number is read. In **sampling without replacement,** a previously selected name cannot be reselected and must be disregarded on any later draw. The population shrinks each time you remove a name, but all names remaining still have the same likelihood of being drawn on the next occasion. Either option is technically acceptable, but survey researchers generally prefer sampling without replacement (because they do not want to use the same sampling units twice or more).

Stratification in Sampling

Simple random sampling is frequently used when the population is known to be homogeneous or its precise composition is unknown. When we know something about the exact composition, we may be able to use a more efficient method of sampling, in which we sample from the different substrates of the population. Professional polling organizations typically use this approach to probability sampling, that is, randomly selecting sampling units (e.g., persons or households) from several subpopulations (termed **strata** or **clusters**) into which the population is divided. For example, if we know the population is 60% female and 40% male (i.e., a ratio of 3 to 2), and that gender is a pertinent variable, we can improve our sampling procedure by selecting subsamples proportionate in size to this 3:2 ratio of females to males.

Called **stratified random sampling,** this is a very efficient way of probability sampling; that is, a separate sample is randomly selected from each homogeneous stratum (or "layer") of the population. The stratum means are then statistically weighted to form a combined estimate for the entire population. In a survey of political opinions, for example, it might be useful to stratify the population according to party affiliation, gender, socioeconomic status, and other meaningful categories related to voting behavior. This method ensures that one will have enough women, men, Democrats, Republicans, and so on to draw descriptive or relational inferences about each respective subgroup. We will have more to say about this method of sampling in a moment.

Area Probability Sampling

A popular variant of this sampling strategy is called **area probability sampling,** because the population is divided into geographic areas (i.e., population clusters or strata). This method is applicable to any population divisible into meaningful geographic areas related to the variables of interest. For example, depending on the variables of interest, meaningful geographic areas might be people living in urban neighborhoods, Inuits in igloos, or nomads in tents. The assumption is that, within each of the areas, the sampling units will have the same probability of being chosen. The sampling procedure can be more complicated than those described above, but the method is cost-effective because the research design can be used repeatedly with only minor modifications (e.g., Fowler, 1993). Suppose a polling organization needed an area probability sample of 300 out of 6,000 estimated housing units in a city, and a good list of all the dwellings in the entire city does not exist (and would be too costly to prepare). Using a city map, the pollsters can instead obtain a sample of dwellings by selecting small clusters of blocks.

To do this in the simplest case, they divide the entire map of the city into blocks of equal size and then select 1 of, say, every 20 blocks for the sample. If they define the sample as the housing units located within the boundaries of these equal-sized sample blocks, the probability of selection for *any* unit is the selection of its block—which is set at 1/20 to correspond to the desired sampling rate of 300/6,000 (Kish, 1965). In other cases, researchers categorize the blocks by taking into account their size or some other factor of interest and then treat this factor as a stratum to sample in a specific way. The procedure can become more complicated as the area gets bigger, but the key requirements are to ensure (a) that all areas will have some chance of selection and (b) that units within the areas are chosen impartially (Fowler, 1993). For the same plan to be used over and over, all that must be altered are the randomly selected units within each area.

Lessons Learned by George Gallup

The late George Gallup, the pioneering survey researcher who founded the Gallup Survey, once noted some of the methodological lessons learned by survey researchers going back to 1936 (Gallup, 1976). That year, Franklin D. Roosevelt (the Democratic presidential candidate) was running against Governor Alfred Landon of Kansas (the Republican candidate). Most people thought Roosevelt would win easily, but a pseudoscientific poll conducted by a current events magazine, the *Literary Digest,* predicted that Landon would win an overwhelming victory. What gave the prediction credence was that the *Digest* had successfully predicted the winner in every presidential election since 1916. Moreover, this time, it announced it had based its prediction on a sample of 2.4 million respondents!

The magazine got these 2.4 million by generating a nonrandom sample of 10 million people from sources like telephone directories, automobile registration lists, and club membership lists; straw vote ballots were then mailed to each name. The lists had actually been compiled for solicitation purposes, and advertising was included with the straw vote ballot (Katz & Cantril, 1937). One problem was that few people in 1936 had a telephone (only one in four households), owned a car, or belonged to a club, so that the final list was biased in favor of wealthy Republican households. Another problem was that there was a large number of nonrespondents, and subsequent analyses suggest that had they responded, the results might have been very different because of the factor of self-selection bias (Squire, 1988); we will return to this problem later.

As it turned out, the election voting was split pretty much along economic lines, the more affluent voting for Landon and the less affluent voting for Roosevelt. The *Digest* predicted that Landon would win by 57% to Roosevelt's 43%, but the election results were Roosevelt 62% and Landon 38% (Freedman et al., 1991). Interestingly, the *Digest* could actually have used the information that the sample was top-heavy in upper-income Republicans to correct its estimate, but it deliberately ignored this information. Instead, the *Digest* proudly proclaimed that the "figures had been neither weighted, adjusted, nor interpreted." After making the largest error ever made by political prognosticators in a presidential election, the *Digest* (which had been in financial trouble before the election) declared bankruptcy.

George Gallup was just getting started in those days. Using his own polling method, he was able to predict that Roosevelt would win (although Gallup was off by 6 percentage points)—as well as to predict what the *Literary Digest* results would be! Gallup's method, called **quota sampling,** was an early precursor of current methods; it assigned a quota of people to be questioned and let the questioner build up a sample that was roughly representative of the population. Now, of course, we use random selection procedures instead of leaving the selection of units to the judgment of the questioner (see also Box 9.5). However, the important lesson that Gallup and other pollsters learned from the *Digest*'s debacle was that large numbers do not, in and of themselves, increase the representativeness of a sample.

BOX 9.5 Bias in Quota Sampling

In early political polling, back in the 1930s, the interviewer would be given ranges of variables and told to identify by sight people who seemed to fit this quota. For example, an interviewer might be told to talk to so many people of ages 21–35, 36–55, and 56 or over. We do not know how much of this interviewing took place on busy street corners and at trolley stops rather than in house-to-house canvassing, but bias might be introduced simply as a consequence of the interviewed individuals' being more accessible than others (Rossi et al., 1983).

In the congressional election of 1942, the pollsters encountered a new problem. They had not reckoned with voter turnout, which was at an all-time low because citizens were changing their places of residence to work in war factories or to enter the military. Gallup's polls correctly predicted that the Democrats would retain control of the House of Representatives, but the margin of victory turned out to be much closer than either he or any other pollsters had predicted. The important lesson learned this time was to give far more attention to the factor of voter turnout in making predictions.

In the 1948 presidential election, Harry S Truman, by luring Democratic defectors back into the fold during the last 2 weeks before Election Day, turned the tide against his Republican opponent, Thomas E. Dewey. However, many public opinion polls predicted that *Dewey* would win. This time, Gallup and other pollsters learned the lesson that political polling had to be done as close to Election Day as possible (see also Box 9.6).

After 1948, the Gallup Survey (and other respected polls) adopted area probability sampling, in which election districts are randomly selected throughout the nation, and then randomly chosen households within these districts are contacted by interviewers. The use of this procedure, and the lessons learned from the mistakes made in previous polls, quickly brought about further improvements. By 1956, the Gallup Survey, based on a little over 8,000 respondents, was able to predict with a margin of error of only 1.7% that Dwight D. Eisenhower would be reelected president. The term **margin of error** means that the prediction, based on the laws of mathematical probability, was that the anticipated percentages would fall within an interval bound by plus and minus 1.7 percentage points. Prudent poll watchers now expect an error of no more than 2 or 3 percentage points in national elections, if the random sampling is properly implemented. In the 2000 election, however, the margin of error of the final polls exceeded the thin difference between the two candidates, George W. Bush and Al Gore, making it impossible to predict the ultimate outcome with a high degree of confidence.

BOX 9.6 Push Polls

Incidentally, don't confuse this legitimate type of polling with what are called "push polls"—an insidious form of negative political campaigning that is designed to push opinions in a particular direction rather than scientifically sample them. Push polls use rumors, lies, innuendoes, and half truths to manufacture negative voter attitudes by posing questions like "Would you be more or less likely to vote for [name of candidate] if you knew he/she had been arrested/failed to pay child support/failed to pay income taxes/falsified his/her résumé?" If you are asked questions like these in a telephone "interview," ask about the sponsors and how the information is being used. The American Association for Public Opinion Research (AAPOR) has campaigned against push polling, including issuing repeated warnings to the public and the media about the iniquity of these pseudoscientific polls. You can help in combating push polls by finding out the name and location of the organization doing the "interviewing" and reporting this information to AAPOR by e-mail at AAPOR-info@goAMP.com.

Point Estimates and Confidence Intervals

Whatever technique is used, survey researchers are usually interested in making point estimates and interval estimates of the population values in question. **Point estimates** are designed to tell them about some particular characteristic of the population. For example, in a survey of a college population, we might want to make a point estimate of the number of seniors who plan to continue their education after graduating. Other examples noted earlier were the number of widgets made by assembly-line workers and the number of cases of tuberculosis contracted on the job. **Interval estimates** tell survey researchers how much the point estimates are likely to be in error (e.g., because of variability in the composition of the population).

Imagine a simple random survey of 100 college students out of a population of 2,500 graduating seniors at a large state university. Each student is asked, "Do you plan to continue your education after you graduate from college, by going on to graduate school, business school, medical school, dental school, or law school?" In answer to the researchers' question, 25 of them reply yes. In order to make a point estimate, the researchers generalize from this sample value to the population of graduating seniors. They multiply the sample proportion replying yes (.25) by the total number of students in the population (2,500). The result leads the researcher to estimate that the true (but unknown) number of graduating seniors planning to continue their education is 625.

How "approximate" is this estimate? The **confidence interval** gives us the answer to this question, as it tells us the probability that the estimated population value is correct within plus-or-minus some specified interval. For example, suppose we want to say with 95% confidence (i.e., 95 chances in 100) that the estimated population value of 625 is correct within plus-or-minus some specified interval (called a *95% confidence interval*). In our example of polling 100 *(n)* graduating seniors, we found .25 (symbolized as *prop*, for proportion) of our sample planning to continue their education. To obtain an approximate 95% confidence interval around *prop*, we compute

$$\text{Lower limit} = prop - 2\sqrt{\frac{prop\ (1 - prop)}{n}},$$

and

$$\text{Upper limit} = prop + 2\sqrt{\frac{prop\ (1 - prop)}{n}}.$$

In our example, $n = 100$, $prop = .25$, and $1 - prop = .75$, so

$$2\sqrt{\frac{prop\ (1 - prop)}{n}} = 2\sqrt{\frac{(.25)(.75)}{100}} = .09,$$

with a resulting lower limit of $.25 - .09 = .16$, and an upper limit of $.25 + .09 = .34$. Applying these proportions to our population *(N)* of 2,500 yields $.16(2,500) = 400$ as the lower limit, and $.34(2,500) = 850$ as the upper limit of our approximate 95% confidence interval for the number of graduating students planning on continuing their education. (In Chapters 10 and 12, we will show how to compute confidence intervals for other important values.)

In this case, the researchers randomly selected individual sampling units, using the population of graduating seniors as a single heterogeneous cluster. In most cases of survey research, however, sampling several strata or clusters is more efficient if the population can be conveniently separated into homogeneous strata. The following case illustrates these advantages and shows what is meant by an unbiased sampling plan in simple random sampling and stratified random sampling.

Benefits of Stratification

Suppose we want to use a random sampling plan to estimate the average hourly production of widgets by teams of assembly-line workers. To keep this example simple, we will imagine that the entire population consists of four teams and that the mean number of widgets produced per hour is

Team A	11.5
Team B	12.5
Team C	13.0
Team D	19.0

14.0 (true population value)

Adding the average hourly production rates (11.5 + 12. 5 + 13.0 + 19.0 = 56.0) and dividing by 4 (56.0/4 = 14.0) tells us that the true population value is 14.0. But for this example, we ask, "How accurate an estimate of the true population value would we obtain by simple random sampling or stratified random sampling?" Finding the answer to this question will reveal what an **unbiased sampling plan** is.

We must initially decide on the size of the sample we wish to use to estimate the population value. To keep it simple, we will define the sample size as any two teams selected at random. For example, were we to randomly select Team A and Team B, we would get a point estimate of 12.0, computed as (11.5 + 12.5)/2 = 12.0. How good is this estimate? The answer, called the **error of estimate,** is defined in this case as the closeness of 12.0 to the true population value of 14.0. We figure this answer out by subtracting the population value from the sample mean, or 12.0 − 14.0 = −2.0. In other words, this particular sample underestimated the true population by 2.0 (the negative difference means it is an underestimate, whereas a positive difference would indicate an overestimate). Table 9.2 lists all possible combinations of two-member samples, the estimates derived from them, and the error of estimate for each sample. The average of the errors of estimate (when we take account of their signs) gives the *bias* of the general sampling plan. Not surprisingly, we see (at the bottom of the last column) that the general sampling plan produces an unbiased estimate—even though there is error associated with individual sample values.

In stratified random sampling (to which we now turn), we would begin by dividing the population into a number of parts. We then randomly sample independently in each part. To get started, notice that the last column in Table 9.2 shows that every simple random sample containing Team D overestimates the population

Table 9.2	Results for All Possible Simple Random Samples of Size Two		
Sample	Sample values	Estimate of population value	Error of estimate
Team A, Team B	11.5, 12.5	12.00	−2.00
Team A, Team C	11.5, 13.0	12.25	−1.75
Team A, Team D	11.5, 19.0	15.25	+1.25
Team B, Team C	12.5, 13.0	12.75	−1.25
Team B, Team D	12.5, 19.0	15.75	+1.75
Team C, Team D	13.0, 19.0	16.00	+2.00
Total		84.00	0.00
Mean		14.00	0.00

			Weighted	Estimate of	Error of
Sample	Stratum 1	Stratum 2	sample values	population value	estimate
1	Team A	Team D	34.5, 19.0	13.375	−0.625
2	Team B	Team D	37.5, 19.0	14.125	+0.125
3	Team C	Team D	39.0, 19.0	14.500	+0.500
Total				42.000	0.000
Mean				14.000	0.000

Table 9.3   Results for All Possible Stratified Random Samples of Size Two

value, and that every random sample without this team underestimates it. If we had reason to suspect this fact before the sampling, we could make use of such information to form strata so that a heterogeneous population is divided into two parts, each of which is fairly homogeneous (Snedecor & Cochran, 1989). One stratum will consist of Teams A, B, and C, and the second stratum will consist of Team D alone, as Table 9.3 shows. This table helps us to see clearly why this general sampling plan is called *unbiased* and also to see the advantages of stratification in probability sampling.

Starting with the first row, notice under "Weighted sample values" that Team A's score is $11.5 \times 3 = 34.5$, whereas Team D's score is not weighted (19.0). The reason we weight Team A's score by multiplying it by 3 is that it is one of three members of Stratum 1. By the same reasoning, we did not weight Team D's score because it is the sole occupant of Stratum 2. To compute the scores under "Estimate of population value," we add Team A's weighted score to Team D's unweighted score and then divide by the total number of members, or $(34.5 + 19.0)/4 = 13.375$. We obtain the "Error of estimate" by subtracting the true population mean from this result, or $13.375 - 14.0 = -0.625$ (which indicates that the Team A + Team D sample underestimates the true population value by a small amount). This table shows the results of all possible stratified random samples of size two. Again, we find (not unexpectedly) that the general sampling plan is unbiased in that the average of the errors of estimate (bottom of last column) is zero.

By comparing the results in Tables 9.2 and 9.3, you will see in quantitative terms the advantages of separating selections from strata of the population. The most extreme errors in Table 9.2 range from −2.00 to +2.00, a difference of 4.00. By contrast, the most extreme errors in Table 9.3 range from −0.625 to +0.500, a difference of 1.125. Notice that fewer samples are possible of size two in Table 9.3 than in Table 9.2. In summary, the error of an individual sample is greater in simple random sampling of a heterogeneous population than in stratified random sampling of that same population divided into homogeneous strata—in this case, by a magnitude of $4.00/1.125 = 3.56$, or more than three times the size. And the potential for error is also greater in simple random sampling than in stratified random sampling. Some forethought—and reliable information, of course—is needed about possible mean differences when one is dividing the population into homogeneous strata; these can pay off handsomely in the utility of stratification.

Estimating Bias Due to Nonresponse

A growing problem in the use of polling methods is that, as surveys proliferate, random samples become harder to obtain because more and more people shut the door or hang up the phone in response to pollsters (see Box 9.7). As a consequence of many individuals' reluctance to be polled, statisticians and survey researchers have devoted considerable effort to studying the possible effects on accuracy of **nonresponse bias** (i.e., an error due to nonparticipation or nonresponse). Not only might this bias result in a smaller **effective sample size** (i.e., the size of the actual final sample) than the researcher planned on for statistical reasons (discussed in a later chapter), but the accuracy of estimates of population values may also be seriously jeopardized when the researcher fails to collect data from a high percentage of those randomly selected to be in the sample.

Table 9.4 illustrates in quantitative terms the basic idea of nonresponse bias, and it also illustrates one way in which researchers who conduct large public opinion polls using mailed questionnaires may attempt to reduce this bias by sending out questionnaires more than once. The data in this table are based on three waves of questionnaires that were mailed out to peach growers in North Carolina (Finkner, 1950). One variable in this study was the number of peach trees owned, and data were available for the entire population of growers for just this variable. As a consequence, it is possible to quantify the amount of the bias due to nonresponse remaining after the first, second, and third mailing (Cochran, 1963, 1977).

The first three rows provide basic data in the form of (a) the number of respondents to each wave of questionnaires and the number of nonrespondents; (b) the percentage of the total population of growers (3,116) represented by each wave of respondents and nonrespondents; and (c) the mean number of trees owned by the respondents in each wave. To calculate the effective sample size after each mailing, we cumulate the number of respondents to that point. Thus, the effective sample size is 300 after the first mailing; 300 + 543 = 843 after two mail-

BOX 9.7   Types of Nonresponse

There are several types of nonresponse. One type occurs when people are not at home, such as when both adults work. Another type is represented by the person who is unable or unwilling to answer questions by the pollster, and a third type by the person who is simply too busy to answer. For example, several years ago, an association of survey researchers reported that 38% of consumers had turned down their interviewers. A typical answer by one person who turned down a telephone request to interview her about where she shops was "It was 7 o'clock, I was putting the kids to bed, and it was zoo time around here, which is when these people call" (Rothenberg,1990, p. A1).

Table 9.4	Example of Bias Due to Nonresponse in Survey Research				
			Response to three mailings		
Basic data	First wave	Second wave	Third wave	Nonrespondents	Total population
1. Number of respondents	300	543	434	1,839	3,116
2. Percentage of population	10	17	14	59	100
3. Mean trees per respondent	456	382	340	290	329
Cumulative data					
4. Mean trees per respondent (Y_1)	456	408	385		
5. Mean trees per nonrespondent (Y_2)	315	300	290		
6. Difference ($Y_1 - Y_2$)	141	108	95		
7. Percentage of nonrespondents (P)	90	73	59		
8. Bias = $(P) \times (Y_1 - Y_2)$	127	79	56		

Source: From p. 4 in *The Volunteer Subject* by R. Rosenthal and R. L. Rosnow. Copyright © 1975. Reprinted by permission of John Wiley & Sons. Based on data from Finkner (1950) and Cochran (1963).

ings; and 843 + 434 = 1,277 after three mailings. To convert the values in row 1 into the percentages in row 2, we divide the row 1 values by the total population size and then multiply by 100 to convert the proportion into a percentage. For example, dividing the number of respondents to the first mailing by the total population value gives us 300/3116 = .096, which, when rounded to .10 and multiplied by 100, tells us that 10% of the growers responded to the first mailing.

The remaining five rows of data are based on the cumulative number of respondents after the first, second, and third mailings. For each wave, five items of information are provided: (d) the mean number of peach trees owned by the respondents up to that point in the survey; (e) the mean number of trees owned by those not yet responding; (f) the difference between these two values; (g) the percentage of the population not yet responding; and (h) the magnitude of the bias (defined in terms of peach trees owned) up to that point in the survey. This last row shows that, with each successive wave of respondents, there was a decrease in the magnitude of the bias (a fairly typical result in such cases). The implication is that increasing the effort to recruit the nonrespondents should lessen the bias of the point estimates.

Furthermore, knowing the magnitude and direction of the nonresponse bias can help us adjust our estimate of the generalizability of the results. To do this, we need to have information about the nonrespondents as well as about the respondents on some variable that is related to our area of interest. The problem for many researchers is that they may not have this information at their fingertips. In other words, they can compute the proportion of population participants (*P*) and the statistic of interest (the point estimate) for these respondents (Y_1), but they may be unable to compute the statistic of interest (the corresponding point estimate) for those who did not respond (Y_2). With the information we do have, we may be in a position to suspect bias but may be unable to give an accurate estimate of its magnitude. We will come back to this problem in a moment (in our discussion of volunteer bias), but one way to minimize nonresponse bias is to try to increase the rate of response.

Improving the Rate of Response

In the case of mail surveys, more nonrespondents may be drawn into the subject sample by one or more follow-up mailings or reminders. Experts who do mail surveys often advise telephoning the nonrespondents if the response rate is still not satisfactory. Professional pollsters attempt to increase the initial rate of participation by using various kinds of incentives and attention-getting techniques, such as using special delivery as opposed to ordinary mail, using hand-stamped rather than postage-permit envelopes, and sometimes including a courtesy gift at the time of the request for participation (Linsky, 1975). In Chapter 5, we discussed the creation of questionnaires; to increase response rates, it is important that the instructions be clear, that the items be easy to read and the layout attractive, and that the task of answering questions not be burdensome (Fowler, 1993; Tryfos, 1996). In the case of telephone surveys, we may be able to increase response rates by sending an informative advance letter that spells out the importance of the study, by pilot-testing probing questions to ensure that the persons contacted will not feel intimidated by them or by the uses to which the data will be put, and by training interviewers and screening out bad ones. One or more follow-up telephone calls on evenings and weekends may also improve the response rate (Fowler, 1993; Tryfos, 1996).

Characteristics of Typical Volunteer Subjects

So far, we have focused on the prototypical survey study. We turn now to a problem that is similar to nonresponse bias, but that may occur in experimental and quasi-experimental studies in which the participants are individually recruited. Most experimenters, for example, do not concern themselves with the particulars of a probability sampling plan when recruiting research participants. One reason for this lack of concern (noted earlier) is that it is often impossible to work within the confines of such a plan. Can you imagine, for example, trying to persuade a randomly selected sample of adults to agree to be assigned to a smoking treatment for many years?

A second reason for experimenters' lack of concern is that, even when random subject selection is feasible, many seem to assume that "people are people" in terms of the psychological factors or mechanisms they are studying. That is, the assumption is that, as long as participants are randomly assigned to treatments, it should make little difference whether those assigned to the experimental and control groups are volunteer subjects (i.e., a self-selected sample) or a random sample of some specified population. In some cases, as we will show next, the use of volunteers may lead to biased conclusions—even when volunteers are randomly assigned to experimental and control conditions (see also Box 9.8). Fortunately, we are able to estimate the direction of the possible bias in many instances (Rosenthal & Rosnow, 1975b; Rosnow & Rosenthal, 1997).

BOX 9.8 The Ubiquitous Volunteer

When scientists recruit volunteers for randomized trials involving risk (e.g., an experiment testing the effects of different diets on cholesterol), it is possible that those already at high risk are the most likely to volunteer. However, volunteer bias is not limited to experimental studies. Suppose a cable television company randomly selects subscribers to be interviewed in a telephone survey. The dissatisfied subscribers might be more likely to go to the trouble to voice their grievances (Tryfos, 1996). The question is how to generalize from these volunteers to the target population.

In particular, we have come to know a great deal about the personal characteristics of the typical volunteers for behavioral and social research, and, in turn, about the nonvolunteers. You may be asking yourself how someone can identify the characteristics of the nonvolunteers (i.e., people who refuse to participate in research). One technique used by researchers who want to compare the characteristics and reactions of volunteers and nonvolunteers is to recruit research subjects from a population for which information is already available on all the potential recruits (e.g., biographical data and psychological test results). Requests for research volunteers are then made some time later—sometimes years later—and those who volunteer are compared with those who do not volunteer on all the items of information in which the investigator is interested. For instance, most colleges administer psychological tests and questionnaires to all incoming students during an orientation period. The results, if they are obtainable by the researchers (i.e., having gotten the IRB's permission, as discussed in Chapter 3), can be used not only to compare those who volunteer with those who do not volunteer for a psychological experiment later that same year, but also to compare the respondents with the nonrespondents to an alumni organization questionnaire sent out years later.

To understand **volunteer bias** (and to explain how it is controlled), we must first know the characteristics of typical volunteers and nonvolunteers. Table 9.5 contains a summary list of nine characteristics of typical volunteers for research participation; they are ranked in the descending order of their approximate accuracy based on the available data (Rosenthal & Rosnow, 1975b). However, the nature of these relationships is context-dependent to a large degree, for example,

1. Volunteer subjects tend to be better educated than nonvolunteers, especially in studies in which personal contact between investigator and respondent is not required.

2. Volunteers are characteristically higher in social-class status than nonvolunteers, but only defined by the respondents' own status rather than by parental status.

Table 9.5	The Typical Research Volunteer

1. Better educated
2. Higher social class
3. Higher IQ scores
4. Higher need for social approval
5. More sociable
6. More arousal-seeking
7. More unconventional
8. More often female
9. Less authoritarian

3. People who volunteer for somewhat less typical types of research (e.g., hypnosis, sensory isolation, sex research, and small-group and personality research) typically score higher on IQ tests than nonvolunteers do.

4. Volunteers tend to be higher than nonvolunteers in need for social approval (i.e., the variable studied by Marlowe and Crowne, discussed in Chapter 6).

5. Volunteers are typically more sociable than nonvolunteers, according to their responses on personality tests.

6. Volunteers tend to be more arousal-seeking than nonvolunteers, especially when the volunteering is for studies of stress, sensory isolation, and hypnosis.

7. Volunteers tend to be more unconventional than nonvolunteers, especially when the volunteering is for studies of sexual behavior.

8. Women are more likely to volunteer for research in general, but they are less likely than men to volunteer for physically and emotionally stressful research (e.g., electric shock, high temperature, sensory deprivation, and interviews about sexual behavior).

9. Volunteers tend to be less authoritarian than nonvolunteers (a characteristic implying that volunteers are typically less rigid thinkers and are likely to put a high value on individual freedom).

Implications for Research Conclusions

Knowing that research volunteers, compared to nonvolunteers, may be brighter (Characteristic 3), higher in approval need (Characteristic 4), less authoritarian (Characteristic 9), and so on, allows us to predict the direction of potential volunteer bias in many situations. As an example, imagine that an educational researcher wants to assess experimentally the validity of a new teaching procedure that is purported to make young children less rigid in their thinking. The researcher asks parents and teachers to volunteer their children or pupils as participants in the investigation because, realistically, it is impossible to draw a random sample for participation. The researcher expects that the children who are volunteered will—

like adults who volunteer themselves—be low in authoritarianism (Characteristic 9). Because people who are low in authoritarianism are also likely to be less rigid thinkers, the researcher suspects that using these volunteered children will lead to a more conservative assessment of the new teaching procedure than if it were possible to use a randomly selected subject sample. The reason is that the experimental group will already be unusually low on the dependent variable (rigidity of thinking). Knowing this, however, the researcher can have greater confidence in the existence of the causal relationship to which the visible evidence in this study points, because that relationship is likely to be even greater in the specified general population.

We can also imagine the opposite type of inferential error in another situation. Suppose a marketing researcher wants to find out how persuasive an advertisement is before recommending its use in a heavily funded television campaign. The researcher finds it most convenient to pilot-test the advertisement on volunteer subjects, who are assigned at random to an experimental group that sees the advertisement or a control group that sees something else that will fill the same amount of time. The researcher knows that volunteer subjects tend to be relatively high in approval need (Characteristic 4), and also (from working in the area and knowing the background literature) that people who are high in approval need are likely to be more influenced than those who are low in approval need (Buckhout, 1965). Putting this information together, the researcher feels it prudent not to make too strong a claim about the causal relationship evidence in this pilot study. Because the volunteers may have overreacted to the treatment in the experimental group, the predicted effect of the new advertisement on the general population may be exaggerated by the pilot study results.

Knowing that biased conclusions are possible in a given situation, researchers can try to avoid this problem. For example, the use of volunteer subjects may lead to biased conclusions in the standardization of a new test. In Chapter 5, we noted that many standardized tests are *norm-referenced;* that is, each person's score can be compared with that of a normative reference group by means of a table of values representing the typical performance of a given group. These "norms" provide a standard of comparison so that we can see how much any person's score deviates from the average of a large group of representative individuals.

For example, if you are planning to apply to law school, you may want to know how much your score on the Law School Admission Test (LSAT) deviates from the scores of other highly qualified college students with similar career plans. In the next chapter, we will explain how to interpret a "standard score," but what is more relevant here is that a crucial assumption of researchers in developing norms for new tests is that the resulting values are representative of the target population. For example, the developers of the LSAT have such information on everyone in the target group because everyone in the group must take this test. However, suppose that a researcher uses volunteer subjects to standardize a brand new intelligence test but wants to use the test and resulting norms in a population consisting of typical volunteers *and* nonvolunteers. Because of Characteristic 3, our best guess is that the researcher's estimates of population norms will be inflated values, because volunteers can be expected to score higher on intelligence tests than nonvolunteers in the same population.

Increasing Participation and Ethical Accountability

Previously, we summarized some of the techniques used to stimulate participation by typical nonrespondents in survey research. Researchers in other areas can use a number of incentives to stimulate participation by typical nonvolunteers (Rosenthal & Rosnow, 1975b; Rosnow & Rosenthal, 1997). Increasing such participation should, in turn, lessen the likelihood of subject selection bias by drawing a more representative subject sample.

One effective recruitment technique is to explain to the potential subjects *why* they will find the research interesting and worthwhile. This approach is based on the finding that persons more interested in the research are more likely to participate. A second technique is to explain the research in a way that is nonthreatening, so that potential participants are not put off by fears of unfavorable evaluation. The basis of this technique is another set of findings that persons who expect to be unfavorably evaluated by the investigator are less likely, and those who expect to be favorably evaluated are more likely, to volunteer. Some other empirically based techniques for stimulating research participation are emphasizing the scientific importance of the research, offering small courtesy gifts to potential participants simply for taking the time to consider participating, and avoiding unnecessary procedures that may be perceived as psychologically or biologically stressful.

A hasty reading of these techniques may give the impression that they are designed only to increase rates of participation. However, there is another, more subtle, benefit. When we tell our prospective participants as much as possible about the significance of the research, avoid doing unnecessary psychologically or biologically stressful research, and so on, it follows that more care and thought probably went into our planning in order to ensure that the study stands up to the scrutiny of critical evaluations. In effect, we are treating the participants as if they were another "granting agency"—which in a sense they are, granting us their time and cooperation. Thus, another benefit of these techniques is that they provide incentives to us, the researchers, to be ethically responsible and humane when we decide what kind of research to do and how to do it (Blanck et al., 1992; Rosenthal, 1994b; Rosnow, 1997).

Pilot Testing as a Final Step

Whatever your research project, whether it involves a survey, a randomized experiment, a single-case experiment, or some other strategy of collecting data directly from people, the final step before implementing the study is to pilot-test the materials. For example, suppose we wanted to study a sensitive topic and were concerned that people would be reluctant to tell the truth (e.g., Lee, 1993). We might pilot-test two or three versions of the questionnaire or interview schedule. If we are concerned about nonresponse bias, we might test different recruitment procedures. Interestingly, even when conducting the actual survey, researchers use embedded randomized experiments on subsets of the sample, and this use of embedded randomized experiments can provide an opportunity to pilot-test different recruitment methods (e.g., Fienberg & Tanur, 1989; Schuman & Presser, 1996; Tanur, 1994). This kind of pilot-testing research can produce valuable information to help us prevent incurably flawed data in future research. As the old saying goes, an ounce of prevention is worth a pound of cure.

Summary of Ideas

1. Probability sampling plans ensure that the selection process will use a random procedure.

2. To be absolutely sure that a sample is representative, we would need to know the particular population values that we are studying. If all of these values were identified, there would be no reason to study the sample.

3. A *biased* sample overestimates or underestimates the true population value; an *unstable* sample is characterized by sampling units that vary greatly from one another.

4. One way to avoid inadequate randomization is to use a table of random digits to select the sampling units.

5. Two options in simple random sampling are (a) sampling with replacement and (b) sampling without replacement (e.g., the wine taster).

6. Area probability sampling is a variant of stratified random sampling in which the strata are geographic clusters.

7. Point estimates are designed to tell us about a particular characteristic of the target population, whereas interval estimates describe how much the point estimates are likely to be in error.

8. As the widget example illustrated, both the error of estimate of an individual sample and the likelihood of making that error tend to be greater in simple random samples than in stratified random samples.

9. In survey research that uses a probability sampling plan, bias due to nonresponse is likely to diminish with each successive wave of respondents (e.g., in the survey of peach growers). Other ways to reduce nonresponse bias in survey research include (a) using reminders and follow-up communications; (b) personalizing the contact; and (c) offering an incentive to respond.

10. As Gallup and other political pollsters have learned from experience, it is best to take the final survey close to election time and to give attention to the factor of voter turnout.

11. On practical, ethical, and theoretical grounds (e.g., the premise that "people are people"), behavioral experimenters tend to pay little attention to whether their participants constitute a random sample of a specified target population.

12. Knowing the relationship between the characteristics of volunteer subjects and the variable of theoretical interest, we can sometimes predict the direction of volunteer bias in experimental and nonexperimental studies.

13. Procedures for stimulating subject participation (e.g., telling people as much as possible about the significance of the research and avoiding psychologically or biologically stressful manipulations) also provide incentives to researchers to act ethically and humanely.

Key Terms

area probability sampling   p. 229
bias   p. 223
clusters   p. 228
confidence interval   p. 233
effective sample size   p. 236
error of estimate   p. 234
interval estimates   p. 232
margin of error   p. 229
nonresponse bias   p. 236
opportunity samples   p. 220
point estimates   p. 232

population   p. 221
probability   p. 221
probability sampling   p. 221
quota sampling   p. 229
random digit dialing   p. 225
random selection   p. 221
representative   p. 221
sample   p. 221
sampling plan   p. 221
sampling without replacement
  p. 228

sampling with replacement
  p. 228
simple random sampling   p. 225
stability   p. 222
strata   p. 228
stratified random sampling
  p. 229
unbiased   p. 222
unbiased sampling plan   p. 234
volunteer bias   p. 239

WEB ACTIVITY

Learn more about survey research at http://www.surveysysem.com/sdesign.htm. For another way to generate random sets of numbers (using either "with replacement" or "without replacement"), visit the Research Randomizer at http://www.randomizer.org. For relevant links to sampling and generalizability issues, visit http://www.trochim.human.cornell.edu/tutorial/TUTORIAL.HTM.

Multiple-Choice Questions for Review

1. Which of the following is most commonly used in public opinion polling? (a) random selection; (b) random assignment; (c) random processing; (d) opportunity sampling

2. A _____ is the total group of participants in which one is interested; a _____ is a segment of the total group that will be studied more closely. (a) universe of subjects, population; (b) population, sample; (c) sample, population; (d) sample, microsample

3. The true population mean is 4. A sample is chosen with the following values: 2, 3, 4, 5, 6. This sample is (a) unbiased; (b) biased; (c) random; (d) nonrandom.

4. The true population mean is 4. Sample A has the following values: 3, 4, 4, 5. Sample B has the following values: 0, 4, 4, 8. Compared to Sample B, Sample A is more (a) unbiased; (b) biased; (c) stable; (d) random.

5. A sampling plan is created in which each member of the population has an equal probability of being selected. This is called a(n) _____ plan. (a) quota sampling; (b) simple random sampling; (c) stratified random sampling; (d) area probability sampling

6. A public opinion pollster divides the population into subpopulations of males and females, and of Democrats and Republicans. She then takes a random sample from each of these subpopulations. This approach is called (a) area probability sampling; (b) stratified random sampling; (c) simple random sampling; (d) quota sampling.

7. A researcher concludes that 1,000 students at a particular college plan to go to graduate school. This is an example of a(n) (a) reliable measure; (b) interval estimate; (c) point estimate; (d) judge's rating.

8. The same researcher states that it is 95% likely that between 900 and 1,100 students at the college plan to go to graduate school. This is an example of a(n) (a) observation measure; (b) confidence interval estimate; (c) point estimate; (d) judge's rating.

9. In some circumstances, people who agree to participate in survey research are noticeably different from people who refuse to participate. This problem is sometimes called (a) lack of randomization; (b) sampling without replacement; (c) instability in sampling; (d) nonresponse bias.

10. Compared to nonvolunteers, those who typically volunteer to participate in psychological research tend to be (a) less authoritarian; (b) higher in arousal seeking; (c) more sociable; (d) all of the above.

Discussion Questions for Review

1. Do you know the answer to the following question asked of a University of Vermont student? Given a true population mean of 12 and the following subjects' scores, (a) which group is measured with greatest stability, and (b) which group is the most biased?

Group 1	Group 2	Group 3
10	10	9
11	12	12
12	14	15
13	16	18

2. Fed up with studying for midterms, four Smith College students—Susan, Valerie, Ellen, and Jane—decide to throw darts at Susan's encyclopedia, which contains one volume for each letter of the alphabet. Because the word *midterm* begins with the letter *M*, the *M* volume is chosen as the target. Each person gets three darts. Susan hits the *M* volume every time; Valerie hits the *N* volume every time; Ellen hits the *L* volume, the *M* volume, and the *N* volume once each; and Jane hits the *M* volume, the *N* volume, and the *O* volume once each. Assuming that each volume of the encyclopedia is the same size, interpret the performance of each person in terms of bias and instability.

3. A Virginia Polytechnic Institute student is interested in the relationship between IQ and sociability. He designs a questionnaire to study this relationship and sends it out to hundreds of people. Twenty percent of the people complete and return the questionnaire. What is a possible source of bias in the results this student will obtain? How would you improve on his design?

4. A University of Kansas student is asked by his instructor to think up experimental cases in which the difference between typical volunteer subjects and nonvolunteers might lead the researcher (a) to overestimate the effectiveness of the experimental treatment and (b) to underestimate the effectiveness of the experimental treatment. Can you help the student? Can you also think of how these situations might be remedied?

5. A University of Michigan student wants to sample the opinions of all graduating seniors on various issues. However, because the graduating class is so large, she decides it would be best to sample a representative group rather than try to contact every one of the graduating seniors. Describe the steps she should take to develop a representative sampling plan, as well as some further steps she might take to deal with the problem of nonresponse bias.

6. An Eastern College student wants to conduct an interview study using married adults who frequent the King of Prussia shopping mall. Because she is worried about volunteer bias, she would like to make every reasonable effort to obtain as representative a sample as she possibly can. What can she do to induce people to participate in her study?

Answers to Review Questions

Multiple-Choice Questions

1. a	**3.** a	**5.** b	**7.** c	**9.** d
2. b	**4.** c	**6.** b	**8.** b	**10.** d

Discussion Questions

1. Group 1 is measured with the greatest stability; its subjects' scores range only from 10 to 13, while Groups 2 and 3 range from 10 to 16 and from 9 to 18, respectively. The means of Groups 1, 2, and 3 are 11.5, 13.0, and 13.5, respectively; therefore, the mean of Group 3 is the most biased.

2. Susan showed no bias with respect to the target volume (her average hit was M, the target volume) and no instability (she hit the same volume each time). Valerie showed a one-volume-away bias, hitting N on average, instead of volume M; she showed no instability, hitting the same volume each time. Ellen showed no bias (her average volume hit was M, the target volume, but she showed a three-volume instability, hitting three adjacent volumes). Jane showed a one-volume-away bias, hitting volume N on average instead of volume M; she showed a three-volume instability, hitting three adjacent volumes. We can summarize the results as follows:

	Bias	No bias
Some instability	Jane	Ellen
No instability	Valerie	Susan

3. Since volunteers or respondents tend to be more intelligent and more sociable than the general population, the correlation between IQ and sociability found in this self-selected sample may be quite different from the correlation we would find in the general population. One way to improve on the design might be to use follow-up questionnaires to increase the representativeness of our sample. Another way to improve on the design might be to try to locate data archives that include data from almost all of a given target population, for example, a college sample all of whom were tested at the time of admission or orientation.

4. In a study of the effects of a placebo on self-reported happiness, volunteers might show a larger placebo effect (i.e., the difference between the placebo and no-treatment condition) than nonvolunteers because volunteers are more likely to want to please the experimenter. In a study of the effects of a treatment designed to increase sociability, volunteers might show a smaller treatment effect than nonvolunteers because volunteers might already score so much higher on sociability that it might be hard to show further changes. Any procedures reducing volunteer bias would help reduce these potential problems.

5. She might draw a random sample of graduating seniors and contact them several times to reduce nonresponse bias. If she knew what characteristics were likely to be highly correlated with questionnaire responses, she might do her random selection within the various strata formed by her subdividing the sample into relatively more homogeneous subgroups.

6. She can try to make her appeal for volunteers as interesting, nonthreatening, and rewarding as possible.

CHAPTER 10

Summarizing the Data

Preview Questions

- How are bar graphs and line graphs used to visualize data?

- How do stem-and-leaf charts work?

- When are means, medians, and modes used?

- How is a confidence interval around a population mean computed?

- Which range should be reported?

- What is the difference between variance and standard deviation?

- What is the purpose of descriptive and inferential measures?

- What is the role of the standard normal distribution?

- Why are z scores called *standard scores*, and how are they used?

The Use of Statistical Procedures

In Chapter 1, we noted that the scientific method, like all methods used to explain specific phenomena, is characterized by a distinctive language particular to the area it represents. So far, we have discussed a number of aspects of the rhetoric of behavioral and social research (e.g., the use of specialized terms, technical definitions, the description of randomized and nonrandomized designs, and the way that theories and hypotheses are articulated). We turn now to statistical analyses, which are also a part of many research reports. The purpose of the remaining chapters is to help you develop an understanding of the proper use and limitations of these methods. Some will be useful as you analyze your results and prepare to write a final report; you should also find them useful beyond the bounds of this course. For example, once you understand the logic of using graphs, descriptive and inferential measures, z scores, probabilities, correlations, and so on, you will be in a stronger position to evaluate claims made on the basis of such information.

If you are learning to use a program such as SPSS, SAS, SYSTAT, or Minitab you will find that the quantitative methods described in the remaining chapters are among the most common statistical tools. When you understand the logic of these methods, you will have a better sense of what your computer churns out. However, these methods are simple enough to use so that all you need to work out the examples presented here is a pocket calculator that can compute the standard deviation and variance of a sample (S, S^2) and a population (σ, σ^2). If your budget permits, you will find calculators that can compute correlations and t tests quite directly; some also give precise p values (so you won't have to search out a table of values) and can be programmed with your favorite formulas. There is also free software that you can download from the Web or even use online, such as the METASTATS software (Foster, 2003) that Mary Jones alludes to in Appendix A.

In this chapter, we review some older and newer procedures to help you summarize and evaluate tendencies of the data. We will begin by showing some ways of graphing data to reveal underlying patterns, with particular emphasis on the use of stem-and-leaf charts. We then review measures that are used to indicate the central or typical value (the mean, median, and mode) and the spread of scores around that value (the range, standard deviation, and variance). In Chapter 9, we showed how to compute and interpret a confidence interval in survey research, and we return to this important concept in order to show how to compute and interpret a confidence interval for an estimated population mean. A valuable piece of information is that population data often take the form of a symmetrical, bell-shaped curve. It permits us to convert scores from distributions of widely differing types to a common metric (by z-scoring them) in order to compare scores based on distributions with widely varying means and standard deviations. In the following chapters, we will show how these concepts provide the basic ingredients of other important data-analytic procedures.

Frequency Distributions for Visualizing Data

It is said that a picture is worth a thousand words. This statement often seems true when one is representing and interpreting research data. With computer programs, it is relatively easy to recast quantitative data into a visual display, but it is important not to overcomplicate the results, as confusion and clutter will elicit vacant staring rather than easy comprehension. If the visual display is properly drawn, it will be informative and easy to understand. Edward R. Tufte (1983), a statistician specializing in graphic designs, suggested that to ensure visual integrity and make it easy for viewers to comprehend, we need to keep in mind three criteria of all good visual displays: clarity, precision, and efficiency. *Clarity* simply means that the data need to be represented in a way that is closely integrated with their numerical meaning. *Precision* means representing the data exactly, and not exaggerating numbers. *Efficiency* means presenting the data in a reasonably compact space, so the viewer or reader is encouraged to think about its substance and is not distracted by unnecessary details (see also Box 10.1).

BOX 10.1   When 1 + 1 = 3 or More

One of Tufte's (1990) mantras is that "confusion and clutter are failures of design, not attributes of information" (p. 53). He mentioned a visual artifact that an eminent design artist described as "one plus one equals three or more" (Albers, 1969). That is, when information is clumsily layered on other information in a visual representation, there is a constant danger that viewers will perceive more facts than the data actually support. The point, Tufte cautioned, is not to fault the viewer for a lack of understanding, but to avoid this situation by thinking hard about how to represent the data clearly, precisely, and efficiently. (Figuratively speaking, of course, sometimes it does seem true that one plus one equals more than the sum of its parts, as in the behavior of a mob or the baking of a cake.) Statistician Howard Wainer (1997), also the author of an excellent book on visual displays, added that "the most important component of a memorable graph is the information it contains" (p. 148). The surest ways to exhibit data badly are to crowd the display with irrelevancies and to use a font that is hard to read, a text full of jargon, or numbers that overburden the viewer with irrelevant or unimportant information (Wainer, 1997).

When you want to emphasize the overall pattern of data, you will find that a **frequency distribution** is useful. Such a "picture" shows the number of times each score or other unit of observation occurs in a set of data. A frequency distribution can take the form of a chart (e.g., a bar graph or a line graph) or a table, such as Table 10.1. This table shows part of the results of an evaluation of a new food product by Elizabeth Street and Mavis B. Carroll (1989). This aspect involved a palatability evaluation, in which Street and Carroll had 50 people taste and evaluate a new food product and a competitive food product (a control) already on the market. Instead of a rating scale with words such as *terrible, very poor, poor, average, good, very good,* and *excellent,* the participants were given a variation of the pictorial scale in Figure 10.1. In the scoring of the results, each of the faces was assigned a number (or score) in the sequence $-3, -2, -1, 0, +1, +2, +3$, with -3 implying the least agreeable and $+3$ being most agreeable. Table 10.1 shows the number (i.e., frequency) of tasters who chose each option in the face scale. For example, in the top row of Table 10.1, we see that only one participant rated the control product -3 (least agreeable), whereas no one gave the new product this "terrible" rating.

Figure 10.2 recasts the results clearly and efficiently as two **bar graphs,** where the height of the solid bars represents the number (frequency) of tasters who chose each option. Notice that the implicit scale values appear on the horizontal axis (called the **x axis**) and the number of tasters appears on the vertical axis (called the **y axis**). Another name for the horizontal (x) axis is the **abscissa**; another name

	Control	New
Score	product	product
−3	1	0
−2	3	1
−1	8	2
0	17	11
+1	15	16
+2	5	13
+3	1	7

Table 10.1   Palatability Evaluation by 50 Tasters of Two Food Products

Source: From *Statistics: A Guide to the Unknown* (3rd ed.) by J. M. Tanur et al., Copyright © 1989 by Wadsworth, Inc., Belmont, California 94002, a division of International Thomson Publishing Inc.

for the vertical (y) axis is the **ordinate.** (To keep these names straight, remember that the "abscissa sits," or rests, on the bottom.) Comparing the two bar graphs allows us immediately to see that the new food product was rated, in general, as more agreeable than the control product. Notice that the tallest bar in the control product group represents tasters who chose the 0 option, whereas the tallest bar in the new product group represents those who chose the +1 option.

Bar graphs are especially useful for representing categories of responses and frequencies (or proportions) within those categories. An efficient way of graphing *changes* in the frequency (or proportion) of scores over time are **line graphs.** An example was shown in Chapter 8, where Figure 8.1 (page 204) is a line graph of up-and-down change in the frequency of subway suicides and suicide attempts from 1980 to 1992 in Vienna, Austria. To find the year in which the

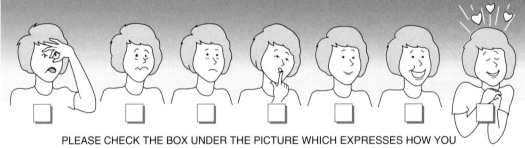

PLEASE CHECK THE BOX UNDER THE PICTURE WHICH EXPRESSES HOW YOU FEEL TOWARD THE PRODUCT YOU HAVE JUST TASTED.

Figure 10.1   **Pictorial taste-test scale (the scores −3 to +3 were assigned the figures from left to right) used in a palatability evaluation study.**

Source: From p. 166 in *Statistics: A Guide to the Unknown,* 3rd edition by J. Tanur et al. Copyright © 1989. Reprinted with permission of Wadsworth, an imprint of the Wadsworth Group, a division of Thomson Learning. Fax 800 730-2215.

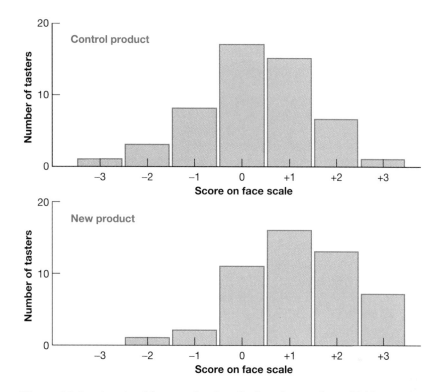

Figure 10.2   **A pair of bar graphs that display the results in Table 10.1.**

number of suicides or suicide attempts increased the most, we find the steepest point and then look at the abscissa to read the year. The value of this visual display is not only that it shows the increases and decreases at a glance, but also that it allows us to compare the change over time in two line graphs before and after the intervention.

Stem-and-Leaf Charts

No hard-and-fast rule requires that graphs always resemble these figures. For example, the **stem-and-leaf chart,** invented by the noted statistician John W. Tukey, provides a clear, precise, and efficient technique for interpreting a batch of data. It is a hybrid between a table and a graph because it presents the original numbers and simultaneously gives an economical summary view of them. It also does not involve any elaborate statistical theory; instead, the chart relies on the creative imagination of the researcher who uses it to test a particular hypothesis or to do exploratory data analysis (Chambers, Cleveland, Kleiner, & Tukey, 1983; Emerson & Hoaglin, 1983; Tukey, 1977).

Stems	Leaves			
8	2	7		
7	0	4	9	
6	2	6	6	9
5	1	2	6	
4	1	7		
3	7			

Figure 10.3   A stem-and-leaf chart of students' ratings of a famous rapper.

Suppose we ask 15 students to rate a famous rapper, known for his social statements and wry political observations, on a scale from 0 ("the most shallow") to 100 ("the most profound"), and we get the following results: 66, 87, 47, 74, 56, 51, 37, 70, 82, 66, 41, 52, 62, 79, 69. Figure 10.3 shows a stem-and-leaf chart of these ratings. The stems are the first digits of these two-digit numbers, and the leaves are the second digits. There are two scores concentrated in the 80s (82 and 87), three scores in the 70s (70, 74, and 79), four scores in the 60s (62, 66, 66, and 69), and so forth. The beauty of the stem-and-leaf chart is that it allows us to see the batch as a whole and to notice (a) how symmetrical the data set is, (b) how spread out the scores are, (c) whether any scores are outside the batch, (d) whether there are small and large concentrations of scores, and (e) whether there are any gaps (Emerson & Hoaglin, 1983). Thus, the stem-and-leaf chart scores high on the criteria of clarity, precision, and efficiency.

As another illustration, in Chapter 8 we discussed a correlational study of the composer Robert Schumann's productivity and his bouts of depression and hypomania (Weisberg, 1994). Returning to Table 8.2 (p. 210), we see the annual rates of musical compositions when he was feeling depressed or hypomanic. Another way of representing these data is shown in Figure 10.4, which plots the rates in adjoining stem-and-leaf charts. Called a **back-to-back stem-and-leaf chart,** this arrangement lets us see at a glance that the rates are spread out more for hypomania than for depression, and that the rates during bouts of depression are concentrated in a single stem.

Depression	Stems	Hypomania
	2	5 8
	1	6
5 5 4 3 1 1 0	0	1 2 4

Figure 10.4   A back-to-back stem-and-leaf chart of Schumann's number of compositions during his bouts of depression and hypomania (Weisberg, 1994).

Percentiles and the Median

So far, the charts we have looked at were used to summarize *all* the data, but researchers also find it useful to summarize part of the batch. For example, there is often a practical value in knowing the point in the distribution below and above which a certain percentage of scores falls, called the **percentile:** 25% of the scores fall below the 25th percentile, 75% of the scores fall below the 75th percentile, and so on. In practice, quantitative summaries of data displayed in stem-and-leaf charts often include a listing of the scores falling at the 25th, 50th, and 75th percentiles.

In most cases, it is highly useful to know the location of the typical score and the spread of scores around that location. We turn to measures of spread in a moment, but one very useful measure of typical location is the 50th percentile, also called the **median** (symbolized as *Mdn*). It is one of several popular measures of **central tendency,** which tells us that it is one measure of the location of central or typical values. The median is the score above and below which half of the scores fall. In other words, the median is the midmost score in a distribution of scores.

For example, when the total number of scores (symbolized as *N*) is an odd number, the median is simply the middle score. Thus, in the series 2, 3, 3, 4, 4, 5, 6, 7, 7, 8, 8, the *Mdn* = 5 because it is in the middle, with five scores below it (2, 3, 3, 4, 4) and five scores above it (6, 7, 7, 8, 8). When the number of scores is an even number (so that there are two midmost scores), the median is computed as half the distance between the two middle numbers. In the series 2, 3, 3, 4, 4, 7, the *Mdn* = 3.5, halfway between the 3 and the 4 at the center of the set of scores (see also Box 10.2).

An easy way to locate the median (the 50th percentile) is to multiply *N* + 1 (where *N* is again the total number of scores in the ordered set) by .50. As reported in the stem-and-leaf in Figure 10.4, Schumann's annual rate of musical compositions was 0, 1, 1, 3, 4, 5, 5 scores when he was depressed. The median is given by .50(*N* + 1), which is .50(7 + 1) = 4th score in this set of seven ordered scores, or *Mdn* = 3 compositions. His annual rate of compositions was 1, 2, 4, 16, 25, 28 scores when he was

---

BOX 10.2   Ties and Medians

Ties create a small problem when one is computing medians. The series 3, 4, 4, 4, 5, 6, 7 has one score below 4 and three above. What shall we regard as the median? A useful procedure is to imagine such a series as perfectly ranked, so that a series 1, 2, 3, 3, 3 is seen as made up of a 1, a 2, a "small" 3, a "larger" 3, and a "still larger" 3. The assumption here is that more precise measurement procedures would have allowed us to break the ties. In the series 1, 2, 3, 3, 3, we regard the "small 3" as the median, because there are two scores below this particular 3 and two above it. In reporting this result, however, we would simply state, "*Mdn* = 3."

hypomanic. The median rate is given by .50(6 + 1) = 3.5th score in this set; that is, the median is halfway between the number 4 and the number 16, or *Mdn* = 10.

We can also use this procedure to locate other percentiles. The 75th percentile is .75(*N* + 1), and the 25th percentile is .25(*N* + 1). In the 0, 1, 1, 3, 4, 5, 5 set, the 75th percentile is .75(8) = 6th score, or 5 compositions. The 25th percentile in this set is .25(8) = 2nd score, that is, 1 lone composition. In the 1, 2, 4, 16, 25, 28 set, the 75th percentile is .75(7) = 5.25th score (i.e., 25% of the distance between the 5th and 6th scores), which gives 25.75 compositions. For these same six scores, the 25th percentile is .25(7) = 1.75th score (i.e., 75% of the distance between the first and second scores), which is 1.75 compositions.

Exploratory Data Analysis

Previously, we mentioned that the stem-and-leaf can be used not only to do hypothesis testing (known as *confirmatory data analysis*), but to do *exploratory data analysis* as well. Exploratory data analysis is detective work because we are looking for clues, and to do it properly, we must look in the right places (Tukey, 1977). Thus, we would not stop with a visual display of the overall batch of data but would also look for patterns in parts of the batch. Let us see how to do this using only the stem-and-leaf chart and the calculation of percentiles.

In the previous chapter, we referred to research on volunteer characteristics. As part of that research, a number of investigators were interested in what kind of volunteers become no-shows (i.e., people who fail to show up for their scheduled research appointments). Suppose we want to estimate the typical number of subjects we need to volunteer to ensure that at least 40 will show up. Some years ago, a literature review (Rosenthal & Rosnow, 1975b) identified 20 studies that had reported the proportion of no-shows. Those proportions are listed in the stem-and-leaf chart in Figure 10.5. The proportion of no-shows (reading from top to bottom) was .42 in one study, .41 in another study, .40 in another study, .38 in another study, and so forth. To continue our detective work, we will compute the 25th, 50th (*Mdn*), and 75th percentiles on these data.

Reading now from the lowest to the highest score in Figure 10.5, the sequence of values is as follows:

(1) .03	(6) .19	(11) .32	(16) .37
(2) .10	(7) .24	(12) .36	(17) .38
(3) .12	(8) .30	(13) .36	(18) .40
(4) .14	(9) .30	(14) .37	(19) .41
(5) .16	(10) .31	(15) .37	(20) .42

and the location of the median is the .50(20 + 1) = 10.5th score. That is, the median is halfway between the 10th score (.31) and the 11th score (.32), or *Mdn* = .32 (i.e., .315 rounded to the nearest even value).

The location of the 25th percentile score is given by .25(*N* + 1), and therefore .25(21) = 5.25th score (i.e., 25% of the distance between the 5th and 6th scores),

Stems	Leaves
.4	0 1 2
.3	0 0 1 2 6 6 7 7 7 8
.2	4
.1	0 2 4 6 9
.0	3

Figure 10.5   A stem-and-leaf chart of the proportion of no-show volunteers in 20 studies (Rosenthal & Rosnow, 1975b).

which gives us .17. The location of the 75th percentile score is $.75(N + 1)$, which we calculate as $.75(21) = 15.75$th score, 75% of the distance between the 15th and 16th scores. In this case, the 15th and 16th scores are both .37, so 75% of the distance between them is zero, and therefore the 75th percentile = .37. To summarize this stem-and-leaf chart in certain key values of the distribution, we would report that (a) the maximum value = .42; (b) the 75th percentile = .37; (c) the *Mdn* (50th percentile) = .32; (d) the 25th percentile = .17; and (e) the minimum value = .03.

What have we learned? The distance between the 25th and the 75th percentiles—called the **interquartile range**—reveals that 50% of the studies that were midmost have values between .17 and .37. From the fact that the median no-show rate of volunteers is .32, a recommendation emerges: If we are counting on 40 volunteer participants to show up for our research, we should probably schedule about 60 (i.e., one third of 60 = 20, and 60 − 20 = 40), or one-half more research subjects than we absolutely need. Of course, this conclusion rests on the assumption that the data in Figure 10.5 are, in fact, typical and that the median no-show rate is still about the same (as the results are relatively old). Findings by Aditya (1996) do seem to support this assumption; in more recent results, he found that the median no-show rate has remained relatively unchanged (still about one third).

The Mode and the Mean

Besides the median, another informative measure of central tendency is the **mode.** It is the score, or category of scores, that occurs most often. In the series 3, 4, 4, 4, 5, 5, 6, 6, 7, the mode = 4. The series 3, 4, 4, 4, 5, 5, 6, 7, 7, 7 has two modal scores (at values 4 and 7) and is thus described as **bimodal** (two modes). For the stem-and-leaf chart in Figure 10.5, we would refer to the modal *category* as the ".30s" (stem of .3 and leaves of 0, 0, 1, 2, 6, 6, 7, 7 ,7, 8). Sometimes, there is no distinct mode, in which case it is better to use another measure to describe the central tendency of the data, such as the median or the ordinary mean.

The ordinary mean (or **arithmetic mean**), frequently called the **mean** for short, is now generally symbolized as *M,* as recommended in the current edition of the publication manual of the American Psychological Association (2001). However, another symbol that some textbooks use for the arithmetic mean is $\overline{X}$. Whether you see M or $\overline{X}$, an arithmetic mean is the sum of the scores ($\Sigma\ X$) divided by the total number (N) of scores in a set (or n for a subset of scores, that is, a sample of scores). Thus, the formula for the mean is

$$M = \frac{\Sigma X}{N},$$

where Σ (the uppercase Greek letter sigma) tells us to "sum" the X scores. In the series 1, 2, 3, 3, 3, the sum of the scores is 12, the number of scores is 5, and therefore, M = 12/5 = 2.4. For the stem-and-leaf values in Figure 10.5, the mean is calculated as the sum of the reported proportions (5.65) divided by 20, which gives M = .28 (i.e., .2825 rounded to .28) as the mean proportion of no-shows (see also Box 10.3).

Reporting more than one measure of central tendency will give readers a clearer idea of the distribution of the data set. When the distribution of scores is symmetrical, all three measures will give the same value. The mode is a good way to show that there were many identical scores, while the median is useful when there are extreme high or low scores because it is unaffected by only a few extreme scores. When scores are tightly bunched, the mean is close to all the scores, though averaging in a few extremely high or extremely low scores may give a misleading picture of the central tendency of the data set.

Figure 10.6 further illustrates these relationships. For example, the (b) curve is a picture of a **symmetrical distribution;** it simply means that there is a correspondence in arrangement on the opposite sides of the middle line. When the right side is not the reverse of the left side of the distribution, this is called an **asymmetrical distribution.** When the mean of the distribution is much larger than the median, the stretched-out tail points conspicuously toward the positive end (a pat-

BOX 10.3 The Mean as the Center of Gravity

You can think of the mean as the "center of gravity" of a distribution of numbers. Suppose you turned the stem-and-leaf on its side and balanced it. The balance point would be the mean (Wilkinson & Engelman, 1996). In Table 10.1, how would you calculate the "balance point" (the mean) of the scores for each of the two food products? You could add up the 50 scores (i.e., −3 to +3 ratings) in each group and divide by 50, which will give M = .22 for the control product and M = 1.18 for the new product. A shortcut procedure for finding the mean of these scores is to multiply each score by its frequency, sum the results, and divide by N.

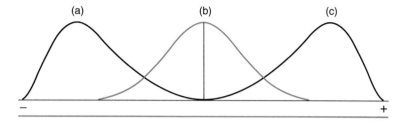

Figure 10.6   **Illustrations of symmetry and asymmetry.**
Only distribution (b) is symmetrical, in that both sides of the middle line are identical. When the long, pointed tail is toward the positive end (i.e., a long right tail) as represented by (a), the distribution is said to be positively skewed. When the long, pointed tail is toward the negative end (i.e., a long left tail) as illustrated by (c), the distribution is said to be negatively skewed.

tern called a **positively skewed distribution**), as illustrated by the (a) curve. When the mean is smaller than the median, the stretched-out tail points toward the negative end (a pattern called a **negatively skewed distribution**), as illustrated by the (c) curve. The (b) curve labeled also shows what we meant when we said that, in a symmetrical (or nonskewed) distribution, the mean, median, and mode all have the same value.

Dealing with Outliers

However, suppose that a few scores lie far outside the normal range. These far-out scores are called **outliers.** When a distribution of scores is strongly asymmetrical because of outliers, researchers generally prefer a **trimmed mean** to an ordinary mean. As mentioned previously, an ordinary mean is very sensitive to extreme values. Trimming implies giving the data set a "light haircut" by cutting off not just the one or more outliers from one side, but the same percentage of the scores from both ends of the series of scores.

Consider this strongly asymmetrical series: -20, 2, 3, 6, 7, 9, 9, 10, 10, 10. The -20 is an outlier that clearly disrupts the homogeneity of the series. To expunge outliers fairly, we trim an equal number of scores from each end. In this case, trimming one score from each end leaves 2, 3, 6, 7, 9, 9, 10, 10. What if we had not given the series a haircut? Would leaving the outlier in have distorted the average by very much? It depends on how the "average" is defined. The trimmed mean = 7.0 and the untrimmed mean = 4.6, so the answer is yes in the case of the ordinary mean (M). The median is unaffected by trimming, so for these scores Mdn = 8 with or without trimming. The mode, which may be affected by trimming, is 10 for the scores before trimming but is bimodal at 9 and 10 after trimming (see also Box 10.4).

BOX 10.4 Misleading Interpretations and Wild Scores

Medians and trimmed means protect us in certain cases from possibly misleading interpretations based on very unusual scores. For example, if we calculated the benefits of a proposed tax plan for 10 families and found 9 of them with a $100 benefit and 1 with a $9,100 benefit, the mean benefit of $1,000 would be highly unrepresentative of the "typical benefit" compared to the trimmed mean, the median, or (in this case) even the mode. Medians and trimmed means also protect us somewhat against the intrusion of certain scores recorded erroneously (called *wild scores*). Imagine the series 4, 5, 5, 6, 6, 6, 7, 7, 8, of which the mean, median, mode, and trimmed mean are all 6. However, suppose we erred and entered the data as 4, 5, 5, 6, 6, 6, 7, 7, 80. Our new (erroneous) mean would now be 14, but our median or trimmed mean would remain unaffected.

The Crude and Extended Range

Besides knowing the central tendency (or "typical value") of a set of scores, researchers also want to know how "spread out" the scores are (called an *interval estimate* in the previous chapter). That is, they also want to know how far the scores deviate from the value of the central tendency measure. Just as there are different measures of central tendency, there are also several different measures of what is alternatively described as *spread, dispersion,* or *variability*. For example, we mentioned the interquartile range (i.e., the distance between the 25th and 75th percentiles), which tells us the variability characteristic of the middle 50% of the scores. Other measures of spread include the range (crude and extended), the variance, and the standard deviation.

We will start with the ordinary **range** (or **crude range**), which is simply the difference between the highest and lowest scores. If you are administering a scale, you will want to report the *potential* crude range as well as the *observed* (or obtained) range. If the potential crude range is very narrow, it may be impossible to produce appreciable differences among the participants; that is, there is a flaw in the design. On the other hand, it does not follow that simply having a very wide potential range will automatically result in a substantial observed range. The way we interpret the range depends on the purpose of the study and the nature of the instruments used.

For example, if you used a scale consisting of 20 five-point items, each item scored from 1 to 5, the potential crude range is from 20 to 100. You would report the crude range (CR) as being the highest score (H) minus the lowest score (L), or $CR = H - L = 80$ points. Using the same method, you would also report the crude range for the observed scores.

BOX 10.5 Which Range Should You Report?

For most practical purposes, you can report either the crude range (CR) or the extended range (ER). However, when measurement is not very precise and when the crude range is small, you will convey a more accurate picture of the actual range when you report the extended range. Suppose you use a 3-point rating scale in your research and all the judges' ratings are at the midpoint value (i.e., 2 on your scale of 1 to 3). The $CR = 2 - 2 = 0$, and the $ER = (2 - 2) + 1 = 1$ (because some of your judges might theoretically have rated nearly as high as 2.5 and some nearly as low as 1.5 had those ratings been possible). To decide which range to report, you can consult the ratio of the CR divided by the ER. This $CR/ER = 0$ in the extreme example just given, and $CR/ER = .90$ if the crude range is 9 and the extended range is 10. With CR/ER as high as .90, it seems reasonable to report either the CR or the ER. With CR/ER much lower, it may be more informative to report only the ER.

A further distinction is made between the crude range and **extended range** (sometimes called the **corrected range**). In the series 2, 3, 4, 4, 6, 7, 9, the crude range is the highest score minus the lowest score, or $CR = 9 - 2 = 7$. The extended range (ER) is a refinement that recognizes that, in more precise measurements, a score of 9 may fall somewhere between 8.5 and 9.5 and that a score of 2 may fall somewhere between 1.5 and 2.5. To adjust for this possibility, we view the extended range as running from a high of 9.5 to a low of 1.5. The extended range is then $9.5 - 1.5 = 8$. The extended range thus adds a half unit at the top of the distribution and a half unit at the bottom of the distribution, or a total of one full unit, and can be computed as $ER = (H - L) + 1$ (see also Box 10.5).

The crude range and the extended range tell us about the extreme scores in a set of scores, whereas the next two measures of spread—the variance and the standard deviation—are based on information from all the scores.

The Variance and the Standard Deviation

The **variance** of a set of scores tells us the deviation from the mean of the scores, but instead of using deviation values directly, it squares the deviations and averages them. In other words, it is the mean of the squared deviations of the scores (X) from their mean (M). The variance of a set of scores is also commonly referred to as the **mean square** (i.e., the mean of the squared deviations), and you will see this term again in our discussion of the F test (which is used in the statistical procedure known as *analysis of variance*). The symbol used to denote the variance of a population is σ^2 (read as "sigma-squared"), and the formula used to calculate the population variance is

$$\sigma^2 = \frac{\Sigma(X - M)^2}{N},$$

where the numerator instructs us to sum the squared deviations of the individual scores from the mean of the set of scores, and the denominator tells us to divide that sum by the total number of scores.

The **standard deviation** is by far the most widely used and reported of all measures of spread around the average. Symbolized as σ, the standard deviation of a population is simply the square root of the population variance. That is,

$$\sigma = \sqrt{\sigma^2},$$

or calculated from the original data as

$$\sigma = \sqrt{\frac{\Sigma(X - M)^2}{N}}.$$

Thus, another name for the standard deviation is the **root mean square,** which is shorthand for the square root of the mean of the squared deviations, as the equation above shows.

If you do not have a calculator that allows you to compute the standard deviation and the variance directly from "raw" (i.e., obtained) scores (and are not using a computer with a statistics package), it is still easy to compute these values with the calculator you use to balance your checkbook. Table 10.2 shows the summary data you need to calculate the variance and standard deviation of the set of raw scores in the first column. You compute the population variance and standard deviation in five easy steps:

Step 1 (in the first column) is to add up the six raw scores ($\Sigma X = 30$), and then to find their mean by dividing the sum by the number of scores ($M = 30/6 = 5$).

Step 2 (in the second column) is to subtract the mean from each raw score. As a check on your arithmetic, you will find that these deviation scores sum to zero, that is, $\Sigma(X - M) = 0$.

Table 10.2 Summary Data for Computing the Variance and the Standard Deviation

Raw scores	$X - M$	$(X - M)^2$
2	-3	9
4	-1	1
4	-1	1
5	0	0
7	2	4
8	3	9
$\Sigma X = 30$	$\Sigma(X - M) = 0$	$\Sigma(X - M)^2 = 24$
$M = 5$		

Step 3 (in the last column) is to square the deviation scores in column 2, and then to add up the squared deviations, which gives $\Sigma (X - M)^2 = 24$.

Step 4 is to compute the population variance (σ^2) by substituting the value obtained in Step 3 in the numerator, and the number of scores in the denominator, which gives you

$$\sigma^2 = \frac{\Sigma (X - M)^2}{N} = \frac{24}{6} = 4.$$

Step 5 is to find the standard deviation, either by obtaining the square root of the value in Step 4, that is,

$$\sigma = \sqrt{4} = 2,$$

or by direct substitution in the formula noted earlier, that is,

$$\sigma = \sqrt{\frac{\Sigma (X - M)^2}{N}} = \sqrt{\frac{24}{6}} = 2.$$

Descriptive and Inferential Measures

Another distinction is that made between descriptive and inferential measures. Suppose we are interested in the variability of the batting averages of a favorite baseball team. We collect the scores of *all* the players and then compute the standard deviation using the formula described above. In this case, the formula used for measuring variability is characterized as a **descriptive measure,** because it describes a *complete population* of scores or events—with Greek letters used to symbolize the particular measure (e.g., σ or σ^2).

As discussed in the previous chapter, researchers are also interested in generalizing from a sample of known scores or events to a population of unknown scores or events, which may be finite or infinite. Suppose we were interested in the variability of major-league baseball players' batting averages. We collect a sample of scores and then make inferences about the variability of scores in the population from which they were drawn. (See also Box 10.6.) The equation we now use to measure variability is characterized as an **inferential measure**—with roman letters used to symbolize the particular measure (e.g., S or S^2).

Except for the denominator and the symbol (Greek or roman), the descriptive and inferential formulas for computing variances (σ^2 and S^2)—and, therefore, standard deviations (σ and S)—are identical. In the descriptive formulas for variances and standard deviations, the numerator is divided by N (as previously shown). In the inferential formulas, the numerator is instead divided by $N - 1$ (because it can be shown statistically that, with repeated sampling, this procedure gives the most accurate inferences). Thus, if you wanted to estimate the variance (σ^2) of a population from a sample, you would use the statistic S^2 (referred to as the **unbiased estimator of the population value of σ^2**) and the following formula:

BOX 10.6 Finite and Infinite

In the baseball example, we are dealing with both a finite sample and a finite population. **Finite** means that all the units or events can, at least in theory, be completely counted. **Infinite,** on the other hand, means "boundless" or "without limits." Suppose, from samples of sand that have been randomly collected, we want to make a generalization about the variability of all the sand at Atlantic City, New Jersey. Here, we are attempting to make an inference from a finite sample to a population of unknown "events" that is regarded as infinite (because of ecological changes and so on).

$$S^2 = \frac{\Sigma(X - M)^2}{N - 1}.$$

Alternatively, if you wanted to estimate the σ of a population from a sample, you would use the statistic S and the following formula:

$$S = \sqrt{S^2} = \sqrt{\frac{\Sigma(X - M)^2}{N - 1}}.$$

For example, if you wanted to generalize from the raw scores in the first column of Table 10.2 to the larger pool (the population) from which the sample of scores was obtained, you would compute

$$S^2 = \frac{\Sigma(X - M)^2}{N - 1} = \frac{24}{5} = 4.8$$

and

$$S = \sqrt{4.8} = 2.19.$$

Confidence Interval for a Mean

In our earlier discussion of survey research (Chapter 9), we introduced the idea of confidence interval estimates, which tell us about the degree to which the point estimates are likely to be in error. The most commonly reported confidence interval estimate (symbolized as CI) is the 95% CI. This interval runs from a value below our obtained point estimate to a value above it, both values having been chosen so that there is a 95% probability that the true (but unknown) population value falls between the lower and upper limits. Because confidence intervals tell us how accurately or precisely we have estimated some quantity (e.g., a specific number of people, a proportion of a population, or a population mean), they are very valuable pieces of information to include in a research report. We turn now to a procedure for obtaining confidence limits around an estimate of a population mean. (In a later chapter, we will describe a procedure for obtaining confidence limits around an estimate of a population effect size.)

Three quantities are required to compute a 95% CI around an obtained estimate of a population mean: n, S, and $t_{(.05)}$, where n is the number of scores upon which the obtained mean (M) is based, and S is the standard deviation of the n scores obtained, computed as

$$S = \sqrt{\frac{\Sigma(X - M)^2}{n - 1}}.$$

If you have had a course in statistics, you know that t is the symbol for Student's t test (discussed in Chapter 13). For this application, all you need to know is how to find the value of $t_{(.05)}$ in order to use it in the formulas described below. Looking at Table B.2 in Appendix B (page 410), you see, at the very top, a row labeled "two-tailed" and a value of ".05" in the fourth column. You know you are looking at the right column if you see 12.706 as the first value (corresponding to what in the far left is labeled "$df = 1$") and 1.960 as the last value (corresponding to "$df = \infty$," the symbol for infinity). We will explain these terms in a later chapter, but for this application the df (which stands for *degrees of freedom*) is defined as $n - 1$ (the number of scores minus 1). We obtain the quantity $t_{(.05)}$ from Table B.2 by looking down the column headed ".05 two-tailed," until we reach the row label indicating the number of df on which our obtained mean was based (i.e., $n - 1$).

Consider the data of Table 10.2 in which $n = 6$ raw scores. These scores are 2, 4, 4, 5, 7, 8, with mean $(M) = 5$ and (as calculated in the previous section) $S = 2.19$. We find that $t_{(.05)} = 2.57$, because $df = n - 1 = 5$, and Table B.2 shows the value 2.57 at the intersection of the column headed ".05 two-tailed" and the row labeled 5 df. To obtain a 95% confidence interval around the estimated population mean, we find

$$\text{Lower limit} = M - \frac{(t_{(.05)})(S)}{\sqrt{n}},$$

and

$$\text{Upper limit} = M + \frac{(t_{(.05)})(S)}{\sqrt{n}}.$$

For our example of Table 10.2, therefore, we find

$$\text{Lower limit} = 5 - \frac{(2.57)(2.19)}{\sqrt{6}} = 5 - 2.30 = 2.70,$$

and

$$\text{Upper limit} = 5 + \frac{(2.57)(2.19)}{\sqrt{6}} = 5 + 2.30 = 7.30.$$

Table 10.3	Values of x and $t_{(x)}$ (for $df = 5$) for Five Different Confidence Intervals	
CI (%)	x	$t_{(x)}$ (for $df = 5$)
99.9	.001	6.87
99	.01	4.03
95	.05	2.57
90	.10	2.02
80	.20	1.48

Because we computed a 95% CI around the obtained estimate of the population mean, we would state that "there is a 95% probability that the estimated population mean falls between the lower and upper limits of 2.70 and 7.30."

Although 95% confidence intervals are the most commonly used, we can choose any size CI we like. We need only replace the quantity $t_{(.05)}$ by the quantity $t_{(x)}$, where x = 1 minus the desired CI. Table 10.3 shows the values of x and $t_{(x)}$ (for $df = 5$) for five different confidence intervals. Values of $t_{(x)}$ are larger for the more demanding confidence intervals (99% and 99.9%), as we would expect in general, but these values of $t_{(x)}$ are especially large (4.03 and 6.87) because of the small sample size in our example ($n = 6$).

The Normal Distribution

When scores on a variety of types of measures (e.g., intelligence test scores, physical performance measures, or scores on an attitude scale) are collected by means of a representative sampling procedure, the distribution of these scores often forms a curve that has a distinct bell-like shape (as shown in Figure 10.7). This curve is called a **normal distribution** because of the large number of different kinds of measurements that are assumed to be ordinarily (i.e., "normally") distributed in this manner.

The normal distribution is particularly useful in providing a mathematical description of populations because it can be completely described from our knowledge of just the mean and the standard deviation. For example, we can say that roughly two thirds of the area of the normal distribution is within one standard deviation of the mean, and so on. More specifically (as represented in Figure 10.7), 68.3% of normally distributed scores will fall between -1σ and $+1\sigma$, 95.4% will fall between -2σ and $+2$, and 99.7% will fall between -3σ and $+3\sigma$. Even though over 99% of the scores fall between -3σ and $+3\sigma$, notice that the tails of the normal curve never do touch down on the abscissa; instead, they stretch into infinity.

One reason the normal distribution is so useful is that, by some simple arithmetic, we can translate raw scores obtained by different measures into standard deviation units. Not only does this process make the different scores comparable, but we can usually estimate what proportion of normally distributed scores in the population can be found in any region of the curve. Because so many measurements are distributed normally in the population, the statistics derived from this bell-

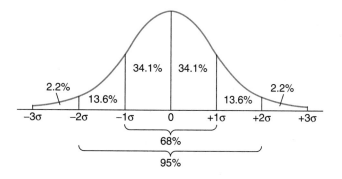

Figure 10.7 **The normal distribution divided up into standard deviation units.**

shaped curve are also very important in the testing of hypotheses. We will return to this topic in Chapter 12, but let us see how you might translate a raw score into a standard deviation unit, or standard score.

Standard Scores

A normal curve with a mean set equal to 0 and standard deviation set equal to 1 is called a **standard normal curve.** Any individual raw score can be put through a statistical translation (referred to as **transformation**) into a **standard score** corresponding to a location on the abscissa of a standard normal curve. A standard score (also called a **z score**) expresses, in standard deviation units, the raw score's distance from the mean of the normative group. We make such a transformation by subtracting the mean of the group (M) from the individual raw score (X), and then dividing this difference by the standard deviation (σ) of the normative group, that is

$$z \text{ score} = \frac{X - M}{\sigma}.$$

For example, scores on the Scholastic Assessment Test (SAT) have a normative group mean of 500 and a standard deviation of 100. Suppose you wanted to transform an individual raw score of 625 into a z score with a distribution mean of 0 and standard deviation of 1. You simply calculate as follows:

$$z = \frac{625 - 500}{100} = 1.25$$

and find that the raw score of 625 corresponds to a z score of 1.25, which tells you how far above the mean (in terms of the standard deviation of the distribution) this score is. To transform the z score back to the original raw score, you multiply the z score by σ and add it to M, which gives you

$$X = (z \text{ score}) (\sigma) + M = (1.25)(100) + 500 = 625.$$

In Table B.1 in Appendix B (see p. 409), you will find a listing of z scores (standardized normal deviates). The z column (with rows ranging from .0 to 4.0) lists z values to one decimal place. The remaining columns (.00 to .09) carry z to two decimal places. The body of the table shows the proportion of the area of the normal distribution that includes and is to the right (i.e., above) the value of any particular z on the abscissa. You can use this information to estimate the proportion of normally distributed scores in the population that are higher (or lower) than the raw score of 625 (corresponding to a z score of 1.25) on the SAT.

Given $z = 1.25$, you simply locate the intersection that corresponds to 1.2 (row 13) and .05 (column 6). That value is .1056, which estimates the proportion of SAT scores including and higher than an obtained score of 625 in the normative group of students taking the SAT. You multiply .1056 by 100 to transform the proportion into a percentage, which tells you that 10.56% of those tested ordinarily score as high as 625 or higher. Thus, you subtract this percentage from 100 to estimate how many ordinarily score lower than 625 (i.e., $100 - 10.56 = 89.44\%$ score lower).

Comparing Standard Scores

Note that the title of Table B.1 refers to "one-tailed" p values. We will have more to say about "one-tailed" (or "one-sided") significance levels in other chapters, but basically the term means that we are concentrating on one part of the normal distribution. In the case of a positive z score, we are focusing on the part from the midpoint (0) to the end of the right tail. If the z were a negative score, we would be concentrating on the part from the midpoint to the end of the left tail. In summary, then, a positive z score is above the mean, a negative z score is below the mean, and a zero z score is at the mean.

It is not necessary for scores on different tests or instruments to be normally distributed for you to transform them into z scores and then compare them in terms of this common metric. For example, by calculating z scores for height and weight, you can tell whether a person is taller than he or she is heavy, relative to others in the normative distribution of height and weight. However, only if they are distributed approximately normally in the population can we estimate from a z score how many scored above or below a given z score. We can do so for SAT scores because they are approximately normally distributed in the population.

As a practical illustration of the utility of z scores, imagine that an instructor has two measures of course grades on five male and five female students, as shown in Table 10.4. One set of scores (X_1) is based on an essay exam of 50 points with $M = 21.2$ and $\sigma = 11.69$, and another (X_2) is based on a multiple-choice exam of 100 points with $M = 68.8$ and $\sigma = 17.47$. The instructor transforms the raw scores into standard scores, with the results shown in the z_1 and z_2 columns. For example, Student 1 received a raw score of 42 on Exam 1, which the instructor converts to a z score by computing $(42 - 21.2)/11.69 = 1.78$. Student 1's score on Exam 1 is

Table 10.4	Raw Scores (X) and Standard Scores (z) on Two Exams				
	Exam 1		Exam 2		
Student ID and gender	X_1 score	z_1 score	X_2 score	z_2 score	Average of z_1 and z_2 scores
1 (M)	42	+1.78	90	+1.21	+1.50
2 (M)	9	−1.04	40	−1.65	−1.34
3 (F)	28	+0.58	92	+1.33	+0.96
4 (M)	11	−0.87	50	−1.08	−0.98
5 (M)	8	−1.13	49	−1.13	−1.13
6 (F)	15	−0.53	63	−0.33	−0.43
7 (M)	14	−0.62	68	−0.05	−0.34
8 (F)	25	+0.33	75	+0.35	+0.34
9 (F)	40	+1.61	89	+1.16	+1.38
10 (F)	20	−0.10	72	+0.18	+0.04
Sum (Σ)	212	0	688	0	0
Mean (M)	21.2	0	68.8	0	0
SD (σ)	11.69	1.0	17.47	1.0	0.98

almost two standard deviations above the mean, but Student 2's score on the same exam is approximately one standard deviation *below* the mean.

The z scores take this information into account, allowing the instructor to make easy comparisons within and across students. Here, the instructor counted the two exams equally to get the average score (in the last column), but it is easy enough to weight them. Suppose she had wanted to count the second exam twice as much as the first exam; she would double the Exam 2 z scores before averaging the two exams and divide by 3 instead of 2. Notice also that the standard deviation (*SD*) at the bottom of the last column is not 1.0; the reason is that the averages of two or more z scores are not themselves distributed as z scores with $\sigma = 1.0$. If the instructor wanted the averages of these z scores to be distributed as z, she would first have to z-score these averages.

Summary of Ideas

1. Clarity, precision, and efficiency are important criteria of graphical integrity when we want to represent numerical data in a visual display.
2. In a frequency distribution, a set of scores is arranged according to incidence of occurrence either in a table or in a figure such as a bar graph or, if we want to show change over time, a line graph.
3. In a stem-and-leaf chart, the original data are preserved with any desired precision so that we can visually detect the symmetry, spread, and concentration of the batch as well as any outliers.
4. A percentile locates a score in a distribution by defining the point below which a given proportion (or percentage) of the cases falls.

5. The median (*Mdn*, or 50th percentile) is the midmost score of a distribution.

6. The mode is the score (or the batch of scores in a stem-and-leaf chart) occurring with the greatest frequency.

7. The mean (*M*) is the arithmetic average of a set of scores.

8. Trimmed means are useful when distributions are strongly asymmetrical and (like medians) can often protect us against the intrusion of wild scores.

9. The range is the distance between the highest and lowest scores (the crude range), sometimes extended (also called *corrected*) to increase precision.

10. The variance (or mean square) is the average squared distance from the mean of all the scores.

11. The standard deviation (or root mean square) is the square root of the variance.

12. Descriptive measures (e.g., σ and σ^2) are used to calculate population values, and inferential measures (*S* and S^2) are used to estimate population values based on a sample of values.

13. A confidence interval (CI) around an estimated population mean tells us how accurately we have estimated the mean within certain lower and upper limits.

14. The normal distribution is a bell-shaped curve that is completely described by the mean and the standard deviation.

15. We calculate standard scores (z scores) by transforming raw scores to standard deviation units.

16. Standard scores permit the comparison (and averaging) of scores from different distributions of widely differing means and standard deviations.

Key Terms

abscissa   p. 249
arithmetic mean (*M*)   p. 255
asymmetrical distribution   p. 256
back-to-back stem-and-leaf
   chart   p. 252
bar graph   p. 249
bimodal   p. 255
central tendency   p. 253
corrected range   p. 259
crude range   p. 258
descriptive measure   p. 261
extended range   p. 259
finite   p. 262
frequency distribution   p. 249
inferential measure   p. 261

infinite   p. 262
interquartile range   p. 255
line graph   p. 250
mean (*M*)   p. 255
mean square (S^2)   p. 259
median (*Mdn*)   p. 253
mode   p. 255
negatively skewed distribution
   p. 257
normal distribution   p. 264
ordinate   p. 250
outliers   p. 257
percentile   p. 253
positively skewed distribution
   p. 257

range   p. 258
root mean square   p. 260
standard deviation   p. 260
standard normal curve   p. 265
standard score (z)   p. 265
stem-and-leaf chart   p. 251
symmetrical distribution   p. 256
transformation   p. 265
trimmed mean   p. 257
unbiased estimator of the
   population value of σ^2 p. 261
variance   p. 259
x axis   p. 249
y axis   p. 249
z score   p. 265

WEB ACTIVITY

See how the mean and median are affected by different distribution shapes by visiting the Rice Virtual Lab in Statistics at http://www.ruf.rice.edu/~lane/stat_sim/index.html and clicking on the Central Tendency radio button. A portal with categorized links to hundreds of statistics-related sites is University of Helsinki statistician Juha Puranen's at http://noppa5.pc.helsinki.fi/links.html.

Multiple-Choice Questions for Review

1. A graph in which the horizontal axis contains the score values, and in which the vertical axis reflects the frequency of a given score, is called a (a) stem-and-leaf chart; (b) cascade plot; (c) data summary graph; (d) frequency distribution.

2. Participants in a study at Iona College are asked to take a test of anxiety. Forty percent of the subjects receive scores lower than 12 on this test. For this sample, the value 12 is considered the (a) mean; (b) 40th percentile; (c) 60th percentile; (d) median.

3. Which of the following is considered a measure of central tendency? (a) mean; (b) 50th percentile; (c) mode; (d) all of the above

4. In a data set consisting of 0, 0, 0, 2, 2, 8, what is the mode? (a) 0; (b) 1; (c) 2; (d) 8

5. In the data set shown above, what is the M? (a) 0; (b) 1; (c) 2; (d) 8

6. In the same data set, what is the Mdn? (a) 0; (b) 1; (c) 2; (d) 8

7. Consider the following set of data points: 0, 1, 2, 3, 4. What is the crude range of these scores? (a) 2.5; (b) 0; (c) 4; (d) 5

8. Formulas that are used to calculate information about a population are called _____. (a) popular; (b) descriptive; (c) inferential; (d) none of the above

9. A standard normal distribution has a mean of _____ and a standard deviation of _____. (a) 0, 1; (b) 1, 0; (c) 1, 1; (d) cannot be determined from this information

10. A DePaul University researcher administers an attitude scale to a group of I/O students. The average score is 2, and the standard deviation is 2. Suppose that you receive a score of 0. What is your z score? (a) 2, (b) −2; (c) 0; (d) −1

Discussion Questions for Review

1. A University of Oregon student conducted a study on anxiety in 11 business executives. Their scores on a standardized test of anxiety were 32, 16, 29, 41, 33, 37, 27, 30, 22, 38, and 33. Can you reconstruct the student's stem-and-leaf chart for these scores? What is the median of these scores, and what are the extended range and the interquartile range?

2. A Fordham University student is interested in studying ways of cutting down noise pollution in Manhattan. Her first step is to buy a machine that will measure the loudness of various sounds. In order to decide which machine to buy, she tests four brands against a standard tone of 85 decibels for five trials each, with the results shown below. Assuming that all the machines have the same price, which should be her first choice?

	Machine A	Machine B	Machine C	Machine D
	76	84	83	85
	82	87	89	81
	78	83	91	93
	84	85	77	89
	80	86	105	77
M	80	85	89	85
S	3.16	1.58	10.49	6.32

Oops . . . she finds that the manufacturer has discontinued her first-choice brand. Which machine would you recommend as a second choice, and why?

3. A Wharton M.B.A. student recorded the following scores for an item on a marketing questionnaire: 22, 14, 16, 24, 13, 26, 17, 98, 11, 9, and 21. What measure of central tendency would you advise him to calculate? Why?

4. A Florida State University student was looking at her grades for the midterm and the final exam. On the midterm she got a score of 58 and the class mean was 52 with a standard deviation of 12. On the final she got a score of 110; the class mean was 100 with a standard deviation of 30. On which test did she do better?

5. A Brandeis University student calls home to tell his family that he just received a score of 2 on a new IQ test. As they wonder why they are spending so much money on his tuition, he reassures them that 2 is his z score. What percentage of the population did he score above?

6. A University of Missouri professor has three sections with three graduate assistants—Tom, Dick, and Harry—each of whom has six students. The time has come to grade papers. In order to ensure uniform grading standards across the sections, the professor instructs the assistants to give an average score of 8.0 (equivalent to B−) on a scale of 1 to 12 (where 1 represents a grade of F, and 12 represents a grade of A). The assistants submit the following sets of grades:

Tom	Dick	Harry
12	8	7
6	8	7
5	10	8
5	7	5
8	8	6
12	7	9

The professor calls in Harry and says, "You have not followed my instructions. Your scores are biased toward having your section do better than it is supposed to." Calculate the means of each section, and then argue the truth or falsity of the professor's accusation. The professor next calls in Tom and Dick and says, "Although both of your sections have a mean grade of 8.0, Tom's scores look more spread out." Calculate, and then compare, the standard deviation of the scores in the sections to decide whether the professor is right. Which is a better grade (relative to one's own section), a 5 in Tom's section or a 7 in Dick's section?

7. Compute the σ, σ^2, S, and S^2 on the no-show data in the stem-and-leaf chart shown in Figure 10.5 (p. 255).

Answers to Review Questions

Multiple-Choice Questions

1. d	**3.** d	**5.** c	**7.** c	**9.** a
2. b	**4.** a	**6.** b	**8.** b	**10.** d

Discussion Questions

1. The stem-and-leaf-plot is

Stem	Leaf
4	1
3	0 2 3 3 7 8
2	2 7 9
1	6

   The median score can be found from .5(N + 1) = .5(12) = 6. Because the sixth score is 32, that is our median. The extended range is the crude range (41 2 16) plus 1 unit, or 25 + 1 = 26. The interquartile range is from the .25(N + 1)th to the .75 (N + 1)th score, or from 27 to 37.

2. Her first choice is Machine B because it shows no bias and the least instability or variability. Her second choice might be Machine D because it shows no bias or Machine A because, although it shows a 5-decibel bias, it measures volume more consistently. As long as she remembers to correct for the 5-decibel bias, she might be well advised to get Machine A.

3. Because of the outlier score of 98, he should prefer the median or a trimmed mean to the ordinary mean. In this example, the mean of the 11 untrimmed scores is 24.6, whereas the median is only 17 and the trimmed mean (trimming by 1 on each end) is 18.2.

4. She did better on the midterm, where the z score = (58 − 52)/12 = .50, than on the final, where the z score = (110 − 100)/30 = .33.

5. He scored above 97.7% of the normative population.

6. The professor is correct in thinking Harry's grading biased. However, the professor is wrong about the direction of the bias. Harry's average grade is a C+ (7) instead of a B− (8). The professor is correct in thinking Tom's grades are more spread out than Dick's grades. The three standard deviations are 3.00, 1.00, and 1.29 for Tom, Dick, and Harry, respectively. Students earning 5s in Tom's section performed the same as those earning 7s in Dick's section; in both cases, z = −1.00

7. The answers are σ = .115, σ^2 = .013, S = .118, and S^2 = .014.

CHAPTER 11

Quantifying and Interpreting Relationships Among Variables

Preview Questions

- What are continuous and discrete variables, and when are discrete variables dichotomous?
- What is the "third-variable problem"?
- Why is the Pearson r measure called the *product-moment correlation?*
- When would you use a rank-order correlation?
- Why is the Spearman rho classified as a product-moment r?
- What is the purpose of the point-biserial r?
- How is dummy coding used to quantify dichotomous variables?
- How is the phi coefficient related to the Pearson r?
- How can you prove that rho, the point-biserial r, and phi are simply cases of the Pearson r?

The Correlation Coefficient

You have seen that researchers view variables not in isolation, but as being systematically and meaningfully associated with or related to other variables. In this chapter, we will elaborate on how, using a single number (called the **correlation coefficient**), you can indicate the strength of association between two variables (X and Y). In particular, we describe correlation coefficients that reflect the degree to which mutual relations between X and Y resemble a straight line (called **linearity**). The **Pearson r** is the correlation coefficient of choice in such situations, with values of 1.0 (positive or negative) indicating a perfect linear relation, and 0 indicating that neither X nor Y can be predicted from the other by use of a linear equa-

BOX 11.1 Galton, Pearson, and *r*

In an earlier chapter, we mentioned Francis Galton's work. One of his many research projects concerned the relationship between traits of fathers and their adult sons. Galton, who was very intuitive about both research methods and statistics, invented a way of measuring the strength of association between the two variables. Inspired by his mentor's statistical thinking, Karl Pearson (1857–1936) perfected Galton's idea into the more general method of correlation that has come to be known as the Pearson *r* (Stigler, 1986).

tion (see also Box 11.1). A positive *r* indicates that an increase in *X* is associated with an increase in *Y,* whereas a negative *r* indicates that an increase in *X* is associated with a decrease in *Y.*

Causation implies correlation (or covariation), but finding that *X* and *Y* are correlated does not tell us *why* they are related. In Chapter 7, we explained that, although covariation is essential evidence for making causal inferences, other requirements of evidence include temporal precedence and the excluding of alternative explanations. One alternative to be considered is whether another variable that is correlated with both *X* and *Y* might explain the observed relationship—called the **third-variable problem.** By way of illustration, mathematician John Paulos (1991) mentioned the high positive correlation between the size of children's feet and their spelling ability. Should we, he asked, use foot stretchers to increase children's spelling scores? The answer, of course, is no, because it is not the length of the children's feet that is the causal variable but the fact that children with bigger feet are usually older, and older children are better educated and therefore spell better. In other words, a third variable (age) can account for the correlation between *X* and *Y.*

We begin by examining what different values of *r* look like. Then we proceed through the steps in computing the correlation coefficient when the raw data have different characteristics (previewed in Table 11.1), such as when the values of *X* and *Y* are continuous or dichotomous. With a **continuous variable,** we can always imagine another value falling between any two adjacent scores, whereas a **dichotomous variable** is divided into two discrete parts (and is more generally referred to as a **discrete variable,** i.e., a variable with two or more distinct or separate parts). For example, a psychophysicist who studies the discrimination of pitch (i.e., the highness or lowness of a tone) might correlate changes in the frequency of sound waves with the differing ability of individuals to discriminate the changes. Both variables are continuous, in that we can imagine a score of 1.5 between 1 and 2, or 1.55 between 1.5 and 1.6. Suppose the researcher also correlated the participants' gender with their abilities to discriminate pitch. Pitch discrimination is a continuous variable, but gender is a discrete variable that is dichotomous (i.e., divided into two separate parts). We can frequently create dichotomies by splitting

Table 11.1	Common Names and Forms of Product-Moment Correlations
Common name	Characteristics of the data
Pearson r	Two continuous variables, such as the correlation of scores on the Scholastic Assessment Test (SAT) with grade point average (GPA) after 4 years of college
Spearman rho (r_s)	Two ranked variables, such as the correlation of the ranking of the top 25 college basketball teams by sports writers (Associated Press ranking) with the ranking of the same teams by college coaches (*USA Today* ranking)
Point-biserial (r_{pb})	One continuous and one dichotomous variable, such as the correlation of subjects' gender with their performance on the SAT-Verbal
Phi coefficient (ϕ)	Two dichotomous variables, such as the correlation of subjects' gender with their yes-no responses to a specific question

variables at the median point (the split is called a **median split;** we will return to this idea when we discuss the binomial effect-size display in the next chapter).

Visualizing the Correlation Coefficient

In addition to the graphics described in the preceding chapter, another informative visual display is called a **scatter plot** (or **scatter diagram**). It takes its name from the fact that it looks like a cloud of scattered dots. Each dot represents the intersection of a line extended from a point on the X axis (the horizontal axis, or abscissa) and a line extended from a point on the Y axis (the vertical axis, or ordinate). To illustrate, Table 11.2 repeats the data that we used in the previous chapter to explain z scores, and we will continue to discuss these data in this chapter. For now, we

Table 11.2	Raw and Standardized Data for Pearson r Correlation Coefficient				
Student ID and gender	Exam 1		Exam 2		Product of
	X_1 score	z_1 score	X_2 score	z_2 score	z_1 and z_2 scores
1 (M)	42	+1.78	90	+1.21	+2.15
2 (M)	9	−1.04	40	−1.65	+1.72
3 (F)	28	+0.58	92	+1.33	+0.77
4 (M)	11	−0.87	50	−1.08	+0.94
5 (M)	8	−1.13	49	−1.13	+1.28
6 (F)	15	−0.53	63	−0.33	+0.17
7 (M)	14	−0.62	68	−0.05	+0.03
8 (F)	25	+0.33	75	+0.35	+0.12
9 (F)	40	+1.61	89	+1.16	+1.87
10 (F)	20	−0.10	72	+0.18	−0.02
Sum (Σ)	212	0	688	0	+9.03
Mean (M)	21.2	0	68.8	0	.90
SD (σ)	11.69	1.0	17.47	1.0	

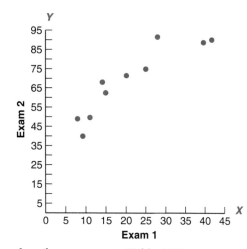

Figure 11.1   Scatter plot of raw scores in Table 11.2.

will concentrate on the raw scores (i.e., the X_1 and X_2 scores) of these 10 students on the two exams. Figure 11.1 displays these scores in the form of a scatter plot.

By way of comparison, Figure 11.2 shows additional scatter plots (each containing 50 dots) that represent different values of the correlation coefficient, including zero and near-perfect rs. However, remember that even a perfect r does not necessarily indicate a cause-and effect relation, as there might be a third-variable explanation (see also Box 11.2). Now imagine a straight line through the dots in Figure 11.2. The higher the correlation is, the more tightly clustered along the line are the dots (and, therefore, the better is the linear predictability). Observe also that the cloud of dots slopes up for positive correlations and slopes down for negative correlations, and that the linearity becomes clearer as the correlation becomes higher. From these diagrams, what would you guess is the size of the Pearson r represented by the data in Figure 11.1?

Calculating the Pearson r

There are many useful formulas for computing the Pearson r correlation coefficient. But the following formula (which defines the Pearson r conceptually) can be used quite generally, and we will use it throughout this chapter to prove that all the correlations listed in Table 11.1 are really Pearson rs in one form or another:

$$r_{xy} = \frac{\Sigma z_x z_y}{N}.$$

This formula indicates that the linear correlation between two variables (X and Y) is equal to the sum of the products of the z scores of X and Y divided by the number (N) of pairs of X and Y scores (see also Box 11.3).

The Pearson r correlation is also called the **product-moment correlation** because the zs (in the numerator) are distances from the mean (also called *moments*)

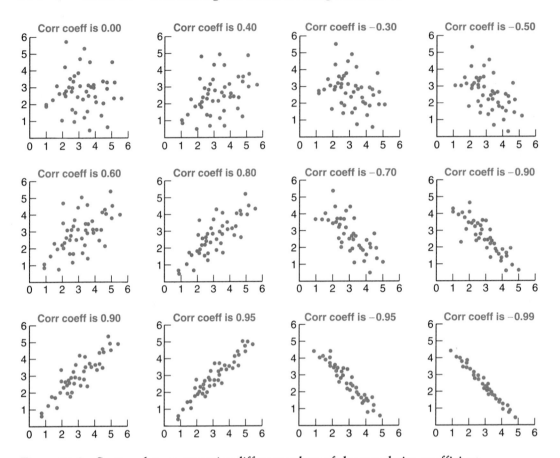

Figure 11.2   **Scatter plots representing different values of the correlation coefficient.**

Source: From *Statistics* (2nd ed., pp. 119, 121), by D. Freedman, R. Pisani, R. Purves, and A. Adhikari, 1991, New York: W.W. Norton. Reproduced by permission of the first author and the publisher.

that are multiplied by each other to form "products." To use this formula, we begin by transforming the raw scores to z scores following the procedure described in the previous chapter. In other words, we calculate the mean and the standard deviation of each column of raw scores and substitute the calculated value in the $(X - M)/\sigma$ formula. In Table 11.2 we see such z scores corresponding to the students' raw scores on Exam 1 and Exam 2. Notice that, for Student 5, the z score for Exam 1 is identical to the z score for Exam 2, even though the raw scores are very different. The reason is that the z scores for Exam 1 were computed from the mean and standard deviation of Exam 1 (21.2 and 11.69, respectively), whereas the z scores for Exam 2 were computed by the use of the mean and standard deviation of that exam (68.8 and 17.47, respectively). Instead of averaging the z scores (as we did in the previous chapter for a very different purpose), the last column in Table 11.2 gives the products of the z scores and their mean, showing that the Pearson r = .90.

BOX 11.2 The Third-Variable Problem

Paulos (1990) also mentioned other fascinating examples of the third-variable problem. For example, there is a positive correlation between milk consumption and the incidence of cancer in various societies. The explanation for this correlation is the fact that people in relatively wealthy societies live longer, and increased longevity increases the likelihood of getting cancer. Indeed, any health practice (such as milk drinking) that increases longevity usually correlates positively with cancer incidence. Another example is the small negative correlation observed between death rates and divorce rates (i.e., more divorce, less death) in various regions of the country. The third variable that explains this correlation is the age distribution of the various regions, as older married couples are less likely to divorce and more likely to die than younger couples.

Although we use the conceptual formula above as a teaching tool in this chapter, it is far easier to obtain the Pearson r by using SPSS, SAS, SYSTAT, Minitab, or a calculator that allows you to punch a few buttons to compute r. But if all you have is the calculator you use to balance your checkbook, another way to compute the Pearson r (which is easier than using the conceptual formula above) is to use the following formula, which is based on raw scores rather than z scores:

$$r_{xy} = \frac{N\Sigma XY - (\Sigma X)(\Sigma Y)}{\sqrt{[N\Sigma X^2 - (\Sigma X)^2][N\Sigma Y^2 - (\Sigma Y)^2]}},$$

BOX 11.3 Linearity and Nonlinearity

The Pearson r is a measure of **linearity** (that is, the mutual relation between two variables resembles a straight line). Thus, a Pearson r near 0 does not automatically imply no relationship; it indicates only that there is no linear relationship. **Nonlinearity** can take many different forms (e.g., U-shaped, J-shaped, and wave-shaped curves). Suppose you were studying the relationship between age and the latency of some response, and you found that latency decreased up to a certain age and then gradually increased. If you plotted the results by means of a line graph, your curve showing this nonlinear relation would resemble a ∪, with age plotted on the abscissa (X axis) and latency of response (from low to high) on the ordinate (Y axis). Other examples of nonlinear relations include curves for learning, extinction, dark adaptation, and response rate as a function of the amount of reinforcement (e.g., Grant, 1956; Malmo, 1959).

	Exam 1		Exam 2		
Student	X	X^2	Y	Y^2	XY
1	42	1,764	90	8,100	3,780
2	9	81	40	1,600	360
3	28	784	92	8,464	2,576
4	11	121	50	2,500	550
5	8	64	49	2,401	392
6	15	225	63	3,969	945
7	14	196	68	4,624	952
8	25	625	75	5,625	1,875
9	40	1,600	89	7,921	3,560
10	20	400	72	5,184	1,440
Sum (Σ)	212	5,860	688	50,388	16,430

Table 11.3   Basic Data for Computing Pearson r from Raw Scores

where N = the number of X and Y pairs of scores, and Σ directs you to sum a set of values. This formula may look difficult, but it is not hard to use. All you need are the sums of the scores and of the squared scores. To illustrate, Table 11.3 shows the basic data you need to compute r from the raw scores in Table 11.2. Substituting these numbers in the formula above gives

$$r_{xy} = \frac{10(16,430) - (212)(688)}{\sqrt{[10(5,860) - (212)^2][10(50,388) - (688)^2]}} = \frac{18,444}{\sqrt{(13,656)(30,536)}} = .90.$$

When using this formula, don't forget to take the square root of the denominator.

Spearman Rank Correlation

Suppose the data are ranks rather than scores on a rating scale. The correlation coefficient is now called the **Spearman rho (r_s)**, but this, as you will see, is nothing more than the product-moment r calculated on numbers that happen to be ranks. Ranked numbers are more predictable, in the sense that knowing only the number of pairs of scores tells us both the mean and the standard deviation of the scores that have been ranked, as long as there are no ties in the ranking. An easy-to-use formula for scores that have been ranked is

$$r_s = 1 - \frac{6(\Sigma D^2)}{N^3 - N}$$

where 6 is a constant value, and N = the number of pairs of scores or ranks. The only new element is D, the difference between the ranks assigned to the two variables being correlated.

To illustrate the use of this formula, Table 11.4 shows a portion of the data collected by Paul Slovic (1987) in his investigation of the perception of risk. He was interested in comparing the judgments people make when they are asked to characterize and evaluate hazardous activities and technologies. This table shows the

Table 11.4	Ordering of Perceived Risk for 30 Activities and Technologies			
Activity or technology	League of Women Voters	Experts	D	D^2
Nuclear power	1	20	−19	361
Motor vehicles	2	1	1	1
Handguns	3	4	−1	1
Smoking	4	2	2	4
Motorcycles	5	6	−1	1
Alcoholic beverages	6	3	3	9
General (private) aviation	7	12	−5	25
Police work	8	17	−9	81
Pesticides	9	8	1	1
Surgery	10	5	5	25
Firefighting	11	18	−7	49
Large construction	12	13	−1	1
Hunting	13	23	−10	100
Spray cans	14	26	−12	144
Mountain climbing	15	29	−14	196
Bicycles	16	15	1	1
Commercial aviation	17	16	1	1
Electric power (nonnuclear)	18	9	9	81
Swimming	19	10	9	81
Contraceptives	20	11	9	81
Skiing	21	30	−9	81
X-rays	22	7	15	225
High school and college football	23	27	−4	16
Railroads	24	19	5	25
Food preservatives	25	14	11	121
Food coloring	26	21	5	25
Power mowers	27	28	−1	1
Prescription antibiotics	28	24	4	16
Home appliances	29	22	7	49
Vaccinations	30	25	5	25
Sum (Σ)	465	465	0	1,828

Source: From "Perception of Risk," by P. Slovic, 1987, *Science, 236,* p. 281. Copyright © by American Association for the Advancement of Science. Reprinted with permission of Paul Slovic and the American Association for the Advancement of Science.

overall rankings made by 15 national experts on risk assessment and 40 members of the League of Women Voters (LWV). We see, for example, that the experts ranked motor vehicles as most hazardous (Rank 1) and skiing as least hazardous (Rank 30), whereas the LWV members ranked nuclear power as most hazardous (Rank 1) and vaccinations as least hazardous (Rank 30). Notice that the sums of the ranks are equal for the two variables (465). The column headed D lists the differences between the ranks. For example, the difference in ranking of nuclear power is computed as $D = 1 - 20 = -19$. The sum of the D scores is always 0. The column headed D^2 shows such differences squared, so that $(-19)^2 = 361$.

The sum of the squared differences (indicated as 1,828 at the bottom of the column headed D^2) is now substituted in the Spearman rho formula:

$$r_s = 1 - \frac{6(1,828)}{30^3 - 30} = .59.$$

In interpreting rank correlations, we use the D scores and the ranks to help us interpret similarities and differences in the results. Here, a positive difference tells us that the LWV members perceived the activity or technology as less risky than did the experts; a negative difference indicates the opposite conclusion. We see, for example, that the two groups of raters disagreed little about the high risks associated with motor vehicles, handguns, and motorcycles (D of +1 or −1). There was little disagreement about the much lower risk associated with power mowers (D = −1), but there was strong disagreement about nuclear power (D = −19), X-rays (D = 15), and mountain climbing (D = −14).

To illustrate that the Spearman rho is a Pearson r calculated on numbers that happen to be ranks, we turn to Table 11.5. The columns containing z scores show the standard scores of the ranks. For example, to find the z score corresponding to the LWV's ranking of nuclear power, we computed

$$z = \frac{X - M}{\sigma} = \frac{1 - 15.50}{8.655} = -1.68.$$

The last column shows the products of the z-scored ranks, with the sum and mean indicated at the bottom. Recalling that the mean of the products is the Pearson r, we see that it is identical to the value we obtained using the Spearman rho formula, that is,

$$r_s = \frac{\Sigma z_x z_y}{N} = \frac{17.82}{30} = .59.$$

Suppose we are working with raw scores that are continuous but we want to recast them as ranks and compute a Spearman rho (see also Box 11.4). Table 11.6 shows how, from our continuing example. The students are ranked from 1 (highest raw score) to 10 (lowest raw score), and again the D score is the difference between these rankings. The sum of the squared differences (indicated as 10 at the bottom of the column headed D^2) is substituted in the numerator of the Spearman rho formula:

$$r_s = 1 - \frac{6(\Sigma D^2)}{N^3 - N} = 1 - \frac{6(10)}{10^3 - 10} = .94.$$

Point-Biserial Correlation

Another special case of the product-moment r is the **point-biserial correlation** (r_{pb}). In this case one variable is continuous, and the other variable is dichotomous with applied values such as 0 and 1 or −1 and +1. The quantification of the two levels of a dichotomous variable is called **dummy coding** when 0 and 1 are used. Dummy coding is a tremendously useful method, for it allows us to quantify

Table 11.5	Ranked and Standardized Data for Spearman Rho Correlation				
Activity or technology	League of Women Voters		Experts		Product of z scores
	Rank	z score	Rank	z score	
Nuclear power	1	−1.68	20	+0.52	−0.87
Motor vehicles	2	−1.56	1	−1.68	+2.62
Handguns	3	−1.44	4	−1.33	+1.92
Smoking	4	−1.33	2	−1.56	+2.07
Motorcycles	5	−1.21	6	−1.10	+1.33
Alcoholic beverages	6	−1.10	3	−1.44	+1.58
General aviation	7	−0.98	12	−0.40	+0.39
Police work	8	−0.87	17	+0.17	−0.15
Pesticides	9	−0.75	8	−0.87	+0.65
Surgery	10	−0.64	5	−1.21	+0.77
Firefighting	11	−0.52	18	+0.29	−0.15
Large construction	12	−0.40	13	−0.29	+0.12
Hunting	13	−0.29	23	+0.87	−0.25
Spray cans	14	−0.17	26	+1.21	−0.21
Mountain climbing	15	−0.06	29	+1.56	−0.09
Bicycles	16	+0.06	15	−0.06	0.00
Commercial aviation	17	+0.17	16	+0.06	+0.01
Electric power	18	+0.29	9	−0.75	−0.22
Swimming	19	+0.40	10	−0.64	−0.26
Contraceptives	20	+0.52	11	−0.52	−0.27
Skiing	21	+0.64	30	+1.68	+1.08
X-rays	22	+0.75	7	−0.98	−0.74
High school and college football	23	+0.87	27	+1.33	+1.16
Railroads	24	+0.98	19	+0.40	+0.39
Food preservatives	25	+1.10	14	−0.17	−0.19
Food coloring	26	+1.21	21	+0.64	+0.77
Power mowers	27	+1.33	28	+1.44	+1.92
Prescription antibiotics	28	+1.44	24	+0.98	+1.41
Home appliances	29	+1.56	22	+0.75	+1.17
Vaccinations	30	+1.68	25	+1.10	+1.85
Sum (Σ)	465	0	465	0	17.82
Mean (M)	15.50	0	15.50	0	.59
SD (σ)	8.655	1.00	8.655	1.00	—

any variable that can be represented as dichotomous. For example, suppose you have performed an experiment in which there were two groups—an experimental and a control group—and you want to correlate group membership with scores on the dependent variable. To dummy-code group membership, you would simply record 1 for experimental and 0 for control. Other examples of dichotomous variables that can be easily recast into 1s and 0s are gender (female vs. male), survival rate (live vs. die), and success rate (succeed vs. fail).

BOX 11.4 Using Rankings for Quick Estimates

Why use rankings when continuous data are available? In most cases, it is preferable to stay with the continuous data and use the Pearson r, but suppose you wanted a quick estimate of the correlation between these six pairs of raw scores:

	Raw score for X	Raw score for Y	Rank of X	Rank of Y
Pair 1	73.8	801.76	2	1
Pair 2	186.2	732.90	1	2
Pair 3	44.4	539.57	3	3
Pair 4	38.6	206.11	4	5
Pair 5	37.5	210.56	5	4
Pair 6	21.8	159.33	6	6

Clearly, it would be tedious to calculate the Pearson r by hand from the raw scores. Transforming the raw scores into ranks and then calculating the Spearman rho on the basis of the values in the last two columns is much easier, although by sacrificing the continuity of the raw scores, we are also missing the fine distinctions. In some situations, however, we may prefer to use rank ordering, such as when judges have no measuring instrument and must resort to rank ordering or when the raw scores include extreme outliers that may result in misleading correlations (i.e., ranked scores never have extreme outliers).

Table 11.6	Raw Data from Table 11.2 Ranked for Spearman Rho Correlation					
	Exam 1		Exam 2			
Student	X_1 score	Rank	X_2 score	Rank	D	D^2
1	42	1	90	2	−1	1
2	9	9	40	10	−1	1
3	28	3	92	1	2	4
4	11	8	50	8	0	0
5	8	10	49	9	1	1
6	15	6	63	7	−1	1
7	14	7	68	6	1	1
8	25	4	75	4	0	0
9	40	2	89	3	−1	1
10	20	5	72	5	0	0
Sum (Σ)	212	55[a]	688	55[a]	0[b]	10

[a]Note that the sum of the ranks is equal for the two variables.
[b]Note that the sum of D is always 0.

Going back to our continuing example in Table 11.2, suppose we want to compare males with females on Exam 1. The scores on that exam were as follows:

Males	Females
42	28
9	15
11	25
8	40
14	20

Although we have two groups of scores, the arrangement does not look like the typical one for a correlation coefficient—where we would expect to see *pairs* of scores (e.g., X_1 and X_2 scores, or X and Y scores). The data arrangement rewritten into a form that "looks more correlational" is shown in Table 11.7.

The first column in Table 11.7 repeats the identification (ID) and gender information, and the next two columns show again the raw and standardized scores for Exam 1. Under "Student's gender," the first column shows the dummy-coded scores for gender, with the female students coded 1 and the male students coded 0. We think of the dummy-coded variable as "femaleness" because 1 and 0 imply the presence and absence of femaleness, respectively. The next column shows the z-score results of standardizing the dummy-coded values. For example, to get the z score for Student 1's gender, we computed

$$z = \frac{X - M}{\sigma} = \frac{0 - 0.5}{0.5} = -1,$$

Table 11.7	Raw, Dummy-Coded, and Standardized Data for Point-Biserial Correlation

Student ID and gender	Exam 1		Student's gender		Product of z scores
	Raw score	z score	Dummy code	z score	
1 (M)	42	+1.78	0	−1	−1.78
2 (M)	9	−1.04	0	−1	+1.04
3 (F)	28	+0.58	1	+1	+0.58
4 (M)	11	−0.87	0	−1	+0.87
5 (M)	8	−1.13	0	−1	+1.13
6 (F)	15	−0.53	1	+1	−0.53
7 (M)	14	−0.62	0	−1	+0.62
8 (F)	25	+0.33	1	+1	+0.33
9 (F)	40	+1.61	1	+1	+1.61
10 (F)	20	−0.10	1	+1	−0.10
Sum (Σ)	212	0	5	0	+3.77
Mean (*M*)	21.2	0	0.5	0	.38
SD (σ)	11.69	1.0	0.5	1.0	

where X = the dummy score of 0 for Student 1, M = the mean of the column of dummy scores (M = 5/10 = 0.5), and σ = the standard deviation (SD) shown at the bottom of that column (0.5).

Notice that, as always, the z scores sum to zero; another sum would signal either a computational or a recording mistake. Observe also that the standard deviation scores within the column of z scores are -1 for a dummy code of 0 and $+1$ for a dummy code of 1, a situation always found when the number of 0 scores equals the number of 1 scores. And finally, the sum of the products of the z scores (shown at the bottom of the last column of data) is $+3.77$. Dividing this value by the number of students (N = 10) gives us the point-biserial r between femaleness and scores on Exam 1, that is,

$$r_{pb} = \frac{\Sigma z_x z_y}{N} = \frac{3.77}{10} = .38.$$

The positive correlation tells us that the female students scored relatively higher on the exam than did the male students. Had the correlation been negative and of the same magnitude, it would have indicated that female students scored relatively lower on the exam than did male students.

Phi Coefficient

Not infrequently, both of the variables to be correlated are dichotomous. In Chapter 8, we noted a hypothetical case in which people who ate a rare hamburger became sick. Going back to Table 8.1 (page 202), suppose we are interested in quantifying the relation between these two variables. We have another special case of the product-moment r, called the **phi coefficient** (symbolized by ϕ, the lower-case Greek letter phi). In this case, both variables are dichotomous (with arbitrarily applied numerical values such as 0 and 1 or -1 and $+1$).

We can find the value of the phi coefficient in several different ways; two of them are shown here. The conceptual procedure, represented in Table 11.8, illustrates why we say that ϕ is another special case of the product-moment r. Under the "Ate burger?" heading, the first column shows the dummy scores of Yes = 1 and No = 0. The next column shows standardized scores corresponding to the dummy-coded values. So, for example, we computed the z score corresponding to Mimi's 1 as

$$z = \frac{X - M}{\sigma} = \frac{1 - .417}{.493} = +1.183.$$

Table 11.8	Dummy-Coded and Standardized Data for Phi Coefficient				
	Ate burger?		Got food poisoning?		Product of
Name	Y = 1; N = 0	z score	Y = 1; N = 0	z score	z scores
Mimi	1	+1.183	1	+1.183	1.400
Gail	0	−0.846	0	−0.846	0.716
Connie	0	−0.846	0	−0.846	0.716
Jerry	0	−0.846	0	−0.846	0.716
Greg	0	−0.846	0	−0.846	0.716
Dwight	0	−0.846	0	−0.846	0.716
Nancy	1	+1.183	1	+1.183	1.400
Richard	0	−0.846	0	−0.846	0.716
Kerry	0	−0.846	0	−0.846	0.716
Michele	1	+1.183	1	+1.183	1.400
John	1	+1.183	1	+1.183	1.400
Sheila	1	+1.183	1	+1.183	1.400
Sum (Σ)	5	0.00	5	0.00	12.012
Mean (M)	.417	0.00	.417	0.00	1.00
SD (σ)	.493	1.000	.493	1.000	.337

Similarly, under the "Got food poisoning?" heading, the dummy coding is again Yes = 1 and No = 0, followed by the corresponding z scores.

The last column in this table shows the mean of the product of the z scores as 1.00, which is the phi coefficient, that is,

$$\phi = \frac{\Sigma z_x z_y}{N} = \frac{12.012}{12} = 1.00.$$

In other words, we have treated phi (ϕ) no differently from any product-moment r calculated on the basis of z scores. The positive correlation tells us that answering yes to the question "Ate burger?" is directly related to answering yes to the question "Got food poisoning?" and the 1.00 tells us that we can predict who got food poisoning perfectly from the knowledge of who ate a burger. If the 1.00 correlation were negative, there would be a perfect inverse relation between eating the burger and getting food poisoning. Thus, when interpreting phi coefficients, we must pay close attention to how the two dichotomous variables were dummy-coded and labeled.

There is an easier way to compute ϕ by using an alternative formula that takes advantage of the fact that the data can be represented in a 2 × 2 table of frequencies (or **counts**), also called a *chi-square contingency table* (more about chi-square in Chapter 15) or simply a "contingency table." You will see this 2 × 2 format in Table 11.9, which shows that all five people who ate the burgers then got food poisoning and that the seven people who did not eat them remained well. Notice

Table 11.9	2 × 2 Contingency Table Coded for Computation of Phi Coefficient		

	Got food poisoning?		
Ate burger?	Yes	No	Totals
No	**A** 0	**B** 7	**(A + B)** = 7
Yes	**C** 5	**D** 0	**(C + D)** = 5
Totals	**(A + C)** = 5	**(B + D)** = 7	

that the cells are labeled A, B, C, and D. With this code, we use the following formula to calculate the phi coefficient:

$$\phi = \frac{BC - AD}{\sqrt{(A + B)(C + D)(A + C)(B + D)}}.$$

Substituting in this formula yields

$$\phi = \frac{(7)(5) - (0)(0)}{\sqrt{(7)(5)(5)(7)}} = \frac{35 - 0}{\sqrt{1,225}} = \frac{35}{35} = 1.00,$$

which (not unexpectedly) is the same result that we obtained using the conceptual formula for the Pearson r.

A Final Note

We will have more to say about the point-biserial correlation (r_{pb}) and the phi coefficient (ϕ) in the following chapters, as correlation coefficients such as r_{pb} and ϕ are very useful indices of the effect size. It is becoming increasingly important in empirical research that scientists report and interpret the effect size, and (as we show in the following chapters) the correlation coefficient is easily computed and interpreted in a wide variety of situations. Of course, the interpretation of the real-life importance of an effect size always depends on the context and the nature of the dependent variable. Nonetheless, the size of the effect is another piece of information that can help you decide whether it is meaningful in a practical or personal way.

Summary of Ideas

1. The Pearson r is a standard index of linear relationship, with possible values running from -1.0 to $+1.0$.

2. The third-variable problem is that another variable that is correlated with both X and Y may be the cause of both (e.g., children's foot size and spelling ability).

3. Scatter plots let us visualize the clustering and slope of dots that represent the relationship between X and Y.

4. The Pearson r, defined as $(\Sigma z_x z_y)/N$, is called the *product-moment correlation* because zs (i.e., standardized distances from the mean) are also known as *moments*.

5. The Spearman rho (r_s) is the Pearson r calculated on scores that happen to be in ranked form (e.g., the data on perceptions of risk).

6. Calculating r on the original unranked scores typically results in a different value for the correlation than calculating r_s on the ranks of the original scores, and calculating r on the original unranked scores is ordinarily preferred.

7. The point-biserial correlation (r_{pb}) is the Pearson r in which one of the variables is continuous and the other is dichotomous (e.g., exam score and student's gender).

8. Dummy-coding the dichotomous variable (e.g., female vs. male, live vs. die, or succeed vs. fail) allows us to calculate r_{pb} by the Pearson r formula.

9. In dummy-coded data, 0 converts to a negative z and 1 converts to a positive z; the particular value of z is computed as $(X - M)/\sigma$.

10. The phi coefficient (ϕ) is the Pearson r where both variables are dichotomous (e.g., "Ate burger?" and "Got food poisoning?").

11. To calculate the correlation between two dichotomous variables, we can (a) dummy-code both variables (e.g., Yes = 1 and No = 0) and then use the corresponding z scores to compute the Pearson r or (b) compute ϕ directly from the 2 × 2 contingency table.

Key Terms

continuous variable   p. 273
correlation coefficient   p. 272
counts   p. 285
dichotomous variable   p. 273
discrete variable   p. 273
dummy coding   p. 280
linearity   p. 272, 277

median split   p. 274
nonlinearity   p. 277
Pearson r p. 272
phi coefficient (ϕ)   p. 284
point-biserial correlation (r_{pb})
    p. 280

product-moment correlation
    p. 275
scatter diagram   p. 274
scatter plot   p. 274
Spearman rho (r_s)   p. 278
third-variable problem   p. 273

WEB ACTIVITY

Guess the correlation for different scatterplots at http://www.noppa5.pc.helsinki.fi/koe/corr/cor1.html.

Multiple-Choice Questions for Review

1. A correlation coefficient reflects the degree of ___ relationship between two variables. (a) linear; (b) curvilinear; (c) any kind of; (d) positive

2. Correlation coefficients range from ___ . (a) 0 to 1; (b) −1 to 0; (c) 1 to 10; (d) −1 to +1

3. A variable (such as gender) with two possible values is called a ___ variable. (a) continuous; (b) dichotomous; (c) quadratic; (d) linear

4. A graph is created in which the X variable is plotted along one axis and the Y variable is plotted along the other axis. Each data point is then represented as a dot in this graph. This kind of graph is called a (a) partial plot; (b) multivariate plot; (c) scatter plot; (d) median-split plot.

5. Another name for the Pearson r is the (a) Spearman rank correlation; (b) product-moment correlation; (c) phi coefficient; (d) point-biserial correlation.

6. Consider the following set of data:

	X	z_x	Y	z_y	$z_x z_y$
	8	1.34	16	1.34	1.80
	6	0.45	12	0.45	0.20
	4	−0.45	8	−0.45	0.20
	2	−1.34	4	−1.34	1.80
Sum (Σ)	20	0.00	40	0.00	4.00

What is the correlation between X and Y? (a) .1; (b) −.1; (c) 1; (d) −1.

7. A distance from a mean is called a(n) ___; the result of two numbers that are multiplied together is called a ___. (a) deviation, sum; (b) deviation, divisor; (c) error, multiplicative index; (d) moment, product

8. A correlation between two variables that are ranked is most specifically called a ___. (a) point-biserial correlation; (b) phi coefficient; (c) Pearson r; (d) Spearman rho

9. A student at Eastern Connecticut University hypothesizes that being female or male is related to one's position on abortion (measured as "prochoice" or "prolife"). To test this hypothesis, the correlation that the student is most likely to use is a (a) Spearman rho; (b) phi coefficient; (c) point-biserial correlation; (d) none of the above.

10. A student at the London School of Economics wants to determine whether political party affiliation (Labour or Conservative) is related to intelligence (measured by an IQ test that yields a series of continuous scores). To test this hypothesis, the student is most likely to use a (a) Spearman rho; (b) phi coefficient; (c) point-biserial correlation; (d) none of the above.

Discussion Questions for Review

1. A St. Bonaventure University researcher administers tests of IQ and reading ability to four high school students. In addition, their grade point averages are obtained from school records, with the following results:

	IQ	Reading	GPA
Student 1	105	13	2.6
Student 2	113	17	3.4
Student 3	87	10	2.0
Student 4	125	19	3.8

The correlation between IQ and reading ability is r = .98. Without doing any direct calculation, the researcher says he knows the correlation between reading and GPA. Do you know this correlation? What about the correlation between IQ and GPA—without any direct calculation?

2. Twenty subjects take part in a University of Minnesota study on the relationship between socioeconomic status (SES: coded as rich = 1, poor = 0) and shyness (coded as shy = 1, not shy = 0).

Given the results shown below, what is the correlation between these two variables? What specific type of Pearson correlation is this?

	SES	Shyness		SES	Shyness
Subject 1	0	1	Subject 11	0	0
Subject 2	0	1	Subject 12	1	1
Subject 3	0	0	Subject 13	0	0
Subject 4	0	1	Subject 14	1	0
Subject 5	1	1	Subject 15	0	1
Subject 6	0	0	Subject 16	1	0
Subject 7	1	1	Subject 17	1	0
Subject 8	1	0	Subject 18	1	1
Subject 9	0	1	Subject 19	0	1
Subject 10	1	0	Subject 20	1	0

3. A student at the University of Waterloo had two judges rate infants' fussiness, with the following results:

	Rater 1	Rater 2
Infant 1	60	30
Infant 2	40	50
Infant 3	30	60
Infant 4	50	40

The interjudge agreement, in terms of r, was not what the student had hoped for: $r = -1.0$. So he got himself two more raters, whose ratings were as follows:

	Rater 3	Rater 4
Infant 1	60	130
Infant 2	40	150
Infant 3	30	160
Infant 4	50	140

What is the agreement, in terms of r, between Raters 3 and 4?

4. A Georgia State University student has a job managing a 200-seat summer-stock theater that is filled to capacity on Saturday nights. To study the effect of staff courtesy on audience enjoyment, she asks the ticket taker to smile at randomly selected patrons. After the show, each member of the audience rates his or her enjoyment of the performance on a 7-point scale. Can you identify the independent and dependent variables and then figure out a way to calculate the correlation between them?

5. A student at California State University at Chico administered two tests to five subjects with the following results:

	Test A	Test B
Subject 1	1	4
Subject 2	2	3
Subject 3	3	2
Subject 4	4	1
Subject 5	5	100

Show a scatter plot of the relationship between the scores on Test A and Test B. Is there anything troubling about this plot? Can you adjust this problem by employing a different version of a Pearson *r*? Show a scatter plot of the revised or transformed scores on Tests A and B. What is the correlation between the tests if you use (a) the original scores and (b) the revised or transformed scores?

6. Two students from Foothill College compared their obtained scatter plots. Which plot is associated with the higher correlation? How can you tell just from inspecting the scatter plots? What are the actual *rs* associated with each plot?

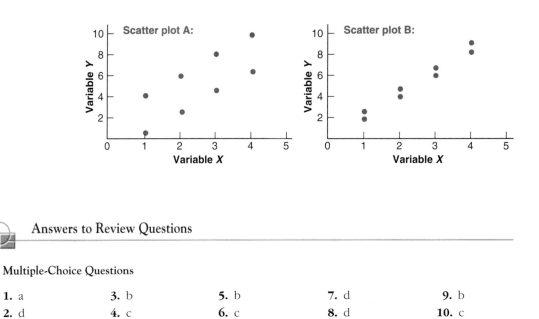

Answers to Review Questions

Multiple-Choice Questions

1. a	**3.** b	**5.** b	**7.** d	**9.** b
2. d	**4.** c	**6.** c	**8.** d	**10.** c

Discussion Questions

1. The correlation between reading ability and GPA is 1.00 because the *z* scores for reading and for GPA are identical. Careful inspection of the original reading and GPA scores shows that the GPA scores are always one fifth the size of the reading scores. If a variable (*X*) is multiplied by any constant (*c*), it yields a new variable (*cX*) that is correlated 1.00 with the original variable (*X*). The reason is that the old scores are multiplied by *c*, the old mean is multiplied by *c*, and the old σ is multiplied by *c*. Thus,

$$\text{old } z = \frac{X - M}{\sigma},$$

and in turn,

$$\text{new } z = \frac{cX - cM}{c\sigma} = \frac{X - M}{\sigma}.$$

As reading ability and GPA have the same z scores, GPA z scores can be substituted for reading z scores, and GPA will be correlated .98 with IQ just as reading is correlated .98 with IQ. You can check this result out by computing z scores for all three variables (IQ, reading, and GPA) and computing the correlations among these three variables.

2. The correlation is −.20, computed by ϕ, the two-dichotomous-variables version of the Pearson r. It can be computed by the z-score method or by the 2 × 2 contingency table method, that is,

$$\phi = \frac{\Sigma z_x z_y}{N}$$

or

$$\phi = \frac{BC - AD}{\sqrt{(A + B)(C + D)(A + C)(B + D)}}.$$

3. The correlation between Raters 3 and 4 is also −1.00. We can compute that directly, or we can notice that Rater 3 rates identically to Rater 1 and that Rater 4 rates identically to Rater 2, except for adding a constant of 100 points to each of Rater 2's ratings. Adding a constant (c) to each score also adds the constant to the mean, so adding a constant to the raw scores does not change the z scores because

$$\text{old } z = \frac{X - M}{\sigma},$$

and

$$\text{new } z = \frac{(X + c) - (M + c)}{\sigma} = \frac{X - M}{\sigma}.$$

4. The independent variable is smiling (scored 1) or not smiling (scored 0). The dependent variable is the rating of enjoyment. For the 200 patrons, we correlate the scores on the treatment variable (1 or 0) with the scores on the 7-point enjoyment scale.

5.

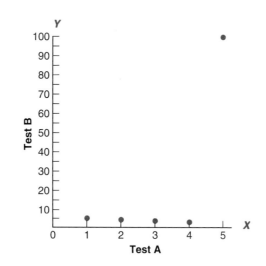

The score of 100 on Test B appears to be an outlier. We can solve the outlier problem by using ranks instead of scores:

Test A		Test B	
Score	Rank	Score	Rank
1	5	4	2
2	4	3	3
3	3	2	4
4	2	1	5
5	1	100	1

Our scatter plot based on ranks is

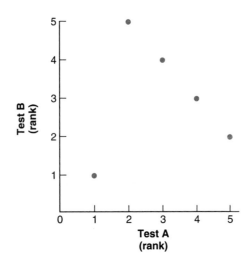

The correlation between Test A and Test B is .69 if we use the original scores; it is .00 if we employ the ranks. A discrepancy that large is unusual and needs to be evaluated further before we can confidently say we "know" the correlation between Test A and Test B.

6. Scatter Plot B is associated with the higher correlation because its points are more tightly clustered around the straight-line relationship between variables X and Y. The correlation between variables X and Y is .83 for Scatter Plot A and .98 for Scatter Plot B.

CHAPTER 12

Statistical Significance, Effect Size, and Power Analysis

Preview Questions

- What is null hypothesis significance testing (NHST)?
- What does statistical power have to do with NHST?
- What does the effect size r tell us?
- How can a large effect size *not* be statistically significant?
- How can a tiny effect still be meaningful and statistically significant?
- What is the purpose of the binomial effect-size display (BESD)?
- What is problematic about reporting effect sizes as squared rs?
- How are confidence intervals for effect size rs computed?

Use of Statistics and Probabilities

Besides describing data (Chapter 10) and measuring relationships (Chapter 11), researchers are often interested in making comparisons using statistical tests such as t (Chapter 13), F (Chapter 14), and chi-square (Chapter 15). In randomized clinical trials, for instance, we want to compare the different groups to see whether there is a difference in success rates in the treatment versus the control group. In Chapter 10, we described another kind of study, in which the subjects rated the palatability of a new food product and a comparison food product already on the market. The new food was rated more favorably on the average than the comparison product. Because these researchers wanted to know whether the difference between the two means might be due to chance, they performed a simple test of statistical significance. Finding the **probability (p value)** associated with the observed difference to be quite small (less than .05), they concluded that the difference between means was "real" and not merely a result of chance (Street & Carroll, 1989). We

293

will examine the reasoning behind this procedure, called **null hypothesis signifi-cance testing (NHST)**.

In recent years, there has been a growing realization that NHST is sometimes misunderstood or misused. For example, p values have sometimes been misconstrued as being indicative of the size, or even the importance, of the effect in question. However, finding that an obtained effect is statistically significant at some specified p level does not automatically reveal that the effect was sizable or important. Nor does the failure to obtain statistical significance at the desired p level tell us that there was no obtained effect, or that the obtained effect was trivial or unimportant. The p value of a significance test (e.g., t, F, or chi-square) is influenced not only by the size of the effect, but by the total number of units or observations (N). As either the size of the effect or the total N increases, the larger is the value of the significance test and the smaller is the p value. Not only does finding a significant p not tell us whether the effect size, the N, or both were responsible in some way, but even if the effect size were responsible, there would still be a lingering question concerning what aspect of this measure was the contributing factor (i.e., was it because the "signal" was large or the "noise" was minimal). We will explain what these concepts mean in the following chapter, where we describe the t test as a signal-to-noise ratio.

However, as researchers usually covet small p values, given an estimated effect size, one way to maximize the "power" of a significance test to detect an expected effect is to figure out in advance how many units (e.g., subjects) will be needed to achieve the desired p level, known as a **power analysis**. A similar analysis is often done after the study is completed, in order to estimate its **effective power** (i.e., its actual power). Later in this chapter, we will illustrate this procedure. The essential point is that it is important to focus your attention not just on p values but on other vital aspects of the results as well, such as the strength of the relationship between X and Y. This relationship is one way of operationally defining the **effect size**. There are other operational definitions of effect size (e.g., R. Rosenthal, 1994a; Rosnow & Rosenthal, 2003; Tatsuoka, 1993), two of which are briefly described in the next chapter (Cohen's d and Hedges's g). However, in this book, we emphasize the use of an indicator symbolized here as $r_{effect\ size}$, which stands for the **effect size correlation**. One reason we prefer r is that it is easy to calculate from t, F, and chi-square statistics that meet certain assumptions (as explained in the following three chapters). Another reason is that the effect size r can be used in situations in which other popular effect-size indices may not make sense, for example, in situations where there are more than two groups and we have predicted a particular pattern of results involving all those groups (Rosenthal, Rosnow, & Rubin, 2000; Rosnow & Rosenthal, 1996a, 2002, 2003). Another reason we prefer the effect size r is that it lends itself to interpretation by a procedure described later in this chapter as the *binomial effect-size display* (or BESD).

The Null Hypothesis in Significance Testing

To help you understand intuitively what NHST and several related concepts mean, we will begin by borrowing an analogy suggested by Wainer (1972). Imagine you are walking along the Atlantic City boardwalk or the Las Vegas strip when a shady character approaches you and whispers he has a quarter that he is willing to sell you for *only* five dollars. What makes the coin worth so much more than its face value? The answer, he tells you, is that this is a quarter with a special property. When properly used, this quarter can win you fame and fortune because it does not always come up heads and tails with equal regularity. Instead, one outcome is more likely than the other. A smart person can, when flipping the coin, bet on the outcome and win a fortune, he says. "It might sound like a cock-and-bull story," he adds, "but flip the coin and see for yourself."

If the coin is not what the street huckster says it is, getting a head or a tail is the result purely of chance. That is, if the coin is simply an ordinary one, then the probability of heads or tails is always one chance in two (see also Box 12.1). Thinking empirically, you accept his challenge and decide to test whether the probability of heads does or does not equal the probability of tails. You flip the coin once and heads appears. You flip the coin again, and again it comes up heads. Suppose you flip the coin nine times and each time it comes up heads. Would you believe him now? If your answer is yes, would you believe him if, in nine tosses, the coin had come up heads eight times and tails once? This is the essential question in NHST. You can be as stringent as you like in setting a rejection criterion, but you *may* eventually pay for this decision by rejecting what you perhaps should not.

The concepts and reasoning involved in NHST evolved out of the ideas and arguments of different statisticians (for an excellent historical overview, see Gigerenzer, et al., 1989). Let us state these ideas more precisely. When you decide to test

---

 BOX 12.1 Probability Revisited

In Chapter 9, we also referred to the concept of probability (see again Box 9.1 on page 222). One important characteristic of probabilities is that if all outcomes are *independent* (i.e., one outcome is not influenced by any other), the sum of all the probabilities associated with a particular event is equal to 1. For example, when you throw a die, there are six possibilities, and (unless the die is loaded) the probability of any particular outcome is therefore 1/6, or .167. Thus, summing all the independent probabilities gives us .167 $\times$ 6 = 1.00. Or instead of throwing a die, suppose you had two fair coins and flipped both at the same time. There are four possible combinations of heads (H) and tails (T): HH, HT, TH, TT. In determining probabilities, the general rule is to count the total number of possible outcomes and then to count the number of outcomes that yield the event you are interested in. The probability of that event is the ratio of the number you are looking for (the favorable event) to the total number of outcomes. For example, the probability of two heads (out of the four possible events) can occur in only one way (HH) and is therefore 1 divided by 4, or .25. The probability of one head (out of these four possible events) can occur in two ways (HT or TH) and is therefore 2 divided by 4, or .5.

whether the probability of heads "does or does not" equal the probability of tails, two hypotheses are implied. One is that the quarter is unbiased (i.e., the probability of heads *does* equal the probability of tails), and the second is that the coin is biased (i.e., the probability of heads *does not* equal the probability of tails). Think of the "experiment" of tossing a coin as a way of trying to determine which of these hypotheses you cannot logically reject. In statistical terms, the name for the first hypothesis is the **null hypothesis** (symbolized as H_0), and the name for the second hypothesis is the **alternative hypothesis** (symbolized as H_1). That is,

> H_0 *(null hypothesis)*: The probability of heads equals the probability of tails in the long run (i.e., the coin is not biased).
>
> H_1 *(alternative hypothesis)*: The probability of heads is not equal to the probability of tails in the long run (i.e., the coin is biased).

Notice that the two hypotheses are *mutually exclusive*; that is, when one hypothesis is true, the other must be false. Experimenters who do NHST are usually interested in testing the specific H_0 (i.e., no difference) against a general H_1 (i.e., some difference). For example, in a between-subjects design with an experimental and a control group, the null hypothesis generally implies no difference in "success rates" between the experimental group and the control group (e.g., no difference in survival rates, performance rates, or however else the outcome variable is defined). The idea behind NHST is to try to reject H_0 and yet be reasonably sure that you will not be wrong in doing so. Hence, there are two kinds of decision risks of general concern in NHST, called *Type I* and *Type II errors*.

Type I and Type II Errors

A **Type I error** implies that one has mistakenly rejected the null hypothesis (H_0) when it is, in fact, true and should not have been rejected. A **Type II error** implies that one has mistakenly failed to reject the null hypothesis when it is, in fact, false and should have been rejected. The risk (or probability) of making a Type I error is called by three different names: **alpha (α),** the **significance level**, and the *p* **value**. The risk (or probability) of making a Type II error is known by one name: **beta (β).** To make the most informed decision, scientists who do NHST would, of course, like to know what each risk is in a given case, so that they can balance these risks in some way.

Let us return with this newfound knowledge to the analogy of the street huckster with the coin for sale. Suppose you decide that you do not want to be wrong more than 1 time out of 20—called the *5% significance level* (see also Box 12.2). You flip the coin 9 times and get 8 heads and 1 tail. To make an informed decision, you need to know about the chances of obtaining this result or a result even more extreme. That is, you need to know the probability of obtaining this result (or a more extreme result) if the null hypothesis is true. Therefore, you think, "If this probability is less than 1/20 (i.e., $p < .05$, where < is read as "less than"), I will reject the null hypothesis and buy the coin; if not (i.e., $p > .05$, where > is read as

---

BOX 12.2 The 5% Solution

The ultimate day-to-day decision about what is a reasonable risk is a personal one. But as you do your literature search, you will notice that many researchers use the .05 level of probability as a critical demarcation point for deciding whether to reject the null hypothesis. The conventional wisdom behind this procedure goes something like this: The logic begins, more or less, with the proposition that one does not want to accept an alternative hypothesis that stands a fairly good chance of being false (i.e., one ought to avoid Type I errors). The logic goes on to state that one either accepts an alternative hypothesis as probably true (not false) or rejects it, concluding that the null is too likely for one to regard *it* as rejectable. The .05 alpha is seen by many scientists as a good "fail-safe" standard because it is convenient (most statistical tables show 5% values) and stringent enough to protect us from too often concluding that the null hypothesis is false when it is actually true.

"greater than"), I will not buy the coin." Because it can be shown that the probability of 8 or 9 heads in 9 tosses is less than 1 out of 20 (*p* approximately .02, or one out of 50), you decide to reject the null hypothesis and buy the coin.

Thus, assuming you have no pangs of conscience about purchasing a crooked coin and using it to win bets, you are doing so for two reasons: (a) because the resultant probability leads you to reject the null hypothesis of a fair coin, with 50% heads, at your chosen significance level (or alpha) of 5%, and (b) because you think that the alternative hypothesis (i.e., the coin is biased) is tenable and that the data (i.e., 8 heads and 1 tail, or 89% heads instead of 50%) support this hypothesis.

Risks of Gullibility and Blindness

This analogy is a simplified one, not exactly a true representation of what goes on in NHST. One reason the coin example falls short is that it is not a relational event; that is, there was only one variable: the result of the coin toss. The scientist who does NHST, however, frequently wants to estimate the probability of claiming that two variables (*X* and *Y*) are related when, in fact, they are unrelated, or that the average "success rate" of one group (e.g., the experimental group) surpassed that of another group (the control group). Type I error can be understood as mistakenly claiming a relationship that does not exist, and it is the likelihood of this risk that initially most interests scientists who rely on NHST. The question that they want answered is "What is the probability of a Type I error?"

Although most scientists who do NHST are not indifferent to the probability of making a Type II error (i.e., failing to claim a relation that truly does exist), many of them do tend to attach greater psychological importance to the risk of making a

Type I error than to the risk of making a Type II error. Of course, we also give greater weight to some decision risks than to others (see Box 12.3), but the reason the scientist attaches greater weight to the risk of making a Type I error is explained in Table 12.1. In the context of the coin example, the risk of making a "Type I error" would imply an *error of gullibility*, or being fleeced by the huckster's claim that an ordinary coin is biased. A "Type II error" implies *blindness*, or the failure to perceive that a not-so-ordinary coin is *really* biased as claimed. Although this analogy is a long stretch, the fact is that scientists are taught to believe that it is far worse to risk being "gullible" than it is to risk being "blind" to a real relationship. Some philosophers characterize this choice as the "healthy skepticism" of the scientific method (Axinn, 1966; Kaplan, 1964).

To show how Type I and Type II error risks would be translated into the tactical language of NHST, we turn to Table 12.2. For researchers, the null hypothesis is usually the assumption that no relationship between two variables is present in the population from which a sample was drawn, or that there is no difference in "success rates" in the different groups or conditions. The researcher considers the possibility of making a Type I error whenever a true null hypothesis is tested. As defined by the upper-left cell in this table (which corresponds to the "gullibility" cell of Table 12.1), a Type I error results when the researcher mistakenly rejects the null hypothesis by incorrectly claiming a relationship that does not exist. As defined by the lower-right cell of Table 12.2 (which corresponds to the "blindness" cell of Table 12.1), a Type II error results when the researcher mistakenly accepts the null hypothesis by failing to claim a relationship that does exist.

Finding and Reporting the Statistical Significance of *r*

Especially when the *p* value is low enough to justify rejecting the null hypothesis, you increase your information about the results by also knowing the effect size. Thus, you need to know not only how to determine the *p* value, but also how to estimate the effect size. We will have much more to say about estimating effect sizes in the remaining chapters, but let us see how you would determine the statistical significance of the effect size *r* and then report what you found. Table 12.3, which contains a portion of a larger table in Appendix B (see Table B.5 on p. 418), shows the *p* levels associated with different values of *r*. The first column lists $N - 2$

Table 12.1	Illustration of Definitions of Type I and Type II Errors	
	True state	
Your decision	The coin is unbiased	The coin is biased
The coin is biased (i.e., it won't come up heads and tails equally)	Type I error (gullibility risk)	No error of inference
The coin is unbiased (i.e., it is an ordinary coin)	No error of inference	Type II error (blindness risk)

BOX 12.3 Innocent or Guilty?

Imagine that a man is being tried for a brutal murder, and suppose that, if convicted, he is likely to be executed. As a member of the jury, you have to vote on whether he is innocent or guilty of the charges against him. If you vote "guilty" and in fact he is not guilty, you may be sending an innocent man to be executed. If you vote "innocent" and in fact he is not innocent, you could be turning a brutal murderer loose in the community. In the United States, it is generally accepted that convicting an innocent person is a more serious risk than permitting a guilty person to go free. The lesson? Just as most scientists who do NHST do not weight Type I and Type II errors equally, in everyday life we also give greater weight to some decision risks than to others.

(where N is the total number of units or observations, for example, the number of subjects), and the other columns indicate the p levels (i.e., Type I error risks). Notice that both one-tailed and two-tailed p levels are given and that the two-tailed ps are always twice the size of the one-tailed. The term **two-tailed p value** implies that the alternative hypothesis (H_1) did *not* specifically predict in which side (or tail) of the probability distribution the significance would be detected. The term **one-tailed p values** implies that the alternative hypothesis requires the significance to be in one tail rather than in the other tail.

As an illustration of how to read Table 12.3 (and Table B.5), suppose you conduct an exploratory study to examine the relationship between people's level of self-esteem (as measured by a standardized personality inventory) and the extent to which they are reported as engaging in gossip (measured by peer ratings). However, you are unsure of the direction this relation will take because (from your literature review) you think that a positive *or* a negative correlation is possible (Foster, 2004; Jaeger, Skleder, & Rosnow, 1998). The reason you are unsure is that some researchers portray the typical gossip as a social isolate, the least popular member of a group, characterized by feelings of little self-worth, social anxiety, and a need for esteem from others, who gossips in order to become the center of attention and to obtain status or esteem from others. By contrast, other researchers characterize the typical gossip as sensitive, curious, social, and involved, a person who gossips out of a need to control or manipulate those perceived to be subordi-

Table 12.2	Implications of the Decision to Reject or Not to Reject the Null Hypothesis (H_0)	
	True state	
Scientist's decision	H_0 is true	H_0 is false
To reject H_0	Type I error	No error of inference
Not to reject H_0	No error of inference	Type II error

Table 12.3	Significance levels of r				
	Probability level (p)				
	.10	.05	.02	.01	two-tailed
$N - 2$	.05	.025	.01	.005	one-tailed
1	.988	.997	.9995	.9999	
2	.900	.950	.980	.990	
3	.805	.878	.934	.959	
4	.729	.811	.882	.917	
5	.669	.754	.833	.874	
10	.497	.576	.658	.708	
20	.360	.423	.492	.537	
30	.296	.349	.409	.449	
40	.257	.304	.358	.393	
50	.231	.273	.322	.354	
100	.164	.195	.230	.254	
200	.116	.138	.164	.181	
300	.095	.113	.134	.148	
500	.074	.088	.104	.115	
1,000	.052	.062	.073	.081	

Note: For a more complete table, see Appendix B, Table B.5. However, notice in Table B.5 that all p values are shown as two-tailed.

nates. As you are unable to predict whether the correlation will be positive or negative, you decide to report a two-tailed (rather than a one-tailed) p value.

Continuing with this example, suppose that, in a total N of 52 subjects, you find that the correlation between self-esteem and the tendency to gossip is $r = .33$. In your literature search, you noticed that effect size correlations of this magnitude were often referred to as "moderate" or "medium-sized" in psychology. That usage is based on certain operational definitions proposed by J. Cohen (1988) for use with the power analysis tables that he developed, where the operational definitions of "small," "medium," and "large" effect sizes for r were approximately .1, .3, and .5, respectively. However, as we will show in a moment, do not assume that a "small" effect is one that is trivial or inconsequential, as the practical importance of an effect depends on the context and the nature of the dependent variable. That the effect size r you obtained was a positive value is consistent with the idea that high gossipers are also higher in self-esteem (whereas a negative r would have implied that the high gossipers were lower in self-esteem). To serve as a helpful (but not critical) alpha, let us assume you chose the conventional 5% significance level. Looking at the intersection of $N - 2 = 50$ and the column labeled .05 two-tailed in Table 12.3, you can see that r must be at least .273 to be beyond the level of risk you chose in order to reject the null hypothesis. As this table shows, the obtained p is somewhere between .02 and .01 two-tailed. That is, $r = .33$ is larger than the listed value for $p = .02$ two-tailed ($r = .322$) and smaller than the listed value for $p = .01$ two-tailed ($r = .354$).

In reporting p values, you have several options. One alternative, which is often used, is to state only that "$p < .05$ two-tailed" (that is, the two-tailed probability of mistakenly rejecting the null hypothesis is less than 1 chance in 20). The problem with this option, however, is that it is imprecise. Were the researcher to report "$p > .05$," we would have no idea whether the p was .06 (which is not very different from .05) or .50 (which is no better than merely flipping a coin). A second alternative is to state that ".01 < two-tailed $p < .02$" (that is, the two-tailed probability of mistakenly rejecting the null hypothesis is "more than 1 chance in 100" but "less than 1 chance in 50"), but it seems wordy and awkward. A third alternative is to state the exact probability, as recommended in the *Publication Manual of the American Psychological Association* (2001, p. 25). There is an exception when the reporting of exact p values may be unwieldy, as in large tables of correlations, in which case the use of a single asterisk(*) to indicate $p < .05$ or a double asterisk to indicate $p < .01$ is recommended by the APA manual (p. 25).

Notice in Table 12.3 that a correlation can be significant at $p = .05$, no matter whether it is a very large correlation or a very small correlation. What counts most in this table is whether the "$N - 2$" is sufficiently large to allow us to detect the particular magnitude of r at the desired level of significance. For example, we see that even an r as small as .062 would be significant at $p = .05$ two-tailed with $N = 1,002$, whereas an r nine times larger would not be significant at the same level with $N = 12$. Thus, only reporting that an effect size r was "significant" does not give us a clue to whether it was as small as .062 (in this table) or as large as 1.0. Furthermore, does it really make any sense to ignore or dismiss a sizable r that was not "statistically significant" ($p > .05$) because the total N was too small? Would it not be more prudent to try to replicate the study with a larger N before concluding that "nothing happened"?

Binomial Effect-Size Display (BESD)

In the following chapters, we will present easy-to-use formulas for obtaining $r_{\text{effect size}}$ from t, F, or chi-square. For now, let us examine how to transform the $r_{\text{effect size}}$ into a convenient display called the **BESD**, shorthand for **binomial effect-size display** (Rosenthal & Rubin, 1982b). The BESD is called a *display* because it converts the "success rates" in experimental and control groups into a 2 × 2 table; it is called a *binomial* (which means "two-term") display because two variables are displayed as dichotomous. To show how the BESD works, we refer to the results in a publicized clinical trial in which the independent variable was whether the subjects received an aspirin every other day, and the dependent variable was whether they experienced a heart attack.

This study reported that heart attack risk is cut in half by aspirin (Steering Committee of the Physicians' Health Study Research Group, 1988). Presumably, the way that aspirin works to reduce mortality from heart attack, or myocardial infarction (MI), is by promoting circulation even when fatty deposits have collected along the walls of the coronary arteries. That is, aspirin makes the transport of blood easier as the arteries get narrower. The finding that heart attack risk is "cut in half" was based on a 5-year investigation of 22,071 male physicians, approximately half of whom (11,037) were given an ordinary aspirin tablet (325 mg) every other day; the remainder (11,034) were given a placebo. Part of the results are shown in Table 12.4.

The top part of this table (labeled A) shows the number of participants in each condition who did or did not have a heart attack. A chi-square (χ^2) test of the statistical significance of these frequencies (using a procedure described in Chapter 15) yielded a p value considerably smaller than the .05 significance level. It was "p is approximately .0000006," which tells us conclusively that the result of NHST was very unlikely to be a fluke or a lucky coincidence. But when we calculate the effect size as a standard phi (ϕ) coefficient (using the procedure described in Chapter 11 for calculating phi on 2 × 2 tables of independent frequencies, or another procedure described in Chapter 15), the result is $r_{effect\ size} = .034$. Before we dismiss this very small-sized r as inconsequential, let us also see what it means in terms of practical importance.

We said that the scientists reported that heart attack risk is cut in half, and let us see how they arrived at this conclusion. In the placebo condition, 189 out of 11,034 subjects had a heart attack, which is 1.7% (i.e., 189/11,034 multiplied by 100). In the aspirin condition, 104 out of 11,037 subjects had a heart attack, which is 0.9% (i.e., 104/11,037 multiplied by 100). Dividing 0.9 by 1.7 tells us that the risk of having a heart attack was cut approximately in half. However, despite this good news, we also see that the percentages are quite small, indicating that relatively few people were actually in jeopardy of having a heart attack (1.3% of the 22,071

Table 12.4   Aspirin's Effect on Heart Attack

A. Myocardial infarction (MI) in aspirin and placebo conditions

Condition	No heart attack	Heart attack	Total
Aspirin	10,933	104	11,037
Placebo	10,845	189	11,034
Total	21,778	293	22,071

B. Binomial effect-size display of $r_{effect\ size} = .034$

Condition	MI absent	MI present	Total
Aspirin	51.7[a]	48.3[b]	100
Placebo	48.3[b]	51.7[a]	100
Total	100	100	200

[a]Computed from 100 (.500 + r/2).
[b]Computed from 100 (.500 − r/2).

Source: Based on results reported in "Preliminary Report: Findings From the Aspirin Component of the Ongoing Physicians' Health Study," by Steering Committee of the Physicians' Health Study Research Group, 1988, *New England Journal of Medicine, 318,* pp. 262–264.

subjects). The question is how to represent the effect size r for the population as a whole and yet not exaggerate its implications.

No measure can capture the full picture, and therefore, it is usually a good idea to explain the implications of medical (and other) results in more than one way. The BESD can be used for this purpose, as it is a standardized display that gives us an idea of the implications of an effect size indexed by a correlation coefficient. Part B of Table 12.4 shows what the effect size r would look like as a BESD. That is, it shows the effect size r to be a simple difference in outcome rates between the experimental (the aspirin) and control (the placebo) groups in a 2 × 2 table with rows and columns always totaling 100 (Rosenthal & Rubin, 1982b). Given a higher success rate in the experimental group than in the control group, the BESD is obtained from any effect size r simply by computation of the treatment success rate as 100(.50 + r/2) and the control condition success rate as 100(.50 − r/2). Since in this study $r/2$ is .034/2 = .017, the r of .034 yields an aspirin success rate (i.e., MI absent) of 100(.50 + .017) = 51.7 and a placebo success rate of 100(.50 − .017) = 48.3. The difference between these rates (51.7 − 48.3 = 3.4) divided by 100 is .034, which is the effect size indexed by r.

Having the rows and columns always sum to 100 makes the values in the A, B, C, D cells easier to interpret and compare as proportions or percentages. This BESD tells us that approximately 3.4% of persons (in a theoretical population that was split into equal halves) who would probably have experienced a myocardial infarction (i.e., given these particular conditions) might not experience MI if they followed the regimen of the aspirin treatment. The BESD preserves the effect size r, but it lets us see that it is equivalent to reducing the heart attack rate from 51.7% to 48.3% in a population in which (theoretically) half the people are given aspirin and half are not, and half have heart attacks and half do not. Remember, however, that the term *success rates* is simply a general expression; in this case, the operational definition of it was "MI absent versus MI present" (whereas the definition in other studies might be success versus failure, improved versus not improved, and so forth).

Many people (including many experienced researchers) might be surprised to learn that an effective biomedical intervention could be associated with an effect size r as small as .034, but certainly the practical importance of this finding is indisputable. In fact, effect size rs smaller than .10 are not at all unusual in biomedical research. In a famous study, called "the biggest public health experiment ever" (Meier, 1988), children who were given the Salk poliomyelitis vaccine were compared with a control group of children who received a simple salt solution (Francis, et al., 1955). There were serious problems with the design and implementation of the experiment, but it was nevertheless concluded that there was "convincing evidence for the effectiveness of the vaccine" (Brownlee, 1955, p. 1010). Interestingly, the effect size r of this "convincing evidence" was .011, which is even smaller than the effect size r in the aspirin study (for further discussion and other examples, see Rosnow & Rosenthal, 2003). One result of our consideration of these small effect sizes is to make us more sanguine about the size of effects in the behavioral and social sciences (Rosenthal, 1995a). (See also Box 12.4.)

BOX 12.4 Effect Size Estimates

Rather than rely on just one study, it is far more informative to summarize the numerical results of a number of studies. In Appendix C, we introduce you to the procedures of meta-analysis, which were created for this purpose. In behavioral medicine, for example, from a meta-analysis of 76 studies, Devine and Reifschneider (1995) estimated an average $r_{effect\ size}$ of .28 for the effect of psychoeducational care on adult hypertensives' blood pressure. In the area of social psychology, from a meta-analysis of 35 studies, Eagly, Ashmore, Makhijani, and Longo (1991) estimated an average r of .32 for the effect of physical attractiveness on attributions of social competence. Effect sizes run the gamut from small to large, but they tend to be especially small (i.e., rs of .10 or smaller) in biomedical drug trials (Rosnow & Rosenthal, 2003).

The Problem in Reporting r^2 as the Effect Size

In your literature search, you may have noticed that some researchers, when reporting the effect size, refer to a squared correlation coefficient. This value (r^2) is also called the **coefficient of determination**, or **proportion of variation explained**. However, the terms *determination* and *explained* are used in a technical sense and, despite the names, do not mean that r^2 explains the causal relation between X and Y. They mean only that r^2 represents the fraction or proportion of the variability shared by X and Y. For example, a positive or negative Pearson r of 1.0—in which case r^2 also equals 1.0—implies that the variation in the Y scores is perfectly associated with the variation in the X scores (and vice versa).

Although r^2 is useful in a number of statistical applications, we do not recommend it as a measure of effect size for two reasons. First, squared correlational indices of effect size lose their directionality (i.e., whether the treatment is helping or hurting, or whether the correlation is positive or negative), and thus are of little use in scientific work for which information on directionality is essential. Second, the implications of r^2 are likely to be misconstrued as being much less important than is often true. For example, if we go back to the aspirin study, squaring $r_{effect\ size} = .034$ suggests there was *no* effect (i.e., $r^2 = .00$)! But when we think of $r_{effect\ size} = .034$ as reflecting a 3.4% decrease in heart attacks (which was the interpretation given in Table 12.4), the effect size takes on practical importance—especially if you can count yourself or a loved one among that percentage (Rosenthal, 1990a, 1990b). In the polio vaccine study, squaring the effect would also make it virtually disappear (i.e., squaring $r = .011$ gives us $r^2 = .000$ or, to four decimal places, .0001).

Therefore, although squaring the effect size r is recommended in a number of textbooks in psychology, Table 12.5 shows the extent to which squaring the

Table 12.5	Increases in Success Rates Corresponding to Values of r^2 and $r_{effect\ size}$			
Coefficient of determination (r^2)	Effect size ($r_{effect\ size}$)	Success rate increased From (%)	To (%)	Differences in success rates
.01	.10	45	55	10% (or .10)
.04	.20	40	60	20% (or .20)
.09	.30	35	65	30% (or .30)
.16	.40	30	70	40% (or .40)
.25	.50	25	75	50% (or .50)
.36	.60	20	80	60% (or .60)
.49	.70	15	85	70% (or .70)
.64	.80	10	90	80% (or .80)
.81	.90	5	95	90% (or .90)
1.00	1.00	0	100	100% (or 1.00)

$r_{effect\ size}$ may be like a magician making a rabbit disappear. Column 1 shows the result of squaring the rs in column 2, and columns 3 and 4 show the percentage increases in success rates (i.e., as revealed by a BESD corresponding to the values in column 2). The final column shows the difference between the values in columns 3 and 4 as a percentage and (in parenthesis) a proportion. The proportions change the percentages back into the values in column 2, reminding us that the difference in "success rates" (e.g., the survival rate, cure rate, improvement rate, or selection rate) is equal to $r_{effect\ size}$.

Statistical Power Analysis

When the null hypothesis has not been rejected in a given study, the reason may be that there was not enough statistical power to reject it, as **statistical power** has to do with the sensitivity of the statistical test (such as t, F, or chi-square) in providing an adequate opportunity to reject the null hypothesis when it warrants rejection (e.g., J. Cohen, 1988; Keppel, 1991; Kirk, 1995; Kraemer & Thiemann, 1987). The purpose of a power analysis is to learn whether there was a reasonable chance of rejecting the null hypothesis, and whether the power should be increased in any future study to increase the sensitivity of the statistical test.

To illustrate, suppose that young researcher Smith conducts an experiment (with $N = 80$) on productivity and finds that Managerial Style A is better than B (the old standard), with p less than .05 and $r_{effect\ size} = .22$. That is, Smith's results are statistically significant at the conventional 5% alpha. Old researcher Jones, the creator of Style B, is skeptical and asks his graduate students to try to replicate Smith's results using 20 available subjects. The graduate students, to Jones's perverse delight, report a failure to replicate Smith's results. Their obtained two-tailed p value, they gleefully tell Jones, is *greater* than .30. Before savoring his victory, Jones tells his graduate students to calculate the effect size of their result. They return with glum faces to report that their effect size is *identical* ($r_{effect\ size}$ = .22) to Smith's.

In other words, Jones's students have found exactly what Smith found, even though the *p* values of the two studies are not very close. The problem, as we now show, is that the students were working with a level of statistical power that was too low to obtain the *p* value reported by Smith. Because of the smaller sample size of 20, it turns out that their power to reject the null hypothesis at .05 two-tailed was about .15, whereas Smith's power of about .50 (using an *N* of 80) was more than three times as great.

You will recall that beta (β) is the probability of a Type II error (i.e., the probability of failing to claim a relationship that does exist). **Power** is simply $1 - β$, or the probability of not making a Type II error. In the language of NHST, *power* refers to the probability of rejecting the null hypothesis when it is false and needs rejecting. For any given statistical test of a null hypothesis (e.g., *t*, *F*, or χ^2), the power of the statistical test is determined by three components: (a) the level of risk of drawing a spuriously positive conclusion (i.e., the *p* level); (b) the size of the study (i.e., the sample size); and (c) the effect size. These three components are so related that when any two of them are known, the third can be determined. Thus, if we know the values for (a) and (c), we should be able to estimate how large a total *N* we need to achieve our desired level of significance.

Table 12.6 provides a compact way of estimating the total number of subjects needed to detect different effect size *r*s at the .05 (two-tailed) significance level. Suppose you decide to work with power = .8 or better, because this happens to be a recommended level (J. Cohen, 1988), and say you anticipate finding a "small" effect ($r_{effect\ size}$ = .10) because of your review of the relevant literature. Given this magnitude of effect (.10) and power (.8), you would need about 800 subjects to reject the null hypothesis at .05 two-tailed. This is a lot of subjects! Had you chosen to work in an area with typically larger effects, your recruitment of subjects would

Table 12.6	Rounded Sample Sizes (Total *N*) Required to Detect Effects at .05 Two-Tailed						
	Effect size correlation ($r_{effect\ size}$)						
Power	.10	.20	.30	.40	.50	.60	.70
.15	85	25	10	10	10	10	10
.20	125	35	15	10	10	10	10
.30	200	55	25	15	10	10	10
.40	300	75	35	20	15	10	10
.50	400	100	40	25	15	10	10
.60	500	125	55	30	20	15	10
.70	600	155	65	40	25	15	10
.80	800	195	85	45	30	20	15
.90	1000	260	115	60	40	25	15

Source: From *Statistical Power Analysis for the Behavioral Sciences* (2nd ed., pp. 92–93), by J. Cohen, 1988 Hillsdale, NJ: Lawrence Erlbaum Associates, Inc. Reprinted by permission of the late Jacob Cohen and Lawrence Erlbaum Associates, Inc.

BOX 12.5 Good News, Bad News, Good News!

As mentioned in Box 12.4, the good news is that most reported experimental effects in behavioral science are quite a bit larger than $r_{effect\ size}$ = .10. They frequently tend to be in the .30 to .50 range, which means that, with power of .80, we would need a total N of 85 ($r_{effect\ size}$ = .30) to about 30 ($r_{effect\ size}$ = .50) subjects. The bad news is that, as explained in Chapter 10, about a third of those who say they will participate as research subjects may be no-shows. Therefore, we may need to multiply our estimated N by 1.5 to compensate for the possibility that a third of the volunteers will not show up. However, the good news is that, in addition to increasing the total N, we may use other techniques to increase power. In the next chapter, you will find a discussion of some other ways to improve statistical power.

have been made much easier. With an effect size r = .30 and power = .8, you would need approximately 85 subjects. With $r_{effect\ size}$ = .50, you would need a total N of only about 30 subjects (see also Box 12.5).

Confidence Interval for an Effect Size

Just as we were interested in confidence intervals for proportions (Chapter 9) and means (Chapter 10), we are also interested in confidence intervals for effect size rs. Suppose you wanted to know the 95% confidence interval (CI) for an effect size r. You would proceed in four steps:

Step 1 would be to consult Table B.6 in Appendix B (p. 419), which is used to transform the $r_{effect\ size}$ to what is called a Fisher z_r (which is a log-based transformation of r). This transformation changes the finite scale of rs (which range from −1.0 to +1.0) into a normal distribution without limits. To distinguish the Fisher z_r from the standard score z noted in previous chapters, we use the subscript r to remind you that this particular z is related to r.

Step 2 would be to substitute the value of N in your study (i.e., the total sample size of your study) in the following expression:

$$\left(\frac{1}{\sqrt{N-3}}\right)1.96,$$

where 1.96 is the standard score z for p = .05 two-tailed, and the other value defines the *standard error* of Fisher z_r. You will find discussions of the standard error in statistics texts, but in general, it refers to the standard deviation of a given statistic. (In the next chapter, where we describe the equation for the t test as resembling a "signal-to-noise" ratio, you can think of the standard error as the more technical definition of noise in the denominator of the t formula.)

Step 3 would be to find the limits of the 95% CI by subtracting (to create the lower limit) the result in Step 2 from, and adding it (to create the upper limit) to, the Fisher z_r transformed effect size in Step 1.

Step 4 would be to consult Table B.7 in Appendix B (p. 420) to transform these lower and upper z_r values back to $r_{\text{effect size}}$ values to define the 95% CI around the effect.

To illustrate, suppose we find that $r_{\text{effect size}}$ = .33 based on a total sample size of N = 80, and we want to compute the 95% CI. The first step would be to look in Table B.6 at the intersection of the row labeled .3 and the column labeled .03, where we find that Fisher z_r = .343.

The second step would be to substitute N = 80 in the expression, that is,

$$\left(\frac{1}{\sqrt{N-3}}\right)1.96 = \left(\frac{1}{\sqrt{77}}\right)1.96 = 0.2234.$$

The third step would be to subtract the result in Step 2 from the result in Step 1 to find the lower limit of z_r (i.e., .343 − .2234 = .1196, rounded to .12), and to add the result in Step 2 to the result in Step 1 to find the upper limit of z_r (i.e., .343 + .2234 = .5664, rounded to .57).

The final step would be to transform both results of Step 3 into effect size rs, which we do by consulting Table B.7. For z_r = .12, we see at the intersection of the row labeled .1 and the column labeled .02 that .119, rounded to .12, is the lower limit of our $r_{\text{effect size}}$ of .33. For z_r = .57, we see at the intersection of the row labeled .5 and the column labeled .07 that .515, rounded to .52, is the upper limit of our $r_{\text{effect size}}$ of .33. We can now say, with 95% confidence, that the population value of $r_{\text{effect size}}$ is between .12 and .52.

To see how the confidence interval is affected by smaller and larger Ns, suppose that the N is 20 instead of 80. Substituting in the expression in Step 2 gives

$$\left(\frac{1}{\sqrt{17}}\right)1.96 = 0.4754,$$

which, when we carry out the remaining calculations, results in a 95% CI from −.13 to .67. A negative effect size r means that the pattern of the observed effect is opposite to that predicted, so in this case, the confidence interval is so wide that it includes unexpected as well as expected directional patterns.

What if we increase the sample to 320? Substituting in the expression in Step 2 gives us

$$\left(\frac{1}{\sqrt{317}}\right)1.96 = 0.1101,$$

BOX 12.6 90% and 99% Confidence Intervals

You need not restrict yourself to a 95% CI if you prefer working with some other interval. The table below shows values of alpha (i.e., p levels), confidence intervals, and the corresponding standard score z for p = .10, .05, and .01 two-tailed:

alpha (α)	.10	.05	.01
Confidence interval (CI)	90%	95%	99%
2-tailed z	1.64	1.96	2.58

For example, if you wanted a 90% CI, you would substitute 1.64 for 1.96 in the formula in Step 2, and if you wanted a 99% CI, you would instead substitute 2.58. Increasing the confidence interval from 95% to 99% will, in turn, widen the confidence interval, and vice versa. (If you ask yourself how wide an interval you would need to be 100% sure about some risky event, you will see intuitively why increasing the confidence level results in a wider confidence interval.)

---

which, when we follow through with the remaining steps, yields a 95% CI from .23 to .42. Thus, we see that working with a smaller N widens the confidence interval, and that working with a larger N shrinks the confidence interval. Because we would prefer a narrower to a wider confidence interval, the lesson is to work with the largest N possible (see also Box 12.6).

Summary of Ideas

1. Three procedures discussed in this chapter that use statistics and probabilities are (a) null hypothesis significance testing (NHST); (b) effect size estimation (and the corresponding BESD and confidence interval); and (c) power analysis.

2. The probability of a particular favorable outcome is the number of favorable events divided by the total number of possible events.

3. The null hypothesis (H_0) and the alternative hypothesis (H_1) are mutually exclusive: When one is true, the other must be false.

4. A Type I error is a mistake in rejecting H_0 when it is true, whereas a Type II error is a mistake in failing to reject H_0 when it is false.

5. The probability of a Type I error is called *alpha* (α), *the significance level*, and the *p value*; the probability of a Type II error is called *beta* (β).

6. The .05 significance level is commonly used by behavioral researchers as a basis for deciding whether or not to reject the null hypothesis.

7. Traditionally, scientists have believed that it is worse to make a Type I error (i.e., an error of gullibility) than to make a Type II error (i.e., an error of blindness to a relationship).

8. When doing NHST, scientists try to see whether they can reject the null hypothesis and yet be reasonably sure that they will not be wrong in doing so.

9. Failure to reject the null hypothesis does not automatically imply "no effect," and therefore, statistical significance should not be confused with the presence or absence of an effect, or with the practical importance of an obtained effect.

10. The binomial effect-size display (BESD) represents the difference in "success rates" (e.g., the survival rate, cure rate, improvement rate, or selection rate) between the experimental and the control condition based on the strength of the effect size correlation ($r_{\text{effect size}}$).

11. Reporting r^2 (the coefficient of determination) as an effect size index can be quite misleading because it conceals directionality and underestimates the importance of the observed effect.

12. Power, defined as $1 - \beta$, refers to the probability of not making a Type II error.

13. Given a particular estimated effect size, we can determine how large the total N must be to achieve any desired level of significance, assuming also a known probability of success (i.e., power).

14. To create a confidence interval around an $r_{\text{effect size}}$, the Fisher z_r transformation is used to locate the upper and lower limits of the r, and then these Fisher z_r limits are translated back into the upper and lower limits of the $r_{\text{effect size}}$.

15. The smaller the N or the higher the desired confidence (e.g., 99% instead of 95%), the wider is the confidence interval.

Key Terms

alpha (α)   p. 296
alternative hypothesis (H_1)
   p. 296
beta (β)   p. 296
binomial effect-size display
   (BESD)   p. 301
coefficient of determination (r^2)
   p. 304
effective power   p. 294

effect size   p. 294
effect size correlation ($r_{\text{effect size}}$)
   p. 294
null hypothesis (H_0)   p. 296
null hypothesis significance
   testing (NHST)   p. 294
one-tailed p value   p. 299
power ($1 - \beta$)   p. 306
power analysis   p. 294

probability   p. 293
proportion of variation
   explained   p. 304
p value   p. 296
significance level   p. 296
statistical power   p. 305
two-tailed p value   p. 299
Type I error   p. 296
Type II error   p. 296

WEB ACTIVITY

Examine how small effects can sometimes be important effects by visiting the Rice University Virtual Lab in Statistics at http://www.ruf.rice.edu/~lane/stat_sim/index.html and then clicking on the Effect Size radio button. Interested in what others, from Aristotle to Yule, have said about probability? Click on Quotes at http://www.mathcs.carleton.edu/probweb/probweb.html. For a really cool portal to all kinds of interesting on-line statistical calculators, click on Statistics at http://www-sci.lib.uci.edu/HSG/RefCalculators3.html (note that there is a hyphen, not a period, after www).

Multiple-Choice Questions for Review

1. "There will be no difference between the experimental group and the control group." This statement is an example of a(n) (a) alternative hypothesis; (b) experimental hypothesis; (c) directional hypothesis; (d) null hypothesis.

2. "The experimental group will score higher than the control group." This statement is an example of (a) H_0; (b) H_1; (c) H_2; (d) H_3.

3. Rejecting the null hypothesis when it is true is called a (a) Type 0 error; (b) Type I error; (c) Type II error; (d) Type III error.

4. Failing to reject H_0 when it is false is called a (a) Type 0 error; (b) Type I error; (c) Type II error; (d) Type III error.

5. A Type II error can be thought of as an error of (a) imprecision; (b) deafness; (c) gullibility; (d) blindness.

6. Scientists usually consider a _____ error more serious than a _____ error. (a) Type I, Type II; (b) null hypothesis, alternative hypothesis; (c) alternative hypothesis, null hypothesis; (d) Type II, Type I

7. A student at Lincoln University conducts a study with 52 subjects and finds the correlation between authoritarianism and prejudice to be $r = .28$. According to Table 12.3, what is the two-tailed significance level associated with this correlation? (a) .10; (b) .05; (c) .01; (d) .001

8. Squaring r yields a statistic known as the (a) coefficient of determination; (b) binomial effect-size display; (c) proportion of variability unexplained; (d) none of the above.

9. A student at Central Arkansas University wants to conduct a study with power of .60 and, from reading previous research, expects to get an effect size r of .20. According to Table 12.6, how many subjects should she obtain in order to reject the null hypothesis at the .05 level two-tailed? (a) 10; (b) 20; (c) 60; (d) 125

10. A student at the University of Alaska expects to find an effect size r of .30 but unfortunately can obtain only 25 subjects. According to Table 12.6, what will the power of his study be? (a) .20; (b) .25; (c) .30; (d) .40

Discussion Questions for Review

1. A Notre Dame University student manipulated the presence or absence of a confederate in a wheelchair on subjects' willingness to sign a petition urging more handicapped parking spaces for public and private buildings. The effect size of the result was $r_{effect\ size} = .40$. Can you create and interpret a BESD for this effect size?

2. A Gallaudet University student was asked by her professor to define the Type II error in the context of the aspirin study (Table 12.4) and to tell how it is related to the power of a test. Do you know the answer? Do you know what factors determine the power of a test of significance?

3. A panicking friend asks a University of Texas student for help with a project she is doing at Southern Methodist University on sex differences in scores on a new test of assertiveness. Her study will involve a randomly sampled group of males and a randomly sampled group of females. She tells the University of Texas student that effect sizes in this area of research have tended to be approximately $r_{effect\ size} = .20$. She wants to present her findings at the Southeastern Psychological Association meeting in New Orleans but worries that the study will not be accepted for presentation unless the group difference reaches a significance level (alpha) of $p = .05$ two-tailed. She also tells

her University of Texas friend that the power level she is seeking for her study is .7. Given all this information, how many male and how many female subjects should the friend advise her to run?

4. A St. Lawrence University student does a study and gets $p = .05$. Exactly what does this p value tell him? What doesn't it tell him that is also important to know?

5. The first three students to complete their course research projects at Minot State College displayed their BESDs to the other students, to inspire them. All three students had developed new methods of teaching vocabulary. What $r_{effect\ size}$ was associated with each of the following BESDs?

Student A:

Method	Above average	Below average
New	75	25
Old	25	75

Student B:

Method	Above average	Below average
New	55	45
Old	45	55

Student C:

Method	Above average	Below average
New	35	65
Old	65	35

6. The Gallaudet University student in Question 2 is also asked by her professor to create a 95% confidence interval for the effect size correlation of .034 in the aspirin study. Do you know how to do it?

Answers to Review Questions

Multiple-Choice Questions

1. d	3. b	5. d	7. b	9. d
2. b	4. c	6. a	8. a	10. c

Discussion Questions

1. The BESD is shown below, and the interpretation would be that the effect size amounts to a 40% difference between rates of petition signing in the wheelchair-present and in the wheelchair-absent condition. The percentages in the BESD are not the raw percentages (rates) in the actual data but are "standardized" so that the values in the margins are equalized (i.e., we assume that half the population was in each condition, and that half the population was in each outcome group).

Condition	Signing petition	Not signing petition	Total
Wheelchair present	70	30	100
Wheelchair absent	30	70	100
Total	100	100	200

2. A Type II error would have occurred if it had been concluded that there was a correlation of zero between taking aspirin and having a heart attack when that correlation was not really zero. The power of a test is the probability that results will be found significant at a given p value when the null hypothesis is false. Power is defined as $1 - $ beta (β), where $\beta = $ the probability of making a Type II error. The power of a test of significance depends on the alpha (α) we set, the actual size of the effect being investigated, and the size of the sample.

3. In Table 12.6, the intersection of the column headed .20 and the row labeled .70 shows the required total N to be 155. Therefore, she should run about half that number of females and half that number of males.

4. It tells him that only 5% of the time would he obtain a result that significant, or more significant, if the null hypothesis (H_0) were really true. It does not tell him about the size of the effect being studied.

5. Since r is simply the difference between the proportions successful in the treatment and the control conditions, the three rs are:

Student A's results   .75 − .25 = .50
Student B's results   .55 − .45 = .10
Student C's results   .35 − .65 = −.30.

Notice that the result for Student C reflects a negative r; the new method is *worse* than the old.

6. Step 1 is to use Table B.6 (on p. 419) to get the Fisher z_r that corresponds to $r_{effect\ size} = .034$, and we find $z_r = .034$ (i.e., not different from r in this particular case). Step 2 is to substitute the N of 22,071 in the expression

$$\left(\frac{1}{\sqrt{N-3}}\right)1.96,$$

which gives us .0132. Step 3 is to subtract this value from .034 to get the lower limit of z_r (.02 rounded), and to add the value to .034 to get the upper limit of z_r (.05). Step 4 is to use Table B.7 (on p. 420) to transform the lower and upper limits of z_r to $r_{effect\ size}$. We can say that, with 95% confidence, the effect size r of aspirin is between .02 and .05 in the population from which the 22,071 subjects were randomly sampled.

CHAPTER 13

The Comparison of Two Conditions

Preview Questions

- What do signal-to-noise ratios have to do with *t* tests?
- What do degrees of freedom (*df*) have to do with *p* values?
- How are *t* tests on independent and related samples computed?
- How is the effect size *r* estimated directly from *t?*
- What are Cohen's *d* and Hedges's *g?*
- Why is *t* said to be the product of the effect size and the study size?
- What are the implications of the relationship above for maximizing *t?*
- What are statistical assumptions of the *t* test?

Comparing Two Means

We have examined the logic of using statistics and probabilities to test hypotheses, and with this chapter we begin our discussion of the three most popular statistical tests: the *t* test (described in this chapter), the *F* test (Chapter 14), and the chi-square (χ^2) test (Chapter 15). The choice of a statistical test is determined by the nature of the research question and the design of the study. If we are interested in comparing the means of two groups (e.g., experimental and control groups), we will find the **t test** (also called **Student's *t***) a convenient and powerful method (see also Box 13.1). It allows us to test the likelihood that the population means represented by the two groups are equal (i.e., the null hypothesis), by setting up a **signal-to-noise ratio**. In this ratio, the "signal" is represented by the difference between the two means, and the "noise" is represented by the variability of the scores within the samples. The larger the signal is relative to the noise, the more likely the null hypothesis is to be rejected.

As you learned previously, it is important not to place the weight of your evaluation of the *practical importance* of an obtained effect on the *p* value, because *p*

BOX 13.1   Student's *t*

The *t* test is called Student's *t* in honor of William Sealy Gosset, its inventor. Gosset worked for Guinness, the famous Irish brewery, which for security reasons prohibited the publication of research done by its staff. Gosset was able to persuade the company to relax this rule for the statistical methods he had developed, and Guinness agreed only on condition that he use a pen name. The name he chose was Student.

---

is an indicator only of statistical significance. You also want to know the effect size and its confidence interval. Of course, although the effect size is mathematically determined by characteristics of the study design and the results, your interpretation of its real-life implications would depend on the context and the nature of the dependent variable (Rosnow & Georgoudi, 1986; Rosnow & Rosenthal, 2003). We will show how to estimate the effect size r ($r_{effect\ size}$) from our knowledge of the value of the *t* test and its associated degrees of freedom (defined in a moment). We will also define two other popular effect size measures (Cohen's *d* and Hedges's *g*) and review how, given what you learned in the previous chapter, you can figure out the 95% confidence interval (or any other level of confidence) for the effect size indicator.

We begin our discussion of the *t* test by explaining how signal-to-noise ratios operate. We will later use this discussion and a relationship conceptually defined as "significance test = effect size × study size" to show how *t* might be maximized. We will describe two general forms of the *t* test, one for use with independent groups (i.e., an independent, or two-sample, *t* test) and the other for use with groups of scores that are not independent (i.e., a paired, or one-sample, *t* test). In the next chapter, we will describe another form of the *t* test, which is used with more than two samples, called a contrast *t*. All of the calculations described in this chapter can be done with a statistical calculator or with a program such as SPSS, SAS, SYSTAT, or Minitab. The same applies to the examples in the remaining chapters; the purpose of these examples is to give you a deeper understanding of the results provided by your calculator or computer, and also to give you conceptual insights into the versatility and limits of these statistical procedures.

Signal-to-Noise Ratios

As an illustration of how *t* tests can be thought of as *signal-to-noise ratios*, suppose a researcher is conducting an experiment on the effect of vitamins on the academic performance of children from families below the poverty level. In Chapter 7, we described the particular statistical plan of this research as a between-subjects randomized design. The researcher has randomly assigned the children to an experimental group (which is administered vitamins at regular intervals) or to a control group (which receives a placebo). The experimenter's working hypothesis is that vitamins will have a positive effect on the children's academic performance, and the null hypothesis is that vitamins will have *no* effect on their academic performance. Table 13.1 and Figure 13.1 show two alternative outcomes of this experiment and help to illustrate the signal-to-noise idea.

We see that the means of the vitamin groups are identical ($M = 15$), as are the means of the control groups ($M = 10$). The only difference between Results A and Results B is that one set of results (B) is more variable. That is, the scores of B are less tightly bunched than the scores of A. When we compare the mean differences *between* the groups ($15 - 10 = 5$), it seems that we should also take into consideration the amount of variability *within* the groups. That is, the 5 points of difference between the groups look larger to us when seen against the backdrop of the small within-group variation of A than when seen against the backdrop of the larger within-group variation of B.

This is the way the *t* test works. It is a test of statistical significance that examines the difference between two means (the *signal*) against the background of the within-group variability (the *noise*). The larger the difference between the means (i.e., the greater the signal), and/or the smaller the within-group variability for any given size of study (i.e., the less the noise), the greater will be the value of *t* (see also Box 13.2). Because large *t*s are associated with differences between means that are more statistically significant, researchers generally prefer larger *t*s. That is, larger *t*s have a lower level of probability (*p* value or alpha), and therefore, in turn, allow researchers to reject the null hypothesis that there is no difference between means.

Comparing Independent Samples

In the example we have been considering, the two groups are presumed to be **independent** of one another; that is, the results in one group are not influenced by the results in the other group. This is also true of Mary Jones's experiment in Appendix A. Had she used a repeated-measures design, the two scores on each sampling unit would not be independent. We will explain the use of *t* tests with nonindependent data in a moment, but when we want to compare independent samples, a general-purpose formula for the *t* test is

Table 13.1   Simple Randomized Design with Alternative Results A and B

	Results A		Results B	
	Vitamins	Control	Vitamins	Control
	13	8	9	4
	15	10	15	10
	17	12	21	16
Mean *(M)*	15	10	15	10

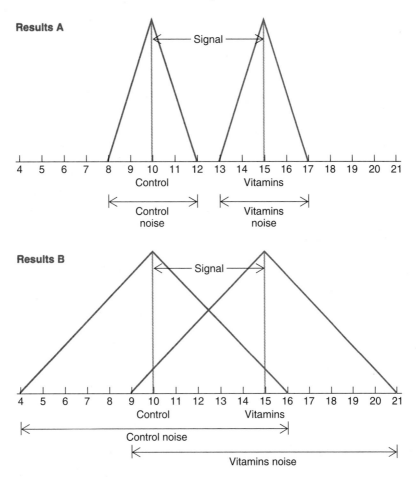

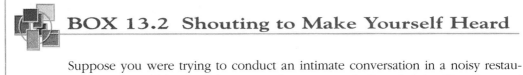

Figure 13.1   Graphical display of the data in Table 13.1
Note that Results A have no overlapping data but that Results B overlap from the scores of 9 to 16.

BOX 13.2 Shouting to Make Yourself Heard

Suppose you were trying to conduct an intimate conversation in a noisy restaurant. You would have to shout to make your words (i.e., the signal) understood over the background din (i.e., the noise). However, if there is not much noise, you can whisper and your communication will be easily picked up. By analogy, *t* tests are more sensitive to differences between groups (i.e., the signal) when the variability within groups (the din) does not overwhelm the magnitude of a real difference.

| Table 13.2 | Basic Data for Calculating t for Results A and B in Table 13.1 |

Results A

	Vitamin group			Control group		
	X_1	$X_1 - M_1$	$(X_1 - M_1)^2$	X_2	$X_2 - M_2$	$(X_2 - M_2)^2$
	13	−2.0	4.0	8	−2.0	4.0
	15	0.0	0.0	10	0.0	0.0
	17	+ 2.0	4.0	12	+ 2.0	4.0
Sum (Σ)	45	0	8.0	30	0	8.0
Mean (M)	15			10		

Results B

	Vitamin group			Control group		
	X_1	$X_1 - M_1$	$(X_1 - M_1)^2$	X_2	$X_2 - M_2$	$(X_2 - M_2)^2$
	9	−6.0	36.0	4	−6.0	36.0
	15	0.0	0.0	10	0.0	0.0
	21	+ 6.0	36.0	16	+ 6.0	36.0
Sum (Σ)	45	0	72.0	30	0	72.0
Mean (M)	15			10		

$$t = \frac{M_1 - M_2}{\sqrt{\left(\dfrac{1}{n_1} + \dfrac{1}{n_2}\right)s^2}},$$

in which M_1 and M_2 are the means of the two independent groups; n_1 and n_2 are the number of units (the number of participants) in each of the two groups; and S^2 is what was called in Chapter 10 the *unbiased estimator of the population variance.* You will find this same formula repeated on the first page of the appendix of Mary Jones's report, along with her calculation of t based on the data she summarized in the body of her report (in her Table 1).

In the formula above, think of S^2 as the "pooled estimate" of the population variance (i.e., a single estimate of the variance associated with both populations from which these two samples were drawn), computed as

$$S^2 = \frac{\Sigma(X_1 - M_1)^2 + \Sigma(X_2 - M_2)^2}{n_1 + n_2 - 2},$$

where X_1 and X_2 are individual raw scores, and the other symbols are defined above. If you want to try your hand with another set of data to check your understanding of this formula, you can try your work with Mary Jones's raw scores.

Table 13.2 provides all the basic data we need to compute t for the two sets of results in Table 13.1. For each group, we compute the sum of the squares of the deviations of the scores from their mean, and we then enter this information in the formula above for S^2. With Results A we find

$$S^2 = \frac{8.0 + 8.0}{3 + 3 - 2} = 4.0,$$

so

$$t = \frac{15 - 10}{\sqrt{\left(\frac{1}{3} + \frac{1}{3}\right)4.0}} = \frac{5}{1.63} = 3.06.$$

Performing these same calculations on Results B gives us

$$S^2 = \frac{72.0 + 72.0}{3 + 3 - 2} = \frac{144.0}{4} = 36.0,$$

and

$$t = \frac{15 - 10}{\sqrt{\left(\frac{1}{3} + \frac{1}{3}\right)36.0}} = \frac{5}{4.90} = 1.02.$$

Not surprisingly, in view of the larger denominator in the t test for Results B (4.90) than for Results A (1.63), the value of t is larger for Results A than for Results B. We expected this effect because of the difference in variability (i.e., the difference in noise levels) between A and B. We can look up the approximate p values corresponding to these results in a suitable table, or if we have a good calculator or are working with a statistics program, we can find the exact p values and report them. As larger ts are rarer events, we expect to find a smaller p associated with Results A than with Results B. However, before we look up these p values, some background information will be useful.

Using the t Table to Find p

Although it is convenient to think of t as a single test of statistical significance, it might also be thought of as a family of curves. The reason is that there is a different curve (each resembles the standard normal distribution) for every possible value of what are called the **degrees of freedom** (symbolized as df) of the t test. In the case we have been considering (the independent t test), the degrees of freedom are defined as $n_1 + n_2 - 2$ (see also Box 13.3). One of the great contributions of the inventor of the t test, William Gosset (Box 13.1), was to figure out by hand (before the invention of the computer) the curve for each number of degrees of freedom. However, instead of having to make our way through scores of different curves, we turn to Table 13.3, which provides a summary of the most pertinent information from these curves for selected p values. This table gives the areas found in one or both tails of the selected t curves. That is, for one-tailed p values, this

Table 13.3	*t* Values Required for Significance at Various *p* Levels				
	Probability level (*p*)				
	.20	.10	.05	.01	two-tailed
df	.10	.05	.025	.005	one-tailed
1	3.08	6.31	12.71	63.66	
2	1.89	2.92	4.30	9.92	
3	1.64	2.35	3.18	5.84	
4	1.53	2.13	2.78	4.60	
5	1.48	2.02	2.57	4.03	
6	1.44	1.94	2.45	3.71	
8	1.40	1.86	2.31	3.36	
10	1.37	1.81	2.23	3.17	
15	1.34	1.75	2.13	2.95	
20	1.32	1.72	2.09	2.84	
25	1.32	1.71	2.06	2.79	
30	1.31	1.70	2.04	2.75	
40	1.30	1.68	2.02	2.70	
60	1.30	1.67	2.00	2.66	
80	1.29	1.66	1.99	2.64	
100	1.29	1.66	1.98	2.63	
1,000	1.28	1.65	1.96	2.58	
∞	1.28	1.64	1.96	2.58	

Note: For a more complete table, see Appendix B, Table B.2.

table gives the areas found in the right-hand tail, while for two-tailed *p*s, it gives the areas found in both tails.

Looking carefully at Table 13.3, we see that for any level of *p*, the value of *t* required to reach that level is smaller and smaller as the degrees of freedom (*df*) increase. In addition, for any *df*, a higher *t* value is required to reach more extreme (smaller) *p* values. One way to think about *t* is that when the null hypothesis of

BOX 13.3 Degrees of Freedom

The origin of degrees of freedom (*df*) has to do in a way with the standard deviation, which in turn depends on the deviations from the mean (i.e., the $X - M$ values). Suppose you have five raw (*X*) scores: 1, 3, 5, 7, 9, with $\Sigma X = 25$ and $M = 5$. The sum of the deviations from the mean has to be zero. That is, $\Sigma (X - M) = 0$ because $(1 - 5) + (3 - 5) + (5 - 5) + (7 - 5) + (9 - 5)$ equals zero. Knowing this, if you were given all but one value, you could easily find the missing value. In other words, one deviation in the group is not free to vary, so one *df* is eliminated. Thus, with a batch of five scores, you have 4 *df* remaining. In the case of a *t* test on two independent samples, you lose one *df* for each group, so that $df = n_1 + n_2 - 2$.

"no difference" or "no effect" is true (i.e., when the means in the population do not differ), the most likely value of t is zero. However, even if the population mean difference were truly zero, we would often find nonzero t values by sheer chance alone. For example, suppose the direction of the effect were predicted, in which case we might use the one-tailed p values. With $df = 8$, we would obtain a t value of 1.40 or greater (favoring the predicted outcome) about 10% of the time (i.e., one-tailed $p = .10$), or of 1.86 or greater about 5% of the time (one-tailed $p = .05$), or of 3.36 or greater about 0.5% of the time (one-tailed $p = .005$).

We are now ready to look up our two ts, and we will assume that the specific direction of the effect was predicted. For this step, we will use the more comprehensive listing found in Table B.2 (see pp. 410–411). The rows show the degrees of freedom, which will be 4 for both sets of results because we eliminate one df in each group (i.e., $df = 3 + 3 - 2 = 4$) when computing an independent t test. We put a finger on the row labeled 4 df and read across the columns until we find a value that is the same as or larger than the obtained value of t. We see that our t of 3.06 is larger than the value listed for $p = .025$ one-tailed (2.776) but smaller than the value listed for $p = .01$ one-tailed (3.747). Thus, the one-tailed p of $t = 3.06$ is less than .025 (i.e., $p < .025$ one-tailed) but greater than .01 (i.e., $p > .01$ one-tailed). We next see that our t of 1.02 is larger than the value listed for $p = .25$ one-tailed (.741) but smaller than the value listed for $p = .10$ one-tailed (1.533). In other words, the one-tailed p for $t = 1.02$ with 4 df is $< .25$ but $> .10$ (see also Box 13.4).

You must decide for yourself whether you will regard any given t as an event rare enough to make you doubt that the null hypothesis is true. Of course, you cannot simply decide, say, that "$p < .20$ is a reasonable risk" and then expect the instructor or others to accept your decision. In psychology, most researchers who do NHST prefer the .05 significance level. By this standard, you would conclude that Results A are "statistically significant" and that Results B are "not statistically significant." Of course (as discussed in the previous chapter), you will also want to examine the effect sizes, confidence intervals, and BESDs when using t tests, as you know that p values alone fail to tell the whole story. Let us review how to obtain this information.

BOX 13.4 The Increasing Stability of *t* Values

Notice also in Table B.2 (and Table 13.3) that the values of t in each column become more stable as the degrees of freedom increase. The reason is that the t distribution gradually approximates the standard normal distribution as the size of the samples is increased. At 30 df, the t distribution is fairly close to that of the standard normal distribution. When $df = \infty$ (infinity), the t distribution gives values identical to those for the standard normal distribution. This information may come in handy if you decide to do a meta-analysis (described in Appendix C), as the implication is that you can look up the p values of zs in the $df = \infty$ row of Table B.2.

Effect Size, CI, and BESD

The procedure for estimating $r_{effect\ size}$ from a t test that compares two groups is simple enough to be performed on any pocket calculator. To reiterate, we will be emphasizing the product-moment r as an index of the effect size, because it can be interpreted by the BESD procedure described in the previous chapter. In the examples we have been discussing, we used the independent (or two-sample) t test on a continuous dependent variable, so our effect size r will be the point-biserial correlation (r_{pb}) described in Chapter 11. That is, our $r_{effect\ size}$ is operationally defined as the correlation between dummy-coded experimental (1) and control (0) group membership and the dependent variable scores. In the case of a paired (or one-sample) t test (discussed in a moment), the statistical meaning of the effect size r is more subtle (see Rosenthal & Rosnow, 1991, pp. 312–314), although we can still calculate $r_{effect\ size}$ from t as described next.

When the significance test is a t test comparing two groups, the corresponding effect size r can be calculated quite simply as

$$r_{effect\ size} = \sqrt{\frac{t^2}{t^2 + df}}$$

where t^2 is the squared value of the t test, and df is defined as $n_1 + n_2 - 2$. In the case of Results A in Table 13.2, with $t = 3.06$ and $df = 3 + 3 - 2 = 4$, we find

$$r_{effect\ size} = \sqrt{\frac{(3.06)^2}{(3.06)^2 + 4}} = .84,$$

which indicates a "jumbo-sized" effect. In the case of Results B, with $t = 1.02$ and the same df, we find

$$r_{effect\ size} = \sqrt{\frac{(1.02)^2}{(1.02)^2 + 4}} = .45,$$

which indicates a substantial effect in spite of the failure of the test to achieve significance at the conventional 5% level. If you turn to the appendix of Mary Jones's report, you will see the same formula and other sample calculations.

We can now create a confidence interval around these effects by following the four easy steps in the previous chapter. To review, with 95% confidence and $r_{effect\ size} = .84$, the first step is to use Table B.6 (page 419) to identify the corresponding Fisher z_r, which in this case is 1.221. In Step 2, we substitute $N = 6$ in the expression

$$\left(\frac{1}{\sqrt{N-3}}\right)1.96$$

and find

$$\left(\frac{1}{\sqrt{3}}\right)1.96 = 1.1316,$$

where 1.96 represents the 95% CI, although we can (as described in the previous chapter) choose another confidence level if we wish). In Step 3, we subtract the value obtained in Step 2 from 1.221 to find the lower limit of z_r (0.0894, rounded to .09) and add 1.1316 to 1.221 to find the upper limit of z_r (2.3526, rounded to 2.35). In the final step, we simply use Table B.7 (page 420) to transform these lower and upper z_r values back into rs. In sum, we are 95% confident that the effect size r in the population is between .09 and .98 (see also Box 13.5).

As we also learned in the previous chapter, had we worked with a much larger N or a less stringent confidence level (e.g. 90% rather than 95%), the interval would not have been this wide. Applying what we learned previously about BESDs, we can now create such displays for the lower and upper limits surrounding the BESD for each obtained $r_{\text{effect size}}$. Table 13.4 shows these BESDs for the results we have seen, and it gives us a clearer sense of the possible practical importance of the effect in question (because it is now encapsulated within the boundaries of the confidence interval). We see that the effect of taking vitamins is important at either extreme of the 95% CI.

Cohen's *d* and Hedges's *g*

Although our own preference is the effect size r (for reasons noted in the previous chapter), two other popular indices of effect size in comparisons of two means are Cohen's *d* (Cohen, 1988) and Hedges's *g* (Hedges & Olkin, 1985). Recalling our discussion of z scores in Chapter 10, you will note that both *d* and *g* are reminiscent of the formula for a z score. **Cohen's *d*** is estimated by the following formula:

$$\text{Cohen's } d = \frac{M_1 - M_2}{\sigma_{\text{pooled}}},$$

BOX 13.5 Crossing Over

Notice at the end of the Results section of Mary Jones's report that she discusses the fact that her 95% CI crossed over into the negative side. There is a special relationship between confidence intervals and the levels on which they are based. Since the width of the confidence interval in percentage units is given by $(1 - \text{two-tailed } \alpha)100$, if an obtained effect size is found significant at the two-tailed α level or at $\alpha/2$ one-tailed, the end of the confidence interval closer to .00 will not cross over the .00 point (i.e., the interval will be entirely on the positive side of .00, or entirely on the negative side of .00). For example, if a 95% CI is entirely between +.00 and +1.00, or entirely between −.00 and −1.00, it will be significant at least at .05 two-tailed or .025 one-tailed. If a 90% CI is entirely between +.00 and +1.00, or entirely between −.00 and −1.00, it will be significant at least at .10 two-tailed or .05 one-tailed.

Table 13.4	BESDs for Results A in Table 13.2	

BESD for lower limit $r_{effect\ size}$ = .09 (95% confidence)

	Improved	Not improved
Vitamins	54.5	45.5
Control	45.5	54.5

BESD for obtained $r_{effect\ size}$ = .84

	Improved	Not improved
Vitamins	92	8
Control	8	92

BESD for upper limit $r_{effect\ size}$ = .98 (95% confidence)

	Improved	Not improved
Vitamins	99	1
Control	1	99

where the difference between two means is divided by the pooled population standard deviation (i.e., the combined standard deviation of the experimental and control group scores). The formula for **Hedges's g** is only slightly different:

$$Hedges's\ g = \frac{M_1 - M_2}{S_{pooled}},$$

where the difference between the two means is now divided by the combined population estimate of the standard deviation of the experimental and control group scores.

If you recall the distinction between descriptive and inferential measures in Chapter 10, the conceptual difference between these two indices is that Cohen's d is a descriptive measure, and Hedges's g is an inferential measure, of the standardized difference (or distance) between two means. On the assumption that the population distributions of the two groups being compared are normal (i.e., bell-shaped), then a d or g of zero would imply that the two distributions overlap one another 100%. The definitions of "small," "medium," and "large" effect-size ds, as suggested by Cohen (1988) for use with his book of power tables, were .2, .5, and .8, respectively. A Cohen's d of .2 tells us that one mean is two tenths of a standard deviation above the other. To estimate the amount of overlap or the amount of gap (or nonoverlap) between two population distributions, we can consult one of Cohen's (1988, p. 22) tables. For instance, given d = .2, there would be 14.7% nonoverlap. With d = .5, there would be 33% nonoverlap; and with d = .8, there would be 47.4% nonoverlap. Because the tails of normal distributions stretch into infinity, there is always some overlap, even if the gap is minimal. For example, with d = 2.0, there is still 19% overlap (or 81% nonoverlap).

There are convenient formulas for converting d or g into an effect size r, or converting r into d or g (Rosenthal, Rosnow, & Rubin, 2000; Rosnow, Rosenthal, & Rubin, 2000); if you would like to learn more about how to do this, see these works. Computing confidence intervals for d and g is a little more complicated than doing so for *r*, but one solution is to (a) convert the *d* or *g* to *r*, (b) use the procedure described in this chapter for obtaining the confidence interval limits of *r*, and (c) finally convert the upper and lower *r*s back to *d* or *r*. There is, however, a further problem in labeling *d* and *g* as small, medium, and large, because the relation between *d*, *g*, and *r* is not a straight line. Though "small" *r*s, *d*s, and *g*s do not run afoul of the labeling convention suggested by Cohen (1988), an *r* of .3 (a "medium" effect) actually corresponds to a *d* of .63, and an *r* of .5 ("large") actually corresponds to a *d* of 1.15 (a "jumbo" effect?). We recommend that you not use these labels in your final paper, but that you report instead the obtained effect sizes and interpret them in the context of your dependent variable.

Maximizing the *t* Test

As alluded to in the previous chapter, the *t* test, like any significance test, can be shown to consist of two components, one having to do with the effect size and the other with the size of the study (i.e., the number of sampling units). The way these two components come together is expressed by the following conceptual relationship:

$$\text{Significance test} = \text{Size of effect} \times \text{Size of study},$$

which tells us that *t* is the product of the effect size (defined, for example, as the effect size *r*, or Cohen's *d* or Hedges's *g*) and the study size (defined, for example, as the total number of units, or *N*). That is, the larger the effect size or the more subjects used, the greater will be the value of *t*. This equation helps us to plan specific ways of maximizing the *t* test in a given situation (i.e., ways of strengthening the power of the *t* test).

For example, here is another formula in which *t* is mathematically broken down into an effect size and a study size component:

$$t = \left(\frac{M_1 - M_2}{S}\right)\left(\sqrt{\frac{n_1 n_2}{n_1 + n_2}}\right),$$

where the effect size is defined as Hedges's *g*, and the study size is defined by the sample sizes of the two groups (n_1 and n_2). This illustration teaches us that we can increase the value of *t* by (a) driving the means further apart, (b) decreasing the variability within groups, or (c) increasing the effective size of the study.

Thus, one way to maximize *t* would be to use a stronger treatment to drive the means of the two comparison groups further apart. For example, were we to investigate the effects of varying amounts of after-school tutoring, we might use 5 hours versus 2 hours of tutoring per week, but certainly not 5 minutes versus 2 minutes per week. Because this strategy would presumably maximize the value of $M_1 - M_2$ in the numerator of Hedges's *g* (i.e., the definition of the effect size component in the conceptual relationship above), it would be a sensible design strategy. Another way to maximize *t* would be to decrease the variability of responses within the two groups, which we could do by decreasing the *S* in the denominator of Hedges's *g* (and thereby strengthen the power of *t*). This is precisely what happened in Results

A, in which the variability of response within groups was substantially less than that in Results B. Two possible ways of decreasing the variability of response would be (a) to standardize the research procedures in order to make them more uniform and (b) to recruit subject samples that were relatively homogeneous in those characteristics that were substantially correlated with the dependent variable. Of course, in using very homogeneous samples, we might be trading generalizability (external validity) for statistical power (statistical conclusion validity). Still another way of strengthening the power of t is by increasing the total sample size, which we discussed in the preceding chapter. Given a total available study size of N (where $N = n_1 + n_2$), it is also prudent to try to keep the sample sizes equivalent in the two groups (i.e., $n_1 = n_2$), because an unequal-n design drains power, and the more unequal the sample sizes, the greater the drain (see Rosenthal & Rosnow, 1991, pp. 304–305).

Comparing Related Samples

So far, we have used t to compare the means of two *independent* groups. That is, we regarded the scores in one group as having no inherent relationship to the scores in the other group. However, suppose we measure the same subjects more than once (e.g., before and after they are exposed to a learning experience) and we want to compare the means of these two measures. Now the two groups of scores are no longer independent because of the repeated measures design, or within-subjects design. A less obvious example of samples that are not independent would occur if the two groups consisted of children who were related by birth, and one member were assigned to Group 1 and the other to Group 2. The common family membership introduces a degree of prior relatedness between the scores in Group 1 and those in Group 2.

When samples that are not independent are compared by the independent t test, the value of the obtained t will be biased (it is usually too small, but also sometimes too large). To avoid this problem, we instead use a **paired t test** (also called a **one-sample t test** or a **correlated t** or **matched t**) for samples that are not independent. To illustrate this approach, we refer to the basic data in Table 13.5, which shows a hypothetical study in which girls were predicted to be more sociable than boys. The scores are the ratings of a judge on a 9-point scale of sociability. What makes this study appropriate for a paired t is that these were six *pairs* of girls and boys, each pair from a different family. When we examine the judge's ratings over these pairs, we find that a child's sociability score is to some degree predictable from family membership. For instance, the column of means shows that the Smith and Jones children were judged (on the average) to be less sociable than the Simpson and Brown children.

In t tests for matched (or correlated) data, we perform our calculations on the difference score *(D)* for each pair of lined-up scores. We use the following formula:

Table 13.5	Basic Data for Paired t Test					
	Group 1	Group 2				
Family	X_1 (girls)	X_2 (boys)	Mean (M_X)	D	$D - M_D$	$(D - M_D)^2$
Smith	4	3	3.5	1	−1	1
Ross	6	4	5.0	2	0	0
Simpson	8	5	6.5	3	1	1
Jones	4	3	3.5	1	−1	1
Hill	6	4	5.0	2	0	0
Brown	8	5	6.5	3	1	1
Sum (Σ)	36	24	30.0	12	0	4
Mean (M)	6	4	5.0	2.0		

Note: The value of M_D is shown as 2.0 at the bottom of the column of differences (D) between Groups I and II (i.e., $D = X_1 - X_2$), and the value of $\Sigma (D - M_D)^2$ is shown as 4 at the bottom of the last column.

$$ t = \frac{M_D}{\sqrt{\left(\frac{1}{N}\right) S_D^2}} $$

in which M_D is the mean of the $D = X_1 - X_2$ scores; N is the number of D scores (i.e., the number of lined-up pairs); and S_D^2 gives us the unbiased estimate of the population value of σ_D^2, with S_D^2 defined by

$$ S_D^2 = \frac{\Sigma (D - M_D)^2}{N - 1} $$

and df now defined as $N - 1$, where N is the number of paired scores. Thus, the paired, or one-sample, t operates by subtracting the values of one of the correlated samples from the corresponding values of the other correlated sample, thereby creating a new *single* sample of difference scores.

Substituting the data in Table 13.5, we find

$$ S_D^2 = \frac{4}{6 - 1} = .80, $$

and

$$ t = \frac{2.0}{\sqrt{\left(\frac{1}{6}\right) .80}} = \frac{2.0}{.365} = 5.48. $$

We can now look up p as a one-tailed value (because we predicted that girls would score higher than boys), also compute the effect size and its confidence interval, and finally display the effect size as a BESD. For the p value, we turn to Table B.2 (p. 410), but we now read across the row labeled 5 df (because the degrees of freedom for a single sample are defined as $N - 1$, or $6 - 1 = 5$). Our obtained t of 5.48 is larger than 4.773 but smaller than 5.893, so one-tailed $p <$ .0025 but $> .001$ (see also Box 13.6). When we calculate the effect size, we find

$$r_{\text{effect size}} = \sqrt{\frac{t^2}{t^2 + df}} = \sqrt{\frac{(5.48)^2}{(5.48)^2 + 5}} = .926,$$

which leads us to conclude that we have another "jumbo-sized" effect in addition to a statistically significant one.

Table 13.6 shows what this imaginary effect will look like as a BESD with equal totals in the margins. The cell values should not be mistaken for the actual frequencies that would be obtained in a random sample; instead, they should be seen as standardized values because of the uniform totals that we imposed on the margins for ease of interpretation. Using the procedure described previously, we can calculate the 95% confidence interval of the effect, which we now find to be between rs of .46 and .99.

Assumptions of the t Test

In the report in Appendix A, Mary Jones refers to an assumption of the t test as **homogeneity of variance.** There are other assumptions of the t test (e.g., Rosenthal & Rosnow, 1991, p. 315), but homogeneity of variance means that the popula-

---

BOX 13.6 How Many Decimal Places?

When you use a calculator to compute statistics, it is a good idea not to scrimp on the number of decimal places in the intermediate calculations, because rounding errors can produce inaccurate results. Suppose you were a NASA engineer trying to figure out how much fuel would be needed to take a manned rocket to Mars. By rounding off the calculations, you might send the astronauts on an impossible mission. However, what if you are puzzling over how many decimals to report in a statistical test. The convention is to report statistical tests (e.g., t, F, χ^2) to two decimal places. What about p values? As noted in the previous chapter, many statisticians report the actual descriptive level of significance because it carries more information than the phrases "significant difference" or "no significant difference at the 5% level" (e.g., Mosteller, Fienberg, & Rourke, 1983; Snedecor & Cochran, 1989). There is something absurd, they would argue, regarding as a "real" effect one that is supported by $p = .05$ and as a "zero" effect one that is supported by $p = .06$. Instead of listing a string of zeros, you can use **scientific notation** as a more compact way to show a very small p value. That is, instead of reporting $p = .00000025$, you report 2.5×10^{-7}, where -7 (i.e., the exponent of 10) tells us to count 7 places to the left of the decimal in 2.5 and make that the decimal place.

Table 13.6	Binomial Effect-Size Display of Results in Table 13.5		
	Sociability		
Gender	More sociable	Less sociable	Total
Girls	96.3	3.7	100
Boys	3.7	96.3	100
Total	100	100	200

tion variance of the two groups is assumed to be equal. When this assumption is seriously violated, the p value may be off, and the effect size r calculated from t may be inflated. How can you determine whether there has been a serious violation of the homogeneity-of-variance assumption? Mary describes one approach, which compares the highest and the lowest estimated population variance by means of the F test. Mary's use of this procedure led her to conclude that the homogeneity-of-variance assumption had, in fact, been violated, and she then used another procedure (called *Satterthwaite's method*) to adjust the degrees of freedom of her t test. The formulas she used are discussed at the end of her report.

However, we do want to note that the most commonly used procedures in this situation involve transformations of the raw data to make the variances more nearly equal, and afterward, the t test is performed on the transformed data. Among the most commonly used transformations are (a) the square root of each score, (b) the log transformation of each score, and (c) the reciprocal value of each score. Another alternative, which is convenient when transformations are not possible (e.g., if you were working with the published data of other researchers), or when a transformation is ineffective, is to replace the pooled S^2 in the denominator of the t formula with the largest S^2. This is a serviceable but conservative procedure (Rosenthal & Rosnow, 1985), as the effect size estimated from t will be smaller (possibly a lot smaller) than the estimate using Satterthwaite's method. To illustrate in the case of Mary Jones's Table 1, where the largest $S = 16,645.07$, and therefore $S^2 = 277,058,355.305$, recalculating t gives us

$$t = \frac{M_1 - M_2}{\sqrt{\left(\frac{1}{n_1} + \frac{1}{n_2}\right)S^2}} = \frac{16,146.67 - 6,990.63}{\sqrt{\left(\frac{1}{15} + \frac{1}{16}\right)277,058,355.305}} = \frac{9,156.04}{5,982.20} = 1.53,$$

which, with $df = n_1 + n_2 - 2 = 29$, has an associated one-tailed $p = .068$ and $r_{\text{effect size}} = .273$.

Summary of Ideas

1. The t test operates like a signal-to-noise ratio used to compare two means relative to the variability of scores within each group.
2. To find a one- or two-tailed p for an obtained t, we need to know the degrees of freedom *(df)* as well as the value of t.
3. Using a one-tailed p implies that we predicted in which side of the t distribution the p value would be situated.

4. In an independent t test, the df are defined as $n_1 + n_2 - 2$ because, in each group, one deviation from the mean is not free to vary.

5. Once we have created a confidence interval for the obtained $r_{effect\ size}$, we can create BESDs to represent the lower and upper limits.

6. Two other popular measures of effect size are Cohen's d (a descriptive measure) and Hedges's g (an inferential measure), both focusing on the standardized difference between two means.

7. Like any significance test, the t test is made up mathematically of two components: the size of the effect times the size of the study.

8. We can maximize the power of the independent t by (a) drawing the means further apart, (b) decreasing the variability within groups, and (c) increasing the effective size of the study.

9. We used a paired t to compare the means of two groups that are not independent, in which case $df = N - 1$, where N is the total number of paired scores.

10. The effect size rs of the t tests described in this chapter can be computed as

$$r_{effect\ size} = \sqrt{\frac{t^2}{t^2 + df}}$$

and the result can then be displayed in a BESD.

11. Several assumptions are made in the use of t tests, and we discussed homogeneity of variance and how, when this assumption is violated, a serviceable but conservative procedure involves adjusting the t formula; Mary's report in Appendix A illustrates another corrective procedure (Satterthwaite's method).

Key Terms

WEB ACTIVITY

Explore the differences between independent and paired t tests by visiting the Rice University Virtual Lab in Statistics at http://www.ruf.rice.edu/~lane/stat_sim/index.html and then clicking on the "t-test" radio button.

Multiple-Choice Questions for Review

1. In a t test, the difference between the two means can be thought of as the (a) significance level; (b) noise; (c) signal; (d) none of the above.

2. In a t test, the variability of scores within samples can be thought of as the (a) significance level; (b) noise; (c) signal; (d) none of the above.

3. A student at Bryn Mawr College conducts a study with 5 subjects in the experimental group and 6 subjects in the control group. She then calculates a *t* test. How many degrees of freedom will be associated with this test? (a) 4; (b) 5; (c) 6; (d) 9

4. A researcher at the University of Saskatchewan computes a *t* test for independent samples. There is a total of 8 subjects, and *t* = 5. What is the appropriate one-tailed *p* value? (a) < .05; (b) < .0025; (c) > .005; (d) < .001

5. A very small *p* value (e.g., .001) automatically means that you have a (a) large effect; (b) moderate effect; (c) small effect; (d) cannot be determined from this information.

6. A student at Williams College conducts a study with an experimental group and a control group. There are 4 subjects in each group. He calculates that *t* = 3. The effect size is the square root of (a) 9/15; (b) 3/13; (c) 3/4; (d) 3/7.

7. Fill in the blanks in the following conceptual equation: Significance test = ___ × ___. (a) *t, r*; (b) *t*, size of study; (c) effect size, size of study; (d) *r*, effect size

8. Which of the following can be used in maximizing *t*? (a) decreasing the difference between the means; (b) calculating *r* instead of *t*; (c) decreasing the variability within groups; (d) all of the above

9. Scores on two variables might not be independent because they were obtained (a) from the same subjects; (b) with a within-subjects design; (c) from brother-sister pairs from the same family; (d) all of the above.

10. A study is conducted in which scores were obtained from 4 subjects on two separate occasions. In other words, there are eight total observations from 4 subjects. The data are analyzed by means of a paired *t* test. How many degrees of freedom will there be? (a) 3; (b) 4; (c) 7; (d) 8

Discussion Questions for Review

1. A Kent State University researcher hypothesizes that marijuana use decreases short-term memory. He brings 5 subjects to his laboratory. Each subject is given a test of short-term memory. Each subject is then given marijuana and administered another test of short-term memory. The results are given below (high scores indicate good memory):

	Test 1	Test 2
Subject 1	5	2
Subject 2	7	5
Subject 3	4	5
Subject 4	8	3
Subject 5	8	4

Can you set up the formula and insert the numbers that would be used to test the hypothesis that the scores on Test 2 are significantly lower than the scores on Test 1? What would be the degrees of freedom? If you found a significant difference and a large effect size, should you conclude that marijuana causes a decrease in short-term memory? Why or why not?

2. A Loyola University student conducted a study comparing the creativity scores of four biology and four history majors. The results were

Biology	History
4	7
6	3
3	5
3	6

Can you set up the formula that would be used to compute a *t* test? What would be the degrees of freedom? How would you compute and interpret the effect size?

3. An experimenter at the University of California at San Diego studied sex differences in nonverbal sensitivity. Her results showed that the women were significantly better than the men at decoding nonverbal cues, with *t* = 2.34, *df* = 62, p < .05 two-tailed, and $r_{effect\ size}$ = .28. Pretend that the experimenter added an additional 60 subjects, randomly selected from the same population as the original sample. When the analysis is recalculated with the extra subjects, should the new *t* be larger, smaller, or about the same size? Should the *p* value be larger, smaller, or about the same size? Should $r_{effect\ size}$ be larger, smaller, or about the same size? Should the 95% confidence interval be wider, narrower, or about the same size?

4. A Santa Fe College student has developed a brief training program that increases sensitivity to nonverbal cues. He plans to compare it to a brief training program that increases sensitivity to people in general. He plans to randomly assign 10 subjects to each treatment, the subjects having been found through newspaper ads. He describes his plan to his professor, who suggests he think hard about trying to obtain a larger *t* than he is likely to get in the planned study. What might the student do to get a larger *t*?

Answers to Review Questions

Multiple-Choice Questions

1. c	**3.** d	**5.** d	**7.** c	**9.** d
2. b	**4.** b	**6.** a	**8.** c	**10.** a

Discussion Questions

1. The difference or change scores (*D*) for the five subjects are −3, −2, +1, −5, −4. The paired *t* can be computed from

$$t = \frac{M_D}{\sqrt{\left(\frac{1}{N}\right)S_D^2}} = \frac{[(-3) + (-2) + (+1) + (-5) + (-4)]/5}{\sqrt{\left(\frac{1}{5}\right)5.30}} = 2.53,$$

obtaining S_D^2 from

$$S_D^2 = \frac{\Sigma(D - M_D)^2}{N - 1}$$

$$= \frac{[(-3) - (-2.6)]^2 + [(-2) - (-2.6)]^2 + [(+1) - (-2.6)]^2 + [(-5) - (-2.6)]^2 + [(-4) - (-2.6)]^2}{5 - 1} = 5.30.$$

The *df* are *N* − 1 = 5 − 1 = 4. Had we found a significant and large change in memory test scores, we would not be able to conclude that the change was due to marijuana use. There was no control group to rule out plausible rival hypotheses. Had we been able to compute the significance level and effect size, we would have used Table B.2 (on p. 410) and found our *t* with 4 *df* to be significant at *p* < .05 one-tailed (but not quite significant at *p* = .025 one-tailed). The effect size would have been computed from

$$r_{\text{effect size}} = \sqrt{\frac{t^2}{t^2 + df}} = \sqrt{\frac{(2.53)^2}{(2.53)^2 + 4}} = .78.$$

2. We would compute t from

$$t = \frac{M_1 - M_2}{\sqrt{\left(\frac{1}{n_1} + \frac{1}{n_2}\right)s^2}} = \frac{4.00 - 5.25}{\sqrt{\left(\frac{1}{4} + \frac{1}{4}\right)2.46}} = 1.13.$$

The df would be $n_1 + n_2 - 2 = 6$, and the effect size could be computed from

$$r_{\text{effect size}} = \sqrt{\frac{t^2}{t^2 + df}} = \sqrt{\frac{(1.13)^2}{(1.13)^2 + 6}} = .42,$$

a very substantial effect size though t is not significant ($p = .30$ two-tailed).

3. From the conceptual equation:

$$\text{Significance test} = \text{Size of effect} \times \text{Size of study},$$

we can see that increasing the size of the study would increase the value of the significance test, and the result would be a smaller (more significant) p value. However, the effect size would not be systematically affected by the addition of more subjects of the same type. To illustrate, we assume the following original ingredients of t:

$$t = \frac{2.585 - 2.000}{\sqrt{\left(\frac{1}{32} + \frac{1}{32}\right)1.00}} = 2.34,$$

and $p = .023$ two-tailed, $r_{\text{effect size}} = .28$. We then add 60 subjects (30 to each group), yielding

$$t = \frac{2.585 - 2.000}{\sqrt{\left(\frac{1}{62} + \frac{1}{62}\right)1.00}} = 3.26,$$

and $p = .0014$ two-tailed, $r_{\text{effect size}} = .28$. Therefore, with nothing changing but n_1 and n_2, we see that t increases, p decreases, and the $r_{\text{effect size}}$ remains unchanged. The 95% confidence interval will shrink with the additional subjects, as illustrated in the previous chapter.

4. The student might try three approaches. First, he might try to drive the means further apart by using a control group that is not as similar to the treatment group. Second, he might use participants who are more homogeneous than the people who answer newspaper ads. Third, he might use larger sample sizes for each condition.

CHAPTER 14

Comparisons on More Than Two Conditions

Preview Questions

- How do F tests apportion variability in the analysis of variance (ANOVA)?

- How are ANOVA summary tables set up and interpreted?

- What is the difference between focused and omnibus statistical procedures?

- When is it appropriate to report an effect size indicator for F?

- What are "tests of simple effects"?

- What are residuals, and what do they have to do with interaction effects?

- What is the purpose of contrast F and t tests?

- What is the difference between effect size rs, contrast rs, and alerting rs?

- What are intrinsically and nonintrinsically repeated measures?

F and t

Although it is generally true that the t test is often used whenever there are only two means to be compared, later in this chapter we will describe how this statistical test can be used to examine a predicted trend in more than two conditions. Another very popular statistic that you are bound to see in your literature search is the F test, which is the primary focus of this chapter. We will see how F tests are signal-to-noise ratios that are used to divide up variability in the procedure called **analysis of variance**, or **ANOVA** (see also Box 14.1). Even if you expect to use a computer to analyze your data, you will find that working through the examples in this chapter will improve your understanding of the information that is provided by your computer program. Furthermore, some of the concepts and formulas in this chapter are so relatively new that they may not yet be available in your computer

BOX 14.1 Comparing Signal Spreads and Noise Spreads

That the F statistic is based on the analysis of variance (ANOVA) implies that we are analyzing variances instead of comparing means. In Chapter 10, we described the variance (S^2 or σ^2) as a measure of the spread of scores around the mean. The strategy of ANOVA in between-subjects (also commonly referred to as *between-group*) comparisons is to compare the spread of scores *between* the conditions ($S^2_{between}$) with the spread of scores *within* the conditions (S^2_{within}). Thus, in the F ratio of $S^2_{between}$ divided by S^2_{within}, you can think of $S^2_{between}$ as the "signal spread" and S^2_{within} as the "noise spread."

program, but they are simple enough to calculate by hand or by using the basic ingredients provided by your computer program.

There is a relationship between F and t that is important to understand. Simply stated, squaring t always produces F, but taking the square root of F does not always produce t. The reason for this conundrum will become clearer as you read this chapter. For the moment, however, all you need to remember is that, when there are only two groups to be compared, taking the square root of F always produces t. Thus, since squaring t always produces F, and you recall that the effect size of t used to compare two means was computed as

$$r_{effect\ size} = \sqrt{\frac{t^2}{t^2 + df}}$$

it follows that, whenever there are only two samples, the effect size of F can be computed as

$$r_{effect\ size} = \sqrt{\frac{F}{F + df}}$$

where df refers to the degrees of freedom "within conditions," obtained by determining the df within each group (or condition) and then adding. When there are more than two samples, the estimation of effect size indicators from F (and t) is more subtle, as we will explain later in this chapter.

Because we cover a great deal of ground in this chapter, it is useful to have an overall sense of the content. We begin by explaining the logic of F tests and the analysis of variance in between-subjects designs, using as our illustration a randomized design with four independent groups. In the illustrative analysis, the F test is what is called an omnibus F (for reasons that are explained shortly). The problem with omnibus statistical procedures is that they are vague and hardly ever address questions of any real interest to researchers. Furthermore, they do not lend themselves to interpretable effect-size indicators (such as r). Thus, we redirect our attention to tests of a more "focused" nature that examine what the APA Publication Manual (2001, p. 26) refers to as "one-degree-of-freedom effects" (called *focused statistical procedures* in this book). The first such procedure we illustrate is the use of t tests after an omnibus F, and then we describe a way of rearranging this particular one-way design into a 2 × 2 design that uses F tests to address three one-degree-of-freedom effects. Another option is to compute contrast t or F tests that allow us to compare the overall pattern of results with a specific prediction in a focused way that is also amenable to interpretable effect-size indicators (and we describe several). Finally, we will turn to the use of contrasts with repeated measures, including research designs that have what are called *intrinsically* or *non-intrinsically repeated measures*.

The Logic of ANOVA

In the previous chapter, we began with a hypothetical case to illustrate the signal-to-noise idea. If we look at another example, we will see that the logic is essentially the same for analysis of variance. In this illustration, we will imagine that an experimenter interested in the effects of nutrition on the academic performance of children decides to use a four-group instead of a two-group randomized design. One group of randomly assigned children gets a hot lunch daily, another group gets free milk, a third group gets a vitamin supplement, and the fourth group gets nothing extra. Once again, imagine two different sets of results of this experiment, as represented by A and B in Table 14.1. We would describe A and B as 1 × 4 ("one-by-four") between-subjects designs because the configuration consists of four independent groups (or samples) in a one-way arrangement.

In examining these results, what conclusions would you be willing to draw on the basis of A compared to B? Note that the outcome in the sample receiving no

Table 14.1 1 × 4 Between-Subjects Design with Alternative Results A and B

Results A:

	Group 1 Zero	Group 2 Milk	Group 3 Vitamins	Group 4 Hot lunch
	8	10	13	17
	10	12	15	19
	12	14	17	21
Mean (*M*)	10	12	15	19

Results B:

	Group 1 Zero	Group 2 Milk	Group 3 Vitamins	Group 4 Hot lunch
	4	6	9	13
	10	12	15	19
	16	18	21	25
Mean (*M*)	10	12	15	19

special nutritional bonus (Group 1) has an average of 10 units of academic performance, whereas the average performance of the sample receiving milk is 12 (Group 2), of that receiving vitamins (Group 3) is 15, and of that receiving hot lunches (Group 4) is 19. By applying the logic about within-group variance described in the previous chapter, we find ourselves feeling more impressed by Results A than by Results B. In Results A, the subjects have never varied in their performance by more than 2 points from the average score of their group. The few points of difference between the mean scores of the four groups look larger when seen against the backdrop of the small within-group variation of Results A, whereas they look smaller when examined against the backdrop of the large within-group variation of Results B.

The analysis of variance provides researchers with a more formal comparison of the variation between the average results per condition and the average variation within the different conditions. In this kind of analysis, as we see next, a ratio (the **F ratio**, or **F test**) is formed. In Chapter 13, we mentioned that one way to think about t is that if the null hypothesis were true, the most likely value of t would be 0. F ratios, on the other hand, usually have values close to 1.0 when the variation between conditions is not different from the variation within conditions (i.e., when H_0 is true); we explain why this is so later. The larger the F ratio becomes, the greater is the dispersion of group means relative to the dispersion of scores within groups. In other words, as with the t, researchers generally prefer larger Fs because they are associated with smaller ps.

Dividing Up the Variance

The calculation of F tests is one purpose of the analysis of variance. A more general purpose is to divide up the variation of all the observations into a number of separate sources of variance. In this illustration of comparing the four samples, the total variation among the 12 scores is broken into two sources: (a) systematic variation between groups or conditions (i.e., the signal) and (b) error variation within groups or conditions (i.e., the noise).

It will be useful here to look again at the basic idea of variance:

$$S^2 = \frac{\Sigma(X - M)^2}{N - 1},$$

where S^2 is the unbiased estimate of the population value of σ^2, and σ^2 differs from S^2 only in that the denominator $N - 1$ is replaced by N. As noted in Chapter 10, the quantity S^2 is also called a **mean square** (abbreviated as MS) because when the sum of the squares—that is, $\Sigma(X - M)^2$—is divided by $N - 1$ (or df), the result is the squared deviation per df, representing a kind of average.

In the analysis of variance, we are especially interested in the numerators of our various S^2 values (e.g., for between conditions and for within conditions). This interest has to do with the additive property of the numerators, or the **sum of**

squares (abbreviated as *SS*) of the deviations about the mean. These *SS* values add up to the total sum of squares in the following way:

Total *SS* = between-conditions *SS* + within-conditions *SS*.

In one-way between-subjects designs, the analysis of variance requires the calculation of the between-conditions *SS* and the within-conditions *SS*. If you are using a calculator to work the examples in this chapter, you might compute the total *SS* as a check on your arithmetic. Before we start crunching numbers, however, let us look at the formulas for each of these three sums of squares.

First, the total *SS* is defined as the sum of squares of deviations of all the measurements from the grand mean. What goes into the total *SS* is given by the following formula:

$$\text{Total } SS = \Sigma(X - M_G)^2,$$

where X is each observation and M_G is the grand mean (i.e., the mean of the condition means).

Second, the between-conditions *SS* is defined as the sum of squares of the deviations of the condition means from the grand mean. This between-conditions value is computed by the following formula:

$$\text{Between } SS = \Sigma[n_k(M_k - M_G)^2],$$

where n_k is the number of observations in the kth condition (and k is *any* particular condition), M_k is the mean of the kth condition, and M_G is again the grand mean.

Third, the within-conditions *SS* is defined as the sum of squares of the deviations of the measurements from their condition means, as given by the following formula:

$$\text{Within } SS = \Sigma(X - M_k)^2],$$

where X is each observation and M_k is again the mean of the condition to which X belongs.

Computing the One-Way ANOVA

We will now use these formulas to compute an overall ANOVA on the scores of Results A in Table 14.1. Table 14.2 provides the basic data for this analysis, with the addition of two new symbols: M_k for the group or the condition mean and M_G for the grand mean.

First, we compute the total *SS*. The formula instructs us to subtract the grand mean from each individual score and then add up the squared deviations:

$$\text{Total } SS = (8 - 14)^2 + (10 - 14)^2 + (12 - 14)^2$$
$$+ (10 - 14)^2 + (12 - 14)^2 + (14 - 14)^2$$
$$+ (13 - 14)^2 + (15 - 14)^2 + (17 - 14)^2$$

Table 14.2	Data for ANOVA Based on Results A in Table 14.1			
	Group 1	Group 2	Group 3	Group 4
	Zero	Milk	Vitamins	Hot lunch
	8	10	13	17
	10	12	15	19
	<u>12</u>	<u>14</u>	<u>17</u>	<u>21</u>
M_k	10	12	15	19

$$M_G = \frac{10 + 12 + 15 + 19}{4} = 14$$

$$+ (17 - 14)^2 + (19 - 14)^2 + (21 - 14)^2$$

$$= 170$$

Next, we compute the between-conditions SS. The formula instructs us to subtract the grand mean from each condition mean and then add up the weighted squared deviations:

$$\text{Between } SS = 3(10 - 14)^2$$
$$+ 3(12 - 14)^2$$
$$+ 3(15 - 14)^2$$
$$+ 3(19 - 14)^2$$
$$= 138$$

And finally, we compute the within-conditions SS. The formula instructs us to subtract the appropriate condition mean from each individual score and then add up the squared deviations:

$$\text{Within } SS = (8 - 10)^2 + (10 - 10)^2 + (12 - 10)^2$$
$$+ (10 - 12)^2 + (12 - 12)^2 + (14 - 12)^2$$
$$+ (13 - 15)^2 + (15 - 15)^2 + (17 - 15)^2$$
$$+ (17 - 19)^2 + (19 - 19)^2 + (21 - 19)^2$$
$$= 32$$

As a check on our arithmetic, we add the sum of squares between conditions to the sum of squares within conditions to make sure their total equals the total sum of squares, that is,

$$\text{Total } SS = \text{between } SS + \text{within } SS$$
$$170 = 138 + 32$$

The ANOVA Summary Table

The results of one-way ANOVAs may be displayed in the form shown in Table 14.3. The rows label the source of variation, in this case the variation between and within conditions. Listed in the SS column are sum-of-squares values for each

Table 14.3	Summary ANOVA Table				
Source	SS	df	MS	F	p
Between conditions	138	3	46	11.50	.003
Within conditions	32	8	4		

Note: The effect size correlation, $r_{\text{effect size}}$, is not reported here because it is not interpretable when the numerator $df > 1$. That is, we compute the effect size of F only when the between-conditions variable is based on a single df (e.g., the situation we find when two means are being compared or, as described later in this chapter, when contrast F tests on more than two groups are computed).

source of variation. The degrees of freedom (df) are listed in the next column (see also Box 14.2). As there were four independent conditions (symbolized as $k = 4$), three of the means were free to vary once the mean of the means (M_G) was determined. We define the degrees of freedom between conditions as

$$df \text{ between} = k - 1,$$

which gives us $4 - 1 = 3$ df between.

We obtain the degrees of freedom within conditions by determining the df within each condition (defined as $n - 1$) and then adding. The reason we have $n - 1$ degrees of freedom within each condition is that all but one score are free to vary within each condition once the mean of that condition is determined, and so we eliminate 1 df within each condition. Thus, the degrees of freedom within conditions are found by

$$df \text{ within} = N - k,$$

where N is the total number of measurements or sampling units and k is the number of conditions, giving us $12 - 4 = 8$ df within.

BOX 14.2 Focused and Omnibus Tests and Effect Sizes

Previously, we alluded to the distinction between omnibus and focused statistical procedures. F tests with 1 df in the numerator are characterized as **focused statistical procedures** because they address specific statistical questions. F tests with numerator $df > 1$ are called **omnibus statistical procedures** because they address diffuse (or unfocused) statistical questions. The rule of thumb is to report effect size indicators for focused statistical procedures and not for omnibus statistical procedures, because effect size indicators are far more clearly interpretable for focused procedures. Because all t tests are intrinsically focused, a further rule of thumb is to report effect size indicators for all t tests. As you get deeper into this chapter, you will have a better understanding of why this is so, and also which F tests have numerator $df = 1$.

The total degrees of freedom (not shown in Table 14.3) are defined as the total number of measurements minus 1, that is,

$$df\text{ total} = N - 1,$$

which gives us $12 - 1 = 11$ df total. After we have computed the df for between and within conditions, we can check our calculations by adding these df to see whether they agree with the df total. In the present case, we have

$$df\text{ total} = df\text{ between} + df\text{ within}.$$

$$11 = 3 + 8$$

The MS column shows the mean squares, which we obtained by dividing the sums of squares by the corresponding df. We divide 138 by 3 to get 46, and we divide 32 by 8 to get 4. These MS values can be seen as the amounts of the total variation (measured in SS) attributable to each df. The larger the MS for the between-condition source of variance (the signal) relative to the within-condition source of variance (the noise), the less likely becomes the null hypothesis of no difference between the conditions. If the null hypothesis were true, the variation per df should be roughly the same for the df between groups and the df within groups. The F value in the next column provides this information. We obtained this F by dividing the mean square between conditions by the mean square within conditions; the result is a signal-to-noise ratio of $F = 46/4 = 11.5$.

To review, F is called the F ratio to reflect the fact that it is a ratio of two mean squares (i.e., two variances, as noted in Box 14.1). The denominator mean square (i.e., the mean square for error) serves as a kind of base rate for noise level, or typical variation. The numerator (i.e., the signal) is a reflection of both the size of the effect and the size of the study. In other words, a numerator MS may be large relative to a denominator MS because (a) the effect is large, (b) the n per condition is large, or (c) both are large. Thus, obtaining large Fs should not be automatically interpreted as indicating the presence of large effects. In the case of F with numerator $df > 1$, the idea of interpreting the effect size is academic, as we can report very clearly interpretable effect sizes only for Fs with numerator $df = 1$.

Using the F Table to Find p

The final value in Table 14.3 is the probability that an F of this size or larger, with this number of degrees of freedom (i.e., 3 in the numerator and 8 in the denominator), might occur if the null hypothesis of no difference among the means were true. In the previous chapter, we noted that there is a different distribution of t values for every possible value of the degrees of freedom. The situation for F is similar but more complicated, because for every F ratio there are *two* relevant df values to take into account: the df between conditions and the df within conditions. For every combination of df between and df within, there is a different curve. As is the case for t, small values of F are likely when the null hypothesis of no difference between conditions is true, but large values are unlikely and are used as evidence to suggest that the null hypothesis is probably false.

Another important difference between t and F curves was alluded to earlier, when we said that the expected value of t is zero when the null hypothesis is true but that the expected value of F is approximately 1 when the null is true. The symmetrical bell shape of t curves means that they are centered at 0, with negative values running to negative infinity and positive values running to positive infinity. However, F curves are positively skewed, with values beginning at zero and ranging upward to positive infinity. In other words, F is intrinsically one-tailed as a test of significance. When the null hypothesis is true, the expected value of F is $df/(df - 2)$, where these df are for within conditions. For most values of df, then, the expected value of F when the null hypothesis is true is a little more than 1.0, as noted in Table 14.4.

Table 14.4 enables us to locate the p value of a given F; a more comprehensive table can be found in Appendix B (see pp. 412–416). In Table 14.4, notice that the critical values of F required to reach the .05 and .01 levels decrease as the df within increase for any given df between. Similarly, the critical values of F decrease as the df between increase for any given df within—except for the special cases of df within = 1 or 2. For df within = 1, there is a substantial increase in the Fs required to reach the .05 and .01 levels as the df between increase from 1 to infinity. For df within = 2, only a very small increase in the Fs is required to reach the .05 and .01 levels as the df between increase from 1 to infinity. In practice, however, there are very few studies with large df between and only 1 or 2 df within.

To look up our F of 11.50 in Table 14.4, we put a finger on the intersection of 3 df between conditions and 8 df within conditions. The two values are 4.07 (the F value required for significance at p = .05) and 7.59 (the F value required for significance at p = .01). Because our obtained F is larger than 7.59, we know that the corresponding p must be less than .01. As implied by the extended table on pp. 412–416, the actual p is approximately .003. Performing the same calculations on Results B in Table 14.1, we would find F to be 1.28 (again with 3 and 8 degrees of freedom). Looking up this value in Table B.3, we find it to be too small to be significant at even the .20 level: The actual p is approximately .35.

What do the more precise p values tell us? The p value of .003 for Results A implies that we would obtain an F of 11.50 or larger (for numerator df = 3 and denominator df = 8) only 3 in 1,000 times if we repeatedly conducted this study under the same conditions and if there really were no overall differences between the four groups (i.e., if the null hypothesis were true). The p value of .35 for Results B implies that we would obtain an F of 1.28 with 3 and 8 df once every 3 times if we conducted the study under *these* conditions over and over, and if the null hypothesis were true. In reporting the p value, there is no need to state that it is one-tailed, because this fact is implicit in F (see also Box 14.3).

Simple Effects and Effect Sizes After an Omnibus F

For the basic data in Table 14.2, knowing that the four groups differ significantly does not tell us whether milk helps in and of itself and whether vitamins help in and of themselves. To address these questions, we need to compare (a) the results

Table 14.4 *F* Values Required for Significance at the .05 (Upper Entry) and .01 Levels

Degrees of freedom within conditions (denominator)	Degrees of freedom between conditions (numerator)						Expected value of *F* when H_0 true
	1	2	3	4	6	∞	
1	161	200	216	225	234	254	—
	4052	4999	5403	5625	5859	6366	
2	18.5	19.0	19.2	19.3	19.3	19.5	—
	98.5	99.0	99.2	99.3	99.3	99.5	
3	10.1	9.55	9.28	9.12	8.94	8.53	
	34.1	30.8	29.5	28.7	27.9	26.1	3.00
4	7.71	6.94	6.59	6.39	6.16	5.63	
	21.2	18.0	16.7	16.0	15.2	13.5	2.00
5	6.61	5.79	5.41	5.19	4.95	4.36	
	16.3	13.3	12.1	11.4	10.7	9.02	1.67
6	5.99	5.14	4.76	4.53	4.28	3.67	
	13.7	10.9	9.78	9.15	8.47	6.88	1.50
8	5.32	4.46	4.07	3.84	3.58	2.93	
	11.3	8.65	7.59	7.01	6.37	4.86	1.33
10	4.96	4.10	3.71	3.48	3.22	2.54	
	10.0	7.56	6.55	5.99	5.39	3.91	1.25
15	4.54	3.68	3.29	3.06	2.79	2.07	
	8.68	6.36	5.42	4.89	4.32	2.87	1.15
20	4.35	3.49	3.10	2.87	2.60	1.84	
	8.10	5.85	4.94	4.43	3.87	2.42	1.11
25	4.24	3.38	2.99	2.76	2.49	1.71	
	7.77	5.57	4.68	4.18	3.63	2.17	1.09
30	4.17	3.32	2.92	2.69	2.42	1.62	
	7.56	5.39	4.51	4.02	3.47	2.01	1.07
40	4.08	3.23	2.84	2.61	2.34	1.51	
	7.31	5.18	4.31	3.83	3.29	1.80	1.05
∞	3.84	2.99	2.60	2.37	2.09	1.00	
	6.64	4.60	3.78	3.32	2.80	1.00	1.00

Note: For a more complete table see Appendix B, Table B.3.

in Group 2 with the results in Group 1 (the zero control) and (b) the results in Group 3 with the zero control. These comparisons are called **tests of simple effects**, and an easy way to do them is by *t* tests. Using the formula for comparing independent means given in the previous chapter, we continue to define s^2 as the pooled value (as described in the previous chapter), although we can now find this value simply from our ANOVA because it is the denominator of our *F* ratio.

To illustrate the test of simple effects using the results in Table 14.2, we substitute the values of Groups 1 and 3 in the general formula for the *t* test:

BOX 14.3 Using *t* to Boost Power

The *F* tests we have looked at so far are all omnibus tests, and we cannot take the square root of an omnibus *F* and get *t*. But taking the square root of a focused *F* (i.e., *F* with numerator df = 1) gives us *t*, and we can then compute and interpret the effect size in the usual way. An interesting characteristic of *F* distributions is that the *p* values, although naturally one-tailed, translate into two-tailed *p* values in *t* curves. Suppose you had a focused *F* and found *p* = .06 in the predicted direction. If you plan to report *t*, you have the option of reporting *p* = .03 one-tailed (because you predicted the direction) or *p* = .06 two-tailed (if you choose a more conservative *p*), but you do not have this option with *F*. There is, of course, not much difference between *p* = .06 and *p* = .03, except that they fall on either side of the coveted *p* = .05.

$$t = \frac{M_3 - M_1}{\sqrt{\left(\frac{1}{n_3} + \frac{1}{n_1}\right)S^2}} = \frac{15 - 10}{\sqrt{\left(\frac{1}{3} + \frac{1}{3}\right)4}} = 3.06,$$

where M_3 is the mean of Group 3; M_1 is the mean of Group 1; n_3 and n_1 are the sample sizes of these groups; and S^2 is the value of the within-conditions *MS* shown in Table 14.3. When we test this *t* for significance, we base our *df* not on $n_3 + n_1 - 2$ (as we did previously), but on *df* equal to the within-conditions *SS* (i.e., 8 *df*) because we are using a pooled estimate of S^2. Referring to Table B.2 (see pp. 410–411), we find the significance of *t* = 3.06 to be less than *p* = .01 but more than *p* = .005 one-tailed. The actual one-tailed *p* is approximately .008 (and the two-tailed *p* = .016, that is, .008 × 2).

Had we planned from the beginning to compute a specific *t* test, we could do so whether our overall *F* was significant or not. That is, we do not have to engage in a kind of "Simon says" game in which we seek "permission" from the *p* value associated with an omnibus test before we examine the effect of interest. However, if we are going to be exploring for large differences that we had not specifically predicted, our *t*-test results are going to be much more interpretable if our overall *F* is significant. The reason is that if we use a lot of *t* tests to go on a "fishing expedition" for significant differences, some of them will turn out to be significant by chance. One procedure that researchers sometimes use to try to avoid an excess of findings of significant *t*s when there are lots of possible *t*s, or the *t* tests were unplanned, is to work with a more conservative level of significance, such as .01 instead of .05, or even .005 or .001 (all listed in Table B.2).

However, we recommend not placing too much emphasis on the significance level and paying more attention to the effect size and its corresponding confidence interval and BESD. To calculate the effect size correlation on our *t*, we use the same formula as before, but we define the degrees of freedom from the groups being compared, that is,

$$r_{\text{effect size}} = \sqrt{\frac{t^2}{t^2 + df}} = \sqrt{\frac{(3.06)^2}{(3.06)^2 + 4}} = .84,$$

where df is based on the fact that there were 3 subjects in Group 3 and 3 subjects in Group 1, and therefore $n_3 + n_1 - 2 = 4$. The confidence interval would be computed as before. In terms of the BESD, this $r_{\text{effect size}}$ of .84 would amount to a difference in success rates of 8% to 92% between nonusers and users of vitamins, respectively (i.e., if half the population used vitamins and half the population showed improved performance).

Two-Way Designs

R. A. Fisher, the British statistician who invented the F test, noticed that it is sometimes possible to rearrange a one-way design to form a two-way design of much greater power to reject certain null hypotheses. We turn now to an analysis of the simplest two-way design, one in which there are two levels of each factor (i.e., a 2 × 2 factorial). An example is essential, and we study again the hypothetical effects of nutrition on academic performance. However, we will slightly change the question we asked earlier about the differences among our four nutritional conditions. Instead we will ask several questions simultaneously:

1. What is the effect on academic performance of the intake of daily milk?
2. What is the effect on academic performance of the intake of daily vitamins?
3. What is the effect on academic performance of both milk and vitamins (i.e., the hot lunch includes both milk and vitamins)?
4. Is the effect of vitamins different when milk is also given from when milk is not given?
5. Is the effect of milk different when vitamins are also given from when vitamins are not given?

We can answer all these questions by using a two-way design of the kind shown in Table 14.5. Notice that this table uses the same scores as those in Table 14.2, which should give you further insight into the two-way factorial by compar-

Table 14.5	Raw Scores of Two-Way Design		
	Milk treatment		
Vitamin treatment	Present	Absent	Row means
Present	17, 19, 21	13, 15, 17	17
Absent	10, 12, 14	8, 10, 12	11
Column means	15.5	12.5	14

Vitamin treatment	Present	Absent	Row means	Row effects
Present	19	15	17	+ 3.0
Absent	12	10	11	−3.0
Column means	15.5	12.5	14	
Column effects	+1.5	−1.5		

Table 14.6 Means and Effects of Results in Table 14.5 — Milk treatment

ing its summary ANOVA with the one-way ANOVA computed previously. Table 14.6 shows the group means of the sets of scores in Table 14.5; Table 14.6 also illustrates how factorial designs allow us to answer more questions than one-way designs. For example, we can learn whether the effect of one of our factors is much the same for each of the two or more conditions of the other factor. As noted earlier, another name for the difference between group means is **simple effects**. Here, a comparison of the differences between the simple effects tells us that there is a two-unit effect (12 − 10 = 2) of milk when no vitamins are given, and that there is a four-unit effect (19 − 15 = 4) of milk when vitamins are given. Similarly, there is a five-unit effect (15 − 10 = 5) of vitamins when no milk is given and a seven-unit effect (19 − 12 = 7) of vitamins when milk is given.

Not only do factorial designs allow us to answer more questions than one-way designs, but having the subjects serve double duty increases the power to reject certain null hypotheses regarding overall effects if the null hypotheses are false. That is, more of the subjects available for the study are able to contribute to the major comparisons (milk versus no milk; vitamins versus no vitamins). In this case, half of all the subjects of the experiment are in the milk conditions instead of the quarter of all subjects that would be in the milk condition in a one-way design. Thus, half the subjects can be compared to the remaining half who received no milk, so that all the subjects of the experiment shed light on the question of the effect of drinking milk. The overall effect (also called a **main effect**) of milk is assessed by a comparison of the milk and no-milk column means (15.5 and 12.5, respectively). At the same time that all subjects are providing information on the milk comparison, they are also providing information on the effect of vitamins. The main effect of vitamins is assessed by a comparison of the vitamin and no-vitamin marginal values in the rows (means of 17 and 11, respectively).

As described next, another advantage of factorial designs is that they allow us to examine **interaction effects** (i.e., assuming they are really of interest to us). They represent the leftover combination of the independent variables after removal of the main effects, and because they are leftover effects, they are called **residuals**. In the 2 × 2 example that we have been discussing, the interaction would be designated as "rows × columns" (stated as "rows by columns") or "vitamins × milk" (stated as "vitamins by milk") to imply this combination. Once you fully understand these ideas, you will have a better sense of when you have actually hypothesized an interaction (in the statistical sense of ANOVA) and when all you are really interested in is the pattern of the cell means and not the residuals (Rosnow & Rosenthal, 1989a, 1991, 1995). (See also Box 14.4.)

BOX 14.4 Cell Means and Residuals

In the past, the idea of residual effects has been a source of confusion even for many researchers, who, when interpreting an interaction, have not examined the residual effects but have confused them with the cell (or condition) means. It is possible, as we illustrated in our discussion of the Solomon design (in Chapter 7), to use a procedure in which we subtract the condition means from one another in order to make the most concise statement about the pretest × treatment interaction. But as we show next, it is also generally true that if you are looking at the cell means, you are not looking at *only* the interaction (Rosnow & Rosenthal, 1989a, 1991, 1995, 1996b).

Effects and the Factorial ANOVA

Earlier, we noted that a general purpose of the analysis of variance is to divide up the variance of all the observations into a number of separate sources of variance. To understand how a two-way ANOVA does its job, we think of the group means (as well as each individual score) as comprising a number of separate statistical elements. In a 2 × 2 design, the group means (and measurements) can be broken into (a) the grand mean, (b) the row effects, (c) the column effects, (d) the interaction effects, and (e) error. We begin by describing how the first four elements (grand mean, row effect, column effect, and interaction effect) are conceptualized in terms of an **additive model** (i.e., a model in which the components sum to the group means.

As noted previously, the **grand mean** (M_G) is the mean of all group means, or $(19 + 15 + 12 + 10)/4 = 14$. As shown in Table 14.6, the **row effect** for each row is the mean of that row minus the grand mean, or

$$\text{Row effect} = M_r - M_G.$$

Thus, the row effects are computed as $17 - 14 = +3.0$ for vitamins present and $11 - 14 = -3.0$ for vitamins absent. The **column effect** of each column is the mean of that column (M_c) minus the grand mean, or

$$\text{Column effect} = M_c - M_G,$$

which gives us $15.5 - 14 = +1.5$ for milk present and $12.5 - 14 = -1.5$ for milk absent. Each set of effects sums to zero when totaled over all conditions, a result that is characteristic of all row, column, and interaction effects.

Not visible in Table 14.6 are the interaction effects (i.e., the residuals, or left-over effects). These effects are what remain after the grand mean, the row effect, and the column effect are subtracted from the group mean. In other words,

$$\text{Interaction effect} = \text{group mean} - \text{grand mean} - \text{row effect} - \text{column effect},$$

so for these data, the interaction effects for the vitamins-plus-milk group (VM), the vitamins-only group (V), the milk-only group (M), and zero control (O) are computed as follows:

	Group mean	−	Grand mean	−	Row effect	−	Column effect	=	Interaction
VM	19	−	14	−	3.0	−	1.5	=	0.5
V	15	−	14	−	3.0	−	(−1.5)	=	(−05)
M	12	−	14	−	(−3.0)	−	1.5	=	(−0.5)
O	10	−	14	−	(−3.0)	−	(−1.5)	=	0.5
Sum	56	−	56	−	0.0	−	0.0	=	0.0

What can we learn about the results of our experiment by studying the above table of effects? The grand mean tells us the general "level" of our measurements and is usually not of great intrinsic interest. The +3 and −3 row effects show us that the groups receiving vitamins (VM and V) did better than those not receiving vitamins (M and O). The +1.5 and −1.5 column effects show us that the groups receiving milk (VM and M) did better than those not receiving milk (V and O). The column of +0.5 and −0.5 interaction effects reveals that the group receiving *both* vitamins and milk (VM) and the group receiving *neither* vitamins nor milk (O) did better than the groups receiving *either* vitamins (V) or milk (M). But although it is slightly better from the viewpoint of the interaction effect alone to receive neither treatment, this statistical advantage in the interaction effect (i.e., 0.5) is more than offset by the statistical disadvantage in the row effect (i.e., −3.0) and the column effect (i.e., −1.5) of receiving neither treatment. (See also Box 14.5.)

BOX 14.5   The Additive Model

We said that the idea of ANOVA is based on an *additive model;* that is, components sum to the group means. You can see this more clearly when you total all four conditions of the two-way table:

	Group mean	=	Grand mean	+	Row effect	+	Column effect	+	Interaction effect
VM	19	=	14	+	3.0	+	1.5	+	0.5
V	15	=	14	+	3.0	+	(−1.5)	+	(−05)
M	12	=	14	+	(−3.0)	+	1.5	+	(−0.5)
O	10	=	14	+	(−3.0)	+	(−1.5)	+	0.5
Sum	56	=	56	+	0.0	+	0.0	+	0.0

The conceptual advantage of the additive structure is that it provides a baseline that allows you to compare row, column, and interaction effects with one another; the statistical advantage is that it makes *F* tests possible.

The Concept of Error

That the mean of each group in a two-way design can be broken down into the grand mean, the row effect, the column effect, and the interaction does not quite tell the whole story—because **error** is omitted. That is, it is not taken into account that the various scores found in each group may be rewritten as a deviation from the mean of that condition. The term *error* takes its name from the idea that the magnitude of these deviations reflects how poorly we have done in predicting individual scores from a knowledge of condition or group membership. A particular score shows a large error if it falls far from the mean of its group but only a small error if it falls close to the mean of its group.

We can now write error as

$$\text{Error} = \text{score} - \text{group mean,}$$

and therefore

$$\text{Score} = \text{group mean} + \text{error,}$$

but

$$\text{Group mean} = \text{grand mean} + \text{row effect} + \text{column effect} + \text{interaction effect,}$$

so

$$\text{Score} = \text{grand mean} + \text{row effect} + \text{column effect} + \text{interaction effect} + \text{error.}$$

Computing the Two-Way ANOVA

Earlier, when we analyzed the results of the present study as a one-way analysis, we computed the total sum of squares as

$$\text{Total } SS = \Sigma \ (X - M_G)^2 = 170,$$

where X is each observation or measurement, and M_G is the mean of all the condition means. We computed the within-conditions SS as

$$\text{Within } SS = \Sigma \ (X - M_k)^2 = 32,$$

where M_k is the mean of the group or condition to which each observation or measurement (X) belongs. For our two-way ANOVA, we may use the same (above) formulas, but we also need to compute the sums of the squares of the rows, the columns, and the interaction.

The sum of squares of the rows is defined as

$$\text{Row } SS = \Sigma \ [nc(M_r - M_G)^2],$$

where n is the number of observations in each condition; c is the number of columns contributing to the computation of M_r (the mean of the rth row); and M_G is again the grand mean. The sum of squares of the columns is defined as

$$\text{Column } SS = \Sigma \ [nr(M_c - M_G)^2],$$

where n is the number of observations in each condition; r is the number of rows contributing to the computation of M_c (the mean of the cth column); and M_G is the grand mean. And finally, the interaction sum of squares is defined as

$$\text{Interaction } SS = \text{total } SS - (\text{row } SS + \text{column } SS + \text{within } SS).$$

With our newfound knowledge about the effects, at the same time that we compute the formulas above we can take apart the individual scores to help us understand better the various terms of the analysis of variance. The ANOVA summary is presented in Table 14.7, and Table 14.8 reminds us where the SS values came from. The only new values in Table 14.8 are those for error, which for each participant is computed as the individual's raw score minus the group mean. Thus, for the VM subject in Table 14.5 who scored 17, we subtract 19 (the mean of this group) to get the error score of -2 in Table 14.8. Beneath each column in Table 14.8 are shown the sums of the listed values (ΣX) and the sums of squares of the listed values (ΣX^2).

In the formula above, the total SS is defined as the sum of the squared deviations between every single score and the grand mean, that is, $(17 - 14)^2 + (19 - 14)^2 + \ldots + (12 - 14)^2 = 170$. Alternatively, we see in Table 14.8 that subtracting the sum of the squared grand means (shown as 2,352) from the sum of the squared scores (shown as 2,522) gives us the same value (i.e., total $SS = 2,522 - 2,352 = 170$). Looking again at Table 14.3, we are reminded that, in the one-way analysis of variance, this total SS is allocated to two sources of variance: a between-conditions and a within-conditions source. In the move from a one-way to a two-way ANOVA, the within-conditions source of variance (i.e., the source attributable to error) remains unchanged (i.e., "Within error" or "Within conditions" $SS = 32$ in Tables 14.3, 14.7, and 14.8). The between-conditions source of variance in the one-way ANOVA (shown in Table 14.3 as 138) is broken down into three components in our two-way ANOVA: a row effect SS, a column effect SS, and an interaction effect SS.

Table 14.8 shows the origin of these values in the individual measurements, and let us also compute them using our formulas. First, we obtain the row effect sum of squares from

$$\text{Row } SS = \Sigma \, [nc(M_r - M_G)^2]$$

$$= [(3)(2)(17 - 14)^2] + [(3)(2)(11 - 14)^2]$$

$$= 108,$$

Table 14.7	Summary Table for Two-Way ANOVA					
Source	SS	df	MS	F	p	$r_{\text{effect size}}$
Vitamins (rows)	108	1	108	27.0	.0008	.88
Milk (columns)	27	1	27	6.75	.03	.68
Interaction	3	1	3	0.75	.41	.29
Within error	32	8	4			

Note: Although the listing of effect sizes for Fs with numerator $df = 1$ is not yet standard, it is a practice strongly recommend by the American Psychological Association's Task Force on Statistical Inference (Wilkinson et al., 1999).

Table 14.8			Table of Effects for Computing ANOVA							
Group	Score	=	Grand mean	+	Row effect	+	Column effect	+	Interaction effect	+	Error
VM	17	=	14	+	3.0	+	1.5	+	0.5	+	(−2)
VM	19	=	14	+	3.0	+	1.5	+	0.5	+	0
VM	21	=	14	+	3.0	+	1.5	+	0.5	+	2
V	13	=	14	+	3.0	+	(−1.5)	+	(−0.5)	+	(−2)
V	15	=	14	+	3.0	+	(−1.5)	+	(−0.5)	+	0
V	17	=	14	+	3.0	+	(−1.5)	+	(−0.5)	+	2
M	10	=	14	+	(−3.0)	+	1.5	+	(−0.5)	+	(−2)
M	12	=	14	+	(−3.0)	+	1.5	+	(−0.5)	+	0
M	14	=	14	+	(−3.0)	+	1.5	+	(−0.5)	+	2
O	8	=	14	+	(−3.0)	+	(−1.5)	+	0.5	+	(−2)
O	10	=	14	+	(−3.0)	+	(−1.5)	+	0.5	+	0
O	12	=	14	+	(−3.0)	+	(−1.5)	+	0.5	+	2
ΣX	168	=	168	+	0	+	0	+	0	+	0
ΣX^2	2,522	=	2,352	+	108	+	27	+	3	+	32

giving us the value shown in the bottom row of Table 14.8.

Next, we obtain the column effect sum of squares from

$$\text{Column } SS = \Sigma[nr(M_c - M_G)^2]$$

$$= [(3)(2)(15.5 - 14)^2] + [(3)(2)(12.5 - 14)^2]$$

$$= 27,$$

again giving the value in Table 14.8.

Finally, we obtain the sum of squares of the interaction from

$$\text{Interaction } SS = \text{total } SS - (\text{row } SS + \text{column } SS + \text{within } SS),$$

which gives us

$$\text{Interaction } SS = 170 - (108 + 27 + 32) = 3$$

and, as anticipated, it is the value shown in Table 14.8.

The logic of computing the degrees of freedom of the two-way ANOVA is the same as that in the one-way analysis, but we must apportion the between-conditions df to the row main effect, the column main effect, and the interaction. The degrees of freedom for rows in Table 14.7 are

$$df \text{ rows} = r - 1,$$

where r is the number of rows (i.e., $2 - 1 = 1$ df). The degrees of freedom for columns are

$$df \text{ columns} = c - 1,$$

where c is the number of columns (i.e., $2 - 1 = 1$). The degrees of freedom for the interaction are

$$df \text{ interaction} = (r - 1)(c - 1),$$

which gives us $(2 - 1)(2 - 1) = 1$ df.

The degrees of freedom for the "Within error" are the same as those in Table 14.3, defined as

$$df \text{ within} = N - k,$$

where N is the total number of observations or measurements and k is the number of groups or conditions (i.e., $12 - 4 = 8$). In other words, this is the number of subjects in each group or condition minus 1 totaled over all groups, or $(3 - 1) + (3 - 1) + (3 - 1) + (3 - 1) = 8$ df within conditions. As a check on the degrees of freedom, we compute the df of the total SS as $N - 1$ (i.e., $12 - 1 = 11$) and find this result to be identical to the sum of the df in Table 14.7 (i.e., $1 + 1 + 1 + 8 = 11$).

As before, we obtain the mean square (MS) values in Table 14.7 by dividing the sums of squares by the corresponding df. For example, we divide 108 by 1 to get 108, and we divide 32 by 8 to get 4 (i.e., the amount of the total variation, measured in SS, attributable to each df). We compute the F ratios by dividing the mean squares for rows, columns, and interaction (the signals) by the mean square within conditions (the noise). Thus, we divide 108 by 4 to get 27.0, and we divide 27 by 4 to get 6.75, and we divide 3 by 4 to get 0.75. Because the effect sizes of F ratios with 1 df in the numerator are readily interpretable, we calculate the effect size of each of these F values by

$$r_{\text{effect size}} = \sqrt{\frac{F}{F + df_{\text{within}}}}.$$

We interpret the results as we would any effect-size correlation, including using the confidence interval and the BESD described in Chapter 11.

Table 14.7 shows precise values of p. The F of 6.75 for the effect of milk could have occurred by chance approximately 3 times in 100, and the F of 27.0 for the effect of vitamins could have occurred by chance far less often, if the null hypothesis were true. By contrast, the F for interaction was so small that it could easily have arisen by chance. However, if the interaction were of interest, we would analyze it as before (i.e., as a comparison between the residuals of the diagonal cells). What we learn from these effect sizes is that both milk and vitamins have a beneficial effect, and that more of the effect is attributable to vitamins than to milk. We can also compute tests of simple effects by using the t procedure described previously.

Contrasts and Correlational Indices

We now describe how to use t and F to make *focused comparisons* (called **contrasts**) of more than two conditions. When using t and F in this way, we use the symbols t_{contrast} and F_{contrast} as a convenient way of differentiating them, but you can refer to them as t and F when you are reporting them in a paper. Contrasts not only address precise predictions but also allow us to compute meaningful effect-size measures when comparing more than two groups.

Table 14.9	Summary ANOVA (Omnibus Fs) for Results A and B in Table 14.1				

Results A:

Source	SS	df	MS	F	p
Between conditions	138	3	46	11.50	.003
Within conditions	32	8	4		

Results B:

Source	SS	df	MS	F	p
Between conditions	138	3	46	1.28	.35
Within conditions	288	8	36		

To illustrate, we refer to the hypothetical data (A and B) that we presented earlier in this chapter (Table 14.1). The overall analysis of variance of each set (A and B) is summarized in Table 14.9. The reason the omnibus F is so much larger for Results A than for Results B is, of course, that the within-conditions variability is much smaller in A than in B. However, saying there was "no difference" between the four groups in Results B would make no sense intuitively, because in Table 14.1 we can clearly see a gradual increment in the scores from Group 1 to Group 4.

Suppose, however, we had hypothesized a linear pattern of regularly increasing means. Because we would get the same omnibus F no matter how the groups were arranged, the omnibus F would be a poor choice to test our hypothesis. A better choice, as we see next, would have been to compute a contrast t or F that was specifically addressed to the predicted linear trend. To do so, we need to state our prediction in simple integers (called **contrast weights**, or **lambda coefficients**, or **λ weights**) that sum to zero (i.e., $\Sigma\lambda = 0$). Since we hypothesized an increasing linear trend in the four groups, we might choose λs of -3, -1, $+1$, $+3$ to represent our prediction. Next, we will compare these weights with the obtained scores using the following formula:

$$t_{contrast} = \frac{\Sigma M\lambda}{\sqrt{MS_{within}\left(\Sigma\frac{\lambda^2}{n}\right)}},$$

where M in the numerator refers to a specific condition mean; MS_{within} in the denominator refers to the within-conditions mean square in Table 14.9; n is the number of observations in the condition; and λ refers to the contrast weight required by our prediction for that condition.

Using this formula with Results A, we find

$$t_{contrast} = \frac{(10)(-3) + (12)(-1) + (15)(+1) + (19)(+3)}{\sqrt{4\left[\frac{(-3)^2}{3} + \frac{(-1)^2}{3} + \frac{(+1)^2}{3} + \frac{(+3)^2}{3}\right]}} = \frac{30}{\sqrt{(4)(6.667)}} = 5.809,$$

which, with 8 *df*, has an associated $p = .0002$ one-tailed. For Results B, applying this same formula yields

$$t_{contrast} = \frac{(10)(-3) + (12)(-1) + (15)(+1) + (19)(+3)}{\sqrt{36\left[\dfrac{(-3)^2}{3} + \dfrac{(-1)^2}{3} + \dfrac{(+1)^2}{3} + \dfrac{(+3)^2}{3}\right]}} = \frac{30}{\sqrt{(36)(6.667)}} = 1.936,$$

which, with 8 *df*, has an associated $p = .044$ one-tailed. The reason that we prefer these results over those in Table 14.9 is that the $t_{contrast}$ addresses the hypothesized linear trend, whereas the omnibus *F*s were not focused on the predicted trend and instead addressed a question that was of little or no interest (i.e., to what extent, quite apart from their particular arrangement, there were overall differences among the groups).

Because squaring these *t*s produces *F*s, we find that $F_{contrast} = (5.809)^2 = 33.74$ for Results A and that $F_{contrast} = (1.936)^2 = 3.75$ for Results B. To obtain the *p* values of these *F*s, we consult Table B.3 with 1 and 8 degrees of freedom. We can also compute these same *F*s from the raw data by first calculating the contrast mean square ($MS_{contrast}$) from

$$MS_{contrast} = \frac{nL^2}{\Sigma\lambda^2},$$

where

$$L = M_1\lambda_1 + M_2\lambda_2 + M_3\lambda_3 + M_4\lambda_4,$$

and then dividing $MS_{contrast}$ by MS_{within}. To illustrate with Results B, we solve for *L* as follows:

$$L = (10)(-3) + (12)(-1) + (15)(+1) + (19)(+3) = 30,$$

and then substitute in the previous equation to find

$$MS_{contrast} = \frac{3 \times 30^2}{(-3)^2 + (-1)^2 + (+1)^2 + (+3)^2} = \frac{2,700}{20} = 135.$$

Our contrast *F*, defined as $MS_{contrast}/MS_{within} = 135/36 = 3.75$, is the same result as before.

Table 14.10 shows the linear contrast sum of squares carved out of the between-conditions sum of squares. That is, since $MS_{contrast}$ has 1 *df* in the numera-

Table 14.10	Linear Contrast Carved Out of Summary ANOVA for Results B in Table 14.1				
Source	SS	df	MS	F	p
Between conditions	138	3	46	1.28	.35
Contrast	135	1	135	3.75	.089
Noncontrast	3	2	1.5	.04	
Within conditions	288	8	36		

tor, it follows that $MS_{contrast} = SS_{contrast}$. New to this table is the noncontrast sum of squares (3), which is simply the remainder after the contrast sum of squares (135) is subtracted from the between-conditions sum of squares (138). The $F_{noncontrast}$ of .04 came from dividing the mean square noncontrast (1.5) by the mean square within (36). Our purpose in generating all this information is to enable us to compute the effect size r for our contrast F from

$$r_{effect\ size} = \sqrt{\frac{F_{contrast}}{F_{contrast} + F_{noncontrast}(df_{noncontrast}) + df_{within}}},$$

with terms defined in Table 14.10. Substituting in this equation for Results B, we find

$$r_{effect\ size} = \sqrt{\frac{3.75}{3.75 + .04(2) + 8}} = \sqrt{\frac{3.75}{11.83}} = .563.$$

The $r_{effect\ size}$ is the correlation between an individual's score on the dependent variable and the contrast weight assigned to the condition to which the individual belongs. There are other correlational indices that are also informative when we want to interpret the meaning of contrasts and are working with more than two groups. You will find a detailed discussion of this approach in Rosenthal, Rosnow, and Rubin's (2000) *Contrasts and Effect Sizes in Behavioral Research* and tutorial introductions in two journal articles (Rosnow & Rosenthal, 1996a; Rosnow, Rosenthal, & Rubin, 2000). There are two more correlational measures that might come in handy.

One is called the **alerting correlation** ($r_{alerting}$) and refers to the correlation between the means and their respective contrast weights. There are inexpensive pocket calculators that allow you to obtain this correlation quickly. Table 14.11 illustrates its calculation in the tabular format of Chapter 11, which in turn illustrated how the product-moment correlation is obtained with the following equation:

$$r_{xy} = \frac{\Sigma z_x z_y}{N},$$

Table 14.11 Alerting Correlation ($r_{alerting}$) Computed from Raw and Standardized Means of Results B in Table 14.1

Groups	Group means Mean	z_1 score	λ weights Lambda	z_2 score	Product of z_1 and z_2 scores
1 (Zero)	10	−1.1795	−3	−1.3416	1.582
2 (Milk)	12	−0.5898	−1	−0.4472	.264
3 (Vitamins)	15	+ 0.2949	+ 1	+ 0.4472	.132
4 (Hot lunch)	19	+ 1.4744	+ 3	+ 1.3416	1.978
Sum (Σ)	56	0	0	0	3.956
Mean (M)	14	0	0	0	.989
SD (σ)	3.3912	1.0	2.2361	1.0	

which tells us to sum the products of the z scores of X and Y and divide by the number of pairs of X and Y scores. Squaring the alerting correlation tells us the proportion of the between-conditions sum of squares (138 in Table 14.10) that can be explained by the particular contrast. If this value approaches 1.0, we can use the following familiar formula to estimate $r_{effect\ size}$ from F:

$$r = \sqrt{\frac{F}{F + df_{within}}},$$

which, in the context of contrast analysis, we refer to more generally as the **contrast correlation** ($r_{contrast}$) rather than (as in our earlier discussion) as the effect size correlation. In two-group designs, however, $r_{contrast} = r_{effect\ size}$, which is why we conveniently called it the "effect size r" when discussing how to use F to compare two groups. In the case of Results B, where $r_{alerting} = .989$, and $r^2_{alerting} = .978$, we find

$$r_{contrast} = \sqrt{\frac{F_{contrast}}{F_{contrast} + df_{within}}} = \sqrt{\frac{3.75}{3.75 + 8}} = .565.$$

Not surprisingly, given the fact that $r^2_{alerting}$ is near 1.0, the contrast correlation is nearly identical to the value of $r_{effect\ size}$ we saw before (i.e., .563).

Intrinsically Repeated Measures

So far in our discussion of statistical tests, whether those tests involved comparing two means (t tests) or more than two groups (F tests), each of our participants, or other units, contributed only a single score, measurement, or observation. However, it often happens in behavioral research that we must measure the participants more than once in order to address the question of interest. We call this **intrinsically repeated measures** research. Suppose, for example, that we wanted to learn the degree to which students' performance on a cognitive task improved over time (i.e., over repeated occasions of measurement). There would be no alternative to measuring the participants repeatedly (i.e., twice, or three times, or more, depending on our specific research question). Our theory might predict, for example, that on a particular cognitive task, students would improve by an equal amount each time they performed the task over four measurement occasions, say, 1 month apart. Table 14.12 shows the results of such a study of three students, and Table 14.13 shows the resulting analysis of variance.

Table 14.12	Cognitive Performance Measured on Four Occasions				
	Occasion of measurement				
Student	First	Second	Third	Fourth	Mean
1	1	3	7	5	4.0
2	0	6	2	4	3.0
3	2	4	6	8	5.0
Mean	1.00	4.33	5.00	5.67	4.0

Table 14.13   Analysis of Variance of Data of Table 14.12

Source	SS	df	MS	$F_{(3,6)}$	p
Between subjects	8.00	2	4.00	—	
Within subjects	60.00	9			
Occasions	38.67	3	12.89	3.62	.08
Occasions × subjects	21.33	6	3.56		

As in any two-way analysis of variance, Table 14.13 shows a row effect (subjects in this example), a column effect (occasions in this example), and an interaction effect (an occasions × subjects interaction in this example). The mean square (*MS*) for subjects tells us how far apart the 3 subjects' means are on average. The mean square for occasions tells us how far apart the four occasions' means are on average. The occasions × subjects interaction mean square tells us how different the subjects effects are on different occasions, or, equivalently, how different the occasions effects are for different subjects. We can think of that as the heterogeneity of the patterns or profiles of four scores among the three subjects. If all 3 subjects showed identical patterns or profiles over the four occasions of measurement, the interaction *MS* would equal zero.

Figure 14.1 shows that the three patterns or profiles are not identical though they do show some similarities. If they were identical, all three profiles would be completely parallel to one another over the four occasions of measurement. Figure 14.2 shows how the three profiles might look if there were no interaction at all.

Although the three profiles of Figure 14.1 are certainly different from one another, they do have in common that for all three, their second, third, and fourth performance scores are all higher than their first score. That fact is consistent with our prediction that performance would improve with each successive measure-

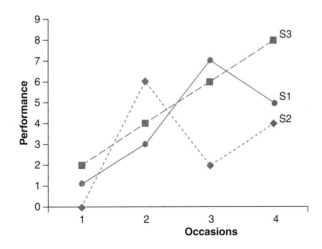

Figure 14.1   Profiles of three subjects' performance measured on four occasions.

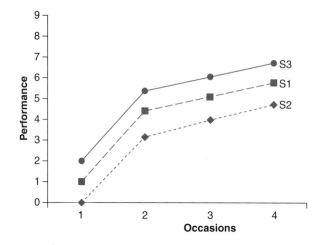

Figure 14.2   **Profiles of three subjects' performance showing zero interaction.**

ment, but it is not quite the same as our prediction. Our prediction had been that students would improve by an equal amount on each occasion of measurement. Using what we have learned about contrasts, we can create a contrast score for each subject. This contrast score, or L score, tells us the degree to which that particular subject behaved in accordance with our prediction. These L scores are simply the sum of the products of the contrast weights, or lambda (λ) weights or coefficients, multiplied by the subject's actual performance, or

$$L = \Sigma Y\lambda = Y_1\lambda_1 + Y_2\lambda_2 + \ldots + Y_k\lambda_k.$$

We form our contrast weights or λs for our occasions of measurement by writing down the value we predict and then subtracting the mean of the four predictions from each individual prediction in order to meet the requirement that, for any contrast, the sum of the λ weights must equal zero.

Suppose our prediction were that, over four occasions, subjects' scores would go from 1 to 3 to 5 to 7. The mean of these four predicted values is 4, which we subtract from each of our four predicted values, yielding weights of -3, -1, $+1$, $+3$. Then, for Subject 1 the L score would be:

$$L = \Sigma Y\lambda = 1(-3) + 3(-1) + 7(+1) + 5(+3) = 16.$$

The analogous L scores for Subjects 2 and 3 are 8 and 20, respectively. We can now compute a one-sample t test on these three L scores using the formula:

$$t_{(df)} = \frac{M_L}{\sqrt{\left(\dfrac{1}{N}\right)S_L^2}},$$

where M_L is the mean of the L scores, N is the number of subjects, S_L^2 is the variance of the L scores, and df refers to the degrees of freedom for the t test, usually $N - 1$. For the data of Table 14.12, then,

$$t_{(2)} = \frac{14.67}{\sqrt{\left(\frac{1}{3}\right)37.33}} = 4.16, p = .027 \text{ one-tailed,}$$

and $r_{\text{contrast}} = \sqrt{\dfrac{t^2}{t^2 + df}} = \sqrt{\dfrac{(4.16)^2}{(4.16)^2 + 2}} = .95.$

There is an alternative to the use of L scores in repeated measures analyses as long as there are at least three occasions of measurement; we can use rs instead. These rs are simply the correlations of the repeated measures with their associated λ weights. Thus, for Subject 1:

Occasion	1	2	3	4
Score (Y)	1	3	7	5
λ	-3	-1	$+1$	$+3$

The correlation of scores with their associated λ s over the 4 occasions is .80. The analogous correlations for Subjects 2 and 3 are .40 and 1.00, respectively. We can now compute a one-sample t test on these three rs as follows:

$$t_{(df)} = \frac{\bar{r}}{\sqrt{\left(\frac{1}{N}\right)S_r^2}},$$

where $\bar{r}$ is the mean of the rs, N is the number of subjects, S_r^2 is the variance of the rs, and df refers to the degrees of freedom for the t test, usually $N - 1$. For the data of Table 14.12, then,

$$t_{(2)} = \frac{.73}{\sqrt{\left(\frac{1}{3}\right).0933}} = 4.14, p = .027 \text{ one-tailed,}$$

and $r_{\text{contrast}} = \sqrt{\dfrac{t^2}{t^2 + df}} = \sqrt{\dfrac{(4.14)^2}{(4.14)^2 + 2}} = .95.$

In this example, the values of t, p, and $r_{\text{effect size}}$ were the same for the L scores and the rs, but it is possible for these values to differ strikingly for L scores versus rs.

Nonintrinsically Repeated Measures

In the repeated measures research we have considered so far, the research question itself *required* that each subject be measured two or more times (i.e., the research was *intrinsically* repeated measures). We turn now to another very common use of repeated measures designs in which it is *not required* in principle that we use a repeated measures design, but the efficiency, precision, and statistical power of the study are increased when several treatments are administered to each of the subjects or other sampling units. We call this **nonintrinsically repeated measures** research.

Consider the following example. We want to compare the effectiveness of four treatment conditions for a rare disorder: a new treatment, the established or standard treatment, a placebo control, and a no-treatment or zero control. But suppose we had available only four patients with the rare disorder. We could randomly assign one patient to each treatment condition, but there is little we could learn from that approach. We would never know whether differences in treatment outcome were due to differences in the four conditions of treatment or simply due to individual differences among the four patients. Treatment conditions would be entirely confounded with individual differences among patients.

Perhaps we could administer all four treatments to all four patients as shown in Table 14.14. All four patients would begin by having no treatment—say, for 1 month—followed by a month of placebo treatment, followed by a month of the standard treatment, followed by a month of the new treatment. That kind of repeated measures design would give us 16 observations, 4 per treatment, instead of just one per treatment, but our results would still be confounded. This time the order of presentation (first vs. second vs. third vs. fourth) would be completely confounded with treatment. We would never be able to disentangle the effects, for example, of being fourth-administered from the effects of the new treatment condition.

There is something we can do to unconfound order effects from treatment effects; we can counterbalance our design by the use of the Latin square described in Chapter 7. Table 14.15 shows the Latin square rearrangement of the conditions shown in Table 14.14. Our four treatments, labeled A, B, C, and D, are all administered to each of our four patients, but each patient is given a different sequence of

Table 14.14	Four Treatments Administered to Each of Four Patients			
	Treatment occasion			
	1	2	3	4
Patient	None	Placebo	Old	New
A				
B				
C				
D				

Note: Treatment condition and order of administration are completely confounded.

Table 14.15	Latin Square Design for the Conditions of Table 14.14			
	Order of administration			
	1	2	3	4
Sequence 1	A	B	C	D
Sequence 2	B	C	D	A
Sequence 3	C	D	A	B
Sequence 4	D	A	B	C

the four treatments. The sequences are arranged so that each treatment occurs once in each row (sequence), and once in each column (order). This arrangement allows us to learn of differences among the four treatments, differences among the four orders of presentation, and differences among the four sequences or subjects. In this design, sequences and subjects are confounded, but since we are rarely interested in either sequence or subject effects, this confounding poses no great problem.

Table 14.16 shows the results of a study of the type we have been discussing and Table 14.17 shows the results of an analysis of variance of these data. We will not describe the details of this analysis here, but they are readily available elsewhere (e.g., Rosenthal & Rosnow, 1991). Here it is enough to note that there is a substantial F for both the order effect and the treatment effect, but we also note that both Fs are omnibus tests, telling us little about what we really want to know about the treatment effect or the order effect. The most efficient way to investigate our treatment effects is by way of the L scores described in the preceding section of this chapter. For each of our patients we compute the appropriate L score. For example, if our prediction had been that placebo would be a lot better than no treatment at all, and that the old treatment was somewhat better than placebo, and that the new treatment was somewhat better than the old treatment, we might have predicted relative outcome scores of 2, 5, 6, and 7, for no treatment, placebo, old treatment, and new treatment, respectively. The mean of these predicted scores is

Table 14.16	Data Obtained for the Latin Square of Table 14.15				
	Order of administration				
	1	2	3	4	Σ
Sequence 1	2	7	10	7	26
Sequence 2	4	8	10	5	27
Sequence 3	6	9	5	8	28
Sequence 4	9	4	8	10	31
Σ	21	28	33	30	112

Treatment sums (each based on 4 scores)

A	B	C	D
16	27	34	35

Table 14.17	Analysis of Variance of the Data of Table 14.16				
Source	SS	df	MS	$F_{(3,6)}$	p
Sequences	3.50	3	1.17	—	
Orders	19.50	3	6.50	4.11	.066
(Sequences × orders)	(67.00)	(9)	(7.44)		
Treatments	57.50	3	19.17	12.13	.0059
Residual (S × O)	9.50	6	1.58		

5, a value we subtract from each prediction to ensure that our contrast weights (λs) will sum to zero.

In this example, then, our contrast weights are −3, 0, +1, +2, respectively. Subject 1 (who is listed as Sequence 1 in Table 14.16) has an L score of 18, computed as

$$L = \Sigma Y\lambda = 2(-3) + 7(0) + 10(+1) + 7(+2) = 18.$$

Subjects 2, 3, and 4 have L scores of 13, 9, and 16, respectively. The t test examining our prediction yields

$$t_{(3)} = \frac{M_L}{\sqrt{\left(\frac{1}{N}\right)S_L^2}} = \frac{14}{\sqrt{\left(\frac{1}{4}\right)15.33}} = 7.15, p = .0028 \text{ one-tailed,}$$

$$\text{and } r_{contrast} = \sqrt{\frac{t^2}{t^2 + df}} = \sqrt{\frac{(7.15)^2}{(7.15)^2 + 3}} = .97,$$

a huge (and highly significant) effect size.

We could, of course, compute L scores for somewhat different predictions or hypotheses. For example, if our prediction had been simply that our two treatment conditions (old and new) would do better than our two control conditions (no treatment and placebo), we might have used contrast weights of +1, +1, −1, −1, respectively, for those four conditions. Had we examined that prediction we would have found L scores of 8, 9, 2, and 7 for Patients 1, 2, 3, and 4, respectively, yielding $t_{(3)} = 4.18$, $p = .012$, and $r_{contrast} = .92$. Had we wanted to investigate the order effect, we could have done so in analogous fashion. For example, had we hypothesized that patients would tend to get better over time, we might have predicted a linear trend with contrast weights of −3, −1, +1, +3. Had we used these weights to investigate order effects, we would have found $t_{(3)} = 2.29$, $p = .053$, $r_{contrast} = .80$. We leave it to our readers to verify that these values are correct!

Summary of Ideas

1. The F test used in a between-conditions ANOVA is a ratio of the spread of mean scores around the grand mean (the signal) to the spread of scores within each condition (the noise).

2. For the special case of the comparison of two groups, $F = t^2$, and in that particular case, we can calculate the effect size correlation for F as

$$r_{\text{effect size}} = \sqrt{\frac{F}{F + df_{\text{within}}}}.$$

3. F tests with numerator $df = 1$ and all t tests are characterized as *focused tests*, whereas F tests with numerator $df > 1$ are called *omnibus tests*.

4. When computing t tests on simple effects after the omnibus F, we define S^2 in the t formula as the MS within (i.e., the pooled error term) in the ANOVA summary table.

5. When computing effect size rs on simple effects after computing the omnibus F, we define df in the $r_{\text{effect size}}$ formula by the size of the groups being compared (i.e., $df = n_1 + n_2 - 2$).

6. In factorial designs, because two or more levels of each factor (independent variable) are administered in combination with two or more levels of every other factor, such factorial designs generally use sampling units more efficiently and address more questions than do ordinary one-way ANOVAs.

7. The error of individual scores (i.e., the deviation of each score from the mean of the group) represents the extent to which the score can be predicted from a knowledge of group membership.

8. The summary table for the factorial ANOVA differs from the summary table for the one-way ANOVA in reflecting the subdivision of the between-conditions SS into main and interaction SS.

9. The additive model is based on the idea that each group mean is the sum of the grand mean, the row effect, the column effect, and the interaction effect. The model thus provides a baseline that allows us to compare these effects with one another.

10. Interaction effects in 2×2 ANOVAs are the effects left over *(residuals)* after the row and column effects are removed from the group means, and removing the grand mean will reveal the pure residuals.

11. Contrast t and F tests are focused procedures that compare *(contrast)* an obtained pattern of means with a predicted pattern expressed in the form of lambda (λ) weights that sum to zero.

12. The alerting r is the correlation between the means and their respective λ weights; the contrast r is the (partial) correlation between the scores on the dependent variable and their respective λ weights with noncontrast sources of variation removed.

13. In two-sample comparisons, the contrast r is equivalent to the effect size r (i.e., the correlation between the scores on the dependent variable and their respective λ weights), but in cases where $k > 2$, the contrast r is usually larger than the effect size r.

14. Squaring the alerting r reveals the proportion of the between-conditions sum of squares that is accounted for by the particular contrast weights (λs). If this value approaches 1.0, we can use the formula in (2) above to estimate $r_{\text{effect size}}$ from F.

15. In intrinsically repeated measures research, we *must* measure the participants more than once in order to address the question of interest. In nonintrinsically repeated measures research, it is *not essential* that we use a repeated measured design, but such a design increases efficiency, precision, and statistical power.

Key Terms

additive model   p. 347
alerting correlation (r_{alerting})
   p. 355

analysis of variance (ANOVA)
   p. 334
column effects   p. 347

contrast correlation (r_{contrast})
   p. 356
contrasts   p. 352

WEB ACTIVITY

Manipulate a data set to see how sums of squares are partitioned in ANOVA by visiting the Rice University Virtual Lab in Statistics at http://www.ruf.rice.edu/~lane/stat_sim/index.html and then clicking on the "ANOVA" radio button.

Multiple-Choice Questions for Review

1. When comparing only two groups, F = (a) t; (b) $2t$; (c) t^2; (d) $t/2$.

2. A "one-way ANOVA" has only one (a) degree of freedom; (b) between-group SS; (c) variance; (d) treatment condition.

3. S^2 is also called (a) sum of squares; (b) σ^2; (c) F ratio; (d) mean square.

4. Total SS = ___ SS + ___ SS. (a) experimental, control; (b) dependent, independent; (c) between, within; (d) all of the above

5. In a two-way factorial, the between SS = (a) main effects SS; (b) main effects SS + interaction SS; (c) main effects SS + interaction SS + error SS; (d) none of the above.

6. A student at the University of Tennessee conducts an experiment with three groups. Each group contains 4 subjects. How many between-conditions degrees of freedom will there be? (a) 2; (b) 3; (c) 4; (d) 11

7. In the study above, what are the total degrees of freedom? (a) 2; (b) 3; (c) 4; (d) 11

8. A student at Southern Illinois University conducts a study with two groups and five subjects in each group. She calculates that F = 5. According to Table 14.4, what is the appropriate p value? (a) $p > .05$; (b) $p < .05$; (c) $p < .01$; (d) cannot be determined

9. A student at the University of Arizona conducts an experiment with four groups. He calculates an F test to examine the overall differences between the groups. He then computes t tests to compare each group to each of the others. These t tests are said to be tests of (a) within-subjects effects; (b) main effects; (c) repeated measures effects; (d) simple effects.

10. Both F with numerator df = 1 and any t test are (a) focused tests; (b) unfocused tests; (c) omnibus tests; (d) diffuse tests.

Discussion Questions for Review

1. From a population of 50 male professional runners, an Ohio State researcher randomly assigns 10 to each of five groups. Each group receives a different brand of running shoe. The brands are coded A, B, C, D, E. Each member of a group receives a new pair of the top-of-the-line shoe made

by the shoe company and then rates the shoe for comfort. Below are the mean comfort ratings (on a scale from 1 to 20) given to the different brands:

Brand	Rating
A	19
B	13
C	17
D	9
E	10

Suppose the researcher performs an analysis of variance, and the within-shoe-brands mean square is 94, whereas the mean square for between-shoe-brands is 188. What is the value of the omnibus F testing the significance of the overall difference among the shoe brands? What are the associated degrees of freedom?

2. A University of Pittsburgh researcher has the following two sets of data, each of which contains three independent groups. The 12 subjects in each set were randomly assigned to the groups; 4 subjects were assigned to each group. The numbers are scores on some dependent measure.

Set A:

	Group 1	Group 2	Group 3
	2	5	11
	3	5	10
	2	4	9
	1	6	10
Mean	2	5	10

Set B:

	Group 1	Group 2	Group 3
	9	11	23
	−6	−10	10
	4	0	−2
	1	19	9
Mean	2	5	10

Which set of data is likely to yield a larger F ratio in an analysis of variance? How can you be sure?

3. A University of Colorado student obtains the following set of means in a study that measures the benefits of vacations in rural versus urban areas for participants who live in rural or urban areas. Higher numbers indicate greater benefits. Figure out the row effects, the column effects, and the interaction residuals, and then decide how they should be interpreted.

	Urban subjects	Rural subjects
Urban vacations	5	3
Rural vacations	11	1

4. A University of Maine student obtains the data shown in Table 14.2 and computes the ANOVA shown in Table 14.3. His primary interest, however, is in whether the hot lunch group performed significantly better than did the average of the remaining three groups. How would you advise him to address his question?

5. A McGill University student who computed a contrast F is advised by her instructor to look at the alerting r before estimating the effect size r from $\sqrt{(F)/(F + df)}$. Why?

6. A University of Maryland-Baltimore County student who used a repeated measures design in his research is advised by his instructor to compute a contrast using L scores. What are they, and how can the student form a set of lambda weights?

Answers to Review Questions

Multiple-Choice Questions

1. c	**3.** d	**5.** b	**7.** d	**9.** d
2. b	**4.** c	**6.** a	**8.** a	**10.** a

Discussion Questions

1. An appropriate table of variance for this study is:

Source	SS	df	MS	F	p
Between brands	752	4	188	2.0	.11
Within brands	4,230	45	94		

The researcher finds F from MS between divided by MS within, and finds df from $k - 1$ for numerator df and $N - k$ for denominator df. The researcher does not report $r_{effect\ size}$ because this is an omnibus F test (i.e., one with numerator $df > 1$).

2. Set A would yield a larger F because its within-condition variability is much smaller than that of Set B. Because the means of Sets A and B are equal, the MS-between results for Sets A and B are equal. Therefore, the results with the smaller MS within will yield the larger F.

3. The following table shows the means, row effects, and column effects (as in Table 14.6):

Type of vacation	Type of subjects Urban (US)	Rural (RS)	Row means	Row effects
Urban (UV)	5	3	4	−1
Rural (RV)	11	1	6	+ 1
Column means	8	2	5	
Column effects	+3	−3		

The interaction effects for each of the four conditions are computed from:

	Group mean	−	Grand mean	−	Row effect	−	Column effect	=	Interaction effect
UV,US	5	−	5	−	(−1)	−	3	=	(−2)
UV,RS	3	−	5	−	(−1)	−	(−3)	=	2
RV,US	11	−	5	−	1	−	3	=	2
RV,RS	1	−	5	−	1	−	(−3)	=	(−2)
Sum	20	−	20	−	0.0	−	0.0	=	0.0

If we disregard matters of statistical significance, these results show that the type of subjects made the largest difference, the type of vacation made the smallest difference, and the interaction made an intermediate amount of difference. The urban subjects benefited more than the rural subjects, the rural vacations were associated with greater benefits than were the urban vacations, and the interaction showed greater benefits for those vacationing in the setting in which they did *not* reside.

4. A *t* test following the *F* would address the question appropriately. The two means to be compared would be the hot lunch mean and the mean of the means of the remaining three groups, that is, $(10 + 12 + 15)/3 = 12.33$. The two required sample sizes, n_1 and n_2, would be the *n* for the hot lunch (i.e., 3) and the *n* for the children in the remaining three groups (i.e., $3 + 3 + 3 = 9$). As in the case of most *t* tests computed after the ANOVA, the S^2 used in computing *t* is the S^2 obtained from the ANOVA, the *MS* within. Thus

$$t = \frac{19 - 12.33}{\sqrt{\left(\frac{1}{3} + \frac{1}{9}\right)4}} = 5.00,$$

and with $df = 8$, $p = .0005$. Whenever we compute *t*, or *F* with 1 *df* in the numerator, we want to know the effect size. So we compute the effect size correlation from

$$r_{\text{effect size}} = \sqrt{\frac{t^2}{t^2 + df}} = \sqrt{\frac{(5.0)^2}{(5.0)^2 + 8}} = .87,$$

which is a jumbo-sized effect. An alternative way to address this question is by means of t_{contrast}, which in this case would involve contrast weights (λs) of $+3, -1, -1, -1$, reflecting our prediction that the hot lunch would be higher than the other three means, which in turn would not differ from each other. As we would expect, the value of t_{contrast} is identical to our sample *t* value of 5.00, that is,

$$t_{\text{contrast}} = \frac{\Sigma M\lambda}{\sqrt{MS_{\text{within}}\left(\Sigma \frac{\lambda^2}{n}\right)}} = \frac{19(+3) + 10(-1) + 12(-1) + 15(-1)}{\sqrt{4\left[\frac{(3)^2}{3} + \frac{(-1)^2}{3} + \frac{(-1)^2}{3} + \frac{(-1)^2}{3}\right]}} = \frac{20}{\sqrt{16}} = 5.00.$$

5. In the context of contrast analysis, the formula she wanted to use to estimate the effect size *r* from her contrast *F* is referred to more generally as the contrast *r* rather than the effect size *r*. However, it can be used to estimate the effect size *r* if the squared alerting *r* approaches 1, as it would imply that there is very little noncontrast variation to be concerned about.

6. *L* scores are the contrast scores for each subject in a repeated measures contrast and are defined as the sum of the products of the contrast weights (the λs) multiplied by the subject's performance scores (the *Y* scores). A convenient way to form a set of λs is to write down your prediction in integers and then to subtract the mean from each integer. For example, if the student had predicted that scores would go from 3 to 9 and then back to 3, he would subtract the mean of 5 from each predicted value, yielding λs of $-2, +4, -2$. Though this step is not required, the student could simplify the computations a little by dividing the contrast weights by 2 to yield the simpler weights of $-1, +2, -1$.

CHAPTER 15

The Analysis
of Frequency Tables

Preview Questions

- What is the purpose of chi-square (χ^2), and how is it computed?
- What is the relationship between χ^2 and the phi (ϕ) coefficient?
- How is an effect size r estimated directly from a 1-df χ^2?
- How are χ^2 tables larger than 1 df interpreted?
- What is the purpose of "standardizing the margins"?

 ## Chi-Square and Tables of Counts

To review, in our discussion of the correlation coefficient (Chapter 11), we said that it could be viewed quite directly as a measure of the degree of relationship between two variables. As noted in Chapter 12, when the number of pairs of scores on which r is computed is small, a very large r (i.e., a substantial effect) may not differ significantly from chance. In that case, although there is a strong relationship between the two variables, effect sizes that substantial occur quite often by chance even if the true correlation is zero. For this reason, we would like to know for any effect size r not only its magnitude but also its confidence interval.

On the one hand, r tells us immediately how "big" a relationship there is between variables, but not how unlikely it is to have occurred by chance. On the other hand, t and F tell us immediately (i.e., with the help of some tables or a computer program or a scientific calculator) how unlikely it is that a given relationship has occurred by chance, but not how "big" the effect is. However, by taking a simple additional step, described in Chapters 13 and 14, we can compute the size of the relationship that a large t or F has convinced us is unlikely to have occurred by chance. Thus, r gives us the size of the relationship and permits us a further assessment of statistical significance, whereas t and F give us statistical significance and permit us a further assessment of the size of the relationship.

The statistic we discuss in this final chapter is the **chi-square**, symbolized as χ^2 and pronounced "ki (rhymes with eye) square." Invented in 1900 by Karl Pearson (who also invented the product-moment r), it is a statistic that, like t and F, tells us (with the aid of a table, computer program, or scientific calculator) how unlikely it is that the relationship investigated has occurred by chance. Also like t and F, chi-square does not tell us immediately about the strength of the relationship between the variables (see also Box 15.1). Just as in the case of t and F, any given value of χ^2 is associated with a stronger degree of relationship when it is based on a smaller number of units or observations. In other words, a relationship must be quite strong to result in a large χ^2 (or t or F) with only a small number of research participants.

We compute χ^2 for tables of independent frequencies (also called **counts**), and therefore χ^2 can be thought of as a comparison of counts. It does its job of testing the relationship between two variables by assessing the discrepancy between the theoretically **expected frequency** (f_e) and the obtained or **observed frequency** (f_o). In other words, it differs from the other significance tests we have examined in that it can be used for dependent variables that are not scored or scaled. In all the earlier examples of t and F, participants' responses were recorded as scores in such a way that some could be regarded as so many units greater or less than other scores. Because chi-square is a comparison of counts, it allows us to deal with categories of response that are not easily scaled, ordered, or scored.

One other important point is that chi-square, like F, can be a focused or an omnibus test. You will recall that all t tests are focused tests, whereas F tests with numerator $df = 1$ are focused and F tests with numerator $df > 1$ are omnibus tests. Chi-squares with 1 df are also focused tests, whereas those with $df > 1$ are omnibus tests. As effect sizes of focused tests are very clearly interpretable and effect sizes of omnibus tests are not, we will explain not only how to compute the

BOX 15.1 Fisher as Detective

In the 19th century, Gregor Mendel, the legendary Austrian botanist, performed experiments that became the basis of the modern science of genetics. Working with garden peas, he showed that their characteristics could be predicted from the characteristics of their "parents." In a famous piece of scientific detective work, Ronald A. Fisher (the inventor of the F test and the null hypothesis) later used the chi-square to ask whether Mendel's data may have been manipulated so that they would seem to be more in line with his theory. Fisher used the chi-square as a "goodness-of-fit" test of Mendel's reported findings compared with statistically expected values, and he found Mendel's data *too perfect* to be plausible. Fisher concluded that Mendel had been deceived by a research assistant, who knew what Mendel wanted to find and who manipulated the data *too* well.

effect size r for a 1-df χ^2, but also strategies for interpreting χ^2 tables of counts when the $df > 1$.

Computing 1-df Chi-Squares

Imagine we wanted to study the food preferences of students who belong to two eating clubs, the Junk Food Junkies (JFJ) and the Green Earthies (GE). We give each student a menu with a choice of one of two meals: a juicy grilled hamburger with onions, pickles, relish, and barbecue sauce on a sesame seed bun (called a Big Jack) or a grilled soyburger with lettuce and tomato on whole wheat bread. Table 15.1 provides the basic data for computing a simple chi-square, a 2 × 2 table. Membership in the clubs is thought of as the independent variable; each club member falls into one and only one of the four possible cells. In Section A, the "observed frequencies" are the number of students in that column (JFJ vs. GE eating club) who chose the alternative listed in that row. Suppose we had hypothesized that Junk Food Junkies will tend to prefer a Big Jack and that Green Earthies will tend to prefer a grilled soyburger. As this table shows, of the members of the Junk Food Junkies, 24 chose a Big Jack, and 12 chose the soyburger, and of the members of the Green Earthies, 13 chose a Big Jack, and 30 chose the soyburger.

The following general formula summarizes the steps we will take in applying chi-square to these data:

$$\chi^2 = \sum \frac{(f_o - f_e)^2}{f_e},$$

Table 15.1 Basic Data for 2 × 2 Chi-Square

A. Observed frequencies (f_o)

Food choice	JFJ	GE	Row sums
Big Jack	24	13	37
Soyburger	12	30	42
Column sums	36	43	79

B. Expected frequencies (f_e)

Food choice	JFJ	GE	Row sums
Big Jack	16.861	20.139	37.000
Soyburger	19.139	22.861	42.000
Column sums	36.000	43.000	79.000

C. $(f_o - f_e)^2/f_e$ values

Food choice	JFJ	GE	Row sums
Big Jack	3.023	2.531	5.554
Soyburger	2.663	2.229	4.892
Column sums	5.686	4.760	10.446

where f_o is the observed frequency in each cell, and f_e is the expected frequency in that cell. This formula instructs us to sum the squared differences between the observed frequencies (f_o) and the expected frequencies (f_e) after first dividing each squared difference by the expected frequency. If the null hypothesis of no relation between the rows and columns is true, we expect the f_o and f_e values to be similar in magnitude. In other words, observed frequencies that are substantially larger and smaller than the expected frequencies are needed to cast doubt on the null hypothesis, because the value of chi-square will be small when the difference $f_o - f_e$ is small.

To use this formula, we must first determine for each of the observed frequencies the number of "expected" entries, that is, the number that would be expected if the null hypothesis of no relationship between the independent and dependent variables were true. To compute this expected frequency (f_e) for each cell, we multiply the column total by the row total where that row and that column intersect in that cell. We then divide this quantity by the grand total of entries. That is,

$$f_e = \frac{(\text{Column total})(\text{Row total})}{\text{Grand total}}.$$

For example, the upper-left cell in Section A of Table 15.1 is at the intersection of the JFJ column and the Big Jack row. The appropriate totals multiplied together and divided by the grand total are $(36 \times 37)/79 = 16.861$. Section B gives all the expected frequencies computed in this way. These values, row by row, are

$$(36 \times 37)/79 = 16.861$$

$$(43 \times 37)/79 = 20.139$$

$$(36 \times 42)/79 = 19.139$$

$$(43 \times 42)/79 = 22.861$$

As a check on our arithmetic, notice that the row totals, the column totals, and the grand total of all the values in Section B are equal to the corresponding totals of the values in Section A. Substituting in the general formula for chi-square, we add up the $(f_o - f_e)^2/f_e$ values (i.e., for each cell, the square of the difference between the observed and expected frequency divided by the expected frequency), which gives us

$$\chi^2 = \frac{(24 - 16.861)^2}{16.861} + \frac{(13 - 20.139)^2}{20.139} + \frac{(12 - 19.139)^2}{19.139} + \frac{(30 - 22.861)^2}{22.861} = 10.446.$$

The $(f_o - f_e)^2/f_e$ values for each cell also appear in Section C of Table 15.1, which underscores the idea that the total of all these values is the chi-square.

Although the formula we have been using to compute χ^2 will work in any situation, there is actually an easier way to compute it directly from the observed frequencies (f_o) in a 2 × 2 table:

$$\chi^2 = \frac{N(\text{BC} - \text{AD})^2}{(\text{A} + \text{B})(\text{C} + \text{D})(\text{A} + \text{C})(\text{B} + \text{D})}$$

Table 15.2	Cells and Margins of 2 × 2 Table

A	B	(A + B)
C	D	(C + D)

(A + C) (B + D)   (N = A + B + C + D)

where the letters are defined in Table 15.2. For the data in Table 15.1, we find

$$\chi^2 = \frac{79[(13 \times 12) - (24 \times 30)]^2}{(37)(42)(36)(43)} = \frac{79(318,096)}{2,405,592} = 10.446.$$

Finding the p Value, Effect Size, and Confidence Interval

As is true of t and F, there is also a different chi-square curve for every value of the degrees of freedom. The degrees of freedom (df) of chi-square are defined as

$$df = (\text{rows} - 1)(\text{columns} - 1),$$

or the number of rows minus 1 times the number of columns minus 1. The larger the χ^2, the less likely are the observed frequencies to differ from the expected frequencies only by chance. Table 15.3 gives a sample listing of χ^2 values with 1 to 5 degrees of freedom for p = .10, .05, and .01. A more comprehensive listing can be found in Table B.4 (see p. 417). Notice that a chi-square must be larger than the degrees of freedom to throw doubt on the null hypothesis.

In this example, the 1-df chi-square of 10.446 is larger than the largest value shown for df = 1 (6.64 for p = .01); the actual p is approximately .001. Thus, a chi-square value this large or larger would occur 1 time in 1,000 repeated samplings if the null hypothesis were true. That is, there is about 1 chance in 1,000 that a chi-square this large would occur if there really were no relationship between organizational membership and food preference (see also Box 15.2).

We now estimate the effect size, and as these are frequency data in a 2 × 2 table, it should be obvious that we will do so by using the **phi coefficient** (φ). In computing phi, we again use the following general formula that was introduced at the end of Chapter 11:

Table 15.3	Chi-Square Values for Significance at .10, .05, and .01		
df	p = .10	p = .05	p = .01
1	2.71	3.84	6.64
2	4.60	5.99	9.21
3	6.25	7.82	11.34
4	7.78	9.49	13.28
5	9.24	11.07	15.09

BOX 15.2 Chi-Square and the Null Hypothesis

Reminiscent of F, all chi-square curves begin at zero and range upward to infinity. You will recall that the expected value of t is zero when the null hypothesis is true, and the expected value of F is $df/(df - 2)$ where df are for the denominator mean square. For chi-square distributions, the expected value (when the null hypothesis of no relation is true) is equal to the df defining that chi-square distribution, that is, (rows $-$ 1)(columns $-$ 1). Thus, for chi-squares based on 2×2, 2×3, and 2×4 tables, the average value of the χ^2 obtained if the null hypothesis were true would be 1, 2, and 3, respectively. The maximum possible value of χ^2 is the total N.

$$\phi = \frac{BC - AD}{\sqrt{(A + B)(C + D)(A + C)(B + D)}},$$

with the letters defined in Table 15.2. Substituting the data in Section A ("observed frequencies") of Table 15.1, we find

$$\phi = \frac{(13 \times 12) - (24 \times 30)}{\sqrt{(37)(42)(36)(43)}} = \frac{-564}{1,551} = .36.$$

Although we see that the numerator of this phi is negative because of the particular arrangement of the cell counts, we also see that Junk Food Junkiness (scored 1 or 0) is positively correlated with Big Jackness (scored 1 or 0). Because the findings are consistent with our hypothesis, we report the phi as a positive effect size (i.e., $r_{effect\ size} = .36$ is in the predicted direction). We can, if we wish, also transform the $r_{effect\ size}$ into a binomial effect-size display (BESD) with uniform row and column totals.

And finally, we compute a 95% confidence interval around the observed effect using the procedure described in Chapter 12 (although we are not limited to a 95% confidence interval and can choose any level of confidence we feel comfortable with). To review, we first consult Table B.6 (p. 419) to convert our $r_{effect\ size} = .36$ into Fisher $z_r = .377$. Step 2 substitutes the value of $N = 79$ in the expression

$$\left(\frac{1}{\sqrt{N - 3}}\right)1.96 = \left(\frac{1}{\sqrt{79 - 3}}\right)1.96 = .2248.$$

In Step 3, we subtract and add this value to the value in Step 1 to find the lower and upper limits of the Fisher z_r values. The lower limit is $.377 - .2248 = .1522$ (rounded to .15), and the upper limit is $.377 + .2248 = .6018$ (rounded to .60). In the final step, we convert these scores back into the metric of the effect size correlation using Table B.7 (p. 420). We have 95% confidence that the $r_{effect\ size}$ is between .15 and .54. Had the total sample size been larger, or had we decided to work with 90% confidence, the interval would have been narrower.

Phi and Chi-Square

If the sample size (N) is not too small $(N > 20)$, and if the smallest expected frequency is not too small (e.g., less than 3 or so), we can test the significance of phi coefficients by chi-square tests, because

$$\chi^2 = (\phi^2)(N).$$

Having satisfied these assumptions in our present data set, we substitute in this equation and find

$$\chi^2 = (.3636^2)(79) = 10.444,$$

which, not surprisingly, is the same value of chi-square that we obtained before (within rounding error).

Notice that the formula above serves as another example of the conceptual relationship described in Chapter 13, that is,

Significance test = Size of effect $\times$ Size of study,

which reminds us that χ^2 (like t and F) is the product of the effect size and the study size. Hence, the larger the effect or the more sampling units in the chi-square table (i.e., the more participants in the study), the greater will be the value of the χ^2. This relationship underscores the importance of doing a power analysis, and it implies that, as in the case of t and F, a relationship must be very strong (i.e., the effect must be substantial) to result in a large chi-square value with only a small number of participants.

More often, we will compute the χ^2 first and then calculate the $r_{effect\ size}$, and as mentioned previously, we report the effect size only when working with chi-squares with $df = 1$. To find the value of the effect size correlation from any 1-df chi-square, we use the following formula:

$$\phi = \sqrt{\frac{\chi^2}{N}},$$

which is our operational definition of $r_{effect\ size}$ for any chi-square with $df = 1$. In our continuing example, substituting in this formula gives us

$$r_{effect\ size} = \sqrt{\frac{\chi^2}{N}} = \sqrt{\frac{10.446}{79}} = .36,$$

which, of course, is the same value of phi that we calculated previously.

Larger Tables of Counts

When there are many cells in a table of counts, a statistically significant chi-square may be more difficult to interpret than in a 2×2 table. Table 15.4 illustrates this situation in a 2×4 table that we created by the addition of two new groups to

Table 15.4	Obtained Frequencies (f_o) for 2 × 4 Chi-Square				
Food choice	PC	MC	JFJ	GE	Row sums
Big Jack	21	8	24	13	66
Soyburger	14	3	12	30	59
Column sums	35	11	36	43	125

Table 15.1. One new group (designated as PC) consists of 35 members of the Psychology Club, and the other new group consists of 11 members of the Mathematics Club (MC). The hypothesis is that psychology and mathematics students are more like Junk Food Junkies than like Green Earthies in choosing grilled beef over grilled soy.

Table 15.5 shows in Section A the expected frequencies (f_e) computed from the obtained counts in Table 15.4. For example, in Table 15.4 we see that 21 of the 35 students who belong to the Psychology Club chose grilled beef. To obtain the expected frequency shown as 18.480 in Table 15.5, we multiply the appropriate row total (shown as 66 in Table 15.4) by the appropriate column total (35) and then divide the product by the total number of observations (125); the result is $(66 \times 35)/125 = 18.480$. Notice that the row and column sums in Section A of Table 15.5 are identical to the corresponding values in Table 15.4.

The calculation of the chi-square with $df = 3$ is accomplished by the general procedure and formula given earlier:

$$\chi^2 = \sum \frac{(f_o - f_e)^2}{f_e},$$

and the entries in Section B of Table 15.5 show the $(f_o - f_e)^2/f_e$ results used in this procedure. The value of this chi-square, then, is the grand total of these cell data, or 14.046. The p value of this chi-square (with 3 df) is approximately .003.

Table 15.5	Expected Frequencies (f_e) and $(f_o - f_e)^2/f_e$ Values				
A. Expected frequencies (f_e)					
Food choice	PC	MC	JFJ	GE	Row sums
Big Jack	18.480	5.808	19.008	22.704	66
Soyburger	16.520	5.192	16.992	20.296	59
Column sums	35	11	36	43	125
B. $(f_o - f_e)^2/f_e$ values					
Food choice	PC	MC	JFJ	GE	Row sums
Big Jack	0.344	0.827	1.311	4.148	6.630
Soyburger	0.384	0.925	1.467	4.640	7.416
Column sums	0.728	1.752	2.778	8.788	14.046

The larger the value of the chi-square, the less likely are the observed frequencies to differ from the expected frequencies only by chance, and this chi-square is interestingly large. However, all it tells us is that *somewhere* in the data the observed frequencies depart noticeably from the expected values. In a way, it reminds us of the case of analysis of variance with $df > 1$ in the numerator of F. That is, a significant omnibus F tells us that there is some difference but not where that difference may be found. To help us interpret chi-square tables with $df > 1$, let us review some of the options available.

Interpreting Large Tables of Counts

One procedure when chi-square $df > 1$ is to inspect closely the $(f_o - f_e)^2/f_e$ results, as these results show which of the cells contributed most to the overall large chi-square. A large cell entry in such a table indicates that the cell in question is "surprising" to us given the magnitude of the row and column totals that are associated with that cell. That is, the cell is "unexpected" in terms of chance or likelihood—not necessarily in terms of our research hypothesis, however. In Table 15.5, the largest values in Section B suggest that Green Earthies reacted in a less likely way than would be expected by chance on the basis of the choices of the other three groups.

A second option for dealing with tables of counts larger than 2 × 2 is to subdivide them into smaller tables. In this procedure, called **partitioning of tables**, we compute additional chi-squares based on portions of the overall table. Either a prior theory or hypothesis or the nature of the obtained results can guide our judgment about which additional chi-squares to compute. The number and size of the subtables are guided by certain statistical rules, and the calculations also call for certain statistical adjustments. If you would like to learn more about partitioning large tables of counts, as well as other strategies for dealing with such tables, you will find a detailed discussion in our advanced text (Rosenthal & Rosnow, 1991, Chapter 23).

For a third option, called **standardizing the margins** (Mosteller, 1968), all that you will need is a pocket calculator and a little patience. This option (which is not as well known as the previous two) will enable you to take the size of the row and column totals (or "margins") into account by setting all the row totals equal to each other and all the column totals equal to each other. This process is, however, different from a BESD, which sets the row and column margins equal to 100. To show how standardizing the margins is done, we illustrate this method with our continuing example.

Taking the Margins into Account

One of the problems of trying to understand the results in tables of counts larger than 2 × 2 is that our eye is likely to be fooled by the absolute magnitude of the frequencies displayed (i.e., the f_o data). Suppose we were to ask of the data in

Table 15.4 which group of students is most overrepresented in the Big Jack category. Our eye notes that Psychology Club members (PC) and Junk Food Junkies (JFJ) have the greatest frequency of occurrence in that category, and thus, we might conclude that one of these groups is most overrepresented in the Big Jack category. Our conclusion would be in error, however. The reason is that we looked only at the interior of the table and not, at the same time, at the sums in the row and column margins.

A look at these margins suggests that the PC and JFJ groups *should* have larger obtained frequencies in the Big Jack category than the Mathematics Club members (MC) because the PC and JFJ groups have more members than the MC group. In addition, there are slightly more students in general in the Big Jack category than in the soyburger category. Taking all these margins into account simultaneously would show us that it is actually the MC students who are most overrepresented in the Big Jack category.

In large tables of counts, "taking the margins into account" becomes a difficult matter without the use of systematic aids to eye and mind. Standardizing the margins allows us to adjust (or "correct") for the unequal column and row margins and thus provides us with a systematic procedure for taking the unequal margins into account. Table 15.6 illustrates the steps taken to adjust for the unequal column and row margins in Table 15.4.

Section A of Table 15.6 shows the results of the first step in this process, which divides each obtained frequency (in Table 15.4) by its column sum. To obtain the "corrected" values for 21 and 14 in Table 15.4, we divided each by 35. To obtain the "corrected" values for 8 and 3 in Table 15.4, we divided each by 11; and so on. These calculations gave us the results in Section A of Table 15.6, where we can see that the column margins have been equalized but that the row margins remain very unequal. To adjust for the latter, we divided each of the new values in Section A by its row margin. To obtain the "corrected" values for .600, .727, .667, and .302, we divided each by 2.296. To obtain the "corrected" values for .400, .273, .333, and .698, we divided each by 1.704. The results appear in Section B of Table 15.6.

Section B has equalized the row margins, at least within rounding error, but the column margins are no longer equal. By now, we know what to do about that: Simply divide each entry of Section B by its new column margin. That process will equalize the column margins but *may* make our new row margins unequal. We repeat this procedure until further repetitions (called *iterations*) no longer affect the margins. For these data, the final results obtained by successive iterations are shown in Section C of Table 15.6, which shows margins equalized within rounding error and allows us to interpret the table entries without worrying about the confusing effects of variations in margins. It clearly shows that, in the Big Jack category, the Mathematics Club (MC) is overrepresented most, whereas in the soyburger category, the Green Earthies (GE) are the ones most overrepresented.

There is one final step we can take to throw the final results into bolder relief: We can show the cell entries as deviations from the values we would expect if there were no differences whatever among the groups in their representation in the Big Jack and soyburger categories. If there were no such differences, and given

Table 15.6	Steps in Standardizing the Margins

A. Results "corrected" for unequal column margins in Table 15.4

Food choice	PC	MC	JFJ	GE	Row sums
Big Jack	.600	.727	.667	.302	2.296
Soyburger	.400	.273	.333	.698	1.704
Column sums	1.000	1.000	1.000	1.000	4.000

B. Results "corrected" for unequal row margins in A (above)

Food choice	PC	MC	JFJ	GE	Row sums
Big Jack	.261	.317	.291	.132	1.001
Soyburger	.235	.160	.195	.410	1.000
Column sums	.496	.477	.486	.542	2.001

C. Final "corrected" results

Food choice	PC	MC	JFJ	GE	Row sums
Big Jack	.517	.657	.589	.238	2.001
Soyburger	.483	.343	.411	.762	1.999
Column sums	1.000	1.000	1.000	1.000	4.000

D. Results in C (above) shown as deviations from an expected value of .500

Food choice	PC	MC	JFJ	GE	Row sums
Big Jack	+.017	+.157	+.089	−.262	+.001
Soyburger	−.017	−.157	−.089	+.262	−.001
Column sums	.000	.000	.000	.000	.000

the margins of Section C, all the values in the table would be .500. In forming our final table, we subtract this expected value of .500 from each entry in Section C; the results are shown in Section D of Table 15.6.

The interpretation of Section D is fairly direct. Besides the big difference between the Green Earthies, who are overrepresented very heavily in the soyburger category, and all the other groups, which are more modestly overrepresented in the Big Jack category, there are other differences that help us to interpret our earlier results. For example, even though some of the sample sizes are too small to be very stable, we can also raise some tentative questions about differences among the three groups overrepresented in the Big Jack category. The Mathematics Club is substantially more overrepresented in the Big Jack category than is the Psychology Club, which is virtually not overrepresented at all. The Junk Food Junkies fall almost exactly midway between the PC and MC groups in their degree of overrepresentation in the Big Jack category.

Because of the small sample sizes, the differences among these three groups (PC, MC, and JFJ) are not significant statistically, but with larger sample sizes they might be. In any case, the purpose of the procedure of standardizing the margins is to highlight the differences among groups, whether these achieve statistical significance or not.

A Journey Begun

The *beginning* in the title of this book is intended to have a double meaning. It not only describes the level of the text but also conveys the idea of a journey. For some students, the journey that you embarked on at the start of this course is now complete. For others, the journey has only just begun. In either case, it should be recognized that, particularly in some of their statistical aspects, the design of experiments and the comparison of research conditions constitute a very specialized and highly developed field. The purpose of Chapters 10–15 was to further your understanding of the logic and meaning of the statistical procedures and concepts associated with the application of the scientific method, an understanding that may have been initiated in a basic statistics course.

A thorough knowledge of the characteristics of both the data obtained and the statistics used is assumed by professional researchers to be an essential aspect of sound scientific practice. Whether the conclusion of this chapter represents the start or the end of your journey in social or behavioral research, you should now have a deeper understanding of the applicability and limits of the scientific method. Many of the procedures you have learned about in these final chapters can be used to address questions you have about the scientific results reported in newspapers and magazines (or that you hear about in chat groups on the Internet) and many everyday questions that can be framed in ways that will allow you to reach beyond other people's conclusions and, using empirical reasoning, decide for yourself what is true.

Summary of Ideas

1. Chi-square (χ^2) is used to test the degree of agreement between the data actually obtained (or "observed") and the data expected under a particular hypothesis (e.g., the null hypothesis).

2. The expected value of chi-square when the null hypothesis is true is equal to the degrees of freedom defining the particular chi-square distribution.

3. The effect size r for 2×2 chi-squares (i.e., focused chi-squares) is phi (ϕ), which is computed directly from chi-square by

$$r_{\text{effect size}} = \phi = \sqrt{\frac{\chi^2}{N}}.$$

4. We compute the confidence interval and use the BESD to interpret the effect size as described in previous chapters.

5. If the sample size is not too small, and if the smallest expected frequency is not too small, we test the significance of the effect size r by $\chi^2 = (\phi^2)(N)$, which reflects the conceptual relationship that significance test = size of effect × size of study.

6. As in the case of t and F, a relationship must be quite strong to result in a large chi-square with only a small number of sampling units.

7. Effect size correlations of .10, .30, and .50 are conventionally referred to as small, moderate, and large, respectively, while "jumbo" effects are substantially larger than .50.

8. One option in interpreting larger tables of counts is to examine the $(f_o - f_e)^2/f_e$ results, because they show which of the cells in the table of counts contributed most to the overall chi-square.

9. A second option is to partition the larger table of counts into smaller (e.g., 2 × 2) chi-square tables.

10. A third option is to standardize the margins (totals) by making all row margins equal and by, at the same time, making all column margins equal.

Key Terms

chi-square (χ^2)   p. 369
counts   p. 369
expected frequency (f_e)   p. 369

observed frequency (f_o)
    p. 369
partitioning of tables   p. 376

phi coefficient (ϕ)   p. 372
standardizing the margins
    p. 376

WEB ACTIVITY

Observe how changes in a 2 × 2 contingency table can affect chi-square by visiting the Rice University Virtual Lab in Statistics at http://www.ruf.rice.edu/~lane/stat_sim/index.html and clicking on the Chi-square radio button and then on the 2 × 2 Contingency Tables link. Your final exams over, papers submitted, and time for a break? Check out http://www.gametheory.net or the Monty Hall Dilemma at http://www.cut-the-knot.com/hall.shtml.

Multiple-Choice Questions for Review

1. Chi-square differs from significance tests such as t and F in that it is specifically designed for use when (a) there are multiple dependent variables; (b) there are multiple independent variables; (c) the dependent variables are not ordered, scored, or scaled beyond two levels; (d) none of the above.

2. Chi-squares are calculated from the differences between _____ and _____ frequencies. (a) expected, obtained; (b) theoretical, operational; (c) between, within; (d) none of the above

3. In the following 2 × 2 table, what is the expected frequency in the upper-left cell? (a) 1; (b) 4; (c) 19; (d) 25

	Democrats	Republicans
Males	4	1
Females	1	19

4. A student at Kutztown University examines a 2 × 2 table of counts and calculates chi-square to be 6. According to Table 15.3, what is the appropriate p value? (a) <.10; (b) <.05; (c) <.01; (d) cannot be determined from this information

5. The same student examines a 4 × 2 table of counts and calculates chi-square to be 6. According to Table 15.3, what is the appropriate p value? (a) > .10; (b)<.10; (c) <.05; (d) cannot be determined from this information

6. The effect size measure typically associated with chi-square is _____. (a) ϕ; (b) f_e; (c) f_o; (d) d

7. $\chi^2 = $ _____ $\times$ _____. (a) ϕ^2, N; (b) row total, column total; (c) rows $-$ 1, columns $-$ 1; (d) none of the above

8. Chi-square tables are also called tables of _____. (a) means; (b) ANOVAs; (c) counts; (d) unequaled margins

9. A study is conducted that yields a 3 $\times$ 4 chi-square table. The overall chi-square is found to be significant. To interpret the results more fully, the researcher decides to examine a table of $(f_o - f_e)^2/f_e$ scores. In this table, the cells with _____ numbers indicate "unexpected" results. (a) small; (b) positive; (c) no; (d) large

10. A study is conducted that yields a 3 $\times$ 4 chi-square table. To interpret the results more fully, the researcher uses a procedure setting the row and column totals equal to each other. This procedure is called (a) partitioning; (b) examining a table of $(f_o - f_e)^2/f_e$ scores; (c) standardizing the margins; (d) binary analysis.

Discussion Questions for Review

1. A clinical psychologist at the University of Alabama examines the relation of three types of psychopathology to socioeconomic status (SES) in 100 subjects. Her table of counts is

SES	Schizophrenic	Neurotic	Depressed
High	5	5	20
Medium	5	15	20
Low	10	10	10

How should she test the hypothesis that this table of counts is significantly different from what would be expected by chance if there were no relation between these variables? How many degrees of freedom will her statistic have? In what way will the p value she obtains address only incompletely her wish to examine the relationship between type of psychopathology and SES?

2. A Brigham Young University student obtained the following data, where the numbers are frequencies (counts). How should she plan to standardize the margins?

Annual carrot consumption	Visual acuity		
	High	Average	Low
11–20 lb.	9	3	1
1–10 lb.	5	8	2
0 lb.	1	8	7

3. A researcher at Rochester Institute of Technology asks 10 engineering students from the freshman, sophomore, junior, and senior classes whether they plan to attend graduate school. The results are

	Frosh	Sophs	Juniors	Seniors
Want advanced degree	7	6	3	1
Want out of school	3	4	7	9

How many degrees of freedom would the chi-square for this table have? How should the researcher calculate the expected frequencies? What is the nature of the relation between year in college and wanting an advanced degree?

4. Three students at the College of New Jersey each conduct the same study with the following results:

	$\chi^2(1\ df)$	N	p
Student 1	2.00	20	.16
Student 2	3.00	30	.08
Student 3	4.00	40	.05

Student 3 claims a significant relationship between the two levels of her independent variable (0, 1) and the two levels of her dependent variable (0, 1). Students 1 and 2 chide her, saying that they have not found a significant effect and that her results are therefore undependable and unreplicable. How should Student 3 reply?

 ## Answers to Review Questions

Multiple-Choice Questions

1. c	**3.** a	**5.** a	**7.** a	**9.** d
2. a	**4.** b	**6.** a	**8.** c	**10.** c

Discussion Questions

1. She would compute a χ^2 for which the df would be (rows − 1)(columns − 1) = (3 − 1)(3 − 1) = 4. Because her χ^2 is based on $df > 1$ (i.e., $df = 4$), its p value will tell her nothing about the nature of the relationship between type of psychopathology and SES. She should therefore consider inspecting the $(f_o − f_e)^2/f_e$ results, partitioning her table, and/or standardizing the margins.

2. Following the procedures of Table 15.6, she would arrive at the approximate solution:

Annual carrot consumption	Visual acuity			
	High	Average	Low	Sum
11–20 lb.	.64	.20	.14	.98
1–10 lb.	.31	.45	.23	.99
0 lb.	.05	.34	.62	1.01
Sum	1.00	.99	.99	2.98

She can display these results as deviations from an expected value of .33 (i.e., the total of 3.00 divided by 9 cells = 3/9 = .33), yielding the following:

Annual Carrot Consumption	Visual Acuity			
	High	Average	Low	Sum
11–20 lb.	.31	−.13	−.19	−.01
1–10 lb.	−.02	.12	−.10	.00
0 lb.	−.28	.01	.29	.02
Sum	+.01	.00	.00	.01

These results show very clearly that high-visual-acuity subjects are relatively overrepresented among high carrot consumers, whereas low-visual-acuity subjects are relatively overrepresented among low carrot consumers. As a corollary, we see that high-visual-acuity subjects are underrepresented among low carrot consumers, whereas low-visual-acuity subjects are relatively underrepresented among high carrot consumers. Unless this was a randomized experiment, the student should be cautious about inferring causality. Although it is possible that eating more carrots leads to better visual acuity, it may also be that better visual acuity leads to finding more carrots in the darker regions of the refrigerator.

3. The *df* for this χ^2 are obtained from (rows − 1)(columns − 1) = (2 − 1)(4 − 1) = 3. The expected frequencies are obtained from

$$f_e = \frac{(\text{Row total})(\text{Column total})}{\text{Grand total}},$$

which, for these data, results in

	Frosh	Sophs	Juniors	Seniors
Want degree	4.25	4.25	4.25	4.25
Want out	5.75	5.75	5.75	5.75

With each advancing year, a greater proportion of students want out, a result shown clearly in the final results, in deviation form, of standardizing the margins:

	Frosh	Sophs	Juniors	Seniors
Want degree	.26	.20	−.10	−.36
Want out	−.26	−.20	.10	.36

Once again, we must be careful in our interpretation of the results. Because this is a cross-sectional study, we cannot distinguish differences in year at college from cohort differences (discussed in Chapter 8).

4. Student 3 should ask that all three students compute the effect size correlation that is associated with their results, using the following formula:

$$r_{\text{effect size}} = \phi = \sqrt{\frac{\chi^2}{N}}$$

When the three students compute their *r*s, they all find exactly the same effect size ($r_{\text{effect size}} = .316$). Student 3 shows thereby that the three studies agree with one another remarkably well.

APPENDIX A

Communicating Your
Research Findings

Research Reports and Poster Presentations

For scientists in all fields, the research process is not complete until results have been reported in a peer-reviewed journal. Students are also required to report their research findings, but the primary audience is usually the instructor. It is exceedingly rare for undergraduates to try to have their research findings published, as the rejection rates of many peer-reviewed journals in psychology and related fields are daunting (70%, 80%, or even higher). Even professional researchers have experienced rejection, and they do not lightly encourage students to strike out on their own without the skilled guidance of an experienced hand. If, however, you are that rare individual encouraged by your instructor to craft a paper for submission to a journal, then your instructor has cautioned you about the precise style required for journal submissions. The standard of most (but not all) psychology journals in the United States is the *Publication Manual of the American Psychological Association* (hereafter called the APA manual), published by the American Psychological Association in 2001; the manual also has a Web site that you can visit to see what is new in APA style (www.apastyle.org). Another useful introduction to various aspects of professional writing in psychology by a prolific author, Robert J. Sternberg of Yale University, who has been successful in all of them, is *The*

Psychologist's Companion (1993). Whether you are writing for a course or professionally, an essential reference for style is Strunk and White's *Elements of Style* (2000), a gem of a book that belongs on every author's desk.

The purpose of this appendix is not to show you how to prepare a journal manuscript, but to show you how to communicate your research findings in a written report for your instructor and, if applicable, in a poster presentation for a wider audience. It is becoming increasingly common for students to present their research results in poster presentations as well as in written reports. If you plan to present a poster at a local or regional meeting, it is important to familiarize yourself with any special requirements or guidelines of the sponsoring organization. Poster presenters are usually expected to bring along written reports as handouts. Although we do not describe how to prepare such handouts in this appendix, you will find further guidance in Rosnow and Rosnow's *Writing Papers in Psychology: A Student Guide to Research Reports, Essays, Proposals, Posters, and Brief Reports* (2003). The tips and guidelines that we list in this appendix were borrowed from that book. Although these guidelines are in the spirit of the APA manual, there are certain departures such as the style of the title page of a research paper for a course and an appendix for your raw data and calculations. The reason for this difference is that you are writing a research report for your instructor to evaluate and grade, and the needs of instructors are different in some respects from journal editors' and reviewers' requirements.

Getting Organized

Before we turn to the steps in writing a report, we begin by discussing the most difficult step for many students: getting started. Clearly, it would be advantageous to get started early to ensure that your task will not be rushed and that you will have ample time to revise and polish your work well before the due date. One reason that students have trouble getting going is that they are unclear about the assignment. Thus, before you do anything else, make sure you know what is expected of you. You can talk with other students to get their impressions, but that approach may stress you out even more. The best person for you to consult is the instructor, teaching assistant, or grader to make sure that you are on the right track. Whether you feel confident or feel you don't have a clue, you will benefit from a meeting.

Besides knowing the form of the final report, here are some questions to keep in mind as you get organized:

- When is the final report due?
- How will it be graded?
- Will there be an opportunity to obtain feedback as the project progresses?
- Is there a specified length for the final report?
- Are intermediate drafts or outlines required, and when are they due?
- Are sample reports available to provide a further idea of what is expected?

Questions about due dates are especially important because missing deadlines—just like unexcused absences on a job—is a sure way to elicit disapproval. If you are someone who has a hard time meeting deadlines, remember that instructors have heard all the excuses. Try keeping a pocket calendar and checking it every morning and evening to see what your responsibilities are for the next several days. If that approach fails, try posting scheduled dates and appointments over your mirror or desk—anywhere you routinely look.

To help you keep on schedule, you can jot down both self-imposed and assigned dates, such as

- Completion of literature search
- Completion of proposal for research
- Completion of ethics review
- Completion of data collection
- Completion of data analysis
- Completion of first draft of research report
- Completion of revised draft(s) of research report
- Submission date

Sample Research Report

Exhibit A.1 shows what a research report submitted as a course requirement looks like. It is a good idea to study this annotated report before you continue. Then, we will focus on each of the following eight parts and provide you with simple guidelines and tips:

Title page

Abstract

Introduction

Method

Results

Discussion

References

End material (e.g., tables, figures, appendixes)

Title Page

We turn now to the structure and form of your research report, beginning with the title page. Notice that the page number in the upper right corner is accompanied (on every page) by the words "Biasing Effects." These words are called *page headers*, and their purpose is to make it easy for the instructor or grader to identify each manuscript page if any pages become separated. The APA rule is that page headers should consist of two or three words from the title. The other kinds of information shown on the title page of Mary's sample paper are her name (the *byline*), the number and name of the course or sequence for which the paper is being submitted, the name of the instructor, and the date the paper will be submitted.

(text continues on p. 398)

Biasing Effects 1

Biasing Effects of Drug-Testing Results on Bail Judgments:

An Experimental Simulation

Mary Jones

Research Report

(Number and Name of Course)

Instructor: Prof. Bruce Rind

(Date Submitted)

The title is
succinct, yet
adequately
descriptive.

The student's
name appears
below the
title.

Insert course
identification
and date.

Pages are
numbered
consecutively,
beginning
with the title
page, and
contain a
short
heading.

Exhibit A.1   Mary Jones's Research Report

Appendix A

Biasing Effects   2

Abstract

The idea for the experiment reported here was originally inspired by a legal discussion regarding the institution of mandatory drug testing of all suspects upon arrest. One side argued that this testing would have biasing effects on bail judgments in legal proceedings, whereas the other side countered that drug information would have no prejudicial effects. Drawing on correspondent inference theory, I hypothesized that harsher bail judgments are more likely when judges are informed that the defendant has tested positive for drug usage than when no testing information is made available. The results of an experimental simulation were in the hypothesized direction, statistically significant, and $r_{effect\ size} = .34$. This report concludes with a brief discussion of methodological limitations of this study and ideas for follow-up research.

Abstract is not indented.

The abstract tells why the research was important and worth doing, what was hypothesized, what the results were, and what else appears in the discussion.

The abstract begins on a new page.

Double spacing leaves one line between each line of type.

Biasing Effects   3

The text
begins on a
new page.

Biasing Effects of Drug-Testing Results on Bail Judgments:

An Experimental Simulation

Serendipity played a hand in the inspiration for this research. While watching TV one evening, I was channel surfing when I happened to see a discussion between lawyers who were arguing over whether drug testing should be performed on all persons arrested. One lawyer argued that the institution of mandatory drug testing would serve as one more weapon for law enforcement officials in fighting the drug war. Another lawyer countered that the institution of mandatory testing could result in threats to individual rights because positive results would unfairly bias judges' decisions on how much bail to impose, even in cases in which there was no connection between drug usage and the crime committed. The response of the first lawyer was that drug information would have no effect on a bail judge's decision. This controversial issue (i.e., whether there might be a biasing effect on bail judgments) whetted my curiosity. To form the basis of a testable hypothesis, I turned to the literature on attribution theory, particularly to an aspect of this work known as correspondent inference theory.

The main task of the bail judge is to set bail at a level that will make it likely that the defendant will appear for trial. In making this decision, the judge is perhaps likely to consider factors suggestive of the defendant's traits, with the idea that some traits should predict the likelihood that the defendant will skip bail or show up for the trial. In social psychology, attribution theory is specifically concerned with factors that influence how observers infer the traits of particular actors (cf. Jones & Davis, 1965; Kelley, 1972) and how this trait information is used to make decisions or judgments regarding actors (Baron & Byrne, 1987). In this vein, Jones and Davis developed a conceptual framework for the description of how observers go about inferring traits of actors, known as *correspondent inference theory.* According to this theory, observers focus

The text
opens with a
repetition of
the title.

The first line
of every
paragraph in
the text is
indented five
to seven
spaces.

Abbreviation
for *id est* ("that
is")

An
ampersand
appears in
parentheses,
where *and* is
used
otherwise.

The opening
paragraph
sets the stage
in an inviting
way.

Leave a
margin of at
least 1 inch
on all four
sides.

Although the
left margin is
even, the
right margin
is ragged.

Citations
buttress the
introduction.

Abbreviation
for *confer*
("compare")

Biasing Effects 4

primarily on certain types of observed behavior to infer traits on the assumption that only certain actions are indicative of traits. Three questions that observers usually ask themselves, according to Jones and Davis, are (a) Was the behavior freely chosen? (b) Did the behavior produce uncommon effects? and (c) Was the behavior low in social desirability?

> Connecting points are lettered for clarity.

The third question seemed particularly relevant to the controversial issue in which I was interested. On the assumption that drug usage is generally held to be low in social desirability (i.e., in our society), it seemed to follow from correspondent inference theory that observers are likely to concentrate on this form of socially undesirable behavior in judging actors' traits. Once observers have inferred traits, they tend to use this information to predict the actors' future behaviors as well as to assess and guide their own actions, decisions, and judgments regarding those actors (Baron & Byrne, 1987). Therefore, I hypothesized that having information about positive results from a drug test is likely to result in harsher bail judgments.

> The introduction concludes with your hypotheses, or theoretical expectations, prior to seeing the findings.

> The introduction gives a concise history and background of the topic, and it leads to the question of interest.

Method

Participants and Study Design

A sample of 31 undergraduate students, including both men and women, participated in this study. With the permission of the instructor and the consent of all the students who participated, an experiment was conducted during a regular class meeting. The students were randomly assigned to either an experimental ($n = 15$) or a control ($n = 16$) condition, and each student received a one-page questionnaire. The questionnaires were mixed together and administered to all students simultaneously. At the conclusion of the study, the students were fully debriefed.

> First-level headings are centered.

> Second-level headings are flush left and italicized.

> The method section, like all the major sections of the text, follow each other without a page break.

> Sample sizes of subgroup are denoted by italicized lower-case n.

The Questionnaire

The questionnaire asked for the respondent's age, sex, year in college, grade point average (GPA), and major. Next came the written

> Second level heading

> Abbreviations are first spelled out.

Biasing Effects   5

instruction to "please read the following paragraph carefully, and then answer the question that follows it." In the experimental condition, the paragraph stated:

> A man was arrested as a suspected burglar. He fit the description of a man seen running from the burglarized house. While in custody the man submitted to a blood test, and it was determined that he had very recently used drugs.

In the control condition, the last sentence in the scenario above was deleted, and the following sentence was substituted:

> The man spent enough time in custody so that he received two meals and made three phone calls.

Immediately after either scenario was the following question: "If you were the bail judge, what bail would you set? Choose a dollar amount from $0 to $50,000."

Results

The overall findings are given in Table 1, which shows that the mean judgment of the students exposed to the drug information was higher than the mean judgment of those exposed to the neutral scenario. Computing the t test on these data yielded $t = 2.08$, $df = 29$, $p = .023$ one-tailed, $r_{\text{effect size}} = .36$, and a 95% confidence interval around the effect size ranging from .01 to .63. One assumption when the t test is used to compare two means is that population variances of the samples are equal, but the estimated population variances in Table 1 are noticeably unequal. Using a standard statistical procedure recommended to me by the instructor, I found that dividing the larger of the two variances (i.e., S^2) by the smaller of the two variances yielded an F ratio that was highly significant, $F(14, 15) = 9.0$, $p = .00013$, implying heterogeneity of variance.

Professor Rind told me about two customary ways of dealing with heterogeneity of variance, one involving transformation of the raw scores and the other, a procedure known as Satterthwaite's method (illustrated in Rosenthal, Rosnow, and Rubin, 2000). Because I was

Appendix A

Biasing Effects 6

doing the calculations by hand, using a programmable scientific calculator downloaded with software developed by Foster (2003), which
computed Satterthwaite's equations automatically, I naturally decided
on the second option. By this method, the t test is calculated in a
slightly different way, and the degrees of freedom are adjusted (all
calculations described in the appendix of this report). Both the t
test result and effect size r were similar to the results above, with
$t = 2.03$, $df = 16$, $p = .03$ one-tailed, $r_{effect\ size} = .34$. In computing
this effect size r from t, I used the original degrees of freedom
($df = 29$) along with the t-test value (1.96) that was associated with
the one-tailed p of .03 for Satterthwaite's adjusted df (Rosenthal et
al., 2000). The 95% confidence interval of the obtained effect size r
ranged from $-.02$ to $.62$, a result that is also similar to the previous result above. The reason that this confidence interval crosses
zero (i.e., it stretches slightly into the negative side) is that the
95% confidence interval has .025 as the one-tailed p, and the obtained p did not quite make the .025 (i.e., it was .03).

Discussion

One fundamental purpose of our criminal justice system is, of
course, to be just and unbiased in all of its aspects. The results of
my experiment were in the hypothesized direction, indicating that
harsher bail judgments were more likely when the "judges" were informed that the defendant had tested positive for drug usage. This
finding implies that the goal of being just and unbiased might be
jeopardized if drug testing and the reporting of its results were
mandated by law. Of course, this biasing effect could be avoided if
judges were not given access to the results of the drug testing.

However, because I was unable to use real judges and had to use
college students, the results may not be applicable to actual bail
judges. Future research could be designed to address this problem of
external validity and also to assess the participants' inferences of
corresponding traits from socially undesirable behavior. In this

Letters used as statistical symbols are italicized: t, F, n, df, S^2, p, and so forth.

The discussion section follows without a page break.

The discussion begins by reminding us of the study's purpose and the main findings.

Mary gives the limitations of the study, which tell the instructor that she has a good understanding of the limited generalizability of the findings.

Biasing Effects   7

study, I merely assumed these inferences from the participants' bail judgments. It is interesting that, although the participants seemingly judged the suspect more harshly when the drug information was included, there was no logical connection between the drug usage and the burglary. Perhaps the participants were drawing on a stereotype to assume that the association was likely, because the media often report property crimes that are motivated by the need to get money to purchase drugs. Future research could use other crime scenarios that are not stereotypically associated with drugs to determine whether biasing effects occur and are general in nature. Finally, it should be emphasized that I am not addressing the legal issue that this kind of testing of someone "innocent until proved guilty" is possibly unconstitutional, that is, on the grounds that it is a violation of civil rights.

Future implications are projected, which tells the instructor that the student has thought about the findings.

Appendix A

Biasing Effects   7

The references begin on a new page.

References

Book with two authors

Baron, R. A., & Byrne, D. (1987). *Social psychology: Understanding human interaction*. Boston: Allyn & Bacon.

Journal article with one author

Foster, E. K. (2003). METASTATS: Behavioral science statistics for Microsoft Windows and the HP49G programmable calculator. *Behavior Research Methods, Instruments, & Computers, 35*, 325-328.

Journal titles are italicized as are volume numbers

Chapter in an edited book

Jones, E. E., & Davis, K. E. (1965). From acts to dispositions: The attribution process in person perception. In L. Berkowitz (Ed.), *Advances in experimental social psychology* (Vol. 2, pp. 219-266). New York: Academic Press.

"Ed." for one editor

Kelley, H. H. (1972). Attribution in social interaction. In E. E. Jones, D. E. Kanouse, R. E. Nisbett, S. Valins, & B. Weiner (Eds.), *Attribution: Perceiving the causes of behavior* (pp. 1-26). Morristown, NJ: General Learning Press.

Page numbers of chapter in edited book

Book with three authors

Rosenthal, R., Rosnow, R. L., & Rubin, D. B. (2000). *Contrasts and effect sizes in behavioral research: A correlational approach*. Cambridge, UK: Cambridge University Press.

Ampersand before the last author's name

Table number
and title are
flush left.

Table 1

Mean, Variability, and Number of Participants in Each Group

Measure	Experimental group	Control group
Mean	$16,146.67	$6,990.63
S	16,645.07	5,549.60
S^2	277,058,355.31	30,798,060.16
n	15	16

Where means
are reported,
an associated
measure of
variability is
also reported.

Tables appear
after the
references in
the APA style.

Tables are
used to
present
information
efficiently.

Appendix A

Biasing Effects   9

Appendix

The following table shows the raw scores (i.e., the individual bail judgments) of 31 college students who were randomly assigned to an experimental or a control group:

Experimental group	Control group
$10,000	$10,000
12,500	4,000
2,000	5,000
50,000	350
20,000	5,000
200	15,000
500	500
30,000	5,000
2,000	500
10,000	1,500
5,000	10,000
10,000	10,000
50,000	20,000
30,000	5,000
10,000	10,000
—	10,000

For my calculations, I used an HP-49G programmable calculator and software that I downloaded from Foster's (2003) METASTATS Web site (www.netaxs.com/~efoster). However, as required by Professor Rind, shown below are the basic equations used, which I got from either the textbook in this course or from Rosenthal et al.'s (2000) more advanced discussion of Satterthwaite's method:

$$t = \frac{M_1 - M_2}{\sqrt{\left(\dfrac{1}{n_1} + \dfrac{1}{n_2}\right)s^2}} = \frac{16{,}146.67 - 6{,}990.63}{\sqrt{\left(\dfrac{1}{15} + \dfrac{1}{16}\right)149{,}682{,}340.575}} = 2.08$$

Although these data are typed, check with your instructor about whether handwritten data are permissible in the appendix of your research paper.

Showing the raw data and the computations of the study helps the instructor to grade the paper fairly.

The appendix of the student's paper begins on a new page.

Appendix A

Biasing Effects   10

$$r_{\text{effect size}} = \sqrt{\frac{t^2}{t^2 + df}} = \sqrt{\frac{(2.08)^2}{(2.08)^2 + 29}} = .36$$

$$t_{\text{Satterthwaite}} = \frac{M_1 - M_2}{\sqrt{\dfrac{S_1^2}{n_1} + \dfrac{S_2^2}{n_2}}} = \frac{16,146.67 - 6,990.63}{\sqrt{\dfrac{277,058,355.305}{15} + \dfrac{30,798,060.16}{16}}} = 2.03$$

$$df_{\text{Satterthwaite}} = \frac{\left(\dfrac{S_1^2}{n_1} + \dfrac{S_2^2}{n_2}\right)^2}{\left[\dfrac{\left(\dfrac{S_1^2}{n_1}\right)^2}{n_1 - 1}\right] + \left[\dfrac{\left(\dfrac{S_2^2}{n_2}\right)^2}{n_2 - 1}\right]}$$

$$= \frac{\left(\dfrac{277,058,355.305}{15} + \dfrac{30,798,060.16}{16}\right)^2}{\left[\dfrac{\left(\dfrac{277,058,355.305}{15}\right)^2}{15 - 1}\right] + \left[\dfrac{\left(\dfrac{30,798,060.16}{16}\right)^2}{16 - 1}\right]} = 16.90$$

As indicated in Rosenthal et al. (2000), I truncated the 16.90 df to the next lower integer, 16. The t of 2.03, with $df = 16$, has a p value of .030 one-tailed. To obtain the effect size correlation, I used the t value of 1.96 associated with the adjusted p value noted above ($p = .030$ one-tailed), and used the original degrees of freedom (29), as indicated in Rosenthal et al.:

$$r_{\text{effect size}} = \sqrt{\frac{t^2}{t^2 + df}} = \sqrt{\frac{(1.96)^2}{(1.96)^2 + 29}} = .34$$

The student has included an explanation of a particular procedure, including the citation of an advanced text that she consulted.

Abstract

Although the *abstract* (or summary) appears on page 2, it is written after you have completed the rest of your paper, as it is a distillation of the important points covered in the body of your report. It tells the reader what your research is about in one succinct paragraph. In the sample report, Mary gives a synopsis of the background of her research, her hypothesis, the way she tested it (by an "experimental simulation"), the results, and a very brief description of the way her discussion section will proceed. The APA rule is that abstracts not exceed 960 characters and spaces (i.e., approximately 120 words), but instructors are usually more lenient about the length of abstracts in student reports. However, one way to conserve characters is to use digits for all numbers, and to abbreviate liberally. Notice that Mary uses the active noun *I* ("I believe … " and "I conclude … "). Not all instructors find this usage acceptable, preferring instead that students use the third person rather than the first person in attributing an action to themselves. For example, referring to yourself as "the experimenter" (third person) rather than as "I" (first person) is preferred by many instructors, although, as the APA manual states (p. 29), it "may give the impression that you did not take part in your own study."

Remember that the purpose of the abstract is to let the reader quickly anticipate what the report is about. With that objective in mind, here are some questions to guide you when planning your abstract:

- What was the problem that I studied or the objective of my study?
- What principal method did I use (a laboratory experiment, a survey questionnaire, judges as raters, etc.)?
- Who were the research participants (i.e., what were their pertinent characteristics)?
- What were the major results?
- What primary conclusions and implications appear in the discussion section?

Introduction

The introduction—the first section after the abstract page—begins by repeating the full title of the paper (not the student's name, however). This section emphasizes linking ideas to past research and should lead into your hypotheses or research questions. Basically, it describes the point of the research and also provides a framework for your later description of the method used. The idea of writing a strong introduction is to lead the reader to the thought, "Yes, of course, that's what this student *had* to do to test this hypothesis." Mary begins by describing a debate she saw on television, which puts her research in a practical light that is both compelling and significant. She develops her hypothesis in such a way that the method section (which follows) will seem a natural consequence of the introduction.

Here are some questions to help you plan the introduction:

- What got me thinking about this study?
- How did I come up with my working hypothesis, and what did I expect to find?
- What terms do I need to define for the reader who may be unfamiliar with this area?

- Do I need to define any terms for special reasons, because they are used differently in different contexts or because I use them in a new way?
- How does the study build on, or derive from, other studies?
- Is each of my hypotheses clearly explained and justified in terms of its logical basis?

Outlining is a good way to organize your thoughts before you begin writing. However, if you did not outline the introduction (or any other section) before you drafted it, a useful trick is to outline the introduction (or the whole paper) after it is written. Just list, in sentence fragments or phrases, the main ideas and what further ideas detail or substantiate the main ideas. This process will show you whether you have proceeded logically or if there are any lapses in logic that need to be corrected.

Method

In the method section, you will describe the procedures used and give a detailed account of the pertinent characteristics of the study participants. Although we use *subjects* and *participants* interchangeably, the APA manual suggests that you call the subjects of the study *participants, individuals, college students, children*, or *respondents*, because the term *subjects* strikes many people as "too impersonal." The APA manual's rule of thumb is to describe the study participants at whatever is the appropriate level of specificity, but to be sensitive to the labels you choose.

A particular problem is avoiding sexist language in describing your study participants. It would be a mistake, for example, to use the word *man* as a general term for both men and women, as the word will create a mental picture that is simply inaccurate (Dumond, 1990). On the other hand, if the subjects were only men, it would be misleading *not* to describe them by sex (and by other relevant distinguishing characteristics, such as age and level of education). When this issue first gained prominence some years ago, writers began to coin contrived words such as *s/he* and *he/she* to avoid sexist language when referring to both sexes. You can avoid awkward terms like these by using plural pronouns when you are referring to both genders. The essential rule, however, is not to mislead people by creating the wrong mental picture.

Notice in Mary's paper that the method section is divided into two parts, each with a side heading. She begins by describing the participants and giving an overall picture of the design of the study; she also tells how the two forms of her questionnaire were distributed so that both she and the participants were blind to which treatment any individual had received. She ends up noting that she debriefed the participants. She then gives a detailed picture of the questionnaire she developed. In other reports, the method section may need more than two parts, depending on how complicated the study is. Notice also that Mary's paper uses two formats of headings: center and flush left. The center heading is used to separate the paper into major sections, is written in uppercase and lowercase letters, and is not italicized. To subdivide the parts of the method section, Mary uses subheadings placed at the left margin, italicized, and typed in uppercase and lowercase. If she had wanted to use a further level of subheadings, they would have been indented, underlined, and followed by a period, with the body of the text then immediately following the heading.

Results

You will describe your data in this section, beginning with the main findings, those most relevant to your hypotheses. Try to strike a balance between being discursive and being overly precise. You might, as Mary does, present the results in a table or a graphic (as described in Chapter 10). Notice that Mary's table appears on a separate page after her reference section, that it is numbered and labeled, and that this labeling includes specific row and column headings. Except for some reports of single-case studies (see the discussion of single-case studies in Chapter 8), you are usually not expected to show individual scores in this section.

Mary's results section tells how she analyzed the data in order to test her hypothesis. She reports the significance test, specifying her p value as one-tailed, and mentions the effect size r and 95% confidence interval. She then mentions that she consulted with the instructor about an appropriate statistical procedure for testing whether the estimated population variances in her Table 1 were homogeneous, and she gives these results as well. Her instructor directed her to an advanced text to find an adjustment procedure once she realized that the homogeneity of variance assumption of her t test had been violated. Though she computed an adjustment using her calculator (and a program that she downloaded from the Web), she gives a good explanation of why she chose this option. The results are presented, and she notes that they are not very different from her original result.

A trick to help you pull the results together before you start writing is to set down a list of your statistical findings. Divide the list into coherent sets of results, and then decide the sequence according to their order of importance or relevance to your hypotheses, questions, and objectives. Experienced authors try to anticipate the questions that readers may have, particularly those about ambiguous results that call for clarification or further analysis. Here are some questions to help you structure this section:

- What were the different results, and what is their order of importance or relevance?
- How can I describe what I found in a careful, detailed way that will make complete sense to someone who is not informed on this topic?
- Have I omitted any necessary details or included superfluous information?
- In reporting my statistical results, am I being sufficiently precise?

Discussion

In the discussion section, you will synthesize and interpret the various parts of your report to form a cohesive unit from the facts you have gathered. Without being overly repetitive, Mary begins by reminding us of the background that she developed in the introduction. She recapitulates her original hypothesis, underscoring the logical continuity of her presentation. Had she gotten any unexpected results, this would be the place to note how serendipity entered into her investigation. She writes "defensively" in that she plays her own devil's advocate by pointing out limitations of her study. She also raises some potential implications and future directions of her research, thus communicating that she has thought about this area.

As you begin to structure this section, here are some questions to consider:

- What was the major purpose of this study, and were there any secondary objectives?
- How do my results relate to that purpose and those objectives?
- Were there any unexpected findings of interest, and how can I describe them to show their relevance to this project and to possible follow-up research?
- How valid and generalizable are my findings, and what are their limitations?
- What can I say about the wider implications of the results?

References

The title page and abstract are on separate pages, and the first page of the introduction (page 3 of Mary's paper) begins on a separate page, but the method, results, and discussion sections follow one another without any page breaks. The reference section also begins on a separate page, and you can now see why complete and accurate notes are crucial. This section is an alphabetized listing of all the sources of information on which you drew. Your notes (e.g., using an index card for each reference) or a running list of sorted references in a file on your computer will now provide the final list. The APA manual requires you to list only those references that you have actually discussed or cited. Mary's paper gives us examples of the style recommended by the APA in referencing books, journal articles, and chapters in edited books; you will find a wide variety of other examples in the APA manual as well as in Rosnow and Rosnow's *Writing Papers in Psychology* (2003). Here is a condensed list of APA rules about referencing:

- List authors' names in the exact order in which they appear on the title page of the publication and by last name, first initial, and middle initial.
- Authors' names are separated by commas; use an ampersand (&) before the last author.
- Give the year the work was copyrighted (the year and month for magazine articles and the year, month, and day for newspaper articles).
- For titles of books, chapters in books, and journal articles, generally capitalize only the first word of the title and of the subtitle (if any) as well as any proper names.
- Italicize (or underline) the title of a book or a journal and the volume number of the journal article.
- Give the city and state of a book's publisher, using postal abbreviations, but you do not need to list state abbreviations for Baltimore, Boston, Chicago, Los Angeles, New York, Philadelphia, and San Francisco.
- If you are listing a foreign city other than Amsterdam, Jerusalem, London, Milan, Moscow, Paris, Rome, Stockholm, Tokyo, or Vienna, you need to list the country as well.

End Material

The APA manual stipulates that tables and figures be placed in the manuscript after the reference section. The traditional purpose of this placement was to make it easier for the copyeditor and the printer to work with the typewritten copy. It is now a common practice, after a paper has been officially accepted for publication, to ask the author to submit a disk containing the manuscript along with a hard copy. The copyeditor then has the option of working with the disk or the hard copy. Many instructors no longer insist that tables and figures be placed after the reference section and are quite amenable to having them inserted in the results section so that they appear along with the narrative that refers to them. Before you do this, however, ask your instructor or grader for permission to put tables or graphics inside the running narrative section.

As illustrated by Mary's paper, many instructors also recommend that the final section of the student's report be an appendix that displays raw materials not described fully in the method section. For example, if you have stimulus materials that can be photocopied, this is the place to include them. Mary's appendix shows her raw data, and it is the place for her to explain the logic of her statistical procedure in more detail than would be appropriate in a results section. Though she used software and a calculator to do her analyses, she gives the formulas she used and shows how the data were plugged into these formulas. The instructor can see that Mary's analyses were done properly and that she has a clear understanding of the procedures. Had there been an error, the purpose of including all this material would be to allow the instructor to trace how far back a mistake in the data analysis goes. As a result, the student will not be penalized for making what might seem a mistake in interpretation or understanding when it is a less serious (but still to be avoided) typographical error or a recording mistake.

Writing and Revising

Now that you know what is expected, it is time to begin writing a first draft. A good way to start is to compose a *self-motivator statement* that you can refer to as a way of focusing your thoughts. Such a statement can be posted over your computer or desk to serve as a guidepost to keep you from wandering off on a tangent. Mary's self-motivator might be "what I know about whether disclosing the results of drug tests influences bail judgments in criminal proceedings."

If you are someone who has trouble getting started, one trick is to begin not at the beginning but with the section you feel will be easiest to write. Once the ideas begin to flow, you can tackle the introductory section. This approach will also bolster flagging spirits, because you can reread the sections you have already written when you begin to feel a loss of energy or determination. Try not to fall into the trap of escaping by napping or watching television. If you recognize these counterproductive moves for what they are, you should be able to avoid them.

Here are some helpful hints to make the writing go more smoothly:

- Find a quiet, well-lighted place in which to write, and do your writing in 2-hour stretches.
- Double-space your first draft so you can get an idea of how long the final (double-spaced) paper will be.
- Double spacing will also give you room for legible revisions if you like to revise your work in the printed version (which we each like to do) as well as on a computer screen.
- Number your printed pages using a header, but number your pages even if you are writing on a note pad.
- Pace your work so that you can complete the first draft and let it rest for at least 24 hours before you revise and polish what will be your final draft.

Layout and Printing

After you have revised your paper and are satisfied with the final version, it is time to prepare it for submission. The final report must not contain any typographical errors or spelling mistakes. To help you catch misspellings, use a spell check. Be sure that the spell check has not missed any misspelled technical terms, however. It may also not catch typos such as a capital *I* when you meant to type *in*, but using a grammar check should catch this kind of mistake (as long as the grammar check doesn't drive you to distraction by querying every phrase and line you write). Put the printed paper aside for a day or two, and then look at it again with a fresh eye. This final reading is called *proofreading* or *proofing*, and it is a last step before you submit your paper.

It is a good idea to proof the paper more than once, because gremlins in a program can sometimes introduce weird changes. Also, you will be surprised how elusive some typos can be; you can stare at them and still not see them immediately. Ask yourself:

- Are there omissions?
- Are there misspellings?
- Are the numbers correct?
- Are the hyphenations correct?
- Are all the references cited in the body of the paper listed in the reference section, and vice versa?

Make sure the print is dark enough to be easily read, as you do not want to frustrate the grader by submitting a paper with type so light or blurry that it taxes the eyes. Use 8½ × 11-inch white paper. The APA manual requires that there be at least 1-inch margins on all four sides of the page, that no typed line exceed 6½ inches, and that there be no more than 27 lines of text on the page. In a student paper, however, these criteria are flexible. Double-space the printout, and print on one side of the paper only, using a page header to number the pages consecutively (described before and illustrated in Mary's paper).

Be sure to back up your work routinely. You never know when somebody may playfully touch a couple of keys and erase all your hard work. It is also a good idea to print a hard copy of each day's labors, so you have a double guarantee that you will not lose your work. When the clean, corrected final draft is completed, make an extra copy—just in case. The original is for the instructor, and the duplicate copy ensures that a spare copy will be readily available if a problem arises.

Notice that Mary's paper leaves the right margin *ragged* (i.e., uneven), which is also a requirement of the APA manual. If this were an article for submission to a journal, although your manuscript would have a ragged right margin, the printed version would appear *justified* (i.e., even on the left and right, as in this book). Now is the time to give your paper a final look, checking to see that all the pages are there and in order, and then to turn it in on schedule. Having adhered to these guidelines, you should feel the satisfaction of a job well done.

Creating a Poster

If you plan to present a poster at a professional meeting, check to see whether the association has particular requirements, such as the number of pages that are permitted. The poster board surface also varies from one sponsoring organization to another but is usually around 4 feet high and either 6 or 8 feet wide. To give you a general idea, Exhibit A.2 shows a template for a poster consisting of six pages. This is usually the bare minimum, so if you have room for additional pages you can plan on including further information. Because you are obviously limited in how much you can say in a six-page poster, it is important to bring along copies of a more complete report to give to anyone who asks for one. On the title page, note your e-mail address and mailing address, so people can get in touch with you if they want to.

Your choice of font size should be determined by the distance from which people will be viewing the posters. The font height should not be less than 3/8 inches, though you might use a bigger font for the title and authors (no less than one inch or, depending on distance, as much as 2–3 inches high). As one instructor cautioned, "Be prepared for being in a cramped area with relatively poor lighting, a lot of distracting noise, and other sensory activity" (Rosnow & Rosnow, 2003, p. 102). Here are further tips from Rosnow and Rosnow's text:

- Use a typeface that is easy to read, such as Arial or Times New Roman, not a fancy one that has squiggles or loops.
- Stand back about 5 feet and see if you can read the poster; the font size should not be less than 24 points.
- Because viewers don't usually want to stand around and study a poster assiduously, use as few words as possible, perhaps emphasizing the main ideas with bullets (as illustrated by Mary's poster).
- Don't overcomplicate tables or figures, and don't use jargon or exotic terms that may be unfamiliar to viewers and turn them away.
- Make your graphics simple so that they are eye-catching, such as a good photo or a good picture.
- Use color for important highlights, but use it sparingly because you are reporting a scientific study, not creating a work of art.
- Try looking at your poster through the eyes of those you want to attract, and also try it out on your instructor and other students for feedback.

Exhibit A.3 shows a poster based on Mary's study and Exhibit A.2's six-page template. You can see that it captures the highlights of her study, but it still would be necessary to read the report to understand the study thoroughly. Thus, it is important to bring along copies of a more complete report rather than simply hand out copies of the poster. However, your handout report should not be the paper you wrote for your instructor, which would be much too long and filled with irrelevant details for poster viewers. The idea is to try to boil down your research to a one-page handout with the information single-spaced on both sides. At the very least, your handout should report group means, sample sizes, and measurement error, as the reader will need this information to reanalyze your results. The idea is to try to anticipate people's questions and to tell them enough so they can come to their own conclusions.

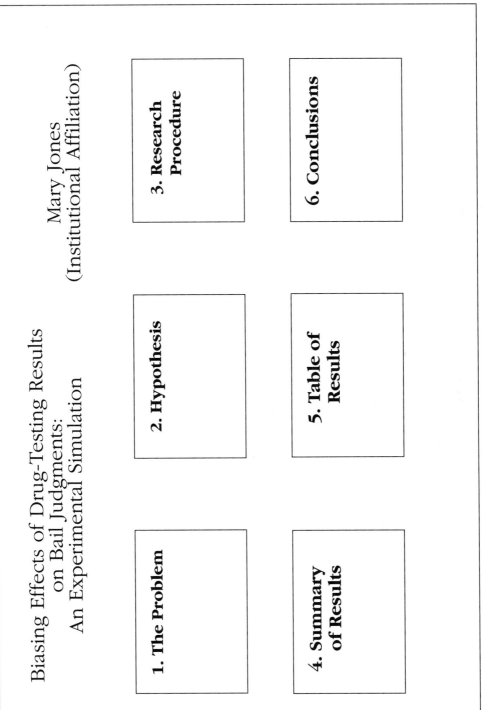

Exhibit A.2   Template for Poster Consisting of 6 Pages Based on Mary's Study in Exhibit A.1.

1. The Problem

Suppose someone arrested for suspicion of burglary is up for bail judgment and the judge knows that the suspect, when arrested, tested positive for drug use. Is the judge likely to order a harsher bail because of this information?

The crime control side has generally argued that mandatory drug testing of all suspects upon arrest will have no biasing effects in legal proceedings, whereas the due process side has argued that drug information will have prejudicial effects.

The purpose of this simulation experiment was to determine whether informing "judges" that the defendant has tested positive for drug usage would result in higher bail judgments.

2. Hypothesis

According to Jones and Davis's (1965) correspondent inference theory, observers focus mainly on certain types of observed behavior of an actor to infer traits because they believe that only certain behaviors are indicative of the actor's traits.

Once observers have inferred these traits, they use this information to predict the actor's future behavior and, in turn, to assess and to guide their own actions, decisions, and judgments regarding the actor.

On the basis of these assumptions, I hypothesized that providing "judges" with the defendant's positive results from a drug test would result in harsher bail judgments than when this information was unavailable.

3. Method

The "judges" in this experiment were 31 undergraduate students, who were randomly assigned to two conditions and asked to read one of two forms of a crime scenario. Both forms stated that "a man was arrested as a suspected burglar" and that "he fit the description of a man seen running from a burglarized house."

In the experimental condition, the story was that, "while in custody, the man submitted to a blood test, and it was determined that he had very recently used drugs." In the control condition, this information was omitted, and the story concluded with the statement that "the man spent enough time in custody so that he received two meals and made three phone calls."

The students were asked to pretend to be the bail judge and to choose a dollar figure from $0 to $50,000 as the amount of bail.

Exhibit A.3   **Mary Jones's Poster Presentation Using the Template in Exhibit A.2.**

(continued)

4. Summary of Results

The results, shown in the table, indicated that the mean judgment of the experimental participants was higher than the mean judgment of the control participants, with $t(29) = 2.08$, one-tailed $p = .023$, $r_{effect\ size} = .36$.

Underlying the use of the t test is the assumption that the population variances are equal, but when I divided the larger of the two associated variances (S^2) by the smaller of the two variances, I found $F(14, 15) = 9.0$, $p = .00013$, implying heterogeneity of variance.

When I used Satterthwaite's procedure, including adjustment of the degrees of freedom to make the t more accurate, the results were not much different: Satterthwaite $t(16) = 2.03$, one-tailed $p = .03$, $r_{effect\ size} = .34$. With 90% confidence, I can say that the population value of the $r_{effect\ size}$ falls between .05 and .58.

5. Mean, Variance, and Number of Participants

Measure	Experimental group	Control group
Mean	$16,146.67	$6,990.63
S	16,645.07	5,549.60
n	15	16

6. Discussion

The results were consistent with the hypothesis that bail judgments would be biased in a harsher direction in the experimental than in the control condition. One possible implication of this finding is that our justice system's goal of being evenhanded and unbiased could be jeopardized if the results of mandatory drug testing were made available to judges prior to their bail judgments.

An important limitation of this study, however, is that the participants were college students, and thus, it might be argued that the results are not generalizable to actual bail judges. Another issue to be explored is whether the students' actual inferences of corresponding traits from socially undesirable behavior drew on a stereotype to assume that there was a likely association between drug usage and information in the burglary scenario.

Exhibit A.3   Mary Jones's Poster Presentation Using the Template in Exhibit A.2.
(*continued*)

APPENDIX B

Statistical Tables

Table B.1	z Values and Their Associated One-Tailed p Values

Second digit of z

z	.00	.01	.02	.03	.04	.05	.06	.07	.08	.09
.0	.5000	.4960	.4920	.4880	.4840	.4801	.4761	.4721	.4681	.4641
.1	.4602	.4562	.4522	.4483	.4443	.4404	.4364	.4325	.4286	.4247
.2	.4207	.4168	.4129	.4090	.4052	.4013	.3974	.3936	.3897	.3859
.3	.3821	.3783	.3745	.3707	.3669	.3632	.3594	.3557	.3520	.3483
.4	.3446	.3409	.3372	.3336	.3300	.3264	.3228	.3192	.3156	.3121
.5	.3085	.3050	.3015	.2981	.2946	.2912	.2877	.2843	.2810	.2776
.6	.2743	.2709	.2676	.2643	.2611	.2578	.2546	.2514	.2483	.2451
.7	.2420	.2389	.2358	.2327	.2296	.2266	.2236	.2206	.2177	.2148
.8	.2119	.2090	.2061	.2033	.2005	.1977	.1949	.1922	.1894	.1867
.9	.1841	.1814	.1788	.1762	.1736	.1711	.1685	.1660	.1635	.1611
1.0	.1587	.1562	.1539	.1515	.1492	.1469	.1446	.1423	.1401	.1379
1.1	.1357	.1335	.1314	.1292	.1271	.1251	.1230	.1210	.1190	.1170
1.2	.1151	.1131	.1112	.1093	.1075	.1056	.1038	.1020	.1003	.0985
1.3	.0968	.0951	.0934	.0918	.0901	.0885	.0869	.0853	.0838	.0823
1.4	.0808	.0793	.0778	.0764	.0749	.0735	.0721	.0708	.0694	.0681
1.5	.0668	.0655	.0643	.0630	.0618	.0606	.0594	.0582	.0571	.0559
1.6	.0548	.0537	.0526	.0516	.0505	.0495	.0485	.0475	.0465	.0455
1.7	.0446	.0436	.0427	.0418	.0409	.0401	.0392	.0384	.0375	.0367
1.8	.0359	.0351	.0344	.0336	.0329	.0322	.0314	.0307	.0301	.0294
1.9	.0287	.0281	.0274	.0268	.0262	.0256	.0250	.0244	.0239	.0233
2.0	.0228	.0222	.0217	.0212	.0207	.0202	.0197	.0192	.0188	.0183
2.1	.0179	.0174	.0170	.0166	.0162	.0158	.0154	.0150	.0146	.0143
2.2	.0139	.0136	.0132	.0129	.0125	.0122	.0119	.0116	.0113	.0110
2.3	.0107	.0104	.0102	.0099	.0096	.0094	.0091	.0089	.0087	.0084
2.4	.0082	.0080	.0078	.0075	.0073	.0071	.0069	.0068	.0066	.0064
2.5	.0062	.0060	.0059	.0057	.0055	.0054	.0052	.0051	.0049	.0048
2.6	.0047	.0045	.0044	.0043	.0041	.0040	.0039	.0038	.0037	.0036
2.7	.0035	.0034	.0033	.0032	.0031	.0030	.0029	.0028	.0027	.0026
2.8	.0026	.0025	.0024	.0023	.0023	.0022	.0021	.0021	.0020	.0019
2.9	.0019	.0018	.0018	.0017	.0016	.0016	.0015	.0015	.0014	.0014
3.0	.0013	.0013	.0013	.0012	.0012	.0011	.0011	.0011	.0010	.0010
3.1	.0010	.0009	.0009	.0009	.0008	.0008	.0008	.0008	.0007	.0007
3.2	.0007									
3.3	.0005									
3.4	.0003									
3.5	.00023									
3.6	.00016									
3.7	.00011									
3.8	.00007									
3.9	.00005									
4.0	.00003									

Source: From *Nonparametric Statistics* (p. 247), by S. Siegel, 1956, New York: McGraw-Hill. Reprinted by permission of McGraw-Hill, Inc.

Appendix B

Table B.2   t Values and Their Associated One-Tailed and Two-Tailed p Values

df \ p	.50	.20	.10	.05	.02	.01	.005	.002	two-tailed
	.25	.10	.05	.025	.01	.005	.0025	.001	one-tailed
1	1.000	3.078	6.314	12.706	31.821	63.657	127.321	318.309	
2	.816	1.886	2.920	4.303	6.965	9.925	14.089	22.327	
3	.765	1.638	2.353	3.182	4.541	5.841	7.453	10.214	
4	.741	1.533	2.132	2.776	3.747	4.604	5.598	7.173	
5	.727	1.476	2.015	2.571	3.365	4.032	4.773	5.893	
6	.718	1.440	1.943	2.447	3.143	3.707	4.317	5.208	
7	.711	1.415	1.895	2.365	2.998	3.499	4.029	4.785	
8	.706	1.397	1.860	2.306	2.896	3.355	3.833	4.501	
9	.703	1.383	1.833	2.262	2.821	3.250	3.690	4.297	
10	.700	1.372	1.812	2.228	2.764	3.169	3.581	4.144	
11	.697	1.363	1.796	2.201	2.718	3.106	3.497	4.025	
12	.695	1.356	1.782	2.179	2.681	3.055	3.428	3.930	
13	.694	1.350	1.771	2.160	2.650	3.012	3.372	3.852	
14	.692	1.345	1.761	2.145	2.624	2.977	3.326	3.787	
15	.691	1.341	1.753	2.131	2.602	2.947	3.286	3.733	
16	.690	1.337	1.746	2.120	2.583	2.921	3.252	3.686	
17	.689	1.333	1.740	2.110	2.567	2.898	3.223	3.646	
18	.688	1.330	1.734	2.101	2.552	2.878	3.197	3.610	
19	.688	1.328	1.729	2.093	2.539	2.861	3.174	3.579	
20	.687	1.325	1.725	2.086	2.528	2.845	3.153	3.552	
21	.686	1.323	1.721	2.080	2.518	2.831	3.135	3.527	
22	.686	1.321	1.717	2.074	2.508	2.819	3.119	3.505	
23	.685	1.319	1.714	2.069	2.500	2.807	3.104	3.485	
24	.685	1.318	1.711	2.064	2.492	2.797	3.090	3.467	
25	.684	1.316	1.708	2.060	2.485	2.787	3.078	3.450	
26	.684	1.315	1.706	2.056	2.479	2.779	3.067	3.435	
27	.684	1.314	1.703	2.052	2.473	2.771	3.057	3.421	
28	.683	1.313	1.701	2.048	2.467	2.763	3.047	3.408	
29	.683	1.311	1.699	2.045	2.462	2.756	3.038	3.396	
30	.683	1.310	1.697	2.042	2.457	2.750	3.030	3.385	
35	.682	1.306	1.690	2.030	2.438	2.724	2.996	3.340	
40	.681	1.303	1.684	2.021	2.423	2.704	2.971	3.307	
45	.680	1.301	1.679	2.014	2.412	2.690	2.952	3.281	
50	.679	1.299	1.676	2.009	2.403	2.678	2.937	3.261	
55	.679	1.297	1.673	2.004	2.396	2.668	2.925	3.245	
60	.679	1.296	1.671	2.000	2.390	2.660	2.915	3.232	
70	.678	1.294	1.667	1.994	2.381	2.648	2.899	3.211	
80	.678	1.292	1.664	1.990	2.374	2.639	2.887	3.195	
90	.677	1.291	1.662	1.987	2.368	2.632	2.878	3.183	
100	.677	1.290	1.660	1.984	2.364	2.626	2.871	3.174	
200	.676	1.286	1.652	1.972	2.345	2.601	2.838	3.131	
500	.675	1.283	1.648	1.965	2.334	2.586	2.820	3.107	
1,000	.675	1.282	1.646	1.962	2.330	2.581	2.813	3.098	
2,000	.675	1.282	1.645	1.961	2.328	2.578	2.810	3.094	
10,000	.675	1.282	1.645	1.960	2.327	2.576	2.808	3.091	
∞	.674	1.282	1.645	1.960	2.326	2.576	2.807	3.090	

(continued)

Table B.2 t Values and Their Associated One-Tailed and Two-Tailed p Values

df	.001	.0005	.0002	.0001	.00005	.00002	two-tailed
	.0005	.00025	.0001	.00005	.000025	.00001	one-tailed
1	636.619	1,273.239	3,183.099	6,366.198	12,732.395	31,830.989	
2	31.598	44.705	70.700	99.992	141.416	223.603	
3	12.924	16.326	22.204	28.000	35.298	47.928	
4	8.610	10.306	13.034	15.544	18.522	23.332	
5	6.869	7.976	9.678	11.178	12.893	15.547	
6	5.959	6.788	8.025	9.082	10.261	12.032	
7	5.408	6.082	7.063	7.885	8.782	10.103	
8	5.041	5.618	6.442	7.120	7.851	8.907	
9	4.781	5.291	6.010	6.594	7.215	8.102	
10	4.587	5.049	5.694	6.211	6.757	7.527	
11	4.437	4.863	5.453	5.921	6.412	7.098	
12	4.318	4.716	5.263	5.694	6.143	6.756	
13	4.221	4.597	5.111	5.513	5.928	6.501	
14	4.140	4.499	4.985	5.363	5.753	6.287	
15	4.073	4.417	4.880	5.239	5.607	6.109	
16	4.015	4.346	4.791	5.134	5.484	5.960	
17	3.965	4.286	4.714	5.044	5.379	5.832	
18	3.922	4.233	4.648	4.966	5.288	5.722	
19	3.883	4.187	4.590	4.897	5.209	5.627	
20	3.850	4.146	4.539	4.837	5.139	5.543	
21	3.819	4.110	4.493	4.784	5.077	5.469	
22	3.792	4.077	4.452	4.736	5.022	5.402	
23	3.768	4.048	4.415	4.693	4.972	5.343	
24	3.745	4.021	4.382	4.654	4.927	5.290	
25	3.725	3.997	4.352	4.619	4.887	5.241	
26	3.707	3.974	4.324	4.587	4.850	5.197	
27	3.690	3.954	4.299	4.558	4.816	5.157	
28	3.674	3.935	4.275	4.530	4.784	5.120	
29	3.659	3.918	4.254	4.506	4.756	5.086	
30	3.646	3.902	4.234	4.482	4.729	5.054	
35	3.591	3.836	4.153	4.389	4.622	4.927	
40	3.551	3.788	4.094	4.321	4.544	4.835	
45	3.520	3.752	4.049	4.269	4.485	4.766	
50	3.496	3.723	4.014	4.228	4.438	4.711	
55	3.476	3.700	3.986	4.196	4.401	4.667	
60	3.460	3.681	3.926	4.169	4.370	4.631	
70	3.435	3.651	3.962	4.127	4.323	4.576	
80	3.416	3.629	3.899	4.096	4.288	4.535	
90	3.402	3.612	3.878	4.072	4.261	4.503	
100	3.390	3.598	3.862	4.053	4.240	4.478	
200	3.340	3.539	3.789	3.970	4.146	4.369	
500	3.310	3.504	3.747	3.922	4.091	4.306	
1,000	3.300	3.492	3.733	3.906	4.073	4.285	
2,000	3.295	3.486	3.726	3.898	4.064	4.275	
10,000	3.292	3.482	3.720	3.892	4.058	4.267	
∞	3.291	3.481	3.719	3.891	4.056	4.265	

Source: From "Extended Tables of the Percentage Points of Student's *t*-Distribution," by E. T. Federighi, 1959, *Journal of the American Statistical Association, 54*, pp. 683–688. Reprinted by permission of the American Statistical Association.

Table B.3 F Values and Their Associated p Values

df_2	p	1	2	3	4	5	6	8	12	24	∞
1	.001	405284	500000	540379	562500	576405	585937	598144	610667	623497	636619
	.005	16211	20000	21615	22500	23056	23437	23925	24426	24940	25465
	.01	4052	4999	5403	5625	5764	5859	5981	6106	6234	6366
	.025	647.79	799.50	864.16	899.58	921.85	937.11	956.66	976.71	997.25	1018.30
	.05	161.45	199.50	215.71	224.58	230.16	233.99	238.88	243.91	249.05	254.32
	.10	39.86	49.50	53.59	55.83	57.24	58.20	59.44	60.70	62.00	63.33
	.20	9.47	12.00	13.06	13.73	14.01	14.26	14.59	14.90	15.24	15.58
2	.001	998.5	999.0	999.2	999.2	999.3	999.3	999.4	999.4	999.5	999.5
	.005	198.50	199.00	199.17	199.25	199.30	199.33	199.37	199.42	199.46	199.51
	.01	98.49	99.00	99.17	99.25	99.30	99.33	99.36	99.42	99.46	99.50
	.025	38.51	39.00	39.17	39.25	39.30	39.33	39.37	39.42	39.46	39.50
	.05	18.51	19.00	19.16	19.25	19.30	19.33	19.37	19.41	19.45	19.50
	.10	8.53	9.00	9.16	9.24	9.29	9.33	9.37	9.41	9.45	9.49
	.20	3.56	4.00	4.16	4.24	4.28	4.32	4.36	4.40	4.44	4.48
3	.001	167.5	148.5	141.1	137.1	134.6	132.8	130.6	128.3	125.9	123.5
	.005	55.55	49.80	47.47	46.20	45.39	44.84	44.13	43.39	42.62	41.83
	.01	34.12	30.81	29.46	28.71	28.24	27.91	27.49	27.05	26.60	26.12
	.025	17.44	16.04	15.44	15.10	14.89	14.74	14.54	14.34	14.12	13.90
	.05	10.13	9.55	9.28	9.12	9.01	8.94	8.84	8.74	8.64	8.53
	.10	5.54	5.46	5.39	5.34	5.31	5.28	5.25	5.22	5.18	5.13
	.20	2.68	2.89	2.94	2.96	2.97	2.97	2.98	2.98	2.98	2.98
4	.001	74.14	61.25	56.18	53.44	51.71	50.53	49.00	47.41	45.77	44.05
	.005	31.33	26.28	24.26	23.16	22.46	21.98	21.35	20.71	20.03	19.33
	.01	21.20	18.00	16.69	15.98	15.52	15.21	14.80	14.37	13.93	13.46
	.025	12.22	10.65	9.98	9.60	9.36	9.20	8.98	8.75	8.51	8.26
	.05	7.71	6.94	6.59	6.39	6.26	6.16	6.04	5.91	5.77	5.63
	.10	4.54	4.32	4.19	4.11	4.05	4.01	3.95	3.90	3.83	3.76
	.20	2.35	2.47	2.48	2.48	2.48	2.47	2.47	2.46	2.44	2.43
5	.001	47.04	36.61	33.20	31.09	29.75	28.84	27.64	26.42	25.14	23.78
	.005	22.79	18.31	16.53	15.56	14.94	14.51	13.96	13.38	12.78	12.14
	.01	16.26	13.27	12.06	11.39	10.97	10.67	10.29	9.89	9.47	9.02
	.025	10.01	8.43	7.76	7.39	7.15	6.98	6.76	6.52	6.28	6.02
	.05	6.61	5.79	5.41	5.19	5.05	4.95	4.82	4.68	4.53	4.36
	.10	4.06	3.78	3.62	3.52	3.45	3.40	3.34	3.27	3.19	3.10
	.20	2.18	2.26	2.25	2.24	2.23	2.22	2.20	2.18	2.16	2.13
6	.001	35.51	27.00	23.70	21.90	20.81	20.03	19.03	17.99	16.89	15.75
	.005	18.64	14.54	12.92	12.03	11.46	11.07	10.57	10.03	9.47	8.88
	.01	13.74	10.92	9.78	9.15	8.75	8.47	8.10	7.72	7.31	6.88
	.025	8.81	7.26	6.60	6.23	5.99	5.82	5.60	5.37	5.12	4.85
	.05	5.99	5.14	4.76	4.53	4.39	4.28	4.15	4.00	3.84	3.67
	.10	3.78	3.46	3.29	3.18	3.11	3.05	2.98	2.90	2.82	2.72
	.20	2.07	2.13	2.11	2.09	2.08	2.06	2.04	2.02	1.99	1.95
7	.001	29.22	21.69	18.77	17.19	16.21	15.52	14.63	13.71	12.73	11.69
	.005	16.24	12.40	10.88	10.05	9.52	9.16	8.68	8.18	7.65	7.08
	.01	12.25	9.55	8.45	7.85	7.46	7.19	6.84	6.47	6.07	5.65
	.025	8.07	6.54	5.89	5.52	5.29	5.12	4.90	4.67	4.42	4.14
	.05	5.59	4.74	4.35	4.12	3.97	3.87	3.73	3.57	3.41	3.23
	.10	3.59	3.26	3.07	2.96	2.88	2.83	2.75	2.67	2.58	2.47
	.20	2.00	2.04	2.02	1.99	1.97	1.96	1.93	1.91	1.87	1.83

(continued)

Table B.3 — F Values and Their Associated p Values

df_2	p	1	2	3	4	5	6	8	12	24	∞
8	.001	25.42	18.49	15.83	14.39	13.49	12.86	12.04	11.19	10.30	9.34
	.005	14.69	11.04	9.60	8.81	8.30	7.95	7.50	7.01	6.50	5.95
	.01	11.26	8.65	7.59	7.01	6.63	6.37	6.03	5.67	5.28	4.86
	.025	7.57	6.06	5.42	5.05	4.82	4.65	4.43	4.20	3.95	3.67
	.05	5.32	4.46	4.07	3.84	3.69	3.58	3.44	3.28	3.12	2.93
	.10	3.46	3.11	2.92	2.81	2.73	2.67	2.59	2.50	2.40	2.29
	.20	1.95	1.98	1.95	1.92	1.90	1.88	1.86	1.83	1.79	1.74
9	.001	22.86	16.39	13.90	12.56	11.71	11.13	10.37	9.57	8.72	7.81
	.005	13.61	10.11	8.72	7.96	7.47	7.13	6.69	6.23	5.73	5.19
	.01	10.56	8.02	6.99	6.42	6.06	5.80	5.47	5.11	4.73	4.31
	.025	7.21	5.71	5.08	4.72	4.48	4.32	4.10	3.87	3.61	3.33
	.05	5.12	4.26	3.86	3.63	3.48	3.37	3.23	3.07	2.90	2.71
	.10	3.36	3.01	2.81	2.69	2.61	2.55	2.47	2.38	2.28	2.16
	.20	1.91	1.94	1.90	1.87	1.85	1.83	1.80	1.76	1.73	1.67
10	.001	21.04	14.91	12.55	11.28	10.48	9.92	9.20	8.45	7.64	6.76
	.005	12.83	9.43	8.08	7.34	6.87	6.54	6.12	5.66	5.17	4.64
	.01	10.04	7.56	6.55	5.99	5.64	5.39	5.06	4.71	4.33	3.91
	.025	6.94	5.46	4.83	4.47	4.24	4.07	3.85	3.62	3.37	3.08
	.05	4.96	4.10	3.71	3.48	3.33	3.22	3.07	2.91	2.74	2.54
	.10	3.28	2.92	2.73	2.61	2.52	2.46	2.38	2.28	2.18	2.06
	.20	1.88	1.90	1.86	1.83	1.80	1.78	1.75	1.72	1.67	1.62
11	.001	19.69	13.81	11.56	10.35	9.58	9.05	8.35	7.63	6.85	6.00
	.005	12.23	8.91	7.60	6.88	6.42	6.10	5.68	5.24	4.76	4.23
	.01	9.65	7.20	6.22	5.67	5.32	5.07	4.74	4.40	4.02	3.60
	.025	6.72	5.26	4.63	4.28	4.04	3.88	3.66	3.43	3.17	2.88
	.05	4.84	3.98	3.59	3.36	3.20	3.09	2.95	2.79	2.61	2.40
	.10	3.23	2.86	2.66	2.54	2.45	2.39	2.30	2.21	2.10	1.97
	.20	1.86	1.87	1.83	1.80	1.77	1.75	1.72	1.68	1.63	1.57
12	.001	18.64	12.97	10.80	9.63	8.89	8.38	7.71	7.00	6.25	5.42
	.005	11.75	8.51	7.23	6.52	6.07	5.76	5.35	4.91	4.43	3.90
	.01	9.33	6.93	5.95	5.41	5.06	4.82	4.50	4.16	3.78	3.36
	.025	6.55	5.10	4.47	4.12	3.89	3.73	3.51	3.28	3.02	2.72
	.05	4.75	3.88	3.49	3.26	3.11	3.00	2.85	2.69	2.50	2.30
	.10	3.18	2.81	2.61	2.48	2.39	2.33	2.24	2.15	2.04	1.90
	.20	1.84	1.85	1.80	1.77	1.74	1.72	1.69	1.65	1.60	1.54
13	.001	17.81	12.31	10.21	9.07	8.35	7.86	7.21	6.52	5.78	4.97
	.005	11.37	8.19	6.93	6.23	5.79	5.48	5.08	4.64	4.17	3.65
	.01	9.07	6.70	5.74	5.20	4.86	4.62	4.30	3.96	3.59	3.16
	.025	6.41	4.97	4.35	4.00	3.77	3.60	3.39	3.15	2.89	2.60
	.05	4.67	3.80	3.41	3.18	3.02	2.92	2.77	2.60	2.42	2.21
	.10	3.14	2.76	2.56	2.43	2.35	2.28	2.20	2.10	1.98	1.85
	.20	1.82	1.83	1.78	1.75	1.72	1.69	1.66	1.62	1.57	1.51
14	.001	17.14	11.78	9.73	8.62	7.92	7.43	6.80	6.13	5.41	4.60
	.005	11.06	7.92	6.68	6.00	5.56	5.26	4.86	4.43	3.96	3.44
	.01	8.86	6.51	5.56	5.03	4.69	4.46	4.14	3.80	3.43	3.00
	.025	6.30	4.86	4.24	3.89	3.66	3.50	3.29	3.05	2.79	2.49
	.05	4.60	3.74	3.34	3.11	2.96	2.85	2.70	2.53	2.35	2.13
	.10	3.10	2.73	2.52	2.39	2.31	2.24	2.15	2.05	1.94	1.80
	.20	1.81	1.81	1.76	1.73	1.70	1.67	1.64	1.60	1.55	1.48

(continued)

Table B.3		F Values and Their Associated p Values									
df_2 / df_1	p	1	2	3	4	5	6	8	12	24	∞
15	.001	16.59	11.34	9.34	8.25	7.57	7.09	6.47	5.81	5.10	4.31
	.005	10.80	7.70	6.48	5.80	5.37	5.07	4.67	4.25	3.79	3.26
	.01	8.68	6.36	5.42	4.89	4.56	4.32	4.00	3.67	3.29	2.87
	.025	6.20	4.77	4.15	3.80	3.58	3.41	3.20	2.96	2.70	2.40
	.05	4.54	3.68	3.29	3.06	2.90	2.79	2.64	2.48	2.29	2.07
	.10	3.07	2.70	2.49	2.36	2.27	2.21	2.12	2.02	1.90	1.76
	.20	1.80	1.79	1.75	1.71	1.68	1.66	1.62	1.58	1.53	1.46
16	.001	16.12	10.97	9.00	7.94	7.27	6.81	6.19	5.55	4.85	4.06
	.005	10.58	7.51	6.30	5.64	5.21	4.91	4.52	4.10	3.64	3.11
	.01	8.53	6.23	5.29	4.77	4.44	4.20	3.89	3.55	3.18	2.75
	.025	6.12	4.69	4.08	3.73	3.50	3.34	3.12	2.89	2.63	2.32
	.05	4.49	3.63	3.24	3.01	2.85	2.74	2.59	2.42	2.24	2.01
	.10	3.05	2.67	2.46	2.33	2.24	2.18	2.09	1.99	1.87	1.72
	.20	1.79	1.78	1.74	1.70	1.67	1.64	1.61	1.56	1.51	1.43
17	.001	15.72	10.66	8.73	7.68	7.02	6.56	5.96	5.32	4.63	3.85
	.005	10.38	7.35	6.16	5.50	5.07	4.78	4.39	3.97	3.51	2.98
	.01	8.40	6.11	5.18	4.67	4.34	4.10	3.79	3.45	3.08	2.65
	.025	6.04	4.62	4.01	3.66	3.44	3.28	3.06	2.82	2.56	2.25
	.05	4.45	3.59	3.20	2.96	2.81	2.70	2.55	2.38	2.19	1.96
	.10	3.03	2.64	2.44	2.31	2.22	2.15	2.06	1.96	1.84	1.69
	.20	1.78	1.77	1.72	1.68	1.65	1.63	1.59	1.55	1.49	1.42
18	.001	15.38	10.39	8.49	7.46	6.81	6.35	5.76	5.13	4.45	3.67
	.005	10.22	7.21	6.03	5.37	4.96	4.66	4.28	3.86	3.40	2.87
	.01	8.28	6.01	5.09	4.58	4.25	4.01	3.71	3.37	3.00	2.57
	.025	5.98	4.56	3.95	3.61	3.38	3.22	3.01	2.77	2.50	2.19
	.05	4.41	3.55	3.16	2.93	2.77	2.66	2.51	2.34	2.15	1.92
	.10	3.01	2.62	2.42	2.29	2.20	2.13	2.04	1.93	1.81	1.66
	.20	1.77	1.76	1.71	1.67	1.64	1.62	1.58	1.53	1.48	1.40
19	.001	15.08	10.16	8.28	7.26	6.61	6.18	5.59	4.97	4.29	3.52
	.005	10.07	7.09	5.92	5.27	4.85	4.56	4.18	3.76	3.31	2.78
	.01	8.18	5.93	5.01	4.50	4.17	3.94	3.63	3.30	2.92	2.49
	.025	5.92	4.51	3.90	3.56	3.33	3.17	2.96	2.72	2.45	2.13
	.05	4.38	3.52	3.13	2.90	2.74	2.63	2.48	2.31	2.11	1.88
	.10	2.99	2.61	2.40	2.27	2.18	2.11	2.02	1.91	1.79	1.63
	.20	1.76	1.75	1.70	1.66	1.63	1.61	1.57	1.52	1.46	1.39
20	.001	14.82	9.95	8.10	7.10	6.46	6.02	5.44	4.82	4.15	3.38
	.005	9.94	6.99	5.82	5.17	4.76	4.47	4.09	3.68	3.22	2.69
	.01	8.10	5.85	4.94	4.43	4.10	3.87	3.56	3.23	2.86	2.42
	.025	5.87	4.46	3.86	3.51	3.29	3.13	2.91	2.68	2.41	2.09
	.05	4.35	3.49	3.10	2.87	2.71	2.60	2.45	2.28	2.08	1.84
	.10	2.97	2.59	2.38	2.25	2.16	2.09	2.00	1.89	1.77	1.61
	.20	1.76	1.75	1.70	1.65	1.62	1.60	1.56	1.51	1.45	1.37
21	.001	14.59	9.77	7.94	6.95	6.32	5.88	5.31	4.70	4.03	3.26
	.005	9.83	6.89	5.73	5.09	4.68	4.39	4.01	3.60	3.15	2.61
	.01	8.02	5.78	4.87	4.37	4.04	3.81	3.51	3.17	2.80	2.36
	.025	5.83	4.42	3.82	3.48	3.25	3.09	2.87	2.64	2.37	2.04
	.05	4.32	3.47	3.07	2.84	2.68	2.57	2.42	2.25	2.05	1.81
	.10	2.96	2.57	2.36	2.23	2.14	2.08	1.98	1.88	1.75	1.59
	.20	1.75	1.74	1.69	1.65	1.61	1.59	1.55	1.50	1.44	1.36

(continued)

Table B.3						F Values and Their Associated p Values						
df_2 df_1	p	1	2	3	4	5	6	8	12	24	∞
22	.001	14.38	9.61	7.80	6.81	6.19	5.76	5.19	4.58	3.92	3.15
	.005	9.73	6.81	5.65	5.02	4.61	4.32	3.94	3.54	3.08	2.55
	.01	7.94	5.72	4.82	4.31	3.99	3.76	3.45	3.12	2.75	2.31
	.025	5.79	4.38	3.78	3.44	3.22	3.05	2.84	2.60	2.33	2.00
	.05	4.30	3.44	3.05	2.82	2.66	2.55	2.40	2.23	2.03	1.78
	.10	2.95	2.56	2.35	2.22	2.13	2.06	1.97	1.86	1.73	1.57
	.20	1.75	1.73	1.68	1.64	1.61	1.58	1.54	1.49	1.43	1.35
23	.001	14.19	9.47	7.67	6.69	6.08	5.65	5.09	4.48	3.82	3.05
	.005	9.63	6.73	5.58	4.95	4.54	4.26	3.88	3.47	3.02	2.48
	.01	7.88	5.66	4.76	4.26	3.94	3.71	3.41	3.07	2.70	2.26
	.025	5.75	4.35	3.75	3.41	3.18	3.02	2.81	2.57	2.30	1.97
	.05	4.28	3.42	3.03	2.80	2.64	2.53	2.38	2.20	2.00	1.76
	.10	2.94	2.55	2.34	2.21	2.11	2.05	1.95	1.84	1.72	1.55
	.20	1.74	1.73	1.68	1.63	1.60	1.57	1.53	1.49	1.42	1.34
24	.001	14.03	9.34	7.55	6.59	5.98	5.55	4.99	4.39	3.74	2.97
	.005	9.55	6.66	5.52	4.89	4.49	4.20	3.83	3.42	2.97	2.43
	.01	7.82	5.61	4.72	4.22	3.90	3.67	3.36	3.03	2.66	2.21
	.025	5.72	4.32	3.72	3.38	3.15	2.99	2.78	2.54	2.27	1.94
	.05	4.26	3.40	3.01	2.78	2.62	2.51	2.36	2.18	1.98	1.73
	.10	2.93	2.54	2.33	2.19	2.10	2.04	1.94	1.83	1.70	1.53
	.20	1.74	1.72	1.67	1.63	1.59	1.57	1.53	1.48	1.42	1.33
25	.001	13.88	9.22	7.45	6.49	5.88	5.46	4.91	4.31	3.66	2.89
	.005	9.48	6.60	5.46	4.84	4.43	4.15	3.78	3.37	2.92	2.38
	.01	7.77	5.57	4.68	4.18	3.86	3.63	3.32	2.99	2.62	2.17
	.025	5.69	4.29	3.69	3.35	3.13	2.97	2.75	2.51	2.24	1.91
	.05	4.24	3.38	2.99	2.76	2.60	2.49	2.34	2.16	1.96	1.71
	.10	2.92	2.53	2.32	2.18	2.09	2.02	1.93	1.82	1.69	1.52
	.20	1.73	1.72	1.66	1.62	1.59	1.56	1.52	1.47	1.41	1.32
26	.001	13.74	9.12	7.36	6.41	5.80	5.38	4.83	4.24	3.59	2.82
	.005	9.41	6.54	5.41	4.79	4.38	4.10	3.73	3.33	2.87	2.33
	.01	7.72	5.53	4.64	4.14	3.82	3.59	3.29	2.96	2.58	2.13
	.025	5.66	4.27	3.67	3.33	3.10	2.94	2.73	2.49	2.22	1.88
	.05	4.22	3.37	2.98	2.74	2.59	2.47	2.32	2.15	1.95	1.69
	.10	2.91	2.52	2.31	2.17	2.08	2.01	1.92	1.81	1.68	1.50
	.20	1.73	1.71	1.66	1.62	1.58	1.56	1.52	1.47	1.40	1.31
27	.001	13.61	9.02	7.27	6.33	5.73	5.31	4.76	4.17	3.52	2.75
	.005	9.34	6.49	5.36	4.74	4.34	4.06	3.69	3.28	2.83	2.29
	.01	7.68	5.49	4.60	4.11	3.78	3.56	3.26	2.93	2.55	2.10
	.025	5.63	4.24	3.65	3.31	3.08	2.92	2.71	2.47	2.19	1.85
	.05	4.21	3.35	2.96	2.73	2.57	2.46	2.30	2.13	1.93	1.67
	.10	2.90	2.51	2.30	2.17	2.07	2.00	1.91	1.80	1.67	1.49
	.20	1.73	1.71	1.66	1.61	1.58	1.55	1.51	1.46	1.40	1.30
28	.001	13.50	8.93	7.19	6.25	5.66	5.24	4.69	4.11	3.46	2.70
	.005	9.28	6.44	5.32	4.70	4.30	4.02	3.65	3.25	2.79	2.25
	.01	7.64	5.45	4.57	4.07	3.75	3.53	3.23	2.90	2.52	2.06
	.025	5.61	4.22	3.63	3.29	3.06	2.90	2.69	2.45	2.17	1.83
	.05	4.20	3.34	2.95	2.71	2.56	2.44	2.29	2.12	1.91	1.65
	.10	2.89	2.50	2.29	2.16	2.06	2.00	1.90	1.79	1.66	1.48
	.20	1.72	1.71	1.65	1.61	1.57	1.55	1.51	1.46	1.39	1.30

(continued)

Table B.3		F Values and Their Associated *p* Values									
df_2 \ df_1	*p*	1	2	3	4	5	6	8	12	24	∞
29	.001	13.39	8.85	7.12	6.19	5.59	5.18	4.64	4.05	3.41	2.64
	.005	9.23	6.40	5.28	4.66	4.26	3.98	3.61	3.21	2.76	2.21
	.01	7.60	5.42	4.54	4.04	3.73	3.50	3.20	2.87	2.49	2.03
	.025	5.59	4.20	3.61	3.27	3.04	2.88	2.67	2.43	2.15	1.81
	.05	4.18	3.33	2.93	2.70	2.54	2.43	2.28	2.10	1.90	1.64
	.10	2.89	2.50	2.28	2.15	2.06	1.99	1.89	1.78	1.65	1.47
	.20	1.72	1.70	1.65	1.60	1.57	1.54	1.50	1.45	1.39	1.29
30	.001	13.29	8.77	7.05	6.12	5.53	5.12	4.58	4.00	3.36	2.59
	.005	9.18	6.35	5.24	4.62	4.23	3.95	3.58	3.18	2.73	2.18
	.01	7.56	5.39	4.51	4.02	3.70	3.47	3.17	2.84	2.47	2.01
	.025	5.57	4.18	3.59	3.25	3.03	2.87	2.65	2.41	2.14	1.79
	.05	4.17	3.32	2.92	2.69	2.53	2.42	2.27	2.09	1.89	1.62
	.10	2.88	2.49	2.28	2.14	2.05	1.98	1.88	1.77	1.64	1.46
	.20	1.72	1.70	1.64	1.60	1.57	1.54	1.50	1.45	1.38	1.28
40	.001	12.61	8.25	6.60	5.70	5.13	4.73	4.21	3.64	3.01	2.23
	.005	8.83	6.07	4.98	4.37	3.99	3.71	3.35	2.95	2.50	1.93
	.01	7.31	5.18	4.31	3.83	3.51	3.29	2.99	2.66	2.29	1.80
	.025	5.42	4.05	3.46	3.13	2.90	2.74	2.53	2.29	2.01	1.64
	.05	4.08	3.23	2.84	2.61	2.45	2.34	2.18	2.00	1.79	1.51
	.10	2.84	2.44	2.23	2.09	2.00	1.93	1.83	1.71	1.57	1.38
	.20	1.70	1.68	1.62	1.57	1.54	1.51	1.47	1.41	1.34	1.24
60	.001	11.97	7.76	6.17	5.31	4.76	4.37	3.87	3.31	2.69	1.90
	.005	8.49	5.80	4.73	4.14	3.76	3.49	3.13	2.74	2.29	1.69
	.01	7.08	4.98	4.13	3.65	3.34	3.12	2.82	2.50	2.12	1.60
	.025	5.29	3.93	3.34	3.01	2.79	2.63	2.41	2.17	1.88	1.48
	.05	4.00	3.15	2.76	2.52	2.37	2.25	2.10	1.92	1.70	1.39
	.10	2.79	2.39	2.18	2.04	1.95	1.87	1.77	1.66	1.51	1.29
	.20	1.68	1.65	1.59	1.55	1.51	1.48	1.44	1.38	1.31	1.18
120	.001	11.38	7.31	5.79	4.95	4.42	4.04	3.55	3.02	2.40	1.56
	.005	8.18	5.54	4.50	3.92	3.55	3.28	2.93	2.54	2.09	1.43
	.01	6.85	4.79	3.95	3.48	3.17	2.96	2.66	2.34	1.95	1.38
	.025	5.15	3.80	3.23	2.89	2.67	2.52	2.30	2.05	1.76	1.31
	.05	3.92	3.07	2.68	2.45	2.29	2.17	2.02	1.83	1.61	1.25
	.10	2.75	2.35	2.13	1.99	1.90	1.82	1.72	1.60	1.45	1.19
	.20	1.66	1.63	1.57	1.52	1.48	1.45	1.41	1.35	1.27	1.12
∞	.001	10.83	6.91	5.42	4.62	4.10	3.74	3.27	2.74	2.13	1.00
	.005	7.88	5.30	4.28	3.72	3.35	3.09	2.74	2.36	1.90	1.00
	.01	6.64	4.60	3.78	3.32	3.02	2.80	2.51	2.18	1.79	1.00
	.025	5.02	3.69	3.12	2.79	2.57	2.41	2.19	1.94	1.64	1.00
	.05	3.84	2.99	2.60	2.37	2.21	2.09	1.94	1.75	1.52	1.00
	.10	2.71	2.30	2.08	1.94	1.85	1.77	1.67	1.55	1.38	1.00
	.20	1.64	1.61	1.55	1.50	1.46	1.43	1.38	1.32	1.23	1.00

Source: Reproduced from Table V of R. A. Fisher and F. Yates, *Statistical Tables for Biological, Agricultural and Medical Research* (6th ed.), 1974, published by Longman Group UK Ltd., London (previously published by Oliver and Boyd Ltd., Edinburgh) and by permission of the authors and publishers. The 0.5% and 2.5% points are reproduced from "Tables of Percentage Points of the Inverted Beta *(F)* Distribution," *Biometrika,* Vol. 33 (April 1943), pp. 73–88, by permission of the Biometrika Trustees, Imperial College of Science, Technology, and Medicine, London, England.

Table B.4 χ² Values and Their Associated p Values

df	.99	.98	.95	.90	.80	.70	.50	.30	.20	.10	.05	.02	.01	.001
							Probability							
1	$.0^3157$	$.0^3628$	$.0^300393$	.0158	.0642	.148	.455	1.074	1.642	2.706	3.841	5.412	6.635	10.827
2	.0201	.0404	.103	.211	.446	.713	1.386	2.408	3.219	4.605	5.991	7.824	9.210	13.815
3	.115	.185	.352	.584	1.005	1.424	2.366	3.665	4.642	6.251	7.815	9.837	11.345	16.268
4	.297	.429	.711	1.064	1.649	2.195	3.357	4.878	5.989	7.779	9.488	11.668	13.277	18.465
5	.554	.752	1.145	1.610	2.343	3.000	4.351	6.064	7.289	9.236	11.070	13.388	15.086	20.517
6	.872	1.134	1.635	2.204	3.070	3.828	5.348	7.231	8.558	10.645	12.592	15.033	16.812	22.457
7	1.239	1.564	2.167	2.833	3.822	4.671	6.346	8.383	9.803	12.017	14.067	16.622	18.475	24.322
8	1.646	2.032	2.733	3.490	4.594	5.527	7.344	9.524	11.030	13.362	15.507	18.168	20.090	26.125
9	2.088	2.532	3.325	4.168	5.380	6.393	8.343	10.656	12.242	14.684	16.919	19.679	21.666	27.877
10	2.558	3.059	3.940	4.865	6.179	7.267	9.342	11.781	13.442	15.987	18.307	21.161	23.209	29.588
11	3.053	3.609	4.575	5.578	6.989	8.148	10.341	12.899	14.631	17.275	19.675	22.618	24.725	31.264
12	3.571	4.178	5.226	6.304	7.807	9.034	11.340	14.011	15.812	18.549	21.026	24.054	26.217	32.909
13	4.107	4.765	5.892	7.042	8.634	9.926	12.340	15.119	16.985	19.812	22.362	25.472	27.688	34.528
14	4.660	5.368	6.571	7.790	9.467	10.821	13.339	16.222	18.151	21.064	23.685	26.873	29.141	36.123
15	5.229	5.985	7.261	8.547	10.307	11.721	14.339	17.322	19.311	22.307	24.996	28.529	30.578	37.697
16	5.812	6.614	7.962	9.312	11.152	12.624	15.338	18.418	20.465	23.542	26.296	29.633	32.000	39.252
17	6.408	7.255	8.672	10.085	12.002	13.531	16.338	19.511	21.615	24.769	27.587	30.995	33.409	40.790
18	7.015	7.906	9.390	10.865	12.857	14.440	17.338	20.601	22.760	25.989	28.869	32.346	34.805	42.312
19	7.633	8.567	10.117	11.651	13.716	15.352	18.338	21.689	23.900	27.204	30.144	33.687	36.191	43.820
20	8.260	9.237	10.851	12.443	14.578	16.266	19.337	22.775	25.038	28.412	31.410	35.020	37.566	45.315
21	8.897	9.915	11.591	13.240	15.445	17.182	20.337	23.858	26.171	29.615	32.671	36.343	38.932	46.797
22	9.542	10.600	12.338	14.041	16.314	18.101	21.337	24.939	27.301	30.813	33.924	37.659	40.289	48.268
23	10.196	11.293	13.091	14.848	17.187	19.021	22.337	26.018	28.429	32.007	35.172	38.968	41.638	49.728
24	10.856	11.992	13.848	15.659	18.062	19.943	23.337	27.096	29.553	33.196	36.415	40.270	42.980	51.179
25	11.524	12.697	14.611	16.473	18.940	20.867	24.337	28.172	30.675	34.382	37.652	41.566	44.314	52.620
26	12.198	13.409	15.379	17.292	19.820	21.792	25.336	29.246	31.795	35.563	38.885	42.856	45.642	54.052
27	12.879	14.125	16.151	18.114	20.703	22.719	26.336	30.319	32.912	36.741	40.113	44.140	46.963	55.476
28	13.565	14.847	16.928	18.939	21.588	23.647	27.336	31.391	34.027	37.916	41.337	45.419	48.278	56.893
29	14.256	15.574	17.708	19.768	22.475	24.577	28.336	32.461	35.139	39.087	42.557	46.693	49.588	58.302
30	14.953	16.306	18.493	20.599	23.364	25.508	29.336	33.530	36.250	40.256	43.773	47.962	50.892	59.703

Source: Reproduced from Table III of R. A. Fisher, *Statistical Methods for Research Workers* (14th ed.), 1973, copyright by Oxford University Press, England. Used by permission of Oxford University Press (originally published by Oliver and Boyd, Ltd.).

Appendix B

Table B.5   r Values and Their Associated p Values

			Probability level		
(N − 2)	.10	.05	.02	.01	.001
1	.988	.997	.9995	.9999	1.000
2	.900	.950	.980	.990	.999
3	.805	.878	.934	.959	.991
4	.729	.811	.882	.917	.974
5	.669	.754	.833	.874	.951
6	.622	.707	.789	.834	.925
7	.582	.666	.750	.798	.898
8	.549	.632	.716	.765	.872
9	.522	.602	.685	.735	.847
10	.497	.576	.658	.708	.823
11	.476	.553	.634	.684	.801
12	.458	.532	.612	.661	.780
13	.441	.514	.592	.641	.760
14	.426	.497	.574	.623	.742
15	.412	.482	.558	.606	.725
16	.400	.468	.542	.590	.708
17	.389	.456	.528	.575	.693
18	.378	.444	.516	.561	.679
19	.369	.433	.503	.549	.665
20	.360	.423	.492	.537	.652
22	.344	.404	.472	.515	.629
24	.330	.388	.453	.496	.607
25	.323	.381	.445	.487	.597
30	.296	.349	.409	.449	.554
35	.275	.325	.381	.418	.519
40	.257	.304	.358	.393	.490
45	.243	.288	.338	.372	.465
50	.231	.273	.322	.354	.443
55	.220	.261	.307	.338	.424
60	.211	.250	.295	.325	.408
65	.203	.240	.284	.312	.393
70	.195	.232	.274	.302	.380
75	.189	.224	.264	.292	.368
80	.183	.217	.256	.283	.357
85	.178	.211	.249	.275	.347
90	.173	.205	.242	.267	.338
95	.168	.200	.236	.260	.329
100	.164	.195	.230	.254	.321
125	.147	.174	.206	.228	.288
150	.134	.159	.189	.208	.264
175	.124	.148	.174	.194	.248
200	.116	.138	.164	.181	.235
300	.095	.113	.134	.148	.188
500	.074	.088	.104	.115	.148
1,000	.052	.062	.073	.081	.104
2,000	.037	.044	.052	.058	.074

Note: All p values are two-tailed in this table.

Source: From Some Extensions of Student's t and Pearson's r Central Distributions, by A. L. Sockloff and J. N. Edney, May 1972, Temple University Technical Report 72–5, Measurement and Research Center. Reprinted with the permission of Alan Sockloff.

Table B.6	Transformations of r to Fisher z_r

Second digit of r

r	.00	.01	.02	.03	.04	.05	.06	.07	.08	.09
.0	.000	.010	.020	.030	.040	.050	.060	.070	.080	.090
.1	.100	.110	.121	.131	.141	.151	.161	.172	.182	.192
.2	.203	.213	.224	.234	.245	.255	.266	.277	.288	.299
.3	.310	.321	.332	.343	.354	.365	.377	.388	.400	.412
.4	.424	.436	.448	.460	.472	.485	.497	.510	.523	.536
.5	.549	.563	.576	.590	.604	.618	.633	.648	.662	.678
.6	.693	.709	.725	.741	.758	.775	.793	.811	.829	.848
.7	.867	.887	.908	.929	.950	.973	.996	1.020	1.045	1.071
.8	1.099	1.127	1.157	1.188	1.221	1.256	1.293	1.333	1.376	1.422

Third digit of r

r	.000	.001	.002	.003	.004	.005	.006	.007	.008	.009
.90	1.472	1.478	1.483	1.488	1.494	1.499	1.505	1.510	1.516	1.522
.91	1.528	1.533	1.539	1.545	1.551	1.557	1.564	1.570	1.576	1.583
.92	1.589	1.596	1.602	1.609	1.616	1.623	1.630	1.637	1.644	1.651
.93	1.658	1.666	1.673	1.681	1.689	1.697	1.705	1.713	1.721	1.730
.94	1.738	1.747	1.756	1.764	1.774	1.783	1.792	1.802	1.812	1.822
.95	1.832	1.842	1.853	1.863	1.874	1.886	1.897	1.909	1.921	1.933
.96	1.946	1.959	1.972	1.986	2.000	2.014	2.029	2.044	2.060	2.076
.97	2.092	2.109	2.127	2.146	2.165	2.185	2.205	2.227	2.249	2.273
.98	2.298	2.323	2.351	2.380	2.410	2.443	2.477	2.515	2.555	2.599
.99	2.646	2.700	2.759	2.826	2.903	2.994	3.106	3.250	3.453	3.800

Source: Reprinted by permission from *Statistical Methods, Eighth Edition* by Snedecor and Cochran © 1989 by Iowa State University Press, Ames, IA 50010.

Table B.7	Transformations of Fisher z_r to r								
z_r	.00	.01	.02	.03	.04	.05	.06	.07	.08	.09
.0	.000	.010	.020	.030	.040	.050	.060	.070	.080	.090
.1	.100	.110	.119	.129	.139	.149	.159	.168	.178	.187
.2	.197	.207	.216	.226	.236	.245	.254	.264	.273	.282
.3	.291	.300	.310	.319	.327	.336	.345	.354	.363	.371
.4	.380	.389	.397	.405	.414	.422	.430	.438	.446	.454
.5	.462	.470	.478	.485	.493	.500	.508	.515	.523	.530
.6	.537	.544	.551	.558	.565	.572	.578	.585	.592	.598
.7	.604	.611	.617	.623	.629	.635	.641	.647	.653	.658
.8	.664	.670	.675	.680	.686	.691	.696	.701	.706	.711
.9	.716	.721	.726	.731	.735	.740	.744	.749	.753	.757
1.0	.762	.766	.770	.774	.778	.782	.786	.790	.793	.797
1.1	.800	.804	.808	.811	.814	.818	.821	.824	.828	.831
1.2	.834	.837	.840	.843	.846	.848	.851	.854	.856	.859
1.3	.862	.864	.867	.869	.872	.874	.876	.879	.881	.883
1.4	.885	.888	.890	.892	.894	.896	.898	.900	.902	.903
1.5	.905	.907	.909	.910	.912	.914	.915	.917	.919	.920
1.6	.922	.923	.925	.926	.928	.929	.930	.932	.933	.934
1.7	.935	.937	.938	.939	.940	.941	.942	.944	.945	.946
1.8	.947	.948	.949	.950	.951	.952	.953	.954	.954	.955
1.9	.956	.957	.958	.959	.960	.960	.961	.962	.963	.963
2.0	.964	.965	.965	.966	.967	.967	.968	.969	.969	.970
2.1	.970	.971	.972	.972	.973	.973	.974	.974	.975	.975
2.2	.976	.976	.977	.977	.978	.978	.978	.979	.979	.980
2.3	.980	.980	.981	.981	.982	.982	.982	.983	.983	.983
2.4	.984	.984	.984	.985	.985	.985	.986	.986	.986	.986
2.5	.987	.987	.987	.987	.988	.988	.988	.988	.989	.989
2.6	.989	.989	.989	.990	.990	.990	.990	.990	.991	.991
2.7	.991	.991	.991	.992	.992	.992	.992	.992	.992	.992
2.8	.993	.993	.993	.993	.993	.993	.993	.994	.994	.994
2.9	.994	.994	.994	.994	.994	.995	.995	.995	.995	.995

Source: Reprinted by permission from *Statistical Methods, Eighth Edition* by Snedecor and Cochran © 1989 by Iowa State University Press, Ames, IA 50010.

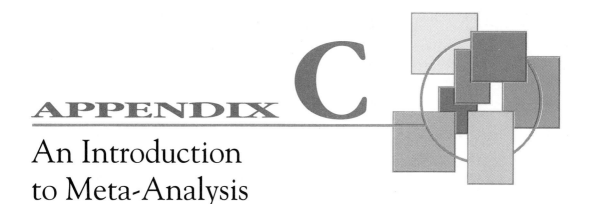

APPENDIX C

An Introduction to Meta-Analysis

Utility of Meta-Analysis

It seems that, almost every time we turn on the television or open a newspaper, we learn about some new biomedical study. Often, we hear that the study reported an effect in one direction whereas others have reported an effect in the opposite direction or an effect that is close to zero. How do researchers resolve this conflicting evidence? An increasingly popular tool, called **meta-analysis** (a term coined by Gene Glass, 1976), is actually a collection of quantitative procedures that are used to sum up a body of related studies and to identify the conditions that might alter the magnitude, and possibly even the direction, of effect sizes. Meta-analysis is a rapidly growing field that has spawned insights in behavioral and social science, policy making, and other areas as well. Although different approaches are used, meta-analysts frequently report the same general kind of information (Rosenthal, 1995b).

The first step in a meta-analysis is to define the independent and dependent variables of interest. The next step is to collect the relevant studies in a systematic way and to collate them by defining specific categories of information. The ensuing steps use both quantitative and graphical procedures (e.g., stem-and-leaf charts) to examine the variability among the obtained effect sizes and use simple statistical formulas to make estimates of the average effect sizes and to determine the significance levels of the combined effects (Rosenthal & DiMatteo, 2001). In this way, meta-analysts seek to develop a meaningful mosaic that reveals patterns in the data and, with the help of moderator variables, explains seemingly contradictory results. Thus, meta-analysis helps researchers to develop a cumulative picture of the research results in a given area rather than requiring them to rely on a single study or on a traditional narrative, non-quantitative review in attempting to understand a phenomenon. Meta-analysis also encourages a deeper understanding of each study, because we have to read each study carefully to extract the essential information.

In this appendix, we give you a sense of some of the procedures that are used to compare and combine effect sizes and to estimate overall p values. If you want to learn more about meta-analysis, you will find an engaging introduction in Morton Hunt's *How Science Takes Stock* (1997) and in Harris Cooper and Larry Hedges's comprehensive *Handbook of Research Synthesis* (1994). Although we focus only on the comparison and combination of two studies in this appendix, you will find procedures for comparing and combining any number of studies in other popular texts and handbooks, including Chalmers and Altman (1995); Cook et al. (1994); H.M. Cooper (1989); Glass, McGaw, and Smith (1981); Hedges and Olkin (1985); Hunter and Schmidt (1990); Light and Pillemer (1984); Lipsey and Wilson (2001); Rosenthal (1991); and Wachter and Straf (1990).

Comparing Two Effect Sizes

Suppose we believe that two studies are conceptually similar, and we also want to compare their effect sizes as further insurance that they constitute a homogeneous set. First, we give the values of $r_{effect size}$ the same sign if both studies show effects in the same direction, but give them different signs if the results are in the opposite direction. Second, we find for each $r_{effect size}$ the Fisher z_r, which (as you learned in Chapter 12) is the log transformation of r found in Table B.6 (p. 419). Third, we substitute in the following formula to obtain the standard normal deviate (z) corresponding to the difference between the Fisher z_r scores:

$$z \text{ of difference} = \frac{z_{r1} - z_{r2}}{\sqrt{\dfrac{1}{N_1 - 3} + \dfrac{1}{N_2 - 3}}},$$

where z_{r1} and z_{r2} are the log transformations found in Step 2 for the $r_{effect size}$ values of Studies 1 and 2, respectively, and N_1 and N_2 are the total sample sizes of Studies 1 and 2, respectively. The final step is to look up the result in Table B.1 (p. 409), which gives us the associated one-tailed p of the z of difference. Let us try some examples.

Example 1. Suppose you have used 100 subjects to try to replicate an experiment that reported a large effect ($r_{effect size}$ = .50) based on only 10 subjects. You observe a moderate-sized effect ($r_{effect size}$ = .31), but it is in the opposite direction of the one previously reported. You code your effect as negative to reflect the fact that it is in the opposite direction, and then you consult Table B.6 (p. 419) to find the Fisher z_r corresponding to each $r_{effect size}$. For r = .50, you find z_r = .549 at the intersection of the .5 row and the .00 column. For r = −.31, you find z_r = .321 at the .3 row and the .01 column intersection, and you code the result as −.321 because your empirical finding was in the "wrong" direction.

Next, from the previous formula, you compute

$$z \text{ of difference} = \frac{(.549) - (-.321)}{\sqrt{\dfrac{1}{7} + \dfrac{1}{97}}} = \frac{.870}{.391} = 2.22$$

as the z of the difference between the two effect sizes. Looking up the p value associated with a z of 2.22 in Table B.1 (p. 409), you find p = .0132 one-tailed, which you can round to .01 one-tailed or .03 two-tailed (i.e., .0132 × 2 = .03 rounded). The p value is small enough to convince you that your result differs from the original one, and because the difference between the r values is obviously large as well as significant statistically, you decide they cannot simply be combined without careful thought and comment. Thus, in describing the results of both studies considered together, you would report the differences between them and try to think of an explanation for their differences.

Example 2. Alternatively, suppose your result is in the same direction as the original one and of a similar magnitude, and you have used the same number of subjects. This time, imagine that the original $r_{\text{effect size}} = .45$ ($N = 120$) and your $r_{\text{effect size}} = .40$ ($N = 120$). Following the same procedure as in Example 1, you find in Table B.6 the z_r values corresponding to these effect size rs to be .485 and .424, respectively. From the preceding formula you compute

$$z \text{ of difference} = \frac{.485 - .424}{\sqrt{\dfrac{1}{117} + \dfrac{1}{117}}} = \frac{.061}{.131} = .47$$

as your obtained z of the difference. In Table B.1 you find the p associated with $z = .47$ to be .3192 one-tailed. Here, then, is an example of two studies that do not disagree significantly in their estimates of the size of the relation between X and Y and are quite similar in magnitude. They can now be routinely combined by means of a simple meta-analytic technique, as shown next.

Combining Two Effect Sizes

Given two effect size rs that are combinable on conceptual and statistical grounds, we can find out the typical (or average) effect size by using the following formula

$$\bar{z}_r = \frac{z_{r1} + z_{r2}}{2},$$

and afterward transforming the resulting Fisher z_r into the metric of an effect size correlation. In this formula the denominator is the number of z_r scores in the numerator; the resulting value is an average Fisher z_r (symbolized here as $\bar{z}_r$, where the bar over the z denotes that it is a mean value). Example 3 shows how this number crunching proceeds.

Example 3. In Example 2, one $r_{\text{effect size}} = .45$ and the other $r_{\text{effect size}} = .40$ (both coded as positive to show that both results were in the predicted direction). You found the Fisher z_r scores corresponding to the effect size rs to be .485 and .424, respectively. From the formula above you compute

$$\bar{z}_r = \frac{.485 + .424}{2} = .45$$

as the average Fisher z_r. Finally, looking in Table B.7 (p. 420), you find that a Fisher z_r of .45 is associated with an r of .422, which is the $r_{\text{effect size}}$ estimate of the two studies combined.

Obtaining an Overall Significance Level

Although meta-analysts are generally more interested in effect sizes than in p values, they might be interested in the overall statistical significance of a set of comparable studies. It is an easy matter to combine the p values and get an overall estimate of the probability that the p values might have been obtained if the null hypothesis of no

Appendix C

relation between X and Y were true. We first obtain an accurate p value for each study (accurate, say, to two digits, not counting zeros before the first nonzero value, such as $p = .43$ or .024 or .0012). That is, if t(with 30 df) = 3.03, we code p as .0025, not as $p < .05$. Extended tables of the t distribution may be helpful here (such as Table B.2 on pp. 410–411), but more helpful still is to use a computer or to have a scientific calculator that spits out accurate ps at the touch of a couple of buttons. For each p, the meta-analyst finds z (not the Fisher z_r, but the standard normal deviate z in Table B.1 of Appendix B). Both ps should also be one-tailed, and we give the corresponding zs the same sign if both studies showed effects in the same direction, but different signs if the results are in the opposite direction.

In our continuing example of working with two studies, the formula we would use to add the two z values is as follows:

$$\text{Combined } z = \frac{z_1 + z_2}{\sqrt{2}}.$$

That is, the sum of the two zs when divided by the square root of the number of zs combined yields a new z. This new z corresponds to the p value of the two studies combined if the null hypothesis of no relation between X and Y is true.

Example 4. As an illustration, suppose we believe that Studies A and B are a combinable set with results in the same direction, but neither is statistically significant. One p is .121, and the other is .084; their zs are 1.17 and 1.38, respectively. From the preceding formula we have

$$\text{Combined } z = \frac{1.17 + 1.38}{\sqrt{2}} = \frac{2.55}{1.41} = 1.81$$

as our combined z. The p associated with this combined z is .035 one-tailed (or .07 two-tailed).

Detective-Like Probing of Reported Data

For our illustrations of meta-analytic comparisons and combinations of effect size rs and ps we have concentrated on the case of only two results. Meta-analysts usually work with scores of results to be coded, compared, and combined, however. The procedures used are quite similar in spirit to the procedures described above, and you will find descriptions in the texts cited earlier—and also some tips on how to estimate effect sizes when published reports provide only limited details. To give you an idea of how this detective-like probing is done, let us say we are interested in knowing the effect size r but all that is provided is that $N = 36$ and $p = .005$ in a 2 × 2 chi-square design. Nevertheless, we can estimate the effect size correlation—in this case phi (ϕ)—because of the relationship of χ^2 to z.

When χ^2 is based on 1 df, then the square root of the χ^2 is equal to z, that is,

$$\sqrt{\chi^2} = z.$$

In Chapter 15, we learned that, if $N > 20$ and the smallest expected frequency is greater than 3 or so, we can test the significance of phi coefficients by

$$\chi^2 = \phi^2 \times N.$$

So it follows that

$$\sqrt{\chi^2} = z = \sqrt{\phi^2 \times N} = \phi \times \sqrt{N},$$

and thus

$$\phi = \frac{z}{\sqrt{N}}.$$

Given this relationship, we find the z associated with the reported $p = .005$ for the 2×2 chi-square (i.e., 1 df χ^2) to be 2.58 in Table B.1 (p. 409). We then substitute $z = 2.58$ and $N = 36$ in the above formula and find

$$r_{\text{effect size}} = \frac{z}{\sqrt{N}} = \frac{2.58}{\sqrt{36}} = .43,$$

which is our approximation of the obtained effect, given the meager ingredients we had to work with.

Here is one more example of the detective-like probing for the effect size (Rosenthal 1994a). Suppose that an experimental report compares a treatment with a control condition but tells us only that p was significant at .05 two-tailed and that $n_1 = n_2 = 16$. That is, $N = 32$ and $df = 30$. From Table B.2 (pp. 410–411), we see that $t = 2.042$ for $p = .05$ (two-tailed) and $df = 30$. Simply by substituting in the formula introduced in Chapter 13, we find

$$r_{\text{effect size}} = \sqrt{\frac{t^2}{t^2 + df}} = \sqrt{\frac{(2.042)^2}{(2.042)^2 + 30}} = .35.$$

The File Drawer Problem

Because many journal editors are reluctant to accept "nonsignificant" results, researchers' file drawers may contain unpublished studies that failed to yield significant results (Bakan, 1967; Sterling, 1959). If there were a substantial number of such studies in the file drawers, the meta-analyst's evaluation of the overall significance level might be unduly optimistic. One solution to this **file drawer problem** is to calculate the number of studies averaging null results that would be required to nudge the significance level for *all* studies (retrieved and unretrieved combined) to the less coveted side of $p = .05$ (Rosenthal, 1979, 1983, 1991). If the overall significance level computed on the basis of the retrieved studies can be brought down to $p > .05$ by the addition of just a few more null results, then the original estimate of p is clearly *not robust* (i.e., not resistant to the file drawer threat).

Table C.1 illustrates the results of such calculations. It shows a table of *tolerance values* in which the rows represent the number of retrieved (i.e., meta-analyzed) studies and the columns represent three different levels of the average statistical significance of the retrieved studies. The intersection of any row and column shows the sum of old and new studies required to bring the p for all studies (retrieved *and* unretrieved) down to the level of being barely "nonsignificant" at $p > .05$. Suppose we meta-analyzed 8 studies and found the average (not the combined, but the mean) p value to be .05. The 64 tells us that it will take an additional 56 unretrieved studies averaging null results to bring the original average $p = .05$ based on 8 studies (i.e., $64 - 8 = 56$) down to $p > .05$. As a general rule of thumb, it has been suggested that we regard as robust any combined results for which the tolerance level reaches

Table C.1	Tolerances for Future Null Results		
Number of studies summarized	Original average significance level		
	.05	.01	.001
1	1	2	4
2	4	8	15
3	9	18	32
4	16	32	57
5	25	50	89
6	36	72	128
7	49	98	173
8	64	128	226
9	81	162	286
10	100	200	353
15	225	450	795
20	400	800	1,412
25	625	1,250	2,206
30	900	1,800	3,177
40	1,600	3,200	5,648
50	2,500	5,000	8,824

Note: Entries in this table are the total number of old and new studies required to bring an original average p of .05, .01, or .001 down to an overall $p > .05$ (i.e., just barely to "nonsignificance").

$5(k) + 10$, where k is the number of studies retrieved (Rosenthal, 1991). In our example of 8 studies retrieved, this means that we will be satisfied that the original estimate of $p \leq .05$ is robust if we feel that there are fewer than an additional $5(8) + 10 = 50$ studies with null results squirreled away in file drawers. Because this table shows a tolerance for an additional 56 studies, we conclude that the original estimate is robust.

Glossary

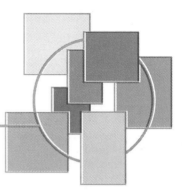

Note: Indicated in parentheses is the primary chapter(s) or appendix where each of the following either appears as a Key Term (listed at the end of the chapter and indicated in boldface within the chapter) or is defined as an important concept or common term.

A-B design Simplest single-case design, in which the dependent variable is measured throughout the pretreatment or baseline period (the A phase) and the treatment period (the B phase). (8)

A-B-A design Single-case design in which there are repeated measures before the treatment (the A phase), during the treatment (the B phase), and then with the treatment withdrawn (the final A phase). (8)

A-B-A-B design Single-case design in which there are two types of occasions (B to A and A to B) for demonstrating the effects of the treatment variable. (8)

A-B-A-B-A design Single-case design in which there are repeated measures before, during, and after treatment (the B phase). (8)

A-B-BC-B design Single-case design in which there are repeated measures before the introduction of the treatments (the A phase), then during Treatment B, during the combination of Treatments B and C, and, finally, during Treatment B alone; the purpose of the design is to tease out the effect of B both in combination with C and apart from C. (8)

abscissa See *x axis*.

abstract Brief, comprehensive summary of the content of a report or paper. (Appendix A)

acceptability stage Stage 3 of discovery, in which a working hypothesis is fashioned according to the criteria of correspondence with reality, a combination of coherence and parsimony, and falsifiability. (2)

accidental plagiarism Unwittingly falling into plagiarism. (3)

accounting for conflicting results One of several possible scenarios for coming up with an acceptable idea. (2)

acquiescent response set The tendency of individuals to go along with any request or attitudinal statement (5)

active deception (deception by commission) Actively misleading the research participants, for example, giving them false information about the purpose of the research, or having them unwittingly interact with confederates. (3)

additive model A model in which the components sum to the group means in ANOVA. (14)

ad hoc hypothesis A conjecture or speculation developed on the spot to explain a result. (1)

alerting correlation ($r_{alerting}$) The correlation between group means and contrast (λ) weights. (14)

alpha (α) Probability of a Type I error. (12)

alpha coefficient See *Cronbach's alpha*.

alternate-form reliability The correlation between two forms of a test with different items that are measuring the same attribute. (6)

alternative hypothesis (H_1) The working hypothesis or the experimental hypothesis (that is, as opposed to the null hypothesis in *null hypothesis significance testing*). (12)

analogical rhetoric or thinking Visualizing one thing in terms of another. (1)

analysis of variance (ANOVA) Subdivision of the total variance of a set of scores into its components. (14)

ANOVA   See *analysis of variance.*

anything-goes view of science   Feyerabend's view that doing research involves a "let's-try-it-and-see" attitude, where anything that works is permissible. (4)

APA manual   *Publication Manual of the American Psychological Association.* (Appendix A)

a priori method   The use of individual powers of pure reason and logic as a basis of explanation (Charles Peirce). (1)

archival material   A relatively permanent repository of data or material. (4)

area probability sampling   A type of survey sampling in which the subclasses are geographic areas. (9)

arithmetic mean (*M*)   Arithmetic average. (10)

artifact   A specific threat to validity, or a confounded aspect of the scientist's observations. (7)

asymmetrical distribution   A distribution of scores in which there is not an exact correspondence in arrangement on the opposite sides of the middle line. (10)

autonomy   The person's "independence," in the context of research ethics, also refers to a prospective participant's right as well as ability "to choose" whether to participate in the study or to continue in the study. (3)

back-to-back stem-and-leaf chart   The back-to-back plots of distributions in which the original data are preserved with any desired precision. (10)

back-translation   See *translation and back-translation.*

bar chart   A graphic form for the distribution of data. (10)

behavior   What someone does or how someone acts. (1)

behavioral baseline   A comparison base, operationally defined as the continuous, and continuing, performance of a single unit in single-case research. (8)

behavioral diaries   Data collection method in which the research participant keeps a record of events at the time they occur. (5)

behavioral science   A general term that encompasses scientific disciplines in which empirical inquiry is used to study motivation, cognition, and behavior. (1)

Belmont Report   The name given to a study developed by a national commission in 1974 to protect the rights and welfare of participants in biomedical and behavioral research. (3)

beneficence   The "doing of good," which is one of the guidelines of the discussed ethical principles. (3)

BESD   See *binomial effect-size display.*

beta (β)   Probability of a Type II error. (12)

between-subjects designs   Statistical designs in which the sampling units are exposed to one treatment each. (7)

bias   Net systematic error. (6, 9)

Big Five factors (OCEAN)   The collective name for five broad domains of individual personality: (a) openness to experience, (b) conscientiousness, (c) extraversion, (d) agreeableness, and (e) neuroticism. (5)

bimodal   Showing two modes (of a distribution). (10)

binomial effect-size display (BESD)   Procedure for the standardized display of the practical importance of an effect size correlation ($r_{\text{effect size}}$) of any magnitude. (12)

bipolar rating scales   Rating scales in which the ends of the scales are extreme opposites. (5)

blind experimenters   Experimenters who are unaware of which participants receive the experimental and control treatments. (7)

byline   The author's name as it appears on the title page of an article. (Appendix A)

causal inference   The act or process of inferring that *X* causes *Y.* (7)

causation   The relation of cause to effect. (7)

ceiling effect   Situation in which the amount of change that can be produced is limited by the upper boundary of the measure. (5)

central tendency   Location of the bulk of a distribution; measured by means, medians, modes, and trimmed means. (10)

central tendency bias   A type of response set in which the respondent is reluctant to give extreme ratings and instead rates in the direction of the mean of the total group. (5)

certificate of confidentiality   A formal agreement between the investigator and the government agency sponsoring the research that requires the investigator to keep the data confidential. (3)

checklists   Method of counting the frequency of occurrence. (4)

chi-square (χ^2) A statistic used to test the degree of agreement between the frequency data actually obtained and those expected under a particular hypothesis (e.g., the null hypothesis). (15)

closed (structured, fixed-choice, or precoded) measures See *structured items.*

clusters See *strata.*

coefficient of determination (r^2) Proportion of variance shared by two variables, and not to be confused with $r_{\text{effect size}}$. (12)

coherence The extent to which things (e.g., components of a theory or hypothesis) "stick together" logically. (2)

cohort A collection of individuals who were born in the same period. (8)

column effects Column means minus grand mean. (14)

concealed measurement The use of hidden measurements, such as a hidden recording device that eavesdrops on conversations. (4)

conceptual definition See *theoretical definition.*

concurrent validity The extent to which test results are correlated with some criterion in the present. (6)

confidence interval The upper and lower bounds of a statistic (e.g., the $r_{\text{effect size}}$), with confidence defined as $1 - \alpha$. (9, 12)

confidentiality Protection of research participants' or survey respondents' disclosures against unwarranted access. (3)

confirmatory data analysis Analysis of data for the purpose of testing hypotheses. (10)

confounded Mixed or confused. (7)

confounded hypotheses (in panel designs) The result when one is unable to separate the effect attributed to one hypothesis from the effect attributed to another hypothesis in cross-lagged panel designs. (8)

constructs Abstract variables, formulated from ideas or images, that serve as explanatory concepts. (2)

construct validity A type of test or research validity that addresses the psychological qualities contributing to the relation between X and Y. (6)

content analysis A method of decomposing written messages and pictorial documents. (4)

content validity A type of test validity that addresses whether the test adequately samples the relevant material. (6)

contingency table A table of frequencies (counts) coded by row and column variables. (11)

continuous variable A variable for which we can imagine another value falling between any two adjacent scores. (11)

contrast correlation (r_{contrast}) The pure correlation between scores on the dependent variable and the lambda coefficients after removal of any other patterns in the data. (14)

contrasts Statistical procedures that address specific questions or predictions in the data, such as testing for a particular trend in the results. (14)

contrast weights See *lambda coefficients.*

contrived observation Unobtrusive observation of the effects of some variable that was introduced into a situation. (4)

control group A condition with which the effects of the experimental or test condition are compared. (1, 7)

convergent validity Validity supported by a substantial correlation of conceptually similar measures. (6)

corrected range See *extended range.*

correlated t See *paired t.*

correlational design A broad class of quasi-experimental designs. (8)

correlational research Another common name for relational research, that is, research in which two or more variables or conditions are measured and related to one another. (1, 8)

correlation coefficient An index of the degree of association between two variables, typically a Pearson r or a related product-moment correlation. (6, 11)

correspondence with reality The extent to which a hypothesis agrees with accepted truths based on reliable empirical findings. (2)

counterbalancing A procedure in which some subjects receive Treatment A before Treatment B, and the others receive B before A. (7)

counts Frequencies. (11, 15)

covariation The principle that, in order to demonstrate causation, what is labeled as the "cause" should be shown to be positively correlated with what is labeled as the "effect." (7)

Glossary

criterion validity The extent to which a measure correlates with one or more criterion variables. (6)

critical incident technique Open-ended method that instructs the respondent to describe an observable action the purpose of which is fairly clear to the respondent and the consequences of which are sufficiently definite to leave little doubt about its effects. (5)

Cronbach's alpha A measure of internal consistency reliability, proposed by L. J. Cronbach. (6)

crossed design Another name for the basic within-subjects design, because the subjects can be said to be "crossed" by treatment conditions. (7)

cross-lagged correlations Correlations of the degree of association between two sets of variables, of which one is treated as a lagged value of the outcome variable. (8)

cross-lagged panel designs Relational research designs using cross-lagged correlations, cross-sectional correlations repeated over time, and test-retest correlations. (8)

cross-sectional design Research design that takes a slice of time and compares subjects on one or more variables simultaneously. (8)

crude range Highest score minus lowest score. (10)

cue words Guiding labels that define particular points or categories of response. (5)

debriefing Disclosing to participants the nature of the research in which they have participated. (3)

deception by commission See *active deception*.

deception by omission See *passive deception*.

decision-plane model A two-dimensional schema of the risks and benefits of doing research. (3)

degrees of freedom (*df*) The number of observations minus the number of restrictions limiting the observations' freedom to vary. (13)

demand characteristics The mixture of various hints and cues that govern the participant's perception of (a) his or her role as research subject and (b) the experimenter's hypothesis. (7)

dependent variable A variable, the changes in which are viewed as dependent on changes in one or more independent variables. (2)

descriptive measures Measures such as σ and σ^2 that are used to calculate population values. (10)

descriptive research An empirical investigation in which the objective is to map out a situation or set of events. (1)

df See *degrees of freedom*.

dichotomous variable A variable that is divided into two classes. (11)

discovery phase Reichenbach's term for the origin, creation, or invention of ideas for scientific justification. (2)

discrete variable A variable taking on two or more distinct values. (11)

discriminant validity Validity supported by a lack of correlation between conceptually unrelated measures. (6)

dispersion Another name for *spread* or *variability*. (10)

double-blind procedures Procedures in which neither the experimenter nor the participants know who has been assigned to the experimental and control groups. (7)

double deception A deception embedded in what the research participant thinks is the official debriefing. (3)

dummy coding Giving arbitrary numerical values (often 0 and 1) to the two levels of a dichotomous variable. (11)

effective power The actual power (i.e., $1 - \beta$) of the statistical test used. (12)

effective sample size The net equivalent sample size that the researcher ends up with. (9)

effect size The magnitude of an experimental effect (i.e., the size of the relation between X and Y. (6, 12, 13, 14, 15, Appendix C)

effect size correlation ($r_{\text{effect size}}$) The magnitude of an experimental effect defined on the basis of the correlation between X and Y. (12, 13, 14, 15, Appendix C)

efficient cause The propelling or instigating condition (i.e., the X that sets in motion or alters Y). (7)

empirical Describing controlled observation and measurement. (1)

empirical reasoning A use of logic and evidence. (1)

error Fluctuation in measurements; also deviation of a score from the mean of the group or condition. (14)

error of estimate Closeness of estimate to actual value. (9)

ethical guidelines A set of principles (such as those discussed in Chapter 3) that help researchers decide what aspects of a study might pose an ethical problem. (3)

ethics The system of moral values by which behavior is judged. (3)

ethnography The study of how people in a cultural setting impose meaning on experiences. (4)

evaluation apprehension The experience of feeling anxious about being negatively evaluated or not positively evaluated. (5, 7)

evaluation, potency, and activity Three primary dimensions of connotative meaning, which are typically measured by a semantic differential. (5)

expectancy control design An experimental design in which the expectancy variable operates separately from the independent variable of interest. (7)

expected frequency (f_e) Counts expected under specified row and column conditions if certain hypotheses (e.g., the null hypothesis) are true. (15)

expedited review The evaluation of proposed research without undue delay. (3)

experimental group A group or condition in which the subjects undergo a manipulation or an intervention. (7)

experimental hypothesis The experimenter's working hypothesis; also an alternative to the null hypothesis. (2, 12)

experimental realism The extent to which the participant is drawn into or is affected by the experimental treatment. (4)

experimental research An empirical investigation in which the objective is a causal explanation. (1)

experimenter expectancy bias Another name for the *experimenter expectancy effect*. (2)

experimenter expectancy effect An experimenter-related artifact that results when the hypothesis held by the experimenter leads unintentionally to behavior toward the subjects that, in turn, increases the likelihood that the hypothesis will be confirmed. (7)

exploratory data analysis A detective-like searching in the data for clues, leads, and insights. (10)

extended range (corrected range) Crude range plus one unit. (10)

external validity The degree of generalizability. (6)

face-to-face interview An interview in which the interviewer and the respondent directly interact with one another face to face. (5)

face validity The extent to which a test seems on its surface to be measuring what it purports to measure. (6)

factorial design Research design with more than one factor and two or more levels of each factor. (7)

fair-mindedness Impartiality. (3)

falsifiability (refutability) The principle (advanced by Karl Popper) that a theoretical assertion is scientific only if it is stated in such a way that it can, if incorrect, be refuted by some empirical means. (2)

$F_{contrast}$ The symbol used in this book to denote an F test (with numerator $df = 1$) that is used to address a focused question or hypothesis (e.g., comparing two groups or conditions). (14)

field experiments Experimental research that is done in a naturalistic setting. (4)

file drawer problem The concern that a substantial number of studies with nonsignificant results are tucked away in file drawers. (Appendix C)

final (teleological) cause The end goal toward which a person or thing presumably tends to strive (Aristotle). (7)

finite Describing the condition in which all the units or events can, at least in theory, be completely counted. (10)

Fisher z_r The log transformation of r, as shown in Table B.6. (12, Appendix C)

fixed-choice measures. See *structured items*.

floor effect Situation in which the amount of change that can be produced is limited by the lower boundary of the measure. (5)

$F_{noncontrast}$ The result of dividing the mean square noncontrast by the mean square within, which is then used to compute an effect size r for $F_{contrast}$. (14)

focused chi-square χ^2 with 1 df (15)

focused statistical procedures Any t test, 1 df χ^2, or F with numerator $df = 1$. (14)

forced-choice scales Measures that use an item format requiring the respondent to select a single item (or a specified number of items) from a pre-sented set of choices, even when the respondent finds acceptable no choice or more than one of the choices. (5)

formal cause   The implicit form or meaning of something (Aristotle). (7)

***F* ratio**   Ratios of mean squares that are distributed as *F* when the null hypothesis is true, where *F* is a test of significance used to judge the tenability of the null hypothesis of no relation between two or more variables (or of no difference between two or more variabilities). (14)

free association method   A method in which the subject tells whatever passes through his or her mind. (2)

frequency distribution   A chart that shows the number of times each score or other unit of observation occurs in a set of scores. (10)

frequency polygon   A line-graph distribution of frequencies of occurrence. (10)

***F* test**   See *F ratio*.

fugitive literature   Hard-to-find literature. (2)

generative   Theories that allow us to generate new hypotheses and observations. (2)

good subject   Research participant who seeks to provide responses that will validate the experimenter's hypothesis. (7)

grand mean (M_G)   The mean of means, or the mean of all observations. (14)

graphic scales   Rating scales in the form of a straight line with cue words attached. (5)

halo effect   A response set in which the bias results from the judge's overextending a favorable impression of someone, based on some central trait, to the person's other characteristics. (5)

Hedges's *g*   An index of effect size in *z*-score-like terms. (13)

history   A plausible threat to internal validity when an event or incident that takes place between the premeasurement and the postmeasurement contaminates the results of research not employing randomization. (7)

homogeneity of variance   Equality of the population variance of the groups to be compared. (13)

hypotheses   Research ideas that serve as a premise or supposition that organizes facts and guides observations. (2)

improving on older ideas   One of several possible scenarios for coming up with an innovative hypothesis. (2)

independent *t*   The *t* test used to compare samples that are independent. (13)

independent variable   A variable on which the dependent variable depends; in experiments, a variable that the experimenter manipulates to determine whether there are effects on another variable, the dependent variable. (2)

inferential measure   Measures such as S and S^2 that are used to estimate population values based on a sample of values. (10)

inferential validity   The implication is that causal inferences made in a laboratory setting are applicable to the real-life experiences they are meant to represent. (1, 6)

infinite   Boundless, or without limits. (10)

informed consent   The procedure in which prospective subjects, who have been told what they will be getting into, give their formal consent to participate in the research. (3)

institutional review board (IRB)   A group set up to make risk-benefit analyses of proposed studies. (3)

instrumentation   A plausible threat to internal validity that occurs when changes in the measuring instrument (e.g., deterioration of the instrument) bias the results of research not using randomization. (7)

intensive case study   An analysis that is characterized by meticulous records and sharp discriminations rather than by the usual casual discriminations and inferences that are associated with our daily encounters with "cases." (2)

interaction effects (residuals)   In factorial designs, condition means minus grand mean, row effects, and column effects. (14)

interaction of independent variables   The mutually moderating effects of two or more independent variables. (2)

interactions   See *interaction of independent variables*.

intercoder reliability   The extent to which raters or judges who do coding of data are in agreement. (4)

interitem correlation (r_{ii})   The relation of the responses to one item with the responses to another item. (6)

internal-consistency reliability Reliability based on the intercorrelation among components of a test, such as subtests or all the individual test items. (6)

internal validity The degree of validity of statements made about whether *X* causes *Y*. (6, 7)

interpreter biases Systematic errors that result when the researcher's interpretation of the observational records is slanted. (4)

interquartile range The difference between the 75th and 25th percentiles. (10)

interval estimates The extent to which point estimates are likely to be in error. (9)

intervention An experimental treatment. (8)

interview schedule A script that contains the questions the interviewer will ask. (5)

intrinsically repeated measures Measurements that *must* be repeated to address the question of interest. (14)

item analysis A procedure used for selecting items (e.g., for a Likert attitude scale). (5)

item-to-item reliability (r_{ii}) The relation of responses to one item with those to another item. (6)

iterations Repetitions. (15)

judges Coders, raters, decoders, or others who assist in describing and categorizing ongoing events or existing records of events. (4)

judge-to-judge reliability (r_{jj}) The relation of one judge's responses to those of another judge. (6)

justification phase Reichenbach's term for the defense or confirmation of hypotheses, theories, or other proposed explanations. (2, 4)

K-R 20 A measure of internal-consistency reliability, developed by Kuder and Richardson. (6)

lambda coefficients (λ weights) Values that sum to zero and are used to state a prediction. (14)

Latin square design A specific repeated measures design with built-in counterbalancing. (7)

lazy writing Papers saturated with quoted material that, with a little more effort, could be paraphrased. (3)

leading questions Questions that can constrain responses and produce biased answers. (5)

leftover effects See *residual effects.*

leniency bias A type of rating error in which the ratings are consistently more positive than they should be. (5)

Lie (L) Scale A set of items in the MMPI that were designed to identify respondents who are deliberately trying to appear "better" than they believe they are. (5)

Likert scales Attitude scales constructed by the method of summated ratings, developed by Rensis Likert. (5)

linearity The mutual relation between two variables that resembles a straight line. (11)

line graph See *frequency polygon.*

logical error in rating A type of response set in which the judge gives similar ratings for variables or traits that are only intuitively related. (5)

longitudinal study Research in which the same subjects are studied over a period of time. (8)

main effect The effect of an independent variable apart from its interaction with other independent variables. (14)

margin of error Interval within which an anticipated value is expected to occur. (9)

margins Row and column marginal values. (12)

Marlowe-Crowne Social Desirability Scale (MCSD) A standardized test that measures social desirability responding and need for social approval. (6)

matched *t* See *paired t.*

matching Design method in which the sampling units are paired on certain relevant variables. (7)

material cause The substance out of which something is made (Aristotle). (7)

maturation A plausible threat to internal validity that occurs when results not using randomization are contaminated by the participants' having grown, for instance, older, wiser, stronger, or more experienced between the pretest and the posttest. (7)

mean (*M*) The arithmetic average of a set of scores. (10)

mean square (S^2), or *MS* Variance. (10, 14)

mean square for error Variance used as the denominator of *F* ratios. (14)

median (*Mdn*) The midmost score of a distribution. (10)

median split Splitting variables at the median point. (11)

mental images Thinking in which images have a hand, which is presumed to be an aspect of the scientific method and explanatory reasoning. (1)

meta-analysis The use of quantitative and graphical methods to summarize a group of similar studies. (Appendix C)

metaphor A word or phrase applied to a concept or phenomenon it does not literally denote. (2)

metaphorical themes Thematic analogies that allow a particular view of the world. (2)

method of agreement If *X*, then *Y*—a statement that implies that *X* is a sufficient condition of *Y* (J. S. Mill). (7)

method of authority The acceptance of an idea as valid because it is stated by someone in a position of power or authority (Charles Peirce). (1)

method of difference If not-*X*, then not-*Y*—a statement that implies that *X* is a necessary condition of *Y* (J. S. Mill). (7)

method of equal-appearing intervals An attitude-scaling technique, developed by L. L. Thurstone, in which values are obtained for items on the assumption that the underlying intervals are equidistant; also called a *Thurstone scale*. (5)

method of self-report The procedure of having the research participants describe their own behavior or state of mind (e.g., used in interviews, questionnaires, and behavioral diaries). (5)

method of tenacity Clinging stubbornly to an idea because it seems obvious or is "common sense" (Charles Peirce). (1)

methodological pluralism The use of multiple methods of controlled observation in science. (1)

methodological triangulation The approach of "zeroing in" on a pattern by using multiple but imperfect perspectives. (4)

microworld simulations The use of computer-generated environments to simulate real-world settings. (4)

Milgram experiments A set of experiments performed by Stanley Milgram in which he investigated the willingness of participants to give "electric shocks" to another subject, who was actually a confederate. (3)

Mill's methods Logical methods (or propositions) popularized by the 19th-century English philosopher J. S. Mill, exemplified by the method of agreement and the method of difference. (7)

minimal risk Studies in which the likelihood and extent of harm to subjects are no greater than those typically experienced in everyday life; such studies are generally eligible for an expedited review. (3)

Minnesota Multiphasic Personality Inventory (MMPI) A structured personality test containing hundreds of statements that reflect general health, sexual attitudes, religious attitudes, emotional state, and so on. (5)

MMPI See *Minnesota Multiphasic Personality Inventory*.

mode The score occurring with the greatest frequency. (10)

moderator variables Conditions that alter the relationship between *X* and *Y*. (2, 8)

MS See *mean square*.

MS$_{contrast}$ The contrast mean square, which is equivalent to the contrast sum of squares. (14)

mundane realism A condition in which the various dimensions of the experiment are very similar to those in the real world. (4)

mutually exclusive Describing the condition: If A is true, then not-A is false. (12)

N The total number of scores in a study, whereas the number of scores in one condition or subgroup is denoted as *n*. (10)

naturalistic observation Research that looks at behavior in its usual natural environment. (4)

necessary condition A requisite or essential condition. (7, 8)

need for social approval The desire to be positively evaluated, or approved of. (6)

negatively skewed distribution An asymmetrical distribution in which the pointed end is toward the left (i.e., toward the negative tail). (10)

nested design Another name for the basic *between-subjects design*, because the subjects are "nested" within their own treatment conditions. (7)

N-of-1 experimental research Another name for *single-case experimental research*. (8)

noise The variability within the samples. (13)

nonequivalent-groups designs Nonrandomized research in which the responses of a treatment group and a control group are compared on measures collected at the beginning and end of the research. (8)

nonintrinsically repeated measures Repeated measures research in which it is not actually essential to use repeated measures, but their use increases the efficiency, precision, and power of the study. (14)

nonlinearity A relation between two variables that does not resemble a straight line. (11)

nonmaleficence Not doing harm, which is one of the guidelines of the discussed ethical principles. (3)

nonreactive observation Any observation that does not affect what is being observed. (4)

nonresponse bias Systematic error that is due to nonresponse or nonparticipation. (9)

nonskewed distribution A symmetrical distribution. (10)

normal distribution A bell-shaped curve that is completely described by its mean and standard deviation. (10)

norm-referenced Indicates that a standardized test has norms (i.e., typical values), so that a person's score can be compared with those of a reference group. (5)

norms Tables of values representing the typical performance of a given group. (9)

no-shows People who fail to show up for their scheduled research appointments. (10)

null hypothesis (H_0) The hypothesis to be nullified; usually states that there is no relation between two or more variables. (12)

null hypothesis significance testing (NHST) The use of statistics and probabilities to evaluate the null hypothesis. (12)

numerical scales Rating scales in which the respondent works with a sequence of defined numbers. (5)

observed frequency (f_o) Counts obtained in specific rows and columns. (15)

Occam's razor The principle that explanations should be as parsimonious as possible (William of Occam, or Ockham). (2)

omnibus chi-square χ^2 with $df > 1$. (15)

omnibus statistical procedures F with numerator $df > 1$, or χ^2 with $df > 1$. (14)

one-group pre-post design (O-X-O) A preexperimental design in which the reactions of only one group of subjects are measured before and after exposure to the treatment. (7)

one-sample t The t test computed on one sample. (13)

one-shot case study (X-O) A preexperimental design in which the reactions of only one group

of subjects are measured after the event or treatment has occurred. (7)

one-tailed p value The p value associated with a result supporting a prediction of a specific direction of a research result, for example, $M_A > M_B$ or the sign of r is positive. (12)

one-way design A statistical design in which two or more groups comprise a single dimension. (14)

open-ended measures Questions or items that offer the respondent an opportunity to express feelings, motives, or behaviors spontaneously. (5)

operational definitions The meaning of a variable in terms of the operations used to measure it or the experimental methods involved in its determination. (2)

opportunistic sampling The selection of units that are available, simply because they are convenient. (4, 9)

opportunity samples See *opportunistic sampling*.

ordinate See *y axis*.

outliers Scores lying far outside the normal range. (10)

page header Two or three words from the title that are typed in the upper-right corner of the manuscript. (Appendix A)

paired t (correlated t or matched t) The t test computed on nonindependent samples. (13)

panel study Another name for a longitudinal study. (8)

paradoxical incident An occurrence characterized by seemingly self-contradictory aspects. (2)

parsimony The degree to which the propositions of a theory are "sparing" or "frugal"; see also *Occam's razor*. (2)

partial concealment Observation in which the researcher conceals only who or what is being observed. (4)

participant observation Studies in which a group or a community is studied from within by a researcher who records behavior as it occurs. (4)

partitioning of tables Subdivision of larger chi-square tables into smaller tables (e.g., into 2×2 tables). (15)

passive deception (deception by omission) The withholding of certain information from the subjects, such as not informing them of the meaning of their responses when they are given a projective test or not telling them the full details of the study. (3)

payoff potential Subjective assessment of the likelihood that the idea will be corroborated. (2)

Pearson _r_ Standard index of linear relationship. (11)

percentile A point in a distribution of scores below and above which a specified percentage of scores falls. (10)

phi coefficient (φ) Pearson _r_ where both variables are dichotomous. (11, 15)

physical traces Material evidence of behavior. (4)

pilot test A way of selecting judges or raters by comparing all recruits in the pool of potential judges for their accuracy of judgments on some relevant criterion. (4)

pilot testing The evaluation of some aspect of the research before the study is implemented. (5)

placebo A substance without any pharmacological benefit given as a pseudomedicine to a control group. (3, 7)

placebo control group A control group that receives a placebo. (7)

placebo effects The "healing" effects of inert substances or nonspecific treatments. (7)

plagiarism Representing someone else's work as one's own. (3)

plausibility stage That phase in the development of a research hypothesis in which the scientist evaluates the plausibility of an initial lead or idea. (2)

plausible rival hypotheses Propositions, or sets of propositions, that provide a reasonable alternative to the working hypothesis. (6)

point-biserial correlation (r_{pb}) Pearson _r_ in which one of the variables is continuous and the other is dichotomous. (11)

point estimates Estimates of particular characteristics of the population (e.g, the number of times an event occurs). (9)

population The universe of elements from which sample elements are drawn, or the universe of elements to which we want to generalize. (9)

positively skewed distribution An asymmetrical distribution in which the pointed end is toward the right (i.e., the positive tail). (10)

posttest-only control-group design An after-only experimental design containing an experimental and a control group. (7)

power (1 − β) In significance testing, the probability of not making a Type II error. (12)

power analysis Estimation of the effective power of a statistical test, or of the sample size needed to detect an obtained effect given a specified level of power. (12)

power of a test The probability, when using a particular test statistic (e.g., t, F, χ^2), of not making a Type II error. (12)

predictive validity The extent to which a test can predict future outcomes. (6)

preexperimental designs Research designs in which there is such a total absence of control that they are of minimal value in establishing causality. (7)

pre-post control-group design Before-after experimental design. (7)

pretest The measurement made before an experimental manipulation or intervention. (5)

pretest sensitization The confounding of pretesting and X, the independent variable of interest. (7)

pretest-treatment interaction The statistical evaluation of pretest sensitization. (7)

principle of the drunkard's search The gathering of data in a convenient place but not a relevant one. (1)

probability The mathematical chance of an event's occurring. (9, 12)

probability sampling The random selection of sampling units so that the laws of mathematical probability apply. (9)

product-moment correlation Standard index of linear relationship, or Pearson _r_. (11)

projective test A psychological measure that operates on the principle that the subject will project some unconscious aspect of his or her life experience and emotions onto ambiguous stimuli in the spontaneous responses that come to mind (e.g, the Rorschach test and the Thematic Apperception Test). (5)

proportion of variation explained See _coefficient of determination._

pseudoscience Bogus claims masquerading as scientific facts. (1)

psychophysics The study of the relationship between physical stimuli and our experience of them. (1)

PsycINFO The American Psychological Association's main database. (2)

p value Probability value or level obtained in a test of significance. (12)

qualitative research Studies in which the raw data exist in a nonnumeric form (e.g., reports of conversations). (4)

quantitative research Studies in which the raw data exist in a numerical form (e.g., observers' or judges' ratings). (4)

quasi-control subjects Research participants who are asked to reflect on the context in which an experiment is conducted and to speculate on the ways in which the context may influence their own and other subjects' behaviors. (7)

quasi-experimental research Study designs that resemble an experimental design (in that there are treatments, outcome measures, and experimental units) but in which there is no random assignment to create the comparisons from which treatment-caused changes can be inferred in randomized designs. (8)

quota sampling A procedure that assigns a quota of people to be interviewed and lets the questioner build up a sample that is roughly representative of the population. (9)

r^2 See *coefficient of determination*.

random assignment A synonym for randomization. (1, 7)

random digit dialing The researcher selects the first three digits of telephone numbers and then uses a computer program to select the last digits at random. (9)

random error The effects of uncontrolled variables that cannot be specifically identified; such effects are, theoretically speaking, self-canceling in that the average of the errors will probably equal zero in the long run. (6)

randomization (random assignment) Random allocation of sampling units to treatment conditions. (7)

randomized experiments Experimental designs that use randomization. (7)

randomized trials Another name for medical experiments that use true randomized experimental designs. (7)

random sampling Selecting a sample by chance procedures but with known probabilities of selection. (1, 9)

random selection Another name for *random sampling*.

range Distance between the highest and lowest score. (10)

rater biases Another name for *rating errors* or *response biases*. (5)

rating errors (response biases) Systematic errors in responses on rating scales. (5)

rating scales The common name for a variety of measuring instruments on which the observer or judge gives a numerical value (either explicitly or implicitly) to certain judgments or assessments. (5)

reactive observation An observation that affects what is being observed or measured. (4)

relational research An empirical investigation in which the objective is to identify relations among variables. (1)

reliability The extent to which observations or measures are consistent or stable. (6)

reliability of components The internal-consistency reliability of the components of a test or inventory.

repeated measures design Statistical design in which the sampling units generate two or more measurements. (7, 14)

replicate To repeat or duplicate a scientific observation. (1)

replication The duplication of a scientific observation, usually an experimental result. (6)

representative Typical, such as when the segment is representative (or typical) of the larger pool. (9)

residual effects Effects left over when appropriate components are subtracted from scores or means. (7, 14)

residuals See *interaction effects, row effects,* and *column effects*.

response biases See *rating errors*.

retest reliability See *test-retest reliability*.

rhetoric The language of a given field, which in science encompasses the proper use of technical terms. (1)

risk-benefit analysis An evaluation of the ethical risks and benefits of proposed studies. (3)

rival hypotheses Competing hypotheses. (4)

rival interpretations Plausible explanations that provide reasonable alternatives to working hypotheses. (4)

root mean square See *standard deviation*.

Rorschach test A projective test that consists of a set of inkblots on pieces of cardboard. (5)

row effects Row means minus grand mean. (14)

Rushton study A field experiment, conducted in a mining company, that raised the ethical issue of fair-mindedness. (3)

sample A subset of the population. (9)

sampling plan A design, scheme of action, or procedure that specifies how the participants are to be selected in a survey study. (9)

sampling units The elements that make up the sample (e.g., people, schools, or cities). (7)

sampling without replacement A type of random sampling in which a previously selected name cannot be chosen again and must be disregarded in any later draw. (9)

sampling with replacement A type of random sampling in which the selected names are placed in the selection pool again and may be reselected in subsequent draws. (9)

scatter diagram See *scatter plot*.

scatter plot (scatter diagram) A visual display of the correlation between two variables that looks like a cloud of scattered dots. (11)

scientific method A general approach or outlook (rather than a single method) emphasizing the use of empirical reasoning. (1)

scientific notation A compact way of reporting numbers with many decimal places. (13)

secondary observation An observation that is twice removed from the source. (4)

segmented graphic scale A rating scale in the form of a line that is broken into segments. (5)

selection A plausible threat to the internal validity of research not using randomization when the kinds of research subjects selected for one treatment group are different from those selected for another group. (7)

self-report measures See *method of self-report*.

self-selection Selection in which the subject chooses for himself or herself whether to enter a treatment condition. (8)

semantic differential method A type of rating procedure in which connotative (or subjective)

meaning is judged in terms of several dimensions, usually evaluation, potency, and activity. (5)

sensemaking The use of ethnographic methodology to explore how people "make sense" of things. (4)

serendipity A lucky or accidental discovery. (2)

signal Information. (13)

signal-to-noise ratio A ratio of information to lack of information, for example, the ratio of the variability between samples (the signal) to the variability within the samples (the noise). (13)

significance level The probability of a Type I error. (12)

simple effects Differences between group or condition means. (14)

simple observation Unobtrusive observation of events without any attempt to affect them. (4)

simple random sampling A sampling plan in which the participants are selected individually on the basis of a randomized procedure (e.g., a table of random digits). (9)

single-case experimental research Studies using repeated measures designs in which $N = 1$ subject or 1 group. (8)

size of the study The number of sampling units. (13)

small-N experimental research Studies using repeated measures designs in which the treatment effect is evaluated within the same subject or a small number of subjects. (8)

socially desirable responding The tendency to respond in ways that seem to elicit a favorable evaluation. (5)

social psychology of the experiment The study of the ways in which the subject-related and the experimenter-related artifacts operate. (7)

Solomon design A four-group experimental design developed by R. L. Solomon as a means of assessing pretest sensitization effects without contamination by pretesting. (7)

Spearman-Brown prophecy formula A traditional equation that measures the overall internal-consistency reliability of a test from a knowledge of the reliability of its components. (6)

Spearman rho (r_s) Pearson r computed on scores in ranked form. (11)

spread Dispersion or variability. (10)

stability The extent to which a set of measurements does not vary. (9)

standard deviation (root mean square) An index of the variability of a set of data around the mean value in a distribution. (10)

standardized measure A measurement (e.g., of ability, personality, judgment, and attitude) that requires that certain rules be followed in the development, administration, and scoring of the measuring instrument. (5)

standardizing the margins Setting all row totals equal to each other and all column totals equal to each other. (15)

standard normal curve Normal curve with mean = 0 and σ = 1. (10)

standard score (*z* score) Score converted to a standard deviation unit. (10)

statistical-conclusion validity The relative accuracy of drawing statistical conclusions. (6)

statistical power See *power.*

stem-and-leaf chart The plot of a distribution in which the original data are preserved with any desired precision. (10)

strata (clusters) Subpopulations (or layers) in survey sampling. (9)

stratified random sampling Probability sampling plan in which a separate sample is randomly selected within each homogeneous stratum (or layer) of the population. (9)

structured items Response items with fixed options. (5)

Student's *t* The pen name used by the inventor of the *t* test, William Sealy Gosset, was Student. (13)

sufficient condition A condition that is adequate to bring about some effect or result. (7)

summated ratings method A method of attitude scaling, developed by Rensis Likert, that uses item analysis to select the best items. (5)

sum of squares (*SS*) The sum of the squared deviations from the mean in a set of scores. (14).

symmetrical distribution A distribution of scores in which there is an exact correspondence in arrangement on the opposite sides of the middle line. (10)

synchronous correlations In panel designs, these correlations represent the degree of relationship of variables at a moment in time. (8)

systematic error The effect of uncontrolled variables that often can be specifically identified; such effects are, theoretically speaking, not self-canceling (in contrast to the self-canceling nature of random errors). (6)

systematic observation Observation that is guided or influenced by preexisting questions or hypotheses. (4)

tally sheets Recording materials for counting frequencies. (4)

***t*contrast** The symbol used in this book to denote a *t* test that is used to address a focused question or hypothesis in a comparison of more than two groups or conditions. (14)

teleological cause See *final cause.*

telephone interview An interview that is conducted by phone rather than face to face. (5)

temporal precedence The principle that what is labeled as the "cause" must be shown to have occurred before the "effect." (7)

test-retest correlations Correlations that represent the stability of a variable over time. (8)

test-retest reliability The degree of consistency of a test or measurement, or the characteristic it is designed to measure, from one administration to another; also called *retest reliability.* (6)

tests of simple effects Statistical tests of differences between group or condition means. (14)

Thematic Apperception Test (TAT) A projective test that consists of a set of pictures, usually of people in various life contexts. (5)

theoretical (conceptual) definition The meaning of a variable in abstract or conceptual terms. (2)

theoretical ecumenism The use of more than one relevant theoretical perspective, in order to foster a holistic picture. (1)

theory A set of proposed explanatory statements connected by logical arguments and by explicit and implicit assumptions. (2)

third-variable problem A condition in which a variable correlated with *X* and *Y* is the cause of both. (11)

three Rs of humane animal experimentation The argument that scientists should (a) *reduce* the number of animals used in research, (b) *refine* the experiments so that there is less suffering, and (c) *replace* animals with other procedures whenever possible. (3)

Thurstone scales See *method of equal-appearing intervals.*

time-series designs Studies in which the effects of an intervention are inferred from a comparison of the outcome measures obtained at different time intervals before and after the intervention. (8)

transformation Conversion of data to another mathematical form. (10)

translation and back-translation Method used in cross-cultural research in which the researcher has one bilingual person translate the questionnaire items from the source to the target language and then has another bilingual person independently translate the items back into the source language. The researcher then compares the original with the twice-translated version to see whether anything important was lost in the translation. (4)

treatments The procedures or conditions of an experiment. (7)

trimmed mean The mean of a distribution from which a specified highest and lowest percentage of scores has been dropped. (10)

t test A test of significance used to judge the tenability of the null hypothesis of no relation between two variables. (13)

two-by-two factorial design A statistical design with two rows and two columns. (7)

two-tailed p value The p value associated with a result supporting a prediction of a nonspecific direction of a research result; for example, either $M_A > M_B$ or $M_B > M_A$ or the sign of r is either positive or negative. (12)

two-way design (two-way factorial) A statistical design in which each entry in the table is associated with a row variable and a column variable. (14)

two-way factorial See *two-way design*.

Type I error The error of rejecting the null hypothesis when it is true. (12)

Type II error The error of failing to reject the null hypothesis when it is false. (12)

unbiased Describing a case in which the values produced by the sample coincide with the "true" values of the population. (9)

unbiased estimator of the population value of σ^2 A specific statistic usually written as S^2. (10)

unbiased sampling plan Survey design in which the values produced by the samples coin-

cide in the long run with the "true" values in the population. (9)

unobtrusive observation Measurements or observations used to study behavior when the subjects are unaware of being measured or observed. (4)

unstructured measures See *open-ended measures*.

validity The degree to which what was observed or measured is the same as what was purported to be observed or measured. (6)

variability See *spread*.

variables Attributes of sampling units that can take on two or more values. (2)

variance (mean square) The mean of the squared deviations of scores from their means in a population or its unbiased estimate. (10)

volunteer bias Systematic error resulting when participants who volunteer respond differently from how individuals in the general population would respond. (9)

wait-list control group The use of a control group in which the subjects wait to be given the experimental treatment until after it has been administered to the experimental group. (8)

Wechsler Adult Intelligence Scale (WAIS) The most widely used of the individual intelligence tests; divided into verbal and performance scores. (6)

wild scores Extreme scores that result from computational or recording mistakes. (10)

within-subjects design Statistical design in which the sampling units (e.g., the research participants) generate two or more measurements. (7)

working hypothesis A testable supposition; also called an *experimental hypothesis* in experimental research. (2)

x axis (abscissa) The horizontal axis of a distribution. (10)

y axis (ordinate) The vertical axis of a distribution. (10)

yea-sayers Respondents who answer questions consistently in the affirmative. (5)

zero control group A group that receives no treatment of any kind. (7)

$\bar{z}_r$ The average Fisher z_r. (Appendix C)

z score See *standard score*.

References

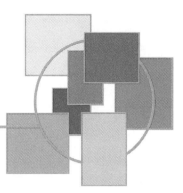

Adair, J. G. (1973). *The human subject: The social psychology of the psychological experiment.* Boston: Little, Brown.

Adair, R. K. (1990). *The physics of baseball.* New York: Harper & Row.

Aditya, R. N. (1996). *The not-so-good subject: Extent and correlates of pseudovolunteering in research.* Unpublished M.A. thesis, Temple University Department of Psychology, Philadelphia.

Aditya, R. N., & House, R. J. (2002). Interpersonal acumen and leadership across cultures: Pointers from the GLOBE study. In R. E. Riggio, S. E. Murphy, F. J. Pirozzolo (Eds.), *Multiple intelligences and leadership* (pp. 215–240). Mahwah, NJ: Erlbaum.

Aiken, L. R., Jr. (1963). Personality correlates of attitude toward mathematics. *Journal of Educational Research, 56,* 576–580.

Ainsworth, M. D. S., Blehar, M. C., Waters, E., & Wall, S. (1978). *Patterns of attachment.* Hillsdale, NJ: Erlbaum.

Albers, J. (1969). *Search versus re-search: Three lectures by Josef Albers at Trinity College, April 1965.* Hartford, CT: Trinity College Press.

Allaman, J. D., Joyce, C. S., & Crandall, V. C. (1972). The antecedents of social desirability response tendencies of children and young adults. *Child Development, 43,* 1135–1160.

Allport, G. W., & Postman, L. (1947). *The psychology of rumor.* New York: Holt, Rinehart & Winston.

American Association for the Advancement of Science. (1988). *Project on scientific fraud and misconduct.* Washington, DC: Author.

American Psychological Association. (1973). *Ethical principles in the conduct of research with human participants.* Washington, DC: Author.

American Psychological Association. (1982). *Ethical principles in the conduct of research with human participants.* Washington, DC: Author.

American Psychological Association. (1992). Ethical principles of psychologists and code of conduct. *American Psychologist, 47,* 1597–1611.

American Psychological Association. (2001). *Publication manual of the American Psychological Association* (5th ed.). Washington, DC: Author.

Anastasi, A., & Urbina, S. (1997). *Psychological testing* (7th ed.). Upper Saddle River, NJ: Prentice Hall.

Anderson, C. A., & Bushman, B. J. (1997). External validity of "trivial" experiments: The case of laboratory aggression. *Review of General Psychology, 1,* 19–41.

Anderson, D. C., Crowell, C. R., Hantula, D. A., & Siroky, L. M. (1988). Task clarification and individual performance posting for improving cleaning in a student-managed university bar. *Journal of Organizational Behavior Management, 9,* 73–90.

Arellano-Galdames, F. J. (1972). *Some ethical problems in research on human subjects.* Unpublished doctoral dissertation, University of New Mexico, Albuquerque.

Arendt, H. (1963). *Eichmann in Jerusalem: A report on the banality of evil.* New York: Viking Press.

Aronson, E., & Carlsmith, J. M. (1968). Experimentation in social psychology. In G. Lindzey & E. Aronson (Eds.), *The handbook of social psychology* (2nd ed., Vol. 2, pp. 1–79). Reading, MA: Addison-Wesley.

Asch, S. E. (1952). Effects of group pressure upon the modification and distortion of judgments. In G. E. Swanson, T. M. Newcomb, & E. L. Hartley (Eds.), *Readings in social psychology* (Rev. ed., pp. 393–401). New York: Holt, Rinehart & Winston.

Atwell, J. E. (1981). Human rights in human subjects research. In A. J. Kimmel (Ed.), *Ethics of human subject research* (pp. 81–90). San Francisco: Jossey-Bass.

Axinn, S. (1966). Fallacy of the single risk. *Philosophy of Science, 33,* 154–162.

Babad, E. (1993). Pygmalion—25 years after interpersonal expectations in the classroom, In P. D. Blanck (Ed.), *Interpersonal expectations: Theory, research,* and applications (pp. 125–153). New York: Cambridge University Press.

Baenninger, R. (1987). Some comparative aspects of yawning in *Betta splendens, Homo sapiens, Panthera leo,* and *Papio sphynx. Journal of Comparative Psychology, 110,* 349–354.

Baenninger, R., Binkley, S., & Baenninger, M. (1996). Field studies of yawning and activity in humans. *Physiology and Behavior, 59,* 421–425.

Bailey, P., & Bremer, F. (1921). Experimental diabetes insipidus. *Archives of Internal Medicine, 28,* 773–803.

Bakan, D. (1967). *On method: Toward a reconstruction of psychological investigation.* San Francisco: Jossey-Bass.

Baldwin, W. (2000). Information no one else knows: The value of self-report. In A. A. Stone, J. S. Turkkan, C. A. Bachrach, J. B. Jobe, H. S. Kurtzman, & V. S. Cain (Eds.), *The science of self-report: Implications for research and practice* (pp. 1–7). Mahwah, NJ: Erlbaum.

Bales, R. F. (1950a). *Interaction process analysis: A method for the study of small groups.* Cambridge, MA: Addison-Wesley.

Bales, R. F. (1950b). A set of categories for small group interaction. *American Sociological Review, 15,* 257–263.

Bales, R. F., & Cohen, S. P. (1979). *Symlog: A system for the multiple level observation of groups.* New York: Free Press.

Baltimore, D. (1997, January 27). Philosophical differences. *The New Yorker,* p. 8.

Barker, P. (1996). *Psychotherapeutic metaphors: A guide to theory and practice.* New York: Brunner/Mazel.

Barlow, D. H. (1984). *Single-case experimental designs* (2nd ed.). New York: Allyn & Bacon.

Barrass, R. (1978). *Scientists must write.* London: Chapman & Hall.

Bartoshuk, L. (2002). Self-reports and across-group comparisons: A way out of the box. *APS Observer, 15:*3, 7, 26–28.

Bauer, M. I., & Johnson-Laird, P. N. (1993). How diagrams can improve reasoning. *Psychological Science, 4,* 372–378.

Baumrind, D. (1964). Some thoughts on ethics of research: After reading Milgram's "Behavioral Study of Obedience." *American Psychologist, 19,* 421–423.

Beck, S. J., Beck, A., Levitt, E., & Molish, H. (1961). *Rorschach's test: Vol. 1. Basic processes.* New York: Grune & Stratton.

Bellack, A. S., Hersen, M., & Kazdin, A. E. (Eds.). (1982). *International handbook of behavior modification and therapy.* New York: Plenum.

Bem, D. J. (1965). An experimental analysis of self-persuasion. *Journal of Experimental Social Psychology, 1,* 199–218.

Bem, D. J. (1972). Self-perception theory. In L. Berkowitz (Ed.), *Advances in experimental social psychology* (Vol. 6, pp. 1–62). New York: Academic Press.

Berelson, B. (1952). *Content analysis in communication research.* Glencoe, IL: Free Press.

Berelson, B. (1954). Content analysis. In G. Lindzey (Ed.), *Handbook of social psychology* (Vol. 1, pp. 488–522). Reading, MA: Addison-Wesley.

Bergum, B. O., & Lehr, D. J. (1963). Effects of authoritarianism on vigilance performance. *Journal of Applied Psychology, 47,* 75–77.

Bernard, H. B., & Killworth, P. D. (1970). Informant accuracy in social network data, Part 2. *Human Communication Research, 4,* 3–18.

Bernard, H. B., & Killworth, P. D. (1980). Informant accuracy in social network data: 4. A comparison of clique-level structure in behavioral and cognitive network data. *Social Networks, 2,* 191–218.

Bernard, H. R. (1994). *Research methods in anthropology: Qualitative and quantitative approaches.* Thousand Oaks, CA: Sage.

Bersoff, D. M., & Bersoff, D. N. (2000). Ethical issues in the collection of self-report data. In A. A. Stone, J. S. Turkkan, C. A. Bachrach, J. B. Jobe, H. S. Kurtzman, & V. S. Cain (Eds.), *The science of self-report: Implications for research and practice* (pp. 9–24). Mahwah, NJ: Erlbaum.

Billow, R. M. (1977). Metaphor: A review of the psychological literature. *Psychological Bulletin, 84,* 81–92.

Biocca, F., & Levy, M. R. (Eds.). (1995). *Communication in the age of virtual reality.* Hillsdale, NJ: Erlbaum.

Blanck, P. D. (Ed.). (1993). *Interpersonal expectations: Theory, research, and applications.* New York: Cambridge University Press.

Blanck, P. D., Bellack, A. S., Rosnow, R. L., Rotheram-Borus, M. J., & Schooler, N. R. (1992). Scientific rewards and conflicts of ethical choices in human subjects research. *American Psychologist, 47,* 959–965.

Blumberg, M., & Pringle, C. D. (1983). How control groups can cause loss of control in action research: The case of Rushton coal mine. *Journal of Applied Behavioral Science, 19,* 409–425.

Bonate, P. L. (2000). *Analysis of pretest-posttest designs*. Boca Raton, FL: Chapman & Hall.

Boorstein, D. J. (1985). *The discoverers*. New York: Vintage.

Bordia, P., & Rosnow, R. L. (1998). Rumor rest stops on the information highway: Transmission patterns in a computer-mediated rumor chain. *Human Communication Research, 25,* 163–179.

Boyatzis, R. E. (1988). *Transforming qualitative information: Thematic analysis and code development*. Thousand Oaks, CA: Sage.

Bradburn, N. M. (1982). Question-wording effects in surveys. In R. Hogarth (Ed.), *New directions for methodology of social and behavioral science: Question framing and response contingency* (No. 11, pp. 65–76). San Francisco: Jossey-Bass.

Braun, H. I., & Wainer, H. (1989). Making essay test scores fairer with statistics. In J. M. Tanur, F. Mosteller, W. H. Kruskal, E. L. Lehmann, R. F. Link, R. S. Pieters, & G. S. Rising (Eds.), *Statistics: A guide to the unknown* (3rd ed., pp. 178–187). Pacific Grove, CA: Wadsworth & Brooks/Cole.

Brehm, S. S., & Kassin, S. M. (1996). *Social psychology*. Boston: Houghton Mifflin.

Brehmer, B., & Dörner, D. (1993). Experiments with computer-simulated microworlds: Escaping both the narrow straits of the laboratory and the deep blue sea of the field study. *Computers in Human Behavior, 9,* 171–184.

Bridgstock, M. (1982). A sociological approach to fraud in science. *Australian and New Zealand Journal of Sociology, 18,* 364–383.

Brody, J. E. (2002, October 22). Separating gold from junk in medical studies. *The New York Times*, p. F7.

Brooks-Gunn, J., & Rotheram-Borus, M. J. (1994). Rights to privacy in research: Adolescents versus parents. *Ethics and Behavior, 4,* 109–121.

Broome, J. (1984). Selecting people randomly. *Ethics, 95,* 38–55.

Brown, R. (1965). *Social psychology*. New York: Free Press.

Brownlee, K. A. (1955). Statistics of the 1954 Polio vaccine trials. [Electronic version]. *Journal of the American Statistical Association, 272,* 1005–1013.

Brunvand, J. H. (2000). *The truth never stands in the way of a good story*. Urbana: University of Illinois Press.

Buckhout, R. (1965). Need for approval and attitude change. *Journal of Psychology, 60,* 123–128.

Burnham, J. R. (1966). *Experimenter bias and lesion labeling*. Unpublished manuscript, Purdue University, West Lafayette.

Buunk, B. P., & Gibbons, F. X. (Eds.). (1997). *Health, coping, and well-being: Perspectives from social comparison theory*. Mahwah, NJ: Erlbaum.

Byrne, D. (1961). Interpersonal attraction and attitude similarity. *Journal of Abnormal and Social Psychology, 62,* 713–715.

Byrne, D. (1971). *The attraction paradigm*. New York: Academic Press.

Byrne, D., Clore, G. L., & Smeaton, G. (1986). The attraction hypothesis: Do similar attitudes affect anything? *Journal of Personality and Social Psychology, 51,* 1167–1170.

Campbell, D. T., & Fiske, D. W. (1959). Convergent and discriminant validation by the multitrait-multimethod matrix. *Psychological Bulletin, 56,* 81–105.

Campbell, D. T., & Kenny, D. A. (1999). *A primer on regression artifacts*. New York: Guilford.

Campbell, D. T., & Stanley, J. C. (1963). *Experimental and quasi-experimental designs for research*. Chicago: Rand McNally.

Cantor, N., & Kihlstrom, J. F. (1989). *Personality and social intelligence*. Englewood Cliffs, NJ: Prentice Hall.

Carr, K., & England, R. (Eds.). (1995). *Simulated and virtual realities: Elements of perception*. London: Taylor & Francis.

Ceci, S. J. (1990). *On intelligence . . . more or less: A bio-ecological treatise on intellectual development*. Englewood Cliffs, NJ: Prentice Hall.

Ceci, S. J. (1996). *On intelligence: A bioecological treatise on intellectual development* (Expanded ed.). Cambridge: Harvard University Press.

Ceci, S. J., & Bruck, M. (1993). Suggestibility of the child witness: A historical review and synthesis. *Psychological Bulletin, 113,* 403–439.

Ceci, S. J., & Bruck, M. (1995). *Jeopardy in the courtroom: A scientific study of children's testimony*. Washington, DC: American Psychological Association.

Ceci, S. J., Peters, D., & Plotkin, J. (1985). Human subjects review, personal values, and the regulation of social science research. *American Psychologist, 40,* 994–1002.

Chalmers, I., & Altman, D. G. (1995). *Systematic reviews*. London: BJM Publishing Group.

Chambers, J. M., Cleveland, W. S., Kleiner, B., & Tukey, P. A. (1983). *Graphical methods for data analysis*. Pacific Grove, CA: Wadsworth.

Chandrasekhar, S. (1987). *Truth and beauty: Aesthetics and motivations in science*. Chicago: University of Chicago Press.

Christie, R. (1951). Experimental naiveté and experiential naiveté. *Psychological Bulletin, 48,* 327–339.

Clark, R. W. (1971). *Einstein: The life and times*. New York: World.

Cochran, W. G. (1963, 1977). *Sampling techniques* (2nd, 3rd ed.). New York: Wiley.

Cohen, J. (1988). *Statistical power analysis for the behavioral sciences* (2nd ed.). Hillsdale, NJ: Erlbaum.

Conant, J. B. (1957). Introduction. In J. B. Conant & L. K. Nash (Eds.), *Harvard case studies in experimental science* (Vol. 1, pp. vii–xvi). Cambridge: Harvard University Press.

Conrath, D. W. (1973). Communications environment and its relationship to organizational structure. *Management Science, 20,* 586–603.

Conrath, D. W., Higgins, C. A., & McClean, R. J. (1983). A comparison of the reliability of questionnaire versus diary data. *Social Networks, 5,* 315–322.

Converse, J. M., & Presser, S. (1986). *Survey questions: Handcrafting the standardized questionnaire*. Beverly Hills, CA: Sage.

Cook, T. D., & Campbell, D. T. (1976). The design and conduct of quasi-experiments and true experiments in field settings. In M. D. Dunnette (Ed.), *Handbook of industrial and organizational psychology* (pp. 223–326). Chicago: Rand McNally.

Cook, T. D., & Campbell, D. T. (1979). *Quasi-experimentation: Design and analysis issues for field settings*. Chicago: Rand McNally.

Cook, T. D., Cooper, H., Cordray, D. S., Hartmann, H., Hedges, L. V., Light, R. J., Louis, T. A., & Mosteller, F. (1994). *Meta-analysis for explanation: A casebook*. New York: Russell Sage Foundation.

Cooper, H. M. (1984). *The integrative research review: A social science approach*. Beverly Hills, CA: Sage.

Cooper, H. M. (1985). Literature searching strategies of integrative research reviewers. *American Psychologist, 40,* 1267–1269.

Cooper, H. M. (1989). *Integrating research: A guide to literature reviews* (2nd ed.). Newbury Park, CA: Sage.

Cooper, H. M., & Hedges, L. V. (Eds.). (1994). *The handbook of research synthesis*. New York: Russell Sage Foundation.

Cooper, M. (1997, February 4). For greedy fugitives, it's "go directly to jail." *The New York Times,* p. B3.

Corsini, R. J. (Ed.). (1984). *Encyclopedia of psychology* (Vols. 1–4). New York: Wiley.

Crabb, P. B., & Bielawski, D. (1994). The social representation of maternal culture and gender in children's books. *Sex Roles, 30,* 69–79.

Crabtree, B. F., & Miller, W. L. (Eds.). (1992). *Doing qualitative research: Multiple strategies*. Thousand Oaks, CA: Sage.

Crancer, J., Dille, J., Delay, J., Wallace, J., & Haybin, M. (1969). Comparison of the effects of marijuana and alcohol on simulated driving performance. *Science, 164,* 851–854.

Cronbach, L. J. (1951). Coefficient alpha and the internal structure of tests. *Psychometrika, 16,* 297–334.

Cronbach, L. J., & Meehl, P. E. (1955). Construct validity in psychological tests. *Psychological Bulletin, 52,* 281–302.

Cronbach, L. J. & Quirk, T. J. (1971). Test validity. In L. C. Deighton (Ed.), *Encyclopedia of education* (Vol. 9, pp. 165–175). New York: Macmillan and Free Press.

Crowne, D. P. (1979). *The experimental study of personality*. Hillsdale, NJ: Erlbaum.

Crowne, D. P. (1991). From response style to motive. *Current Contents: Social and Behavioral Sciences, 23*(30), 10.

Crowne, D. P., & Marlowe, D. (1964). *The approval motive: Studies in evaluative dependence*. New York: Wiley.

Cryer, J. D. (1986). *Time series analysis*. Boston: PWS-Kent.

Csikszentmihalyi, M., & Larson, R. (1984). *Being adolescent: Conflict and growth in the teenage years*. New York: Basic Books.

Danziger, K. (1988). A question of identity: Who participated in psychological experiments? In J. Morawski (Ed.), *The rise of experimentation in American psychology* (pp. 35–52). New York: Oxford University Press.

Darley, J. M., & Latané, B. (1968). Bystander intervention in emergencies. *Journal of Personality and Social Psychology, 8,* 377–383.

Davis, J. D., Gallagher, R. L., & Ladove, R. (1967). Food intake controlled by blood factors. *Science, 156,* 1247–1248.

Davison, G. C. (2000). Case study. In A. E. Kazdin (Ed.), *Encyclopedia of psychology* (Vol. 2, pp. 46–48). New York: Oxford University Press & American Psychological Association.

Day, D. D., & Quackenbush, O. F. (1942). Attitudes toward defensive, cooperative, and aggressive wars. *Journal of Social Psychology, 16,* 11–20.

Denzin, N. K., & Lincoln, Y. S. (Eds.). (1994). *Handbook of qualitative research*. Thousand Oaks, CA: Sage.

Denzin, N. K., & Lincoln, Y. S. (2000). The discipline and practice of qualitative research. In N. K. Denzin & Y. S. Lincoln (Eds.), *Handbook of qualitative research* (2nd ed., pp. 1–28). Thousand Oaks, CA: Sage.

Department of Health and Human Services. (1983). Protection of human subjects. *Code of Federal Regulations, 45*, Section 46.115.

DePaulo, B. M., & Kashy, D. A. (1998). Everyday lies in close and casual relationships. *Journal of Personality and Social Psychology, 74*, 63–79

DePaulo, B. M., Kashy, D. A., Kirkendol, S. E., Wyer, M. M., & Epstein, J. A. (1996). Lying in everyday life. *Journal of Personality and Social Psychology, 70*, 979–995.

Devine, E. C., & Reifschneider, E. (1995). A meta-analysis of the effects of psychoeducational care in adults with hypertension. *Nursing Research, 44*, 237–245.

De Vos, G. A., & Boyer, L. B. (1989). *Symbolic analysis cross-culturally: The Rorschach test*. Berkeley: University of California Press.

de Wolff, M. S., & Van Ijzendoorn, M. H. (1997). Sensitivity and attachment: A meta-analysis on parental antecedents of infant attachment. *Child Development, 68*, 571–591.

Diener, E. (2000). Subjective well-being. *American Psychologist, 55*, 34–43.

DiFonzo, N., Bordia, P., & Rosnow, R. L. (1994). Reining in rumors. *Organizational Dynamics, 23*, 47–62.

DiFonzo, N., Hantula, D. A., & Bordia, P. (1998). Microworlds for experimental research: Having your (control and collection) cake and realism too. *Behavior Research Methods, Instruments, & Computers, 30*, 278–286.

Dorn, L. D., Susman, E. J., & Fletcher, J. C. (1995). Informed consent in children and adolescents: Age, maturation and psychological state. *Journal of Adolescent Health, 16*, 185–190.

Downs, C. W., Smeyak, G. P., & Martin, E. (1980). *Professional interviewing*. New York: Harper & Row.

Dumond, V. (1990). *The elements of nonsexist language*. New York: Prentice Hall.

Eagly, A. H. (1978). Sex differences in influenceability. *Psychological Bulletin, 85*, 86–116.

Eagly, A. H., Ashmore, R. D., Makhijani, M. G., & Longo, L. C. (1991). What is beautiful is good, but. . .: A meta-analysis review of research on the physical attractiveness stereotype. *Psychological Bulletin, 110*, 109–128.

Ebbinghaus, H. (1885). *Über das Gedächtnis: Untersuchungen zur experimentellen Psychologie*. Leipzig, Germany: Duncker & Humblot.

Egan, T. (2003, Jan. 3). Search for Bigfoot outlives the man who created him. *The New York Times*, pp. A1, A16.

Emerson, J. D., & Hoaglin, D. C. (1983). Stem-and-leaf displays. In D. C. Hoaglin, F. Mosteller, & J. W. Tukey (Eds.), *Understanding robust and exploratory data analysis* (pp. 7–32). New York: Wiley.

Entwisle, D. R. (1961). Interactive effects of pretesting. *Educational and Psychological Measurement, 21*, 607–620.

Ericsson, K. A., & Simon, H. A. (Eds.). (1993). *Protocol analysis: Verbal reports as data* (Rev. ed.). Cambridge: MIT Press.

Esposito, J. L., Agard, E., & Rosnow, R. L. (1984). Can confidentiality of data pay off? *Personality and Individual Differences, 5*, 477–480.

Exline, J. J. (2002). Stumbling blocks on the religious road: Fractured relationships, nagging vices, and the inner struggle to believe. *Psychological Inquiry, 13*, 182–189.

Exner, J. E. (1993). *The Rorschach: A comprehensive system* (3rd ed., Vol. 1). New York: Wiley.

Eysenck, H. J. (1952). The effects of psychotherapy: An evaluation. *Journal of Consulting Psychology, 16*, 319–324.

Eysenck, H. J. (1961). The effects of psychotherapy. In H. J. Eysenck (Ed.), *Handbook of abnormal psychology* (pp. 697–725). New York: Basic Books.

Fairbanks, L. A. (1993). What is a good mother? Adaptive variation in maternal behavior of primates. *Current Directions in Psychological Science, 2*, 179–183.

Federighi, E. T. (1959). Extended tables of the percentage points of Student's *t* distribution. *Journal of the American Statistical Association, 54*, 683–688.

Ferster, C. B., & Skinner, B. F. (1957). *Schedules of reinforcement*. New York: Appleton-Century-Crofts.

Festinger, L. (1954). A theory of social comparison processes. *Human Relations, 7*, 117–140.

Festinger, L. (1957). *A theory of cognitive dissonance*. Evanston, IL: Row Peterson.

Festinger, L. (1962). *A theory of cognitive dissonance*. Stanford, CA: Stanford University Press.

Festinger, L., Gerard, H., Hymovitch, B., Kelley, H., & Raven, B. H. (1952). The influence process in the presence of extreme deviates. *Human Relations, 5,* 327–346.

Festinger, L., Schachter, S., & Riecken, H. (1956). *When prophecy fails.* Minneapolis: University of Minnesota Press.

Feyerabend, P. (1988). *Against method* (Rev. ed.). London: Verso.

Fienberg, S. E., & Tanur, J. M. (1989). Combining cognitive and statistical approaches to survey design. *Science, 243,* 1017–1022.

Fine, G. A., & Deegan, J. G. (1996). Three principles of Serendip: Insight, chance, and discovery in qualitative research. *Qualitative Studies in Education, 9,* 434–447.

Fine, G. A., & Turner, P. A. (2001). *Whispers on the color line: Rumor and race in America.* Berkeley: University of California Press.

Finkner, A. L. (1950). Methods of sampling for estimating commercial peach production in North Carolina. *North Carolina Agricultural Experiment Station Technical Bulletin, 91* (whole).

Fischer, K. W., Pipp, S. L., & Bullock, D. (1984). Detecting developmental discontinuities. In R. N. Emde & R. J. Harmon (Eds.), *Continuities and discontinuities in development* (pp. 95–121). New York: Plenum.

Fisher, R. A. (1973). *Statistical methods for research workers* (14th ed.). New York: Hafner.

Fisher, R. A., & Yates, F. (1974). *Statistical tables for biological, agricultural, and medical research* (6th ed.). London: Longman.

Fisher, R. J. (1993). Social desirability bias and the validity of indirect questioning. *Journal of Consumer Research, 20,* 303–315.

Fiske, D. W. (2000). Artifact in assessment. In A. E. Kazdin (Ed.), *Encyclopedia of psychology* (Vol. 1, pp. 245–248). New York: Oxford University Press & American Psychological Association.

Flanagan, J. C. (1954). The critical incident technique. *Psychological Bulletin, 51,* 327–358.

Forrest, D. W. (1974). *Francis Galton: The life and work of a Victorian genius.* New York: Taplinger.

Fossey, D. (1981). Imperiled giants of the forest. *National Geographic, 159,* 501–604.

Fossey, D. (1983). *Gorillas in the mist.* Boston: Houghton Mifflin.

Foster, E. K. (2003). METASTATS: Behavioral science statistics for Microsoft Windows and the HP49G programmable calculator. *Behavior Research Methods, Instruments, & Computers, 35,* 325–328.

Foster, E. K. (2004). Research on gossip: Taxonomy, methods, and future directions. *Review of General Psychology, 8,* in press.

Fowler, F. J., Jr. (1993). *Survey research methods* (2nd ed.). Newbury Park, CA: Sage.

Francis, Jr., T., Korns, R. F., Voight, R. B., Boisen, M., Hemphill, F., Napier, J., & Tolchinsky, E. (1955). An evaluation of the 1954 poliomyelitis vaccine trials—summary report. *American Journal of Public Health, 45*(5), 1–63.

Franke, R. H., & Kaul, J. D. (1978). The Hawthorne experiments: First statistical interpretation. *American Sociological Review, 43,* 623–643.

Freedman, D., Pisani, R., Purves, R., & Adhikari, A. (1991). *Statistics* (2nd ed.). New York: Norton.

Frey, J. H. (1986). An experiment with a confidentiality reminder in a telephone survey. *Public Opinion Quarterly, 50,* 26–269.

Friedman, H. (Ed.). (1998). *Encyclopedia of mental health* (Vols. 1–3). San Diego, CA: Academic Press.

Fuerbringer, J. (1997, March 30). Why both bulls and bears can act so bird-brained: Quirky behavior is becoming a realm of economics. *The New York Times,* Section 3, pp. 1,6.

Funke, J. (1991). Dealing with dynamic systems: Research strategy, diagnostic approach and experimental results. *German Journal of Psychology, 16,* 24–43.

Gallup, G. (1976, May 21). *Lessons learned in 40 years of polling.* Paper presented before National Council on Public Polls.

Galton, F. (1869). *Hereditary genius.* London: Macmillan.

Gantt, W. H. (1964). Autonomic conditioning. In J. Wolpe, A. Salter, & L. J. Reyna (Eds.), *The conditioning therapies* (pp. 115–126). New York: Holt, Rinehart & Winston.

Gardner, H. (1985). *Frames of mind: The theory of multiple intelligences.* New York: Basic Books.

Gardner, H. (Ed.). (1993). *Multiple intelligences: The theory in practice.* New York: Basic Books.

Gardner, H., Kornhaber, M. L., & Wake, W. K. (1996). *Intelligence: Multiple perspective.* Ft. Worth, TX: Harcourt Brace.

Gardner, M. (1957). *Fads and fallacies in the name of science.* New York: Dover.

Garfield, E. (1989a). Art and science: 1. The art-science connection. *Current Contents, 21*(8), 3–10.

Garfield, E. (1989b). Art and science: 2. Science for art's sake. *Current Contents, 21*(9), 3–8.

Gazzaniga, M. S., & LeDoux, J. E. (1978). *The integrated mind*. New York: Plenum.

Gentner, D., Holyoak, K. J., & Kokinov, B. N. (Eds.) (2001). *The analogical mind: Perspectives from cognitive science*. Cambridge: MIT Press.

Gentner, D., & Markman, A. B. (1997). Structure mapping in analogy and similarity. *American Psychologist, 52,* 45–56

Gibson, E. J., & Walk, R. D. (1960, April). The visual cliff. *Scientific American, 202*(4), 64–71.

Gigerenzer, G. (1991). From tools to theories: A heuristic of discovery in cognitive psychology. *Psychological Review, 98,* 254–267.

Gigerenzer, G., Swijtink, Z., Porter, T., Daston, L., Beatty, J., & Krüger, L. (1989). *The empire of chance: How probability changed science and everyday life*. New York: Cambridge University Press.

Gilgun, J. F., Daly, K., & Handel, G. (Eds.). (1992). *Qualitative methods in family research*. Thousand Oaks, CA: Sage.

Gillespie, R. (1988). The Hawthorne experiments and the politics of experimentation. In J. Morawski (Ed.), *The rise of experimentation in American psychology* (pp. 114–137). New York: Oxford University Press.

Gilovich, T. (1991). *How we know what isn't so: The fallibility of human reason in everyday life*. New York: Free Press.

Glass, G. (1976) Primary, secondary, and meta-analysis of research. *Educational Researcher, 5,* 3–8.

Glass, G., McGaw, B., & Smith, M. L. (1981). *Meta-analysis in social research*. Beverly Hills, CA: Sage.

Gniech, G. (1976). *Störeffekte in psychologischen Experimenten*. Stuttgart: Kohlhammer.

Goldberg, L. R. (1993). The structure of phenotypic personality traits. *American Psychologist, 48,* 26–34.

Goldman, B. A., & Mitchell, D. F. (1995). *Directory of unpublished experimental mental measures* (Vol. 6). Washington, DC: American Psychological Association.

Goldman, B. A., & Mitchell, D. F. (2003). *Directory of unpublished experimental mental measures* (Vol. 8). Washington, DC: American Psychological Association.

Goldman, B. A., Mitchell, D. F., & Egelson, P. (Eds.). (1997). *Directory of unpublished experimental mental measures* (Vol. 7). Washington, DC: American Psychological Association.

Goldman, B. A., Osborne, W. L., & Mitchell, D. F. (1996). *Directory of unpublished experimental mental measures* (Vols. 4–5). Washington, DC: American Psychological Association.

Goldman, B. A., Saunders, J. L., & Busch, J. C. (1996). *Directory of unpublished experimental mental measures* (Vols. 1–3). Washington, DC: American Psychological Association.

Gombrich, E. H. (1963). *Meditations on a hobby horse*. London: Phaidon.

Goodenough, W. H. (1980). Ethnographic field techniques. In H. C. Triandis & J. W. Berry (Eds.), *Handbook of cross-cultural psychology: Methodology* (Vol. 2, pp. 29–55). Boston: Allyn & Bacon.

Gould, M. S., & Shaffer, D. (1986). The impact of suicide in television movies: Evidence of imitation. *New England Journal of Medicine, 315,* 690–694.

Grant, D. A. (1956). Analysis-of-variance curves in the analysis and comparison of curves. *Psychological Bulletin, 53,* 141–154.

Greco, M., Baenninger, R., & Govern, J. (1993). On the context of yawning: When, where, and why? *Psychological Record, 43,* 175–183.

Greenwald, A. G. (1980). The totalitarian ego: Fabrication and revision of personal history. *American Psychologist, 35,* 603–618.

Gross, A. E., & Fleming, I. (1982). Twenty years of deception in social psychology. *Personality and Social Psychology Bulletin, 8,* 402–408.

Gross, A. G. (1990). *The rhetoric of science*. Cambridge: Harvard University Press.

Gubrium, J. F., & Sankar, A. (Eds.). (1993). *Qualitative methods in aging research*. Thousand Oaks, CA: Sage.

Guilford, J. P. (1954). *Psychometric methods* (2nd ed.). New York: McGraw-Hill.

Guilford, J. P. (1967). *The nature of intelligence*. New York: McGraw-Hill.

Gulliksen, H. (1950). *Theory of mental tests*. New York: Wiley.

Hagenaars, J. A., & Cobben, N. P. (1978). Age, cohort and period: A general model fo the analysis of social change. *Netherlands Journal of Sociology, 14,* 58–91.

Hall, J. A. (1984). *Instructor's manual to accompany Rosenthal/Rosnow: Essentials of behavioral research*. New York: McGraw-Hill.

Hall, R. V., Lund, D., & Jackson, D. (1968). Effects of teacher attention on study behavior. *Journal of Applied Behavior Analysis, 1,* 1–12.

Hallett, T., & Fine, G. A. (2000). Ethnography 1900: Learning from the field research of an old century. *Journal of Contemporary Ethnography, 29,* 593–617.

Hantula, D. A., Stillman, F. A., & Waranch, H. R. (1992). Can a mass-media campaign modify tobacco smoking in a large organization? Evaluation of the Great American Smokeout in an urban hospital. *Journal of Organizational Behavior Management, 13,* 33–47.

Harré, R., & Lamb, R. (Eds.). (1983). *Encyclopedic dictionary of psychology.* Cambridge: MIT Press.

Harris, B. (1988). Key words: A history of debriefing in social psychology. In J. Morawski (Ed.), *The rise of experimentation in American psychology* (pp. 188–212). New Haven, CT: Yale University Press.

Harrower, M., & Bowers, D. (1987). *The inside story: Self-evaluations reflecting basic Rorschach types.* Hillsdale, NJ: Erlbaum.

Härtel, C. E. J. (1993). Rating format research revisited: Format effectiveness and acceptability depend on rater characteristics. *Journal of Applied Psychology, 78,* 212–217.

Hartmann, G. W. (1936). A field experiment on the comparative effectiveness of "emotional" and "rational" political leaflets in determining election results. *Journal of Abnormal and Social Psychology, 31,* 99–114.

Haviland, J. B. (1977). Gossip as competition in Zinacantan. *Journal of Communication, 27,* 186–191.

Haywood, H. C. (1976). The ethics of doing research . . . and of not doing it. *American Journal of Mental Deficiency, 81,* 311–317.

Hedges, L. V., & Olkin, I. (1985). *Statistical methods for meta-analysis.* New York: Academic Press.

Heise, G. A., & Miller, G. A. (1951). Problem solving by small groups using various communication nets. *Journal of Abnormal and Social Psychology, 46,* 327–331.

Hersen, M., & Barlow, D. H. (1976). *Single-case experimental designs: Strategies for studying behavior change.* Oxford: Pergamon Press.

Higbee, K. L., & Wells, M. G. (1972). Some research trends in social psychology during the 1960s. *American Psychologist, 27,* 963–966.

Hineline, P. N., & Lattal, K. A. (2000). Single-case experimental design. In A. E. Kazdin (Ed.), *Encyclopedia of psychology* (Vol. 7, pp. 287–289). New York: Oxford University Press & American Psychological Association.

Hirsh-Pasek, K., & Golinkoff, R. M. (1993). Skeletal supports for grammatical learning: What infants bring to the language learning task. In C. Rovee-Collier & L. P. Lipsitt (Eds.), *Advances in infancy research* (Vol. 8, pp. 299–315). Norwood, NJ: Ablex.

Hirsh-Pasek, K., & Golinkoff, R. M. (1996). *The origins of grammar: Evidence from early language comprehension.* Cambridge: MIT Press.

Hogan, R., Hogan, J., & Roberts, B. W. (1996). Personality measurement and employment decisions. *American Psychologist, 51,* 469–477.

Hollon, S. D., Thase, M. E., & Markowitz, J. C. (2002). Treatment and prevention of depression. *Psychological Science in the Public Interest, 3*(2), 39–77.

Holsti, O. R. (1969). *Content analysis for the social sciences and humanities.* Reading, MA: Addison-Wesley.

Holyoak, K. J., & Thagard, P. (1997). The analogical mind. *American Psychologist, 52,* 35–44.

Hoover, K., & Donovan, T. (1995). *The elements of social scientific thinking* (6th ed.). New York: St. Martin's Press.

Houts, A. C., Cook, T. D., & Shadish, W., Jr. (1986). The person-situation debate: A critical multiplist perspective. *Journal of Personality, 54,* 52–105.

Hoyt, W. T. (2000). Rater bias in psychological research: When is it a problem and what can we do about it? *Psychological Methods, 5,* 64–86.

Hult, C. A. (1996). *Researching and writing in the social sciences.* Boston: Allyn & Bacon.

Hume, D. (1739–1740). *A treatise of human nature.* Oxford, UK: Clarendon Press. (Republished 1978 by Oxford University Press.)

Hunt, M. (1997). *How science takes stock: The story of meta-analysis.* New York: Russell Sage Foundation.

Hunter, J. E., & Schmidt, F. L. (1990). *Methods of meta-analysis: Correcting error and bias in research findings.* Newbury Park, CA: Sage.

Imber, S. D., Glanz, L. M., Elkin, I., Sotsky, S. M., Boyer, J. L., & Leber, W. R. (1986). Ethical issues in psychotherapy research: Problems in a collaborative clinical trials study. *American Psychologist, 41,* 137–146.

Iversen, I. H., & Lattal, K. A. (1991). *Techniques in the behavioral and neural sciences: Vol. 6. Experimental analysis of behavior.* Amsterdam: Elsevier.

Iversen, L. L. (2000). *The science of marijuana.* Oxford, UK: Oxford University Press.

Jaeger, M. E., & Rosnow, R. L. (1988). Contextualism and its implications for psychological inquiry. *British Journal of Psychology, 79,* 63–75.

Jaeger, M. E., Skleder, A. A., & Rosnow, R. L. (1998). Who's up on the low down: Gossip in interpersonal relationships. In B. H. Spitzberg & W. Cupach (Eds.), *The dark side of close relationships* (pp. 103–117). Hillsdale, NJ: Erlbaum.

Jammer, M. (1966). *The conceptual development of quantum mechanics.* New York: McGraw-Hill.

Janis, I. L., & Mann, L. (1965). Effectiveness of emotional role-playing in modifying smoking habits and attitudes. *Journal of Experimental Research in Personality, 1,* 181–186.

Johnson, G. (2002, September 24). Here they are, science's 10 most beautiful experiments. *The New York Times,* Section F, p. 3.

Johnson, M. L. (1953). Seeing's believing. *New Biology, 15,* 60–80.

Johnson-Laird, P. N. (1983). *Mental models: Towards a cognitive science of language, inference, and consciousness.* Cambridge: Harvard University Press.

Johnson-Laird, P. N., & Byrne, R. M. J. (1991). *Deduction.* Hillsdale, NJ: Erlbaum.

Johnston, J. M., & Pennypacker, H. S. (Eds.). (1993a). *Readings for strategies and tactics of behavioral research* (2nd ed.). Hillsdale, NJ: Erlbaum.

Johnston, J. M., & Pennypacker, H. S. (1993b). *Strategies and tactics of behavioral research* (2nd ed.). Hillsdale, NJ: Erlbaum.

Jones, E. E., & Gerard, H. B. (1967). *Foundations of social psychology.* New York: Wiley.

Jones, J. H. (1993). *Bad blood: The Tuskegee syphilis experiment* (Rev. ed.). New York: Free Press.

Jones, M. B., & Fennell, R. S., III (1965). Runway performance in two strains of rats. *Quarterly Journal of the Florida Academy of Sciences, 28,* 289–296.

Judd, C. M., & Kenny, D. A. (1981). *Estimating the effects of social interventions.* Cambridge: Cambridge University Press.

Jung, C. G. (1910). Ein Beitrag zur Psychologie des Gerüchtes. *Zentralblatt für Psychoanalyse, 1,* 81–90.

Jung, C. G. (1959). A visionary rumor. *Journal of Analytical Psychology, 4,* 5–19.

Jung, J. (1969). Current practices and problems in the use of college students for psychological research. *Canadian Psychologist, 10,* 280–290.

Kagay, M. R.. (1996, December 15). Experts say refinements are needed in the polls. *The New York Times,* p. 34.

Kahane, H. (1989). *Logic and philosophy: A modern introduction* (6th ed.). Belmont, CA: Wadsworth.

Kahneman, D., Slovic, P., & Tversky, A. (Eds.). (1982). *Judgment under uncertainty: Heuristics and biases.* New York: Cambridge University Press.

Kahneman, D., & Tversky, A. (1973). On the psychology of prediction. *Psychological Review, 80,* 237–251.

Kanner, L. (1943). Autistic disturbances of affective contact. *Nervous Child, 2,* 217–250.

Kaplan, A. (1964). *The conduct of inquiry: Methodology for behavioral science.* Scranton, PA: Chandler.

Karney, B. R., & Coombs, R. H. (2000). Memory bias in long-term close relationships: Consistency of improvement. *Personality and Social Psychology Bulletin, 26,* 959–970.

Kashy, D. A., & DePaulo, B. M. (1996). Who lies? *Journal of Personality and Social Psychology, 70,* 1037–1051.

Katz, D., & Cantril, H. (1937). Public opinion polls. *Sociometry, 1,* 155–179.

Kazdin, A. E. (1976). Statistical techniques for single-case experimental designs. In M. Hersen & D. H. Barlow (Eds.), *Single case experimental designs: Strategies for studying behavior change* (pp. 265–316). Oxford, UK: Pergamon Press.

Kazdin, A. E. (1980). *Research design in clinical psychology.* New York: Harper & Row.

Kazdin, A. E. (1992). *Research design in clinical psychology* (2nd ed.). Boston: Allyn & Bacon.

Kazdin, A. E. (Ed.). (2000). *Encyclopedia of psychology* (Vols. 1–8). New York: Oxford University Press & American Psychological Association.

Kazdin, A. E., & Tuma, A. H. (Eds.). (1982). *Single-case research designs.* San Francisco: Jossey-Bass.

Kelley, H. H., & Thibaut, J. W. (1969). Group problem solving. In G. Lindzey & E. Aronson (Eds.), *The handbook of social psychology* (2nd ed., Vol. 4, pp. 1–101). Reading, MA: Addison-Wesley.

Kelman, H. C. (1968). *A time to speak: On human values and social research.* San Francisco: Jossey-Bass.

Kendall, P. C., Howard, B. C., & Hays, R. C. (1989). Self-referent speech and psychopathology: The balance of positive and negative thinking. *Cognitive Therapy and Research, 13,* 583–598.

Kenny, D. A. (1979). *Correlation and causality.* New York: Wiley.

Kenny, D. A., & Campbell, D. T. (1984). Methodological considerations in the analysis of temporal data. In K. Gergen & M. Gergen (Eds.), *Historical social psychology* (pp. 125–138). Mahwah, NJ: Erlbaum.

Kenny, D. A., & Campbell, D. T. (1989). On the measurement of stability in over-time data. *Journal of Personality, 57,* 445–481.

Keppel, G. (1991). *Design and analysis: A researcher's handbook* (3rd ed.). Englewood Cliffs, NJ: Prentice Hall.

Kerner, O., et al. (1968). *Report of the National Advisory Commission on Civil Disorders.* New York: Bantam.

Kidder, L. H. (1972). On becoming hypnotized: How skeptics become convinced: A case of attitude change? *Journal of Abnormal Psychology, 80,* 317–322.

Kidder, L. H., Kidder, R. L., & Snyderman, P. (1976). *A cross-lagged correlational analysis of the causal relationship between police employment and crime rates.* Paper presented at the meeting of the American Psychological Association, Washington.

Kilborn, P. T. (1994, January 23). Alarming trend among workers: Surveys find clusters of TB cases. *The New York Times,* pp. A1, A16.

Kimble, G. A. (1989). Psychology from the standpoint of a generalist. *American Psychologist, 44,* 491–499.

Kimmel, A. J. (Ed.). (1981). *Ethics of human subjects research.* San Francisco: Jossey-Bass.

Kimmel, A. J. (1988). *Ethics and values in applied social research.* Beverly Hills, CA: Sage.

Kimmel, A. J. (1991). Predictable biases in the ethical decision making of American psychologists. *American Psychologist, 46,* 786–788.

Kimmel, A. J. (1996). *Ethical issues in behavioral research: A survey.* Oxford, UK: Blackwell.

Kimmel, A. J. (2004). *Rumors and rumor control: A manager's guide to understanding and combatting rumors.* Mahwah, NJ: Erlbaum.

Kirk, R. E. (1995). *Experimental design: Procedures for the behavioral sciences* (3rd ed.). Pacific Grove, CA: Brooks/Cole.

Kirk, R. E. (2000). Randomized experiments. In A. E. Kazdin (Ed.), *Encyclopedia of psychology* (Vol. 6, pp. 502–505). New York: Oxford University Press & American Psychological Association.

Kish, L. (1965). *Survey sampling.* New York: Wiley.

Kleinmuntz, B. (1982). *Personality and psychological assessment.* New York: St. Martin's Press.

Klohnen, E. C., & Mendelsohn, G. A. (1998). Partner selection for personality characteristics: A couple-centered approach. *Personality and Social Psychology Bulletin, 24,* 268–278.

Klopfer, B., & Kelley, D. M. (1942). *The Rorschach technique.* New York: World Book.

Koffka, K. (1935). *Principles of gestalt psychology.* New York: Harcourt Brace.

Köhler, W. (1929). *Gestalt psychology.* New York: Liveright.

Kolata, G. B. (1986). What does it mean to be random? *Science, 231,* 1068–1070.

Kolodner, J. L. (1997). Educational implications of analogy: A view from case-based reasoning. *American Psychologist, 52,* 57–66.

Komaki, J., & Barnett, F. T. (1977). A behavioral approach to coaching football: Improving the play execution of the offensive backfield on a youth football team. *Journal of Applied Behavior Analysis, 10,* 657–664.

Kordig, C. R. (1978). Discovery and justification. *Philosophy of Science, 45,* 110–117.

Koshland, D. E., Jr. (1988). Science, journalism, and whistle-blowing. *Science, 240,* 585.

Kosslyn, S. M. (1994). *Elements of graph design.* New York: W. H. Freeman.

Kraemer, H. C., & Thiemann, S. (1987). *How many subjects? Statistical power analysis in research.* Newbury Park, CA: Sage.

Kragh, H. (2002, August). Paul Dirac: Seeking beauty. *Physics World,* pp. 27–31.

Kratochwill, T. R., & Levin, J. R. (Eds.). (1992). *Single-case research design and analysis: New directions for psychology and education.* Hillsdale, NJ: Erlbaum.

Kraus, S. J. (1991). Attitudes and the prediction of behavior: A meta-analysis of the empirical literature. *Personality and Social Psychology Bulletin, 21,* 58–75.

Krippendorff, K. (1980). *Content analysis: An introduction to its methodology.* Beverly Hills, CA: Sage.

Kuhn, T. S. (1962). *The structure of scientific revolutions.* Chicago: University of Chicago Press.

Kuhn, T. S. (1977). *The essential tension.* Chicago: University of Chicago Press.

Labaw, P. (1980). *Advanced questionnaire design.* Cambridge, MA: ABT Books.

La Greca, A. M. (Ed.). (1990). *Through the eyes of the child: Obtaining self-reports from children and adolescents.* Boston: Allyn & Bacon.

Lakoff, G., & Johnson, M. (1980). *Metaphors We Live By.* Chicago: University of Chicago Press.

Lana, R. E. (1969). Pretest sensitization. In R. Rosenthal & R. L. Rosnow (Eds.), *Artifact in behavioral research* (pp. 119–141). New York: Academic Press.

Lana, R. E. (1991). *Assumptions of social psychology: A reexamination.* Hillsdale, NJ: Erlbaum.

Lana, R. E., & Rosnow, R. L. (1972). *Introduction to contemporary psychology.* New York: Holt, Rinehart & Winston.

Latané, B., & Darley, J. M. (1968). Group inhibition of bystander intervention in emergencies. *Journal of Personality and Social Psychology, 10,* 215–221.

Latané, B., & Darley, J. M. (1970). *The unresponsive bystander: Why doesn't he help?* New York: Appleton-Century-Crofts.

Lavelle, J. M., Hovell, M. F., West, M. P., & Wahlgren, D. R. (1992). Promoting law enforcement for child protection: A community analysis. *Journal of Applied Behavior Analysis, 25,* 885–892.

Lavrakas, P. J. (1987). *Telephone survey methods: Sampling, selection, and supervision.* Beverly Hills, CA: Sage.

Lazarsfeld, P. F. (1978). Some episodes in the history of panel analysis. In D. B. Kandel (Ed.), *Longitudinal research for drug abuse* (pp. 249–265). New York: Hemisphere Press.

Leary, D. E. (Ed.). (1990). *Metaphors in the history of psychology.* Cambridge: Cambridge University Press.

Lee, R. M. (1993). *Doing research on sensitive topics.* London: Sage.

Lewin, T. (1994, January 7). Prize in an unusual lottery: A scarce experimental drug. *The New York Times,* pp. A1, A17.

Lewis-Beck, M., Bryman, A., & Liao, T. F. (2003). *Encyclopedia of research methods for the social sciences.* Thousand Oaks, CA: Sage.

Li, H., & Wainer, H. (1998). Toward a coherent view of reliability in test theory. *Journal of Educational and Behavioral Statistics, 23,* 478–484.

Li, H., Rosenthal, R., & Rubin, D. B. (1996). Reliability of measurement in psychology: From Spearman-Brown to maximal reliability. *Psychological Methods, 1,* 98–107.

Light, R. J., & Pillemer, D. B. (1984). *Summing up: The science of reviewing research.* Cambridge: Harvard University Press.

Likert, R. A. (1932). A technique for the measurement of attitudes. *Archives of Psychology, 140,* 1–55.

Linsky, A. S. (1975). Stimulating responses to mailed questionnaires: A review. *Public Opinion Quarterly, 39,* 83–101.

Lipsey, M. W., & Wilson, D. B. (2001). *Practical meta-analysis.* Thousand Oaks, CA: Sage.

Liss, M. B. (1994). Child abuse: Is there a mandate for researchers to report? *Ethics and Behavior, 4,* 133–146.

Loftus, E. F., & Palmer, J. C. (1974). Reconstruction of automobile destruction: An example of the interaction between language and memory. *Journal of Verbal Learning and Verbal Behavior, 13,* 228–238.

London, P. (1970). The rescuers: Motivational hypotheses about Christians who saved Jews from the Nazis. In. J. Macaulay & L. Berkowitz (Eds.), *Altruism and behavior* (pp. 241–250). New York: Academic Press.

Loomis, J. M., Blascovich, J., & Beall, A. C. (1999). Immersive virtual environments as a basic research tool in psychology. *Behavioral Research Methods, Instruments and Computers, 31,* 557–564.

Mahler, I. (1953). Attitude toward socialized medicine. *Journal of Social Psychology, 38,* 273–282.

Main, M., & Solomon, J. (1990). Procedures for identifying infants as disorganized/disoriented during the Ainsworth Strange Situation. In M. T. Greenberg, D. Cichetti, & E. M. Cummings (Eds.), *Attachment in the preschool years* (pp. 121–160). Chicago: University of Chicago Press.

Malmo, R. B. (1959). Activation: A neuropsychological dimension. *Psychological Review, 66,* 367–386.

Mann, L. (1967). The effects of emotional role playing on smoking attitudes and behavior. *Journal of Experimental Social Psychology, 3,* 334–348.

Mann, L., & Janis, I. L. (1968). A follow-up study on the long-term effects of emotional role playing. *Journal of Personality and Social Psychology, 8,* 339–342.

Mann, T. (1994). Informed consent for psychological research: Do subjects comprehend consent forms and understand their legal rights? *Psychological Science, 5,* 140–143.

Marks, G., & Miller, N. (1987). Ten years of research on the false-consensus effect: An empirical and theoretical review. *Psychological Bulletin, 102,* 72–90.

Martin, D. (2001, March 25). Charles Johnson, 76, proponent of flat earth. *The New York Times,* p. 44.

Maurer, T. J., Palmer, J. K., & Ashe, D. K. (1993). Diaries, checklists, evaluations, and contrast effects in measurement of behavior. *Journal of Applied Psychology, 78,* 226–231.

Maxwell, S. E., & Delaney, H. D. (2000). *Designing experiments and analyzing data: A model comparison perspective.* Mahwah, NJ: Erlbaum.

McClelland, D. C., Atkinson, J. W., Clark, R. A., & Lowell, E. L. (1953). *The achievement motive.* New York: Appleton-Century-Crofts.

McCrae, R. R., & Costa, P. T., Jr. (1997). Personality trait structure as a human universal. *American Psychologist, 52,* 509–516.

McGuire, W. J. (1964). Inducing resistance to persuasion: Some contemporary approaches. In L. Berkowitz (Ed.), *Advances in experimental social psychology* (Vol. 1, pp. 191–229). New York: Academic Press.

McGuire, W. J. (1969). Suspiciousness of experimenter's intent. In R. Rosenthal & R. L. Rosnow (Eds.), *Artifact in behavioral research* (pp. 13–57). New York: Academic Press.

McGuire, W. J. (1973). The yin and yang of progress in social psychology: Seven koan. *Journal of Personality and Social Psychology, 26,* 446–456.

McGuire, W. J. (1997). Creative hypothesis generating in psychology: Some useful heuristics. *Annual Review of Psychology, 48,* 1–30.

McNemar, Q. (1946). Opinion-attitude methodology. *Psychological Bulletin, 43,* 289–374.

Meier, P. (1988). The biggest public health experiment ever: The 1954 field trial of the Salk poliomyelitis vaccine. In J. M. Tanur, F. Mosteller, W. H. Kruskal, E. L. Lehmann, R. F. Link, R. S. Pieters, & G. R. Rising (Eds.), *Statistics: A guide to the unknown* (3rd ed., pp. 3–14). Pacific Grove, CA: Wadsworth.

Menges, R. J. (1973). Openness and honesty versus coercion and deception in psychological research. *American Psychologist, 28,* 1030–1034.

Merriam, S. B. (1991). *Case study research in education.* San Francisco: Jossey-Bass.

Merritt, C. B., & Fowler, R. G. (1948). The pecuniary honesty of the public at large. *Journal of Abnormal and Social Psychology, 43,* 90–93.

Merton, R. K. (1948). The self-fulfilling prophecy. *Antioch Review, 8,* 193–210.

Merton, R. K. (1968). *Social theory and social structure.* New York: Free Press.

Michener, W., Rozin, P., Freeman, E., & Gale, L. (1999). The role of low progesterone and tension as triggers of perimenstrual chocolate and sweets craving: Some negative experimental evidence. *Physiology and Behavior, 67,* 417–420.

Milgram, S. (1963). Behavioral study of obedience. *Journal of Abnormal and Social Psychology, 67,* 371–378.

Milgram, S. (1974). *Obedience to authority: An experimental view.* New York: Harper & Row.

Milgram, S. (1977). *The individual in a social world: Essays and experiments.* Reading, MA: Addison-Wesley.

Milgram, S., Mann, L., & Harter, S. (1965). The lost-letter technique: A tool of social research. *Public Opinion Quarterly, 29,* 437–438.

Miller, A. I. (1986). *Imagery in Scientific Thought: Creating 20th Century Physics.* Cambridge: MIT Press.

Miller, A. I. (1996). *Insights of Genius: Imagery and Creativity in Science and Art.* New York: Springer-Verlag.

Miller, G. A., & Newman, E. B. (1958). Tests of a statistical explanation of the rank-frequency relation for words in written English. *American Journal of Psychology, 71,* 209–258.

Miller, N., & Pollock, V. E. (1994). Meta-analytic synthesis for theory development. In H. Cooper & L. V. Hedges (Eds.), *The handbook of research synthesis* (pp. 457–484). New York: Russell Sage Foundation.

Miller, P. V., & Cannell, C. F. (1982). A study of experimental techniques for telephone interviewing. *Public Opinion Quarterly, 46,* 250–269.

Millham, J., & Jacobson, L. I. (1978). The need for approval. In H. London & J. E. Exner (Eds.), *Dimensions of personality* (pp. 365–390). New York: Wiley.

Mitchell, J. (1985). *Eccentric lives and peculiar notions.* New York: Harcourt Brace Jovanovich.

Mook, D. G. (1983). In defense of external invalidity. *American Psychologist, 38,* 379–387.

Morse, J. M. (Ed.). (1993). *Critical issues in qualitative research methods.* Thousand Oaks, CA: Sage.

Mosteller, F. (1968). Association and estimation in contingency tables. *Journal of the American Statistical Association, 63,* 1–28.

Mosteller, F., Fienberg, S. E., & Rourke, R. E. K. (1983). *Beginning statistics with data analysis.* Reading, MA: Addison-Wesley.

Murphy, K. R., Jako, R. A., & Anhalt, R. L. (1993). Nature and consequences of halo effect: A critical analysis. *Journal of Applied Psychology, 78,* 218–225.

Myers, D. G. (2000). The funds, friends, and faith of happy people. *American Psychologist, 55,* 56–67.

National Commission for the Protection of Human Subjects of Biomedical and Behavioral Research. (1979). *The Belmont report: Ethical principles and guidelines for the protection of human subjects of research.* Washington, DC: Government Printing Office.

National Heart Institute. (1966). *The Framingham heart study: Habits and coronary heart disease.* Public Health Service Publication No. 1515). Bethesda, MD: National Heart Institute.

Neisser, U., Boodoo, G., Bouchard, T. J., Jr., Boykin, A. W., Brody, N., Ceci, S. J., Halpern, D. F., Loehlin, J. C., Perloff, R., Sternberg, R. J., & Urbina, S. (1996). Intelligence: Knowns and unknowns. *American Psychologist, 51,* 77–101.

Neisser, U., & Fivush, R. (Eds.). (1994). *The remembering self: Construction and accuracy in the self-narrative.* Cambridge: Cambridge University Press.

Neuringer, A. (1992). Choosing to vary and repeat. *Psychological Science, 3,* 246–250.

Neuringer, A. (1996). Can people behave "randomly?" The role of feedback. *Journal of Experimental Psychology: General, 115,* 62–75.

Neuringer, A., & Voss, C. (1993). Approximating chaotic behavior. *Psychological Science, 4,* 113–119.

Nisbet, R. (1976). *Sociology as an art form*. London: Oxford University Press.

Nisbett, R. E., & Wilson, T. D. (1977). Telling more than we can know: Verbal reports on mental processes. *Psychological Review, 84,* 231–259.

Norwick, R., Choi, Y. S., & Ben-Shachar, T. (2002). In defense of self-reports. *APS Observer, 15:*3, 7, 24.

Nouri, H., Blau, G., & Shahid, A. (1995). The effect of socially desirable responding (SDR) on the relation between budgetary participation and self-reported job performance. *Advances in Management Accounting, 4,* 163–177.

Nunnally, J. C., & Bernstein, I. H. (1994). *Psychometric theory* (3rd ed.). New York: McGraw-Hill.

Offer, D., Kaiz, M., Howard, K. I., & Bennett, E. S. (2000).The altering of reported experiences. *Journal of the American Academy of Child & Adolescent Psychiatry, 39,* 735–743.

Omodei, M. M., & Wearing, A. J. (1995). The Fire Chief microworld generating program: An illustration of computer-simulated microworlds as an experimental paradigm for studying complex decision-making behavior. *Behavior Research Methods, Instruments, & Computers, 27,* 303–316.

Ones, D. S., Viswesvaran, C., & Reiss, A. D. (1996). Role of social desirability in personality testing for personnel selection: The red herring. *Journal of Applied Psychology, 81,* 660–679.

Oppenheimer, R. (1956). Analogy in science. *American Psychologist, 11,* 127–135.

Orne, M. T. (1959). The nature of hypnosis: Artifact and essence. *Journal of Abnormal and Social Psychology, 58,* 277–299.

Orne, M. T. (1962). On the social psychology of the psychological experiment: With particular reference to demand characteristics and their implications. *American Psychologist, 17,* 776–783.

Orne, M. T. (1969). Demand characteristics and the concept of quasi-controls. In R. Rosenthal & R. L. Rosnow (Eds.), *Artifact in behavioral research* (pp. 143–179). New York: Academic Press.

Orne, M. T. (1970). Hypnosis, motivation, and the ecological validity of the psychological experiment. In W. J. Arnold & M. M. Page (Eds.), *Nebraska Symposium on Motivation* (pp. 187–265). Lincoln: University of Nebraska Press.

Osgood, C. E., Suci, G. L., & Tannenbaum, P. H. (1957). *The measurement of meaning*. Urbana: University of Illinois Press.

Overton, W. F. (1991a). Historical and contemporary perspectives on developmental theory and research strategies. In R. Downs, L. Liben, & D. Palermo (Eds.), *Visions of aesthetics, the environment, and development: The legacy of Joachim Wohlwill* (pp. 263–311). Hillsdale, NJ: Erlbaum.

Overton, W. F. (1991b). The structure of developmental theory. In H. W. Reese (Ed.), *Advances in child development and behavior* (Vol. 23, pp. 1–37). New York: Academic Press.

Pargament, K. I. (2002). The bitter and the sweet: An evaluation of the costs and benefits of religiousness. *Psychological Inquiry, 13,* 168–181.

Parker, K. C. H., Hanson, R. K., & Hunsley, J. (1988). MMPI, Rorschach, and WAIS: A meta-analytic comparison of reliability, stability, and validity. *Psychological Bulletin, 103,* 367–373.

Parloff, D. N. (Ed.). (1995). *Ethical conflicts in psychology*. Washington, DC: American Psychological Association.

Paul, E. F., Miller, F. D., & Paul, J. (Eds.). (2000). *Why animal experimentation matters: The use of animals in medical research*. New Brunswick, NJ: Transaction Publishers.

Paulhus, D. L. (1991). Measurement and control of response bias. In J. P. Robinson, P. R. Shaver, & L. S. Wrightsman (Eds.), *Measures of personality and social psychological attitudes* (pp. 17–59). San Diego, CA: Academic Press.

Paulos, J. A. (1990). *Innumeracy: Mathematical illiteracy and its consequences*. New York: Vintage Books.

Paulos, J. A. (1991, April 24). Math moron myths. *The New York Times OP-ED,* p. 25.

Pearl, J. (2000). *Causality: Models, reasoning, and inference*. Cambridge, UK: Cambridge University Press.

Peirce, C. S. (1966). *Charles S. Peirce: Selected writings (Values in a universe of chance)*. (P. P. Weiner, Ed.). New York: Dover.

Pelz, D. C., & Andrew, F. M. (1964). Detecting causal priorities in panel study data. *American Sociological Review, 29,* 836–848.

Pera, M., & Shea, W. R. (Eds.). (1991). *Persuading science: The art of scientific rhetoric*. Canton, MA: Science History.

Pessin, J. (1933). The comparative effects of social and mechanical stimulation on memorizing. *American Journal of Psychology, 45,* 263–270.

Pfungst, O. (1911). *Clever Hans (The Horse of Mr. von Osten)*. New York: Holt. (Reissued by Holt, Rinehart & Winston, 1965, edited and introduction by R. Rosenthal.)

Phelps, E. A., O'Connor, K. J., Cunningham, W. A., Funayama, E. S., Gatenby, J. C., Gore, J. C., & Banaji,

M. R. (2000). Performance on indirect measures of race evaluation predicts amygdala activation. *Journal of Cognitive Neuroscience, 12,* 729–738.

Phillips, D. P., & Carstensen, M. S. (1986). Clustering of teenage suicides after television news stories about suicide. *New England Journal of Medicine, 315,* 685–689.

Phillips, D. P., & Glynn, L. M. (2000). Field study. In A. E. Kazdin (Ed.), *Encyclopedia of psychology* (Vol. 3, p. 370). New York: Oxford University Press & American Psychological Association.

Phillips, D. P., & King, E. W. (1988). Death takes a holiday: Mortality surrounding major social occasions. *Lancet, 2,* 728–732.

Phillips, D. P., Lesyna, K., & Paight, D. J. (1992). Suicide and the media. In R. W. Maris, A. L. Berman, J. T. Maltsberger, & R. I. Yufit (Eds.), *Assessment and prediction of suicide* (pp. 499–519). New York: Guilford.

Phillips, D. P., & Paight, B. A. (1987). The impact of televised movies about *suicide:* A replicative study. *New England Journal of Medicine, 317,* 809–811.

Phillips, D. P., & Smith, D. G. (1990). Postponement of death until symbolically meaningful occasions. *Journal of the American Medical Association, 263,* 1947–1951.

Pierce, C. A., & Aguinis, H. (1997). Using virtual reality technology in organizational behavior research. *Journal of Organizational Behavior, 18,* 407–410.

Platt, J. (1992). Cases of cases. . .of cases. In C. C. Ragin & H. S. Becker (Eds.), *What is a case? Exploring the foundations of social inquiry* (pp. 21–52). Cambridge, UK: Cambridge University Press.

Popper, K. R. (1934). *Logik der Forschung.* Vienna: Springer-Verlag.

Popper, K. R. (1961). *The logic of scientific inquiry.* New York: Basic Books.

Popper, K. R. (1963). *Conjectures and refutations: The growth of scientific knowledge* (Rev. ed.). London: Routledge.

Popper, K. R. (1972). *Objective knowledge: An evolutionary approach.* Oxford: Oxford University Press.

Postman, L., Bruner, J. S., & McGinnies, E. (1948). Personal values as selective factors in perception. *Journal of Abnormal and Social Psychology, 43,* 142–154.

Ragin, C. C. (1992). Introduction: Cases of "What is a case?" In C. C. Ragin & H. S. Becker (Eds.), *What is a case? Exploring the foundations of social inquiry* (pp. 1–17). Cambridge, UK: Cambridge University Press.

Ragin, C. C., & Becker, H. S. (Eds.). (1992). *What is a case? Exploring the foundations of social inquiry.* Cambridge: Cambridge University Press.

Ramachandran, V. S. (Ed.). (1994). *Encyclopedia of human behavior* (Vols. 1–4). Orlando, FL: Academic Press.

Rand Corporation. (1955). *A million random digits with 100,000 normal deviates.* New York: Free Press.

Randhawa, B. S., & Coffman, W. E. (Eds.). (1978). *Visual learning, thinking, and communication.* New York: Academic Press.

Raudenbush, S. W. (1984). Magnitude of teacher expectancy effects on pupil IQ as a function of the credibility of expectancy induction: A synthesis of findings from 18 experiments. *Journal of Educational Psychology, 76,* 85–97.

Reed, S. K. (1988). *Cognition: Theory and applications* (2nd ed.). Pacific Grove, CA: Brooks/Cole.

Regis, E. (1987). *Who got Einstein's office? Eccentricities and genius at the Institute for Advanced Study.* Reading, MA: Addison-Wesley.

Reichenbach, H. (1938). *Experience and prediction.* Chicago: University of Illinois Press.

Rensberger, B. (2000). The nature of evidence. *Science, 289,* 61.

Riessman, C. K. (Ed.). (1993). *Qualitative studies in social work research.* Thousand Oaks, CA: Sage.

Rind, B., & Bordia, P. (1996). Effect on restaurant tipping of male and female servers drawing a happy, smiling face on the backs of customers' checks. *Journal of Applied Social Psychology, 26,* 218–225.

Roberts, C. W. (Ed.). (1997). *Text analysis for the social sciences: Methods for drawing statistical inferences from texts and transcripts.* Mahwah, NJ: Erlbaum.

Roberts, R. M. (1989). *Serendipity: Accidental discoveries in science.* New York: Wiley.

Robin, H. (1993). *The scientific image: From cave to computer.* New York: W. H. Freeman.

Robinson, J. P., Shaver, P. R., & Wrightsman, L. S. (Eds.). (1991). *Measures of personality and social psychological attitudes.* San Diego, CA: Academic Press.

Roethlisberger, F. J., & Dickson, W. J. (1939). *Management and the worker.* Cambridge: Harvard University Press.

Rosenbaum, M. (1986a). Comments on a proposed two-stage theory of relationship: First repulsion; then attraction. *Journal of Personality and Social Psychology, 51,* 1171–1172.

Rosenbaum, M. (1986b). The repulsion hypothesis: On the nondevelopment of relationship. *Journal of Personality and Social Psychology, 51,* 1156–1166.

Rosenbaum, P. R., & Rubin, D. B. (1983). The central role of the propensity score in observational studies for causal effects. *Biometrika, 70,* 41–55.

Rosenberg, M. J. (1969). The conditions and consequences of evaluation apprehension. In R. Rosenthal & R. L. Rosnow (Eds.), *Artifact in behavioral research* (pp. 279–349). New York: Academic Press.

Rosengren, K. E. (Ed.). (1981). *Advances in content analysis.* Beverly Hills, CA: Sage.

Rosenhan, D. L. (1973). On being sane in insane places. *Science, 179,* 250–258.

Rosenthal, R. (1966). *Experimenter effects in behavioral research.* New York: Appleton-Century-Crofts.

Rosenthal, R. (1973). Estimating effective reliability in studies that employ judges' ratings. *Journal of Clinical Psychology, 29,* 342–345.

Rosenthal, R. (1976). *Experimenter effects in behavioral research* (Enlarged ed.). New York: Irvington.

Rosenthal, R. (1979). The "file drawer problem" and tolerance for null results. *Psychological Bulletin, 86,* 638–641.

Rosenthal, R. (1982). Conducting judgment studies. In K. R. Scherer & P. Ekman (Eds.), *Handbook of methods in nonverbal behavior research* (pp. 287–361). New York: Cambridge University Press.

Rosenthal, R. (1983). Meta-analysis: Toward a more cumulative social science. In L. Bickman (Ed.), *Applied social psychology annual* (Vol. 4, pp. 65–93). Beverly Hills, CA: Sage.

Rosenthal, R. (1985). From unconscious experimenter bias to teacher expectancy effects. In J. B. Dusek (Ed.), *Teacher expectancies* (pp. 37–65). Hillsdale, NJ: Erlbaum.

Rosenthal, R. (1987). *Judgment studies: Design, analysis, and meta-analysis.* Cambridge: Cambridge University Press.

Rosenthal, R. (1990a). Evaluation of procedures and results. In K. W. Wachter & M. L. Straf (Eds.), *The future of meta-analysis* (pp. 123–133). New York: Russell Sage Foundation.

Rosenthal, R. (1990b). How are we doing in soft psychology? *American Psychologist, 45,* 775–777.

Rosenthal, R. (1990c). Replication in behavioral research. *Journal of Social Behavior and Personality, 5,* 1–30.

Rosenthal, R. (1991). *Meta-analytic procedures for social research* (Rev. ed.). Newbury Park, CA: Sage.

Rosenthal, R. (1993). Interpersonal expectations: Some antecedents and some consequences. In P. D. Blanck (Ed.), *Interpersonal expectations: Theory, research, and applications* (pp. 3–24). Cambridge: Cambridge University Press.

Rosenthal, R. (1994a). Parametric measures of effect size. In H. Cooper & L. V. Hedges (Eds.), *The handbook of research synthesis* (pp. 231–244). New York: Russell Sage Foundation.

Rosenthal, R. (1994b). Science and ethics in conducting, analyzing, and reporting psychological research. *Psychological Science, 5,* 127–134.

Rosenthal, R. (1995a). Progress in clinical psychology: Is there any? *Clinical Psychology: Science and Practice, 2,* 133–150.

Rosenthal, R. (1995b). Writing meta-analytic reviews. *Psychological Bulletin, 118,* 183–192.

Rosenthal, R., & DiMatteo, M. R. (2001). Meta-analysis: Recent developments in quantitative methods for literature reviews. *Annual Review of Psychology, 52,* 59–82.

Rosenthal, R., & Fode, K. L. (1963). The effect of experimenter bias on the performance of the albino rat. *Behavioral Science, 8,* 183–189.

Rosenthal, R., Hall, J. A., DiMatteo, M. R., Rogers, P. L., & Archer, D. (1979). *Sensitivity to nonverbal communication: The PONS test.* Baltimore: Johns Hopkins University Press.

Rosenthal, R., & Jacobson, L. (1968). *Pygmalion in the classroom: Teacher expectation and pupils' intellectual development.* New York: Holt, Rinehart & Winston.

Rosenthal, R., & Lawson, R. (1964). A longitudinal study of experimenter bias on the operant learning of laboratory rats. *Journal of Psychiatric Research, 2,* 61–72.

Rosenthal, R., & Rosnow, R. L. (Eds.). (1969). *Artifact in behavioral research.* New York: Academic Press.

Rosenthal, R., & Rosnow, R. L. (1975a). *Primer of methods for the behavioral sciences.* New York: Wiley.

Rosenthal, R., & Rosnow, R. L. (1975b). *The volunteer subject.* New York: Wiley.

Rosenthal, R., & Rosnow, R. L. (1984). Applying Hamlet's question to the ethical conduct of research: A conceptual addendum. *American Psychologist, 39,* 561–563.

Rosenthal, R., & Rosnow, R. L. (1985). *Contrast analysis: Focused comparisons in the analysis of variance.* Cambridge: Cambridge University Press.

Rosenthal, R., & Rosnow, R. L. (1991). *Essentials of behavioral research: Methods and data analysis* (2nd ed.). New York: McGraw-Hill.

Rosenthal, R., Rosnow, R. L., & Rubin, D. B. (2000). *Contrasts and effect sizes in behavioral research: A correlational approach.* Cambridge: Cambridge University Press.

Rosenthal, R., & Rubin, D. B. (1978). Interpersonal expectancy effects: The first 345 studies. *Behavioral and Brain Sciences, 3,* 377–386.

Rosenthal, R., & Rubin, D. B. (1979a). Comparing significance levels of independent studies. *Psychological Bulletin, 86,* 1165–1168.

Rosenthal, R., & Rubin, D. B. (1979b). A note on percent variance explained as a measure of the importance of effects. *Journal of Applied Social Psychology, 9,* 395–396.

Rosenthal, R., & Rubin, D. B. (1982a). Comparing effect sizes of independent studies. *Psychological Bulletin, 92,* 500–504.

Rosenthal, R., & Rubin, D. B. (1982b). A simple general purpose display of magnitude of experimental effect. *Journal of Educational Psychology, 74,* 166–169.

Rosenzweig, S. (1933). The experimental situation as a psychological problem. *Psychological Review, 40,* 337–354.

Rosnow, R. L. (1980). Psychology of rumor reconsidered. *Psychological Bulletin, 87,* 578–591.

Rosnow, R. L. (1981). *Paradigms in transition: The methodology of social inquiry.* New York: Oxford University Press.

Rosnow, R. L. (1983). Von Osten's horse, Hamlet's question, and the mechanistic view of causality: Implications for a post-crisis social psychology. *Journal of Mind and Behavior, 4,* 319–338.

Rosnow, R. L. (1986). Shotter, Vico and fallibilistic indeterminacy. *British Journal of Social Psychology, 25,* 215–216.

Rosnow, R. L. (1989, May). Die macht des Gerüchts. *Psychologie Heute,* pp. 20–24.

Rosnow, R. L. (1990a). The researcher's worst friend. In P. Chance & T. G. Harris (Eds.), *The best of Psychology Today* (pp. 260–264). New York: McGraw-Hill.

Rosnow, R. L. (1990b). Teaching research ethics through role-play and discussion. *Teaching of Psychology, 17,* 179–181.

Rosnow, R. L. (1991). Inside rumor: A personal journey. *American Psychologist, 46,* 484–496.

Rosnow, R. L. (1993). The volunteer problem revisited. In P. D. Blanck (Ed.), *Interpersonal expectations: Theory, research, applications* (pp. 418–436). New York: Cambridge University Press.

Rosnow, R. L. (1997). Hedgehogs, foxes, and the evolving social contract in psychological science: Ethical challenges and methodological opportunities. *Psychological Methods, 2,* 345–356.

Rosnow, R. L. (2001). Rumor and gossip in interpersonal interaction and beyond: A social exchange perspective. In R. M. Kowalski (Ed.), *Behaving badly: Aversive behaviors in interpersonal relationships* (pp. 203–232). Washington, DC: American Psychological Association.

Rosnow, R. L. (2002). Experimenter and subject artifacts. In N. J. Smelser & P. B. Baltes (Eds.), *International encyclopedia of the social and behavioral sciences.* Amsterdam: Pergamon.

Rosnow, R. L., & Aiken, L. S. (1973). Mediation of artifacts in behavioral research. *Journal of Experimental Social Psychology, 9,* 181–201.

Rosnow, R. L., Esposito, J. L., & Gibney, L. (1987). Factors influencing rumor spreading: Replication and extension. *Language and Communication, 7,* 1–14.

Rosnow, R. L., & Fine, G. A. (1974, August). Inside rumors. *Human Behavior,* pp. 64–68.

Rosnow, R. L., & Fine, G. A. (1976). *Rumor and gossip: The social psychology of hearsay.* New York: Elsevier.

Rosnow, R. L., & Georgoudi, M. (Eds.). (1986). *Contextualism and understanding in behavioral science: Implications for research and theory.* New York: Praeger.

Rosnow, R. L., Goodstadt, B. E., Suls, J. M., & Gitter, A. G. (1973). More on the social psychology of the experiment: When compliance turns to self-defense. *Journal of Personality and Social Psychology, 27,* 337–343.

Rosnow, R. L., & Rosenthal, R. (1970). Volunteer effects in behavioral research. In K. H. Craik, B. Kleinmuntz, R. L. Rosnow, R. Rosenthal, J. A. Cheyne, & R. H. Walters, *New directions in psychology* (No. 4, pp. 211–277). New York: Holt, Rinehart & Winston.

Rosnow, R. L., & Rosenthal, R. (1976). The volunteer subject revisited. *Australian Journal of Psychology, 28,* 97–108.

Rosnow, R. L., & Rosenthal, R. (1988). Focused tests of significance and effect size estimation in counseling psychology. *Journal of Counseling Psychology, 35,* 203–208.

Rosnow, R. L., & Rosenthal, R. (1989a). Definition and interpretation of interaction effects. *Psychological Bulletin, 105,* 143–146.

Rosnow, R. L., & Rosenthal, R. (1989b). Statistical procedures and the justification of knowledge in psychological science. *American Psychologist, 44,* 1276–1284.

Rosnow, R. L., & Rosenthal, R. (1991). If you are looking at the cell means, you're not looking at *only* the interaction (unless all main effects are zero). *Psychological Bulletin, 110,* 574–576.

Rosnow, R. L., & Rosenthal, R. (1995). "Some things you learn aren't so": Cohen's paradox, Asch's paradigm, and the interpretation of interaction. *Psychological Science, 6,* 3–9.

Rosnow, R. L., & Rosenthal, R. (1996a). Computing contrasts, effect sizes, and counternulls on other people's published data: General procedures for research consumers. *Psychological Methods, 1,* 331–340.

Rosnow, R. L., & Rosenthal, R. (1996b). Contrasts and interactions redux: Five easy pieces. *Psychological Science, 7,* 253–257.

Rosnow, R. L., & Rosenthal, R. (1997). *People studying people: Artifacts and ethics in behavioral research.* New York: W. H. Freeman.

Rosnow, R. L., & Rosenthal, R. (2002). Contrasts and correlations in theory assessment. *Journal of Pediatric Psychology, 27,* 59–66.

Rosnow, R. L., & Rosenthal, R. (2003). Effect sizes for experimenting psychologists. *Canadian Journal of Experimental Psychology, 57,* 221–237.

Rosnow, R. L., Rosenthal, R., & Rubin, D. B. (2000). Contrasts and correlations in effect size estimation. *Psychological Science, 11,* 446–453.

Rosnow, R. L., & Rosnow, M. (2003). *Writing papers in psychology: A student guide to research reports, essays, proposals, posters, and brief reports* (6th ed.). Belmont, CA: Wadsworth/Thomson Learning.

Rosnow, R. L., Rotheram-Borus, M. J., Ceci, S. J., Blanck, P. D., & Koocher, G. P. (1993). The institutional review board as a mirror of scientific and ethical standards. *American Psychologist, 48,* 821–826.

Rosnow, R. L., Skleder, A. A., Jaeger, M. E., & Rind, B. (1994). Intelligence and the epistemics of interpersonal acumen: Testing some implications of Gardner's theory. *Intelligence, 19,* 93–116.

Rosnow, R. L., Strohmetz, D., & Aditya, R. (2000). Artifact in research. In A. E. Kazdin (Ed.), *Encyclopedia of psychology* (Vol. 1, pp. 242–245). New York: Oxford University Press & American Psychological Association.

Rosnow, R. L., & Suls, J. M. (1970). Reactive effects of pretesting in attitude research. *Journal of Personality and Social Psychology, 15,* 338–343.

Ross, L., Greene, D., & House, P. (1977). The "false-consensus effect": An egocentric bias in social perception and attribution processes. *Journal of Experimental Social Psychology, 13,* 279–301.

Rossi, P. H., Wright, J. D., & Anderson, A. B. (1983). Sample surveys: History, current practice, and future prospects. In P. H. Rossi, J. D. Wright, & A. B. Anderson (Eds.), *Handbook of survey research* (pp. 1–20). New York: Academic Press.

Rothenberg, R. (1990, October 5). Surveys proliferate, but answers dwindle. *The New York Times,* pp. A1, D4.

Rozelle, R. M., & Campbell, D. T. (1969). More plausible rival hypotheses in the cross-lagged panel correlation technique. *Psychological Bulletin, 71,* 74–80.

Rozin, P., Fischler, C., Imada, S., Sarubin, A., & Wrzesniewski, A. (1999). Attitudes to food and the role of food in life in the U.S.A., Japan, Flemish Belgium and France: Possible implications for the diet-health debate. *Appetite, 33,* 163–180.

Rubin, D. B. (1973). The use of matched sampling and regression adjustment to control bias in observational studies. *Biometrics, 29,* 184–203.

Rubin, D. B. (1974). Estimating causal effects of treatments in randomized and nonrandomized studies. *Journal of Educational Psychology, 66,* 688–701.

Rubin, D. B., & Thomas, N. (1996). Matching using estimated propensity scores: Relating theory to practice. *Biometrics, 52,* 249–264.

Rubin, Z. (1974). Jokers wild in the lab. In J. B. Maas (Ed.), *Readings in Psychology Today* (pp. 25–27). Del Mar, CA: CRM Books.

Russell, M. S., & Burch, R. L. (1959). *The principles of humane experimental technique.* London: Methuen.

Saks, M. J., & Blanck, P. D. (1992). Justice improved: The unrecognized benefits of aggregation and sampling in the trial of mass torts. *Stanford Law Review, 44,* 815–851.

Sales, B. D., & Folkman, S. (Eds.). (2000). *Ethics in research with human participants.* Washington, DC: American Psychological Association.

Sartre, J.-P. (1956). *Being and nothingness.* New York: Washington Square Press.

Saxe, L. (1991). Lying: Thoughts of an applied social psychologist. *American Psychologist, 46,* 409–415.

Schachter, S. (1968). Obesity and eating. *Science, 161,* 751–756.

Schacter, D. L. (1999). The seven sins of memory: Insights from psychology and cognitive neuroscience. *American Psychologist, 54,* 182–203.

Schaeffer, N. C. (2000). Asking questions about threatening topics: A selective overview. In A. A. Stone, J. S. Turkkan, C. A. Bachrach, J. B. Jobe, H. S. Kurtzman, & V. S. Cain (Eds.), *The science of self-report: Implications for research and practice* (pp. 105–121). Mahwah, NJ: Erlbaum.

Schlaifer, R. (1980). The relay assembly test room: An alternative statistical interpretation. *American Sociological Review, 45,* 995–1005.

Schuler, H. (1982). *Ethical problems in psychological research.* New York: Academic Press.

Schultz, D. P. (1969). The human subject in psychological research. *Psychological Bulletin, 72,* 214–228.

Schuman, H., & Presser, S. (1996). *Questions and answers in attitude surveys: Experiments on question form, wording, and content.* Thousand Oaks, CA: Sage.

Scott, W. A. (1968). Attitude measurement. In G. Lindzey & E. Aronson (Eds.), *The handbook of social psychology* (2nd ed., Vol. 2, pp. 204–272). Reading, MA: Addison-Wesley.

Scott-Jones, D., & Rosnow, R. L. (1998). Ethics and mental health research. In H. Friedman (Ed.), *Encyclopedia of mental health* (Vol. 2, pp. 149–160). Palo Alto, CA: Academic Press.

Sears, D. O. (1986). College sophomores in the laboratory: Influences of a narrow data base on social psychology's view of human nature. *Journal of Personality and Social Psychology, 51,* 515–530.

Shadish, W. R., Cook, T. D., & Campbell, D. T. (2002). *Experimental and quasi-experimental designs for generalized causal inference.* Boston: Houghton Mifflin.

Shaw, M. E., & Wright, J. M. (1967). *Scales for the measurement of attitudes.* New York: McGraw-Hill.

Sherman, S. J., Presson, C., & Chassin, L. (1984). Mechanisms underlying the false consensus effect: The special role of threats to the self. *Personality and Social Psychology Bulletin, 10,* 127–138.

Shermer, M. (1997). *Why people believe weird things: Pseudoscience, superstition, and other confusions of our time.* New York: W. H. Freeman.

Sidman, M. (1960). *Tactics of scientific research: Evaluating experimental data in psychology.* New York: Basic Books.

Sieber, J. E. (1982a). Deception in social research: 1. Kinds of deception and the wrongs they may involve. *IRB: A Review of Human Subjects Research, 3,* 1–2, 12.

Sieber, J. E. (Ed.). (1982b). *The ethics of social research* (Vols. 1–2). New York: Springer-Verlag.

Sieber, J. E (1983). Deception in social research: 2. Factors influencing the magnitude of potential for harm or wrong. *IRB: A Review of Human Subjects Research, 4,* 1–3, 12.

Sieber, J. E. (1992). *Planning ethically responsible research.* Newbury Park, CA: Sage.

Sieber, J. E. (1994). Scientists' responses to ethical issues in science. In W. Shadish & S. Fuller (Eds.), *The social psychology of science* (pp. 286–299). New York: Guilford.

Sieber, J. E., & Saks, M. J. (1989). A census of subject pool characteristics and policies. *American Psychologist, 44,* 1053–1061.

Siegel, S. (1956). *Nonparametric statistics.* New York: McGraw-Hill.

Sigall, H., Aronson, E., & Van Hoose, T. (1970). The cooperative subject: Myth or reality? *Journal of Experimental Social Psychology, 6,* 1–10.

Silverman, D. (1993). *Interpreting qualitative data: Methods for analyzing talk, text, and interaction.* Thousand Oaks, CA: Sage.

Silverman, I. (1977). *The human subject in the psychological experiment.* New York: Pergamon.

Simonton, D. K. (2000). Archival research. In A. E. Kazdin (Ed.), *Encyclopedia of psychology* (Vol. 1, pp. 234–235). New York: Oxford University Press & American Psychological Association.

Singer, E., Hippler, H.-J., & Schwarz, N. (1992). Confidentiality assurances in surveys: Reassurance or threat? *International Journal of Public Opinion, 4,* 256–268.

Singer, E., Von Thurn, D. R., & Miller, E. R. (1995). Confidentiality assurances and response: A quantitative review of the experimental literature. *Public Opinion Quarterly, 59,* 66–77.

Skinner, B. F. (1938). *The behavior of organisms: An experimental analysis.* New York: Appleton-Century-Crofts.

Skinner, B. F. (1948a). Superstition in the pigeon. *Journal of Experimental Psychology, 38,* 168–172.

Skinner, B. F. (1948b). *Walden II.* New York: Macmillan.

Slife, B., & Rubinstein, J. (Eds.). (1992). *Taking sides: Clashing views on controversial psychological issues* (7th ed.). Guilford, CT: Dushkin.

Slovic, P. (1987). Perception of risk. *Science, 236,* 280–285.

Smart, R. G. (1966). Subject selection bias in psychological research. *Canadian Psychologist, 7a,* 115–121.

Smelser, N. J, & Baltes, P. B. (Eds.). (2002). *International encyclopedia of the social and behavioral sciences* (Vols. 1–26). Amsterdam: Pergamon.

Smith, C. (1980). *Selecting a source of local television news in the Salt Lake City SMSA: A multivariate analysis of cognitive and affective factors for 384 randomly-selected news viewers.* Unpublished doctoral dissertation, Temple University School of Communication, Philadelphia.

Smith, C. P. (Ed.). (1992). *Motivation and personality: Handbook of thematic content analysis*. Cambridge: Cambridge University Press.

Smith, M. B. (2000). Moral foundations in research with human participants. In B. D. Sales & S. Folkman (Eds.), *Ethics in research with human participants* (pp. 3–10). Washington, DC: American Psychological Association.

Smith, M. L., & Glass, G. V. (1977). Meta-analysis of psychotherapy outcome studies. *American Psychologist, 32,* 752–760.

Smith, T. W. (1997, April 20). Punt, pass and ponder the questions. *The New York Times,* p. 11.

Snedecor, G. W., & Cochran, W. G. (1989). *Statistical methods* (8th ed.). Ames: Iowa State University Press.

Sockloff, A. L., & Edney, J. N. (1972). *Some extensions of Student's t and Pearson's r central distributions*. Technical Report 72–5. Temple University Measurement and Research Center, Philadelphia.

Solomon, R. L. (1949). An extension of control group design. *Psychological Bulletin, 46,* 137–150.

Solomon, R. L., & Howes, D. (1951). Word frequency, personal values, and visual duration thresholds. *Psychological Review, 58,* 256–270.

Sommer, R. (1968). Hawthorne dogma. *Psychological Bulletin, 70,* 592–595.

Sonneck, G., Etzersdorfer, E., & Nagel-Kuess, S. (1994). Imitative suicide on the Viennese subway. *Social Science and Medicine, 38,* 453–457.

Sperry, R. W. (1968). Hemisphere deconnection and unity in conscious awareness. *American Psychologist, 23,* 723–733.

Squire, P. (1988). Why the 1936 *Literary Digest* poll failed. *Public Opinion Quarterly, 52,* 125–133.

Stanley, B., Sieber, J. E., & Melton, G. B. (1987). Empirical studies of ethical issues in research: A research agenda. *American Psychologist, 7,* 735–741.

Stanley, J. C. (1971). Test reliability. In L. C. Deighton (Ed.), *The encyclopedia of education* (Vol. 9, pp. 143–153). New York: Macmillan & Free Press.

Stanovich, K. E. (1986). *How to think straight about psychology*. Glenview, IL: Scott, Foresman.

Steering Committee of the Physicians' Health Study Research Group. (1988). Preliminary report: Findings from the aspirin component of the ongoing physicians' health study. *New England Journal of Medicine, 318,* 262–264.

Sterling, T. D. (1959). Publication decisions and their possible effects on inferences drawn from tests of significance—or vice versa. *Journal of the American Statistical Association, 54,* 30–34.

Stern, S. E., & Faber, J. E. (1997). The lost e-mail method: Milgram's lost-letter technique in the age of the Internet. *Behavior Research Methods, Instruments, & Computers, 29,* 260–263.

Sternberg, R. J. (1985). *Beyond IQ: A triarchic theory of human intelligence*. Cambridge: Cambridge University Press.

Sternberg, R. J. (1990). *Metaphors of mind: Conceptions of the nature of intelligence*. Cambridge: Cambridge University Press.

Sternberg, R. J. (1993). *The psychologist's companion: A guide to scientific writing for students and researchers* (3rd ed.). Cambridge: Cambridge University Press.

Sternberg, R. J. (1997). The concept of intelligence and its role in lifelong learning and success. *American Psychologist, 52,* 1030–1037.

Sternberg, R. J. (2000). Research dissemination. In A. E. Kazdin (Ed.), *Encyclopedia of psychology* (Vol. 7, pp. 76–80). New York: Oxford University Press & American Psychological Association.

Sternberg, R. J., & Detterman, D. K. (Eds.). (1986). *What is intelligence? Contemporary viewpoints on its nature and definition*. Norwood, NJ: Ablex.

Steuer, J. (1992). Defining virtual reality: Dimensions determining telepresence. *Journal of Communication, 42,* 73–93.

Stigler, S. M. (1986). *The history of statistics: The measurement of uncertainty before 1900*. Cambridge: Belknap/Harvard.

Stone, A. A., Turkkan, J. S., Bachrach, C. A., Jobe, J. B., Kurtzman, H. S., & Cain, V. S. (Eds.). (2000). *The science of self-report: Implications for research and practice*. Mahwah, NJ: Erlbaum.

Stone, P., Dunphy, D., Smith, M., & Ogilvie, D. (1966). *The General Inquirer: A complete approach to content analysis*. Cambridge: MIT Press.

Street, E., & Carroll, M. B. (1989). Preliminary evaluation of a new food product. In J. M. Tanur, F. M. Mosteller, W. H. Kruskal, E. L. Lehmann, R. F. Link, R. S. Pieters, & G. R. Rising (Eds.), *Statistics: A guide to the unknown* (3rd ed., pp. 161–169). Pacific Grove, CA: Wadsworth & Brooks/Cole.

Strickland, B. R. (1977). Approval motivation. In T. Blass (Ed.), *Personality variables in social behavior* (pp. 315–356). Hillsdale, NJ: Erlbaum.

Strohmetz, D. B., & Rosnow, R. L. (1994). A mediational model of artifacts. In J. Brzeziński (Ed.), *Probability in theory-building: Experimental and non-experimental approaches to scientific research in psychology* (pp. 177–196). Netherlands: Rudopi.

Strunk, W., Jr., & White, E. B. (2000). *The elements of style* (4th ed.). Boston: Allyn & Bacon.

Stryker, J. (1997, April 13). Tuskegee's long arm still touches a nerve. *The New York Times*, p. E4.

Suls, J. M., Martin, R., & Wheeler, L. (2000). Three kinds of opinion comparison: The triadic model. *Personality and Social Psychology Review, 4,* 219–237.

Suls, J. M., & Miller, R. L. (Eds.). (1977). *Social comparison processes: Theoretical and empirical perspectives.* Washington, DC: Hemisphere.

Suls, J. M., & Rosnow, R. L. (1988). Concerns about artifacts in psychological experiments. In J. Morawski (Ed.), *The rise of experimentation in American psychology* (pp. 163–187). New York: Oxford University Press.

Susman, E. J., Dorn, L. D., & Fletcher, J. C. (1992). Participation in biomedical research: The consent process as viewed by children, adolescents, young adults, and physicians. *Journal of Pediatrics, 121,* 547–552.

Symonds, P. M. (1925). Notes on rating. *Journal of Applied Psychology, 9,* 188–195.

Tan, D. T. Y., & Singh, R. (1995). Attitudes and attraction: A developmental study of the similarity-attraction and dissimilarity-repulsion hypotheses. *Personality and Social Psychology Bulletin, 21,* 975–986.

Tanur, J. M. (Ed.). (1994). *Questions about questions: Inquiries into the cognitive bases of surveys.* New York: Russell Sage Foundation.

Tanur, J. M., Mosteller, F., Kruskal, W. H., Lehmann, E. L., Link, R. F., Pieters, R. S., & Rising, G. R. (Eds.). (1989). *Statistics: A guide to the unknown* (3rd ed.). Pacific Grove, CA: Wadsworth & Brooks/Cole.

Tatsuoka, M. (1993). Effect size. In G. Keren & C. Lewis (Eds.), *A handbook for data analysis in the behavioral sciences: Methodological issues* (pp. 461–479). Hillsdale, NJ: Erlbaum.

Taylor, S. J., & Bogdan, R. (1998). *Introduction to qualitative research: A guidebook and resources* (3rd ed.). New York: Wiley.

Tedlock, B. (2000). Ethnography and ethnographic representation. In N. K. Denzin & Y. S. Lincoln (Eds.), *Handbook of qualitative research* (2nd ed., pp. 455–486). Thousand Oaks, CA: Sage.

Thurstone, L. L. (1929). Theory of attitude measurement. *Psychological Bulletin, 36,* 222–241.

Thurstone, L. L. (1929–1934). *The measurement of social attitudes.* Chicago: University of Chicago Press.

Tolman, E. C. (1959). Principles of purposive behavior. In S. Koch (Ed.), *Psychology: A study of a science* (Vol. 2, pp. 92–157). New York: McGraw-Hill.

Tourangeau, R. (2000). Remembering what happened: Memory errors and survey reports. In A. A. Stone, J. S. Turkkan, C. A. Bachrach, J. B. Jobe, H. S. Kurtzman, & V. S. Cain (Eds.), *The science of self-report: Implications for research and practice* (pp. 29–47). Mahwah, NJ: Erlbaum.

Treadway, M., & McCloskey, M. (1989). Effects of racial stereotypes on eyewitness performance: Implications of the real and rumored Allport and Postman studies. *Applied Cognitive Psychology, 3,* 53–63.

Tryfos, P. (1996). *Sampling methods for applied research: Text and cases.* New York: Wiley.

Tufte, E. R. (1983). *The visual display of quantitative information.* Cheshire, CT: Graphics Press.

Tufte, E. R. (1990). *Envisioning information.* Cheshire, CT: Graphics Press.

Tukey, J. W. (1977). *Exploratory data analysis.* Reading, MA: Addison-Wesley.

Turkkan, J. S., & Brady, J. V. (2000). Placebo effect in research design. In A. E. Kazdin (Ed.), *Encyclopedia of psychology* (Vol. 6, pp. 210–212). New York: Oxford University Press & American Psychological Association.

Tversky, A., & Kahneman, D. (1974). Judgment under uncertainty: Heuristics and biases. *Science, 185,* 1124–1131.

Vickers, B. (Ed.). (1996). *Francis Bacon: A critical edition of the major works.* Oxford, UK: Oxford University Press.

Wachter, K. W., & Straf, M. L. (Eds.). (1990). *The future of meta-analysis.* New York: Russell Sage Foundation.

Wainer, H. (1972). Draft of Appendix for R. E. Lana & R. L. Rosnow's *Introduction to contemporary psychology.* New York: Holt, Rinehart & Winston.

Wainer, H. (1990). *Computerized adaptive testing: A primer.* Hillsdale, NJ: Erlbaum.

Wainer, H. (1997). *Visual revelations: Graphical tales of fate and deception from Napoleon Bonaparte to Ross Perot.* Mahwah, NJ: Erlbaum.

Wainer, H., & Thissen, D. (1993). Combining multiple-choice and constructed-response test scores: Toward a Marxist theory of test construction. *Applied Measurement in Education, 6*(2), 103–118.

Walker, C. J., & Beckerle, C. A. (1987). The effect of anxiety on rumor transmission. *Journal of Social Behavior and Personality, 2,* 353–360.

Walker, C. J., & Blaine, B. (1991). The virulence of dread rumors: A field experiment. *Language and Communication, 11,* 291–298.

Wallis, W. A., & Roberts, H. V. (1956). *Statistics: A new approach.* New York: Free Press.

Weaver, C. (1972). *Human listening.* Indianapolis: Bobbs-Merrill.

Webb, E. J., Campbell, D. T., Schwartz, R. F., & Sechrest, L. (1966). *Unobtrusive measures: Nonreactive research in the social sciences.* Chicago: Rand McNally.

Webb, E. J., Campbell, D. T., Schwartz, R. F., Sechrest, L., & Grove, J. B. (1981). *Nonreactive measures in the social sciences* (2nd ed.). Boston: Houghton Mifflin.

Webber, R. A. (1970). Perception of interactions between superiors and subordinates. *Human Relations, 23,* 235–248.

Weber, R. P. (1985). *Basic content analysis.* Beverly Hills, CA: Sage.

Wechler, J. (Ed.). (1978). *On aesthetics on science.* Cambridge: MIT Press.

Weick, K. E. (1968). Systematic observational methods. In G. Lindzey & E. Aronson (Eds.), *The handbook of social psychology* (2nd ed., Vol. 2, pp. 357–451). Reading, MA: Addison-Wesley.

Weick, K. E. (1995). *Sensemaking in organizations.* Thousand Oaks, CA: Sage.

Weinberger, D. A. (1990). The construct validity of the repressive coping style. In J. L. Singer (Ed.), *Repression and dissociation: Implications for personality theory, psychopathology, and health* (pp. 337–386). Chicago: University of Chicago Press.

Weiner, B. (1991). Metaphors in motivation and attribution. *American Psychologist, 46,* 921–930.

Weisberg, R. W. (1994). Genius and madness? A quasi-experimental test of the hypothesis that manic-depression increases creativity. *Psychological Science, 5,* 361–367.

Werner, H. C., & Kaplan, B. (1963). *Symbol formation: An organismic-developmental approach to language and the expression of thought.* New York: Wiley.

Weschler, L. (1988, January 18). Onward and upward with the arts. *The New Yorker,* pp. 33–56.

Westen, D., & Rosenthal, R. (2003). Quantifying construct validity: Two simple measures. *Journal of Personality and Social Psychology, 84,* 608–618.

Wheeler, L., Martin, R., & Suls, J. (1997). The proxy model of social comparison for self-assessment of ability. *Personality and Social Psychology Review, 1,* 54–61.

White, L., Tursky, B., & Schwartz, G. (Eds.). (1985). *Placebo: Clinical phenomena and new insights.* New York: Guilford Press.

White, T. L., Leichtman, M. D., & Ceci, S. J. (1997). The good, the bad, and the ugly: Accuracy, inaccuracy, and elaboration in preschoolers' reports about a past event. *Applied Cognitive Psychology, 11,* S37–S54.

Wickesberg, A. K. (1968). Communication networks in a business organization structure. *Journal of the Academy of Management, 11,* 253–262.

Wiggins, J. S. (Ed.). (1996). *The five-factor model of personality.* New York: Guilford Press.

Wilcox, B., & Gardner, D. (1993). Political intervention in scientific peer review: Research on adolescent sexual behavior. *American Psychologist, 48,* 972–983.

Wilkinson, L., & Engelman, L. (1996). Descriptive statistics. In L. Wilkinson (Ed.), *SYSTAT 9: Statistics I* (pp. 205–225). Chicago: SPSS Inc.

Wilkinson, L., and the Task Force on Statistical Inference. (1999). Statistical methods in psychology journals. *American Psychologist, 54,* 594–604.

Willis, G., Brittingham, A, Lee, L., Tourangeau, R., & Ching, P. (1999). *Responses errors in children's surveys of immunization.* Vital and Health Statistics, Series 6, No. 8, Hyattsville, MD: National Center for Health Statistics.

Wolman, B. B. (Ed.). (1977). *International encyclopedia of psychiatry, psychology, psychoanalysis, and neurology* (Vols. 1–12). New York: Van Nostrand Reinhold.

Wood, J. (1989). Theory and research concerning social comparisons of personal attributes. *Psychological Bulletin, 106,* 231–248.

Woodrum, E. (1984). "Mainstreaming" content analysis in social science: Methodological advantages, obstacles, and solutions. *Social Science Research, 13,* 1–19.

Wyer, R. S., Jr., & Srull, T. K. (Eds.). (1989). *Advances in social cognition: Vol. 2. Social intelligence and cognitive assessment of personality.* Hillsdale, NJ: Erlbaum.

Yin, R. K. (1989). *Case study research: Design and methods.* Newbury Park, CA: Sage.

Zajonc, R. F. (1965). Social facilitation. *Science, 149,* 269–274.

Zechmeister, E. G., & Nyberg, S. E. (1982). *Human memory: An introduction to research and theory.* Monterey, CA: Brooks/Cole.

Zipf, G. K. (1935). *The psycho-biology of language.* Boston: Houghton Mifflin.

Zipf, G. K. (1949). *Human behavior and the principle of least effort.* Reading, MA: Addison-Wesley.

Name Index

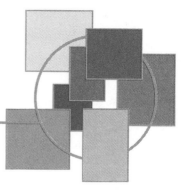

Subject Index

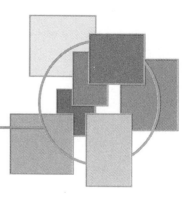

CHAPTER 14
Sums of squares and degrees of freedom in ANOVA:

$$\text{Total } SS = \Sigma(X - M_G)^2 \qquad df \text{ total} = N - 1$$

$$\text{Between } SS = \Sigma[n_k(M_k - M_G)^2] \qquad df \text{ between} = k - 1$$

$$\text{Within } SS = \Sigma(X - M_k)^2 \qquad df \text{ within} = N - k$$

CHAPTER 14
Mean squares and F ratio in one-way ANOVA

$$MS_{between} = \frac{\text{Between } SS}{df \text{ between}} \qquad MS_{within} = \frac{\text{Within } SS}{df \text{ within}} \qquad F = \frac{MS_{between}}{MS_{within}}$$

CHAPTER 14
Row, column, and interaction sums of squares and degrees of freedom in two-way ANOVA:

$$\text{Row } SS = \Sigma[nc(M_r - M_G)^2] \qquad df \text{ rows} = r - 1$$

$$\text{Column } SS = \Sigma[nr(M_c - M_G)^2] \qquad df \text{ columns} = c - 1$$

$$\text{Interaction } SS = \text{total } SS - (\text{row } SS + \text{column } SS + \text{within } SS) \qquad df \text{ interaction} = (r - 1)(c - 1)$$

CHAPTER 14
Mean squares and F ratios in two-way ANOVA:

$$MS_{rows} = \frac{\text{Row } SS}{df \text{ rows}} \qquad F_{rows} = \frac{MS_{rows}}{MS_{within}}$$

$$MS_{columns} = \frac{\text{Column } SS}{df \text{ columns}} \qquad F_{columns} = \frac{MS_{columns}}{MS_{within}}$$

$$MS_{interaction} = \frac{\text{Interaction } SS}{df \text{ interaction}} \qquad F_{interaction} = \frac{MS_{interaction}}{MS_{within}}$$

CHAPTER 14
Contrast t on more than two independent groups:

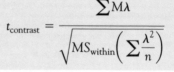

$$t_{contrast} = \frac{\Sigma M\lambda}{\sqrt{MS_{within}\left(\Sigma\frac{\lambda^2}{n}\right)}}$$

CHAPTER 14
$r_{contrast}$ from $t_{contrast}$ or $F_{contrast}$ on more than two groups:

$$r_{contrast} = \sqrt{\frac{t_{contrast}^2}{t_{contrast}^2 + df}} = \sqrt{\frac{F_{contrast}}{F_{contrast} + df_{within}}}$$

CHAPTER 14
$r_{\text{effect size}}$ *from* F_{contrast} *on more than two groups:*

$$r_{\text{effect size}} = \sqrt{\frac{F_{\text{contrast}}}{F_{\text{contrast}} + F_{\text{noncontrast}}(df_{\text{noncontrast}}) + df_{\text{within}}}}$$

CHAPTER 14
Contrast t on more than two repeated measures:

$$t_{(df)} = \frac{M_L}{\sqrt{\left(\frac{1}{N}\right)S_L^2}},$$

CHAPTER 15
Chi square and expected frequency:

$$\chi^2 = \sum \frac{(f_o - f_e)^2}{f_e} \quad \text{and} \quad f_e = \frac{(\text{Column total})(\text{Row total})}{\text{Grand total}}$$

CHAPTER 15
2 × 2 chi-square (1 df):

$$\chi^2 = \frac{N(BC - AD)^2}{(A + B)(C + D)(A + C)(B + D)}$$

CHAPTER 15
Effect size of 1 df chi-square:

$$r_{\text{effect size}} = \phi = \sqrt{\frac{\chi^2}{N}}$$

APPENDIX C
Comparing two effect sizes:

$$z \text{ of difference} = \frac{z_{r1} - z_{r2}}{\sqrt{\frac{1}{N_1 - 3} + \frac{1}{N_2 - 3}}}$$

APPENDIX C
Combining two effect sizes:

$$\bar{z}_r = \frac{z_{r1} + z_{r2}}{2}$$

APPENDIX C
Combining two significance levels:

$$\text{Combined } z = \frac{z_1 + z_2}{\sqrt{2}}$$